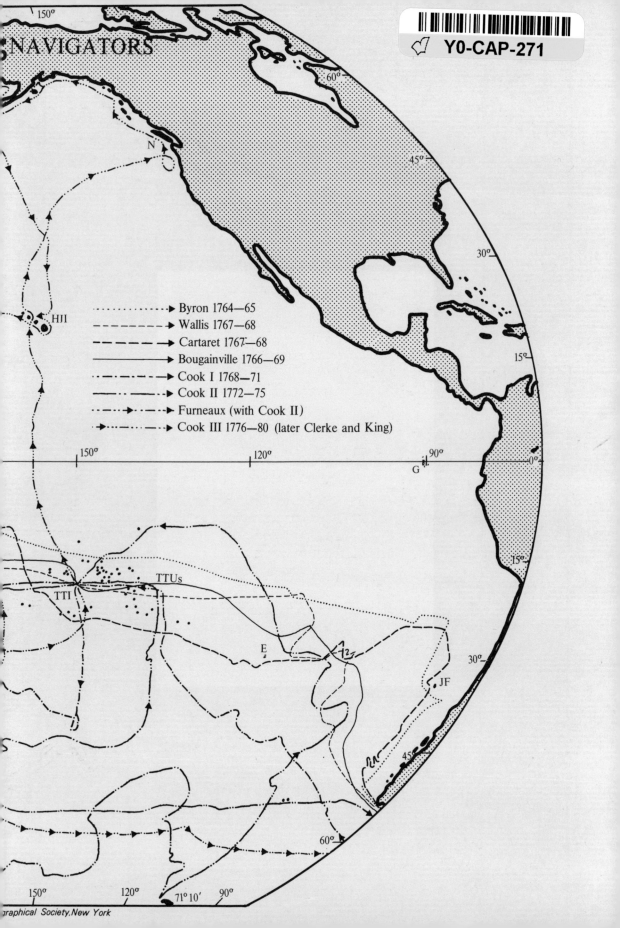

NAVIGATORS

........▸ Byron 1764—65
– – –▸ Wallis 1767—68
– ·– ·▸ Cartaret 1767—68
———▸ Bougainville 1766—69
–·–·–▸ Cook I 1768—71
–··–··▸ Cook II 1772—75
–·▸–·▸ Furneaux (with Cook II)
▸··–··▸ Cook III 1776—80 (later Clerke and King)

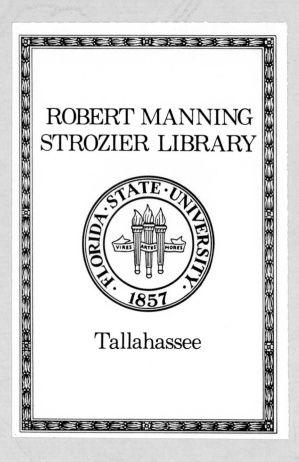

Paradise
Found and Lost

BY THE SAME AUTHOR

Burma Setting, 1943

The Compass of Geography, 1953

India and Pakistan: A general and regional geography, 1954, 3rd ed. (revised with A. T. A. Learmonth) 1967; Indian ed. 1985; translated into Russian 1957 as *Indiya i Pakistan*

Australia, New Zealand and the Pacific, 1956, 3rd ed. 1969

The Fijian People: Economic Problems and Prospects, 1959; translated into Fijian as *Na Kawa I Taukei*

Let Me Enjoy: Essays, partly geographical, 1965

Australia, 1968

The Pacific since Magellan: I. The Spanish Lake, 1979

The Pacific since Magellan: II. Monopolists and Freebooters, 1983

EDITED WORKS

The Changing Map of Asia (jointly with W. G. East), 1950, 5th ed. 1971

Peter Dillon of Vanikoro: Chevalier of the South Seas, by J. W. Davidson, 1975

The Pacific since Magellan, Volume III

Paradise Found and Lost

O. H. K. Spate

To any meditative Magian rover,
this serene Pacific once beheld,
must ever after be the sea of his adoption...
Thus this mysterious divine Pacific zones
the whole world's bulk about; makes
all coasts one bay to it; seems
the tide-beating heart of earth.

Herman Melville,
Moby Dick, CX

University of Minnesota Press. Minneapolis

Published by the University of Minnesota Press
2037 University Avenue Southeast, Minneapolis MN 55414.
Published simultaneously in Canada
by Fitzhenry & Whiteside Limited, Markham.

Printed in Australia by Macarthur Press

LIBRARY OF CONGRESS
Library of Congress Cataloguing-in Publication Data

Spate, O.H.K. (Oskar Hermann Khristian), 1911–
    Paradise found and lost / O.H.K. Spate.
    p. cm.—(The Pacific since Magellan ; v. 3)
    Bibliography: p.
    Includes index
    ISBN 0 8166 1715 5 : $59.50
    1. Oceania—History. I. Title. II. Series: Spate, O.H.K.
(Oskar Hermann Khristian), 1911–   Pacific since Magellan ; v. 3.
DU 28.3.S68 1988
990—dc19

To the Memory of my Mother
Olive
and to her grandchildren
Alastair, Andrew, and Virginia
finis coronat opus

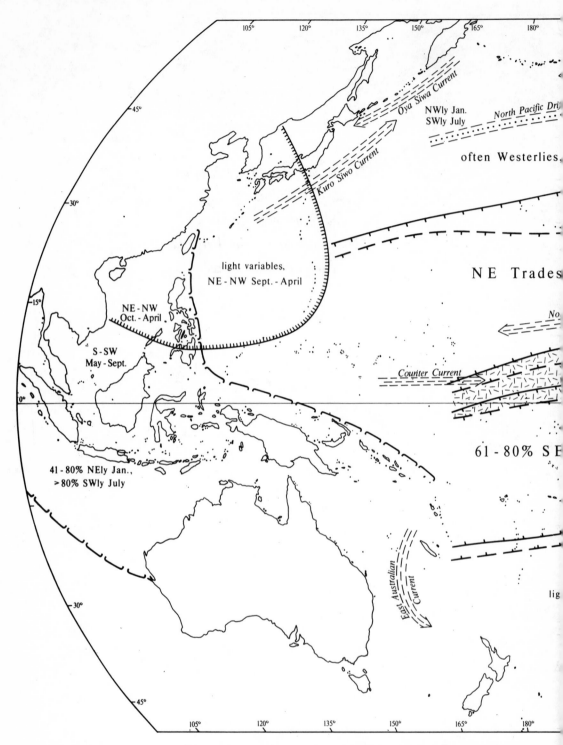

Figure 2. PACIFIC WINDS AND CURRENTS. 1, Approx. limits of Trade Wind belts, April–September; 2, same in October–March; 3, approx. trend of main currents; 4, of main drifts; 5, encloses area dominated by Southeast Asian monsoons; 6, areas of high typhoon risk, especially July–October; 7, belt of calms and light airs (Doldrums).

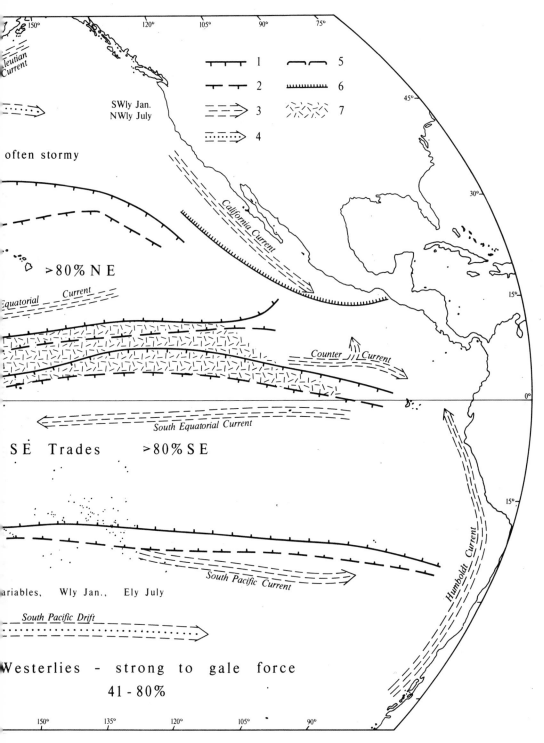

Figures indicate frequency of prevalent wind in total observations, excluding calms. Central meridian 165°W. Compiled from *Fiziko-Geograficheskiy Atlas Mira* (Moscow 1964), Plates 40–1; British Admiralty Charts 5215, 5216. Base map by courtesy of American Geographical Society, New York.

PREFACE

Thus far, with rough and all unable pen,
Our bending author hath pursued the story,
In little room confining mighty men,
Mangling by starts the full course of their glory—

Thus far, and alas, no farther. When I started on this work, some fifteen years ago, I had in my mind's eye half a dozen places between 1894 and 1939 to ring the curtain down with dramatic effect. But my reach has exceeded my grasp by far, and it is obvious that the Pacific *since* Magellan is a misnomer. 'The desire and pursuit of the whole' is but a golden dream. Yet the pursuit is its own reward, and has its delights as well as its drudgeries.

Reviewers have once more been more than generous; to be bracketted with Fernand Braudel is exceedingly flattering to the ego. This last volume posed much more complex problems of organisation than the first two; I can only hope that my attempted solution, separating a relatively austere chronology from more discursive discussions of general problems of the Pacific in the 'contact' phase, has given some coherence to a very multiplex story.

The first two chapters form an attempt to redeem the promise, in the Preface to *The Spanish Lake*, to say more of the great Oceanic diaspora. These chapters were in fact the first of the whole work to be written, but it seemed better to hold them over to the beginning of the present volume, which deals essentially, in one major aspect, with the first really substantial contacts between European and Pacific peoples. They have of course been extensively revised to take into the reckoning recent work on Pacific prehistory and anthropology, which includes some excellent general surveys which, had I waited, would have saved me much arduous searching for scattered articles in sometimes obscure and dusty journals.

But another major aspect of the present volume is geopolitical; once more, this is a history of the Pacific, rather than the Pacific peoples; thought I hope I have said enough of the Islanders to show some empathy. It has therefore seemed unnecessary, even had I the time and space to do so, to go into detail on the rise of the Pomares, Kamehahas, Tubous whose dynasties grew into the more or less viable 'Missionary Kingdoms' of the nineteenth century, in the making of which Euroamericans also played a large part. The flourishing of these political structures lies outside the chronological limits of this volume, and their dynastic detail is the province of more specialised works, on which, as will be apparent, I have drawn heavily for illumination of general themes.

This volume, like *Monopolists and Freebooters*, though to a lesser extent, is double-ended: The general narrative closes at the end of the century, with Vancouver—for twenty years the internecine wars of Europe precluded much activity in the Pacific—but the economic activity of Europeans in the Ocean, small-scale as it was, had a certain momentum of its own. It has to be taken into account in the last two decades of the eighteenth century, but to cut its discussion off at 1800 would be altogether too drastic an amputation. For a variety of reasons, 1825 or thereabouts seems a more appropriate terminus for the economic discussion; by this time Sydney and Honolulu are beginning to stand on their own feet, or at least to become significant, if small and peripheral, components of the global economy.

'My days among the Dead are past'—but over the years they have come alive. The dreamy idealists Mendaña and Quiros, tough ruthless Coen, Dampier of the enquiring gaze, the Forsters trapped between their self-esteem and the harsh realities of shipboard life—these and many others are to me not names in the histories but real people, their elements mixed of greatness and littleness, knowing both despair and hope, servitude and grandeur. I can only hope that for my readers also, I have been able to give them some semblance of life.

And now, like Gibbon at Lausanne, I must say farewell to an old and constant friend, albeit a much-demanding one. My wife has shared this friendship, immeasurably lightened its demands and enhanced its joys, and been an unfailing source of sustenance and strength. No words can adequately express what her support has meant to me over these Pacific years.

O.H.K.S.

Canberra
14 November 1986

ACKNOWLEDGEMENTS

My greatest debt is to The Australian National University, materially for the continuation of a Visiting Fellowship, morally for the interest and encouragement of so many people, from the Chancelry to the Tea Room of the Coombs Building. I must mention particularly Professor R. Gerard Ward, Director of the Research School of Pacific Studies, Professor Anthony Low, the former Vice-Chancellor, and the successive heads of the Department of Pacific and Southeast Asian History, Professor Gavan Daws and Dr Anthony Reid. In that Department, I must mention particularly Honore Forster, Robert Langdon, Dorothy Shineberg and Nicholas Thomas; Julie Gordon, Karen Haines, Elizabeth Kingdom, and Dorothy McIntosh of the clerical staff have been most helpful.

Outside the Department, Dr Peter Bellwood of the Faculties, Professors Jack Golson and Roger Keesing in Pacific Studies, and Dr Barry Smith of Social Sciences have read chapters or sections of this volume; they are not responsible for any remaining errors. Manlio Pancino of the cartographical section in the Department of Human Geography has re-drawn my crude maps with skill and care. The ANU has lost the first fine careless raptures of its early days—naturally given the current freezing economic climate and its own quantitative growth—but it remains a splendid place in which to work as a scholar.

Special thanks are due to Captain H. M. Denham and the Hon. Clive P. Gibson, London, and Herr Peter Rheinberger, Liechtenstein, for the generous permission for Plates III, XII and XVIII.

Outside ANU but within Australia I must thank Dr Alan Frost of La Trobe University; Dr Howard Fry of the James Cook University, Townsville; Messrs Frank Horner and R. J. King of Canberra; and Mme Marie-Laure Marcel, Cultural Counsellor at the French Embassy.

Overseas, courteous replies to requests and inquiries were received from Mr Fergus Clunie, Fiji Museum; Mme Marie-Françoise Demongeot, Bibliothèque Publique, Dijon; Professor John Dunmore, Massey University, Palmerston North, New Zealand; Dr J. R. H. Gibbons, University of the South Pacific, Fiji; Dr Rüdiger Joppien, Kunstgewerbemuseum, Cologne; Major Dr Rui Carita, Funchal, Madeira; Surgeon Vice-Admiral Sir James Watt, London.

I have had always courteous assistance from the staffs of the following Libraries: in Australia, the ANU and National Libraries in Canberra, the Mitchell and the New South Wales Libraries in Sydney; and in the United States, the Library of the University of California, Riverside Campus, and the Australian National Gallery.

Lastly, it is becoming, and also a great pleasure, to express my gratitude to my most meticulous of editors, Pat Croft. Our friendship has only strengthened through the stresses of three volumes.

CONTENTS

MAPS

PLATES

PRELIMINARY DATA

1. BIBLIOGRAPHICAL

References

For a work cited more than once, the full title, with place and date of publication, is given at first citation in each chapter, with a short title in brackets: J. R. Forster, *Observations made during a Voyage round the World* (London 1778) [*Observations*]. The original date of reprinted works, if not given in the text, is indicated in the notes, but where several places of publication appear on a title page, only the first is normally shown. It is worth noting that when the place of publication is Berkeley, this usually implies the University of California Press; Amsterdam, N. Israel; Harmondsworth, Penguin or Pelican.

Occasionally a very cumbersome title or sub-title has been slightly shortened, and in journal articles sub-titles are omitted when they seem to add nothing.

Abbreviations

One work is so often cited that it is referred to by editor's name and volume number only:

Beaglehole   J. C. Beaglehole, *The Journals of Captain James Cook on his Voyages of Discovery*, Hakluyt Society Extra Series 34–7, Cambridge:

I.   *The Voyage of the* Endeavour, *1768–1771* (1955, reprint with addenda and corrigenda 1968)
II.   *The Voyage of the* Resolution *and* Adventure, *1772–1775* (1961, reprint 1969)
III.   *The Voyage of the* Resolution *and* Discovery, *1776–1780* (1967)
IV.   *The Life of Captain James Cook* (London 1974)

Abbreviations for periodicals and series are self-explanatory except for:

HS 1st (2nd) Ser.   Publications of the Hakluyt Society, First Series 1847–99, Second Series 1899+ (serial number also given)
JPH   *Journal of Pacific History*
JPS   *Journal of the Polynesian Society*

Chartered Companies:

EIC	East India Company
RAC	Russian–American Company
RCF	Real Compãnía de Filipinas
SSC	South Sea Company
VOC	Vereenigde Oost-Indische Compagnie

Provenance of periodicals:

Great Circle	Dept of History, University of Western Australia, Nedlands, WA 2009
Historical Studies	Dept of History, University of Melbourne, Parkville, Vic. 3052
Jnl Pacific History	Dept of Pacific and Southeast Asian History, RS Pacific Studies, Australian National University, Box 4 GPO, Canberra, ACT 2601
Jnl Polynesian Soc.	Dept of Anthropology, University of Auckland, Private Bag, Auckland, New Zealand
Pacific Studies.	Institute for Polynesian Studies, Brigham Young University—Hawaiian Campus, Laie, Hawaii 96762, USA

Other bibliographical points

Translations are by myself, except when quoted from previously Englished works, as acknowledged in the notes or made clear by context.

It seems impossible to compile a short select bibliography which would not be invidious, and unless it were expanded into a *catalogue raisonné* of inordinate length a full alphabetical listing of sources gives equal weight to a sketchy article and a serious and substantial study. The gathering of all the most significant sources for Bligh, for example, in one or two lengthy notes, with comments, seems to me more useful than spreading them over several pages of an alphabetical list.

Only rarely, and then by reason of the non-availability of the specific works, have quotations from other authors been accepted unchecked. I have indicated by whom I have been led to a particular work; for any inadvertent omission of such acknowledgement I offer my apologies.

2. GENERAL

Dates

Dates are New Style except when dealing with Russian activities. Times for shipboard events are in 'ship time', the day running for twenty-four hours from noon on the previous day by civil time; thus from midnight to noon on 1 April is the first of the month by both ship and civil time, but at noon ship time moves to 2 April.

Money

Very roughly indeed, for the period of this volume, £1 = 4½ dollars (Spanish or American) = 20 French livres. Given the great inflation since the eighteenth century, it is pointless to attempt the conversion of sums of money into modern equivalents. Monetary figures given in this volume are given for what they are worth, and that is as contemporary indices or orders of magnitude.

Non-English names and terms

Spellings of place-names usually conform to those in *Webster's Geographical Dictionary* or are those of my sources. Accents are given for Spanish names except those in such common use in English that this seems pedantic; they are of course retained in quotations, personal names, and titles of books or articles.

In Russian names, the termination *–ov* is used for persons, but for places I follow the Hungarian 1:2,500,000 World Map which uses *–of*: thus Aleksandr Baranov but Baronof Island.

Terms such as *marai, tapu, mana* are italicised at first appearance, thereafter in Roman. Their meaning is given (sometimes by context) at first appearance or main treatment, and this can be found from the Index.

Polynesian spellings

Modern forms of Polynesian names are used, giving those of contemporary accounts where this seems desirable for clarity. Glottal stops are omitted: 'The hamzah, represented by an inverted comma and indicating a glottal closure, has been omitted . . . because it is almost impossible to be consistent in its use'—K. Luomala, *Maui-of-a-thousand-tricks* (Honolulu 1949), 15; for an example, see note 42 to Chapter 7 below. The stop is retained in quotations from other authors.

There is one important exception: it is convenient to distinguish between the Hawaiian Islands as a group or a sociopolitical entity, and the main island, and this is easily done by referring to that island as Hawai'i.

Changes in place-names

Over the past 170 years, several places have changed their names. It would be absurdly anachronistic to use Guangszhou for Canton; on the other hand, Sandwich Islands for Hawaii seems pedantic, as Cook's name has not been current for a century or so, unlike his New Hebrides. In general I have used eighteenth-century forms, but Australia is used for New Holland and Tasmania for Van Diemen's Land where the context is geographical rather than historical. It may be noted that the Ellice Islands are now Tuvalu; the Gilberts, Kiribati; Ile de France, Mauritius; the New Hebrides, Vanuatu; Palau, Belau.

Shipping tonnages

Before 1773, a ship's tonnage generally meant 'tons burden', much the same as carrying capacity or deadweight tonnage, expressed in units of 40 cu. ft (1.13 m³). Measurement tonnage (length × breadth × depth of hold ÷ 100 or 94) was used in government contracts, and it was not until after compulsory registration of shipping was introduced in 1786 that the old 'tons burden' was completely replaced by measurement or register tons. By 1775 the carrying capacity of a ship would more often than not exceed its measured tonnage. See R. Davis, *The Rise of the English Shipping Industry In the Seventeenth and Eighteenth Centuries* (Newton Abbot 1962), 74–9, 372–3.

Plates

Every effort has been made to trace the owners of the copyright in the plates, but this has not always been possible. Apologies are offered for any inadvertent omissions.

'Photo ANU' in Plate captions indicates that the prints were prepared by RSSS & RSPACS Photographic Unit, Australian National University.

Maps

In this volume the scale changes, and it is unfortunately not possible to show practically every place mentioned in the text on a map, as it was in the first two volumes; I hope that Figure 6 does so for one key area. Perhaps the most handy general map of the Pacific Ocean is that published by the National Geographic Society, Washington, DC, USA, which has insets of the main island groups.

Special usages

'Oceania' (Fig.3) refers to Polynesia, Micronesia and Melanesia except for interior New Guinea.

'Straits' unless otherwise stated or clearly implied means the Straits of Magellan; 'Cape', the Cape of Good Hope; 'Islands' (except for named groups such as the Falkland Islands), those of Oceania. 'Galleon' or 'Galleons' when given an initial capital refers to those on the Manila-Acapulco run, as distinct from galleons in general.

Strictly speaking the name 'Juan Fernández' is that of the group of Chilean islands comprising Mas-a-Tierra ('Nearer land'), Santa Clara, and Mas Afuera ('Further out'), of which only the first is inhabited; but in normal usage, both ancient and modern, the term unless qualified always signifies Mas-a-Tierra alone, and is so used here.

A distinction is made between the shores of oceans or seas and the coasts of islands or landmasses.

'Discovery' refers to the first sighting and recording by and for Europeans; this is a matter of convenience, and is not meant to detract from the undoubted priority of Islanders in all but a tiny handful of the Ocean's multitudinous islands.

Chapter 1

THE PEOPLING OF THE PACIFIC

You yoke the Aleutian sealrocks with the lava
and coral sowings that flower the south,
Over your flood the life that sought the sunrise
faces ours that followed the evening star,
The long migrations meet across you . . .

The Oceanian realms

The vast span of the island-studded Pacific has been conventionally divided, like Gaul, into three parts. Polynesia was so named by de Brosses 'because of the multitude of islands which it includes'; the name came into English with Callender's plagiarism of him, *Terra Australis Cognita*, in 1766. Early in the nineteenth century it was firmly established, along with Malte-Brun's Oceania for the whole expanse of the South Pacific and the analogous coinages of Micronesia, from the tiny size of most of its component islands, and Melanesia, from the prevailing black colour of its people (Fig.3).[1] By the end of the century this usage had hardened into a view that definable areas were inhabited by discrete peoples whom some thought to represent 'the three major divisions of mankind, the Mongoloid in Micronesia, the Negroid in Melanesia in oceanic guise, the Caucasoid in Polynesia in modified form.'[2]

Since 1900 an immense amount of research has shown, as usual, that the reality is not so simple as the schema; there are overlaps and blendings, particularly on the marches of Melanesia and Polynesia. The diversities within 'Melanesia' are such that some authorities see the term as little more than an expedient catch-all which should be scrapped, and while the general cultural unity of Polynesia is generally recognised, it is now usual to see within it two sub-entities, East and West, the division lying between Samoa and the Society Islands, with Hawaii in the eastern sector. It would be strange if there were no such differentiation over so wide a space so fragmented into island groups. Conversely, there is increasing archaeological and linguistic evidence for an early 'community of culture' transcending the traditional frontier with Melanesia.

Robinson Jeffers, 'Continent's End', in *Roan Stallion* (1924);
quoted courtesy of Random House, Inc., New York.

1

With these modifications, however, the old tripartite division remains a convenient breakdown of the vast Oceanian area, and in some aspects corresponds to broad differences in social structure and *mores*, even in these days of almost complete Christianisation and the recognition of common interests in the various agencies which link the newly independent states of Melanesia and Polynesia.

Theories of origins

'Origins', not origin; paticularly in the border zone between eastern New Guinea and Fiji, race, language, and archaeological elements interdigitate and overlap. We may begin with the actual distribution of languages, basically divided into Austronesian tongues and 'others'. These others occupy all of New Guinea except for some Austronesian coastal pockets, and extend eastwards into the Santa Cruz group, between the Solomons and Vanuatu; altogether there are over 700 of them. They antedate the Austronesian languages, their first entry into New Guinea having taken place some 15,000 years ago.[3]

The Austronesian languages were once called Malayo–Polynesian, since they are found in Malaysia and the islands from Taiwan to Madagascar. Austronesian speakers are generally believed to have reached northwestern New Guinea about 3500 B.C., but had relatively little impact along the northern coast, perhaps because there were already solidly entrenched Papuan horticultural population already there.[4] Apart from one enclave in the extreme west, Austronesian languages in New Guinea are confined to pockets in the southeast and adjacent islands. The area between the southeastern Solomons and Fiji is the domain of a group of languages known as Eastern Oceanic, and from its parent stock, about 2000 or 3000 years ago, there broke off the great group of Polynesian languages, which cover everything east of Fiji to Hawaii, Easter Island and New Zealand. There are also a few outliers, reverse eddies, as far west as Kapingamarangi, halfway between New Ireland and the Carolines.

Over this immense area, enormously greater than that of Europe or Australia, but, excluding New Zealand, with only about 115,000 km² of dry land parcelled out into hundreds of islands, the resemblances in speech are so strong that Horatio Hale, an early but still well-regarded observer, uses 'Polynesian Languages' and 'Polynesian dialects' interchangeably; Cook's people in 1778 were astonished to find that at Hawaii they could trade in the same language as at Tahiti, 3200 km to the south, and they had a similar experience in New Zealand.[5]

The massive island of New Guinea stands apart. Its peoples display an astonishing variety of physical types as of languages, and their nearer origins in Southeast Asia have never been doubted. The first entry of Australoid people into New Guinea probably took place long before that of the Papuan speakers, probably during the late Pleistocene glaciation,

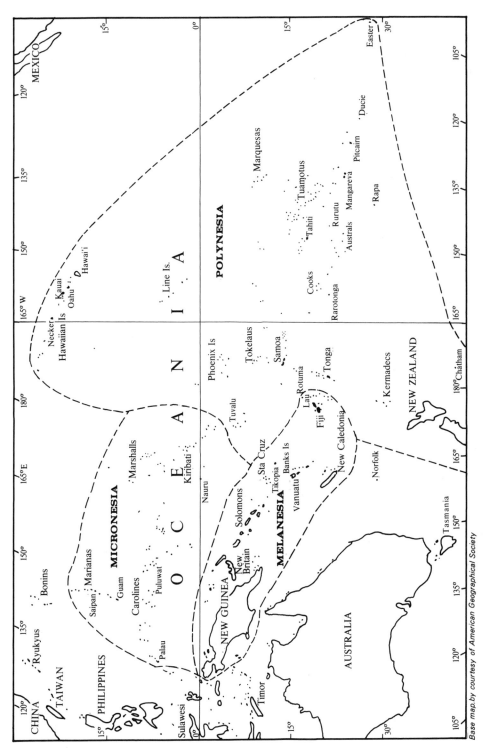

Base map by courtesy of American Geographical Society

Figure 3. OCEANIA.

when vast masses of oceanic water were locked up in the ice-caps, leaving only relatively minor water barriers between the islands. Nevertheless, since the Sunda Shelf between Malaya and Borneo and the Sahul Shelf between Australia and New Guinea were not joined, these hunter-gatherers were probably the first blue-water navigators. They had to cross a minimum of 70 km of open sea, thousands of years before Cyprus, only 80 km from Asia Minor, was settled. This 'crossing of the major biogeographic barrier of Wallace's Line marked mankind's first real step into the Pacific'; settlement gradually spread until the stage was set for the Austronesian expansion into Oceania itself, beginning some 4000 or 5000 years ago.[6]

From the beginnings of European contact, the riddle of the Islanders had fascinated seamen and scholars, the lay and the learned alike: how had men and women reached these spots of land, so remote that they ought to have been empty, but were not? The first serious discussions took place in the great cabin of Cook's *Endeavour* over two centuries ago.[7] The orthodox consensus ever since has been for an origin in Southeast Asia, with migration or drift more or less directly into the Pacific. Fundamental to the argument is the strong affinity of Polynesian with languages spoken from Madagascar to Taiwan; this has never been seriously challenged. The net effect of recent research has been to confirm the traditional view, with modifications; but within it there is room for divergences, nor, on other than the linguistic front, has it been unchallenged.

There have been many aberrant propositions, offshoots of the classical schema or of the grandiose extreme Diffusionist view that all things civilised were born of the Nile, to be carried by the Children of the Sun ever eastward, across the Old World and the Ocean to the Mexican and Andean plateaus. The most remarkable of the earlier students of the problem was Horatio Hale of the great Wilkes expedition of 1838–42. Hale based himself mainly on linguistics, but treated oral genealogies and traditions respectfully but not uncritically. He anticipated glotto-chronology and on the settlement sequence within Polynesia his arguments often coincided with contemporary views. Unfortunately his sobriety in the handling of traditions was not always followed by his successors.

Although Sir Peter Buck, as well known by his Maori name Te Rangi Hiroa, naturally attached much weight to the traditions of his maternal ancestors, he did so with more finesse than some European weavers of hypotheses. His books, especially *Vikings of the Sunrise*, gave a large and genial view of the ancestral achievements, though one too well argued and too well based on the distributional facts—as then known—to be dismissed as simply pious ethnocentrism. His major divergence from orthodoxy was in his insistence that the entry was probably by Micronesia, not Melanesia; in which, however, he was followed by Alexander Spoehr in the 1950s and by William Howells today.[8]

Some of the direct challenges to the standard view were mere fanciful curiosities: theologically inspired linkages between the Maori and the Old Testament Israelites; Fornander's elaborate derivation from a Middle Eastern 'Cushite-Arabian' civilisation'; the more precise Mormon thesis that in 58 B.C. Hawaii was settled by Amerinds springing from a Hebrew colony in Mesoamerica; appeals to a mythical lost continent, argued soberly by J. A. Moerenhout in the 1830s and by Jules Garnier forty years later, but fantastically in our century by people who have not their excuse of writing before the geological absurdity of such a notion was established.

Not precisely a challenge but rather a very complex refinement with a drastic change of emphasis is Heine-Geldern's theory, based largely on a study of adze-types, which places the initiation of what were to become Oceanic cultures in China, with migrations from advanced bases in Japan and Taiwan by the Micronesian route and through Melanesia, with many reverse eddies. There is increasing interest in possible Chinese influences and links with the North Pacific.[9] And there is an intriguing hint, based on genetic data, that 'some of the old sites in South America may have originated from descendants of people from the Pacific.'[10]

The debate must be not so much whether trans-Pacific contacts were made but whether they were of sufficient scale or continuity as to make a significant input into pre-Colomban cultures. There is no doubt that through the ages drift voyages from eastern Asia brought many people to northwestern America, and there are many parallels, some remarkably close, between Sinic and Mesoamerican cultures; but could these chance arrivals have included so many highly-skilled specialists (with their tools), in a vast range of techniques, as would be needed? Yet the evidence for *some* influence seems irrefutable. Far more widely publicised is the challenge presented by Thor Heyerdahl.[11] It is difficult to distil the essence of Heyerdahl's views from his enormous and sometimes slightly archaic agglomeration of evidence, but the core may be put thus: the basic elements in Oceanic culture are 'an earlier substratum from Peru', deliberate explorers, who were overlaid by people from the Pacific Northwest of America, originally from Asia but driven from their new homes by tribal warfare and carried by winds and currents to Polynesia, in the first instance Hawaii.[12] The second of these hypotheses (which has become rather obscured by Heyerdahl's fixation on Easter Island) was adumbrated long ago, by William Ellis, and may have its point of origin in Fr Martínez de Zuñiga's *Historia de las Islas Filipinas* of 1803.[13]

Heyerdahl has one indubitably strong argument: in relevant latitudes, winds and currents favour westwards crossings of the Pacific and disfavour eastwards ones. Polynesian visits to South America, returning for instance

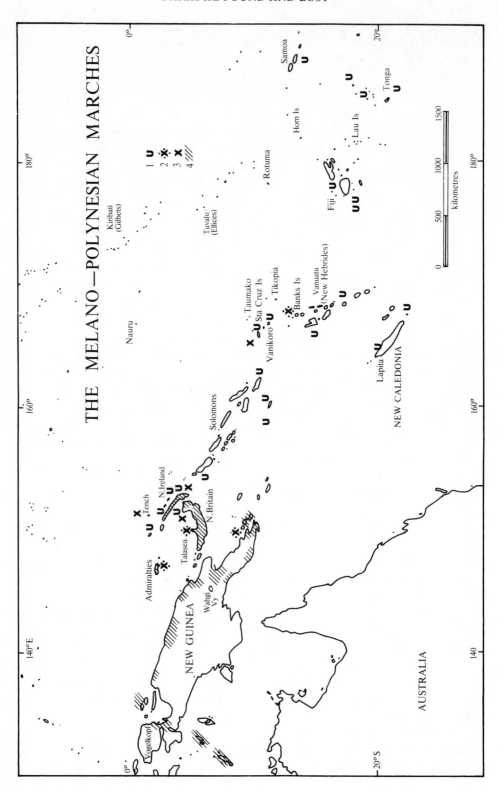

THE MELANO–POLYNESIAN MARCHES

with the sweet potato, are thus inherently very improbable. He is abundantly right in stressing time of transit (varying with winds and currents) against mere flat map distance, though he rather forgets this when hypothesising return voyages.

He and others have demonstrated that balsa rafts of considerable burden, with centre-boards and sails, are of good sea-keeping capacity and capable of some windward sailing, though his crews were very small.[14] But while he scores some telling points, both negative and positive, one cannot help feeling that by and large his arguments fall short of scientific logic. It seems for instance very odd to cite the absence of pottery in both the Pacific Northwest and Polynesia as suggesting a link between them, while positing a considerable influence in Polynesia by Andean cultures with their great ceramic tradition.[15]

On the whole it seems fair to say that while his theories, modified for a different point of entry, might give acceptable solutions for a few distributional problems, there are more in which his views are inadequate or beside the point; in total his arguments are less convincing than those based on the archaeology and linguistics of Polynesia itself. It is to Heyerdahl's very great credit that he has himself published papers by co-workers some of which tend to undermine his own views. His daring appeal to adventure, physical and intellectual, has opened our minds to possibilities where we saw only impossibilities.

Some problems of distributions

Recent research on biogeographical distributions leaves a number of questions very open, but—with the important exception of the sweet potato—it does not lend much support to the idea of trans-Pacific contacts on a very significant scale.[16]

An important question is whether certain cultivated plants are indigenous or of ancient establishment in the Islands, or are of recent introductions. Cultivated cottons could well have resulted from post-Columban contacts, but there are puzzling occurrences of 'wild' cottons on isolated Wake Island and Hawaii, though these may have been accidentally introduced by Europeans. In the Marquesas cotton of some sort 'was established before any possible introduction by European missionaries' (but does this include Mendaña?), possibly however one of the 'wild' forms which were pretty certainly growing on several Polynesian islands 'long before the eighteenth century visitors.'[17] Gourds were known in Southeast Asia long

◀ *Figure 4.* THE MELANO-POLYNESIAN MARCHES. 1, Lapita pottery; 2, obsidian sources (note that in Santa Cruz obsidian came not only from nearby Banks Is. but also from Talasea and the Admiralties); 4, enclaves of Austronesian languages. Compiled from maps in P. Bellwood, *Man's Conquest of the Pacific*, and J. D. Jennings (ed.), *The Prehistory of Polynesia*.

before the Pacific migrations, but the *Lagenaria* species was used in Mesoamerica also long before human beings arrived in Polynesia, so that
Heyerdahl may be warranted in keeping it on his list of possible American
imports. The coconut, however, with whose supposed American origin
he makes much play, has been found in fossil form on the north coast
of New Guinea and on Aneityum, Vanuatu, in both cases dating from
about 5000 years ago. An Indo-Pacific origin seems indicated, and from
a careful study of the viability of the nuts in sea-water R. G. Ward
concluded that the coconut could hardly have crossed the Pacific unaided
by man. This is perhaps a hint of a possible contact, almost certainly
one-way if at all, from Oceania to Mesoamerica.[18]

There is little difference of opinion as to the ancestral home of *Ipomea
batata*, the sweet potato, without which 'the agricultural exploitation which
accompanied the last phase of Polynesian expansion could not have been
effected'.[19] Almost all authorities hold that it is definitely an American
plant. Douglas Yen, perhaps the most eminent, thinks that it came to
Polynesia possibly as early as A.D. 400, but to Asia by the Manila Galleons
and to western Melanesia from Brazil, at Portuguese hands. Donald Brand
argues strongly that it reached India via Portugal in the earliest sixteenth
century and was soon spread by Asian traders into Indonesia, reaching
the Pacific later on; this view faces insuperable archaeological objection.[20]
A review by Patricia O'Brien supports Yen in his first two propositions
but suggests that the spread into Melanesia was from the east.[21] Natural
spread, by drifting or bird-carried seeds, has also been suggested.

Important for the argument for the antiquity of *Ipomea* in the Pacific
is its adaptation, in the New Guinea Highlands and in New Zealand,
to marginal climatic conditions. In relatively cool New Zealand the crop
changed from a perennial into an annual, necessitating the development
of storage techniques; pits which can hardly have been for anything but
storing sweet potatoes are found there from A.D. 1100–1200.[22] This seems
conclusive against an introduction after 1492.

Ironically, all the three authors named above agree that the similarity
of the Maori name *kumara* (and variants) to the Peruvian *cumar* is not
evidence, but fortuitous; this has been something of a hallowed linkage
in much writing on the problem.[23] Nevertheless, Brand himself 'would
not be greatly surprised if the plant had come from South America 'a
few centuries earlier', and *Ipomea batata* holds its place as the firmest
evidence for a significant cultural importation from South America. But
again, unless contacts were few and fleeting, it is more than surprising
that maize (much easier to transfer over long distances) should not have
been transported also.[24] Incas with no corn, no pots?

Whatever extraneous elements may have entered, there can be little
or no doubt that the general cast of the agriculture that developed in
the Melano-Polynesian hearth resembles that of the shifting swidden

cultivators of Southeast Asia. It was strongly dependent on fruits and on roots and tubers such as taro, yam, and kumara, and presumably its initiators or early carriers were east of Wallace's Line before rice farming came to dominate the lowlands of Southeast Asia. Thence came also pigs, dogs and chickens. But time and adaptations to differing local environments led to many local variations, some of a remarkably intensive nature.[25]

Human biology has also been called upon to testify to Oceanic origins. At one time blood groups were thought to offer promising leads, and to indicate migration from America. But the populations were very small, many of them isolated for long periods, so that random genetic drift had full scope, and even the proponents of serological studies advised much caution in drawing conclusions from often confusing data.[26]

The same factors of small, often minute, size and isolation mean that a mere handful of new arrivals could have large demographic effects. Robert Langdon has put forward a convincing case, based on the finding of early sixteenth century cannon in the Tuamotus, for the survival of castaways from Loaysa's ship *San Lesmes*, lost in 1526; these men could have contributed to the light pigmentation of some people seen by Quiros in the Tuamotus and by Wallis in Tahiti.[27] The great eighteenth century explorations, still more the beachcombing phase *circa* 1790–1825, gave ample opportunity for blood mixture, or contamination if that term be preferred.[28] 'Purity of blood' is likely to be a slippery concept.

Highly sophisticated techniques, baffling to the layman, are now being applied to the regional populations. Although 'The weakness of genetic analysis is that... only the contemporary genetic profile is observed' and hence it can say nothing on the timing of ethnic inputs, it does pinpoint elements in the present populations which would otherwise go unobserved. Some of the linkages indicated may seem rather obvious, as that the Fijian profile includes both Melanesian and Polynesian elements, but others are more subtle and surprising, for example the virtual absence of a Polynesian genetic influence in Nauru, where the links are Melanesian and Filipino.[29] No one group of studies 'holds the key' to the riddles of human occupance of Oceania, but we may expect that future genetic explorations will prove highly relevant.

The archaeological record: Micronesia to West Polynesia

The last thirty or forty years have seen striking advances in the archaeology of Australia and the South Pacific. Interpretation is very vulnerable to change as new sites are excavated, but there is one objective certainty: thanks to radiocarbon and other dating techniques, as far east as Tonga and Samoa we can now think in terms of three or four millenia rather than ten or twelve centuries; in the west, much more.

In the eastern Melanesian islands, Fiji and western Polynesia, the earliest archaeological evidence is often associated with a type of pottery known as Lapita ware (Fig.4). It has decorated motifs which show affinities with those of pottery in Indochina and Taiwan, though this has been discounted.[30] The intervening Micronesian area is less known archaeologically, but the pottery, and shell artefacts from Marianas, may indicate a connection. This might seem to support Howells's revival of the Micronesian entry, but the data are scant indeed. Obviously, the reproach of no archaeological depth is particularly applicable to the tiny scraps of land, often no more than a lens of sand three or four metres thick, on the atolls which form the majority of Micronesian islands. Howells rather neatly turns some of the marked discontinuities, for instance the absence of pigs, by appeal to the atoll ecology, an exceedingly narrow base for agriculture. His hypothesis is summed up in four seductive maps, but has failed to gain general acceptance.[31]

A recent study suggests a new time-scale for the initial expansion into the Pacific.[32] Owing to the rapid post-glacial rise of sea level as the ice-caps melted, beginning about 18,000 years ago, all Lapita coastal sites more than 4000 years old would have been submerged. The inference is for much earlier occupation of eastern Melanesia, when water-gaps were narrow and many present islands were part of much larger land-masses. The transgressing waters meant diminishing land resources and enforced migrations, with a turn to marine resources and increased maritime skills.

The positive evidence for such earlier occupation is slight, naturally so since much of the relevant area is submerged. The Misisil cave in New Britain was certainly inhabited 11,000 years ago or more; there are the mysterious 'tumuli' of the New Caledonian Ile des Pins, apparently man-made and possible 8000–10,000 years old. Most intriguing is a report, as yet unconfirmed, of fire-blackening and arranged coral blocks on the floor of an under-water cave in Tuvalu at a depth of 40–45 metres; from the rate of rise of sea level, if this is confirmed as evidence of human occupance it must be at least 8000 years old.[33] This may be the beginning of a serious revision of accepted views.

This must be left unresolved. In keeping with this new slant, however, but perhaps paradoxically in relation to older views, evidence of human occupation in New Guinea points to settlement in the Highlands much earlier than on the coast. By about 7000 B.C. people in the Wahgi Valley had developed an elaborate system of water-control ditches which indicate an agriculture based on taro; ground stone tools date from around 8000 B.C.[34] This remarkably intensive development is not matched on the coast, nor of course in Australia, where the antiquity of man has been pushed back to 40,000 years at the minimum. The skilled gardeners of the Highlands were isolated behind some of the most savagely-dissected and jungly terrain in the world, and there is a discontinuity with 'Island Melanesia'.

Lapita has been seen 'as the founding culture in much of Island Melanesia, as it is in Polynesia'[35] though there is debate as to how much of it is an indigenous growth and how much derived from Southeast Asia. The idea that the culture was one of atoll reef-fishers and gatherers, 'strand-loopers', has fallen into disfavour, and there is a tendency to stress the Lapita people's capacity as seafarers and traders. On Watom Island, off New Britain, Lapita ware is associated with flakes of obsidian from the volcanic peninsula of Talasea on the bigger island, and Talasea obsidian has been found with Lapita ware on Gawa in the Santa Cruz group; from the Admiralty Islands obsidian reached Malo in Vanuatu. Obsidian flakes from Talasea have been found on the Ile des Pins. This involves transport for a total distance of 2700 km, with several stretches of open sea, over two millenia ago.[36]

In Fiji and New Caledonia the Lapita ceramic style was succeeded, in the last four or five centuries B.C., by pottery with incised decoration, and that again by plainer forms, which in these areas survived until European contact. So much seems agreed, but in Tonga and Samoa (where Lapita-like sherds were found in a now submerged site) the art of pottery died out, perhaps about the beginning of our era; the pots seen by early European visitors to Tonga were imported from Fiji.[37]

There are many gaps in the record, and conflicting interpretations of it. The littoral orientation of Lapita culture was overstressed; there was an increasing, though far from complete, trend to agriculture, paralleled by decline in pottery and shell-middens. It is consistent with such an evolution that inland sites are found early in the Samoan record, and shell-middens are few or absent, though some may have been lost by submergence.[38]

That the Polynesians sprang from these marches with Melanesia seems in some sort the consensus. Debate will persist, on broad outlines as well as details, but it may be that the Polynesians did not so much *come* thither as *become* there; the general trend of recent research is to shuffle aside 'races' and 'migrations' as formal entities, in a mode which it is not fanciful to call Existentialist.[39] From this hearth or melting-pot, however, they spread out over the vast Oceanic distances.

The Matter of Hawaiki

So much for West Polynesia; but this still leaves the Matter of Hawaiki—the dispersal into the uttermost eastern isles. The word 'Matter' is given an initial capital because the story is enshrined in a great cycle of epic and romance, a *gesta* vaster in range and more marvellous in event than medieval Europe's Matters of Troy, of Arthur, or of Charlemagne.

It is impossible in these pages to give any adequate impression of the beauty and power of the Polynesian myths: the begetting of the gods by the coition of Rangi, Sky-father, with Papa, Earth-mother, and of how Tane, god of trees and birds, with mighty effort broke the close embrace of his parents, lifted the sky, and gave to all created beings light, air, room to move; the begetting of men and women by Tane on the bodies of his Earth-formed-maid and their daughter the Dawn-maid.[40] More mundane in one sense, no less poetic in another, are the traditions of the voyagers from ancestral Hawaiki, who 'fished for islands' until in the far south Maui hauled up the giant sting-ray which we call the North Island of New Zealand.[41]

The chants of these seafarers, interspersed through their sagas, are unfortunately as obscure as historical data as they are noble as poetry. Here again it is impossible to represent adequately the permutations of scholarly and unscholarly exegesis; for example

> Let us, therefore, have done with these uncertain, unsatisfactory, and futile attempts of men to settle America by Behring's Straits, and let us follow the right way, which is God's own way, [from Malaya] by the Isles of the Southern Pacific Ocean [to] Copiapo, in Chile, a few hundred years after the deluge.[42]

Sublime certitude!

As with Polynesian languages, so with the legends: there are strong family resemblances between the various recensions, but naturally details of names, genealogies, events, differ from group to group of the Islands. Perhaps the most developed voyaging tradition is the Maori version as presented by Peter Buck; as a record of events it is now in disrepute, but may stand as reflecting a widely-held popular view. While not discounting the role of sporadic small parties, under younger sons of chiefs impelled by domestic discords to leave their country for that country's good, and setting out with a hope rather than a conviction of happy landings, Buck places much more reliance on formally organised expeditions with definite goals, using sailing directions from earlier reconnaissances.

After the legendary catch of Maui—surely the *ne plus ultra* of anglers' stories—the actual discovery of New Zealand is ascribed to Kupe, who about A.D. 925 chased a squid into the remote south and returned to his central Polynesian base with sailing directions for the new land. The grand event in these traditionary chronicles is the coming of the 'Great Fleet' in the twelfth century, following Kupe's directions and bringing wives and cultivated plants; the canoes are listed by name in a splendid poem. They chose separate stretches of coast and parcelled out the land. One canoe was first blown to the Kermadecs—uninhabited when Euro-peans came upon them, but with traces of Polynesian visits.[43]

A common feature in all these traditions is reference to an ancestral home, called Hawaiki in Maori but elsewhere, in accordance with regular phonetic rules, styled Avaiki, Havai'i, Havaiki, Hawai'i, Savai'i: 'It will be found that this is, so to speak, the key-word which unlocks the mystery of the Polynesian navigations.'[44] These are the optimistic words of Horatio Hale in 1846; but, as Percy Smith remarked,

> With laudable pride and affection, with a strong belief in the sacredness, the beauty, the prolificness of the Fatherland, the Polynesians have carried this great name Hawaiki in their wanderings, and have applied it to many of their later homes.[45]

Smith goes on to give a list (incomplete) of eighteen possible original homes, beginning with Java or Jawa and even hinting at Ava in Burma.

Obviously and naturally, the name meant different things in different places. To Buck, Hawaiki is definitely Raiatea, to Sharp equally definitely Samoa, and so on. For Smith the trail lay westwards to India; Heyerdahl after asserting, without evidence, that 'the known Polynesian migratory period of about 1200–1300 A.D. was principally centred just in Hawaii', goes on to fix Hawaiki with deadly precision in Hakai Straits, British Columbia... though later in the same volume he seems to opt for a Maori Hawaiki in Peru. A comment is apt: '[Elsdon] Best credited the Maori with memories of the snow-crested Himalayas... memories which Heyerdahl transfers to the flanks of the Andes.'[46]

The Matter of Hawaiki forms a magnificent body of poetry which, like the Matter of Arthur's Britain, has a historical referend—if only it could be found. It cannot be taken too literally (that way academic madness lies) but there seems a substantiality within it that cannot be too lightly dismissed. We shall return to the navigational problems involved in this maritime expansion.

The archaeological record: East Polynesia

Kindred as East and West Polynesia are, they have distinct cultural kits: 'One-piece shell fishhooks, tanged adzes, stone pounders, and stone *marae* with courts and platforms: all these things are absent in islands to the west'.[47] Our old guide Lapita has faltered; indeed, east of Samoa there is no pottery at all except for a total (to 1980) of twelve sherds in the Marquesas.[48] This is puzzling, and not least on Heyerdahl's theory of origins in South America, where the cultures were so intensely ceramic. Even if the potter's art withered away for lack of raw material, one might surely expect some trace of ceramic imports to survive—at least, or not least, on Easter Island, in the unlikely event that it was the point of entry.

Although 'populous migrations' are now not usually accepted, the general view still looks to one island group as the primary dispersal centre for East Polynesian culture, rather than 'a tremendously complicated network of voyages... each diffusing culture traits'. That does not rule out local inter-island or inter-group contact by both genuinely purposive and accidental voyages, for which there is much evidence. But voyagers who fetched up on a sizeable populated island would as a rule arrive with much poorer material equipment than their 'hosts', and so might not exercise much cultural influence—if indeed they received a friendly welcome. Lack of suitable resources to use new techniques, the hold of existing values and satisfactions, ethnocentrism—such factors could influence the acceptance or rejection of both material and intangible elements; modern proponents of 'development' are familiar with traditional reluctances (not always without sound reason) to doing things in the most 'efficient' way.[49]

Although the Polynesians 'came into' the groups east of Tonga, instead of 'becoming' there, it does not follow that the first area settled was the primary dispersal point for East Polynesia. Radiocarbon dates in themselves do not say much, if anything, about process, and must always be interpreted in the stratigraphical context. The main contenders for the primary position (whether or not we still like to call it Hawaiki) seem to be the Societies and the Marquesas, and the tendency seems to be in favour of the latter. Speaking very roughly, the general view of modern archaeologists is of advance from a forward base in the Tonga-Samoa area, settled by 1100–1000 B.C., to the Marquesas by A.D. 300 and thence to Easter Island and Hawaii a century or two later, and to the Societies by A.D. 600, whence New Zealand was reached by A.D. 800. There may well have been secondary dispersal from the Societies later, to Hawaii and again New Zealand.

The arguments depend upon the meticulous analysis of differing assemblages of cultural property, from fishhooks to *marae* (temple complexes), from phonemes to myths. There is no consensus, except the commonsense one that much more must be done before a true consensus is reached. The apparent priority of the Marquesas, for example, may in reality reflect the environmental contrast between that group and the Societies, which may give the former the edge in preservation of readily interpretable evidence. The reefless cliffed coasts of the Marquesas, with rock-shelters and dunes at the mouths of deep narrow valleys, have decently stratified sites, so that 'Early radiocarbon dates and excellent typological sequences are by no means hard to find.' In total the Societies may have yielded many more artefacts, but there are few well-stratified sites, since the long-settled coastal strips have been continually disturbed, making the archaeological structure much harder to interpret. And everywhere 'Many artefacts exist in museums, but without context.'[50]

K. P. Emory bases himself largely on the marae,[51] stone religious structures, basically arrangements of courts and terraces leading to a high platform (*ahu* or *tuahu*). Some are truly imposing; in Tahiti Wallis saw one being built with a court 81 by 112 metres and an 11-step pyramid

Plate I. THE GREAT MARAI IN TAHITI. The length of the base was 82 metres, of the topmost tier 56, height about 16. From J. Wilson, *A Missionary Voyage to the South Pacific Ocean*, 1799. Photo ANU.

over 15 metres high; 'the size of marae was the constant index of political standing.'[52] In Hawaii and the Marquesas the variety of arrangement of the basic members is almost bewildering. Marae are found in most of Polynesia, but not in New Zealand, where the name was used for the village green or plaza, though there are a few sacred sites, marked by unworked stones or slabs but significantly known as tuahu.

Of particular interest is the Hawaiian Necker Island, 480 km WNW of Kauai. On this barren scrap, only 1.2 km long, Emory found the remains of no fewer than thirty-five marae of Tuamotuan-Tahitian type. The island could hardly support many people permanently, and the suggestion is of deliberate visits, possibly pilgrimages, 960 km there and back and mostly out of sight of land, with a tiny landfall.[53] Yet, though the Necker marae, as well as Hawaiian tradition, point back to Tahiti, there are fourteen stone images in Hawaii which point to the Marquesas.

This example may serve as an illustration of the complexities in the quest for a primary dispersal centre or 'homeland'. The question must

still be left open, but there is no doubt as to the ultimate receiving ends:
New Zealand, Hawaii, Easter Island.

New Zealand

Basic to cultural evolution in New Zealand are the geographical factors
of large size and cool climate. The North Island alone has more land
below 300 metres above sea level than all the rest of Polynesia plus Fiji
and New Caledonia; and although from about A.D. 1000 to 1600 the
climate was warmer than it is today, several staple plants of the Islands
could not be grown—breadfruit, coconut, bananas. Yam and taro had
a footing, but the sweet potato (kumara) was the main cultivated crop.
Perhaps as important as any cultivated food was the indigenous bracken
(*Pteridium esculentum*), usually referred to as fern-root.[54] Kumara is frost-
sensitive; cold winters enforced the use of storage pits. Ecological know-
how was advanced; there were names for fifty soil-types, and one tribe
had named 280 plants.[55]

While there is little doubt that the initial settlement took place between
A.D. 800 and 1000—which is consistent with Maori tradition—and while
it is no longer held that there was an earlier population of 'Moriori',
there is debate about the actual nature of the culture in the early phase,
often called 'Moa-hunter' or Archaic as opposed to the later 'Classic'
culture. Janet Davidson has suggested that this division is too simple to
accommodate varying rates of change and regional differentiation, and
has proposed a tripartite scheme: Settlement to A.D. 1200, Expansion
and Rapid Change 1200–1500, Transitional from 1500 to 1769.[56]

Be that as it may, the giant moa and its relatives would obviously
provide a very good source of protein—while they survived, which in
the extreme south was until the late seventeenth century, much later
than elsewhere.[57] It may be hazardous to argue from the absence of the
short stone club or *patu*, so common in contact times, that the earlier
phase was fairly peaceful, basically a society of hunter-gatherers; spears
and clubs, like digging-sticks, can be made of wood, and so perish without
trace. But the striking proliferation of stockaded hill-forts or *pa* does
point to an increasingly violent society from the fifteenth century onwards.
The number of pa is extraordinary; in the effectively occupied part of
North Island, that under 300 metres, they are of the order of one to
every 10–15 km², and in some areas even more numerous.[58]

The society which Cook found in New Zealand was very different
from that of the settlement phase. Apart from the pa and the patu, witnesses
to the escalation of warfare, and ornaments in jade or greenstone, its
most remarkable material expression was a splendid art, most richly
manifested in tattooing and fine wood-carving for the beams and façades
of houses and the prows of canoes. It is marked by highly convoluted
curvilinear motifs and stylised anthropomorphic figures; with the strong

emphasis on military skills and virtues, it may not be fanciful to associate this flowering of decorative art with the martial pride of a turbulent tribal aristocracy.

This culture might be called classic without a capital; its coming— if it was that and not a 'becoming'—has been seen as conforming to the traditional version that 'the new Hawaiki immigrants brought with them (or returned to get) the all-important sweet potato'; on this view agriculture was an 'economic weapon' in its expansion.[59] On the other hand, the adjustments enforced by climate—seasonal cropping and winter storage of kumara—seem to demand some considerable time, and it is now thought that 'kumara and other cultivated plants were probably introduced by New Zealand's earliest settlers.'[60] Groube has suggested that these new techniques were most likely to be developed 'in the most climatically tolerant zone, the Northland [north of Auckland], precisely where canoe stories are rare.' Some canoe traditions indicate arrival on an already occupied coast, and direct penetration into the higher (and cooler) inland, but this would scarcely be feasible without the new storage devices. Building on these biogeographical factors Groube, like Simmons, logically if unromantically demotes 'Hawaiki' to Northland.[61]

It would be over-simple to account for the escalation of warfare by straightforward 'pressure on land'; the lowlands could have supported, by swidden cultivation using available techniques, a greater population than that at European contact. More important than the question of the total area notionally available are those of how rapidly it could be cleared and how soon more would be needed by a given expanding group. The labour demand for building the multitudinous pa implies a rapid increase of population, and given the plentiful summer rain of North Island, burning for cultivation or to induce a prolific growth of fern-root could be very difficult.[62] With a run of climatically bad years it might well seem more economical (and much more enjoyable) to raid another group's land than painfully to clear more of one's own;[63] this quite apart from questions of prestige, which ranked very high indeed in Maori values. The path of the defeated, as elsewhere in Polynesia, was at best into exile.

Hawaii

Hawaii is *sui generis* in the Polynesian world; not so much in material culture as in the degree of centralised political organisation, to such an extent that Wittfogel could include it, albeit rather marginally, in his study of hydraulic despotisms. The final form of the Hawaiian State was certainly affected by direct European influences, but both traditional and archaeological evidences suggest that the trend to formal quasi-monarchical rule, initially over a single island, set in some centuries earlier; the Europeans 'were only the midwives.'[64]

The terrestrial environment is relatively massive and diversified. The eight main islands have an area of over 16,000 km², with 10,415 km² in Hawai'i itself, the base whence Kamehameha I had by 1810 extended his rule over all except Kauai. All the islands are volcanic and there is a marked contrast between their wet and ruggedly dissected windward aspects and the drier southwestern slopes with wider valleys and even a few quite extensive plains. There are only a few fringing reefs, and no barrier reefs enclosing lagoons, but the terrain provides ecological niches which could support dense local populations. At the time of European contact the population was probably between 200,000 and 250,000, and some estimates go higher.[65]

Initial settlement was perhaps as early as A.D. 500–600; by 1200–1400 inland expansion was well under way, and a century or so later wet taro was being grown on stone-faced terraces. Taro was also grown without irrigation, and other staples were sweet potato, coconuts, bananas, breadfruit; there are extensive areas parcelled out into long fields with earth or dry-stone walls following the contours. The very limited scope for reef and lagoon fishing was offset by the building of great stone-walled fishponds, up to 200 hectares in area; stone was also used for revetting saltpans and for paving or marking pack-trails.

The architectural heritage of Hawaii is not confined to such utilitarian structures. There were very numerous temples (*heiau*, corresponding to marae), some of great size, up to 162 by 59 metres, and of all degrees of complexity in layout; peculiar to Hawaii were their 'oracle towers', obelisks of scaffolding covered with bark cloth, within which priests ascended to communicate with the deities. Also unique, at least in scale, is the 'City of Refuge' near Kealakekua Bay on Hawai'i; with massive walls four metres high it looks more like a fort than the sanctuary that it was.[66]

These elaborations reflect the political sophistication of the Hawaiian hierarchy, a sophistication fittingly and strikingly symbolised by the incomparable featherwork, mainly in bright reds and yellows, reserved for the rich cloaks and crested helmets of the higher chiefs: a truly imposing regalia. 'Aloha', leis, surfing, and these badges of pride sum up the popular image of traditional Hawaii; we shall return to look at the social reality.

Ultima Thule: Easter Island

Easter Island, otherwise Isla de Pascua or Rapanui,[67] is about 1600 km from Henderson, the nearest Polynesian island known to have been inhabited, twice as far from the Societies and the Marquesas, and 3600 from its possessor, Chile. It is reefless and has no resemblance to the popular stereotype of a 'South Sea Isle'; from the air, rolling downlands of yellowish grass, broken by rocky volcanic outcrops, give an oddly Scottish effect, except for the great crater of Rana Kao, which however can produce

Plate II. EASTER ISLAND STATUES. The bodies of these great monoliths are virtually buried in slumped quarry debris. By courtesy of Dr Peter Bellwood, ANU.

a very fine chill Scotch mist. On the ground, the delusion fades; the few trees are bananas, guavas, coconuts, eucalypts, citrus, and by the re-erected statues one kicks up worked flakes of obsidian at almost every step.

Ever since the reports of González, Cook, and La Pérouse, speculation on the origin of the great statues has built up a mystique, and despite the definitely Polynesian character of the language, artefacts and social structure, it is perhaps going too far to say that 'when we turn from such special features as scripts and statues to Easter Island culture as a whole, the strangeness and mystery quickly dissipate.'[68] That begs the question, which is precisely statues and script. It can hardly be said that Thor Heyerdahl has dispelled the mystery; rather his tangle of inferences has added to it. Like Andrew Sharp and Robert Langdon, he has the heretic virtue of sharpening orthodox wits. The discussion here can only be an outline of a great mass of argument.[69]

Easter Island society was initially disrupted by the Rapanui themselves well before serious European contact. At some time between 1680 and Cook's arrival in 1774 the traditional rivalry of the east and the west in this island of only 160 km², of 'Long-ears' and 'Short-ears', culminated in the violent overthrow of the former, symbolised by the physical over-throwing of most of the statues. The Pascuenses (Easter Islanders) had reached an astonishing level of cultural achievement, but at the heavy cost of environmental degradation, notably an almost complete deforestation. 'In a typically human fashion, their success seems to have carried with it the seeds of its own destruction. In the horrifying disintegration . . . is reflected in microcosm the dilemma of twentieth century man.'[70]

Heyerdahl held that the Long-ears represented the older more aristocratic culture of the island, and were in fact from Peru, probably led by people of Caucasoid type; a recent linguistic study claims that there may have been an original non-Polynesian population.[71] It is at any rate certain that by Cook's time there had been a breakdown of society, and the agitated history of the Pascuenses in the next century was utterly devastating. After Peruvian slavers had carried off about a thousand people for the guano workings, the fifteen who were repatriated brought back smallpox, and in 1867 only 111 Pascuenses were left on the island. Annexation by Chile in 1888 brought at least stability, and by 1972 the indigenous population had reached 1355.[72]

Drawing from Peruvian traditions recorded by Sarmiento de Gamboa and others, Heyerdahl claims that the Spaniards had two widely separated bearings from Peru to Easter Island, so that 'the ancient Peruvians were able to pinpoint Easter Island's exact position' through cross-bearings— an island 24 km long and some 3500 km distant! At two months' sail was a barren island with 'three high mountains', then an island called

Qüen, and ten days beyond that a still larger one. To Heyerdahl the first island is indubitably Sala-y-Gomez, which has indeed three summits towering to 30 metres—not likely to impress a man living in sight of the Andes as 'high'—and indeed Heyerdahl himself calls it 'an unimpressive islet almost awash in stormy weather'. The only source for this story is the interrogation, under threat of death, of an Indian centenarian; the only specific voyage cited is that of Túpac Inca Yupanqui, which even if authentic and even if it reached some island whence it brought back many *black* prisoners, seems centuries late for Heyerdahl's purposes.[73]

A valuable by-product of the heresies of Heyerdahl and Sharp has been a strengthening of work on 'primitive' navigation. Whatever may be thought of Túpac's fleet carrying 20,000 men, Heyerdahl has shown that the combination of balsa, sail and centre-boards produces craft capable of lengthy sea-keeping and some windward sailing. It is no longer thought that all the cultures of the South American littoral were land-bound, and it is known that some used sails not borrowed from the Spaniards.[74] It does not follow that the requisite voyages were made.

Again, while Heyerdahl's insistence on the role of winds and currents is unexceptionable, the data he relies upon appear out-of-date. Recent oceanographical analysis has not been confined, as formerly, to reports from areas of regular ocean traffic, but depends upon the dynamics of ocean masses as established by 'about sixty thousand observations made by research vessels... which cover the entire area of the Pacific in a rather equal and uniform way,'[75] and have refined the hitherto accepted circulation map. In particular, a west-east South Equatorial Counter-current and a west-east South Pacific Current have been found; and there are of course temporary but significant reversals due to exceptional weather conditions. Heyerdahl's east-west transoceanic 'escalators' are thus not so reliable as he assumed. In any case, voyages from South America, drift or navigated, would be far more likely to fetch up in the Marquesas or Tuamotus than at Easter Island, as is shown both by computer simulations and by the actual tracks of Heyerdahl and his successors.[76] This would seem a more economical approach to the question of South American contacts than the highly dubious pinpointing of Easter Island.

The archaeological record is generally taken to disclose three phases: from about A.D. 400 to the twelfth or thirteenth century; then a Middle Period until the Poike war about 1680; finally the Late Period of dis-integration.[77] The first two are distinguished by changes in the style of the ceremonial platforms or *ahu*. The problem is whether such massive structures were beyond the building capacity of Polynesians, and whether the resemblances to Peruvian masonry are so close as to enforce a belief that the techniques were brought from America. On the former point, the ahu bear a general resemblance in form and function to marae, and most of the techniques can be matched elsewhere in Polynesia. On the latter, many of Heyerdahl's parallels seem overly fine-drawn, and some of his dating is suspect. Some American influence there may be, but in general the Heyerdahlian picture seems considerably overdrawn.[78] Some archaeological evidence is unequivocal: fishhooks are of Polynesian type, and an analysis of 875 adzes leads to the conclusion that 'only the Marquesas demonstrate enough similarities to suggest a specific relationship.[79]

Much less clear is the botanical evidence. It is odd that if the Spaniards in 1770 were offered Chili peppers, the Forsters—trained and keen botanists—should have seen none in 1774. The presence of the *totora* reed (*Scirpus*) in the crater of Rana Kao is puzzling; but the plant is not limited to Easter Island and South America. The Hawaiian and Rapanui names for it are similar, and the Easter Island form is earlier than the Hawaiian. There may have been a pre-human dissemination by birds.[80]

The brooding power and grandeur of the statues—and the conspicuous presence of some of them on the porch of the British Museum[81]—have meant that for the generality of people they *are* Easter Island, symbols of inscrutable mystery.

There are in all some 600 statues, but in general they are not so gigantic as popular impression goes, though big enough; most of them are three to five metres high, and there is an unfinished monster, still lying in the quarry, of twenty metres. The stone from which they are cut is a fairly easily worked volcanic tuff. There is really no difficulty about their transport and erection, as La Pérouse's engineer saw, though this too has been blown up into a 'mystery'. Transport was by skids, sledges, rollers, levers, perhaps fork-lifts to ease them forward (the island once carried enough timber); erection by easing them up a temporary ramp or wedging stones beneath them, as Heyerdahl showed by actual experiment on the island. There are plenty of analogues for the process, from Egypt and Stonehenge onwards; in Peru, but also in Tonga.[82] The great magnet for the cyclotron at the University of Melbourne was moved in by the ancient technique of ramp, rollers, and levers. Since the great figures were most probably designed to display the *mana*, the sacred power of chiefs, clan rivalries as well as the major clash of 1680 may have been involved in their overthrow.[83] Let us leave these giant images standing in their forsaken majesty, gazing unseeing into space, abiding our question.

Still less amenable to our question are the remarkable writings—the only ones from Polynesia—preserved on wooden boards. They may have been simply mnemonic, aids to memorising genealogies, but by the time they came to European notice their significance had been lost; the suggestion that the script is clumsily imitative of European writing, briefly glimpsed when chiefs were induced to 'sign' the Spanish proclamation of annexation in 1770, is hardly convincing. The strangest feature is that the lines are arranged in 'reversed boustrophedon', alternately from right to left and left to right.[84]

The symbols themselves have been deciphered to reveal chants and genealogies in a Polynesian-type language,[85] but the riddle remains. If reversed boustrophedon is, as has been claimed, a 'natural solution' why is it so rare that Heyerdahl can claim that the only other example anywhere is among the Cuna Indians of Panama? (It is a pity that he, who illustrates so much, should not have given us two lines of Cuna.) Others have gone even further afield, to Mohenjo-daro on the Indus, and the climax is surely reached in the assertion that the writing retains 'traces of Egyptian, Chinese, and Palestinian script'.[86] To the layman much of the discussion seems as obscure as the script itself, which remains perhaps the only true 'mystery of Easter Island'.

Golson's extremely careful analysis of the archaeology discountenances the existence of two distinct ethnic groups. Yet his conclusion is cautious: 'the simple view of Easter Island as an Eastern Polynesian colony begs a number of questions.'[87] But Heyerdahl also begs questions, and argues in circles, sliding too easily from 'might have' to 'must have' to 'did'. The data make it probable that there were contacts between South America and Polynesia—one must never forget the sweet potato—and to postulate Polynesian voyages to South America is against all oceanographic probability. Contacts from South America would be much more likely by way of the Tuamotus and Marquesas than by Easter Island.

The devoted research and polemic of over thirty years have not validated Heyerdahl's bold assertion that on Easter Island 'Where South America and its early megalithic high-cultures end, Polynesian and Pacific Island prehistory begins.' The research of others has shown that Polynesian prehistory began much earlier, and far to the west. It is strikingly put, and it is true, that 'man spoke in Peru... along the open beaches—when no word had yet been uttered inside the roaring breakers of Polynesia';[88] but this truth is a truism that cannot bear the weight that Heyerdahl places upon it.

Vikings or drifters?

Nothing in Oceania more greatly impressed early European visitors than the ingenuity and seaworthiness of the local sailing craft, which unluckily they often called 'canoes'. This usage is too hallowed by time to be displaced, but it gives a misleading impression of flimsiness and crudity. Most workaday craft, used for lagoon or inshore fishing, were indeed canoes on any definition, and the larger and more elaborate types were derived from them so that in one sense the term may be accurate enough; but they were certainly not what is commonly implied by the words 'any rude craft in which uncivilized people go upon the water.'[89]

The Micronesian *proa* or *prau* was strictly a single-hulled outrigger; Tahitian *pahi*, Fijian *drua*, Tongan *tongiaki* were double-hulled. These were carvel-built, tightly stitched or lashed together with coconut fibre (coir or sennit). Voyaging canoes were decked, and had deckhouses, sometimes substantial, on a platform straddling the hulls. Cook saw a pahi of 33 metres building—0.6 metre longer than his own *Endeavour*—and as late as 1939 a 30-metre outrigger was built in Kiribati, but most ocean-goers were half to two-thirds this size.[90] They could sail to windward with much the same facility, or lack of it, as a contemporary European brig. Sail type varied; East Polynesia used spritsails, but in contact times the 'Oceanic lateen' was spreading from Micronesia through Fiji as far as Samoa. In Fiji the marriage of this Micronesian rig with Tongan-Samoan hull forms produced the drua (Plate III), with an upwind capacity that rendered return voyages to Tonga easier and greatly enhanced the traffic between these two groups. As for speed, this was comparable and sometimes superior to that of European vessels.[91]

Such vessels could keep the sea for a considerable time, and carry a considerable cargo. Sharp reckons that the 250 warriors with whom George Vason travelled in a Tongan canoe, around 1800, were the equivalent by weight of: 30 humans, 2 boars, 3 sows, 12 piglets, 10 dogs, 20 rats (perhaps not on manifest!), 100 breadfruit and banana plants, 12 tons sundries—'A double canoe one-third of the size would have been ample for viable settlement.' Lewis estimates that a large voyaging canoe could carry provisions for a month or six weeks; given favourable winds and currents such craft could make 160–240 km in a day's run, giving a range of 4800–7200 km, enough to take them to 'the furthest outposts of Polynesia.'[92] Clearly, if by 'canoe' we mean 'any rude craft', to use the term for such vessels approaches an abuse of language.

Small wonder, then, that some enthusiasts have given the impression that the vast expanse of Oceania was criss-crossed by a net of regular long-distance traffic flows; nor that there was a reaction, forcefully expressed in Andrew Sharp's rejection of the concept of deliberate navigation leading to the discovery of outlying islands, or at least discovery and return. It is fair to say that while Sharp was not quite so rigorous either in fact or in logic as he asserted, he did impel a serious reassessment. This has involved the study of indigenous navigational lore and mariners' training; actual experiment by voyaging without benefit of European instruments (in one case not even a clock); and computer simulation of drift voyages.

There is virtually no problem and no debate as to voyaging between groups as close as Tonga and the Laus (eastern Fiji), about 370 km apart; here crossings were virtually habitual. The range of geographical knowledge naturally varied greatly from place to place; the classic case is

Plate III. A FIJIAN FLEET. The drawing of Bauan drua off Ovalau was made about 1854-5; those of fifty years earlier would have been rather smaller but similar in construction and rig, hardly 'Any rude craft...'! By courtesy Captain H. M. Denham, London; photo Fiji Museum, Suva.

the 'chart' made by Tupaia of Raiatea for Cook—'cartogram' would
be a better term, since distances are only relative and a linguistic misunderstanding resulted in some islands north of the latitudinal axis being
placed south of it. 'When all allowance has been made, however, the
scope of the map remains impressive... virtually all major islands from
Rotuma to the Marquesas are represented', a range of 43° of longitude,
almost 4700 km.[93] Tupaia's own travels seem to have been confined to
the Societies and perhaps Samoa, plus Rurutu (Hiti-roa) in the Australs,
480 km south of Tahiti with no intervening islands.

The latitudinal range of Tupaia's knowledge is less impressive: 15°,
about 1650 km. This of course is precisely what we should expect in
the region of the Trades and the Equatorial Currents; a similar pattern
is strikingly displayed in maps of computer-simulated drift. Equally to
be expected is the predominantly east to west set of these drifts; the
simulations show over 20 per cent probability of drifts from Rapa and
Pitcairn reaching the Australs and Tuamotus respectively.[94]

On the other hand, west-east voyages were certainly possible. While
some ardent Polynesianists have undoubtedly exaggerated the strength
and persistence of westerly winds in the zone of the North Equatorial
Countercurrent, there is no doubt also that Heyerdahl, for example, has
underestimated this factor. The hurricanes of December–March have also
a strong southwesterly component, and the recently identified South
Equatorial Countercurrent and South Pacific Current must also be taken
into account. Out of 125 examples of accidental voyages in the South
Pacific whose beginnings and ends are known, about twenty-four finished
east of their origins, while some have a strong meridional component.[95]

Sharp's book set off a polemic in which the acerbity was at least in
part due to his own angularity. His thesis is that the Islands were settled
by accidental one-way voyages, mainly of fishing or trading parties blown
away by storms. Even if at initiation these voyages were intentional,
as of voluntary or enforced exiles, they were random and unnavigated.
The voyagers were not 'at the mercy of winds and waves' since they
could steer for any land they might see: 'this was exploration, although
the actual sighting of land, like all discovery, was of necessity by chance.'[96]
Set against Sharp's general tone, the disclaimer about winds and waves
seems thin.

Sharp takes a narrow view of 'navigation'; to him 'it implies that
the existence and location of one's objective is known, and a course
set for it.'[97] This begs a question: 'it all depends on what you mean'
by *known*. One could argue plausibly, on Sharp's terms, that the first
voyage of Columbus was not a 'navigation'; more pertinently, that for
much of the Polynesian realm the existence of islands over the horizon
was a more than reasonable expectation, while on past experience there

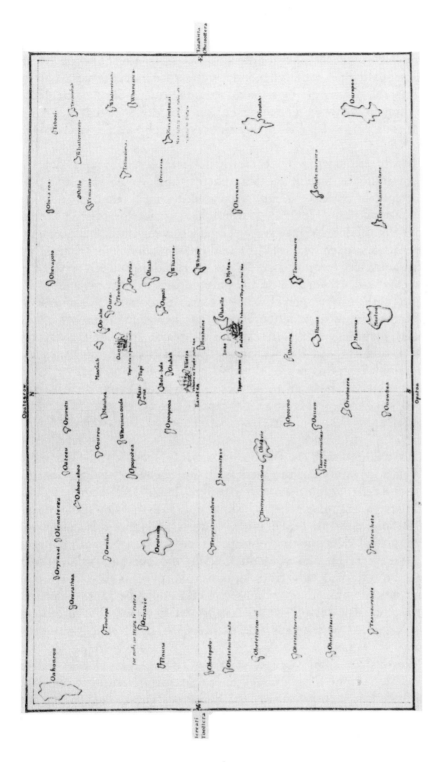

Plate IV. TUPAIA'S CHART. From R. A. Skelton (ed.), *Charts and Views* accompanying *The Journals of Captain James Cook*, Hakluyt Society, 1969. By permission of the British Library. Photo ANU.

was no reason to believe in limitless wastes of empty ocean. It is clear, from recorded practice, that Polynesian seamen 'lost' by tempest could pull themselves through by navigation in a calculated direction. Sharp does allow for deliberate exploration: voyages in the hope of finding new lands, impelled perhaps by legend; by pressure on resources; by tribal and clan quarrels; or simply by a desire for adventure—surely a neglected factor in human history. The distribution of domesticated plants and animals through the Islands surely involves deliberate, well-stocked voyaging.[98]

A deliberate explorer will certainly deliberately navigate. Whether he finds anything or not is another matter; and at the terminal point accident comes into play—though it was not chance that led Cook to the east coast of New Holland; it was chance that his precise landfall should be at Point Hicks. Voyages may be purposive in intent but accidental in the event, as indeed was that of Columbus in 1492, or Bouvet's in 1739 to the remotest scrap of land in the world. To disagree with Sharp is not to agree with Heyerdahl on the pinpointing of Easter Island.

To begin with, Sharp seems nearly always to convey the impression that the target islands of a deliberate voyage *were* pinpoints. But islands are not flat shapes in flat static spaces of paper sea; they are three-dimensional, and the sea has its signs. David Lewis demonstrates that we should think in terms not of discrete points but of screens or 'island blocks'; even low islands can be detected by various signs at a distance of some 48 km, and circles of this radius often overlap to form much larger target areas—a very different pattern from a scatter of dots on a map.

Oceanian navigational craftsmanship, unduly scouted by Sharp, was embodied in a 'Mystery' in the mediaeval European sense—the mastery of art and craft through a mass of traditional lore—and it was carefully handed down in training schools ashore and afloat. On some islands complex markers were used to set initial courses, and there was an immense store of empirical data on the motions of the stars, seasonal change in wind and weather, bird movements, swells and currents, island loom, clouds and the reflected light from lagoons, phosphorescence, wave patterns. Who would think that a man's testicles could be a most sensitive balance to detect the set of swells?[99]—and yet it seems obvious enough once one is told. The sea was not pathless, to those who could read it.

Some non-instrumental voyages, such as that of the *Hōkūle 'a* from Hawaii to Tahiti, come fairly enough under Sharp's strictures on the great difference between sailing towards the definitely known and sailing into the void. But David Lewis sailed with Tevake of Santa Cruz (Ndeni) between Vanikoro and Taumako, and with the Carolinian Hipour from Pulawat to Saipan and back, involving stretches of 725 km out of sight of land. Admittedly from known to known, but these experienced Islander pilots revealed things, in the heavens and in the sea, not dreamt of in Sharp's philosophy.[1] The signs and wonders of the deep are manifold, and even though we allow a 'sensual and emotional familiarity with the sea', reading them is not a matter of a 'mysterious instinct or sixth sense', which Sharp rightly scorns, but of senses not dulled by civilised shortcuts. We have learnt to read, and forgotten memory; to make maps, and are lost without them; to compute, and may soon be unable to add up. We might remember Quoodle.[2]

On specific points of sea practice Sharp is not always sure-footed,[3] but he is undoubtedly right in discounting far-fetched speculation and flimsy inferences as to extremely long-distance two-way voyages, involving the accurate calculations needed for latitude sailing to make a precise landfall. Nor need we delay over the claims for nautical instruments such as the Hawaiian 'sacred calabash' alleged to have been used to determine latitudes; this has been beautifully exploded as 'a suitcase and not a primitive sextant.'[4] Despite the ingenuity of the instructional models used for training seamen, the dismissal of high claims for Polynesian abstract astronomy—as distinct from star-lore—is supported by Åkerblom's careful study, and must be accepted.

In general, therefore, Sharp may be justified in underplaying return voyages, certainly for the real ends of the earth, Hawaii, New Zealand, Easter Island. On the other hand, there is increasing evidence of a higher capacity for deliberate navigation, in Sharp's own sense, than he would allow, and covering greater distances. In some cases there is probably some point in Sharp's implication (or assertion) that those who disagree with him are subjective romantics, given to wishful thinking—but this has a double edge; subconscious iconoclasm can also be subjective.

There is an important psychological factor. If people had arrived in west-central Polynesia by relatively short island-hops from the west, then their inherited presumption from experience would be that more islands would lie further east, at manageable intervals, indefinitely: that was their world. Again, they would have gained experience in the techniques of transporting live plants and animals. So in times of stress, from internal conflict or natural crisis, why not try? Since the direction of further effort was westwards—to windward—it would seem reasonably easy to return: upwind into the unknown, downwind back to the known. Of course it did not always work, but dead men tell no tales; failures were 'unlikely to be reported back to alter the image of the home community... The greatest significance of Tupaia's map may be that it shows that his image of his own world was of Tahiti surrounded on all sides by a screen of islands.'[5]

More concretely, the inferences to be drawn from the computer simulations strongly support Sharp in one way—they indicate that for the outer trio, Hawaii, Easter Island, New Zealand, returns were unlikely indeed; in all probability settlement was by one or several one-way voyages, and archaeology seems to support this. For these islands, this is not a startling conclusion; with all respect for Te Rangi Hiroa, one may feel that to believe otherwise is more than a shade romantic.

In another aspect the computer findings are negative for Sharp's views. The possibilities of drifts to Hawaii are slight, and return drifts would be more likely to the Marshalls, in Micronesia, than to anywhere in Polynesia. Drifts either to or from New Zealand are also very unlikely, but there are at least low possibilities of return drifts, and possibly knowledge of 'these southern islands and their zenith stars' might have filtered back to tropical Polynesia, 'and if so the information necessary for later navigated voyages would have been made available in "Hawaiki" '. Both for New Zealand and Hawaii, then, initial settlement would seem to call for deliberate exploring voyages. As for Easter Island, of 2208 simulated drifts from Polynesia only three even came within 320 km of the island, and 'since the likelihood of a drift or accidental voyage from South America is virtually nil', the Rapanui 'stem from spontaneous creation on that island or reached there from elsewhere in Polynesia having intentionally followed an east[wards] course... We prefer the latter hypothesis'.[6]

There remains a problem which seems neglected in the literature. At the time of European contact, the heroic age of really distant voyaging was far in the past: why? The most probable explanation lies in a general climatic deterioration in the first couple of centuries of our millennium, such as was a major factor in the ending of voyages to Greenland by the Vikings of the North. For Polynesia this would have meant stronger Trade Winds, weaker westerly components, more storms.[7] There is obviously a wide field for research here, in the first instance palaeoclimatic; but the oral traditions suggest the cessation of really far-flung voyaging about this time.

The saga stands, a majestic achievement of skill and courage.

Chapter 2

OCEANIA ON THE EVE

Or to burst all links of habit—there to wander far away
On to island after island at the gateways of the day.
Larger constellations burning, mellow moons and happy skies,
Breadths of tropic shade and palms in cluster, knots of Paradise.
Droops the heavy-blossom'd bower, hangs the heavy-fruited tree—
Summer isles of Eden lying in dark-purple spheres of sea...
There the passions cramp'd no longer shall have scope and breathing-space...

The Romantic vision of the South Seas finds a suitably lush expression in Tennyson's lines, a vision still held by the more naive of today's tourists, even if they do not propose, as the poet does (momentarily), to take some savage woman and to rear a dusky race. Islands such as Tahiti, with its towering crown of Orohena, are beautiful beyond description; but the more numerous coral isles are flat, many are scantily vegetated, and the drier ones are unlovely places. The passions, or some of them, were as much cramped by hierarchy, ritual and 'good form' as in Victorian England—after all, *taboo* is an Oceanian word—and 'links of habit' were strong to the point of tyranny. This chapter seeks to present at least some lineaments of life in Oceania on the eve of substantial European intrusion into the summer isles of Eden. The picture is perforce much simplified, even stylised.

The Oceanic environment

On various reckonings of its boundaries, the Pacific Ocean covers between 150 and 180 million km²; the lower figure is 27 per cent of the earth's surface. Immense areas in the north and east are utterly empty, and even in the island realms of Oceania the ratio of land to sea is low indeed. New Guinea and New Zealand aside, the Pacific Islands have a total land area roughly equivalent to that of England or New York State, but fragmented and sub-fragmented into literally thousands of islands. The 1156 islets of the Marshalls, strung out in two lines each nearly 1000 km long, have an actual land area of about 180 km², on average 16 hectares each.[1]

Basically, the Islands fall into three main types: high volcanic islands, coral atolls, and the few tabular raised coral reefs such as Nauru and

---

Alfred Tennyson, *Locksley Hall* (1842)

Tongatapu; there are of course combinations of these elements. The high islands of Melanesia, and Polynesian New Zealand, west of the 'andesite line' marking the edge of the Australian geotectonic plate, are in effect the crests of complexly folded mountain ranges, with sedimentary and ancient metamorphic rocks intruded by granites; they are thus essentially 'continental' islands.[2] The truly oceanic high islands are formed of successive outpourings of basalt from huge ranges on the ocean floor; Mauna Kea in Hawai'i rises from a base nearly 5500 metres below sea level to 4200 above it.

Coral reefs can also be classified, rather roughly, into three main types: fringing, in contact with the land; barrier, parallel to the coast but separated from it by a lagoon; and atolls. Atolls are reefs of corals and similar organisms more or less completely enclosing a lagoon; they are rarely the neat circles of the schoolbooks. Many carry elongated islets built of debris from the reef itself, piled up by wave action, especially during storms.[3] Naturally these are most common on the windward, that is generally the eastern, aspects of the atolls; conversely, passes through the reefs are usually to leeward. Reef-building corals can flourish only in clear water at 18–23°C, and are inhibited or destroyed by sediment or by fresh water; hence barrier reefs may be broken opposite river mouths.[4]

The reef is a prolific supplier of marine products, but the land environment of atolls is very poorly endowed. The islets of rubble and sand rarely rise more than five metres above the seas; the soil is exclusively calcareous, and so porous that any organic materials are quickly leached out, except in those islands so arid as to develop a crust of guano from the droppings of nesting birds. There is no surface drainage, only a lens of fresh water formed by rain seeping down to rest on the denser salt water permeating the coral basement.[5] (The scarcity of potable water is to some extent offset by the presence of coconuts.) Hurricanes, droughts, great waves (tsunamis) produced by submarine earthquakes can all but annihilate these tiny footholds of terrestrial life.

Some islands, such as the phosphate or guano islands of the equatorial Phoenix and Line groups, are practically desert. On the high islands, relief produces a marked rain-shadow on leeward slopes; Kauai (Hawaii) has, or had in 1945, the distinction of having both the driest and the wettest stations in Oceania: 559 mm on the leeward side, 12,090 mm on the windward.[6] In the Carolines and Marshalls from July to October, and from December to March in a belt from the Solomons through Samoa and south to 30°S, tropical cyclones (typhoons or hurricanes) bring peril to Islands life. In the Tuamotus a hurricane in 1903 took 517 lives— over a tenth of the population—and in 1889 the course of Samoan history was changed by the storm which destroyed six rival warships, German and American, in Apia Harbour.[7]

The natural vegetation of Oceania is very dominantly Indo-Malaysian; only in Hawaii and a few eastern islands are there any American affinities. Plant distribution, until human times, was by wave- wind- or bird-borne seeds; of 212 species on Juan Fernández, only thirteen could not be accounted for by such transportation.[8] This spread of inert plant material from Asia, against the general trend of winds and currents, of course took very many millenia.

Great areas in New Guinea and the Solomons are still occupied by dense rain forest corresponding reasonably well to the popular image of 'jungle'. There are outliers in Fiji and Samoa, but elsewhere in the high islands generations of shifting agriculture have produced secondary forest with areas of scrub or grassland, such as the *talasiga* or 'burnt country' of the drier northwest of Viti Levu (Fiji); the grasslands of the New Guinea Highlands are also man-made.

As is natural in an island realm, there is a strong tendency, in both flora and fauna, to endemism, that is the occurrence of species confined to a single island or group; the birds of the Galápagos, differing from island to island, gave Charles Darwin one of the first clues to his evolutionary hypothesis. Again naturally, both flora and fauna grow progressively poorer from west to east: 129 species of *Ficus* in New Guinea, twenty-five in New Caledonia, four in Tonga, only one in the Tuamotus; there are over 2000 known species of orchids in New Guinea, four in the Marquesas.[9]

The most striking feature of the natural flora of the drier coral islands is its poverty: a few grasses, low bushes and herbs, few trees or none. From the sea, the prospect is pleasing enough, but it is simply formed by the wall of introduced coconut palms. Apart from the pandanus (screwpine) and portulaca, probably all food plants are human introductions, and for the all-important taro the soil itself has been formed by patient composting. Things are different in the wetter islands of the east, especially the larger Carolines; here there is real forest, and something like the 'summer isles of Eden' may still be found; but generally speaking, on the atolls east of Kiribati what lushness there is has been created by generations of skilled gardeners.

Common to both high and low islands is the littoral flora. Tidal mangrove flats may be quite extensive on the larger islands west of Samoa—one must drive fifty-five km from Suva to find a good sandy beach—but the low islands rarely have enough soil and water to produce enough mud. The strand vegetation and the narrow strip of 'beach forest' behind it are remarkably uniform; herbs and bushes, including portulaca and the convolvulus 'beach morning-glory', with pandanus, casuarina and hibiscus as the most prominent plants in the beach forest.

Few land animals can be carried very far by waves or winds, and it is not surprising that the non-marine fauna of Oceania is very limited indeed. Probably the most important faunal boundary is about 170°E; anopheline mosquitoes have not penetrated east of that meridian, so that Fiji and Polynesia are malaria-free. While *Anopheles* may also carry the embryo of the filariasis worm, this affliction has a strikingly different form on either side of 170°E; to the east, where a different mosquito, *Aedes variegata*, is the carrier, filariasis much more often results in the horrible malformations of elephantiasis.[10]

The high islands are for the most part deeply dissected, and lowlands are rare; only the largest carry rivers big enough to form broad valleys such as that of the Sigatoka, or even small lowlands such as the Rewa delta, both on Viti Levu. They still offer much richer and more diversified ecological niches than do the low coral isles, and there is an environmental carry-over into the differing ways of living of the two types, and even in some degree into the social structures. But in both alike, Neolithic men and women showed great adaptability and ingenuity in making the best of their generally limited natural resources.

The harvest of land and sea

The agriculture of Oceania was based on roots and fruits; its pioneers did not bring rice from its cradle in Southeast Asia, and indeed horticulture is a more appropriate term than agriculture, which has immemorial associations with fields and grain.

The area cultivated at any one time or place was small, but labour was intensive, and loving, and except in times of dearth, brought on by natural calamity or war, the people were better fed than many of their cash-cropping descendants who eat largely out of tins.[11] The small plots were minutely subdivided, or carried very mixed plantings, permitting a spread of work and yields through the year and ensuring against a complete failure of food production. At a given time most of the plots would have been resting as fallow on a rotation of up to fifteen years; this is swidden, slash-and-burn, or shifting cultivation. The mixed plantings could include various legumes or pulses, bananas, some types of yams, sugar-cane, gourds, arrowroot, and cordylines, of which the roots were a source of sweetening and the leaves valuable for thatching and in earth-oven cooking. Sweet potatoes were grown separately, in well-tended mounds. Another important plant was *Piper methysticum*, a pepper whose root, chewed or ground, was mixed with water to make *kava* (Fijian *yaqona*), an excellent convivial beverage essential to many ceremonies, especially in Fiji and Samoa, and well described as 'one of the greatest and least harmful of the world's great tranquillisers'.[12]

The major staples were two tree crops, coconuts and breadfruit, and two roots, yam and taro. Yams were not very important east of Samoa;

they are labour-demanding and need light, relatively dry, and well-tilled soils; with very careful attention, and much magic, the tubers of the Great Yam (*Dioscorea alata*) might reach a length of three metres, and in Melanesia this species still retains an important role in ritual and competitive display. As a 'dry' crop it was symbolic of masculinity, while water-loving taro represented femininity; yams were men's care, taro women's, a distinction which might well seem validated by the phallic shape of the yam tuber and the yonic or vulviform of the taro leaf.[13]

The taros are arums and thrive only in a moist habitat; they were grown in clearings in the wetter rain forest and in swampy patches, and also in irrigated terraces, sometimes quite elaborate, from New Caledonia to Hawaii. On atolls, where irrigation was impossible, the giant *Cystosperma* was grown in man-made swamps; pits were dug down to the fresh-water lens and a compost was built up from all available vegetable waste—in Kiribati, in basket-work caissons, the result being a pot-plant up to three metres high, with leaves as big as a bath-towel and corms weighing 70 or 80 kg.[14]

Yams if properly stored could be kept for some months; but in general tubers and roots were perishable and, unlike grain, wasted a great deal of space in storage and carriage, so that it was impossible to accumulate a long-term easily transportable surplus; they had to be used up or else rot. This was a factor in the ceremonial exchanges and distributions of produce which were central to social life.

Breadfruit (*Artocarpus*, a giant mulberry) was widespread; in Truk and Tahiti it was the staple, and in the Marquesas so dominant that failure of the rains meant devastating famine. The tree is very prolific, producing yearly up to 150 large spherical fruits weighing from two to five kg each; it may stay in bearing for fifty years. The starchy fruit when baked stayed good for some weeks, or it could be fermented in covered pits, like little silos, to form a dough which would keep for months. The trees had further uses, providing timber for building or canoe hulls, gum for caulking and bird-lime, and an inner bark which could be beaten into a fine white 'cloth'. Nothing in the vegetable realm impressed early European observers more than this handsome tree, so ornamental and yet so generously productive of a ready-made equivalent to the staff of life; Joseph Banks rhapsodised that 'in Otaheite, where Love is the Chief Occupation', there was ample spare time for its exercise, since a man 'by planting 4 breadfruit trees, a work which cannot last more than an hour, does as much for his generation as a European who with yearly returning toil cultivat[es] corn for his family, and this Leisure is given up to Love.'[15]

As a universal provider, however, the breadfruit was outclassed by the coconut, without which human life could hardly have been sustained on small atolls, where today the consumption per head is at least five or six nuts daily.[16] Untreated, the nut gave both food and drink; its flesh could be creamed for a condiment, while the 'heart', the young frondlets around the terminal bud, made an excellent salad. The trunk provided timber for houses, small canoes, canoe-rollers, spears and fending; the leaves supplied thatch, wrapping, fans and mats; the dried husk was used for very strong cordage (sennit or sinnet), tinder, kindling and caulking; the shells served as bowls and bottles, and even, according to William Ellis, for trepanning.[17] The palm could grow on poor calcareous soils and was remarkably tolerant of salinity; if in Tahiti *Artocarpus* was the Tree of Love, in the low isles *Cocos nucifera* was truly the Tree of Life.

Also important were bananas, wild and cultivated, in some of the Societies rivalling breadfruit as a staple, and the sweet potato, especially in New Guinea and Hawaii and particularly in New Zealand where it was a staple along with the root of the indigenous bracken. It goes without saying that Melanesia, with its richer flora, was better-found than Polynesia in minor forest products for food and artefacts, and that only in the larger Melanesian islands could hunting, except for feral pigs, be of much account as a source of food. In New Zealand, however, rats and birds were taken for the pot; elsewhere in Polynesia fowling was for sport or for much-prized red and yellow feathers rather than for food.

This intensive gardening left little place for animal husbandry. Leaves, fruits and nuts could provide vitamins, but the basic vegetable foods were sugary or starchy carbohydrates lacking in protein; the deficit was made up from many marine organisms and 'cottage livestock'—pigs, chickens, and dogs. In Melanesia pigs were and are of enormous significance in the rituals of feasting and exchange which lie at the heart of social life; in Polynesia the attitude is rather more mundane, but the omnivorous pig is invaluable as 'a sort of bank for the storage of an unconsumable surplus of vegetable foods' and a converter of carbohydrates into protein.[18] Many groups had pigs before European explorers brought them, but the breeds were small, although a diet of coconut, taro, sweet potato and odd food scraps rendered their flesh very palatable.

Dogs were perhaps more often reared for food than as domestic companions; they had the same diet as pigs, and unprejudiced Europeans found that dogs so fed, and cooked like pork—wrapped in leaves and placed on hot stones covered with earth—were excellent eating.[19] Small stock was very unequally distributed; all three animals are still scarce on many atolls, where both pigs and poultry do seem to have been the gift of Europe. Easter Island had only chickens, important in gift exchange.[20] In any case, except in the interiors of the more massive western islands, animal protein was available much more abundantly from the sea and the reef than from dry land.

'In no part of the world, perhaps, are the inhabitants better fishermen; and, considering their former entire destitution of iron, their variety of fishing apparatus is amazing.'[21] The Islanders had a very intimate knowledge of fishy habits and habitats. In Truk and Ponape alone the following methods were used: pole-and-line; trolling from canoes; framed handnets; casting nets; long-handled nets for flying-fish lured at night by torches; seines; baskets set on the lagoon floor like lobster-pots; spearing; fish drives; fish weirs on fringing reefs; poison.[22] Melanesia added traps lined with thorns, plunge-baskets, and kites which jiggled the bait along on the water surface. Spinners with lures, generally of pearl-shell, were used in Micronesia and the Solomons; Polynesians elaborated extremely ingenious and beautiful bonito spinners, with blunt hooks designed not to pierce the quarry's jaw but to hold it just long enough to yank the fish in at top speed, no time being lost by unhooking—most elegant micro-engineering.[23]

Hooks in many functional forms are important diagnostics in Oceanian archaeology, and Bengt Anell has brought out the marked limitation of some types of gear to Melanesia and the possible ultimate affinities of the Polynesian compound hooks to earlier forms in northeastern Eurasia, points which might be cited in favour of a Micronesian entry.[24] Turtle and (rarely) coconut shell were used for hooks, sometimes also stone, but most were shaped from molluscan shells or from bone—including human bone, 'the most offensive use to which the bones of an enemy could be applied'. Twigs and roots of trees were twisted or bound into suitable shapes and allowed to grow into shark hooks which might be forty cm long, 'such frightful things, that no fish, less voracious than a shark, would ever approach them.' Nets ranged from mere hand-scoops to seines seventy-five metres long, 'seldom possessed by any but the principal chiefs' who organised their co-operative manufacture; the first wetting of such a net was an occasion of high ceremony. Magic and ritual were essential to success.

Apart from sea-fishing proper, for anything from albacore and shark to flying-fish, there was the wealth of beach, lagoon, and reef: shrimps, crayfish, crabs (and also the tree-climbing landcrabs); amongst bivalves, mussels, oysters, cockles, and the giant clam *Tridacna*, their shells providing basins, spoons, scrapers, ornaments and cutting tools; delicious sea-urchins; octopuses, enticed from their coral crannies by cowrie-shell lures; turtles, sacred and reserved for chiefs,[25] as often were albacore and other big fish. They were also tapu to women.

Artefacts and arts

Before the European takeover, which brought with it demands from Church and State for concentration, most Polynesians lived not in recognisably discrete villages (though there were some) but in little homesteads spread through the gardening areas, separate but not so far distant from each other as to be really 'dispersed settlement'; here and there might be some thickening of the stipple, for instance around the seat of a great chief. Although there might be a continuous belt of settlement around an island, this was continuous only in a physical, not a social, sense; it was segmented by the boundaries of the various land-holding groups, which tended to run from the coast to the centre, like the wedges of a pie. (This gave each group access to each of the productive zones— reef, lagoon, coastal lowland, bush; such layouts, transverse to the ecological zoning, are found in many countries.) Of course this is a notional model, but it was quite often approached in reality, with variations enforced by accident of topography and history. In New Guinea and New Zealand the whole scale of things was different; the terrain was much more diversified and so were settlement patterns, ranging from tiny shifting hamlets to large nucleated villages.[26]

Except for marae and a few other stone buildings, architecture was vegetal: timber frames, matting walls, thatched roofs, though the frames might be placed on blocks of stone or coral. 'Bamboo and thatch' does not mean that a building was rude or 'primitive'; nobody could think that who has seen the towering polychromatic façade of a New Guinea *haus tambaran* or 'spirit-house', still more the cunning engineering of its internal structure designed to withstand high hill-top winds, or a great Fijian *bure* (Plate V). The Reverend William Ellis complained of the Tahitian 'wide unpartitioned buildings, by no means favourable to domestic comfort and Christian decency',[27] but such dwellings if properly maintained (an important qualification) were very well adapted to their environment climatically and aesthetically, and to their purposes of family living and hospitality, both 'open plan'; and if they very rarely harboured much privacy, they were certainly not without domestic comfort.

The Oceanians had 'No Sort of Iron',[28] but they wrought marvels of utility and beauty from wood, stone, shell and bone with tools of stone and shell, and sharks' teeth as gravers. Handtools as well as houses and canoes were held together by sennit lashings of intricate elegance. Many raw materials were used for plaiting and splendid basketry: coconut and pandanus leaves, reeds, bamboo, were fashioned into sleeping-mats, sails, screens, even body-wrappers and 'ponchos'; fine mats were prominent in ceremonial presentations and exchanges and as emblems of prestige. Cloth—*ahu* in Tahiti, *tapa* in Hawaii (the most generally used term today), *masi* in Fiji—was made by beating out the inner bark of the paper mulberry and other trees with wooden mallets; the bark was resinous, and so narrow strips could be felted together into bolts nearly 200 metres long.

The finest tapa was very soft and white; designs were stamped or impressed with vegetable dyes. Mat-making and cloth-beating were in the main women's tasks, often in a sociable working-bee, and ladies of high rank took pride in the corresponding refinement of their handiwork; Ellis has a delightful vignette of the 'Queen' of Eimeo (Moorea) and her ladies pounding away, and highly amused by the effect of the din on her visitor: at a distance the noise was not disagreeable, 'indicating the abode of industry and peace; but in the cloth-houses it is hardly possible to endure it'.[29] Like the mats, cloth was conspicuous in presentations and displays of wealth.

Display was also provided by personal adornment. Many societies practised tattooing, and in New Zealand the ribbed and vigorously swirling patterns achieved a remarkable dynamism; in Hawaii the art of feather-work reached its height. Design of a very high order was also shown in wood-carving, whether for utilitarian bowls, boxes, and canoe-bailers, or for ceremonial objects and weaponry; William Morris would have felt at home.[30] In Melanesia the makers of masks produced bizarre but powerful masterpieces.[31] But perhaps the triumphs of material aesthetic achievement in Oceania were the magnificent war canoes, as we see them in the paintings of William Hodges or John Webber.

But then the making of canoes was in the highest degree involved with magical and religious significance. Some were sacred to a god, and these needed human sacrifices at their launchings; everywhere boat-builders, like the architects of marae, commanded high prestige. The various crafts had their own chants and spells; 'Every phase in the construction of a large canoe was surrounded by magico-religious ritual' and 'A craftsmen careless of ritual is also careless of workmanship.'[32] This held good for all skilled workers, by hand or brain; for gardeners, for fishermen, for poets.[33] Prayer as well as patience was needed for the marvels of workmanship with tools of stone or shell, and there was little distinction between sacred and mundane: carpenters and priests shared the honorable name of *tohunga* or man of eminent skills.[34] There was a religious component even in sports such as archery.[35]

But the most inspiriting creative achievements of the Pacific peoples must surely be found in the arts, often interwoven, of oratory, song, dance and drama. The Oceanic Muse commanded a wide range of genres: rhythmic work-chants; bardic narratives weaving genealogy and myth into wild and noble tales of gods, demi-gods, and mortal heroes; praises of ancestral deeds, panegyrics of chiefly lines; invocations to mighty deities like Tangaroa and Oro; simple personal prayers; cosmic reflections; spells and charms; ballads and war-songs; direct or metaphoric erotic verse; formal ode and taut jeering epigram.[36] Some modes were enhanced by settings and dance, often by torchlight, *son et lumière*.

A certain invidious eminence in the dance has indeed been accorded to the South Seas ever since the first European reports, half-shocked half-delighted, of the Tahitian dancing by enticing young ladies in topless crinolines. This has obscured recognition of the deep social significance of the dance throughout Oceania and of its range of settings and purposes, far beyond the *hula*—dances for prowess in love or war, for fertility, but also dances symbolising the spiritual relationship betwen humankind and the all-embracing Earth Mother. Religious exegesis could blend with secular narration into an indefinitely extensible ballet, reaching far back into the ancestral past and returning to lively comment on current affairs; an impressive achievement intellectually, and even today, usually in sadly diminished form, an impressive spectacle in both Melanesia and Polynesia. No wonder that in the Marquesas 'the master of chants was outranked only by the chief and the inspirational priest.'[37]

So far the picture seems one of a Sidneian Arcadia in which an easy elegance was the rule of life. It was not so; classic Polynesia deserved the name 'the Age of Elegance' no less, probably more, than did the Regency and Reign to which Arthur Bryant applied that ticket; but it too had its underside:

> old Polynesia had two faces, one of them ghastly. Warface, over-population, infanticide, starvation, oppressive taboos, heavy obligation to chiefs, human sacrifice, cannibalism, and slavery decimated society, and natural disasters of hurricanes and/or *tsunami* devastated the islands.[38]

With wonderful resilience, or nonchalance, humankind can push to the back of its mind natural disaster, can live and be cheerful under the shadow of a volcano or of nuclear war; and yet the fear is there, lurking. In Oceania, fear was a constant: the creeping internal fear of sorcery and of malign spirits who must be bought off by more sorcery or by sacrifice. Tribal warfare was endemic, and the penalties for the losers were often cruel and bloody in the extreme.

There were mitigations. In Melanesia 'Big-Men' dominated by a Tammany boss's code of generous hand-outs; in more hierarchical Polynesia there was a code of reciprocity, *noblesse oblige*, in theory rather like the sentimentalised picture of the Squire's Merrie England, and in practice perhaps much the same: as Oliver sums up the Tahitian precepts for the good chief, the just and benevolent Lord, 'as I interpret these remarkable guidelines for tribal "good government", the "goodness" had to do mainly with benefits to the chief.'[39] And, almost literally, the Devil took the hindmost.

Nevertheless, all debits debited, the Oceanic achievement, with limited resources, was very considerable. It has been said that while Pacific people could work very hard on occasion, 'their work was mostly physical, without the mind being greatly stretched.'[40] The design of a *haus tambaran*; the complex devices of the Melanesian trading rings; the building and navigation of the great ocean-going canoes; the diplomatic protocol, matching that of post-Renaissance Europe in its niceties; the elaboration of ceremonial and customary social controls; the superbly organised spectacles of song and dance; the subtle cosmogonies—these seem to me reasonably mind-stretching activities.

Kin and land

'The land is the people; break up the land and you break up the people'[41]— a succinct statement of a basic feeling which runs through all Oceania, through all the wearisome complexities of kinship systems and land tenures. Land *ownership*, as conceptualised by Europeans, is an almost meaningless term; *rights* in the use of land a term of potency. Land was held not individually but by groups of kinsmen; but it was as a rule occupied and worked by individuals and their close relatives. There was a prescriptive right to cultivate garden land, but this was not perpetual; it was more in the nature of an informal lease to be varied as circumstances varied. The surrounding bush was in a sense common land, though not worked in common but rather held as a joint stock which could be drawn upon by group members at need, whether for forest products or cultivation. This was nominally with the consent of the group, in practice generally with that of the chief or the elders, as representing the common good.[42]

Harold Brookfield expresses the rationale admirably: notionally the cultivator and his heirs had rights in perpetuity, but family needs vary through time, and with shifting cultivation a family needs right of access to more land than it currently works. 'Flexibility of allocation and protection of individual right are both necessary', and could not be secured by individual tenure; but 'Behind and around individual title is a continuing group title, to used and unused land alike', and, 'the individual's rights mesh . . . into those of the group.'[43] For long-lived tree crops, as a rule the usufruct belonged to the planter wherever he planted them, but normally permission to do so would be sought from any interested parties, and first-fruits would be presented.[44]

In the more hierarchical societies, commoners' use of land was subject to more or less direction by the chiefs, who could for example either prescribe or proscribe the raising of a particular crop, sometimes in response to genuine social need or ecological constraint, sometimes to meet personal ambitions by the display of wealth or power. The chief initiated communal enterprise and was responsible for the fair allocation of land. In some places, however, there was at least an incipience of feudalism. In irrigable Hawaii there was a definitely proprietary attitude to land by the more powerful chiefs, whose traditional functions of distributing land and mobilising resources for prestations and ceremonies were largely carried out by officials, the collectors of tribute; in effect the genial custom of first-fruits was transformed into an arbitrary tax.[45] The 'communism' of Islands society is a myth.[46]

'Take me to your Leader'

The classic portrayal of contrast between Melanesian societies and those of Micronesia and Polynesia was made by Marshall Sahlins. In Melanesia, except for Fiji, New Caledonia and the New Guinea Highlands (no mean exceptions!), political units were very small kin-residence groups, villages or mere hamlets which simply repeated a strongly egalitarian pattern. There were no wide political structures, or hardly any, no permanent hierarchies, and power or rather influence was exercised by 'Big-Men' who built up clientèles by displays of calculated generosity, especially through ceremonial feasting. Intense rivalry meant that they had to keep up their positions by putting on bigger and better performances, and this meant drawing on their clients for support in the amassing of material goods for public giveaways. Sooner or later a Big-Man was likely to find himself charging his followers more than the traffic would bear; his faction would dissolve and eclipse ensued. The Big-Man's authority was achieved, not inherited or ascribed, and so was personal to himself; there was 'a flux of rising and falling leaders', and obviously this set 'ceilings on the intensification of political authority.'[47]

In Polynesia, on the other hand, there were pyramids of lower and higher chiefs culminating in a paramount who might control a whole island or more; since the high chiefs were of divine descent they had inherited sanctity. A chief was a true holder of officer and title, which descended to his heirs, not a temporary *primus inter pares* like a Big-Man; the power of command, in Polynesia was 'socially assigned to office and rank.' Of course privilege carried responsibilities, for the correct conduct of the ceremonies necessary for prosperity, for good governance, for liberal feasting, and there was an ethos of generosity. And chiefs, like Big-Men, could overstrain the system or could lose prestige and position through personal failings; but the political structure remained.

Sahlins also attempted an evolutionary classification of Polynesian societies, based on their degree of class-stratification, which in turn was correlated with the productive capacities of the various island units: 'the greater the productivity, the greater the distributive activities of the chief, and the greater his powers.' And this depended directly on the number of people in the given unit.[48] Sahlins then worked out relativities in detail, ranking Hawaii, Tonga, Tahiti and (less assuredly) Samoa as the most stratified societies, and some atolls as the least; a result entirely expectable on gross empirical grounds. Working with 'status level' as his criterion, Irving Goldman produced a classification into Traditional, Stratified and Open Societies; his placing is very similar to that of Sahlins, especially at the top end.[49]

These analyses of a mass of most complex data are an agreeable change from the almost tribally-solipsist approach of some anthropologists; both have a somewhat determinist and 'cultural materialist' cast. Sahlins indeed, with refreshing elasticity of mind, has notably changed his stance; but despite himself 'his early work lives a life of its own today.'[50] Seminal as his earlier views have been, they have not escaped questioning, especially of the rather too pat Melanesian/Polynesian antithesis.

Empirically, the assertion that the Big-Man had always to struggle for the power and influence that the chief received by birthright seems too stark. On a broad view the dichomoty has some validity, but in detail it seems overdrawn, overlooking some aspects of leadership in both realms, and many exceptions: 'It is clear that ascription and achievement are not polar opposites, but a matter of emphasis in particular contexts.'[51] Being the son of a Big-Man did not make one in turn a Big-Man, but it certainly helped (where doesn't it?), and being the son of a high chief certainly gave one a strong presumption of inheriting, but did not guarantee a peaceful succession or long continuance in office.[52] Moreover, quite apart from the admitted and annoying exceptions in Fiji and New Caledonia, plausibly ascribed to Polynesian influence, many Melanesian societies 'emphasized ascription in one form or another and... demonstrated hereditary succession to leadership office'; the degrees of ascription and achievement overlap along a continuum, and 'in most respects New Caledonian and Maori leadership were more like each other than either was like the leadership stereotype' for its own cultural realm.

From a different angle, using linguistic reconstructions, Andrew Pawley analyses the term *ariki* (= chief) and its cognates to show that ' "the Polynesian institution of *ariki* chieftainship" is the continuation of a Proto-Oceanic—that is to say a Proto-Melanesian tradition.' Chieftainship is too widespread in Melanesia to be explained away as borrowing from Polynesia, and there is not 'one law for Polynesians and another for Melanesians.'[53] Finally, Jonathan Friedman queries Sahlins's use of productivity estimates to assess the degree of stratification, finding it tautologous and in some cases empirically unsound. One may also wonder whether Sahlins makes sufficient allowance for the inescapable sketchiness of his demographic data; he takes the pre-contact population of Tahiti as 180,000, while Douglas Oliver makes it 36,366—a discrepancy which seems to make even the roughest quantification pointless.[54] Again, the evolution of societies is not always 'progressive' to a more sophisticated order, as seems implied in Sahlins's approach; the decadence of Easter Island society, long before its devastation by Peruvian slavers, is a terrible exemplar. Friedman argues that 'the simple dichotomy Melanesia/Polynesia is incorrect and that the same kinds of tendencies may cross-cut the supposed cultural and/or evolutionary boundary.'[55]

Chiefs and commoners

All Polynesian societies had chiefs, although in some, such as the Maori, most men could claim to be chiefs of a sort, and in some the chief's way of life differed but little from that of the common herd. Chieftainship descended by male primogeniture, although females could succeed in certain circumstances. An excessively incompetent chief might be deposed, or rather barred from political activity, since he retained the title and he alone could carry out certain essential rituals. Sacred and secular jurisdictions were in fact divided in some islands, and in Tonga the 'King' or Tui Tonga who once had exercised both temporal and spiritual functions, by Cook's time was confined to religious duties, while another Tui was the nominal political leader, and a third the effective executive ruler.[56] Such untidiness greatly confused early European visitors, who thought in terms of sovereignty located in one precisely designated crowned head.

Atoll societies were as a rule relatively simple, without too great a differential between chiefs and commoners; chiefs received deference but rarely exaggerated homage and total submission.[57] On high islands the lines between chiefs—*ariki, aliki, alii, arii*—and their subjects were generally much sharper; sheer numbers probably accounted for much of this, and over the generations the multiplicity of ramifying or segmenting kin-groups meant that, despite a traditional affinity, the highest chiefs (*ariki nui*) became greatly distanced from ordinary members of the clan or tribe. This is setting aside the possible origin of major aristocratic houses in conquest from without, a view now generally discarded except on a local scale, but recently given a new twist by Sahlins.[58]

There were grades of chieftainship, depending on genealogical closeness to the putative Founding Father or on the extent of power; in some island groups there was an intermediate class, the *rangatira* or *raatira*, who in Tahiti might be equated with gentry or yeomen. Below them was the mass of ordinary folk, of some worth as tillers of the soil but 'persons without distinction', and below these the worthless—those at the very tail of the most junior of junior lines, slaves taken in war, or the *kauwa*, the untouchables of Hawaii, who may have been the descendants of people outcast for grave sins against the intricate social and moral codes.[59] Such people provided the bodies for human sacrifices.

There was no full-time artisan class as such, but really skilled people were acknowledged as specialised experts in their crafts. The social status of craftsmen was in general determined by their inherited rank, and could be high or low, while some crafts had associations usually referred to as guilds, though perhaps they were nearer to the fraternities than the guilds of medieval Europe—that is, clubs for worship and feasting rather than rings for trade regulation and quality control. In the absence of money, payment was by subsistence on the job plus donatives in kind; much craft work was not 'commercial employment' but service owed to a chief and participation in a community project. Thus for the making of a great Hawaiian feather cloak 'the whole social system—gods, chiefs, priests, and commoners—was activated and called upon at different stages.

Only a chief with the support of his *kahuna* (priests and craftspeople) had access to the necessary feathers and workers.'[60]

Once more, ritual was essential; magic and technique overlapped; the canoe-builders of Samoa, great sticklers for custom, had their expertise 'reinforced by the belief in their magical power to make a canoe unlucky, if they were not satisfied with the generosity of their employer.'[61] Court and cult also demanded their servants: retainers and waiting-women for chiefs and their wives; the fledgling bureaucracy of land-stewards or bailiffs (*konohiki*) in Hawaii; soothsayers and shamans; the orators or 'talking chiefs' (*tulafale*) of Samoa; bards or rhapsodists such as the *orero* of Tahiti, who were 'required to have tireless lungs and a fool-proof memory' to deliver, non-stop and word-perfect, lengthy chants to the crowds in the marae.[62]

Chiefs themselves had very important religious functions and their authority was underpinned by belief in their divine descent; but their prestige was still 'subject to abrogation by assassination, deposition or defeat in war', and hence the need for special mediators with the super-natural, priests whose role would be less vulnerable to political accident.[63] Priests, like craftsmen, could come from many ranks of society, and some ministered to their own craft only, especially in Hawaii 'where every craft and every status had its own cult and its own priests.'[64] In fact the heads of all social groups, down to the household, probably had some religious function as intermediaries with the gods or at least a familial tutelary god (the saying of grace before meals by European fathers of families is a faint analogy, or vestige), but there was a specialised priesthood charged with more public duties such as the delivery of oracles and the taking of auguries, especially for war. Recruitment, as in the crafts, was largely hereditary, but there was a training or novitiate; we can see why the two groups were bracketed as tohunga. Some priests were attached to marae; as the equivalent of a simple parson of the parish for the humbler shrines, for the greater temples one might almost say as a cathedral chapter: Tahitian high priests were indeed compared to bishops,[65] and it is clear that high chief and high priest were normally closely associated in governance.

Chiefs: tapu *and* mana

Their ascribed divinity hedged Polynesian chiefs within a sheltering net-work of prohibitions, *tapu* or *tabu*, whence our 'taboo'. The general effect of tapu might be summed up as *noli me tangere*, don't touch me, and the extreme of chiefly untouchability seems to have been reached in Hawaii, where 'Not even the shadow of a person was to fall on the person or possession of a high chief', or in Tahiti where even the sounds making up the royal names were tapu, so that ordinary words containing them had to be changed for the duration of the reign. Chiefly privilege extended to preferential treatment in the after-life.[66]

Persons or things under tapu were regarded as charged with a potentially highly dangerous force, and so must be approached or handled only with the utmost precaution; hence the usual equation of the word with 'prohibited'. Contact with a tapu'd person or object could contaminate, so that there was a connotation of impurity; yet since tapu was ultimately of divine origin, it could also be sacred—the term implied 'a sanctity demanding ritual avoidance'. Which of these aspects was dominant depended on circumstances, and there were degrees of intensity.[67]

Tapu was so to say inherent and permanent in the persons and property of high chiefs, and indeed in Tahiti it could be imprinted on the soil by the mere footfall of a paramount chief, who had consequently to be carried about on men's shoulders, lest his tracks disrupt the coutryside.[68] As well as tapu on bodily contacts there were many tapu relating to food, especially to enforce sexual segregation while eating and to reserve certain foods, such as turtles, for chiefs and/or males. Many tapu were local and *ad hoc*; there were of course rules and rituals for lifting them when the time came. The sanctions for violation could be secular and immediate, even death if a powerful chief were involved, or more usually were supernatural and delayed, in the form of disease and again perhaps death; after all, the chief had the best sorcerers at call.[69] To early Europeans some tapu were intelligible as keeping women and the lower classes in their places, but the bewildering variety of local and temporary tapu often seemed utterly capricious, mere 'haphazard superstitions, sacraments of savagery'; but ships' captains and even missionaries soon found the uses of placing 'taboos' on their own accounts.[70] It is not surprising that many affrays stemmed from witting or unwitting breaches of tapu.

Tapu on places could be permanent, or permanent for certain classes—women were as a rule barred from marae—but not only chiefs but also quite ordinary people could protect their plantings, trees, reefs and fishing-grounds by temporary tapu, marking the limits with strips of cloth or plaited leaves. An important form of tapu, *rahui* in Tahiti, banned the consumption of designated foods, and might be backed by dangerous spells. Typical occasions for food tapu were to accumulate stocks for the feasts which accompanied chiefly births, marriages and deaths; to allow recovery after the devastation of war, drought or hurricane; or to build up stores to feed workers on a big project like building a marae. They might, however, be imposed simply to guard against over-fishing or to conserve stocks against an expected dearth.[71]

Apart from any direct economic benefits, tapu was an important factor in social control and, more positively, it helped in canalising collective energies; for a big job, such as the piecing together of a huge seine, the artefact, the tools, the workers and the work-place were all tapu: an effective discipline on the shop-floor.

Plate V. A FIJIAN CHIEFLY HOUSE. By Conway Shipley, 1851. This splendid structure, 38 metres long, belonged to Tanoa, high chief of Bau and father of King Cakobau. By permission of the Pitt-Rivers Museum, Oxford.

As we have seen, even a deposed chief retained his ritual functions, which came to him by virtue of his divine descent; but he would have lost most if not all of his *mana*. This is a most difficult and elusive concept, with many English renderings: psychic power (vague, and hence perhaps the favourite), divine force, totemic principle, miracle, authority, prestige, 'not only a force, a being; it is also an action, a quality, and a state'.[72] Some writers on mana verge upon a metaphysical mysticism; Firth and Oliver protest against the assumption that the word means much the same wherever it is found; the former sees it as an anthropological term of art which may have little in common with its actual usage by Islanders. Yet there is no doubt that it was and is a word of power, whatever the local nuances.

Chiefly mana was an inherited quality, and yet it was not entirely inherent nor inalienably fixed; it could be added to by success in affairs, or diminished, even destroyed, by failure; and although it was an index of power, it was an index not based on a simple mechanical assessment of resources. It combined material strength and *la gloire*: Napoleon had a mighty mana until 1812 and finally lost it in 1815. A man's personal effort could enhance his mana, and people of low degree could gain mana by resolute action in a time of troubles.

Behind the concept lay the belief that the chief, owing to his divine descent, was in much closer touch with the all-potent world of spirits than ordinary men could be; and it had the very practical significance that a chief's mana affected, one might almost say controlled, weather, crops, fishing, health and disease—in sum, the welfare of his people. On Tikopia, Firth found that the people recognised no mana 'alone of itself' but a mana of the rain, of food, and so on. Mana could be conceived of as a quality but not as a metaphysical abstraction; the people were content with the concrete results. He thus arrived at a pragmatic definition (for Tikopia) in terms of the upshot of material happenings (crops, fishing, cure of sickness, death by bewitchment), the personal attributes of chiefs, and the volition of spiritual beings who granted or denied mana to the chiefs.[73] The concept thus sustained the position of chiefs and enhanced their ancestrally-derived power; the occasional failure of one chief to deliver the goods hardly imperilled the institution of chieftainship. The small island of Tikopia was spared the endemic wars which ravaged many islands, but one can see how the concept could carry over into martial situations.

Mana attached to objects as well as persons; the possessions of a chief naturally partook of his mana. Canoes, in which so much capital and ritual were invested, definitely possessed mana, and it has been suggested that tools which long retained their pristine effectiveness thereby acquired it.[74] Finally, at least among the Maori, the term when applied to land seems to have approached the European idea of sovereignty.[75]

Reciprocity and exchange

In principle, Polynesian chiefs, at least in the more stratified societies, had rights not only to customary first-fruits and to labour services for personal as well as communal purposes, and to special objects such as turtles and fine mats, but could levy on the goods of commoners, at times to the point of spoliation.[76] On the other hand, the chief had reciprocal obligations; apart from being organiser of victory, patron of the arts, and co-ordinator of public works, he was responsible for the general welfare, and many of the goods which flowed up to him flowed down again.

His life-style was often much richer than the commoner's, but though he apparently had great possessions, much of his wealth was as it were in trust and passed quickly through his hands, in largesse to his people, 'financing' (that is, feeding) the large contingents withdrawn from their own gardens for big public works, and in presentations to his retainers and experts or to visiting notables. Particularly for artefacts such as fine mats, the chiefly court was a centre of demand, but also, by redistribution, of supply.

The economic ethos, if one may coin a paradoxical term, demanded generosity from the chief, but this depended on the willing flow of goods from his subjects; the return downwards might not be the full equivalent of what came up, but then the managing director was entitled to his fee, the kin shared in the glory of (seemingly) self-regardless liberality, and moreover 'by thus supporting communal welfare and organising communal activities, the chief creates a common good . . . a public economy greater than the sum of its household parts.'[77]

A major vehicle for redistribution was the feast, which was far more than an occasion for uninhibited eating: in one Solomons tribe 'Two words are used for feasts . . . the meaning of the first is "eating", of the second "fame",[78] and this succinct formula could be echoed throughout Oceania. There were many occasions: chiefly births, marriages, deaths and other ritual-demanding happenings; planting and harvest; calendrical events such as the rising of the Pleiades; the start and the end of communal building projects; political purposes—mobilising allies or celebrating peace, honouring embassies. Feasts could be truly spectacular; at one Maori feast in 1844, with some 3400 guests, there was a wall over a metre high, built up of 11,000 baskets of potatoes topped with 9000 dried sharks. Such Gargantuan celebrations carried a clear message from the donors: ours is the wealth, the power, the mana.[79]

Underlying all this was the complex philosophy of gift exchange, which has been called 'the primitive way of achieving the peace that in civil society is secured by the State.'[80] Gift exchange circulated goods in two modes, straight reciprocity and pooling for redistribution, but these merge; pooling was an organised system of ultimately reciprocal exchanges.

Although exchange had 'the appearance of being free and spontaneous', in reality there was calculation. There was a social compulsion to give, and to return at least the equivalent—if possible more, to set up a counter—obligation. The sanctions for repayment were exclusion from the system, loss of good repute and prestige ('face'), fear of witchcraft. Any appearance of overt bargaining or reckoning would have been terribly bad form, unless for some political reason it was desirable to force on a breach. Otherwise no open dissatisfaction would be shown; yet the accounts were kept, mentally but strictly.[81]

All this presents a genial picture of societies based, in their economic life, on forms of mutual aid, albeit with some loading, scarcely excessive, in favour of the directing chiefs. It may often have been so, but in general this is probably too theoretical and rosy a view. In Tahiti, Oliver states that in many or most cases redistribution was largely confined to a clique of retainers at the top, only token amounts going far down, and that most rahui were imposed not for social ends but for the good of the imposers. In Hawaii the development of political structures covering ever larger areas, with ever-increasing distances and tiers of authority between top and bottom, led to a cycle of centralisation and exaction, palace revolts and peripheral revolts. Even on peaceful Tikopia the system of fraternal reciprocity showed signs of cracking under the stress of hurricane-generated famine, and there were rumours of wars.[82] Elsewhere, there were wars.

War and cannibalism

Any illusions about a Pacific, and pacific, Golden Age before Europeans introduced grog and muskets could hardly survive a brief tour of the clustering pa of New Zealand or the ring-forts of Fiji, so strikingly reminiscent of Britain's Iron Age forts. Perhaps the most classic examples of endemic warfare are from Mangareva (Tuamotus) and Mangaia (Cooks). Mangareva carried perhaps 3000 people on 28.5 km² of poor land, where 'under extreme duress [the people] resorted to fresh meat cannibalism . . . Hunger has been described as a common cause of war.' And yet it seems too simple to see the wars just in terms of land hunger; for if so, why should winning tribes ravage and even destroy the breadfruit and coconut groves on the lands they conquered? On Mangaia wars were so ferocious that the normal Polynesian pattern of authority was subverted: 'temporal power was the reward of war and not of hereditary descent'.[83]

Economic factors may not have ranked high among the ostensible causes of war, though in so far as wealth was power they might underlie them. Most Islands wars were straight struggles for power, for the assertion of superior mana, and the humiliation of the enemy by devastating their land might be more satisfying than the economic gain of taking it over unravaged. After this indemnity for their impudent defence, the surviving vanquished might be suffered to exist on their own land, or some of it, paying tribute; or they might not. However, since alliances often shifted rapidly, the 'final solution' was rarely applied.

In principle all the able-bodied males of a tribe, except some priests, were bound to follow their chief to the wars, but subchiefs of a realistic turn of mind might inhibit a high chief from entering upon a chancy war; so also might the priests, who were essential for the necessary rituals and as oracular and oratorical morale-boosters. An important part of mobilisation was the ceremonial summons to carefully cultivated allies. Preliminaries might involve human sacrifices; the bodies could be used for auguries, doubtless sometimes rigged. The forces included women auxiliaries to bring up supplies and look after the wounded, and there were not a few Amazon combatants. The main weapons were clubs, spears, rasps of sharks' teeth or stingray spines, and stones expertly thrown or slung.

There must have been a decidedly feudal air about the assembly of numerous small contingents in various panoplies of war. Much warfare was small-scale bush fighting, but pitched combats with regular orders of battle also took place. There were 'shapers of battle' who marshalled the forces, but once the lines had met, perhaps after single combats by noted warriors, the action seems as a rule to have been a hand-to-hand mêlée without much general direction.[84] As for naval warfare, we know that there were fleets of scores of war-canoes, but Europeans saw only reviews; probably the canoes were used in the Roman manner, as fighting stages.

There were drawn or indecisive battles, and these might be succeeded by a negotiated peace, celebrated of course with much dancing and feasting; but if one side broke, it was usually pursued with ferocity. Women and children were slaughtered, perhaps with frightful mutilation before or after death; houses were burnt, groves and gardens wrecked. The remnants of the defeated, if not reduced to vassaldom or slavery, sought refuge in inland fortresses or remote and wild terrain, perhaps to emerge and fight another day, or voyaged into exile, to discovery or death.

The aftermath of battle was a significant context for cannibalism; to eat a slain foe was the extreme expression of revenge, or it might be a sympathetic magic to gain more strength, more mana. This was not the only reason for anthropophagy; hunger or lack of other animal protein drove men to eat other men, and there was also ritual cannibalism, as on the deaths of Marquesan chiefs or prophets. Not all Islanders were cannibals; Tahitians did not indulge, but Fijians were notorious, especially in missionary appeals for funds to rescue the children of perdition.[85] Undoubtedly accounts of cannibal orgies were vastly heightened for religious propaganda or money-grubbing sensationalism; the taller tales

speak more of the inner fantasies of their tellers than of 'savage life'.
Walter Arens is justified in pointing out that few accounts (not, as he
seems to imply, none) can be sheeted home to reliable eye-witnesses,
but he passes far too lightly over the Polynesian evidence, which is too
compelling to warrant his scepticism.[86]

Humans, spirits, and gods

The distinction between magic and religion is often a thin one, and in
Oceania unreal; there was a continuum between the spirits of the home
and the garden and the bush, the immediate agents of death or calamity
or prosperity, to the great cosmic deities of the creation myths. The
former were to be placated or enlisted as allies by magical rites and
spells, the latter worshipped in what even European minds sometimes
saw as a truly religious mode; their servants, however benighted, were
real priests, not just witch-doctors or sorcerers, though there was much
overlap. Between such mighty deities as Tangaroa, the maker of man,
and the spirit who watched over the family yam-patch, there swarmed
a host of godlings, tutelaries of a tribe or a cult or a craft. A Marquesan
proverb ran 'To every island its gods: to every fisherman his god.'[87]

In a spirit-dominated world, myriads of natural omens affected day-
to-day doings, and deliberately-sought auguries (as by divination from
sacrificed animals or men) exercised strong influence on public and private
actions; as well as the formal oracles promulgated by accredited priests,
there were the utterances of persons possessed or inspired by spirits. Magic
was therefore essential for the control of nature and for protection against
unknown but suspected supernatural malevolences and the sorcery of
human enemies, and again for the encouragement or cajoling of whatever
benevolences might be.

The use of magic did not of course preclude intense practical application
and technical skill in, say, gardening and navigation, based on a rich
inherited knowledge of natural phenomena: one planted at the right time
for the rains. But it was also empirically known that the rains did not
always come at the right time for the planting, for reasons unknown
but in all probability due to the displeasure of gods or spirits, touchy
beings whom it was all too easy to offend inadvertently; and 'Hence
we have the entry of magic upon the economic stage, the attempt to
control the ungovernable'.[88]

One form of mediation between man and the supernatural is through
occult societies. In Melanesia secret societies were widespread, but in
Polynesia the most known (or notorious) association, the Arioi of the
Society Islands, was anything but secret; since it numbered perhaps up
to one-fifth of the population, how could it be?

This was a society open to both sexes and all ranks; candidates faced a long probation in the lowest of seven grades, unless they were chiefs of standing, who could enter well up the ladder. These prentice years were devoted to meticulous drilling in song, dance, and lyrical and satiric drama; for the main on-duty occupation of the Arioi was the giving of elaborate entertainments, often on tour round the islands. In some respects the Arioi resembled a freemasonry, and these tours were valued as a counter to inter-tribal or island antipathies; although they were often warriors—their patron Oro was the god of battles—their visits could lead to at least the suspension of tribal wars. Against this their maintenance and plundering habits could impose a severe strain on their hosts.

Only the lower ranks of Arioi engaged in the more strenuous performances; the seniors lent ease and dignity to the proceedings. The entertainments had very strong and explicit sexual content; according to the Reverend William Ellis, Ariori privileges included automatic entry at death to a lascivious Paradise,[90] and in this life, besides receiving lavish material gifts, they ran to free and frequent copulation amongst themselves. But the most startling Arioi practice was infanticide; to have killed a child was probably not a prerequisite for entry, but retention of membership nearly always involved the destruction of any offspring of their genial activities;[91] indeed, to have a child and let it live seems to have been a method of resigning for those who felt that for them the heyday in the blood was tame.

Yet the Arioi were more than just 'strolling players and privileged libertines'; for all their lasciviousness, the performance had a strong religious component, presenting 'the two main principles, Tangaroa and the matter with which he united, the creation of the world, of the gods, and of the elements ... the lives of the demi-gods or hereos, these being followed by love-scenes'—the same zest for vigorous living and love-making as was displayed in the Greek Olympus by its

> gods, in sundry shapes
> Committing heady riots, incests, rapes ... .[92]

The great Gods of Polynesia by some reports seem to have been like the Lucretian deities, aloofly at ease in an Empyrean above any concern for the human world, with at their head a Deist First Cause who set the world spinning and then sat back; this at least for Tangaroa in Tahiti, where he was regarded as 'too far above the things of this world ... to interest himself in the fate of men', wherefore he had no temples and few worshippers, 'although all were zealous in celebrating his glory, power, and works'. And yet the same early authority says that 'the gods were not merely concerned with the important events of life, for there was not a single action, enterprise, or event' with which they were not involved; in effect, a sparrow 'shall not fall on the ground' without divine cognisance.[93] At all events the gods were very ready to take offence if their due offerings and ceremonials were neglected.

In Samoa also Tangaroa held a unique position, but elsewhere Tane was held to have been the maker of men, and there were rivals: Oro, son of Tangaroa and god of war; Hiro, a shifty Ulysses, patron of seamen and thieves; the only half-divine Maui 'of a thousand tricks', the fisher of islands.[94] The details of the pantheon were fluctuant from archipelago to archipelago.

We are left with an impression of the great impersonal forces of the Cosmos dramatically personified: Gods created in man's much magnified image. A great and wild poetry for the heavens and the deeps of ocean; and here on Middle-Earth a civilisation racked by brute fear and dark sorceries and cruel wars, yet with much tenderness and joy, a graceful aesthetic and a tough realism co-existing in a very human mix.

Chapter 3

THE TASK AND THE TOOLS

The pilots now their rules of art apply,
The mystic needle's devious aim to try.
The compass plac'd to catch the rising ray,
The quadrant's shadows studious they survey!
Along the arch the gradual index slides
While Phoebus down the vertic circle glides...
Their sage experience thus explores the height
And polar distance of the source of light:
Then through the chiliads triple maze they trace
Th'analogy that proves the magnet's place.

Europe and the Pacific in 1700

Before the eighteenth century, the Oceanic Pacific had not been subject to European incursion, but merely to forays that passed through and stayed not, leaving no doubt on a score or so of islands memories of a mysterious apparition, a few tools and trinkets, perhaps a few babies, from the visits of Mendaña and Quiros.[1] The Manila Galleon routes were desert tracks, with the one oasis of Guam; the buccaneers found nothing new, apart from the shadowy and suspect 'Davis Land'. Le Maire and Tasman did indicate the existence of other oases, but their voyages were only traverses made as quickly as might be.

Only in 1764, with Byron, beings the era of incursions, mainly State-run expeditions formally organised and, from Cook onwards, taking their time about it. The rivals, Britain, France and Spain, were ostensibly concerned for the advancement of knowledge, but always with keen eyes to the main chance in commercial and geopolitical advantage. By 1780–90 the main lineaments of the island groups had been established, and with the founding of Sydney in 1788 incursion was succeeded by invasion: whalers, traders, missionaries, transient as individuals, formed an economic and social force that had come to stay.

But in 1700 European knowledge of the Pacific was practically confined to its margins, and even then with two great gaps—all the north from southern Japan to California, all the eastern coast of New Holland, were

---

W. Falconer, *The Shipwreck* (London 3rd ed. 1769); the
operation described is checking magnetic variation with azimuth
compass and log tables (chiliads).

55

terrae incognitae. Exploitation of the known margins was well advanced, by Spanish colonisation or by the East India Companies; but real knowledge was very unequal, or unequally accessible, and largely confined to the selvedge. The Pacific shores of Spanish America were to all intent no more open to the outside inquirer than were those of China or Japan. The great succession of Spanish historians of the Indies were of academic interest, but away from the Caribbean very little indeed was known of *current* conditions. Apart from sports such as the English priest-errant Thomas Gage, the reporters were buccaneers on raids or on the run, and very few had anything like Dampier's objective and inquiring spirit. It is perhaps not too much to say that not until the Frenchman Frézier in 1716 was there a full, informed and accessible report by a neutral observer; and Frézier's admirable observations dealt only with the littoral of Chile and Peru.[2]

Yet, however inadequate or distorted the information on the content of the Pacific littorals, their outlines (apart from the gaps mentioned) were known; the maps were there. It was far otherwise with the truly Oceanic Pacific.

Although in the two and a half centuries between Magellan and Cook there may have been as many as 450 European crossings of the Pacific,[3] the vast majority of these were by Manila Galleons on their fixed route, which even on its southern west-bound limb passed north of all the Islands except Hawaii and the Marianas. By visit or by native report the Spaniards knew of the western Carolines; further east some of the Marshalls and a few of the Gilberts (Kiribati) had been sighted. But knowledge was so vague that some islands were 'discovered' more than once.[4]

In the southern Marianas four islands were indeed well known: Saipan, Rota, Tinian, Guam. They exercised a magnetic attraction for scurvy-ridden crews, buccaneers or privateers, following the westward track of the Galleon. Despite Legaspi's annexation of Guam in 1565 and its annual use as a way-station by the Galleon from Acapulco, actual colonisation began only in 1668; but interlopers were keenly aware of the value of the group, which was visited by Drake, Cavendish, van Noort, Spilbergen and the Nassau Fleet before 1668, and after by the buccaneers Eaton and Swan (with Dampier), the privateers Rogers and Clipperton, and Commodore Anson. In an odd way Guam was almost neutral, 'welcom[ing] any ships that come, friend or foe, in times of war or peace';[5] though given Spanish weakness on the spot this was doubtless from necessity not choice.

Elsewhere information was scrappy indeed. The northern coast of New Guinea was known by 1545, and in 1606 Torres sailed through the strait named after him; but the insularity of New Guinea, though sometimes suspected, was not part of the stock of common European knowledge in 1700.[6] Tasman in 1644 was instructed to discover whether there was a passage south of the island, but turned back just too soon; a year earlier, however, his great if well-distanced circumnavigation of New Holland set limits to any hypothetical protrusion of that landmass north and east into the Pacific.

East of New Guinea a total of five or six score islands and atolls, out of thousands, had been seen by Europeans before 1700; landings had been made on two or three dozen. Mendaña and Quiros had been in the Marquesas, Tuamotus, Solomons, Santa Cruz and Espíritu Santo, Le Maire had added the northern Tongan outliers, Tasman had added New Zealand, Tonga itself, and the merest glimpse of Fiji. In the remoter east, tiny Henderson and Ducie, beyond Pitcairn, had astonishingly enough been seen by Quiros; but the land, or cloud, seen by Edward Davis in 1681 could not be, as has been thought, Easter Island. Considering the multitude of islands, the list of sightings is not long; and some of the most important—the Society, Samoan, and Hawaiian Islands, and New Caledonia, had not been seen by Europeans, as of record, by 1700.[7]

But what, apart from vague outlines and dots on maps, was actually *known*? The answer must be, 'not much'. Of those visitors who returned to report, only Mendaña and Quiros had made more than the briefest landings, and the total of their three stays was forty-eight weeks. For practical men and practical purposes, their lyrical estimates of Pacific potentialities were heavily discounted by the extraordinary vagueness of their longitudes.

Anything more, by 1700 or even 1750, had to be picked out from the journals of less dedicated voyagers. One can get something of their flavour from the marginal notes scattered through de Brosses:

> Solomon isles, rich in gold... Perfidy of islanders... copulation of turtles... there is no people which habitually nourishes itself on human flesh... History of the solitary on Juan Fernandez which has given rise to the romance of Robinson Crusoe ['which one still reads willingly']... Docility of the people... Their women paint themselves... Treachery of the women... Description of the bird of Paradise... Bad people of the thousand Isles...

There is of course more in the text; some travellers, from Pigafetta to Dampier, were good and alert obervers; but it does not amount to much.

Perhaps the thing that most struck the seamen was the handiness of the canoes; for the rest, the 'Indians' were by and large judged by their readiness to exchange fresh provisions for trade trinkets. Yet we have already, long before Bougainville's Nouvelle Cythère, a few faint and scattered hints of the carefree Good or Noble Savage, in Gonneville and Le Maire, along with savages less noble by far, whom yet 'we should not consider as pure animals', even if they seem just that. After all, 'every animal, man as well as brute, is born equally savage' and will remain so if left to himself; but even amongst brute beasts, how many are capable of domestication!⁸ There is hope, but the Enlightenment has still some way to go.

There was also a persistent *leit-motif*, a known and dominant route— round South America and then up the Chile-Peruvian coast, or with the Trades across the Ocean, on either course striking into the Galleon track from New Spain to Guam. Beyond these known corridors were only spots of islands, shifting and fragmented bits of coasts. But in the commercial rivalries of the later seventeenth century, in the turmoil of the Spanish Succession and its aftermath, pressures were building up towards the second and greatest European opening of the Pacific, beginning with State initiatives but fulfilled by wider and freer economic enterprise than that of the old Crown and Company monopolies. The chief fuglemen were John Campbell, Charles de Brosses and his plagiarist John Callender, and Alexander Dalrymple. But before discussing, in the next chapter, the alliance of geophysics and geopolitics of which they were the theorists, we must look at the technical resources for the great achievement of the disclosure and enclosure of the Ocean.

Sails, steering, and water supply

The ships of Cook and Bougainville were far more efficient machines for navigation than were those of Mendaña, Drake, and Tasman. The trend in the later seventeenth century was towards cleaner lines, away from the towering after-castles, gorgeous with Baroque gilding and tower-ing, unfunctionally, to the glory of a Vasa, a Stuart, a Bourbon; the result was a ship almost flush-decked but for a low poop.⁹ The tendency was also to reduce the size but increase the number of the propulsive square sails. Although the 'ship' in the restricted technical sense was a three-master, the maid-of-all-work brig, square-rigged on two masts, came to its floreat in the eighteenth century; but the nomenclature for the variant rigs of the smaller craft was in such licentious flux that even experts sometimes give up.¹⁰

Merchantmen and warships ceased to be as interchangeable as in Armada days.¹¹ At one extreme was the box-like Dutch *fluyt* or fly-boat, designed to maximise cargo-space and minimise the crew required, a relatively shallow-draft vessel, flat-bottomed and taking the ground well; colliers such as Cook's *Endeavour* followed the same principles. But this was at the expense of speed; the hulls of warships had to have the bulky strength to carry heavy guns, but also narrower underwater lines for speed. For exploration, warships had the disadvantages of relatively deep draught and limited space for stores on voyages lasting for years, and they needed many more men.

Plate VI. THE *ENDEAVOUR* AT WHITBY. By T. Luby, 1768. The barque is the *Earl of Pembroke* before she was commissioned as Cook's *Endeavour*. By permission of National Library of Australia, Canberra.

Men-of-war or merchantman, handling qualities were greatly improved early in the eighteenth century by a number of seemingly minor changes in rig. The square sails were of course the propellants, and the increase in their number broke up the total surface of sail into smaller units easier for the men to handle and so enabling the amount of canvas set to be more quickly adjusted to changes in the wind. But besides these propulsive sails, at either end of the ship were 'voiles d'évolution' or balancing sails, the set of which supplemented the action of the narrow rudder. Forward, seventeenth century ships carried a spritsail, too close to the water to be very effective, underneath the bowsprit, and above it a spritsail topsail, 'an awkward contraption' very liable to be carried away.[12] These inefficient sails were replaced by much handier fore-and-aft jibs, in the Royal Navy between 1702 and 1715. At the stern the effective but clumsy lateen mizzen yielded to a spanker or driver, a quadrilateral sail carried on a gaff and much more easily set. 'The practical effect of all these changes in sail plan was to make ships lighter on the helm and easier to handle; to give them better performance when closehauled on a wind . . . and to save labour.'[13]

There was also a most useful change in the steering mechanism. The rudder was originally moved by a horizontal tiller which in heavy weather required the strength of several men; in large vessels the tiller came in on the lower deck, and steering by orders shouted from above was obviously unsatisfactory. To overcome this, the tiller was provided with a whipstaff, a lever passing up to the quarterdeck. This was mechanically inefficient and really useful only in good weather, since it could be wrenched from the helmsman's grasp by a sudden heavy sea. Around 1700–5 some designer thought of running lines from a yoke on the rudder to a drum on the quarterdeck, which could be rotated by a wheel. This device, soon widely adopted, provided a readier response of helm and helmsman, and even in rough weather needed only two men at the wheel, in good weather only one.[14]

Long-distance navigation, especially within the tropics, was hampered by the recurrent need of careening a ship to get rid of weeds and barnacles and to coat the bottom with various compositions hopefully effective against teredos and other marine borers; Le Maire's *Eendracht* was but one of the ships lost by fire as a result of 'breaming', burning off the weed with brushwood fires. In the sixteenth century sheathing with lead plates had been tried, but proved too expensive, heavy, and unreliable; builders fell back on a wooden outer sheathing with an inner lining of tar and hair. Another widely used method was 'filling', studding the sheathing with flat-headed nails driven in so closely that their rust formed an inverted carapace for the hull; this was effective, but favoured the growth of weed and so reduced speed.

The British Admiralty experimented with copper sheathing in 1761–3, and the *Dolphin*, the third ship so treated, went twice round the world. This was effective against both worm and weed, but the bolting of the plates to the timbers, and fittings such as rudder-pintles, were seriously corroded by the electrolytic reaction of copper and iron, which could be avoided by using copper for bolts and pintles, but at increased cost. It was not until the late 1770s that copper bottoms came into general naval use, to the enhancement of speed and the longevity of hulls.[15] One obstacle to the use of copper sheathing in remoter seas was the absence of ports with repair facilities; for this reason neither Cook's ships nor Bougainville's had copper sheaths; they were 'filled'.

A major problem on long voyages was the supply of water and cooking fuel; replenishment of both was a necessary obsession of captains—it was the insistence of La Pérouse's second in command, de Langle, on taking on more water that led to his own death at Samoan hands. Various methods were tried to purify putrid water; on his second voyage Cook had a 'Tin Machine . . . a most excellent contrivance' in which water fell through a succession of perforated trays, and the wind at least blew away the stench.[16] Projected devices to distil fresh water from salt were numerous; many worked well enough on a small pilot scale. In March 1768, approaching the Tuamotus and Tahiti, Bougainville ran his 'cucurbite' for twenty-two days; it produced 233 litres per day, about 1 litre per man, and he was happy with it as a supplement.[17]

In England, Joseph Priestley recommended passing easily-made carbon dioxide through seawater, and Cook was directed to try it, but seems to have done so half-heartedly. Dr James Lind, famous as a writer on scurvy, devised a still, and was public-spirited enough not to object too strongly when another naval surgeon took the credit—and a cash prize— for a remarkably similar invention. This also was tried by Cook, on his second voyage, and on one occasion he secured 145 litres in a day. He thought it useful on the whole, but inadequate, as it could produce— if there were plenty of fuel—enough water to support life, but not health. But on the third 'I laid it aside as a thing attended with more trouble than profit.'[18]

Despite their theoretical simplicity and promising start, distilling devices had limitations which prevented general acceptance. They made heavy demands on storage for wood or coal; they could not be used in heavy weather, and were thought, probably justly, to carry an extra fire risk; and of course by the time water was running short, so was wood to fuel them. Those who gave them a fair trial returned favourable verdicts, but only as a useful adjunct to the main supply.

One of the most dreaded hazards of the sea, fire, was considerably mitigated by Benjamin Franklin's invention of the lightning-conductor in 1752; this won almost immediate acceptance. At Batavia in 1770 Cook was warned by thunder to run up an 'Electrical Chain' which in his opinion saved the *Endeavour* from the shattering of the mainmast suffered by a Dutch Indiaman lying close by.[19]

The explorers' ships

Table 3.I, despite its gaps, sets out some salient points about the ships used by the explorers of the Pacific from Byron to Baudin. Under 'type' the first word is that of official listing, the bracketed word that of the actual type if different. 'Ship' is used in the strict sense of a fully square-rigged 3-master, but terms 'sloop' and 'bark' are rather indefinite, being often used for 'any small vessel that did not fit specifically into a recognised class of minor warship';[20] Malaspina's and Baudin's corvettes were similar to frigates but smaller. Gabarres were storeships, and so in effect were flutes, the term generally implying a warship without her guns mounted.

The figures for 'men' are the total complements at sailing, including supernumeraries such as scientists—twenty-three with Baudin—but excluding stowaways and seamen recruited during the voyage. The *Duff* was unique in that supernumeraries—missionaries—outnumbered crew by six to one, and included six women. There was also one woman with Bougainville, Jeanne Baré, who came aboard disguised as manservant to the botanist Commerson; had Banks sailed on Cook's second voyage, Jeanne might have had a rival in 'Mr Burnett', a young lady who waited for him at Teneriffe, in vain.[21]

It is very unlikely that Cook himself chose the *Earl of Pembroke*, destined for fame under the name *Endeavour* (Plate VI), since the Admiralty bought her, apparently before he was considered for her command, specifically for her roominess, practically a *sine qua non* for a long exploring voyage when all liquid and many dry provisions had to be carried in casks or barrels, very wasteful of space. But he certainly approved of her purchase and had a large say in the choice of her successors. All four were Whitby-built cats, bluff-bowed colliers (and Cook began his maritime career in the North Sea coal trade); very sturdy vessels, capacious and long-enduring, capable of being easily and safely grounded.[22]

Cook himself pointed out the advantages of such vessels, as against frigates and all other types, for long-distance exploration; yet it is a striking fact that, despite his immediate recognition as first among the seamen-explorers of his time, his preference for a stout carrier was followed not by his compatriots but by the Frenchmen La Pérouse and D'Entrecasteaux. However, this was only after Bougainville's compromise of a frigate ill-matched with a bulky but slow storeship had forced him to scamp his voyage.[23] Moreover, between Cook and Flinders the only British voyage to have discovery as a main purpose was Vancouver's, and he was also charged with a diplomatic task. Bligh's voyages were

Table 3.1 SHIPS ON MAJOR PACIFIC VOYAGES 1764–1803

	Commander	Ships	Type	Tons	Guns	Men
1764–65	BYRON	Dolphin	frigate	511	24	190
		Tamar	sloop		16	115
1767–68	WALLIS	Dolphin	frigate	500	32	150
1767–68	CARTERET	Swallow	sloop		18	86
1766–69	BOUGAINVILLE	Boudeuse	frigate	510	26	232
		Etoile	flute	480		116
1768–71	COOK I	Endeavour	bark	365	6	106
1769–70	SURVILLE	St Jean Baptiste	ship	650	36	194
1770	GONZÁLEZ	San Lorenzo	ship		64	c.480?
		Sta Rosalia	frigate		26	c.265?
1771–73	MARION DUFRESNE	Mascarin	flute	140	22	
		Mqs de Castries	flute	100	16	
1771–73	BOENECHEA	Aguila	frigate		24	266
1772–75	COOK II	Resolution	sloop (bark)	462	12	125
		Adventure	sloop (bark)	340	10	88
1774–75	BOENECHEA and ANDIA	Aguila	frigate		22–26	231–266
		Júpiter	bark (paquebot)			
1775–76	LÁNGARA	Aguila	frigate		22–26	231–266
1776–80	COOK III	Resolution	sloop (bark)	462	12	114
		Discovery	sloop (bark)	340	8	72
1780–81	MOURELLE	Princesa	frigate			
1785–88	LA PÉROUSE	Boussole	frigate (flute)	c. 450		120
		Astrolabe	frigate (flute)	c. 450		124
1787–89	BLIGH I	Bounty	ship	215	4	46
1789–94	MALASPINA	Descubierta	corvette	306		104
		Atrevida	corvette	306		104
1790–91	EDWARDS	Pandora	frigate		24	160
1790–92	MARCHAND	Solide	ship	300		50
1791–93	D'ENTRECASTEAUX	Recherche	frigate (gabarre)	500		113
		Espérance	frigate (gabarre)	500		106
1791–93	BLIGH II	Providence	ship			
		Assistant	brig			27
1791–95	VANCOUVER	Discovery	sloop (ship)	340	10	101
		Chatham	brig	130		45
1796–98	WILSON	Duff	ship			62
1800–03	BAUDIN	Géographe	corvette	350	30	124
		Naturaliste	corvette	350(—)	20	121
1801–03	FLINDERS	Investigator	sloop	334	10	88

in a sense commercial, or at least cargo seeking, and Edwards's in the *Pandora* was purely naval.

For completeness we may mention the shipping of Russians and Spaniards in the North Pacific. The earlier official voyages of Bering and his lieutenants were carried out in small, brig-like vessels; later on brigantines and hookers were used. Unofficial voyages began in *shitiki*, distant descendants of Volga river craft, very clumsy sailers. They were superseded by 'Okhotsk galliots', broad-beamed and almost keelless, rigged with a single square sail and a jib. Marginal as they were to both the Ocean and modernity, it is astonishing that such rude craft could master the waters, alternately stormy and fog-bound, of the 2000 km long Aleutian chain.[24]

More sophisticated, but still inferior by metropolitan standards, were the Spanish vessels built at San Blas, which anticipated Cook at Vancouver Island. These ships were schooners and 'frigates', but the largest of the latter, the *Santiago*, was only 225 tons with six guns, when European frigates carried from twenty-four guns upwards; they might perhaps be better equated with armed brigs or barks. Nevertheless, despite poor maintenance and supply and appalling losses from scurvy, they made possible the Spanish thrust to the north.[25]

Instruments and charts

Alongside the improvements in the mariner's prime tool of trade, his ship, there were radical changes in the theory of navigation and in his navigational kit, resultants of the linked progress of physical science and precision instruments: 'at no period perhaps was the general progress of the sciences more closely bound with that of navigation'. Telescopes, verniers, micrometres, logarithms—all seventeenth century inventions—greatly facilitated the measurement of a degree of latitude, a fundamental datum. In 1756 the surveys of the Académie Royale des Sciences, in Quito, Lapland and France, confirmed Newton's deduction of the polar flattening of the globe and established the mean length of a minute of arc on the meridian as 6080 feet, which is still the British nautical mile and very close indeed to the true figure of 6076 feet or 1852 metres.[26]

Theoretical as this may seem, it was of immediate practical significance in estimating the day's distance run, essential, along with the course set, in the Dead Reckoning of a ship's position. On the old figure of 5000 feet, which went back through Ptolemy to Posidonius (*c*. 135–51 B.C.), forty-two feet run out in half a minute on the log-line (first described by William Bourne in 1574) corresponded to a rate of one mile per hour—hence reckoning in knots, not 'knots per hour'; but now the interval between knots on the line had to be raised to fifty-two feet. Yet the traditional reckoning of sixty miles to a degree—one mile to one minute of arc—'was too convenient a one to be sacrificed, and the nautical mile parted company with the [statute] mile practically without discussion.'[27]

Adoption of improvements was far from automatic; as late as 1789 Dutch East Indiamen ignored log-and-line in favour of the crude old assessment of speed by timing an object floating parallel to the ship's side.[28] The pioneers of navigational theory were bitter about the rude rejection of 'starre shooters and sunne shooters' by bluff skippers who knew the sea, but conversely many works were clogged with needless mathematics that 'by frightening [the seaman] must actually have delayed his progress.'[29] Conservatism coexisted with fanciful speculation, as the history of the compass shows,[30] and of course some innovations excellent in theory simply could not stand up to shipboard conditions, at least not without much modification. Cook, no 'copper-bottomed, bevel-edged bigot' in such matters, asked for one of Dr Gowin Knight's improved azimuth compasses for his first voyage, but reported that, allowing for his own ignorance of how to adjust it, he thought it 'by far too Complex an Instrument ever to be of general use at Sea'; nevertheless, with further improvements Knight's compasses became in time practically standard at sea.[31]

The most striking instrumental innovation before Byron's voyage was John Hadley's quadrant of 1731: 'quadrants had been used by sailors for three centuries; but it was a quadrant with a difference', allowing for altitudes to be taken within one minute of arc 'independent of any disturbance by the motion of the ship.'[32] Its advantages over the old back-staff, in ease and accuracy of observation, were manifest. In the 1750s Captain John Campbell developed Hadley's quadrant into a sextant; angles could be read over an arc of 120°, against the quadrant's 90°, and accurately down to 10″. Indeed, the more delicate sextant was usually reserved for the tricky observation of lunar distances, the quadrant being accurate enough for routine latitude shots.

Although the seventeenth century did see marked advances in marine charting, there was no revolution comparable to that brought about in topographical mapping by military demands on land. The increasing size of armies meant longer lines of battle and more attention to transport and terrain; the increasing range and power of cannon led to the subtle geometry of Vaubanian fortification; and by 1700 these factors had combined to produce maps of amazing detail, accuracy and beauty. At sea, perhaps the main advance between 1600 and 1700 was the supersession of the old plane chart by the Wright-Mercator projection, in which a rhumb or compass-bearing appears as a straight line. But if there was no revolution, there were detail improvements through the century, perhaps culminating in the great atlas of Mercator charts of western Europe, Le Neptune françois of 1693. Under the impulsion of the Académie des Sciences and the Cassinis, France was taking the cartographical lead from Holland.[33]

The precision afforded on land by carefully measured bases was far more difficult to attain at sea. The usual 'running traverse' by taking compass bearings from prominent points as the ship passed along the coast depended for accuracy on knowing the speed of the ship, and the flux of tides and currents in coastal waters meant that as a rule fixes could only be approximate. 'The plotting of a close sounding cover, a prime necessity if charts were to become more accurate and reliable, was still not practicable.'[34] Hadley's quadrant could be used for horizontal as well as vertical bearings, but was not taken up for coastal surveys until the 1760s; the station pointer, a simple instrument which gave a rapid solution of resection problems, came in the next decade.

Edmond Halley made some very notable contributions to nautical science and marine cartography. His two voyages in H.M.S. *Paramore*, 1698–9 and 1699–1700, are generally regarded as the first to be sent out by a government for a scientific purpose and nothing more; that purpose was 'to improve the knowledge of the Longitude and the variation of the Compasse'. The result was the first printed map with isolines, and the first published map showing lines of equal magnetic variation or isogonals. The first version covered only the Atlantic, but the widely used World Chart of 1702 took in the observations of other voyagers as far east as the Marianas, leaving the South Sea blank for lack of data.[35]

Much earlier Halley had spent his twenty-first year on St Helena, charting southern hemisphere stars for the Royal Society; the island was cloudy and this was 'an employment that obliged me to regard more than ordinary the Weather.' Here again the result was a cartographical novelty, a cartogram showing the Trade Winds and Monsoons. As a map, it was perhaps bettered by William Dampier's of 1699; but Dampier, though a most excellent empirical observer, made no attempt at explanation, while Halley's text and map together formed a pioneer induction into maritime meteorology.[36] When we add that as Astronomer Royal Halley advised John Harrison, whose timekeeper was at last 'to discover the Longitude', we must conclude that he had indeed deserved well of the republic of seafarers.

The longitude found

'To discover the Longitude': the phrase had become a symbol of impossibility, like ropes of sand or silk purses from sows' ears. The basic problem was simple enough; since the earth rotates through 360° in twenty-four hours, one hour corresponds to 15°, and all that was needed was to compare one's local time with that of a point of departure of known longitude or at some fixed meridians.

But it was impossible to carry with one the standard time of say Ferro or Greenwich, since no clock had been produced capable of running consistently as sea; even Christiaan Huyghens's pendulum clock (1657) was vulnerable to the ship's motion, and moreover the gravity constant, on which the time of the pendulum's swing depended, was found to vary with latitude. It was of course possible to predict astronomical events such as eclipses and to time them locally against their time at places of known longitude, available in almanacs; but these were infrequent, and again the observational instruments were not accurate enough to give the needed precision. Galileo's discovery of Jupiter's satellites, with occultations three or four times a week, raised hopes, and indeed they proved useful on land; but again the telescopes needed for their exact observation were quite unmanageable at sea.[37]

The Paris Observatoire Royale dates from 1672, the Greenwich Royal Observatory from 1675,[38] and from now on the general use, going back to Ptolemy, of Ferro in the Canaries as the prime meridian began to yield to one or other of these sites. In Britain the loss of Admiral Sir Clowdisley Shovel and 2000 men, in thick weather off the Scillies—a disaster wrongly ascribed to mistaken longitudes[39]—led to the formation of a Board of Longitude which could make grants for research and award prize money up to £20,000, an immense sum for the times. There was a host of wild schemes, but also some solid work, before the skill and persistency of the London clockmaker John Harrison produced spring-driven chronometers which could meet the Board's demand of an error of no more than two minutes of time, half a degree, in a voyage to the West Indies and back. Harrison's earlier pedestal models were too heavy and cumbersome to be practicable on board ship, and it was not until 1759 that he produced a more convenient timepiece in watch form, the famous 'H4'.

With this instrument Harrison's son sailed for the West Indies in 1761, and early in the voyage demonstrated its value by correctly predicting a landfall for the morrow, when all the rest on board thought they were still over 1°30', 140 km, from their first port of call, Madeira—certainly a good place to celebrate![40] A party on the Board of Longitude, led by Nevil Maskeleyne, Astronomer Royal, favoured the alternative method of lunar distances; the prize money was grudgingly doled out, the elder Harrison not being fully paid until 1775, a year before his death at eighty-three.[41]

This was after Cook had taken a facsimile of H4, made by Larcum Kendall, on his second voyage, and reported that 'it has exceeded the expectations of its most zealous advocate and being now and then corrected by Lunar observations has been our faithful guide through all the vic-issitudes of climates.'[42] Across the Channel there was an alternative script, with Ferdinand Berthoud and Pierre Le Roy in the roles of Harrison and Kendall; the British had an edge in priority, but the margin was narrow.[43]

At the same time the lunar distance method, known in theory for centuries and occasionally attempted in practice, was put on a new footing by Tobias Mayer, a young German mathematician who never saw the sea. The irregularities of the moon's motion are such that Sir Isaac Newton declared that they formed the only problem that ever made his head ache;[44] Mayer produced complete and accurate tables of the moon's angular distance from the sun and certain fixed stars. These were adapted by Maskelyne and printed in his *The British Mariner's Guide* of 1763, without acknowledgement, and with acknowledgement in the first annual issue of *The Nautical Almanac*, 1766, which gave the figures for every three hours of 1767. Cook did not have a mechanical timekeeper on his first voyage, as is sometimes stated, but he did have the *Almanac*, an invaluable time-saver.

Even with this aid, however, 'A foolscap sheet of calculations was needed for each of several sets of observations... All this could be swept away if accurate Greenwich time could be carried on board ship.'[45] But the chronometer did not immediately sweep the board. The timepieces were extremely costly, required the greatest care in handling and against accidental damage, and were too complex for mass production; it took Kendall over two years to copy H4. Lunar distances required only the tables, a sextant, training in the calculations, and patience. They remained the standard method of determining longitude at sea until well into the nineteenth century—indeed, the tables survived in *The Nautical Almanac* until 1908, on the eve of radio time signals.[46]

Nevertheless, by the time of Cook's second voyage two reliable methods were known for the overcoming of that ancient impossibility, the Discovery of the Longitude. Better ships and better navigational tools were available than ever before; and new motivations were to lead to a second Age of Discoveries.

Chapter 4

TERRA AUSTRALIS QUAERENDA

Non pas trop loin de là, peut-on voir le visage
D'une autre Nymphe, encore incognue et sauvage?
L'on dit, que seulement Magellanus un jour
En sa bouche une fois la baisoit par amour,
Sans taster plus avant ses membres incognuz...

And, Southern witch, whose glamour drew de Quiros
O'er half the earth for one unyielded kiss...

Arnold Wood engagingly begins his *Discovery of Australia* with a Greek
Utopian tale of about 350 B.C.: beyond the Ocean Sea surrounding Europe,
Asia and Libya, lay a fourth part of the earth, where everything was
on a grander scale than in Hellas.[1] From Francis Bacon on, the Pacific
was the home of Utopias, and the dream of an Austral land seduced
alike *philosophes* and hard-headed propagandists for Trade and Empire.

The idea of a 'Fourth World' (sometimes styled fifth, to allow for
America), had a lively existence well before Quiros; Mercator's world
maps, especially that of 1569 which became standard, publicised a vast
landmass sweeping up from Tierra del Fuego to Beach and Locach and
the rest of the misbegotten progeny of Polo, perhaps joining New Guinea
or perhaps not, and thence sinking down to the Land of Parrots and
Tierra del Fuego again. Mercator also set out the doctrine that such
a landmass was necessary to compensate the Northern Hemisphere's
preponderance of land over sea and so to maintain the balance of the
globe.[2]

To this abstract geophysical necessity the quenchless zeal of Quiros
gave form, life, and high colour; he had had at least a Pisgah-sight of
the Promised Land, which flowed with much more than milk and honey.
The French had not only Quiros but their own pioneer, the Norman
Paulmyer de Gonneville who, fired by Portuguese discoveries, set out
in 1503 and found a genial country whose people 'asked only to lead
a joyous life, without much work, living by fishing and the chase and

---

From the 1598 French edition of Mercator's *Théâtre de l'Univers*,
cited in A. C. Taylor, *Le Président de Brosses et l'Australie* (Paris
1938), 22; Bernard O'Dowd, 'The Bush', in *Collected Poems*
(Melbourne 1944), 204.

what their land gave them of itself'—an early prefiguration of *le mirage tahitien*. Unluckily, the account of his voyage, published in 1663 by a descendant of the Indian prince whom he had brought back and married into his own family, left the location of this noble country wide open— so open that it could be placed anywhere from Virginia to Madagascar. This very vagueness was useful—Gonneville's Land could be fitted into anybody's scheme—and in France the story was influential far into the eighteenth century.[3] After all, Gonneville and Quiros were the two men who had really been to Terra Australis, or near it.

For an authoritative statement we may turn to Bernhard Varenius's *Geographia Generalis* (1650), a work of such prestige that the 1712 Cambridge edition was directly sponsored by Isaac Newton and Richard Bentley— with notes to bring it into line with Newtonian rather than Cartesian physics. Varenius does not use the term 'Terra Australis', but he accepts the Mercator tradition, while stressing the *incognita* aspect. He notes that salt water does not freeze as easily as fresh, but does not draw the inference that sea-ice indicated a nearby landmass, which was to become a favourite argument, but he does stress that islands, especially when clustered, were such indicators.[4] Without much direct argument, then, the man who is still regarded as a father of modern geography, or at least a grandfather, could be taken as buttressing the orthodoxy of Terra Australis.

The theory of Terra Australis

The eighteenth century saw a change in geographical outlook, from the mathematical and cosmographical Ptolemaic approach, still ruling in the dry synthesis of Varenius, to an interest more localised to the earth as the home, the dominion, of Man; one might say back to the more humanistic geography of Strabo.[5] 'Problematic features of the globe were coming to be understood with respect to the terrestrial system, rather than to the design of the heavens.'[6] New synthesisers, especially in France, demanded co-ordinated assaults on the vast blanks on the map—interior Africa, the North Pacific, the Northwest Passage, Terra Australis. All these, plus the Patagonian Giants, figured in the appeal of Moreau de Maupertuis, who as President of the Berlin Academy listed them in his *Lettre sur le Progrès des Sciences* (1752) addressed to Frederick the Great.

There had been one recent voyage in search of the Southland, directly inspired by the Gonneville story, that of de Lozier Bouvet, who on 1 January 1739 found a few square kilometres of ice-capped lava in 54°26′S, which he named, for the day, Cap de la Circoncision, sure that it was a headland of the Southern Continent. It is now Bouvet Island, the only scrap of land on the earth's surface which is literally a thousand miles from anywhere.[7] Bouvet sailed east along the pack for some 1600 km, seeing nothing but ice and fog.

His discovery, such as it was, caught the imaginations of Maupertuis, Buffon, de Brosses, Philipe Buache. Maupertuis prided himself on leading the Lapland geodetic expedition (1736–7), and chided Bouvet for lack of persistence, remarking airily that ice was no invincible obstacle; he was not the only savant thus to presume towards seamen. He may well have deserved Voltaire's savage ridicule in the *Histoire du Dr Akakia*; but he was the catalyst for Charles de Brosses to write his very significant *Histoire des Navigations aux Terres Australes*, in which good work he was powerfully seconded by Buffon.[8]

Buffon also took a cavalier attitude towards seamen whose observations, particularly on the cold of the Southern Hemisphere (which were in general correct), did not square with his theories; but he admitted that Bouvet had shown the difficulty of access to the Continent. However, the ice itself was a sure sign of land; since seawater did not freeze, the great bergs could only be formed in great estuaries, which implied extensive highlands, within which one might expect to find men grouped in societies. This river-born ice could not be a continuous barrier; somewhere there must be a way in.[9] This view was widely accepted, and bedevilled discussion of the Austral problem until the sensible account of ice formation by J. R. Forster, based on observations made on Cook's second voyage. This voyage pushed any possible Southern Continent well beyond 60°S, into what we now know as Antarctica, whose existence was still rather doubted by Rainaud in 1894, on the eve of the great wave of South Polar exploration.[10]

As for Buache, a grand systems-monger, as Broc says he abhorred a vacuum, and in 1744 produced a map which compartmented the Pacific by mainly submarine mountain chains, 'a new world... delineated all the more minutely since it was hypothetical.' But he did at least separate New Holland as the 'Continent Austral', distinguishing it from the 'Terres Antarctiques', which by analogy with the North Polar regions he provided with a Mediterranean, the 'Mer Glaciale Antarctique'.[11]

This was the school in which de Brosses was formed.[12] The importance of his *Histoire* was that for the first time the fragmented references to an Austral Continent, previously scattered in individual narratives or buried in massive compilations, were brought together, logically arranged, and accompanied by analyses of the advantages and problems of discovery and colonisation: 'the most weighty combination of history and propaganda as yet devoted to the enterprise of the South Sea.'[13] John Campbell had indeed collected and commented, in the twenty kilograms of his *Navigantium*, the necessary materials, but in a far less structured way.[14] To bring order into his discussion de Brosses arranged his sixty-five voyages in three regional groups: *Magellanie*, for the Atlantic sector; *Australie* for the south Indian Ocean ('Australinde' might have been better); and for the Pacific *Polynesie*, a name with a great future.[15] The gibe that he used three of his five Books for recounting voyages and only two for thinking is pointless;[16] the presentation of data as a preliminary to their analysis was logical.

On the theoretical side de Brosses was conventional enough, citing Buffon on the doctrine of balance. More than a third of the globe was unknown—all beyond the Antarctic Circle and all that lay between it and the three southernmost known points, the Cape of Good Hope, Tierra del Fuego, and Patenta Island off New Guinea. (It seems odd that New Zealand and New Holland were omitted, but he was thinking of known continental terminations.) It was not possible that in such an immensity there should not be one or more landmasses sufficient to counterpoise northern Asia and 'keep the globe in equilibrium in its rotation'. The argument was to be elaborated by Alexander Dalrymple, who calculated that in the critical zone from the Tropic of Cancer to 50°N there were 4880 square degrees of land to 4840 of water. In the matching southern zone, only 1060 square degrees of land were known, a deficiency of 3820 in the necessary counterweight. They must be somewhere, and the voyages of Tasman, Halley and Bouvet made it clear that the great bulk of them must lie in the Pacific.[17]

On ice, de Brosses again followed Buffon, and improved on him: 'The more land, the more ice; consequently, the more ice the more land', so instead of being regarded as an insurmountable obstacle, ice should be an encouragement. However, although Bouvet should be sent out again, this ice objection really held only for Magellanie; all Polynesie lay open.[18] There was another component in the theory of Terra Australis. While he admitted the awkwardness of the nomenclature, de Brosses's 'Terres Australes' stretched as far north as New Guinea (thus taking in New Holland), which for Varenius was a peninsula of the Southern Continent.[19] But the latter had said flatly that nothing was known of it beyond its bare existence; and here the theory of 'climates' came to the rescue of projectors. 'Climate' in this context had not its modern meaning, but was a term applied to latitudinal divisions of the globe, delimited by hours of daylight, and in each hemisphere there were twenty-four climates between the Equator and the Polar Circle. By analogy, one could deduce the likely properties of unknown lands lying in a given climate, and it could fairly be claimed that the fifth and sixth climates—Mediterranean latitudes, about 31–41°—were those most favourable to human activities and comforts (including the vine!).

The equation was happily applied to the Southern Continent, especially to Nuyts Land in South Australia, in proposals addressed in 1717 by J.P. Purry to the Governor-General at Batavia. Nothing happened, but alongside Quiros's rapturous testimonials to the tropical riches of Espíritu Santo, John Campbell and Emanuel Bowen placed on the shores of the Great Australian Bight the seductive legend: 'NB. *This is the Country seated according to* Coll: Purry *in the best Climate in the world.*'[20]

Planning for Terra Australis

If Bouvet was the unlucky precursor in the actual search for Terra Australis, John Campbell was the predecessor in propaganda. One suspects that de Brosses owed more than a patriotic Frenchman would care to admit to this spokesman for the aggressive British merchantry;[21] not that de Brosses was averse to mercantilism—he held shares in the Compagnie des Indes, of which Bouvet was an official—but his whole tone was monarchical. The enterprise was one for Princes, whereas Campbell thought that one of the great Companies should undertake it—if not the East India, then the South Sea might be induced to live up to its name, and if it refused, then even the Royal African; but if these corporations failed in their patriotic duty, surely there was enough foresight and risk capital in England for private enterprise to engage in so great a public good.[22]

The two men were of course very different in background and status; de Brosses a *savant* at least verging on a *philosophe*, Campbell a very competent hack-writer; but there was a remarkable convergence in their ideas. Both canvassed much the same avenues of entry into the South Sea; both relied heavily on Quiros and thought Dutch reticence about austral lands neighbouring their holdings was evidence of their value; both regarded ice as a sure sign of land; both thought that the terrors of Cape Horn could be overcome; both gave high priority to the seizure of Juan Fernández as a base (and here de Brosses speaks lovingly of his boyhood delight in Robinson Crusoe). As for settlement, Campbell in the end strongly recommends Van Diemen's Land, after earlier favouring New Britain, which was de Brosses's final choice.[23]

Bouvet had proposed a colony in Quiros's Tierra Austrialia del Espíritu Santo, which on Vaugondy's map (in de Brosses's *Histoire*) was shown impacted into northeast New Holland. The possession of French forward bases in Ile de France (Mauritius) and Pondicherry, and Dampier's 'excellent principle' of approaching the unknown by the known, in this case Papua or Gilolo, influenced de Brosses in opting for New Britain.[24]

Both *Navigantium* and *Histoire* are at bottom inputs into the cold war of mercantilism. Campbell, while not eschewing rhetoric and even in places a rough bulldog eloquence, is as one might expect more down-to-earth, and more aggressive. Terra Australis would be a compensation for the loss of the Asiento for supplying slaves to Spanish America, and the occupation of Juan Fernández 'must prove wonderfully advantageous, considering the Opportunity they would have of vending' Dampier's 'strong well-limbed Negroes' of New Britain to Chile and Peru. This seems his only reference to native peoples, except for the remark that even though they might be savages, they could probably provide valuable commodities in exchange for 'those Trifles, which we know, from Experience, such Savages naturally admire.'[25]

This eye to the main chance was not at all wanting in de Brosses: what openings the Terres Australes might give for unloading onto the untutored Indian glass beads, cheap cloth, paper, brandy, hardware, and 'our little mirrors at 7 francs the dozen'! But we must avoid the greed and cruelty of the old Spaniards, which led them to 'contemptuously cut the throats of millions of Indians, as vile beasts of another colour'. The greater glory for a sovereign would be to create new nations, as the ordered societies of Latin Europe had tamed the wild northerners and made those savages into men; after all, we Europeans once lived in caves and woods like the Australians, and used stone tools.

In marked contrast to Campbell, de Brosses argued for conciliation of the natives. Easy does it; some savages seemed curiously averse to accepting the benefits of civilisation, but if only two could be induced to wear European clothes, the rest would come to desire them, for 'Do not the passions reign in remote solitudes as in the great world?'—an impeccably Enlightenment remark. But it would be inadvisable to let missionaries loose upon them too soon; their so laudable zeal might compromise the future by reckless affronts to things the people most revere. Temporal blessings first, and above all no force: 'Planting the Cross with the sword is contrary to Christian charity.' These moral homilies were preceded by much-needed advice never to cut down coconut trees for the nuts, and succeeded by amusing and generally sensible hints on the bestowal of place-names.[26]

Campbell's appeal for colonisation appears crude commercialism compared with de Brosses's broad philosophical approach, backed by a rather quaint sociology. However, while he stressed the benefits of purely scientific exploration, de Brosses like Campbell had a strongly materialistic geopolitical motivation. If Campbell was writing in the flush of Anson's triumphant homecoming, de Brosses was close to the opening of the Seven Years' War, and began by asserting that the search for new venues for trade and colonisation was for France a matter not of her interests merely, but of necessity 'at a time when a neighbouring power visibly affects the universal monarchy of the sea', and affirmed, in the purest vein of mercantilism, that while the projected colony must have some necessary industries, this must be 'within the restriction imposed by the great known principle, that every colony must remain in entire dependence upon its metropolis.'[27]

The advantages to the home society were elaborated. The fear of depopulation was a myth; the more populous the colonies, the more they would consume, hence the more work at home, and the multiplying of occupations would multiply men. Agriculture, as opposed to mining, promoted a greater population and hence a greater marine, and it dealt in tangible and not conventional wealth (*biens physiques & non conventionels*)—a physiocratic touch.[28] But besides the economic gains, the colonies would provide valuable social benefits.

Even a private house needed its drains, and since galleys had become obsolete the State needed a channel to get rid of noxious human elements without wasting them on the gallows. For the female half of the populace, unfitted for forced labour, there existed no punishment between death and banishment (which was futile) except a useless 'momentary chastisement by the rod'. Unmarried mothers who murdered their babies were so often unfortunate rather than really wicked; in truly sad cases (one is cited) transportation should be an allowable alternative to death. The men could be assigned to farmer settlers who could not yet afford African slaves; and when his term was out, a convict with some talent might make a little fortune. As for the women, they 'above all will provide by their fecundity the first and most necessary production that a colony needs.'[29] Except perhaps for a modest degree of humanitarianism, there was nothing new in all this—Moll Flanders and Manon Lescaut had gone to America the hard way[30]—but when the real Austral Continent was settled, it was as a convict colony such as de Brosses had advocated.

The piratical Scot John Callander put de Brosses into English under the bold title *Terra Australis Cognita* without so much as naming him as a source—he gave merely occasional references to 'the *French* writer, from whom we have drawn many helps'. Most of his few additions to de Brosses were lifted word by word from Campbell editorial comment and all; the plagiarism is one of the most impudent on record.[31] (True, de Brosses himself cribbed from David Hume, but that is another, and amusing, story.)[32] Writing after the Seven Years' War and not at its beginning, Callander had an advantage over his victim, and made the ignoble most of it: 'VAIN are the repeated exhortations of the *French* writer, addressed to a nation' which had gone down in defeat, and with sadistic emphasis he closed with de Brosses's own closing words on 'the glory of my sovereign, and the prosperity of my native country.'[33] Nevertheless, for the English reader Callander's three quartos were probably more to the point than Campbell's two enormous and daunting folios.

Alexander Dalrymple's two collections on Terra Australis really came too late to affect the issue greatly; Cook would have sailed with or without them. Dalrymple was inferior to de Brosses as a writer, nor is his work so well organised as the Frenchman's. His Pacific volumes put the case for Terra Australis with uncritical force, relying too heavily on Quiros, and typographical exuberance, as in the dedication 'To—THE MAN—who *Emulous* of MAGALHANES' should discover the Continent—not, as at first sight one is tempted to think, a pointer to himself.

He seems 'constitutionally incapable' of distinguishing between 'the continent's existence [and] the desirability of its existence'.[34]

Dalrymple's most important contribution is in detail—the prominence he gave to Torres's discovery of his Strait, which had been almost lost to sight, though not so totally as is often stated or implied. He gave a map showing Torres's track to Joseph Banks, who took it with him on the *Endeavour*; but Cook also had de Brosses's book with Vaugondy's similar map, and on the whole this carried more weight in his mind. As for Dalrymple's companion Atlantic volume, that was a curiosity chiefly notable for the constitution for his projected colony, so Utopian as to admit women to 'Publick Office . . . on the same footing as the men.'[35]

On all counts, de Brosses must be given pride of place among the proponents of Terra Australis; more practical than the theorists, he had a far broader and more elevated outlook than the commercial projectors. He was in quite close contact with Dalrymple and hence had some influence on the revival of British influence in the Pacific apart from his disguised influence via Callander,[36] but naturally his most direct impact was in France.

Strangely, he does not seem to have been read by Yves de Kerguelen, who in 1772 discovered in the South Indian Ocean a land which he thought to be indubitably Terra Australis, and reported on 'in terms which would not have disgraced Baron Munchausen himself', only to be discredited when he returned the next year. He then found it a bleak and barren land, Cook's '*Island of Desolation*', which still bears Kerguelen's name. This was a contribution, though a negative one, in that his fiasco 'finally persuaded the French' (so enamoured of Gonneville's Land) 'that *Terra Australis* was a fiction'.[37]

But if Kerguelen did not profit from de Brosses, a greater man and navigator did. On his return from arduous campaigning in Canada, the young Louis-Antoine de Bougainville received from his brother the welcoming, and welcomed, gift of the *Histoire*, which was to point his way to Nouvelle Cythère and around the world. The volumes became 'his code, his breviary.'[38]

Science or Empire?

The achievement of de Brosses was to meld diverse currents of motivation: the quest for knowledge, the scientific reasoning of Dampier, Buffon, Maupertuis; the rapt vision of the disciples of Quiros and Gonneville; the commercial realism of Campbell—he combined 'a solid common sense with a generous idealism.' But neither pure scientific curiosity nor pure commercialism would suffice to induce governments or the great Companies to launch the costly enterprises proposed to them.[39] These motives played their part, and one cannot of course draw sharp boundaries; any one discovery might have scientific, commerical and political bearings. But underlying science and trade, cementing the great exploratory achievements together, was the geopolitical imperative of Empire.

By 1760 there were a formidable body of theory and opinion about the South Sea, and some facts; but the facts were 'island groups whose names shift with every whim of cartographic fashion... squiggles of coastline which hint at intriguing but still unproven lands... the straight-jacket of winds and currents which pushed the tracks of sailing ships into a narrow belt';[40] and the data had been collected haphazard, on voyages predatory or commercial. Except for the Russians in the north, there had been since Tasman only one Pacific voyage, Dampier's to New Britain, which had discovery as its prime aim. With the same exceptions, no exploration had been undertaken by the State—one cannot count Anson as an explorer.

There had been two voyages under corporate auspices—Roggeveen's for the Dutch West India Company, Bouvet's (Austral if not Pacific) for the Compagnie des Indes; and both were initiated from outside or below. The former had ultimate commercial exploitation in view, while Bouvet, though inspired by Gonneville, had as his first objective the finding of way-stations for the Compagnie between Senegal and Ile de France, the known bases on this long stretch being in actually or potentially hostile hands—Dutch at the Cape, British at St Helena, Portuguese in Brazil.[41] Private not public enterprise then, and little of it, and the advancement of knowledge ran a poor second to the advantage of trade.

From Byron's circumnavigation of 1764–6, however, there were marked changes; in organisation, the major voyages being state-run under naval command in King's Ships, and later in the scope of objectives, observation by experts in the field sciences being added to the fixing of positions and the mere general reconnaissance of new lands, while artists as well as scientists were carried to ensure a full graphic record. The organisation of science had now become an important concern of the State; the London Royal Society retained autonomy, but all the great capitals from Lisbon to St Petersburg had their Academies of Sciences, Boards of Longitude or hydrographic commissions, Schools of Mining and Engineering, 'formally attached to the state and implementing royal policy.'[42]

In the field, the learned Jesuit of a former age was giving place to the savant sponsored by an Academy, often trained at a German university, Uppsala or Leyden—rarely the Sorbonne or Oxbridge—or in some government agency, notably the technical branches of the army or navy.[43] The Academies and the specialised schools were deeply involved in the planning of discovery—the participation of the Royal Society and sister bodies of nine countries in the 1761 and 1769 observations of the Transits of Venus was only the most famous example, with 270 observers at places ranging from Finland and Philadelphia to Baja California and Tahiti.[44]

Instructions to navigators became more and more detailed; those to Byron do not reach six pages and say nothing at all about any but routine nautical observations, those to La Pérouse cover *inter alia* chemistry, horticulture, meteorology, *materia medica* and human anatomy—but not anthropology; that was to come later still, with Nicolas Baudin. Observations in natural history had generally been left to the surgeon, or in French ships the chaplain—botany was still part of medical training as supplying herbal drugs for *materia medica*—but the new professionalism meant their replacement by experts.[45]

No voyages in the South Sea before Bougainville carried any official scientists or artists; in the north the Russians, with Steller and Delisle de la Croyère on Bering's voyage, were well ahead. But Bougainville, himself a noted mathematician, had the astronomer Véron and the botanist Commerson, while on his three voyages Cook carried altogether fifteen scientists and artists, some of them of high repute then as now: Banks, Solander, Sparrman, the Forsters, and among the artists Hodges and Webber. By the end of the century the unfortunate Baudin was saddled with twenty-three. The seniors had their own servants and a vast amount of impedimenta; La Pérouse's ships and Malaspina's were almost floating laboratories. Housing these supernumeraries and their gear was an eternally messy problem, the source of frictions rising to hatreds. The 'Great' cabin (the *Endeavour's* was about 5 by 5.5 metres), the main working space, was always grossly overcrowded; Banks's vignette of himself and Solander working at a table littered with seaweed and barnacles is most untypically pleasant.[46]

Commanders on the whole found the scientists interesting and instructive nuisances, reluctantly amenable to ship's discipline. Captains had to keep a watchful eye on wind and weather and tide; they wanted to see what lay around the next headland and were ever anxious to avoid embayment; the naturalists were ever anxious to linger botanising in the bay. Science was a new profession, seamanship an old one, and naturalists were jealous of their recent dignity. 'What treasures of firmness and tact were needed in the leaders responsible for these little floating communities, shut in on themselves for two or three years!'; and tact was often wanting on both sides. J. R. Forster's private journal is at times horrifying in its outbursts of frustration and anguish, and some of his attacks on Cook are bitter, yet their relations were genial compared with the deadly hate between Baudin and his naturalist François Péron, whose official account constantly, obsessively, denigrated his commander but mentioned him by name twice only, in the nominal roll and in the report of his death.[47] This was an extreme case—both were very cantankerous men—but eloquent of the potential for discord. There were exceptions, of course; Cook got on very well with the cheerful Banks, but then he owed Banks the deference due to superior social position, while Banks owed him the deference due to a man sixteen years older.

The complete dependence on government funding (Banks was exceptional) 'sparked tensions between savant and paymaster, between the ethos of... a free market in knowledge and national advantage.' It is naive to see with Carrington 'a noble rivalry, concerned with the increase of knowledge... differ[ing] greatly from the mean exclusive struggle for monopoly which had marked earlier exploration'; such a notion could not survive a reading of Martin-Allanic's densely detailed account of the murky atmosphere of intrigue and espionage surrounding Bougainville's expedition.[48] There were always secret instructions, enjoining Acts of Possession in likely places. Towards the end of a voyage logs and journals were impounded for the scrutiny of the naval authorities—the *cause célèbre* was that of the Forsters, who overcame the ban by publishing in effect a version of Johann Reinhold's journal under the name of his son, who did not hold himself bound by agreement on publication signed by his father.[49] Naturally, major voyages were often succeeded by a rush of unauthorised 'quickies'.

There were it is true exchanges of information, mainly astronomical, and what J.-P. Faivre has called the 'Venusian year' of 1769 certainly saw a remarkable international effort. But even in a paper published under the auspices of UNESCO, Faivre had to admit that this was exceptional, and that alongside co-operation there was a cold war of espionage, deliberate disinformation, suborned documents; the exploration of the Pacific was in a sense a collective work of the maritime powers, but more by convergence than by true collaboration.[50] At bottom the stance was one of competition, though not so intense and bitter as today's rivalries in space. It is true also—and again this can be said of today— that the personal relations of scientists in the warring camps were often cordial. But the answer to 'Science or Empire?' must be 'Empire and Science', in that order (Plate VII).

When appealed to in the names of science and humanity, governments could be brought to behave with rather more decency than those of our own age; Banks, in time of war, secured the release of scientists detained on both sides of the English Channel. The safe-conducts given to Cook by Benjamin Franklin and the French government during the American War marked a high point; but Madrid ordered his arrest should he put in at a Spanish port, and the security of a safe conduct could be fragile; a slight technical flaw in his papers sufficed to keep Matthew Flinders in detention at Ile de France for over six years.[51]

Basically, then, the explorations of the Pacific represented a sparring for position by the superpowers of that day, Britain and France, in the disclosure of a new world, as the superpowers of today spar for position

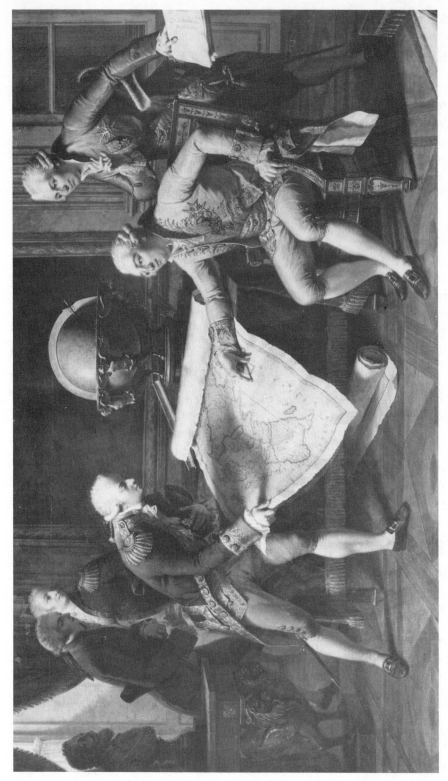

Plate VII. EMPIRE AND SCIENCE. This painting by Mansiaux, in the Musée de Versailles, shows Louis XVI giving his instructions to La Pérouse. By permission and © Musées Nationaux.

in the new world of space. In both cases, scientific endeavour was and is at once a cover and a weapon.

> With existing British strengths, the combined effect [of Campbell's proposals] would be a very pretty British stranglehold on the extra-European commerce of the globe . . . Eighteenth century Englishmen studied exploration partly for its scientific appeal but chiefly in order to learn how to out-distance the French.[52]

Across the Channel, the geopolitical ambition of Choiseul, with Bougainville as his executive agent, was dominant. Beyond such mundane objectives as a stronger place in the China trade and an entry into the spice trade, he aimed at compensation for the loss of Canada, a revitalisation of national morale, a turning of national energies towards the sea[53]— in short, a *revanche* on those waves which Britannia ruled. But the end of the Seven Years' War released British energies as well.

There is an entertaining sidelight on this rivalry in a report of the French Ambassador in London on a meeting with the First Lord of the Admiralty: 'Mylord Sandwich repeated to me at least twenty times' that Cook's second voyage could have 'one motive only, that of curiosity, without any plan of settlement whatsoever.' This was difficult to believe: such expense for a voyage of curiosity? The object was said to have been the discovery of the Pole; would that have taken it to Tahiti? The *Resolution* was to go out again—'You will surely never guess the object of this voyage', the return of Omai to Tahiti. The Ambassador hoped to have Cook to dinner, and to pump him about 'this voyage around the Pole, which he avoided so often and so long.'[54]

We may let an intelligent contemporary, neither Gaul nor Briton, have the last word: Ambrosio O'Higgins, then Governor of Concepción, reporting La Pérouse's visit. To the chagrin of the local merchants, there had been no hint of contraband, and the French seemed to have no thoughts beyond an enthusiastic search for an exact knowledge of the Globe and all that it held of use to humankind—

> That, as it should seem, is the philosophy of these admirable men; but still, it is not to be supposed that they will set aside their nations' interests by neglecting . . . to appropriate for colonisation at an opportune time (though, for the nonce, it would be only in their mind's eye) some island of suitable resources . . .

Or almost the last word: unknown to O'Higgins, one of these admirable philosophic men had his mind's eye fixed not on some South Sea isle but on the weakness and the possibilities of subversion of Chile itself . . .[55]

The Utopian Pacific

Alongside the geographers, the merchants, the theoreticians and practitioners of Science and Empire, men who at their most speculative dealt,

or tried to deal, in real data plotted on real maps, there lived another
tribe: the dreaming founders not of trading colonies but of ideal, or
sometimes satiric, commonwealths, who found in Terra Australis or
thereabouts a fitting locale for their wild imaginings. Individually, with
the giant exception of Lemuel Gulliver's *Travels into Several Remote Nations
of the World*, their works may seem, and often are, mere curiosities;
collectively, they form an impressive body of writing, reflecting new
tendencies in social and political theory and religion, or to the orthodox
irreligion. Terra Australis, incognita and imaginary as it was, has therefore
a definite place in the history of ideas. It is not too much to claim it
as a hatchery for some at least of the ideas which were to descend on
France in 1789; or, to adopt a kindlier metaphor and not to repudiate
the Enlightenment, a seed-bed of ideas which came to fruition, so far
as they ever did, in the Revolution.

Sir Thomas More's original Utopia was located nowhere in particular,
and rightly so in view of its name. The only clue is that the traveller
who returned from that strange country, Raphael Hythlodsy, had sailed
on Vespucci's last voyage,[56] and made his way eventually to Taprobane.
So at any rate More's Nowhere was somewhere in the Austral hemisphere;
Bougainville's naturalist Philibert Commerson thought he had found it,
literally, in Tahiti.[57] In 1629 Francis Bacon placed his New Atlantis firmly
in the Pacific: 'We sailed from Peru ... for China and Japan, by the
South Sea'.

The heroic age of Utopia in Terra Australis or the South Sea ran
from Gabriel de Foigny in 1676 to Restif de la Bretonne in 1781; during
this period eleven imaginary voyages to the Southland appeared in France
alone.[58] Asia was too civilised for the implacement of an imaginary state,
though social criticism by the vehicle of an Oriental traveller reporting
on Europe was common—Montesquieu's *Lettres Persanes* had many imita-
tors; America was becoming too well known, Africa was a desert; Terra
Australis, even in its avatar of New Holland, was at once concrete and
vague. It also provided the isolation necessary for Utopians to maintain
the purity of their particularities—those who had any contact at all with
the outside world, usually for technological espionage, regulated it more
strictly than a modern People's Republic, and the traveller reached them
only by some abrupt rupture of continuity, usually shipwreck.[59] There
was also a deeper psychological factor, a mythos: the constant image,
coming down from Graeco-Roman times, of the felicities of 'sweet golden
climes' in the far South as against the raw harshness of Boreal Europe.[60]
And there were always the Arcadias of Quiros and, for the French,
Gonneville.

Basically all Utopias are a protest against society as it is; the rich
harvest in France at this time when Utopic writing was slack in England

may mean that the English had had their bourgeois revolution and had not yet seen through it.[61] One need not detail the standard features: mastery over nature, a changeless centralised polity, mathematical settlement patterns, gerontocracy, brain-washing education, sexual choice in elaborate group introductions, and so on.[62] There was nearly always a Venerable Sage who does all the talking, itself a venerable tradition going back to the Socrates of Plato's *Republic* and persisting even in William Morris's *News from Nowhere*, that refreshing exception to the general intolerability of Utopias.

The classics are Foigny's *La Terre Australe connue* (or *Les Avantures de Jacques Sadeur*), in part at least a send-up of Quiros; Denis Vairasse's *L'Histoire des Sévarambes* (1677-9), and Simon Tyssot de Patot's *Voyages et Avantures de Jacques Massé* (1710), which is also a tale of intrigue and Rider Haggard adventure.[63] The curious reader is warned that these lands of earthly delights are also often curiously flat, literally so in Foigny, whose 'Australians'—he seems to have been the first to use the word— have levelled their mountains.

The authors were all firm Deists. Their foundation was Cartesian and their tone materialistic, disguised a little by high-falutin' moralising. They presented a 'natural religion' with civic ceremonies like Robespierre's Feasts of Reason; immortality, if allowed at all, they saw as collective, death as a peaceful passage into the world-soul. All this was highly subversive, an underground literature of dissent; most titles bore fictitious imprints. And they were not without influence, both direct literary influence and an indirect sapping of conventional moral standards.[64]

Vairasse, in close touch with the Whig opposition to Charles II, was especially significant, and has been given a place in the protohistory of Socialism. His book ran to twenty-two editions, ten of them in translation, by 1787, and was ascribed to Bayle, Leibnitz (!) and Algernon Sydney. From it Voltaire took hints for *Candide* and Rousseau almost certainly had it at hand when outlining the *Discours sur l'inegalité*. Already in 1719 *Robinson Crusoe* was described as being in the manner of *Jacques Massé* and the *Histoire des Sévarambes*; opinion is divided as to any debt of Defoe to Vairasse, but his direct influence on Swift has been plausibly claimed. Respectable company so far, but Kant mentioned him alongside Plato and More![65]

Vairasse took care to give verisimilitude by linking the adventures of his Captain Siden with a real shipwreck, that of the *Gulden Draak* on the west coast of New Holland in 1656. This was a form of realism prefiguring that of Swift, who placed his cunning balance of dominant dystopia with utopic elements entirely in the Pacific: Lilliput probably in the Tasman Sea (and not as shown in his map), Brobdingnag near Alaska, Laputa east or south of Japan, Houyhnhnmland somewhere south of Alaska.[66]

The great circumnavigations made the Pacific a real place, less adapted to Utopian purposes, but there were some attempts to capitalise on the new information. We may pass over, for the time, Diderot's *Supplément* to Bougainville, but two works call for some comment. The first is the greatest of French austral romances, Nicolas Edmé Restif de la Bretonne's *La Découverte australe Par un Homme-volant ou le Dédale français: Nouvelle très-philosophique.*[67]

This is one of the great crazy books of the world. All was grigrist to Restif's mill, which worked with the frenzy of the auto-didect. He had read them all: Lucian, More, Cyrano de Bergerac, Swift, de Maillet of *Telliamed*, our Deist trinity Foigny Vairasse and Tyssot, Rousseau were only a few of those who contributed to his most eclectic philosophy, pantheistic, materialist, irrational but with yearnings after reason, vitalist, evolutionary from moss to Man 'nuance à nuance'.[68]

We cannot even outline Restif's amazing geography and more amazing natural history, nor the complex steps, or rather flights, by which the French Daedalus provided a vast archipelago in high southern latitudes with a Citizen King, prefiguring by eight years the first fine raptures of Louis XVI as King not of France but of Frenchmen; though this model monarch prudently reserved to the Royal House the right of flight, which would certainly have been convenient for Louis in 1791.[69] Restif's monarchy had odd links with the real world: it planned to carry off Jean-Jacques Rousseau to act as adviser, and its aerial scouts kept a close watch on Cook's ships sailing south from the New Hebrides lest they should light upon some colony of the Austral Empire and corrupt its perfect polity.[70]

Daft; but in this weird gallimaufry lay all the program of the Enlightenment: the civic religion of all good men, confederation instead of war, the philosopher king freely granting a nicely tempered liberty. But not only the Enlightenment's overt policies, but also its dark underside: the secret longings to give play to passion, to escape from the public intellectual stance of cold rationalism, and yet not to repudiate rationality. A tragic dilemma, which still grips those who both think and feel: 'Passion and Reason, selfedivision cause.'[71]

Finally, 'the most perfect instance of Tahitian Utopias'[72] was written by no less a personage than the Marquis de Sade, inset in his novel *Aline et Valcour* (1793); a sentimental or indeed *larmoyant* book, with much conventional prating about Virtue, and, for Sade, relatively few horrors. One of its heroes, Sainville, tracking down his abducted wife (*de facto*) was told that a lady resembling her had sailed from the Cape with Cook (!), passing as the wife of a lieutenant on the *Discovery*. Following up this clue by sailing for Tahiti via New Zealand, he found near Davis Land an island with a most benevolent and democratic monarch and all the usual, almost compulsory, appurtenances of an Enlightenment Utopia: voluntary isolation from the outside world, symmetrically planned towns, uniform housing and clothing, no luxury, Deism, liberty but not licence in sex, communal education, egalitarianism. 'In a word, nothing reminded me of the golden age so much as the gentle and pure manners of this good people.' Not at all what we expect from Sade! But savage irony.

What have all these wild romancings to do with Pacific History? On the surface, in the sense of actual events in the Pacific, very little; and yet they were part of the critical thinking of the century which in so many fields—science, economics, industry, politics—laid the foundations of our modern world. Side by side with more sober geographical speculations, they were a part of what Terra Australis, the South Sea, the Pacific meant in the minds of men ill-informed indeed, but eager either to grasp its reality or to make of it an ideality. As Garagnon has well said, to the French Australia was 'a detour between France as it was and France as it should be ... all these utopias were blueprints for reform, for action.'[73] Terra Australis as yet incognita was important not only as a spur to the mundane efforts which brought the British to Botany Bay in 1788, but also to the intellectual movement which brought the French to the Bastille in 1789. Not only what happened in the Pacific but also what was thought or dreamt about the Pacific must be counted into its history.

Chapter 5

CHRONOLOGY I: THE CIRCUMNAVIGATORS: BYRON THROUGH COOK

... por mares nunca dantes navegados ...

After Abel Tasman's circumnavigation of Australia, at a distance, in 1642–3, and the voyage of Martin Fries to the Kuril Islands in the latter year, there was a lull of over a century in Pacific discovery. Such voyages as took place were devoted to rapine (the buccaneers and Anson), commercial espionage (Sir John Narborough's Chilean expedition of 1670–1), or commerce, licit or illicit, by the Manila Galleon or the traders from St Malo to the South American west coast during the War of the Spanish Succession. There was one partial exception; Jacob Roggeveen in 1722 had the Great South Land as his objective, and did discover some islands, but his motive was basically commercial.

In 1763 the Treaty of Paris ended the Seven Years' War; of the two great rivals, Great Britain had definitely secured the advantage over France in two continents. Canada had been conquered and was to be held, and in India the tiny French holdings were to be mere unfortified trading posts, while against these French losses the English East India Company had acquired or was acquiring sizeable territories—the Northern Circars (Sarkars), once French, and above all Bengal. France remained however a Great Power, and it was not to be expected that she would not seek compensations; her authoritarian government had to maintain its prestige. Unless Europe was to be plunged into another round of costly wars—and Louis XV's France however strong on *la gloire* was weak on finance—compensation could be found only overseas; but where?

The game had been lost in India, in the East Indies the Dutch were entrenched, and British and Dutch between them controlled the approaches to East Asia, where China was too big to tackle and French commerce had never been able to compete very effectively at Canton. Atlantic North America was now firmly under British sway, Atlantic South America was held either by Britain's client Portugal or by France's ally Spain; and indeed the first attempt at securing compensation, Bougainville's

---

'over those never-navigated seas'—Luis Vaz de Camões, *Os Lusiadas*, I.1.

colony in the Falklands, foundered on the necessity of maintaining the Family Compact between the Courts of Versailles and Madrid. There remained the great unknown of the South Sea, to which Bougainville now turned.

But it was also not to be expected that the old enemy, Britain with her strong navalist tradition and her aggressive merchantry, would stand meekly by while French seamen 'called a New World into existence to redress the balance of the Old.' The French diversion in the Falklands enabled perfidious Albion to steal a march over her rival; in the year that Bougainville founded his colony, Byron sailed on a geopolitically motivated circumnavigation, and set off the great series of voyages which were to unveil every corner of the scarcely known Pacific and make of its peoples a vibrant element in the European imagination.

Commodore the Hon. John Byron

H.M.S *Dolphin* and H.M.S *Tamar* (Capt. Patrick Mouat); from the Downs, 21 June 1764, to the Downs, 9 May 1766.

The *raison d'être* of Byron's voyage was strategic, and every effort was made to conceal his destination, even to appointing him ostensibly Commander-in-Chief, East Indies. The objective was to find bases in the South Atlantic at Pepys's Island and 'His Majesty's Islands called Falklands Islands', a somewhat premature designation. Thence he was to visit Drake's New Albion and search for a passage to Hudson's Bay.

Byron reached Port Desire in Patagonia on 18 November 1764 and after searching for the non-existent Pepys's Island went to the Straits for wood and water, anchoring on 21 December near Cape Virgins where he met the famous Giants, to whom 'The Stoutest of our Grenadiers would appear nothing'. On 12 January 1765 he sighted the Falklands, but apart from a plenty of anti-scorbutics and the fine harbour of Port Egmont, where 'all the Navy of England might safely ride', he was not impressed. Byron took possession, although he thought (mistakenly) that Richard Hawkins had done so in 1593; he did not know that Bougainville had claimed them for France nine months earlier, and left a colony.

Leaving the Falklands on 28 January, Byron picked up the storeship *Florida* at Port Desire and took her into the Straits, where he was much intrigued by meeting a French ship; he did not learn that she was Bougainville's, on his second Falklands voyage. Byron declined her proffered assistance, and 'was in great hopes she would have run ashore', a charitable sentiment tactfully omitted by Hawkesworth. From Port Famine he sent the *Florida* home with a despatch remarking laconically that 'Our Ships are too much disabled for the California Voyage'.

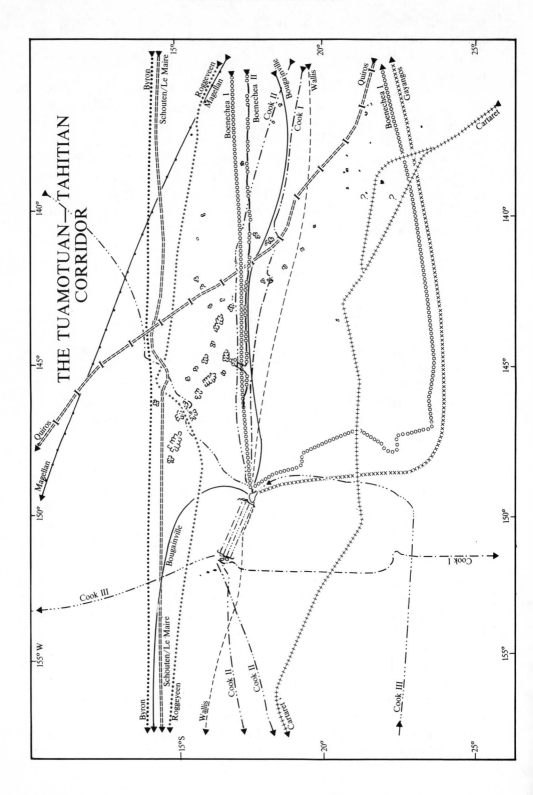

THE TUAMOTUAN–TAHITIAN CORRIDOR

His plan was 'to run over for India by a new Track'. Leaving the Straits on 9 April he watered at Mas Afuera, thought of looking for Davis Land, and decided to steer for the Solomons. On 22 May he hauled northwards to get the 'true Trade' and then set westwards again. Between 7 and 14 June he sighted Tepotu and Napuka, Takaroa and Takapoto, and either Manihi or Takaroa, all in the Tuamotus, landing only on Takaroa, where were found the remains of Roggeveen's *Africaansche Galei*. He now noted the absence of a great swell from the southwest and vast flocks of birds flying south; had it not been for an earlier failing of the winds and present sickness, Byron flattered himself that he would probably have found Terra Australis. As it was, he pressed on to Pukapuka and on the 24th reached Atafu in the Tokelaus.[1]

He thought that he was now in the Solomons, but became convinced that the French charts of them were wrong. As water was beginning to run short, he turned north for the Marianas, and on 4 July sighted 'Byron's Island' in Kiribati.[2] After what he described, with exaggeration, as certainly 'the longest, hotest, & most dangerous Run that was ever made by Ships', he reached Tinian on 30 July. He spent two months there, finding it not so pleasant as in Anson's account; sailing on 1 October, he reached Batavia on 28 November. He stayed only twelve days, fearing its notorious unhealthiness; by 14 February 1766 he was at Cape Town, and left for home early in March.

Around the world in little over twenty-two months; much the fastest circumnavigation till then, but achieved only by flagrant disregard of his instructions. Beyond his mere say-so about the condition of his ships (which seems belied by the smooth Pacific crossing and the *Dolphin*'s second voyage under Wallis), there seems no excuse for the jettisoning of the Californian mission; it was probably an over-ambitious project, but Byron did not even try. Throughout his journal one sees a tendency to exaggerate dangers and difficulties; perhaps his gruelling experiences after the *Wager* mutiny affected him,[3] but this disposition contrasts markedly with those of his successors. Nor were the results of his 'new Track' impressive; only Napuka, Tepoto, Atafu and Byron's Island were new discoveries; a slim haul. Gallagher argues that but for his northwards turn in May he would have anticipated Wallis at Tahiti, but this is only a might-have-been, and even so the argument is confused.[4]

Apart from taking possession of the Falklands, the main achievement of the voyage was a new lease of life for the dubious legend of the

◀ *Figure 5.* THE TUAMOTUAN-TAHITIAN CORRIDOR. Cartaret's 'Bishop of Osna-burg's I.' may have been either Mururoa (H. Wallis, *Cartaret*, I. 153) or Tematangi (A. Sharp, *Discovery*, 110), hence the alternative routes. Cook's tracks in Societies are diagrammatic. For island identifications, see Fig. 6. Mercator projection.

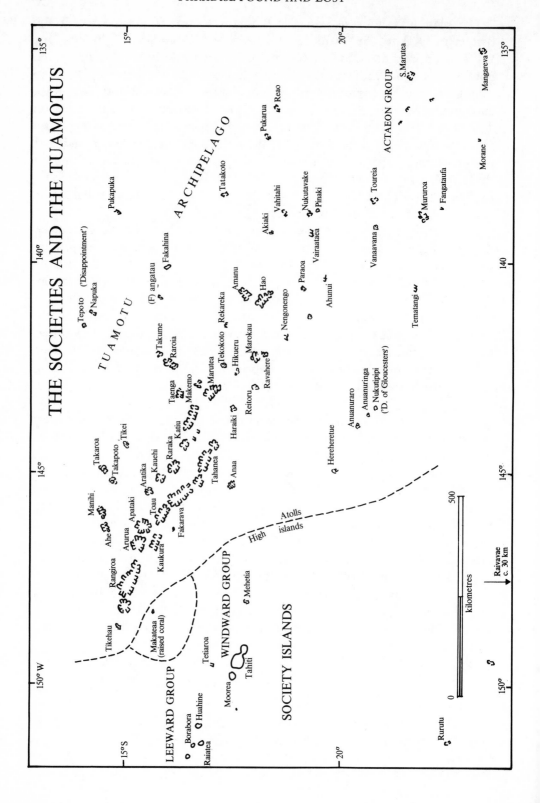

THE SOCIETIES AND THE TUAMOTUS

TUAMOTU ARCHIPELAGO

LEEWARD GROUP

WINDWARD GROUP

SOCIETY ISLANDS

ACTAEON GROUP

High   Atolls
islands

Borabora
Raiatea   Huahine
Moorea
Tahiti
Mehetia
Tetiaroa
Makatea
(raised coral)
Tikehau
Rangiroa
Ahe
Manihi
Arurua
Apataki
Kaukura
Toau
Takaroa
Takapoto
Tikei
Aratika
Kauehi
Raraka
Katiu
Makemo
Fakarava
Tahanea
Taenga
Marutea
Anaa
Haraiki
Reitoru
Ravahere
Marokau
Hikueru
Tekokoto
Rekareka
Takume
Raroia
Tepoto ('Disappointment')
Napuka
Pukapuka
(F)angatau
Fakahina
Tatakoto
Amanu
Hao
Nengonengo
Ahunui
Paraoa
Akiaki
Vahitahi
Nukutavake
Pinaki
Vairaataea
Vanaavana
Toureia
Mururoa
Fangataufa
S.Marutea
Morane
Mangareva
Reao
Pukarua
Hereheretue
Anuanuraro
Anuanuringa
Nukutipipi
('D. of Gloucesters')
Tematangi

Rurutu

Raivavae
c. 30 km

0   kilometres   500

150° W   145°   140°   135°

15°S

20°

150°   145°   140   135°

15°

20°

Patagonian Giants. This ancient mariner's tale had a good run, from Magellan to Le Maire, but later travellers had discounted it. Byron gave no measurements, beyond saying that a man of 6 feet 2 inches was comparatively 'a mere shrimp'; other accounts were less discreet, and Hawkesworth *more suo* heightened the tale, sparking off a lively controversy on both sides of the Channel. Bizarre as it seems, it is likely that His Britannick Majesty's Government sought to divert attention from the serious business of the Falklands by playing up this tall story.[5]

Captain Samuel Wallis

H.M.S *Dolphin* and H.M.S *Swallow* (Capt. Philip Cartaret, till 10 April 1767); from the Nore, 3 August 1766, to the Downs, 28 May 1768.

Wallis's voyage was a follow-up of Byron's; the Falklands apparently safely netted, attention might turn to the continent which Byron thought lay south of his track past the Tuamotus. Wallis's instructions were to sail westwards from the Horn for 100–120° of longitude, as nearly as possible in the latitude of that cape. The land once found, he was to return by the Falklands; if he found no land, or was driven too far north, he might return by the East Indies.[6]

By 17 December 1766 Wallis reached Cape Virgins, where he took a measuring-rod to the Giants, who proved only tall men.[7] The passage of the Straits took seventeen weeks of foul and perilous weather. The *Swallow* was not copper-bottomed like the *Dolphin*; under-officered and ill-equipped, she was in bad shape and lagged constantly, and Cartaret urged that she should be sent home, even under Wallis, while Cartaret carried on in the *Dolphin*—an impossible proposition for any commander. When on 10 April 1767 they at last reached Cape Pilar at the exit of the Straits, the *Dolphin* lost sight of her consort, in sailing conditions which gave plausible reason for not waiting or returning for her. To Cartaret, who had other grievances over supplies, this was plain desertion; to Wallis, a happy accident.[8]

Once free in the Pacific, Wallis was unable to steer a directly westwards course, but he did keep well to the west of any previously recorded voyage, sailing over the reputed lands of Davis and Juan Fernández (not of course the island of that name). By early June he was in the Tuamotus, sighting Pinaki or Nganati, Nukutavake, Vairaatea, Paraoa, Manuhangi and Nengonengo; all except Vairaatea, Quiros's San Miguel, were new.[9] On the 17th Wallis passed the bold volcanic cone of Mehetia, which was to become a landmark for ships making for the great discovery of next day: his King George III's Island, our Tahiti.

◀*Figure 6.*   THE SOCIETIES AND THE TUAMOTUS. Cf. Fig. 5. Mercator projection.

The *Dolphin's* stay of five weeks in Matavai Bay was a cardinal event in Pacific history. The initial reception was peaceful, if thievish, but menaces and actual attacks led to fighting, stones against guns, and the loss of many Tahitian lives. Possession was taken by 'right of Conquest' and asserted by a pendant hoisted ashore; the Tahitians were seen to pile propitiatory offerings around it, as well they might. After this relations became not only peaceful but cordial, and when the strange visitors departed 'Queen' Purea shed many tears. Wallis thought this remarkable, and well he might.

This large, extremely beautiful, fertile and well-populated island was at first taken to be 'the long wishd for Southern Continent', or at least an outlier. Refreshed and with his sick recovered, Wallis sailed on 27 July, perhaps playing Aeneas to Purea's Dido. He passed Moorea and three minor islands, and by mid-August was at Niuatoputapu and Tafahi in northern Tongan waters; these were Le Maire's Verraders and Cocos. At this last he decided to make for Tinian, which he reached on 19 September; the only discoveries en route were Uvea, and Rongerip in the Marshalls.[10] A month at Tinian, three weeks at Batavia, and then he sailed for the Cape and England.

Wallis's achievement lies in one word: Tahiti. His discovery did not really initiate the legend of an almost-Paradise; its flowering had to wait for Bougainville and Commerson, though there are hints in Wallis's dull and Robertson's lively journals, and more in Hawkesworth's recension. Yet even apart from the happy chance that Tahiti was well placed for observing the 1769 Transit of Venus, which brought Cook thither, an island so well-endowed as an intra-Pacific base could not fail to become a magnet, and a focus for European rivalries. Within eight years of Wallis's landfall, Tahiti had been 'possessed' by three powers—Britain, France and Spain. The Tahitians' thieving of iron seems trivial.

Captain Philip Cartaret

HMS *Swallow*; from Cape Pilar, 15 April 1767, to Spithead, 10 March 1769.

Cartaret's appeal to be allowed to carry on in command of the *Dolphin*, or to serve in her as Lieutenant, was due to no lack of courage or confidence; indeed, it was inspired by his conviction of fitness for the task, based on his Pacific experience with Byron. The sequel showed that he was so fitted. He did not clear Cape Pilar until 15 April, four days after the separation from Wallis. He decided to replenish his water at Juan Fernández; he reached Mas Afuera on 9 May and the main island next day, to meet a rude shock—Spanish colours on a substantial fort. Having only English colours (almost incredible official parsimony), he wisely returned to Mas Afuera, where he watered with great difficulty. Leaving on 25 May he steered for the islands of SS Felix and Ambrose, thinking that in British hands they might be a useful counterpoise to Juan Fernández. He did not find them, but was the first to suggest that they were Davis's legendary land.[11]

It was impossible to avoid northing, but when Cartaret did turn west it was on a course south of previous tracks. This led him to his first discovery, on 2 July: Pitcairn, minuscule but to become big with the *Bounty* legend. On 11–12 July he picked up a handful of Tuamotuan atolls, and on 12 August came to, and recognised, Mendaña's Santa Cruz, now Ndeni.[12] Here the Master's stupidity in cutting down a coconut palm resulted in a nasty affray; Cartaret's tribute to the 'Heroick defenders of their country' is inexplicably omitted by Hawkesworth. This was near disaster; of his scurvy-ridden company, four men died by arrows, including the Master; with his death, only Cartaret and his Lieutenant, Erasmus Gower, could navigate, and he had to abandon his idea of discovering to the south.[13]

Survival now depended on the lives of two men; they would have to hasten for the East Indies, since the Southeast Monsoon would fail in ten weeks or less. Cartaret therefore pressed on for New Britain, skirting just north of the Solomons (Fig.7) but out of sight of them until Ndai, Malaita, and Buka off the northern tip of Bougainville; owing to the confusion of the charts he failed to recognise them as the Solomons.[14] Beyond Buka he was in waters already explored, by the Spaniards seeking the return route from the Philippines to New Spain and by Le Maire. New Britain was sighted on 26 August and at last his people were able to rest and refit.

He landed at Gower's Harbour and English Cove on what he thought was New Britain but was actually the southern end of New Ireland. There were huts, but no inhabitants; precautions were taken against their possible return to find the havoc wrought on their palms, cut down in scores for the nuts and 'cabbage'-tops.[15] The crew was desperately weak, but mustered strength to careen and repair. Cartaret spent a week at English Cove, taking possession before sailing on 9 September.

One significant discovery remained to him, of water not land. Forced by wind and current to enter Dampier's St George's Bay, he had no choice but to press ahead in hope of a passage, encouraged by the strong set into the opening. A passage there was, St George's Channel separating New Ireland from New Britain;[16] Cartaret also found the Duke of York's Islands, still so named, and recognised the separation of New Ireland and New Hanover by Byron Strait. There was more fighting with islanders in the Admiralties (Cartaret's name) but no new discoveries, except possibly Tobi in the Carolines, and finally on 15 December he reached Makassar.

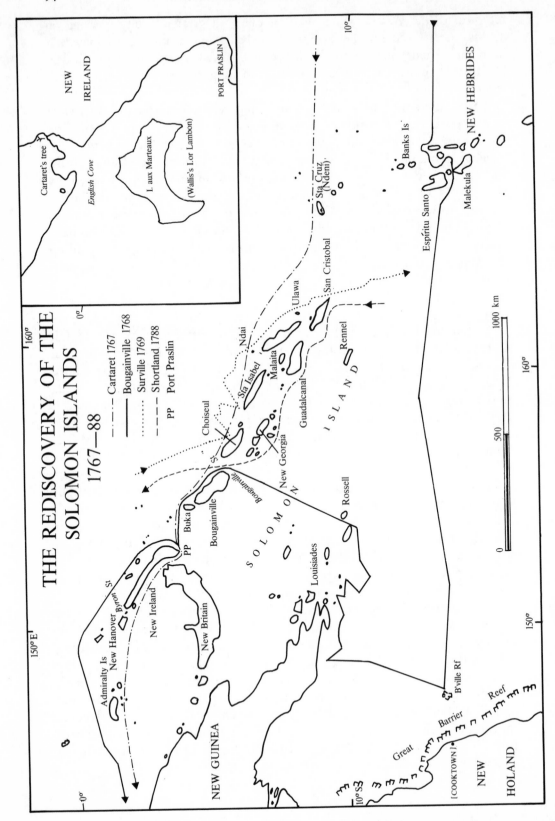

THE REDISCOVERY OF THE
SOLOMON ISLANDS
1767–88

Cartaret 1767
Bougainville 1768
Surville 1769
Shortland 1788
PP   Port Praslin

NEW IRELAND

Cartaret's tree
English Cove
I. aux Marteaux
(Wallis's I. or Lambon)
PORT PRASLIN

10°

NEW HEBRIDES

Banks Is

Sta Cruz
(Ndeni)

Espíritu Santo

Malekula

0°

160°

Ulawa
San Cristobal
Ndai
Malaita
Rennel
Sta Isabel
Choiseul
St
New Georgia
Guadalcanal
I S L A N D

Buka
Bougainville
Bougainville
PP
S O L O M O N
Rossell
Louisiades

Admiralty Is
New Hanover
Byron St
New Ireland
New Britain

NEW GUINEA

B'ville Rf
Great
Barrier
Reef
[COOKTOWN]
NEW HOLAND

10° S

150°E

0°

150°

160°

0   500   1000 km

His reception was inhospitable or worse; the Dutch were deeply suspicious, and Cartaret carried a chip on both shoulders; he did indeed enter into contacts with dissident local rajas through an English adventurer.[17] The Dutch held him up in or near Makassar for over five months, there was a grudging reception and more delay at Batavia, and not until he reached the Cape on 23 November 1768 did he find a friendly welcome. The last leg was marked by a meeting, north of Ascension Island in the Atlantic, with a French ship which 'shot by us as if we had been at anchor'. They spoke; it was Bougainville's *la Boudeuse*. Both sides were chary of exchanging information.[18]

Cartaret's geographical contribution was respectable, not outstanding; he had shaved off a slice of the area where Terra Australis might be; found Pitcairn, insignificant at the time; and cleared up the relationships of New Britain, New Ireland and New Hanover. But when we consider the inadequacies of 'this miserable Tool', the *Swallow*, his voyage must rank high for an 'industrious valour' as much to his credit as the disregard of his claim to advancement was to the Admiralty's discredit. He was left for ten years without a ship.

Capitaine de vaisseau (ad hoc) Louis-Antoine de Bougainville

La Boudeuse and *l'Etoile* (P.–N. Duclos Guyot); from Nantes, 15 November 1766, to St Malo, 16 March 1769.

Bougainville's voyage was a move for French *revanche* after the loss of Canada, in the defence of which he had played a gallant part.[19] Mathematician and soldier, he missed no chance of sea-training, and was an active adherent of the energetic Choiseul, who was Minister for War and Marine as well as running foreign affairs. The search for compensation led first to the Falklands, where Bougainville was authorised to make a private settlement, which he did in 1764. This naturally led to complication with the Spaniards, and he had to hand over to them his little colony. The whole first year of the voyage was taken up by the cession; as he was planned to be back in France by early 1769, this loss of time was a major factor in his relative lack of results in the Pacific.

Bougainville was to search for new lands suitable for colonisation, to open up a new route to China, and to seek spice-plants to be taken to Ile de France. After such defeats as Quiberon Bay, the French navy badly needed to regain confidence and prestige, and Bougainville's company of 338 represented an investment to this end of 5.5 to 6 per cent

◀ *Figure 7.* THE REDISCOVERY OF THE SOLOMON ISLANDS 1767–88. Inset from Taillemitte, *Bougainville*, I. 370, and Bougainville, *Voyage round the World* (London 1772), Plate III. The Ile aux Marteaux was so named for the hammer-oysters found there.

of its strength. One of his company, the Prince of Nassau-Siegen, put it well: a brilliant exploit by the Marine would turn the nation's thoughts more strongly to the sea. Numa Broc is blunter: it would save face.[20]

Bougainville left Montevideo on 14 November 1767, entering the Straits on 4 December, and confirmed Wallis's scaling-down of the Giants. Clearing the Straits, on 26 January 1768, after a difficult passage, he held a generally northwestwards course, well to the east of Wallis's, until about 32°S, then west with some northing across 'Davis Land' until he struck into the corridor already sailed by Le Maire, Roggeveen, Byron and Wallis (Fig.5). This brought him to the Tuamotus, his 'Archipel Dangereux', where between 22 and 26 March he picked up a number of atolls.[21] On 2 April he saw the sharp cone of Mehetia—'pic de la Boudeuse' or, oddly, 'le Boudoir'—and beyond it Tahiti. The ships closed with the island on the 4th, not at Matavai but at Hitiaa Bay on the exposed northeast coast (Fig.8) where on the 6th they made a difficult entry into the lagoon—a 'detestable anchorage'.

Detestable physically—they lost six anchors—but humanly it seemed Camões's Ilha dos Amores; a young girl came on board the *Boudeuse* and carelessly dropped her only garment, 'and the capstan was never hove with more alacrity'.[22] The *Etoile* had no such luck; she was boarded by a chief, Aotourou (Ahu-toru) who looked round for women and soon spotted Commerson's valet Jean Baré—correctly Jeanne!—who left in confusion.[23] The welcome was warm indeed; true, there was 'assassination'; by some soldiers, but Bougainville ironed the suspects and threatened death, and Nassau-Siegen's aristocratic diplomacy smoothed things over. Counting with stones, the Tahitians showed Bougainville that a stay of nine days would be more acceptable than eighteen, and he left on 16 April, taking with him Aotourou.

Before leaving he took possession of 'Nouvelle-Cythère' and the 'Bourbon Archipelago'. His procedure seems most irregular; an inscription and a bottle with the signature of the witnesses were buried, close on midnight, no 'Indians' being around—surely beneath the dignity of His Most Christian Majesty.

Passing north of Moorea, in early May Bougainville sighted and 'possessed', from afar, Manua, Tutuila and Upolu in Samoa, all seen by Roggeveen; he called them the Navigators' Islands, some trading being done with canoes. Le Maire's Hoorn Islands ('l'enfant Perdu') were seen on the 11th, and now, instead of edging away to the northwest to clear New Guinea, Bougainville boldly carried on west to the New Hebrides, his Grandes Cyclades. Here, between 22 and 28 May, he sighted Maewo ('Aurora'), Pentecost, Aoba (where he landed) and Malekula, all probably seen by Quiros; he recognised Quiros's Espíritu Santo. Hopes of landing were frustrated when one of his boats reacted to two arrows, which fell short, with a heavy fusillade.

If Espíritu Santo were not, as Vaugondy and Bellin showed it, part of New Holland, all geographers accepted that the Austral Continent must lie near it. They had passed Quiros's supposed position; where was his great land? did it touch New Guinea? Continuing on the same latitude would soon show them. By this time they were eating rats, and some of Bougainville's staff were highly critical of this bold decision. On 4 June they saw Diane Reef, an outlier of the Great Barrier; two days later long lines of breakers forbade any further westwards search. Unlike Cook, Bougainville was approaching the Barrier head on, and it would have been madness to risk his crews simply to check on the cartographers, even though he was sure that land lay beyond the reefs.[24] His northward turn on 6 June is commemorated by the name Bougainville Reef.

At daybreak on 10 June they saw ahead a very high and beautiful land—the Papuan coast of Orangerie Bay, about 300 km ESE of Port Moresby. Bougainville thought that to the west there might be a passage between New Holland and New Guinea, but this was problematical,[25] and he dared not risk it. There followed a most hazardous navigation along what is still called the Louisiade Archipelago, until on 26 June he rounded 'cap de la Délivrance' on Rossell Island. And now they ate two dogs from the Straits and, tearfully, a favourite milch-goat.[26]

New Guinea, bugbear of navigators, had been rounded, but deliverance from privation was not yet. Bougainville was approaching the Solomons, but failed to recognise these notoriously wandering islands. He came up between Mendaña's San Marcos, to which he gave its present name Choiseul, and a larger island which he left nameless but which is now Bougainville. The Melanesians were not at all like 'les bons Cythéréens'; after a smart attack from Choiseul a grilled human jaw-bone was found in a canoe. Desperate for refreshment, Bougainville made for New Britain and at last, on 6 July, found an anchorage free of hostile warriors. He had been preceded: there was a scrap of lead in the beach, bearing the words HORD HERE ICK MAJESTY'S—a relic of Cartaret's stay, as was also perhaps the absence of any useful plants but a very few 'cabbage-trees' swarming with enormous ants.

Cartaret's plate did not stop Bougainville taking possession of 'Port Praslin', which was on New Ireland not New Britain; he could not know that Cartaret had sailed between the two. The stay, in almost continuous rain, was disappointing, but at least the sick got some rest. On 26 July he sailed, north of New Ireland and the Admiralties, before coming down to New Guinea, still in desperate straits: 'There has been much dispute on where hell is, but in simple truth we have found it.'[27] But on 1 September they were well received by the Dutch at Buru—Bougainville's force was stronger than Cartaret's—and now at last they could eat... . Bougainville stayed briefly at Batavia: and a month at Ile de France; from the Cape he was consciously chasing Cartaret, and caught up with him on 15 February 1769.

Bougainville was given an impossible timetable for an ambitious voyage; he was instructed to leave China by late January 1768, but owing to the Falklands complication that was when he left the Straits. His ships were ill-matched and ill-provisioned. The voyage was carried out with determination and skill, but the results were disappointing: no Southern Continent, no route to China, no spices. Most of the islands seen were not new to Europeans, but as a result of Bougainville's only major deviation from the standard corridor there was at least the good negative finding that Quiros's Terra Australis was not where the geographers had put it; and the width of the Pacific was 'establish[ed] for the first time with certainty' by the observation of a solar eclipse at Port Praslin.[28] Bougainville had taken possession, for what it was worth, all over the place, his most notable 'acquisition' being a New Guinean strip from 126° to 150°E (Paris)—from the Admiralties to Sulawesi![29]

It has been said, by a Frenchman, that 'the results of Bougainville's voyage were above all literary.'[30] The French navy did gain experience and prestige, there was a new French interest in the South Sea; Nouvelle-Cythère was more than a geographical datum. Bougainville's glowing account and Commerson's dithyramb made it a potent hallucinatory symbol, men and women displayed in the naked simplicity of their natural goodness.[31]

Lieutenant James Cook (I)

HMS *Endeavour*; from Plymouth, 16 August 1768, to the Downs, 13 July 1771.

The ostensible centre-point of Cook's first voyage was to observe the Transit of Venus from Tahiti, but there would be no point in confining so distant an expedition to this single aim. Additional instructions directed him to search for the suspected southern continent between Wallis's track and 40°S; not finding it, he was to make for the east coast of New Zealand. If he did find it, he was 'with the Consent of the Natives to take possession of Convenient Situations in the Country'.

Alexander Dalrymple, the champion of Terra Australis, was recommended by the Royal Society to lead the expedition, but this foundered on his insistence that he must have sole command and the Admiralty's insistence (doubtless with the unhappy precedents of Halley and Dampier in mind) that only a naval man could command a King's Ship.[32] James Cook was only a Master, but well regarded by both Admiralty and Royal

Society for his excellent hydrographical and astronomical work in Newfoundland; he was to be assisted by Charles Green of Greenwich Observatory. Other scientific interests were to be looked after by a wealthy
young botanist, Joseph Banks, who was accompanied by a suite of seven,
including a Swedish colleague, Daniel Solander, and two artists.

By 14 November 1768 Cook reached Rio de Janeiro, where a suspicious
Viceroy very grudgingly allowed him some facilities. He sailed on 7
December; departing from precedent his Instructions were to sail by Cape
Horn, not the Straits. He entered Strait Le Maire on 14 January 1769;
only sixteen days later he was only 30' east of the longitude of Cape
Pilar. He now sailed generally northwest, to the west of Wallis's track,
which brought him on 4 April to the Tuamotus, where his only new
island was Ravahere. On the 13th he anchored in Matavai Bay.
    Cook and Banks were to stay at Tahiti three months, observing not
only the Transit but a new floral realm, new manners and customs. Cook
immediately issued strict trading rules; as Wallis had found, a free market
would lead to serious pilfering by the crew, especially of iron, and inflation.

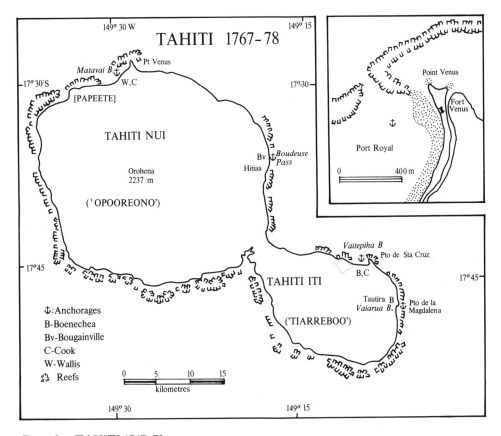

Figure 8. TAHITI 1767–78.

The 'Dolphins Queen' Purea had lost much of her old authority, and at first it was difficult to know with whom to deal. A site for the observatory was found in 'Fort Venus' and Cook tried to explain that the occupation would be temporary—'Whether they understood us or no is uncertain but no one appear'd the least displeased'. The Tahitians may have felt more unease when the stockaded fort was armed with two guns and six swivels, but by then it was too late. The Transit was duly observed on 3 June; the results were not so precise as could be wished, but for once Beaglehole seems less than just to his hero when he says roundly that they were a failure. They were very significant, if not crucial, in the evaluation of the world-wide corpus of observations which determined the sun's distance from the earth to within 1 per cent.[33]

Relations with the Tahitians were mostly amicable indeed, although there was the usual thieving, and one shooting, and once Cook seized canoes in retaliation for theft, with dubious justice. He learnt that European ships had recently visited—Bougainville's, though they were thought to be Spanish—and Cook and Banks had a jolly six-day tour all round the island. Meanwhile the ship's company enjoyed abundant sexual amenity.

They left Tahiti on 13 July, taking with them a chief, Tupaia, and his boy servant Taiata; Tupaia was to be of great value as an interpreter in New Zealand and a guide in the islands neighbouring Tahiti, which Cook called the Society Islands, on account of their contiguity and not, as is still sometimes stated, for the Royal Society.[34] Landings were made on Huahine, Tahaa and Raiatea ('Ulitea'), where Cook took possession. On 10 August he stood southwards in search of the Southern Continent; nothing was found except, on the 14th, the small island of Hitiroa or Rurutu. In 40°S, as instructed, he steered for New Zealand; a heavy swell from the south gave no promise of land in that direction.

Landfall was made on 6 October near Poverty Bay in North Island and the next seven months were spent in the production of a map of both islands in which the only serious errors were the mistaking of Banks Peninsula for an island and the converse for Stewart Island. Cook spent three weeks careening and refreshing at Ship Cove in Queen Charlotte Sound; here they found clear evidence of Maori head-hunting and cannibalism, and Banks 'suppos[ed] they live intirely on fish dogs and Enemies.' The Maori were obviously a militant people; the hill-forts testified to that, and affrays alternated with very friendly passages, in which Tupaia acted as interpreter. Cook took possession of both islands; at Mercury Bay (North Island) there is no mention of the Consent of the Natives; at Queen Charlotte Sound they consented to a mark that would show any visiting ship that Cook had been there.

This circumnavigation meant, in Banks's words, 'the total demolition of our aerial fabric called continent.' Cook's Instructions gave him the option of returning by either Cape, Good Hope or Horn. A direct course to the Horn would remove any lingering doubts as to Terra Australis, while no major discoveries were likely on the Cape of Good Hope route, against the Westerlies. The ship was not in a good state for a winter voyage either way in high latitudes. Consulting his officers, Cook decided on a fruitful compromise; he would go by Good Hope but sail northabout New Holland.

On 1 April 1770 he left New Zealand at Cape Farewell; on the 19th land was seen south of Cape Howe.[35] Cook proceeded up the coast until on the 29th he anchored in what he first called Sting Ray Bay but later, after Banks had been at work, Botany Bay. A few Aborigines made gestures of defiance till driven off by small shot; they avoided any close approach and were utterly indifferent to presents. Their fate lay a generation ahead.

He left on 6 May, passing and naming but not entering Sydney's Port Jackson, and on the 15th named the easternmost point of Australia Cape Byron. He was soon well within the Great Barrier Reef, and on 11 June the *Endeavour* struck on coral. She was got off next day and the leak was fothered;[36] with great difficulty they entered Endeavour River, near Cooktown, for repair. Here some contact was made with the shy Aborigines, and a strange beast was shot, the first recorded 'kanguru'. Leaving this refuge on 4 August, Cook got outside the Barrier, but was borne in upon it and only with great peril re-rentered through Providential Channel.[37] Navigation within the Barrier was hazardous, but on 23 August he rounded Cape York into Endeavour Strait, after landing on Possession Island and formally claiming the whole coast by the name of New South Wales.[38] There was no question of the Consent of the Natives; by the lights of the day the country appeared unimproved by man and so *terra nullius*.

Perhaps from Dalrymple's map, more probably from Vaugondy's, Cook was reasonably assured of a passage westwards; by it he reached Batavia on 11 October. The Dutch were presumably becoming used to weary British circumnavigators, and he was given every facility for speedy repair, more badly needed than he had realised. But his stay, till 27 December, was disastrous. Hitherto he had lost only two men, none from scurvy; Batavia cost him thirty lives from malaria and dysentery, including those of the artist Sydney Parkinson, the astronomer Charles Green, Bank's assistant Hermann Spöring, Tupaia and Taiata.

Venus observed, and the most massive body of scientific and social data yet brought back from the South Sea; the outline of eastern New Holland no longer conjectured but established; some 8700 km of coastline there and in New Zealand charted with remarkable accuracy; two large dents in the supposed Southern Continent—great results from a single voyage, prelude of greater to come.

Commander James Cook (II)

HMS *Resolution* and HMS *Adventure* (Comdr Tobias Furneaux); from Plymouth, 13 July 1772, to Spithead, 30 July 1775 (*Adventure* in July 1774).

Cook's second voyage was born of his first; in a 'Postscript' to his journal he had outlined a voyage which should settle Terra Australis once for all, using the Cape approach to get into the Westerlies for a circumnavigation in high latitudes, with Queen Charlotte Sound as an advanced base. This apart, the plan was remarkably like Bouvet's of 1740–1 (Fig.9),

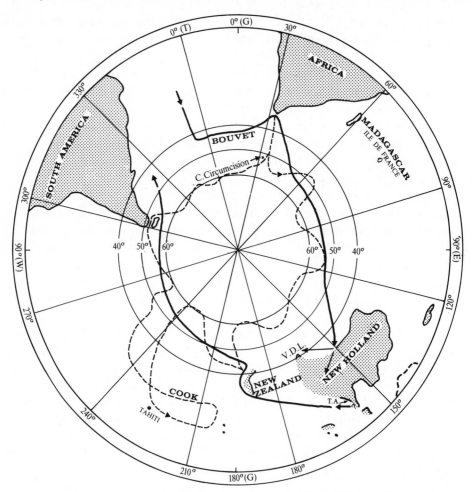

Figure 9. BOUVET AND COOK. Outlines from Cook's sketch in Portfolio of Charts and Views in Hakluyt Society edition of Cook's *Journals*, Plate XXV, but New Holland and New Zealand shown according to pre-Cook knowledge, and Dalrymple's non-existent Gulf of San Sebastian omitted. Solid line = Bouvet's plan for a second voyage and broken line = Cook's. N. L., Nuyts Land; V. D. L., Van Diemen's Land; T. A., Bouvet's probable conception of Quiros's Tierra Australia. (T), (G), Teneriffe, Greenwich.

whose Cap de la Circoncision was given in the Instructions as a marker both outwards and on the return;[39] in the event Cook remarkably exceeded his own design. The experience of the Great Barrier Reef indicated that two ships would be desirable.

With the Falklands crisis settled, the times were propitious, and Cook got his two ships, Whitby-built barks like the *Endeavour*, renamed *Drake* and *Raleigh*; to avoid a needless provocation to Spain, they became, most fittingly, *Resolution* and *Adventure*. For the first time, chronometers were taken on a circumnavigation, Larcum Kendall's facsimile of Harrison's H4 and an Arnold with Cook, two Arnolds with Furneaux, in charge of the Greenwich astronomers William Wales and Charles Bayly. The artist William Hodges, on the *Resolution* had a fine gift, anticipating Turner's, for the strange lights of sea and sky and ice. Banks was to have come as naturalist, but withdrew when the Admiralty condemned his top-heavy deckhouse for his gear and suite of fifteen persons; he was replaced by Johann Reinhold Forster and his son George, the father a fine scientist but cross-grained in the extreme.[40]

After three weeks at the Cape, Cook sailed for Cape Circumcision on 30 October 1772; the first iceberg was seen on 9 December and a few days later the first pack, which Cook, in common with most geographers (but not J. R. Forster), took to imply a landmass behind it. On 1 January 1773—Day of the Circumcision, the anniversary of Bouvet's discovery in 1739—he was south of the erroneous position given him for the 'cape'; Bouvet must have been mistaken (Fig.7). He turned east, then south for the first known crossing of the Antarctic Circle (16 January), coming to about 120 km from the real Antarctica before standing NE for 'the land said to have been lately discovered by the French'—Kerguelen's. He passed well to the south of it, and again there was ice but no land; it could not be the Continent. After a long run, 90–150°E, roughly on 60°S, he bore away from the ice for New Zealand, reaching Dusky Sound, in the extreme southwest, on 26 March. This was a wild country of fiords with only a couple of Maori families to give the Forsters their first view of primitive life; they were not greatly impressed. Cook left on 11 May and a week later was at Queen Charlotte Sound, where he found the *Adventure*, which had lost touch off Kerguelen and skirted the east coast of Van Diemen's Land, without however settling the question of its insularity.[41]

With winter at hand, Cook decided on a tropical cruise in the gap between his previous tracks to and from Tahiti. On 4 June he passed through Cook Strait and held east as far as the longitude of the Tuamotus before turning north; no land, and Terra Australis seemed less and less likely. In the old corridor (Fig.5) he added Tekokoto, Marutea and Moto-tunga to previous discoveries,[42] and anchored again in Matavai Bay on

26 August. The welcome was warm but trade was poor—there had been local war—and on 1 September he left for Huahine and Raiatea, where pigs and provender were in good supply. When he sailed, on 17 September, he took with him a young man 'Oddidy' (Hitihiti or Mahine), while Furneaux gave passage to the more famous Omai.

Cook liked known bases—and unknown tracks between them; his return to New Zealand was circuitous. He made first for Tasman's Amsterdam, but avoiding the tracks of previous navigators. This brought him on 27 September to the atoll of Manuae-Auoto ('Hervey Island') in what is now the Cook group, and on 2 October to Eua, Tasman's Middelburg. The well-cultivated prospect and the welcome were delightful, but Cook (*noblesse oblige*, no doubt) was the only one to venture on kava. At Tongatapu next day the welcome was as warm, but with spring Cook was eager for another summer traverse in the south, and left on the 7th. New Zealand was sighted two weeks later, and, after a storm in which the *Adventure* finally separated, he anchored in Queen Charlotte Sound on 3 November.

The stay at Ship Cove saw a practical demonstration of Maori cannibalism; amidst the general abhorrence, that of Oddidy 'shone with a superior lustre', to the great edification of the Forsters—an offset to his ready indulgence with the girls.[43] Before leaving on 25 November Cook buried a bottle under a marked tree for Furneaux, not fixing a rendezvous but mentioning Easter Island and Tahiti as possible points of call. Five days after Cook sailed Furneaux arrived. His stay also was marked by cannibalism, ten of his men being killed and eaten.[44] After this loss, he was probably wise not to chase after Cook; he sailed on 23 December for the Horn, came quite close to Cape Circumcision without finding it, and reached England a year before Cook.

Cook's next stage, New Zealand to New Zealand via the Antarctic, Easter Island, the Marquesas, Tahiti, Tonga, the New Hebrides and New Caledonia, in eleven months, was by itself a voyage of unprecedented originality and scope. He began with two great loops which took him down to the Antarctic Circle, up to 47°51'S, then in a lunge to 71°10' (30 January 1774), by far the deepest penetration southwards yet made.[45] This was the most perilous and gruelling part of the voyage, and bitter were the tirades of J. R. Forster against 'A cruise . . . shocking to humanity', wilfully prolonged for one man's vain pride.[46] The Southern Continent, if as Cook thought likely it did exist, must lie beyond vast fields of pack-ice, flecked and girdled by giant bergs. Even to Cook's resolution, this was clearly *non plus ultra*. Most men would have considered their task performed, and well performed, but characteristically he did not take the easy course for the Horn and home. He had a good ship, a healthy crew, sufficient stores, and to the north there was much still unknown or dubiously placed on the maps.

The first new objective was the country supposed to have been discovered by Juan Fernández in the sixteenth century; there was not the
least sign of land anywhere near the positions given by Dalrymple. Cook
now made for Easter Island, sighted on 11 March after 103 days with
no glimpse of land; he was too ill to go ashore, but his officers and
the Forsters provided reasonable accounts of an island marked, apart from
the statues, mainly by poverty. Leaving on the 16th, Cook sailed for
the Marquesas, anchoring on 8 April at Mendaña's port on Dominica
(Hiva Oa). After only four days he left for Tahiti, picking up en route
four Tuamotuan islands ('Palliser's Islands') of which Toau and Kaukura
were new to Europeans.

Cook anchored in Matavai Bay on 22 April; he had intended merely
to check the chronometers, but the prosperity so lacking eight months
earlier had returned, the welcome was rapturous, and he decided to prolong
his stay. There was the usual thieving, and on one occasion Cook resorted
to the formal flogging of a chief, but the great event was the assembly
of a fleet to attack rebellious Eimeo (Moorea): 160 big double canoes,
as many smaller craft, with an estimated 7760 men—a magnificent sight,
which led Cook and the Forsters to exaggerated conjectures of the total
population.

The Eimeo war hung fire, and Cook sailed on 14 May, calling at Huahine
and Raiatea; amply supplied, he resolved to check Quiros's discoveries.
Leaving Raiatea on 4 June, he found uninhabited Palmerston Island on
the 16th and five days later Niue, where his landing was resisted, whence
his unflattering name Savage Island. Very different was the welcome
at Nomuka (Tasman's Rotterdam) on 17–29 June, which earned for the
Tongan group the name Friendly Islands. On 3 July the first (and very
brief) European landing was made in Fiji, on tiny Vatoa (Turtle Island);
the few inhabitants retired from the beach, and Cook came to the rather
hasty conclusion that the Fijians were a docile people.

Cook's landfall on 17 July on what he called the New Hebrides was
Bougainville's, Maewo; between then and 31 August he sailed right down
the chain and back again, sighting all its islands (Fig.10).[47] Relations with
the people were mixed but mostly poor; Malekula was hostile, on Eromanga what seemed a determined attempt to seize a boat led to heavy
firing, but with little loss of life. The longest stay, 15–19 August, was
on Tana; here again there were warning shots and a nasty affair in which
a Tannese was killed;[48] but there was also some guardedly friendly intercourse, and J. R. Forster made some vulcanological observations which
enabled him to criticise the great Buffon. Returning up the west side
of the chain, Cook passed between Malekula and Espíritu Santo to come
upon the latter from the east—he named Cape Quiros—and so, unlike
Bougainville, to enter Quiros's Bay of SS Philip and James. La Austrialia

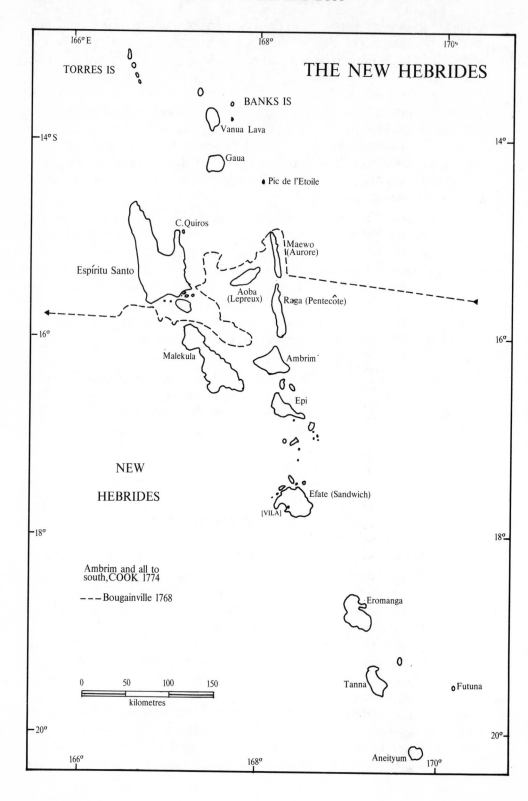

166° E   168°   170°

TORRES IS

THE NEW HEBRIDES

BANKS IS

Vanua Lava

14° S   14°

Gaua

Pic de l'Etoile

C.Quiros

Maewo (Aurore)

Espíritu Santo

Aoba (Lepreux)

Raga (Pentecôte)

16°   16°

Malekula

Ambrim

Epi

NEW

HEBRIDES

Efate (Sandwich)

[VILA]

18°   18°

Ambrim and all to
south,COOK 1774

– – – Bougainville 1768

Eromanga

0   50   100   150

kilometres

Tanna

Futuna

20°   20°

166°   168°   Aneityum   170°

del Espíritu Santo, in Cook's own phrase 'the only remains of Quiros's continent', was no longer tacked on to New Holland; it had at last reached its true abiding-place. Cook's chart of the islands was still used in the 1890s.

The Forsters thought, with horror, that Cook now meant to sail directly across 'the South Sea in its greatest breadth'; in fact he was making for New Zealand to prepare for a final summer cruise, homewards by the Horn. He had not gone far before he sighted, on 4 September, a land of which there was no hint in charts or tradition: New Caledonia.[49] He came upon it at Balade, near its northeastern tip. The people were shy, poor, and, astonishingly, 'not in the least addicted to pelfering'; the men were naked except for penis-cases, the women, according to George Forster, amused themselves innocently by leading the sailors on and then slipping off.[50] They had no animals at all, and a beef-bone left from the crew's al fresco supper made them suspect their visitors of man-eating.

Cook ran down the east coast, and on the southern tip and the off-lying Isle of Pines saw the giant Araucaria trees, which the Forsters, against the unlettered seamen, took to be basalt columns; a mistake these savants were rather slow to admit. Cook left on 1 October, and nine days later saw Norfolk Island with its tall pines; his report of their assumed value for masts and yards had some significance for the founding of Australia. On the 17th he made his New Zealand landfall, the cone of Mount Egmont. At Queen Charlotte Sound his bottle had been taken, and once an alarming rumour of a recent wreck had been discounted, the Maori left him in no doubt that this had been done by Furneaux. By 11 November Cook was ready for the last phase of this complex voyage.

On 17 December land was sighted south of Magellan's Cape Deseado at the entrance to his Straits; a week's stay (20–28th) among the Tierra del Fuegians of Christmas Harbour gave the Forsters ample data to attack at once the philosophers of primitive happiness and the vices of civilisation. Cook entered Strait Le Maire on the 30th, and with the New Year 1775 was stretching across the South Atlantic; he did not find Dalrymple's non-existent Gulf of San Sebastian, but did find the grim shores of South Georgia,[51] the South Sandwich Islands, and Southern Thule—well-named, probably by J. R. Forster. 'Bouvet's discovery was yet before us... to be clear'd up'; alas, this was not done with absolute certainty until 1898.[52] By 21 February Cook was convinced that Bouvet had been deceived by ice and clouds; in fact he was very close to Bouvet Island, Cape Circumcision, and with this his Instructions were fulfilled to the letter. They had been more than fulfilled in the spirit.

◀ *Figure 10.*   THE NEW HEBRIDES

On sighting Tierra del Fuego Cook wrote 'I have now done with the SOUTHERN PACIFIC OCEAN, and flatter myself that no one will think that I have left it unexplor'd'. The last nail had been driven into the already heavily-studded coffin of Terra Australis (Fig.13); the icy limits of any possible Antarctic Continent had been outlined; Quiros's Tierra Austrialia definitely fixed, the New Hebrides completely charted, New Caledonia discovered. Kendall's chronometer H4 had been a faithful guide. The Forsters especially had gathered extensive observations which they were to organise methodically and, despite their rhetorical moralising, to analyse perceptively.

Magellan must always have the prime honour of first daring the utterly unknown Pacific. That said, Cook's second voyage was incomparable.

Captain James Cook, F.R.S. (III)

H.M.S *Resolution* and H.M.S *Discovery* (Comdr Charles Clerke);[53] from Plymouth, 12 July 1776 (*Discovery* 12 August, joining at the Cape), to the Thames, 7 October 1780.

A revival of British interest in the Northwest Passage, inspired in part by impatience at the Hudson Bay Company's apparently do-nothing monopoly and also by the counterpart to the mythical Terra Australis, the mythical open Polar Sea, received added impetus from the publication in 1774 of an English version of Jacob von Stählin's account and map of the Russian discoveries. Already in that year Daines Barrington, FRS and friend of Sandwich the First Lord, Banks, Cook, and as long as possible of J. R. Forster, was projecting a voyage to be undertaken when Cook returned. After that return Cook had been appointed Fourth Captain of Greenwich Hospital, 'a fine retreat and a pretty income', but with 'limits far too small for an active mind like mine', for which 'the whole Southern hemisphere [had been] hardly big enough'.[54]

Cook read his own mind well; yet in February 1776 he had spent six of the preceding eight years in two extremely wearing voyages, and even Sandwich, 'Jemmy Twitcher' and not the most delicate of men, was decently diffident about ordering him out again so soon. But at a small dinner—Sandwich, Cook's early patron Admiral Sir Hugh Palliser, the Admiralty Secretary Sir Philip Stephens, high company for a farm-worker's son—Cook was asked for his advice. This seems to have been the catalyst for his hardly suppressed desires; he volunteered.

The plan was for Cook to go out by the Cape and check the discoveries of Marion du Fresne and Kerguelen, which might prove Indian Ocean analogues of the Falklands; then by New Zealand to Tahiti to take Omai home, a reasonable cover story. He was then to sail to Drake's Nova Albion (California) and coast northwards, not wasting time by inspecting inlets below 65°N, but thence to search diligently for an opening to

Hudson's Bay—Dampier's recommended approach, which Byron had so signally failed to pursue. Should he not find an opening in his first season, he should try again next summer for either a Northwest or a Northeast Passage, after wintering at Petropavlosk.

Undue reliance was placed on von Stählin's map, which replaced G. F. Müller's Alaskan peninsula and long chain of close-set Aleutian Islands by an open island-strewn sea (Fig.12). Müller's version of 1758 in fact corresponded better with reality, and so the more logical approach would have been from Canton, as Barrington had suggested. But von Stählin's version had the imprimaturs of the St Petersburg Academy and the Royal Society; its author claimed that it was 'a very accurate little Map', though he guaranteed no positions. Actually it was totally fallacious.[55]

Considering the general thrust of the Passage lobby's propaganda, one may wonder whether the voyage was quite so innocent of commercial or strategic intent as Beaglehole infers. In 1774 that much-advertised key to the South Sea, the Falklands, had slipped from British hands; there might be compensation in the north, where French Canada was no longer an obstacle and Drake's Nova Albion was a card up the sleeve. It is noteworthy that Russian cooperation seems to have been counted upon, but the Bourbon Powers were suspicious: perhaps Omai and the Passage were blinds? There was even a minor flurry in the French foreign office over diplomatic gossip that Cook was bound for Kamchatka to assist in an Anglo-Russian conquest of Japan. Cook was enjoined most carefully not to trespass on Spanish holdings; just two weeks before he sailed San Francisco was founded to forestall any Russian advance, and ever-nervous Madrid took no chances with a possible third player; Mexico was instructed that if Cook called at a Spanish port, he was if possible to be arrested.[56]

Leaving the Cape on 30 November 1776 and passing between Marion's 1772 discoveries, Marion and Prince Edward Island, Cook was off Kerguelen by Christmas Eve. He sailed round the north and east coasts, not seen by the French; with his earlier voyage south of that dreary island, Kerguelen's great land was destroyed. On 26 January 1777 Cook anchored for four days in Furneaux's Adventure Bay in Van Diemen's Land; the timid Tasmanians fled abruptly when Omai fired a musket to show off. By 12 February the ships were in the old home from home, Queen Charlotte Sound. Maori whom Cook thought of as old friends were strangely reluctant to meet him; they feared retaliation for the deaths of Furneaux's men, but were reassured when it became clear that Cook saw no point in applying European notions of justice, so long after the event, to probably unpremeditated killings.

Cook left Ship Cove on 25 February; his Instructions called for leaving the *Societies* a month earlier. He was relying on the Westerlies to give him sufficient easting before turning north into the Trades for Tahiti;

but it was now the season of variables east of North Island, and the winds failed him. On 30–31 March he discovered Mangaia, Atiu and Takutea in the Southern Cooks; a landing party on Atiu was politely but firmly kept all day cooped up in the crowd not far from the beach. Very little supply could be had, and none at hostile Manuae (6 April). The *Resolution* was heavily loaded with livestock bought at the Cape as gifts for the Islands, water was short, and Cook reluctantly decided to make not for Tahiti but Tonga. Uninhabited Palmerston Island was reached on 14 April, and here some victuals were found for man and beast; but for the first time, apart from the Forster's complainings, there was criticism of Cook's navigation.[57]

On 2 May Cook reached Nomuka, by the 14th he had exhausted its stocks and set off for the Haapai group,[58] a hazardous navigation made at the importunity of chief Finau ('Feenough'), who was anxious to keep this company of consumers away from his own island Vavau. After another brief call at Nomuka, Cook reached Tongatapu on 10 June, staying a month. Five days at Eua, and on 17 July he sailed for Tahiti—four months behind schedule.

This prolonged interlude enabled Cook and his surgeon William Anderson to gain a good deal of insight into Tongan society, although of course its intricacies could not be unravelled in eleven weeks. Tongan thievery was elegantly ingenious, and Cook resorted to rough measures: flogging, and slashing of men's arms to ensure recognition. Clerke shaved their heads, and this ridicule had some effect; and some officers commented adversely on Cook's harshness. Trade was lively, until at the end only girls were in good supply; quantities of red feathers were obtained, of high value in Tahiti. There were entertainments by both parties—dances, fireworks, wrestling (Tongans now and then politely losing), feasting. Friendly Islands indeed; and yet the genial Finau may have plotted a general massacre of Cook's company.[59] In Tonga Cook heard of Fiji, only three days' sail away, and Samoa, and saw Fijians. His original timetable was in ruins, but if it were set back one year, as in effect it had been, he had time to make a push for one or the other, and one feels that the Cook of 1770 or 1775 would have done so.[60]

En route to Tahiti Cook discovered Tubuai in the Australs on 8 August, and on the 12th anchored at Vaitepiha Bay, Tahiti, where he received a reasonably accurate account of the arrival, and failure, of the Spanish mission. On the 24th he was at Matavai Bay, where Omai's Tongan stock of red feathers and an equestrian dash in a suit of armour (from the Tower of London!) offset for a while his lowly rank. The Eimeo war was on and Cook refused a request to assist in it, though he did attend a human sacrifice for its success. At Eimeo a goat was stolen, and Cook, who seems to have been living on his nerves, exacted an indiscriminate and disproportionate penalty in burned and wrecked houses and canoes; at Huahine a man lost his ears for theft of a sextant.

The livestock were disposed of, with much relief, and it only remained to dispose of Omai. He was landed on Huahine on 30 October and took possession of a little house, thoughtfully built without nails, for his strange medley of European treasures, which included an organ, a jack-in-the-box, and 'electrical machine', and assorted firearms.[61] Cook spent a full month at Raiatea, during which he seized the very helpful chief Orio and his family as hostages for the return of deserters.[62] The attempted desertions reflected not only desire for the fleshly delights of the Islands but some sense of strain amongst the company now facing a long voyage into the inhospitable boreal seas. After a brief call at Borabora (8 December) Cook set out for Nova Albion, ten months after due date. The delays were due largely to bad luck with the winds, yet there seem signs in Cook of a loss of his usual urgent drive; though once on the American coast—a new world to conquer—the Cook of old was for a while reborn.

On 24 December the crews received an acceptable gift, the turtles of scrub-covered Christmas Island in the Line group. Then on 18 January 1778 high land was seen to the northeast: Oahu, and soon after Kauai and Niihau, the westernmost of the larger islands of Hawaii, his Sandwich Islands (Fig.11). This was unexpected; Cook had already issued winter

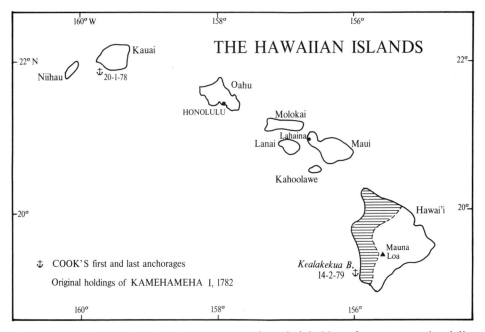

Figure 11.   THE HAWAIIAN ISLANDS. Kamehameha's holdings from R. S. Kuykendall, *The Hawaiian Kingdom*, I. 33 and map.

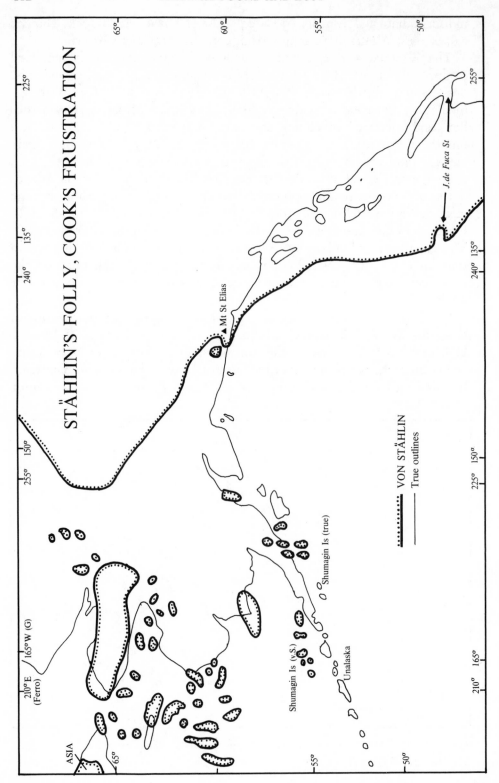

STÄHLIN'S FOLLY, COOK'S FRUSTRATION

clothing. He could not make Oahu, but had very pleasant visits on the other two, despite the shooting of a Hawaiian by Lieutenant John Williamson, a self-righteous critic of some of Cook's punitive measures. The Captain himself was astonished to be greeted by full prostrations, and also to find the language and customs so similar to those of Tahiti: how had this nation spread itself so widely? Trading seemed remarkably honest—some of the lower deck thought differently—and Cook did not know, then, that his precautions against communicating venereal disease were ineffectual. He thought that these islands, so close to the Galleon route to Manila, might be useful to the Spaniards.

On 2 February the voyage was resumed, and on 7 March the American coast was sighted at Cape Foulweather (Cook's name still stands) in Oregon. Progress was slow, but on the 22nd Cook sighted Cape Flattery, the south head of Juan de Fuca Strait, but, night falling, he did not see the Strait itself and wrongly wrote it off as non-existent. On the 29th he entered a harbour which was to become the centre of a new fur trade and an international crisis: Nootka Sound on Vancouver Island.

The Indians here were filthy, light-fingered (they had some iron and wanted more), and with sound business instincts—so sharp that 'not a blade of grass but had its seperated owner' who demanded payment. No wonder that, according to the New Englander John Ledyard, Cook remarked of one 'This is an American indeed!'.[63] One man had a couple of silver spoons; Cook thought that the iron, and presumably the spoons, had come by tribe-to-tribe trading and were no evidence of a Spanish visit, but the spoons at least had almost certainly been filched from Juan Pérez's *Santiago* in 1774.[64]

Most of the stay at Nootka was devoted to repairs and replacing masts. On 26 April Cook sailed on what was to prove a most wearisome and frustrating search for the Passage. Weather compelled him well offshore as he passed the alleged position of de Fonte's fabled strait; Cook did not believe in it, but regretted not being able to check. He made land again at 55°20′N—almost exactly Chirikov's landfall in 1741; there followed weeks of investigating a most dangerous coast, bafflingly indented and island-strewn. Cook's Instructions indeed were to begin such a search at 65°N, but then the inlets pointed north and one might lead him to Bering Sea and that latitude. After passing Bering's Mount St Elias on 9 May the coast trended west and then southwest—Kenai Peninsula (Fig.15); Müller might have been right. But then, just where von Stählin's map indicated, it turned north again in a wide opening, now Cook Inlet.

◀ *Figure 12.* STÄHLIN'S FOLLY, COOK'S FRUSTRATION. Cf. Plate XVI and Fig. 21 in Spate, *Monopolists and Freebooters*. It will be seen that almost the only accurate placing on Stählin's map is Mt St Elias.

Many thought that this was the passage; Cook did not, but 'to satisfy other people's he went up it (25 May–5 June) until his judgement was confirmed at Turnagain River.

There was a trifling skirmish, no shooting, and some trading with Indians whom Cook thought might be Eskimos; and then on 19 June, in the Shumagins, some Indians handed in a neat box in which, after they had left, was found a note in Russian; only '1776' and '1778' could be made out. The coast, islands or mainland, still trended southwest; von Stählin was wrong. Fog was now added to the other perils. At last (28 June) Cook found a way through the Aleutian screen, at Unalaska Island; here he watered at 'Samgoonoodha Harbour', now English Bay. Another Russian note was received.

Cook now passed out of the Pacific proper into the Bering Sea. There was no Passage in Bristol Bay, north of the Alaskan Peninsula, and after taking possession of the country (rather boldly, in view of the obvious Russian presence) he pushed on to Bering Strait, naming Cape Prince of Wales, the westernmost point of the American mainland, on 9 August. In the Arctic Ocean he stretched as far east as Mys Schmidta on the Siberian side and west to Icy Cape on the American; his farthest north was 70°44′ on 18 August. At every point a field of ice barred the way north, and the coasts were drear and desolate.

By 3 October he was back at Unalaska, and here at last made contact with the Russians, introduced by salmon loaves sent by the local factor Grigoriev Ismailov. Corporal Ledyard volunteered to seek him out, with Indian guides, and brought back three fur-traders, followed by Ismailov himself.[65] Over the bottles, relations were cordial, if linguistically limited Ismailov declared non-existent a third of von Stählin's islands, and Cook now took his measure of the latter: 'A map that the most illiterate of his illiterate Sea-faring men would have been ashamed to put his name to.' That he took so long in reaching this conclusion has been seen as another sign of the stress he was undergoing.[66]

Hawaii was obviously more agreeable than Kamchatka for wintering, and on 26 October Cook sailed south to a landfall on Maui a month later. To the distress of his crews he did not land immediately, mainly in order to regulate the trade.[67] He sailed round Hawai'i itself, and not until 17 January 1779 did he come into port on its western coast, at Kealakekua Bay.

His reception surpassed anything yet experienced. By the accident of timing, Cook had arrived at the festival-tide of Lono, the harvest-god, and was taken as his avatar: presentations, prostrations, a wild abandon of jubilee. But after a while the strain of food offerings on the grandest scale began to tell; very friendly chiefs asked when their visitors might be leaving, '& seemd well pleas'd that it was to be soon.' Cook took the hint, sailing on 4 February.[68]

Had this been all, the voyage might have been another triumph; but the *Resolution*'s repairs in England had been scamped, and very soon after leaving her foremast was sprung in a gale. On 11 February Cook returned to a changed Kealakekua Bay; the old spirit of joyous worship was replaced by apprehension and tension. An attempt to seize the person of the chief Kalaniopuu to secure the return of a stolen cutter led to an affray in which Cook was killed, 14 February 1779. Some of his remains were returned a few days later; the mast was repaired, not without heavy fighting, and on the 22nd the ships left the Bay.

What followed was anti-climax, and yet heroic. Many a good officer might have thought that Cook had now disposed of the Passage as well as Terra Australis, and sailed for home; but Clerke, now in command, despite his illness determined to complete the search, if completed it could be. He sailed for Kamchatka, where he was received, and thence repeated Cook's fruitless voyagings along the ice-edge. Returning, he died of consumption off Kamchatka on 22 August, and was buried at Petropavlosk with all honour—'not more than he deserv'd but all that we could pay'. Nothing could exceed the kindness of the Russians; the Governor, Magnus Behm, gave the crews 400 pounds of tobacco, of which they had long been starved, and they offered to have their grog stopped that they might make him some return in kind; a pleasing touch in a sad ending.[69] It was left to John Gore to take the ships home by Macao and the Cape.

The voyage inevitably failed in its main objective, and was marked by tragedy in the fullest Greek sense; for there can be little doubt that at the end Cook had been touched by *hubris*. It is also all but certain that his judgement and control had been sapped by disease. Yet when he sailed he was under forty-eight, and tough, and in those days before routine medicals there could have been scarce any reason to doubt that he would return with more laurels. But for that sprung mast, Sandwich's little dinner, so often condemned, might now be hailed as the happiest of inspirations—though again, had Sandwich administered the naval dock-yards more conscientiously, the mast might not have sprung.

Nor were the achievements small. The American and Arctic navigation was a great feat of seamanship; the voyage was remarkable for the range and intensity of its ethnographic observations. It marks too the convergence of the three great drives to Pacific America, British, Russian and Spanish (and, with Ledyard, the Yankee!). The high prices received at Macao for sea otter pelts gave birth to the Pacific fur trade. The discovery of Hawaii revealed a new base for voyaging, which in little over three decades was to become a node of whaling and trading activity. The voyage, marred as it was, ranks still among the greatest.

Chapter 6

CHRONOLOGY II: FRENCHMEN AND SPANIARDS 1769–1776

The man who finds an unknown country out,
By giving it a name, acquires, no doubt,
A gospel title . . .
A beam in proper form transversely laid
Of his Redeemer's cross the figure made;
His royal master's name thereon engrav'd,
Without more process, the whole race enslav'd,
Cut off that charter they from nature drew,
And made them slaves to men they never knew.

Jean-François-Marie de Surville

St Jean-Baptiste; from Pondicherry, 2 June 1769, to Callao, 9 April 1770.

The rationale of this muddled and unhappy voyage was a strange mixture of commerical and geographical speculation. The Compagnie des Indes, usually shaky, was nearing collapse with the virtual demise of French power in India after the Seven Years' War, nor could the near-bankrupt government bail it out. French colonies and French merchants remained in India, however, and the end of the Compagnie's monopoly left the field free for 'country trade', to which redundant officers and seamen naturally turned. Amongst them was the able and experienced Surville, who even before the formal dissolution of the Compagnie in 1769 had secured the financial backing of the Governor of Pondicherry, Jean Law de Lauriston (nephew of the famous or infamous financier John Law) and of the wealthy Jean-Baptiste Chevalier, Governor of Chandernagor. Late in 1766 Surville obtained the Compagnie's licence to build the 650-ton *St Jean-Baptiste* at Nantes, and then brought her to India to be fitted out for a large-scale trading voyage. The details of financing and of the lading need not concern us, but the total investment was around £150,000 in contemporary values, an immense sum for the day.[1]

The original intention seems to have been to trade in Manila and the East Indies and to attempt to break into the Dutch monopoly in Japan. This straightforward commercial motivation was cut into by rumours of a fabulously rich island recently discovered by the British in the South

Charles Churchill, *Gotham* (London 1764), Book I.

Sea; it even had a colony of Jews, so doubtless good business could be done.[2] Nobody knew where this marvellous island was, but somehow— Dunmore suggests by a phonological confusion of 'Wallis' and 'Davis' in French—it became identified with our old and elusive friend Davis Land.

After leaving Pondicherry the *St Jean-Baptiste* called at Malacca and Trengannu, but the Pacific voyage proper may be taken as beginning at the Bashi (Batan) Islands north of Luzon. The people were friendly and many pigs were obtained, the last substantial supply of fresh provisions for a voyage which was to take another seven months. Three men deserted, and Surville carried off three islanders as replacements; they were treated very kindly, and his second, Guillaume Labé, thought that Surville was much too soft with them.

To Labé's distress, Surville was remarkably secretive about his plans. They left the Bashis on 24 August 1769; by September they were in the Carolines, looking for Sonsorol, but their charts were inadequate and they were using Dampier's longitude, 3° out, for their departure from the Bashis.[3] Winds were poor, scurvy had already struck, and they saw no land until, on 7 October, they sighted 'Ile de la Première Vue'— Bougainville's Choiseul. On the 13th they anchored at 'Port Praslin'— not Bougainville's, but in some small islands at the western end of Mendaña's Santa Ysabel (Fig.7). Although Surville, a humane man, was at pains to cultivate friendship, a watering party suffered an attack which was repelled with heavy loss from French musketry.[4] A young lad, Lova Saragua, was captured by using two Malagasy crewmen with their heads powdered to look like the lime-dressed hair of the locals; Surville fed him at his own table, and he became probably the first Melanesian to reach Europe.

Port Praslin was left on 21 October; on the 27th 'Ile Inattendue' (Ndai, Cartaret's Gower) was seen, and passing Malaita Surville tried to trade at 'Ile des Contrariétés'—Ulawa, between Malaita and San Cristobal— but the islanders seemed too threatening. On 6–7 November Surville thankfully cleared the Solomons, naming two islands at the eastern end of San Cristobal 'Iles de Déliverance.[5] None of his islands were new to Europeans, and Surville did not recognise them as the Solomons; he gave them the name 'Arsacides', drawn from the article in Diderot's *Encyclopédie* on the Assassins of the Levant.

Neither he nor Labé knew where they were; they were not even sure whether they had passed east or west of New Britain, and there was no sign of Quiros's Tierra Austrialia, though by their dead reckoning they had sailed over it. They had in fact been sailing straight for the New Hebrides, but unluckily turned SSW when only 130 km away. They had more bad luck when they sailed just north of New Caledonia without seeing it. They were now in dreadful plight—twenty-eight men died of scurvy in as many days. Surville at last took Labé into confidence; they read Tasman and decided to run south to 35° and make for New Zealand along the parallel—with misgivings, for although Tasman had reported a fine country, the most striking specific was the name of Murderers' Bay. On 12 December they made landfall near Hokianga Harbour, in the long northern arm of North Island.

This was a lee shore, there were breakers on Hokianga Bar, and no shelter along Ninety Mile Beach. Working north through a gale, they rounded Cape Maria van Diemen on the 16th; but for this gale, which blew Cook offshore, they would have met the *Endeavour*. Once in the lee of the land the sea became smooth, and on the 17th they anchored in 'Lauriston Bay', now Doubtless Bay, so named by Cook only nine days earlier. With Port Praslin and Tasman in mind, the French were wary of the surprising friendliness of the Maori, but relations soon became amicable; Surville tactfully observed local etiquette and was careful to obtain permission for felling trees. Much help was given by the chief Ranginui in a storm which stranded a yawl; Surville thought it lost, but when he was about to leave saw some Maori carrying it off. Unable to regain it, in his anger he burned huts and canoes and carried Ranginui off.

They sailed on the last day of 1769. They had obtained only a few greenstuffs; there were only two anchors left, and of the 194 men who had sailed from Pondicherry, sixty-two were dead. Surville's instructions forbade calling at Spanish settlements in America, but a council decided that this was the only possible course, in great hope that 'the feelings of humanity [of] the gentlemen who rule there' would afford them succour. And this course might yet bring them to Davis Land; they gave up this dream early in March.

The crossing was miserable. Ranginui died of scurvy on 24 March 1770, the day they sighted Mas Afuera; with only two boats left it was too hazardous to risk a landing on Mas a Tierra.[6] At last on 4 April they made landfall and on the 7th dropped anchor at Chilca, south of Callao. Next morning Surville tried to land, and in his heavy full uniform was drowned on the bar. Labé took the ship to Callao; her sick were looked after, but the bureaucratic clutches of the humane 'gentlemen who rule there' held her for precisely three years. On 7 April 1773 the *St Jean-Baptiste* cleared Callao; she did not reach France until August.

Humanly and financially, the voyage was a disaster; eighty men had died including all of the fifty Indian lascars. The bigger backers got about half their money back by an auction of the cargo; Labé lost his life's savings, Surville's wife her dowry. But geographically the results were not negligible.

Surville's track across the Pacific, roughly between 35 and 40°S, cut another slice off Terra Australis. It should have sunk Davis Land once and for all; instead it led to González's voyage, but after that very little more was heard of the old buccaneer legend. More importantly, though Surville did not recognise his Arsacides as the Solomons, academic geographers did.

First in the field was J.–N. Buache de Nerville, nephew of the famous Philippe Buache, who in 1781 produced a *Mémoire sur l'existence et la situation des îles de Salomon*. It was clear from Mendaña that the Solomons lay not far west of Santa Cruz; Cartaret, Bougainville and Surville had all found a group of large islands between Santa Cruz and New Guinea; and comparison of their accounts of the people, especially Surville's, with that of Mendaña made the identification all but certain.

The matter was brought to a head by the voyage of John Shortland, taking two of the transports of the First Fleet from Port Jackson to China, northabout New Guinea. This led to his discovery (August 1788) of a large island which still retains the name he gave it, New Georgia. The editor of his journal gratuitously remarked that the French had seen very few points in this region, and that 'for the form and location of the rest ... we are indebted entirely to the researches of our own countryman'.[7] This very brash assertion naturally produced a Gallic response, from Claret de Fleurieu; it was decisive, and may be aptly summed up in its title: *Découvertes des François en 1768 et 1769 dans le Sud-Est de la Nouvelle-Guinée et reconnaissance postérieure des mêmes terres par des navigateurs anglois qui leur ont imposé des nouveaux noms.*[8] Fleurieu did not discount the British contribution, nor gloat unduly, but he did point out that the British must or should have known of Surville by 1783, and on the identification he did a thorough detective job. Perhaps the most notorious of the South Sea's wandering islands were now firmly pinned down; only Alexander Dalrymple, that stern defender of lost causes, remained unconvinced.[9]

Capitán de Navío Don Felipe González y Haedo

San Lorenzo and *Santa Rosalia* (Don Antonio Domonte); from Callao, 10 October 1770, to Chiloé, 15 December 1770.

The arrival of the *St Jean-Baptiste* at Callao aroused the deep suspicions of the energetic Viceroy Manuel de Amat y Jumient.[10] What was this David [*sic*] Land Surville had sought? Was it perhaps one of the islands Byron had found? If so, the ancient enemy must be forestalled. Amat therefore sent out two ships, of 64 (or 70) and 26 guns—as Fleurieu said, 'an armament sufficient to subjugate all the Archipelagos of the *Great Ocean*, but not too good [*peu propre*] to explore them'.[11] González's Instructions were to seek for the island in 27–28°S, and if it were colonised to expel the intruders if possible; if impossible, to report back at once.

If it were inhabited by indigenes, they should with all gentleness be brought under the powerful protection of the King of Spain. He was also to examine the Chilean coast in about 50–52°S.

The voyage itself was uneventful. On 15 November 1770 González sighted Easter Island, which he named 'San Carlos'. Landing parties found the people very poor, docile and timorous, great beggars—surprisingly, there is no reference to thieving. Few women were to be seen; perhaps women and goods were held in common? They were intelligent and could be easily domesticated and converted to 'any religion which might be put before them.' From the sea the great statues were taken for pyramidal shrubs, an inverse error to the Forsters' in New Caledonia, but after closer inspection the Spaniards' description of them was much better than Roggeveen's. On the 20th possession was taken by 250 men in military order; three crosses were erected, and chiefs and priests were induced to set their hieroglyphic marks on the formal document.[12]

González sailed on 21 November. He was not sure that this was really David Land and cruised about, going as far as 4° westwards without seeing any land. A council decided not to risk the Chilean exploration, in view of the lack of charts or sailing directions for this hazardous coast; probably a wise decision with such big ships. They therefore made for Chiloé, reaching Callao in March 1771.

The first reaction in Lima was euphoric: 'We have reverted to the spirit of discovery and conquest of the sixteenth century.'[13] Amat, convinced that David Land had indeed been found, received instructions to send a second expedition, to colonise and convert; but new information, albeit confused, came in of the British discovery of Tahiti—a new menace, or opportunity.[14] He thought that the investigation of both Tahiti and San Carlos could be carried out in a single voyage, but it became apparent that the latter was really only Roggeveen's Easter Island. David, or Davis, Land sank into the cloud-banks which had probably given it birth.

Marc-Joseph Marion du Fresne

Mascarin and *Marquis de Castries* (A.-B.-M. du Clesmeur); from Port Louis, Ile de France, 18 October 1771, to Port Louis, 8 April 1775.

Like Surville, Marion du Fresne was an officer of the Compagnie des Indes left unemployed by its dissolution; and his voyage was similarly speculative, and disastrous. Bougainville's protégé Aotourou (Ahu-toro, or by name-exchange with him Poutavery) had reached Ile de France on his homeward journey to Tahiti, but there was no provision for his onwards transport. Marion, backed by a local magnate René Magon, offered to return Aotourou in the course of an exploring and trading voyage; he would meet the costs from trading profits, but would need the loan of two ships and large advances for fitting-out and lading. The plan was to sail southeast from the Cape for Gonneville's Land—its last serious appearance—and thence to Tahiti by Van Diemens Land and New Zealand, returning by Quiros's Tierra Austrialia—and the Spiceries.[15]

Relief from the Aotourou dilemma; perhaps a new continent and bases on a new route (actually Tasman's sweep!) outflanking the Dutch in the Indies; the spices so dear to the heart of the improving Intendant of Ile de France, Pierre Poivre—it is no wonder that Marion got his ships and stores. It was to prove a bad bargain.

An outbreak of smallpox on Ile de France led to a hurried departure, lest Aotourou should fall a victim; but on 6 November 1771, off Madagascar, he did die of that disease. Marion's instructions were to return to Port Louis if smallpox appeared on the ships,[16] and Aotourou's death destroyed the ostensible reason for the voyage. But his was the only case and business was business; far too much had been invested for a tame return to be tolerable, and Marion pressed on to the Cape.

Thence he sailed eastwards (28 December) and between 13 and 21 January 1772 made his only discoveries, Cook's Prince Edward Islands, one of which bears Marion's name, and the Crozets, named for his second on the *Mascarin*. Windswept and treeless, they were hardly Gonneville's well-favoured land, but they might be headlands or offliers of the Southern Continent. To us with our knowledge of sub-Antarctic conditions it may seem astonishing that men could think of fine countries in these desolate regions, but it must be remembered that these islands lie in 46°S, equivalent to Rochefort or La Rochelle in France, and on the analogy of 'climates' should be as genial.

Serious exploration was made impossible by a collision, probably due to the incompetence of du Clesmeur, who owed his command to being nephew of the Governor of Ile de France. Timber was needed for remasting, and it was decided to make for Van Diemens Land. Early in February they passed north of the land which Kerguelen was to discover one week later, and on 3 March sighted Van Diemens Land, anchoring on the 6th off Forestier Peninsula. There was a slight brush with the Aborigines— this was only the second European visit—but no water or suitable timber was found, and after three days Marion set course for New Zealand.

The landfall, on 25 March, was the smooth snowy cone of 'Pic Mascarin', Cook's Mount Egmont. Like Surville, Marion made north; he looked in vain for water and timber at Three Kings' Islands, and missed Surville's Lauriston Bay; one can only speculate on his reception by Ranginui's tribe. On 4 May he anchored in the Bay of Islands. Enough basic Polynesian had been gained from Aotourou for communication with the Maori; all was amity, and Marion was allowed to cut down some kauri trees, at

a masting camp deep in the bush. Crozet, recalling Tasman's Murderers'
Bay, clucked anxiously over his commander's neglect of security; Marion,
who had imbibed romantic ideas from Commerson at Ile de France, was
quite at home, and completely blind to any thought that after five weeks
he might be outstaying his welcome. On 12 June he went ashore with
a fishing party; on that day and the next he and some thirty men were
massacred.[17] Crozet and du Clesmeur took a bloody revenge; after taking
possession of 'France Australe' they sailed from 'Treachery Bay' on 12
July. En route to Guam they sighted several islands in Tongan waters,
but these were not new or are not identifiable.[18]

The results of Marion's voyage were succinctly and brutally summed
up: 'It is unfortunate that it has cost the King 400 to 500 thousand livres
to have a bankrupt massacred in New Zealand...'.[19] There was nothing
to show but five bleak islands and some first-hand information about
the Maori, including the experience of massacre which, by Crozet's report,
momentarily shook Jean-Jacques Rousseau himself.

Capitán de Navío Don Domingo de Boenechea (I)

Aguila; from Callao, 26 September 1772, to Valparaiso, 21 January 1773.

After González's return to Lima there came the shocking news of the
British discovery of 'George's Island' or Otaheite, which the Viceroy
Amat persisted in attributing to 'the English astronomers Solander and
Banks' in their voyage 'under the pretext of observing the Transit of
Venus'.[20] He also persisted in 'holding firmly to the belief' that the English
were 'in actual occupation' of 'some outpost in the midst of these Seas';
at any rate, it was essential to make sure.[21] The Viceroy was dissatisfied
with González's rather cursory report on San Carlos (Easter Island), and
although its colonisation was deferred, Boenechea was instructed to make
a more thorough examination of the island. Two Franciscans, sent to
make a spiritual reconnaissance, had also the more mundane assignment
of reporting on the best defensible site on San Carlos for some fifty
people. Tahiti also was to be carefully investigated. Amat's Instructions
breathe humanity and good sense; a few likely lads might be brought
to Peru, of their own free will, but on no account any women, and
the Padres were warned against reckless baptisms or other measures which
might lead to 'ultimate failure of highly catholic ambitions.'

Boenechea's sealed orders, when opened, gave the option of taking either
Tahiti or San Carlos first, and in council with his officers he decided
on that order. On 28 October he came to Tauere in the Tuamotus, a
new discovery, then to Haraiki and Anaa, both seen by Bougainville.
On 6 November he was off Mehetia,[22] where an 'Indian' came on board
and guided them to Tahiti itself. Landfall was on the 8th, though it was

not until the 19th that Boenechea found a satisfactory anchorage at 'Puerto de la Magdalena' (Vaiurua) on the southeastern peninsula of Tahiti-iti (Fig.8).

The people were friendly, indicating an anchorage in a way that suggested they had seen frigates before, and there were other evidences of European visits, including hatchets of English make. It must have been disconcerting to see French and Spanish colours greeted with silent indifference, the Union Jack with loud shouts. The Spaniards behaved with scrupulous correctness; their reports, though admiring, were more restrained than those of their predecessors, and they were less appreciative of Tahitian womanhood, but then they were only seven weeks from home comforts. Boenechea does not seem to have taken possession, but despite his obvious lack of European priority he renamed Tahiti for the Viceroy—Isla de Amat.[23]

Having wooded, watered, and made minor repairs, always in great amity with the Tahitians, Boenechea left on 20 December, with four willing young passengers, for a brief look at Moorea. While he was searching for a way through the reefs, the *Aguila* had struck on a coral patch, and the leak was gaining. Repair would obviously be impossible at harbourless San Carlos; despite the explicit instructions for a landing on that island, he sailed direct for Valparaiso.

A competent and limited reconnaissance, no more; but no more was intended. The voyage was intended to confirm or dispel the Viceroy's apprehensions of an English colony, and to gain the information for a more serious Spanish effort, and as far as Tahiti was concerned it did so.

Capitán de Navío Don Domingo de Boenechea (II) and Teniente de Navío Don Tomás Gayangos

Aguila and *Júpiter* (storeship; Don José de Andía y Varela); from Callao, 20 September 1774, to Callao, 8 April 1775.

Boenechea's journal of his first voyage was sent to Spain and submitted to an eminent naval authority, Juan de Lángara. He took a more sober view than Amat; the islands were of no use to Spain as a way-station and had few resources; the only reason for other powers to occupy them would be as bases for contraband, but they offered no opening for this. Lángara therefore advised against colonisation, but 'those hapless natives' would be gladdened by knowing that the Catholic King could help them on the path to salvation, so a small religious mission should be sent.[24]

Boenechea was therefore ordered to return to Tahiti, taking with him the two survivors of the four young men brought to Lima, and two Recollect Fathers. To carry their stores and a pre-fabricated house the 'paquebot' *Júpiter* was chartered, to sail under her owner Andía y Varela, an able Chilean merchant seaman. The *Júpiter* lost contact before the Tuamotus were reached, and although she was only a few hours behind the *Aguila* at 'San Narcisco' (Tatakoto, 29 October, a new discovery), the ships did not see each other there or at the rendezvous, Anaa. Boenechea discovered one more atoll, 'San Julian' (Tahanea),[25] before making Mehetia and Tahiti itself on 13 and 14 November. The next day Andía, who had already reached Tahiti, rejoined, and on the 27th the ships anchored in Vaitepiha Bay, 'Puerto de Santa Cruz', in the Tautira district of Tahiti-iti; Cook had been there four months earlier.

Before finally anchoring they had called at Vaiurua, just down the coast; this was the home of Pautu, one of the lads returning from Lima, and he was rapturously welcomed. Boenechea's reception in Tautira was thus prepared for, and was extremely friendly, especially on the part of the 'Cacique' Vehiatua and the overlord Tu. Every assistance was given not only for provisioning but also in finding and preparing a site for the mission house; on their part the Spaniards showed a becoming respect for marae. Pautu, baptised Tomás, insultingly 'went native' again, and a sailor was badly hurt in a fight with a Tahitian; but things were smoothed over and by the last day of the year the Padres were safely installed. According to Andía, they were already nervously wishing themselves in Lima.[26]

On New Year's Day 1775 the Most Holy Cross was set up before the mission house, with salutes of musketry and cannon and celebration of the Mass. On the 5th the mission was formally inaugurated, and El Rey Don Carlos III's gracious and powerful protection was offered to and accepted by Tu and Vehiatua. Tahiti had now been 'possessed' thrice in eight years; Corney rather grandly suggested that this last proceeding should be styled 'The Convention of *Hatutira*, 1775'.[27]

On the 7th the ships left for a short cruise through the Society Islands, returning to Puerto de la Santa Cruz on the 20th. Boenechea, stricken with sudden illness, died on the 26th, Gayangos taking command. On the 28th he sailed for home; two men tried to desert, but 'an infinite number of Indians' attempted to stow away. The only incident on the return was the discovery, on 5 February, of Raivavae ('Santa Rosa') in the Australs.

Apart from the settling-in of the Padres and the soon forgotten 'treaty' with Tu and Vehiatua, the most notable feature of this voyage—and of the other Spanish visits—was the absence of bloodshed. Of course the Tahitians knew the effect of firearms, and had paid dearly for that knowledge; but it was not without reason that Andía contrasted the 'forebearance and gentleness' of his country with the 'harshness and wanton behaviour' of the British.[28]

Teniente de Navío Don Cayetano de Lángara y Huarte

Aguila; from Callao, 27 September 1775, to Callao, 15 February 1776.

The purpose of this voyage was simply to bring supplies for the maintenance of the Mission; a purpose frustrated by the missionaries themselves.[29]

The voyage itself calls for no comment. Lángara found nothing new in the Tuamotus, and anchored at Puerto de Santa Cruz on 3 November. It immediately became clear that the Viceroy's warning against reckless excess of zeal had been utterly superfluous.

On what criterion Fathers Jéronimo Clota and Narciso González were selected for the Mission it is impossible to discern, but one must suspect that it was on the time-honoured principle that these two were the two whom their superiors could most gladly spare. The pair did nothing whatsoever towards conversion of the lost souls around them; in fact, they rarely stirred outside their house. To be fair, they may have feared less for their lives than lest they should suffer the fate of Diderot's Chaplain, who fell into fleshly sin.[30] The fact remains that the net result of their missionary presence was *minus* two converts, since not only Tomás (Pautu) relapsed, but also—despite his high sponsorship—his comrade baptised as Manuel de Amat. One feels that the Padres' interpreter, whom they do not condescend to mention by name, would have made a much better apostle than these professionals.

This young man, the marine Máximo Rodríguez, had energy, shrewdness, humour and good-humour, practicality and lively curiosity. He became a great favourite with the Tahitians, and put in some pointed anti-British propaganda. The contrast between his active mind and the torpor of his superiors is neatly brought out by a diary entry; after a sixteen-day tour all round Tahiti-nui, Rodriguez returned to base and 'found nothing noteworthy except the *Padres*' lack of interest in my journey.'[31]

The return of the *Aguila* meant one thing to these timorous messengers of Grace: home. They made this very clear to Lángara, who had no option but to take them back to answer to higher authority, which very properly relegated them to disgraced oblivion. Rodríguez, equally properly, was commissioned Sub-Lieutenant.

Although Lángara left the house in care of local chiefs and promised to return with fresh clerics, this was the end of Spanish activity in Tahiti. It was not the end of interest; Lángara brought back tangible evidence that Amat's fears were not quite groundless—medals distributed by Cook and depicting George III with the *Resolution* and *Adventure* on the reverse. On his third voyage Cook added a second inscription to the Spanish cross, stressing British priority; when this became known in Madrid, it produced an order of 1782 that the insolent addendum should be erased and, if possible, the Mission should be renewed. But in Peru it was the time of the great revolt of Túpac Amaru; the Viceroy Teodoro de Croix, summarising his reign in 1790, reported that ships and money had been lacking, and passed on to his successor the hope that this might be 'one of the glorious undertakings reserved for Your Excellency's activity and zeal...'.[32] But we have left the days of Carlos III and Jose de Gálvez for those of Carlos IV and Godoy, and this is the last glimmer of what had been so briefly 'la Isla de Amat'.

Chapter 7

COMMENT ON COOK

Our soules, whose faculties can comprehend
The wondrous Architecture of the world:
And measure euery wandring plannets course,
Still climing after knowledge infinite
And alwaies mouing as the restles Spheares,
Will vs to weare our selues and neuer rest...

I whose ambition leads me not only farther than
any other man before me, but as far as I think it
is possible for man to go...

The work

In the history of the Pacific James Cook's achievement is central and commanding. Its literature is commensurate; a bibliography of 1970 has 4808 entries, and there followed a decade of bicentenaries, each with a new crop of monographs and symposia; as Holmes remarks, an axe rather than a pruning-knife is needed to cut through the thickets of print.[1] This literature is as voluminous as it is numerous; five of the basic books— the journals of Cook, Banks and the Forsters, Beaglehole's *Life* and J.R. Forster's *Observations*—run to 11,822 pages. Lesser journal-keepers have a different importance, often not so much as witnesses to fact as indices to feelings, to the morale and morals of the ships' companies. Heinrich Zimmermann and, despite his borrowed fables and his own rhodomontades, John Ledyard are of value as giving a lower deck view, and as outsiders—German and American—they are not completely wrapped up in the Royal Navy mystique. Even John Marra's anonymous catchpenny publication is at least evidence that not all Cook's people saw him as a benevolent father figure and a stainless hero.[2]

To begin with Cook's strictly geographical contributions: the coasts of New Zealand and eastern New Holland charted; New Caledonia, most of the New Hebrides and Hawaii added to the maps; outer limits set to any Antarctic continent; the shores of Bering Sea explored and the Arctic Ocean penetrated, so that the 'standard' maps of Müller and von

---

C. Marlowe, *The First Part of Tamburlaine the Great* (London 1590),
II.vii; James Cook, *Journal*, 30 January 1774.

Stählin were replaced by a far closer approximation to reality. Quantitatively, this is impressive enough; but as important was the quality of Cook's charting. He made mistakes—Stewart Island a peninsula, Banks Peninsula an island—and 'He consistently missed the best harbours' (Papeete, Auckland, Wellington, Jervis Bay, Port Jackson), 'though in every separate case there is an obvious and sufficient reason.'[3] But whenever winds and weather enabled him to keep close to the coast his charting attained an accuracy unusual hitherto on a first survey, though as a direct result of his influence not so unusual after him; his ships were an intensive training school for a generation of seamen. One factor fostering such accuracy, as Beaglehole points out, is that his own training in the coastal trade and in the Newfoundland survey meant that he was not so reluctant to keep close inshore as a deep-water Royal Navy officer might be; another was his use of the cat-built collier, which could take the ground safely, unlike the frigate with its sharper lines.[4]

The North Sea work was pilotage as much as navigation, but as a navigator in the fullest sense Cook's record is outstanding. The observation of the Transit of Venus was not the failure it has sometimes been rated; on the second and third voyages Cook had the advantage of 'Mr Kendall's watch', and although it was to be long before chronometers became standard equipment, it was his lengthy and rigorous testing of them in the Pacific, with many checks against longitudes fixed by lunar distances, that ensured their ultimate acceptance. On the *Endeavour* Cook received instruction from the official astronomer Charles Green and later he had the able services of William Bayly and William Wales, but he was a capable astronomer in his own right.[5]

Another great geographical result was negative, the destruction of Terra Australis Incognita (Fig.13); but it was not altogether a small thing to have refuted so decisively a position held for centuries. It could even be put positively:

> It is now discovered beyond all doubt that the same Great Being who created the Universe by his *fiat*, by the same ordained our earth to keep a just poise, without a corresponding Southern continent...
> He stretched out the North over the empty space, and hangeth the earth upon nothing.
> Job 26:7.[6]

The immediate economic effects of Cook's third voyage were neatly summed up by his editor John Douglas: extension of whaling into the South Atlantic; 'We may soon expect to hear' of the Russians expanding eastwards in America—and they founded Kodiak in the year that these words were published; 'the fresh mine of wealth discovered in the furs

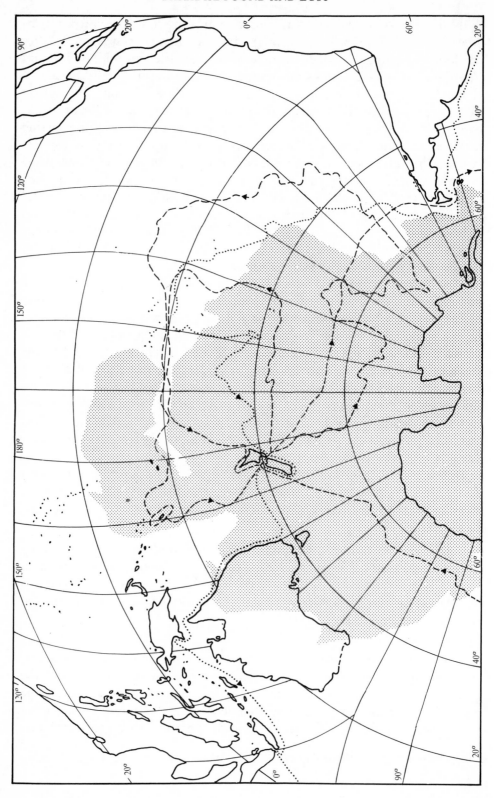

of King George's Sound [Nootka]'—and James Hanna opened this trade in 1785.[7]

Besides the astronomical and strictly geographical findings, other scientific results of the voyages were remarkable. Cook himself had no training in the field sciences, still less in the as yet embryonic social sciences; but he was a man who could learn much and quickly through osmosis of mind to mind in the great cabin. He was fortunate that his scientific companion on the first voyage was not Johann Reinhold Forster but Joseph Banks, whose gaiety and charm (and the assurance given by wealth) contrasted with the crabbed nature of Forster, ever struggling and anxiety-ridden. Yet, despite the Forsters' bitter complaints of insult and malevolence from the ship's company and of inhuman Antarctic traverses merely for the greater glory of Cook, their records also offer evidence of co-peration and even cordiality.

The main burden of work in the field sciences—botany, zoology, geology—fell upon Banks and Solander on the first voyage, on the Forsters on the second, on Cook's surgeon William Anderson on the third. These sciences were crystallising out of an undifferentiated 'natural history' or 'natural philosophy', and the observations and collections made on the voyages formed a massive contribution to 'Enlarging the Sphere of Contemplation'. In one field at least Cook took issue, from his own observation and the influence of J. R. Forster, with the conventional wisdom enunciated by the great Buffon—the origin of polar ice. The professional's discussion was the more thorough and coherent, but both Cook and Forster could be credited with pioneer work in glaciology.[8]

Aside from economics, social science could hardly be said to exist as such, but still there had always been 'Manners and Customs' which in principle could be observed by anyone of intelligence. The Earl of Morton, President of the Royal Society, 'offered to the consideration of Captain Cooke [sic], Mr Banks, Doctor Solander' Hints, some of ineffable triteness, which did however include faint foreshadowings of J.-M. Degérando's The Observation of Savage Peoples of 1800, the first manifesto of anthropology.[9]

Here Cook himself was a practitioner, and amateur, as they all were, but a shrewd observer not given to grandiose generalisations. Unlike all other expeditions since those far-off days of Mendaña, Cook's Oceanic traverses were interrupted by sojourns in Tahiti and Tonga, sometimes lasting for months; time enough to learn the language, and then there

◀ Figure 13.   COOK'S DEMOLITION OF TERRA AUSTRALIS. Dotted line, Cook's first voyage; pecked line, his second; stipple, maximum extent of Terra Australis Incognita, after Belga, Florianus, Hondius, Janssonius, Mercator and Visscher. Bartholomew's Lotus projection. Original by Richard I. Ruggles, in H. Friis (ed.), The Pacific Basin, reproduced by courtesy of the American Geographical Society, New York.

was the unexpected bonus that something like the same tongue was spoken from New Zealand to Hawaii, from Tonga to Easter Island. It was too soon for anthropology, but not for ethnography, and 'the moment in history when Cook approached Vahitahi Atoll in the Tuamotu Archipelago can be seen as marking the beginning of Pacific ethnography.'[10]

'The opening of the Pacific is therefore to be numbered amongst those factors contributing to the triumph of romanticism and science';[11] today this may seem an odd collocation, but the boundary between the two cultures was not then drawn tightly.[12] Banks's artists were hired to be empirical, applied; but in those days a certain non-utilitarian elegance did not come amiss in scientific illustration, and the artists—and still more the engravers who broadcast their art—were not free from the conventions of their craft. Not least of the legacies of Cook's voyages is the treasury of graphic illustration created on them: landscapes, birds, beasts, men and women. In his classic *European Vision* Bernard Smith has skilfully explicated the achievements of this art, and its limitation, the distortion of reality induced by neo-classic tradition or romantic imagination, both idealising; and the subtle moulding of sensibility through the portrayal of a new world of nature and humanity.

William Hodges stands out, in the ravishing paintings of Tahitian canoes against their superb mountain back-drop, the eeriness of Easter Island, the Antarctic ice-islands, the water-spouts, the aery sweep of clouds around Table Mountain—surely not surpassed before his time, nor after it but for Turner—in the rendering of sea and shafts of sun and tumult in the heavens. Hodges and George Forster inspired the young Alexander von Humboldt to undertake those great journeys which led to the grand synthesis of *Cosmos* and the foundation of modern geography.[13] Had Cook's voyages yielded no more, he would still have deserved well of the republic of learning; and there was much more.

To his contemporaries, that 'more' would have included the conquest of scurvy, a claim until recently accepted without query. It can be admitted only with large reservation; Cook accomplished not so much its conquest as its avoidance. We shall return to this distinction in Chapter 9.

The man

'James, ye son of a day labourer' was born on 27 October 1728 in the Yorkshire village of Marton, a little south of Teesmouth; he died on 14 February 1779 at Kealakekua Bay, Hawai'i, a Fellow and Medallist of the Royal Society, a Post-Captain in His Britannick Majesty's Navy, and possessor of a name which rang from side to side not only of all Europe but of all the navigated seas of the world. Such an ascension would be noteworthy in any age; in the hierarchical and deferential rural

England of the Hanoverians it was extraordinary. Yet in many aspects James Cook seems an archetypal ordinary Englishmen, transcending his origins through that type of genius which has been described as an infinite capacity for taking pains. His watchword was indeed Thorough, until the last fatal lapse into impatience.

When Cook was eight, his father was advanced to be in effect farm-manager for Thomas Skottowe, one of the local gentry, who was sufficiently struck by the boy's intelligence to pay his modest school fees.[14] At eighteen he was indentured for three years to John Walker, a Whitby Quaker engaged principally in the collier trade from Tyneside to London. For centuries this had been regarded as an outstanding 'nursery of seamen': a hard school but a thorough, offering intensely practical experience in the North Sea, home waters but not the less hazardous for that. Cook, 'the industrious apprentice' if ever there were one, supplemented this shipboard training with solid study in the Walkers' home; but above all he learnt to hold, in Beaglehole's unforgettable phrase, 'the line of coast alive in the mind.'[15] Walker, like Skottowe, had an eye for intelligence and character, and in 1755 offered Cook the command of his own ship; instead of accepting, on 27 June Cook unpredictably volunteered into the Royal Navy as an Able Seaman.[16]

This was a strange decision. The Seven Years' War was brewing; it was a time when most respectable seamen would be desperate to escape the press-gangs, but as master of a ship Cook would have been exempt from the press.

Of course, amongst the riff-raff and starvelings dragged aboard by the press a really able and experienced seaman would stand out and might secure promotion, and in fact Cook became master's mate a month after joining his first ship; but that the tradition of Skottowe and Walker should continue and lead to real advancement was a gamble. Fortunately they found a successor in Captain Hugh Palliser, under whom Cook spent most of his first two years in the Navy. At the end of that time he was promoted Master; not a commissioned rank but a post of key importance in the working of a ship, responsible above all for its navigation.[17]

Cook's North American service began at the siege of Louisburg, where he had the luck to fall in with Samuel Holland, a military engineer who, with his Captain, John Simcoe, gave him instruction in 'Spherical Trigonometry, with the practical part of Astronomy.' So equipped, he had an important post in the indispensable charting of the St Lawrence for the attack on Quebec, a service in which the topographical intelligence had to be gathered as you went along, under fire. By the time the campaign was over, Cook was highly regarded as an expert cartographer, and from 1763 to 1768 was in charge of surveying the intricate and alternately fog-bound and ice-menaced skerries of Newfoundland. His winters were spent in England, working up the data, and on 21 December 1762 he married Elizabeth Batts of Barking, a happy though much-interrupted union. Nine days later Lord Colville, commodore on the North American station,

> beg[ged] leave to inform their Lordships, that from my experience of Mr Cook's Genius and Capacity, I think him well qualified for the Work he has performed, and for greater Undertakings of the same kind.[18]

Colville can hardly have imagined how much greater those undertakings were to be.

Why Cook, why a mere Master? Though allotted only one ship against two for previous circumnavigations, the undertaking was obviously more demanding than an Atlantic survey, which might well be assigned to a Master; and after the war there could have been no lack of competent commissioned officers on half-pay, but most of the old Pacific hands were at sea when preparations began, and the exploring record of Byron and his companion Mouat was dubious, not to mention Byron's constant harping on dangers and distresses. But it was not inevitable that Cook should be chosen, it only looks so now; nor indeed that he should return in triumph—it might have been left for scuba divers to find generations later his bones, or at least his ship.[19]

Reporting on the Newfoundland survey had made Cook personally known to Philip Stephens, Secretary to the Admiralty, and on his recommendation, warmly backed by Palliser, on 15 May 1768 James Cook, technically only seconded from his Newfoundland post, was commissioned Lieutenant in command of the Endeavour bark.[20]

As to what manner of man Cook was, we know much and little; much about the seaman and scientist, little about the man himself except as displayed in his professional activity, and this although we have records from men in close contact with him on every day of the nine years during which he left his mark on nearly half of the earth's surface.

So we have a few anecdotes and sketches by his companions, notably Samwell, Zimmermann, and (read with due caution) the Forsters; but as to his domestic life, practically nothing except the admiring but unspecific memories of his widow. Three or four letters to John Walker give glimpses of a relaxed Cook; when he emerged from obscurity to walk, wine and dine with the Great, he comported himself well, and perhaps he owed this to the natural good manners of a Quaker household. Not that he shows much sign of religious feeling, except for the naming of Providential Channel, and he could swear vigorously enough—Sparrman was shocked by his unQuakerly 'Goddamns' in a crisis.[21]

Beaglehole sought to get behind the homages and the tributes, their numbing rhetoric, and the flag-wagging of 'Men Who Made the Empire' hagiography; he saw Cook's innermost quality as a passionate professionalism and a stubbornness, yet 'patience is the other side of stubborn-ness.'[22] While there is much common to all attempted analyses of 'Cook the Man', all we can say is that beneath the surface of the exemplary professional, there were depths; but the soundings are few.

In some ways Cook seems to measure up—or down—to the stereotype of the model scientist: impersonal, unimaginative, totally objective, pas-sionless except in the pursuit of knowledge but there indefatigable and persevering to the end, with a steely nerve and an unceasing curiosity so great that, flat against the *mores* of his time and rank, he was willing to strip to the waist to gain access to a Tongan ceremony, to the scandal of at least one of his officers.[23] As a discoverer, he displayed an almost faultlessly matched blend of prudence and daring; and his reflections on his work show a mind at once lively and judicious.

He had some wit, little humour, but he could be genial off-duty company. Was he a hard man, or humane? He seems to have flogged about the ordinary rate—more than the alleged 'monster' Bligh—and yet nearly all his coevals stress his humanity; all that this means is that he was mixed, as was his age (and ours)—an age of gross brutalities but also of *A Sentimental Journey* and *The Man of Feeling*. Nor were other responsible navigators of his time less averse than he to the shedding of Island blood. The present inhabitants of peaceful Niue are entitled to resent being damned with Cook's name of 'Savage Island' because their ancestors warded off the monstrous menace of white strangers from the sea; but conversely, how was Cook to know that the skilled Niuean spearmen 'may have *intentionally* controlled the near miss' from five paces?[24] Empathy should work both ways. It may at least be said that until the third voyage, Cook endeavoured to act with moderation in tricky circumstances.

His daemon, Duty, made Cook drive himself hard—and his crews; yet his concern for their welfare was always clear, and we need not think that it was solely in the interests of efficiency; here again that Quaker background in Whitby may have counted. At least until the stresses, as much internal as external, of the third voyage sapped his control over his always hasty temper, he was a just man, and this the lower deck appreciated. With few exceptions, those who sailed with him came to admire, respect, love him. A standard refutation of that Olde English myth that only 'gentlemen' can lead.

What was it that brought James Cook, in his own words, 'from a prentice boy in the Coal Trade to a Commander in the Navy' and—*not* in his own words—to a secure place among the immortals? As with that other austere man, in many ways his fellow, Robert E. Lee, it is difficult to see the real human being through the pearly haze of hagi-ography. How to bring out that Marvellian 'industrious valour' without freezing 'a legend out of life, A blank-verse statue'?[25] How to find the key opening the door into the true, the inner man?

Perhaps he himself gave the clue in that quiet but iron-hard remark 'I, whose ambition...'. Surely here is fire beneath the ice, a deep-hidden fire welling, rather than bursting, out this once. Yet he also maintained proportion and control also: he knew when to turn back, in 71°10′S or 70°44′N, and was 'not sorry to meet with this interruption' of the Antarctic ice, an honourable release from perils. Only on Hawai'i did this saving prudence desert him.

The question remains: when, how, did the prentice boy realise that there was greatness in him?

Up to the first voyage there seems nothing to distinguish James Cook (did anyone after childhood call him Jim or Jemmy?) from any other able young man from the lower ranks who had the luck to fall in with officers intelligent enough to recognise his intelligence. In charge of the Newfoundland survey he is assured enough, with the quiet pride of the skilled technician, master of his craft. In his first major command he is palpably nervous (who of his origins wouldn't be?) in his exchanges with the Viceroy at Rio de Janeiro, and disguises this by appeals, uncharacteristic but quite in the high-flown Iberian manner, to his dignity and that of 'the King my Master'. This is not surprising; what might surprise is that after his return to 'the Honour of an hour's Conference with the King' (an hour, for the son of a labourer!), success did not go to his head: 'I may however venter to assure you that the Voyage has fully answered the expectation of my Superiors...'.[26] Was ever a flatter, more official, evaluation, by its achiever, of a great achievement? Of all the world's great heroes, perhaps the most commonplace, and perhaps all the greater for that.

Here, it may be, it was precisely his inferior station in life that saved him—one can only imagine what a Byron (Admiral or Poet) or a Dalrymple would have made of such a success, what he would have demanded for his due as a gentleman, what rows and what intrigues if he didn't get it! But for Cook, he had come very far, he had done great things, yet he was not of the Great or even gentry; a manly but not a magniloquent profile was indicated, and anyhow the farm-worker's son, Yorkshire at that, did not have it in him to be magniloquent. Yet now he was aware of his capabilities, he desired a second voyage, and his stance was just right to get it. On that voyage, when he turned back from 71°10′S, he must have known himself destined to a rare degree of greatness, though we cannot imagine him putting such a thought into written words. It was a happy solution to the problem of humanising the Hero that Beaglehole, the man skilled in words, at such moments remained silent and let Cook, the man of simple direct words only, speak for himself.

The first voyage was a first masterpiece; the second was a crisply confident and unmatched achievement; the third goes beyond maturity, into decline.

Towards Kealakekua Bay

Barely four weeks out, the *Resolution* very nearly struck on a reef in the Cape Verdes; even Cook admitted that 'our situation for a few Minutes was very alarming', and William Anderson filled a couple of agitated pages on what seemed to him most negligent seamanship. Ominous perhaps; but it seems to inflate such an incident to say that 'The trust of the whole ship's company suffered a severe shock',[27] when Gilbert and Cook's own Lieutenant Gore mentioned it with the utmost casualness, and Ledyard not at all.

Beaglehole suggested that the investigation of Kerguelen Land was perhaps 'a lapse of proportion' contributing to Cook's failure to reach northwest America in 1777;[28] but after all, he had been instructed 'to examine [those islands] thoroughly' without spending too much time, and six days, one watering and one a needed Christmas break for the crews, do not seem too much. By no fault of his own, Cook was a month behind schedule on leaving the Cape, and these six days cannot have much affected his chance of reaching America in the first season, 1777.

The first serious delay was due to the unforeseeable failure of the Westerlies east of New Zealand; Cook could not make enough easting to reach Tahiti before the livestock, a floating farmyard of gifts from the King, 'Farmer George', for the princes of the Islands, would be dead of thirst or starvation; even the severest shipboard critic of his navigation admitted that 'the isles of Amsterdam and Rotterdam [Tonga] were now our only resource.'[29]

So a verdict of acquittal here; what is inexplicable is the failure to seek out such fine islands as Fiji and Samoa, credibly reported and quite close. It is true that for modern ethnohistorians the weighty observations of Cook and Anderson on Tongan society are compensation for the missing of two or three high islands, and indeed it might be that Cook was shifting to a Forsterian stance, more interested in people than in outlines on the chart; one might find hints in this direction. But this is pure speculation, and it is more likely that we have here a first indication of staleness, a loosening of grip. One can hardly see the Cook of seven or five years earlier failing to track down such challenging and enticing clues.[30]

Less doubtful is the evidence for an increasing loss of self-control. Cook was still capable of tact and generosity, but more and more he failed to rein in his naturally hot temper and to balance scrupulously the scales of justice or even advantage. On the second voyage, the Forsters' censures had been sporadic and rather muted, but now the officers' journals criticise and even condemn the harsh and arbitrary measures that Cook resorted to against Tongan and Tahitian thieving; his flogging, arm-slashing, ear-clipping are deplored with more or less severity by Anderson,

Burney, Gilbert, King, Rickman, and even the most loyal Zimmermann. In the Friendly Islands, Ledyard even alleged that as a result of 'the full assertion of extreme power . . ., before we quite Tongataboo we could not go anywhere in the country upon business or pleasure without danger.'[31]

At Moorea, Cook's reaction to the theft of a single goat was a bout of indiscriminate destruction of canoes and houses. He regretted 'this troublesome, and rather unfortunate affair'; but congratulated himself on his moderation and was pleased when Omai, telling the tale to other Islanders, improved the terrorist effect by multiplying the losses tenfold. Few of his officers shared his complacency.[32]

There were signs also that Cook was losing touch with his people. As a rule he was rather reserved about his plans, but Zimmermann says that 'On occasion he made very fine speeches' to the crew, and at Tahiti he put it to them that in the bitter northern seas they would really need their grog, so would it not be better to forgo it now, when in comfort, rather than risk short allowance in the nipping cold? It was their choice. He threw in the bait of shares in the £20,000 reward for finding the Northwest Passage, and on Saturday nights they could still have 'full allowance to drink to their female friends in England, lest among the pretty girls of Otaheite they should be wholy forgotten.'[33] Alas, under growing stress Cook forgot the humour and humanity of this little pep-talk. The crews also were feeling the strain of the long voyage, and when he abandoned this sweet reasoning for arbitrary fiats on food and—more important—drink, there was real unrest, in his eyes virtually mutinous.

There had been murmurings, unknown to Cook, about spruce beer at Nootka; in the Arctic Sea he had thought that walrus meat was fine—few agreed, and a midshipman remarked that his captain's taste 'was, surely, the coarsest that ever mortal was endued with' (an excellent enduement, surely, for an explorer!). Matters nearly came to a head during the six weeks 'hovering on the edge of Paradise' in sight of Hawai'i with landing precluded by Cook's rational desire to control trading (which was active, by canoe) and the crews, by some inexplicable oversight on his part, still on needlessly short rations. Although he tried to fool himself into believing that beer from sugar-cane 'was esteemed by every man on board' as ersatz grog, 'when the Cask came to be broached not one of my mutinous crew would even so much as taste of it'; he cut off the grog ration altogether, and recorded his spluttering indignation at the hidebound conservatism of the sailors he had saved from scurvy.[34] 'Spluttering': the last adjective one could have applied to the Cook of old, but warranted by the defensive outpouring in his Journal.

There are other indications that, at fifty, the strain on Cook's body was wearing away the fine edge of his mind. He had been seriously ill on the second voyage with a 'Billious colick' which is likely to have been due to 'a heavy ascaris (roundworm) infestation of the intestine', perhaps brought on by his notorious readiness to try any local foods. The Forsters thought him close to death; in convalescence all he could eat was a favourite Tahitian dog of Johann Reinhold's.[35]

The ramifications of such a deep infection might well account for the indisputable deterioration in Cook's personality and powers on the third voyage; not only the outbursts of violence in Tonga and the Societies, but also the loss of keenness shown by the failure to seek out Fiji and Samoa, the almost trance-like state in which he received his investiture as a deity on Hawai'i, his indecisions and hasty errors of judgement in the last days. Bowel inflammation would allow 'colonization by coliform bacteria which could interefere with the absorption of the B complex of vitamins and probably other nutrients.' Cook's numerous symptoms, physical and psychological, are consistent with such a diagnosis; and since some greenstuffs also may inhibit vitamin B absorption, Watt suggests that medical historians may have concentrated unduly on the antiscorbutic vitamin C. Most paradoxically, 'It is therefore possible to conclude that Cook fell victim to his own passionate conviction that health at sea was to be found only in the nutrients provided by fresh provisions.'[36]

Apotheosis on Hawai'i

The word 'apotheosis',[37] so often loosely misused, is strictly applicable to Cook's experience when he at last landed on Hawai'i on 17 January 1779. The theatre of his vesting with divinity was Kealakekua Bay (Fig.14): its stage was the heiau (temple) Hikiau at Kakooa where the backdrop, the great lava cliff (Pali) running southeastwards from the royal village of Kowrowa (modern Kaawaloa), trended away from the shore.[38]

Never had there been a reception like this; hundreds of canoes, thousands of people, and as Cook set foot on the beach these masses prostrated themselves abjectly; those with him sensed that this was an act of worship. An old priest, Koa, and a younger, Keliikea,[39] took Cook and Lieutenant James King to a circle of crude images on the heiau; Koa appeared to address them all despitefully, except a central one covered with red cloth. To this 'he prostrated himself, & afterwards kiss'd [it], & desird the Captn to do the same, who was quite passive, & sufferd Koah to do with him as he chose.' There were gifts, chanted antiphons, and at last great shouts from the crowd of 'Orono! Orono!'.[40]

In fact, Cook's approach around Hawai'i parallelled in timing (November–January), direction (clockwise), and terminal (Hikiau) the great annual procession honouring Orono or Lono, the akua or god of fruitfulness and peace; and the yards and sails of his ships simulated, on a giant scale, Lono's processional banners. This makahiki season was something of a Saturnalia for the usually rigorously oppressed commoners; tapu (Hawaiian kapu) was relaxed, and the fighting chiefs who lorded it during the eight months subject to Ku, god of war and human sacrifice, took a lower profile. But if Cook had never yet received a welcome so rapturous and so complete in its submission, 'There never had been a makahiki season like this, and the priests of Lono made the most of it.'[41]

The priests obligingly tapu'd a site at Hikiau for the tented observatory—did this seem a heiau of the strangers?—and indeed King says that more privacy was provided than was desired; not a woman would approach. This was made up for by those afloat, Cook's own attempted tapu against girls on the ships having long since gone by the board. Provisions poured in, with no hint of payment. A week later, the Bay was deserted; there was a tapu to be lifted next day, when the 'King' of Hawai'i, Terreeoboo or Kalaniopuu,[42] would come to Kowrowa. He duly arrived on the 25th and spent several hours on the *Resolution*, returning on the morrow for a state visit in three great double canoes, his own crowded with his

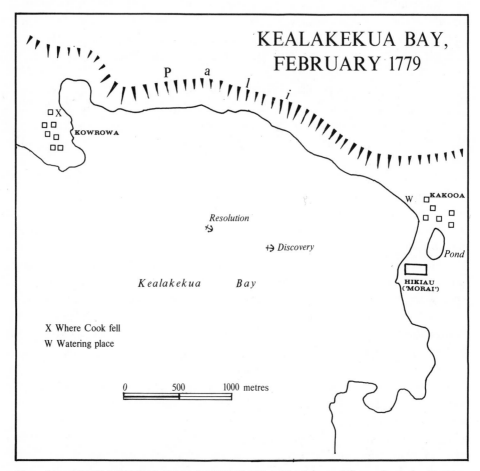

Figure 14. KEALAKEKUA BAY, FEBRUARY 1779. Adapted from charts by E. Riou and (?) W. Bayly.

chiefs in magnificently glowing feather cloaks. Kalaniopuu landed at Hikiau and threw his own cloak around Cook, laying half a dozen more at his feet, and the two great arii sealed their friendship by a formal exchange of names. Later, Cook reciprocated with a linen shirt and his own sword.

So far, one or two trifling misunderstandings about tapu apart, all had gone merrily as a marriage bell. Zimmermann thought darkly that the death of William Watman was ominous, as showing the Hawaiians that their visitors were mere mortals; but it seemed rather to become a symbol of human solidarity. According to King it was at Kalaniopuu's request that Watman was buried on the Morai; and this first Christian ceremony in Hawaii was followed by three nights of Polynesian rituals at the grave.[43]

It seemed as if nothing could be denied Lono. Cook asked King, whose affable manners and linguistic ability cast him as intermediary, to arrange the purchase of the rickety fence around the heiau, for fuel; King at first had 'some doubt about the decency' of this, but Koa raised no objection and asked no payment; he even allowed the removal of all the wooden images except the central one, of Ku.

That this action had any sacrilegious import is doubtful. Ledyard told an incredible story of an outrageous forced purchase; Zimmermann thought that there was secret indignation, a factor in later hostility. The American missionary Sheldon Dibble, bitterly hostile to Cook, cited Ledyard but admitted that 'after repeated enquiries I cannot find that the people attached much importance to that circumstance'—a large admission from one who traduced Cook for unchastity. Later, T. G. Thrum cited Hawaiian evidence that 'This class of carved images' were not tapu but could be and were used for Cook's purpose—firewood.

Most recent writers, if they discuss the matter at all, seem to follow Thrum; but Brossard accepts Zimmermann's view of hidden discontents, and calls Cook's action 'an inexplicable psychological error'. Let Sahlins have the last word; the makahiki would end about 31 January, Ku would return, the fence and images 'would be completely refurbished for Ku rites', and the main image, reclaimed by Koa, was Ku's. Later the action was reinterpreted as a breach of tapu.[44]

But the honeymoon was nearing its end; Kalaniopuu and his chiefs were asking pointedly when their guests might be leaving, and there were broader hints; theft, rare at first, was increasing. Apart from the material strain of feeding nearly 200 sailors, there were less tangible factors in the chiefs' anxiety. In the cycle, Lono's makahiki was a period of priestly dominance; now it was ending, it was high time that Lono should return to the heavens. The chiefs were reassured, Kalaniopuu gathered a last grand presentation, and on 4 February Cook sailed, promising to return next year. 'Everything was proceeding historically right on ritual schedule'[45]—so far. For a week later there occurred a violent break in the ritual continuum: Lono's unscheduled return.

Death of a god

In Sahlins's model

> the Captain and the King, Cook and Kalaniopuu, representing respectively Lono and Ku, were natural rivals for Hawaiian power... In late January 1779, the ascending political curve of Ku... intersected with the declining course of Lono (Cook) [who] obliged by leaving almost at the precise end of the Makahiki period... A few days later, however, the ritual calendar intersected with another field of causation: the *Resolution* unfortunately sprung her foremast...

The return broke the rules; Cook now became 'hors catégorie'.[46]

Ku the warrior was in the ascendant, the whole atmosphere had changed; Samwell alone discounted this, all others remarked on jeers, tension, downright hostility.[47] The girls indeed were as willing as ever through all the tumults, and the friendly priests at Hikiau readily tapu'd a site for repair of the mast. But theft became rampant, the armourer's tongs were stolen twice—the Hawaiians kept a close eye on the smithy—long daggers were in demand, and at least one was home-made.[48] There was stone-throwing, and Cook was tricked into a wild-goose chase after stolen goods. Chiefs seemed implicated, and in a nasty scuffle the friendly arii Parea was struck with an oar, and young Vancouver was roughed up.

Cook contemplated using force, lest the Hawaiians should imagine they had the advantage, and ordered firing with ball if there were more stone-throwing or insolence. On the 14th, three days after arrival, the *Discovery's* cutter, an essential boat, was missing; the cable had been cut. Cook at once ordered boats to blockade the Bay and seize canoes. The standard version, stemming from King, is that from the first he also intended to take Kalaniopuu and his young sons hostage; Gavan Kennedy argues plausibly that this was a belated afterthought, and its hasty implementation, with only the marine Lieutenant Molesworth Phillips and nine men, led directly to disaster.[49]

Probably about 7.30 a.m. they landed at Kowrowa and strode up the path to Kalaniopuu's house; Cook himself carried a gun with small shot in one barrel and ball in the other. Off the point were a launch under Lieutenant John Williamson, the senior officer, a pinnace under Henry Roberts, and a small cutter. The gathering crowd seemed peaceable enough, and after some parley Kalaniopuu agreed to come with Cook; but the unprecedented show of armed force was alarming,[50] and there were protests. News now came that the very friendly chief Kalimu had been killed by fire from one of the blockading boats;[51] distressed, and distracted by the pleas of women and warriors, Kalaniopuu sat down on the ground—in itself a shocking posture for a great chief surrounded by his warriors. Men began putting on heavy war-mats, and Cook realised that he could not secure his hostages without using violence, and his handful of marines was an insufficient force. At Phillips's suggestion they were ordered out of the milling crowd and formed into a rough line at the water's edge. Clearly the plan had failed, and Cook began to follow them.

In face of threatening gestures, he fired with small shot, useless against a war-mat, and a general melée began. Cook fired ball, and killed his man; he ordered the marines to fire, but before they could reload they were overrun. In the confusion, the boats gave little help; four marines were killed, and with them died James Cook, whether by stabbing or clubbing or forcible drowning hardly matters.

On the *Resolution* 'a general silence ensued throughout the ship for the space of near half an hour: it appearing to us something like a Dream that we could not reconcile ourselves to ...'.[52]

It was not easy, either, to reconcile themselves to the thought that their commander had been wretchedly supported, especially by Williamson. That strange man claimed that Cook had waved to him to take the launch further offshore; Roberts more reasonably took the gesture as an order to cease firing and come in to bring off the marines. On no hypothesis creditable to him is Williamson's conduct explicable; during the struggle he kept his launch well away, and was even said to have threatened to shoot 'the first man that pull'd a stroke' to bring her closer in. Although Phillips, his bitter enemy, is reported to have said that it was extremely doubtful whether anything could have saved Cook's life, it seems beyond question that the disgraceful failure even to attempt to rescue the bodies, which was possible, must be laid to Williamson's account.[53]

In King's carefully smoothed out version, so often uncritically followed, the pacific interpretation of Cook's gesture is improved upon. He half-hints, in flat contradiction of Phillips who was at his Captain's side, that the marines fired without Cook's orders, so that 'It is not improbably that his humanity ... proved fatal to him.' From King this version entered the iconography with John Webber's painting, and became part of the hagiography.[54]

That was for the future; now, for the shocked men in the ships, and especially for Clerke who, ill as he was, had to take command, the most pressing concern had to be for the indispensable mast being repaired at Hikiau. King, whom Cook had sent there to reassure the priests that no harm was intended, had only six marines, and the noise of firing across the Bay provoked alarm and agitation on both sides. This was seen from the *Discovery*, and she dispersed the crowd around the heiau, with no injuries, by two beautifully aimed shots. Clerke now sent Bligh to Hikiau to bring off the precious timepiece; before he could tell King 'the Shocking news that Captain Cook was kill'd, we saw it in his and the Sailors looks.' King posted the reinforcements on the heiau—ironically, the removal of the old fence had weakened it as a strongpoint—and left Bligh in command with strict orders to act on the defensive. He had hardly reached the ships when he heard musketry; it was vital to protect the mast, and Bligh's notion of defence was never passive. On this, Clerke decided that the only safe course was to bring off the mast, which was done by a strong force.

It was now 11.30 a.m.; after four crowded and emotionally racking hours, there was time for deliberation. The lower deck was hot for revenge, and even Clerke had a passing desire to land with fire and sword. But apart from humanitarian arguments against violence—the attack seemed unpremeditated—there were prudential ones. The Hawaiians had proved tougher than had been thought; firearms would in the end prevail, but it would be pitting scores against hundreds, and the loss of even a few men would be crippling. Clerke kept his head admirably; seeking a cooling-off period, he steered the debate away from reprisals. It was decided to demand the return of the bodies, or at least of Cook's.[55] By now the Hawaiians knew what firearms meant.

The mission was deputed to King and Burney. They could not risk landing—the beach looked militant—but Koa swam to the boats and parleyed with a now distrustful King. Brossard gives Koa a key role; he had staked his reputation on the godhead of Cook, but even a god should respect the forms, which this 'Lono' by returning had failed to do. Koa, convinced that Cook was 'un akua impossible', an impostor, and anxious lest he himself should be exposed as a false prophet, had fostered alarms and discontents leading to the fatal affray, and now was trying to entrap King and Clerke.[56] At last a friendly and reliable chief, saying he came from Kalaniopuu, told King that Cook's body, taken upcountry, would be returned next day.

So ended the first day; the uneasy night was marked by a 'prodigious number' of fires and much howling ashore; the morning by conches blowing and large parties marching over the hills. Koa turned up with gifts and blandishments, presumably spying; he was fobbed off. After dark Keliikea came out—he was nearly shot by a sentry—and called for King; he brought a piece of Cook's thigh, the bones being in Kalaniopuu's keeping. It was now Ku's cycle, chiefs and priests were at variance, the priests still friendly to the departed Lono's people—except, Keliikea warned, Koa, 'our mortal and determined enemy'.

The 16th was a day of stalemate, provocative insults met by warning gunfire, on the 17th more cannonading was called for to protect watering parties, and at last it was thought necessary to burn some houses, an action which became a general conflagration of the priestly village of Kakooa where the still friendly Keliikea lived; so enthusiastic were the sailors that the boats returned with two Hawaiian heads stuck on their bows.[57]

Finally on the 20th the mast was stepped, and a delegation from Kalaniopuu brought peace-offerings and what remained of Captain James Cook: the scalp, the skull, the long bones and the hands, identifiable by a scar from Newfoundland days. This stripping away of the flesh, except for the hands, was not 'evidence of a savage and unrelenting barbarity; so far from this, it was the result of the highest respect they could show him', and it is possible that the other bones were regarded as sacred until the revolt against tapu in 1819, and then hidden by the priests.[58]

Next day the fragmented remains were committed to the sea; on 22 February 'we sail'd out of the bay, receiving as we passed the shore many affectionate farewells.'

Questions remain. Can the undeniably close correlation between the model of the Lono cycle and the actual events be coincidence, or can it be given some causative value? Does Sahlins fall into an unwarranted cultural determinism? Did it have to happen that way? What if the foremast had not sprung, if Kalimu had not been chancely killed, if Cook had pulled the wrong (or right) trigger? Who can tell who actually gave what orders, when? Just when, why, did the Hawaiians nerve themselves to deicide? Was this Koa's doing? How far was Cook himself responsible for his death?

This last question was discomforting in the extreme, and it is not surprising that some of those close to him, notably Burney and Samwell, should have resorted to spirited but implausible special pleading to repel suggestions that Cook was not in full control of himself on his last day. Some not so close differed—Ledyard, with hindsight, spoke of Cook 'blinded by some fatal cause', not perceiving or brashly disregarding 'every symptom of mischief'. Others thought that had ball been used earlier, the lesson would have been heeded; instead Cook staked everything on the Hawaiians scattering before a whiff of musketry or even, as he said, a single musket; they did not, and everything fell to pieces. Clerke saw this delusion as the fatal factor.[59] It seems indubitable that Cook's mind and temper had been worn by physiological and mental stress to a dangerous degree of irritation, leading to a final breakdown not of nerve but of judgement. But to have admitted human blundering would have been to blur the image of a man without flaw, and hence the smooth artifice of King's official account.

Hubris? The ineluctable acting out of the myth? Or the ascaris worm?

Apotheosis at large

No less than the achievement of Cook's life, the manner of his death ensured that his posthumous career would be enshrined in a multitude of literary and graphic creations, ranging from the epic (or would-be) to unintentional farce. The first full-dress treatment of the first voyage was Hawkesworth's, in a prose which had Johnson's ponderosity without his pungency and resonance. He told the story in the first person, yet freely interpolated his own substantive reflections on the events. This, shocking by modern editorial standards, did not worry his readers so much as his scouting of Divine Providence; and he was blamed for lush Tahitian scenes—unjustly since he was 'following copy', Banks's journal. Hence his literary reputation, almost on a par with Johson's was paradoxically 'destroyed by the book which also preserved his name for posterity.'[60]

At this stage, however, for the public at large Cook was second fiddle to Banks and Solander; Horace Walpole for instance condemned these two, not Cook, for bringing 'European recklessness' to 'that poor little speck Tahiti', and on the Continent the voyage was generally credited to their names—as late as 1983 there is an echo of this.[61] There was an outbreak of verse pamphlets, drearily sentimental or drearily salacious, mostly on the alleged amours of Banks and 'Queen Oberea' and (later on those of Omai); there are perhaps a dozen couplets decent, in both senses, in the lot.[62]

Even after the triumphant second voyage, whatever seamen and geographers may have thought, for the men (and the ladies) about Town, for 'philosophers', Cook's achievement bulked less than the furore over that long-desired exhibit, the Natural yet civil man, Omai. However, despite the acrimony over the publication of George Forster's narrative, as literature the best account of all, Cook entered upon his own in Germany, and his standing was enhanced by George's tribute, old passion spent, *Cook der Entdecker: Versuch eines Denkmals* in his translation of the third voyage: a man 'so well acquainted with the whole globe that he bore it in his hand as though it were the imperial orb.'[63]

That voyage of course brought with it the glory of martyrdom—and commercial exploitation. Both are found in P. J. de Loutherbourg's spectacular pantomine *Omai: Or. A Trip Round the World* (1785), with exotic but carefully researched settings and costumes. Its final scene had a great backdrop of Cook borne into the heavens above Kealakekua Bay by Britannia and Fame; a Parisian counterpart was engagingly respectful of *la pudeur anglaise*.[64] There was another outpouring of bad verse, the most widely-read piece being probably the delightfully daft elegy by the Swan of Lichfield.[65]

Somewhat more serious are the formally rhetorical eulogies, a baroque art-form still lingering in continental academies. Conventions of Virtue and Valour triumph over mere fact in these stylised raptures; but they fostered a new Vision of Greatness, associated not with wars and conquests but with the peaceful spread of knowledge, human welfare, and social trade. They thus helped to fashion 'a new kind of hero, one admirably adapted to the needs of the new industrial society of Europe in its global expansion'; although it is going too far to style Cook 'the prototypical hero of European imperialism', a role long since filled by Vasco da Gama. Anna Seward's absurd *Elegy* and the inept tribute of the Poet Laureate Pye conform to this model of the wise, modest, austere, benevolent, and yet daring Hero of Humanity.[66]

Cook had also his detractors; Alexander Dalrymple, though sometimes critical, should not be counted amongst them, as he often is.[67] National and political antagonism was responsible for the distortions of a French pseudo-philosophical work of 1801, in which 'the terrible Cook' was endowed with 'the atrocious soul of a Cromwell' and committed outrages at which humanity shuddered over that single and infamously celebrated goat. It was not chauvinism but religious conviction which led so good an Englishman as William Cowper to condemn Cook for having allowed himself to be worshipped: 'God is a jealous God', and His vengeance had repaid the sacrilege.[68]

When, however, religious fanaticism combined with nationalist prejudice, the result was devastating to Cook's reputation in Hawaii itself. Evangelism did not always mean fanaticism; visiting Kealakekua Bay, the Reverend William Ellis also saw in Cook's death 'an overruling Providence', but his fair and balanced reflections end with the point that Cook had opened the way not only for the philosopher and the merchant, but also for 'the missionary in his errand of mercy...'. But this, and even Cowper's measured reprobation, are as dust before the merciless rantings of the American missionaries Sheldon Dibble and Hiram Bingham. The former stated that Cook 'gave countenance to the evil' of sexual intercourse and himself fornicated with a princess; the latter spoke of him as a contemptible worm whose example 'left the nation confirmed in superstition darker than before, encouraged in adultery and violence more destructive'. These libellous excesses were very faithfully dealt with in J. J. G. Stokes's refutation, but their distortions, especially in the 1867 vernacular version of Samuel Kamakau, held sway in Hawaii for the rest of the century.[69]

Until Beaglehole, 'all descriptions and judgements of [Cook's] three great voyages... rested on a pathetically weak basis of original documentation';[70] there was no edition of any of the original journals, free of the embellishments of Hawkesworth and Douglas, until Wharton's *Endeavour* edition in 1893.[71] Between Kippis in 1788 and Kitson in 1907, only one biography was published embodying any substantial original research, that by the

Reverend George Young in 1836. There were of course swarms of retellings and rehashings, more or less (usually less) conscientious, many in the Men Who Made the Empire mould, stirring and highly patriotic and moral entertainment for British (and colonial) Youth. Amazingly, while the Paris Société de Géographie devoted 140 pages to its Special Meeting on 14 February 1879, the Royal Geographical Society gave the centenary just one page—reporting the Paris meeting![72] Not until 1914 did Cook join those heroes of Empire whose bronze effigies litter central London. Cook was there, he was great, but merely an image taken for granted and paraded when appropriate as a forerunner of dominion over palm and pine.

A forerunner of dominion in Australia he certainly was, but for much of last century he was neglected in that country. Apart from a plaque set up near the landing by Governor Brisbane in 1822, there seems to have been no memorial before 1859, when an English immigrant put up a pump in Geelong to shame the locals. His pump-priming took some little time, but by 1879 Sydney had two statues, largely owing to the patriotic efforts, not untinged by an eye to his own fame, of Sir Joseph Carruthers, sometime Premier of New South Wales. The indifference of the nineteenth century was replaced in the twentieth by an absurd emphasis on Cook as the Founder-Father of Australia, which he was not. As Jillian Robertson points out, after 1770 Cook visited New Zealand four times and Tahiti thrice, but never returned to mainland Australia.[73] (He had of course no particular reason for doing so, and some against— too little water in the south, too many reefs in the north.) His description of it is much less than enthusiastic. But a father figure was needed, and although objectively Banks should have been the man (James Matra being too obscure), he had not Cook's fame, and still less the inestimable advantage, in a self-styled egalitarian society, of humble birth.

Entrancing as the task would be, it is impossible to trace here the literary legacy of James Cook; a few titles may be cited, simply to give some idea of the range of relevant material. In his own century, his demolition of Terra Australis did not entirely disconcert Utopists; we have noted *Hildebrand Bowman* and *La Découverte australe*. Poetical tributes included those in Jacques Delille's *Les Jardins* and the epic *Oceania* (in German hexameters) of the Danish poet Jens Baggesen, understandably abandoned after the British bombardment of Copenhagen in 1807.[74]

Legions of poetasters have hymned Cook, few poets; perhaps the matter-of-factness of the man stands in the way. It is difficult to recall any memorable work by a poet of stature, even in Australia, where the exaltations and miseries of Quiros's melancholy questing have had symbolic and even mythic value.[75] Rex Ingamells devoted a whole book to Cook in his 'epic' *The Great South Land*; his reach far exceeded his grasp. There is indeed Kenneth Slessor's *Five Visions of Captain Cook*, but even here the real focus of the poem seems not so much on Cook, the provider of the setting, as on the memories of the blind veteran of his voyages, Alexander Home.[76] But the vast sub-literature, in verse and prose, would surely be worth exploring, not for intrinsic merit but for the light it would throw on changing modes and attitudes.

Nor has Cook had a notable career on the stage; innumerable appearances in pageants and reconstructions of landings, but here again there may be little for a dramatist to catch hold of in a man so balanced; and if Cook is protagonist, who stands against him? One would have to make Koa, anachronistically, into a patriot. (There might be some good comedy in the Forsters.) Nevertheless, the moral issues involved in his actions give scope for treatment, on stage or screen, rather than in the three- or five-act drama, and there have been some interesting experiments; one would like to know more of the tragedy *La Cokiado* presented in Malaga in 1796! A warning should be given that Jean Girardoux's shrewd and delightfully witty *Supplément au Voyage de Cook* bears no relation to any actual person or event.[77]

These remarks may seem, indeed they are, snippets, but they have a serious purpose: to show that the legacy deserves more coherent study than is possible here. This century has seen the flowering of interest in Cook as a man, not just a monument; but although the historical facts are established, and despite the proliferation of bicentennia in the seventies, there is still a wide field of inquiry in the people and the writings associated with James Cook. But this will be not so much in the traditional vein of nautical history and formal biography; rather the seas which still await more thorough charting are those of psychology indigenous and intrusive and their interaction; the social and geoeconomic consequences, within and without the Pacific, of the great opening; aesthetics; the history of ideas. Still, for his century, he must remain a central figure.

Chapter 8

CHRONOLOGY III: AFTER COOK

> ...to survey this coast would be an almost endless
> task tho' indispencably nesecary to finish the geography
> of north America trading vessels to this coast will
> make considerable advances towards this but it can
> thuroughly done intill it is done at some national
> expence whose Commanders are uninterested by commerce.

The locus of Pacific exploration now shifts in large measure to the North; and the multiplicity of voyages compels a departure from the layout of the preceding chronological chapters. The epigraph above is borne out by the record. While there was much unsystematic discovery by private Russian enterprise, records are scanty, until the Billings expeditions (1786–92) under Imperial auspices, and the aim of G. I. Shelikov was not so much exploration as exploitation by his fur-trading monopoly, which was the direct progenitor of the Russian-America Company (RAC), opposite number to the Hudson's Bay Company.[1] After Cook's men had shown the profit of selling sea otter skins in China, there was any amount of private British enterprise, but coordination had to wait upon Vancouver's official surveys of 1792–4. Typically, all Spanish voyages were State undertakings, politically not commercially motivated. *Per contra*, all American voyages were strictly private. Of the two significant French voyages, that of La Pérouse in 1786–7 was official, Marchand's in 1791–2 private.

The situation is rather different if we turn to the important landward approach to the northeast Pacific. The first penetration to the coast, in 1793, was made by a servant of the Montreal-based North West Company, but on his own initiative. The magnificent transcontinental crossing by Meriwether Lewis and William Clark in 1804–6 was perhaps the first great governmental undertaking by the United States of America, a concept worthy of Alexander Hamilton, paradoxically inspired by his opponent, the arch-agrarian defender of 'small government' Thomas Jefferson.[2] There is food for thought in the varying national styles displayed in this bare record.

Robert Haswell, mate of Boston sloop *Washington*, off Queen Charlotte Islands, June 1789, in F. W. Howay (ed.), *Voyages of the "Columbia"* (Cambridge, Mass., 1941), 99–100.

The Russians in the North

P. K. Krenitzin and M. D. Levashov in 1766-8 and P. Zaikov in 1774-9 at last put the Aleutians on the map with reasonable accuracy (Fig.15), but there was now a new urgency. Despite the cordial receptions at Petropavlosk, the visits of Cook, Clerke, and especially La Pérouse were alarm-signals showing the vulnerability of the Russian position; distance and obscurity no longer seemed adequate defences. One response was in effect a new Great Northern Expedition, ironically under Joseph Billings, once a seaman on Cook's last voyage, now a captain in the Russian Navy.[3] During the preparations Billings met at Iakutsk an old shipmate, John Ledyard on his astonishing attempt to cross Siberia; James Burney, who knew both, remarked sardonically that if the Empress Catherine 'had understood the characters of the two men' she would probably have recalled Billings and replaced him by Ledyard.[4]

The expedition fell into two parts; the first was a futile attempt to replicate Dezhnev's exploit in sailing from the Arctic to Anadyr. The Pacific phase began in September 1789 when Billings and Gavril Sarychev sailed from Okhotsk in two poorly manned ships. One was wrecked immediately, with the other, *Slava Rossii* (Glory of Russia), they wintered at Petropavlosk. Next year, after a brief search for mysterious foreign ship reputed to be prowling around Alaskan waters,[5] they reached She-likhov's station at Old Kodiak, fifty Russians were settled, and Montagu Island, again wintering in Kamchatka. The next season was spent in the Bering Sea; Billings set off on a painful but informative land journey in the Chukchi country, leaving Sarychev to take the *Slava Rossii* to Unalaska, where he wintered, wracked by scurvy, before returning to Petropavlosk in June 1792.

The results were hardly brilliant.[6] There were no discoveries of much note, though many positions were more accurately fixed than heretofore and a good deal of scientific and especially ethnographic information was gathered. Two notable results were official confirmation of the appalling atrocities inflicted on the Aleuts by the fur traders, or robbers, and the pinpointing of the risks to Imperial prestige inherent in their far-ranging but very thin and utterly unregulated expansion.

Such reports were grist to the mill of a remarkable entrepreneur, Grigorii Ivanov Shelikhov, and his son-in-law and Court agent Nikolai Petrovich Rezanov, who had long been agitating for a monopolistic company, on the lines of the EIC, to control the trade. As the sea otters were eliminated from nearer Aleutian waters, the trade became more capital-intensive: longer voyages, stouter ships, more provisioning. She-likhov was able to mask his private ends with a show of patriotic and civilising purpose, emphasising 'for the record' schools and Christian missions. In 1784 he made Kodiak a secure base; his success may be gauged

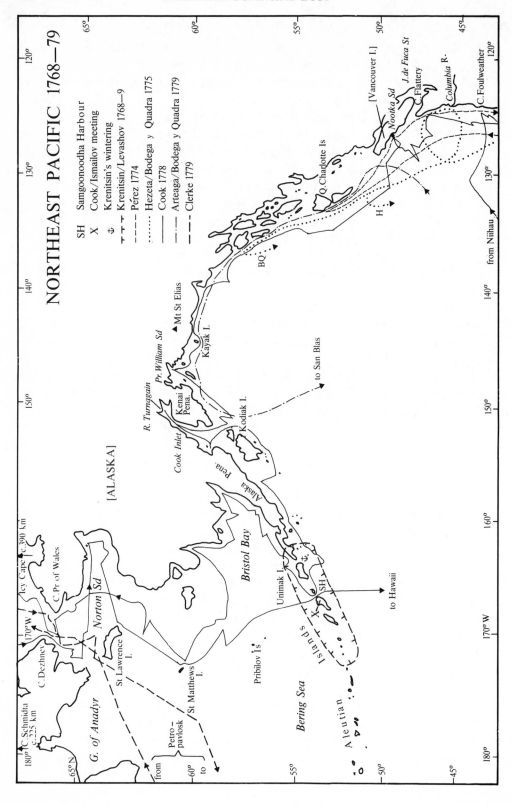

NORTHEAST PACIFIC 1768–79

SH   Samgoonoodha Harbour
X   Cook/Ismailov meeting
⚓   Krenitsin's wintering
⊤–⊤ Krenitsin/Levashov 1768–9
– – – Pérez 1774
...... Hezeta/Bodega y Quadra 1775
——   Cook 1778
–·–· Arteaga/Bodega y Quadra 1779
– – – Clerke 1779

by John Meares's sour note that in Cook Inlet his officer 'met with Russian and Kodiak hunters, who followed him from village to village, and had got entire possession of the river.'[7]

Tough and unscrupulous as he was, Shelikhov had grandiose colonising visions, and he did at least see the need of conservation, if not of sea-otters at least of his workforce, and did something to mitigate the savage oppression of the Aleuts and other tribes. He died before his Rossisko-Amerikanskaia Kompaniia received its charter, through a maze of intrigue, in 1799; it flourished under his dynamic successor, Aleksandr Baranov, who—not without hard fighting against Indians now armed with muskets by British and Boston traders—established in 1799–1804 a new base at Novo-Arkhangel'sk (now Sitka) on the island which bears his name. Thence the RAC reached out to Fort Ross in California in 1812, and even, briefly and almost farcically, to Hawaii.[8] All this was exploitation, not exploration; yet exploration was to come into its own with the series of circumnavigations, from Krusenshtern and Lisianski in 1803–6 to Lütke in 1826–9, which were closely linked with the problems of supply to Russian America.

The Spaniards in the North, to 1779

If Shelikhov married commerce and politics in plans which envisaged expansion down to 40°N, the Spanish response to the Russians, Cook, and La Pérouse, with a glance at the Americans, was almost entirely political and defensive; but it was an aggressive defence, as shown by the orders to arrest Cook, if possible, and to take possession at points *north* of any European settlements that might be found.[9] Political discussion is reserved for Chapter 13, but this background of apprehension must be borne in mind as the motivating force in Spanish exploration.

The first voyage was by Juan Pérez in the *Santiago*, at 225 tons the pride of the San Blas fleet.[10] Neither ship nor crew was suitable, nor was San Blas a good base, and Pérez did not try very hard. He sailed on 25 January 1774, but with a lengthy stop at San Diego took four months to reach Monterey, leaving on 11 June. Not until 18 July did he make a landfall; next day he sighted the capes marking Dixon Entrance, north of the Queen Charlotte Islands. He turned back in about 55°30'N; he had been instructed to go as far as 60°. On 8 August he anchored off an inlet which he named San Lorenzo, the famous Nootka Sound. He did not enter, and next day was blown off; by the 27th he was back in Monterey. Pérez made no landings, and for its purposes of checking the Russians and staking-out Spanish claims, the voyage was a signal failure.

◀ *Figure 15.* NORTHEAST PACIFIC 1768–79. Cf. Fig. 18. Tracks of Cook and Clerke after Beaglehole; Spanish tracks approximate; area of Krenitsin's exploration indicated.

The poverty of local resources was such that for the next round the Viceroy Antonio de Bucareli had to call on Madrid for six young and promising naval officers, one of whom, Juan Francisco de Bodega y Quadra, was to make a great name.[11] Of the six, Bruno de Hezeta was to command the *Santiago*, Manuel Manrique the tiny schooner *Sonora*. Quadra volunteered so that she might have a second officer; three days out of San Blas, Manrique had to be sent back, mad. Quadra took over, with the experienced pilot Francisco Antonio Mourelle.

The instructions were to go to 65°N. They sailed on 16 March 1775; Quadra and Mourelle turned down Hezeta's suggestion that the *Sonora* should turn back and take refuge in Monterey. In mid-July they were off the present Washington State, where a watering party was killed by Indians; the hesitant Hezeta now wished to return, most of his crew being scurvy-stricken. There can be little doubt that the separation of Quadra and Mourelle on 1 August was voluntary—a most constructive desertion! Left alone, Hezeta made landfall on Vancouver Island, then turned back, on the 17th sighting but not investigating the mouth of the Columbia River—a missed opportunity indeed. He was safe in Monterey on 29 August.

Quadra and Mourelle pushed on. They saw Cook's Mount Edgcumbe, near Sitka, on 15 August; a week later, looking for de Fonte's legendary passage, they were forced south, and they found the Entrada de Bucareli on Prince of Wales Island, now Bucareli Bay or Sound, which was to bulk large in Spanish plans. Another effort brought them to 58°30′, and then they had to give over; many of their supplies had been left on the *Santiago*, and scurvy was rife. Returning, they narrowly missed the entry to Juan de Fuca Strait and anchored at Monterey on 7 October; Quadra and Mourelle had to be carried ashore. A most gallant voyage in a wretchedly leaky and over-crowded 11-metre schooner.

The next voyage was in direct response to Cook's third, but the demands on San Blas for supply ships to Alta California were such that Quadra had to bring a ship from Guayaquil, the *Favorita*. He was to command her, with Mourelle as pilot, while Ignacio de Arteaga had overall command in the San Blas-built *Princesa*. The delay meant that Cook, whom they were intended to intercept, was on the coast a year before the Spaniards.

The ships sailed from San Blas on 11 February 1779, and despite separation by storms both reached Bucareli Bay on 3 May—a marked contrast to Hezeta's hesitations and Pérez's dallying. Some weeks were spent in a careful examination of the Bay and its surroundings, presumably with a view to future colonisation; there were some clashes with Indians. On 1 July they sailed, and on the 9th saw high snowy land to the north; they passed Kayak Island, where Bering and Steller had landed, and Mount St Elias, crossing the mouth of Prince William Sound to anchor on 21 July at 'Puerto Santiago', Port Etches on Hinchinbrook Island. There was no hope of reaching 70°N, as instructed, since the inlet was girdled by high mountains; they left on 28 July, reaching Kenai Peninsula on 1 August. The return, compelled by scurvy, began on the 7th, and after another separation they reached San Francisco in October and San Blas, in company, on 21 November. Detail had been added to the Bucareli Bay area, and possession taken in several places, but for the most part they had followed in Cook's tracks; the voyage though competent and useful for Spanish purposes was hardly outstanding.

International preoccupations, especially Spain's involvement in the American War of Independence, enforced a cessation of activity on the coast, and when peace returned the running was made by a very mixed lot of adventurers in the fur trade and a massive French intervention under La Pérouse.

The French: La Pérouse and Marchand

French interest in the South Sea was not extinguished by the limited success of Bougainville and the failure of Kerguelen; in 1774 a young naval officer, Louis de Latouche-Tréville, enlisted Cook's support for a scheme to explore the Ocean north and east of the Marquesas and then the south coast of New Holland. This was lost to sight in the American War, and another project for a colony in Van Diemens Land was too wild to get off paper. Terra Australis found a last defender, appropriately in a Baron de Gonneville, who thought that perfidious Albion, like the Dutch, had designedly concealed the possibilities.[12]

But in the post-war euphoria a truly prestigious expedition was decided upon, in conscious emulation of Cook.[13] Louis XVI himself, a keen geographer taught by Philippe Buache, took an intelligent interest in its planning.[14] No expedition of the century, except perhaps Malaspina's, was better-found, whether in ships, stores, instruments, seamen or scientists, than that which sailed from Brest on 1 August 1785 under Jean-François Galaup de la Pérouse in the *Astrolabe* and Paul-Antoine de Langle in the *Boussole*; at every point in the planning the lessons of Cook had been taken to heart, and the total cost was 1,000,000 livres, an immense sum for the always shaky French finances.[15] La Pérouse had gained renown in 1782 by a brilliant raid on the British posts in Hudson's Bay, with de Langle as his second; this experience might be useful in the cold foggy waters of the North Pacific.

After an approach by the Dutch commercial adventurer Willem Bolts, now a thorn in the side of his old employers the EIC, for a fur trading venture to Northwest America, the project took definite form early in 1785; the fur trade remained an important objective, but in Fleurieu's hands the scientific aspect came to the fore. He, the Geographer Royal Jean Buache and the King himself worked out a most comprehensive plan, which included the uncertain islands in the South Atlantic and South

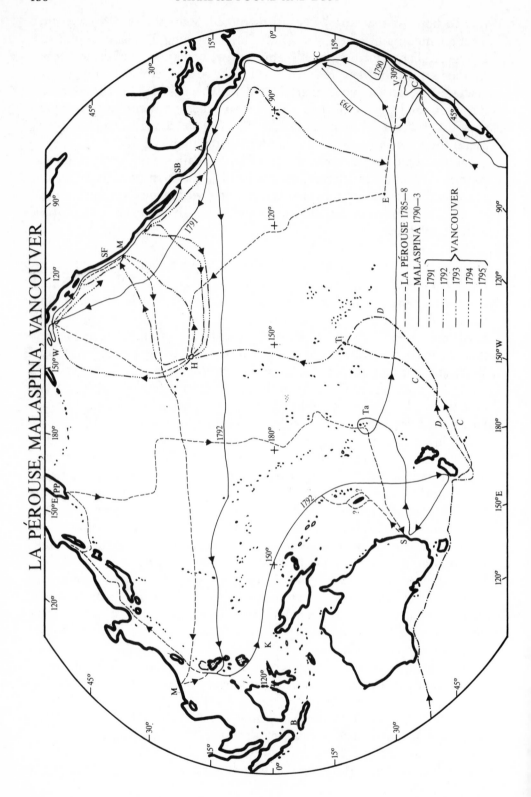

Pacific; New Holland and New Zealand; the west coast of New Caledonia, not seen by Cook; Tahiti, the Marquesas and Hawaii; Northwest America; the waters north of Japan which Cook had left unexplored.[16] The manners and physiques of peoples and all aspects of the natural sciences were to be examined—there were even 'small aerostatic balloons' to check on winds in the upper air (they seem to have been used to amuse the Chileans). Trade goods included fifty-two plumed helmets and 1,000,000 assorted pins.[17]

Although it is often said that the primary tasks of the voyage were scientific, 'Political and Commercial Objects' came first in the detailed instructions, followed by investigations into the China trade (the French at Canton were going through a lean time) and the fur trade. Reports were to be made on all European commerce and possessions, 'which may be interesting... in a military point of view'; likely places for French settlement were to be noted. It was to be an affair of prestige, if possible surpassing Cook. Brossard is direct: 'a voyage which would without doubt have an air [une allure] of discovery in such little known seas as the North Pacific, but before all a commercial and political objective.' Much of the programme was simply espionage, and the military expert, the engineer Monneron, was diligent.[18]

La Pérouse passed Cape Horn on 1 February 1786; he had wisely been given much discretion, and equally wisely spent little time looking for the supposed sightings of Drake and Juan Fernández. He put into Concepción for three weeks, sailing on 17 March for Easter Island, where some statues were precisely measured—his engineers saw no difficulty in erecting them—and thence not to Tahiti as the plan provided (he thought it too well known) but to Hawaii in order to reach Northwest America in full summer; he also wished to check the 'los Majos' and 'La Mesa' of Anson's Spanish map, which he thought were Hawaii displaced eastwards. He was at Maui at the end of May and sighted Mount St Elias on 24 June.

On 2 July he anchored at 'Port des Français', now Lituya Bay, hoping to find a river that might connect with the Great Lakes—Buachian geography. La Pérouse was soon disillusioned with this slab-sided fiord; every prospect displeased and local man was vile, though he did provide furs. Here the first tragedy occurred; twenty-one men were drowned when, owing to the rashness of their officer, their boats were capsized in a squall. He thought that the inlet might do for a French factory,

◀ Figure 16. LA PÉROUSE, MALASPINA, VANCOUVER. C, D, tracks of Chatham and Discovery from New Zealand to Tahiti. Limitations of space preclude representation of all Vancouver's passages on the northwest American coast. Base map by courtesy of the American Geographical Society, New York.

if that were worthwhile, and bought, or thought he did, a little island for a cenotaph to his lost men, the only Act of Possession of the voyage.[19]

On 31 July La Pérouse left Port des Français and proceeded south along what he correctly deduced was a screen of islands, not a mainland. He could not linger to explore this maze; time pressed, as he needed to reach China at the season of the southeast monsoon to take him towards Kamchatka, and he had concluded that de Fonte's tale of waterways across North America was 'fabricated in England'—as it was, though with no serious intent—and that whatever closet geographers might say, there was no Northwest Passage. On 14 September the ships anchored at Monterey, the first outsiders to visit Alta California. La Pérouse's comments on its polity, civil and religious, were friendly but critical, in the Enlightenment or rather Physiocrat manner—what the country really needed was real colonisation, a more open economy, and agricultural development.[20]

The ships left Monterey on 24 September on a course designed to avoid the Manila Galleon track. This led to the discovery of uninhabited Necker Island, 480 km WNW of Kauai, and to near-disaster on the neighbouring French Frigate Shoals. They made a landfall on Asunción, a barren black cone in the northern Marianas, and passing north of Luzon reached soundings in Chinese waters on New Year's Day 1787. At Macao the furs from Port des Français were sold for the benefit of the crews, not very profitably; La Pérouse thought that French ventures in the fur trade would be too risky.[21] After a month at Macao and six weeks at Cavite and Manila, his judgement on Chinese administration was most unfavourable and on Spanish rule in the Philippines scarcely less scathing; again a freer economy and the Physiocrat recipe of agricultural development were needed.[22]

On 9 April he sailed northwards; bad weather off the Pescadores forced him to go east of Taiwan and through the Ryukyus. Quelpart (Cheju do or Saishu To) was sighted on 21 May, and on the 25th both Korea and Japan were in view from Tshushima Straits. La Pérouse closed with the Japanese coast at Noto Peninsula and on 6 June stood across for Tartary, first seen on the 11th in 42°55′N, west of Vladivostock. The major geographical contribution of the voyage lay ahead, 'the only part of the globe which had escaped the indefatigable activity of Captain Cook.'[23]

Patience was sorely needed when weaving from side to side of the narrow fog-shrouded gulf of Tartary. The ships crept slowly up the mainland coast, meeting no inhabitants, until on 7 July they were in sight of both Tartary and 'Segalien', though still in some doubt whether the land to the east was Sakhalin or Yezo (Hokkaido). At last they met the Ainu people, physically nasty but morally good; their information left little doubt of the insularity of Sakhalin, though much about a passage northwards for large ships. At their farthest north, on 26 July in 51°44′, just south of the Amur delta, the boats found only six fathoms; even were there a way through, for small craft, time pressed for the desired exploration of the Kurils.[24] La Pérouse turned back, rounded the southern tip of Sakhalin on 11–14 August and sailed between that island and Hokkaido. Still plagued by heavy fogs, he recognised Iturup and Urup as Fries's Staten Landt and Compagnie Landt (1643) and reached Petropavlosk on 7 September.

La Pérouse did not completely fill up the gaps in these Tartarian seas; Sakhalin and Hokkaido were definitely distinguished, but the latter, 'Jesso', could still be thought of as several islands, and the question of an unimpeded passage between Sakhalin and the mainland was still open. Vancouver's lieutenant William Broughton replicated La Pérouse's voyage in 1797, adding little; he was 'fully convinced that there was no opening to the sea in this [northern] direction'. As late as the Crimean War a small Russian squadron escaped from a trap through the northern exit, unknown to the blockading British and only definitely known to the Russians five years earlier.[25] Nevertheless, La Pérouse's map was a vast improvement; and it is also notable that only in the Gulf of Tartary, two years out from Brest, that there were even symptoms of scurvy.

La Pérouse's reception by the Russians, who expected him, was more than genial; in a touching gesture, he restored the little memorial to Charles Clerke. He received from Paris notice of his promotion to Commodore, and instructions to hasten to New Holland to check on reported British activity. He therefore abandoned his plan of going to New Zealand by Guam and the Solomons, sending his Russian interpreter Barthélemy de Lesseps (uncle of the canalbuilder) across Siberia with his journals to date.[26] On 30 September the ships left Avacha Bay and struck into the Pacific on an entirely new track.

This brought him to Tau, most easterly of the Samoan group, on 6 December, and on the 9th he anchored at 'Manoua', really Tutuila, which had been sighted by Roggeveen and Bougainville. Here another tragedy befell; against La Pérouse's wishes, de Langle insisted in taking on more fresh water as a guard against scurvy. Relations with the Samoans had been amicable, with a few slight jostlings; but the watering party was attacked and lost twelve dead, including de Langle and the naturalist Lamanon, with twenty wounded. La Pérouse took no revenge, for fear of slaying the innocent; but his views, formed at Lituya Bay, of the inherent badness of the Good Savage were confirmed, and he was bitter against the philosophers who idealised the 'natural man'; on the eve of his death, Lamanon had told La Pérouse that 'these men are more worthy than we.'[27]

La Pérouse passed on, sighting Savaii, Manono and Apolima, new discoveries, and then by Schouten's Cocos and Traitors' Islands (Tafahi and Niuatoputapa) until by year's end he was at Vavau, which had been discovered by Francisco Maurelle in 1781 on a voyage from Manila to San Blas. He cleared the Tongan group at Tasman's Pylsart (Ata) on 1 January 1788; no landing on Norfolk was possible, and by the 24th he saw the masts of British ships in Botany Bay. Arthur Phillip had arrived six days earlier, and was engaged in shifting the embryo colony to Port Jackson.

Cordialities were accepted in the spirit in which they were proffered; 'Europeans are all fellow-countrymen at such a prodigious distance' from home.[28] Two of Phillip's officers promised all aid in their power; in their straightened circumstances, as La Pérouse well understood, this could amount to no more than a hearty *bon voyage*, but Phillip agreed to forward the despatches informing his Minister that he would explore the islands from New Caledonia to New Guinea and proceed by Torres Strait to reach Ile de France in December. On 10 March the ships sailed; then, but for a few fallacious rumours, there was silence for thirty-eight years. The only other French voyage of importance in the North Pacific was that of Etienne Marchand, who got his serious information on the sea-otter trade not from La Pérouse but from a British captain, Nathaniel Portlock, in 1788 at the Cape. Marchand received the backing of a Marseilles firm, who built a 300-ton ship, copper-bottomed not nailed, well-equipped and well-named the *Solide*. Despite the desire for speed to get ahead of the intensifying competition, sailing was delayed by the uncertainties of the Nootka crisis, and on 14 December 1790 Marchand left Marseilles.[29]

He stopped only at the Cape Verdes before rounding the Horn and watering in the Marquesas (12–20 June 1792). His 'Iles de la Révolution' were Uapou, Tahuata, Nukuhiva and a couple of near-by islands; all but the islet had been seen and patriotically christened by the Yankee trader Joseph Ingraham the year before; they were to be 'discovered' and rebaptised by Richard Hergest, in Vancouver's supply-ship *Daedalus*, the year after.[30] Marchand's relations with the Marquesans were friendly; he took possesion—for the King in his log, for the Nation in his book!— and left bottled copies of the act in care of three generations, an aged and a mature man and a young girl.[31] One may suspect that the bottles soon found other uses.

On 7 August he made landfall at Cape Edgecumbe and spent a few days trading, probably in Sitka Sound. Going down the Queen Charlottes he found that 'where the English have reaped, there remains nothing for the gleaner', and decided to try the 'still almost unknown' Barkley Sound, south of Nootka, only to meet a trader coming out. He therefore made at once for China with what furs he had, to be ahead of competitors.

Marchand left the coast on 8 September and after calling at Hawaii reached Macao on 25 November. Bad luck again; the sale of furs in southern Chinese ports had just been prohibited. Sailing on 6 December he arrived at Toulon on 14 August 1792—a remarkably brisk circumnavigation, twenty months, with only one death, from apoplexy. The furs were sent to Lyons for sale, and ruined in the 1792 siege.

There was one other French voyage to the coast, by the shadowy *Flavie*. She was met at Nootka by Galiano and Valdés in July 1792; her captain alleged that as well as furs he was looking for La Pérouse; as the Spaniards drily hinted, she seemed somewhat off course...[32]

Seeking La Pérouse: d'Entrecasteaux

La Pérouse was expected in France by mid–1789; that year passed, and the next, with no news. Fleurieu, now Minister of Marine, and the Société d'Histoire Naturelle brought the matter before the National Assembly and the King. They acted quickly; perhaps it was a relief, in that time of troubles, to have a national object on which Frenchmen could unite. Two ships were placed under the command of Joseph-Antoine Bruny d'Entrecasteaux, who had made a notable voyage from Ile de France to China against the monsoon. His 'frigates' were really gabarres, bulky carriers of 450–500 tons, slow and lacking in manoeuvrability. Provisioning, in the disturbed state of French dockyards, was poor. Even more serious, the invidious distinction as to status and promotion between noble *officiers rouges* and plebeian *officiers bleus*, though recently abolished, still rankled, and the ancient tension was rapidly widening into a political rift; the ships sailed just two months after the King's flight to Varennes, when lines were being drawn ever more sharply. The scientists, particularly the Jacobin botanist La Billardière, first chronicler of the voyage, as sons of the Enlightenment were enemies of the Ancien Régime.[33]

La Pérouse's last letter from Botany Bay indicated a wide area for the search, roughly the Melanesian seas. These were to be approached by the south of New Holland; La Pérouse's tracks were to be picked up in Tonga. The ships sailed from Brest on 29 September 1791, d'Entrecasteaux in the *Recherche* and Jean-Michel Huon de Kermadec, an old friend from the China voyage, in the *Espérance*. Cape Town was reached on 17 January 1792, and here depositions were received from Ile de France, made by two French merchant captains. They deposed that John Hunter, who had met La Pérouse at Botany Bay, while returning to England from Sydney had seen Admiralty Islanders wearing what appeared to be French uniforms. Though sceptical of these certainly garbled reports, d'Entrecasteaux felt that he could not ignore them, and decided to go to the Admiralties by the north of New Guinea.[34]

Sailing in mid-February, d'Entrecasteaux found that he would not be able to get east of Timor before the Southeast Monsoon set in; he therefore reverted to the original plan, calling at Amsterdam Island (St Paul) and

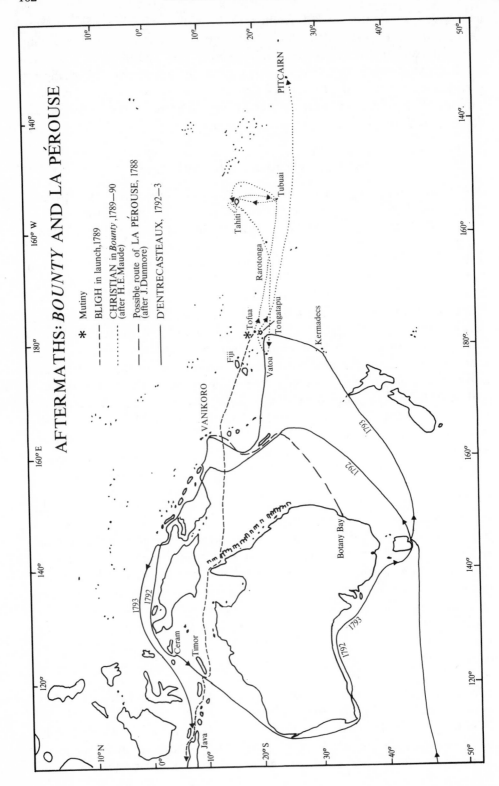

AFTERMATHS: *BOUNTY* AND LA PÉROUSE

* Mutiny

------- BLIGH in launch,1789

········ CHRISTIAN in *Bounty*,1789—90
(after H.E.Maude)

— — — Possible route of LA PÉROUSE, 1788
(after J.Dunmore)

——— D'ENTRECASTEAUX, 1792—3

watering in Van Diemens Land, where he explored Dentrecasteaux Channel, part of which had been seen by Bligh, and Bruny Island (21 April–28 May). The southern reefs of New Caledonia were reached on 16 June, and here the real search began, or should have done; both La Pérouse's letter and d'Entrecasteaux's instructions specified the island.[35] Since Cook had charted the east coast La Pérouse would probably have taken the west, and d'Entrecasteaux duly worked up it; but he seems to have been shaken by a narrow escape from wreck at the start, and to have missed chances of finding a pass through the barrier reef. (Fig.17).

The northern reefs were cleared on 3 July and d'Entrecasteaux passed through the Solomons and Cartaret's St George's Channel to reach the Admiralties at the end of July; so eager were the crews that trees stranded on the reefs were taken for ship's timbers—but there were enough for a whole fleet, and the reported French accoutrements turned out to be native belts and ornaments.[36]

After refreshing at Amboyna d'Entrecasteaux again took up the old plan, exploring the southwest of New Holland (Recherche Archipelago, Esperance Bay) until on 2 January 1793, at the Head of the Bight, he was forced to give up thoughts of seeking a passage between Van Diemens Land and the continent by water shortage; they had a sea-water still but it needed too much fuel, 'for when water is scarce on board ship, wood is never abundant.'[37] He therefore made for the south of Van Diemens Land, anchoring in Recherche Bay on the 21st.

It is most unlikely that, as Rossel hinted, the British needed the spur of d'Entrecasteaux to make them explore Bass Strait, though doubtless his maps, which fell into their hands after the expedition broke up, were studied with interest and profit;[38] but his work might have provided a basis for later French claims, and certainly drew attention to Van Diemens Land's attractions for settlement. After amicable contact with the Tasmanians, whose family affection suggested that here was 'an image of the first state of society',[39] d'Entrecasteaux left Adventure Bay on 27 February and sailed by Cape Maria van Diemen and the Kermadecs for Tonga, reached on 23 March; again there was no trace nor tradition of La Pérouse, though he had been, very briefly, at Vavau and Tongatapu. Passing through the southern New Hebrides (Vanuatu) and north of the Loyalties, d'Entrecasteaux again ignored the Isle of Pines, inexplicably unless he was looking for Cook's harbour at Balade as the only known safe port in New Caledonia. There he anchored on 21 April.

Morale had been good on the first New Caledonian visit; now it came under stress. Much was due to the disillusionment of finding that the people described by Cook and the Forsters as friendly and honest were

◀ *Figure 17.* AFTERMATHS: *BOUNTY* AND LA PÉROUSE.

now sunk in wretchedness, famished and disease-ridden, thievish and, when they had the numbers, aggressive; they were also cannibals. On the west coast d'Entrecasteaux had speculated that the guarding reefs were to protect Cook's pacific people from intruders; now he saw them as a barrier to keep the savages in and 'to prevent anyone coming to be devoured by them'![40] Tribal wars and drought were probably responsible for the change; drought made watering far more difficult than on Cook's visit. And now d'Entrecasteaux was plunged into melancholia by the death of his old comrade Huon de Kermadec. It was more than a private loss; de Kermadec was respected by all, but his replacement, Alexandre d'Auribeau, though a fine seaman was too proud of his noble birth, a rigid Royalist, and austere.

On 13 May they cleared the D'Entrecasteaux Reefs north of New Caledonia, and on the 19th, near Santa Cruz, sighted an island which they named for the *Recherche*; a savage irony, for it was Vanikoro, where, only five years earlier, La Pérouse's ships had met their end. Almost certainly there were survivors on the island, quite certainly there were relics. So near had d'Entrecasteaux come, unwittingly, to his goal.

The search had failed, but important geographical work still lay ahead. From 25 June to 9 July they were in the Solomons, and then came to Bougainville's Louisiades, sighting Rossel Island on the 11th and from here to new Britain the map is still scattered with French names: Renard, Deboyne, Bonvouloir, D'Entrecasteaux, Trobriand, Lusançay Islands; Huon Gulf; Willaumez Peninsula. But the end was near; d'Entrecasteaux, still under the shock of de Kermadec's death, himself died off the Admiralties on 20 July. Command fell to d'Auribeau, with Rossel in the *Recherche*; but the former was seriously ill, and for much of the remaining voyage Rossel was effectively in command of an expedition racked by scurvy, dysentery, and bitter dissensions.

They reached Surabaya in Java on 19th October, but the Dutch kept them outside for a week. The inhospitable delay was soon explained by the devastating news of France at war, her King and Queen guillotined. After dreary squabbles with the Dutch and his seditioners, on 17 February 1794 d'Auribeau hoisted the white banner of the monarchy, no longer contaminated by the National tricolour in the canton. The expedition dissolved, most of the Republicans making their way to already revolutionised Ile de France, the Royalists by long and painful odysseys to Europe. The Dutch eventually took over the ships.[41]

No trace of La Pérouse had been found, the end was disaster; but, despite hesitations at New Caledonia, the scientific and geographical results were considerable. The expedition left lasting memorials in French names on the coasts of Australia and Tasmania, in New Caledonia, above all in the hazardous seas east of New Guinea.[42]

In August 1826 an adroit Irish sailor of fortune, Peter Dillon, arrived in Calcutta. On his voyage from Chile he had called at Tikopia to look up a Prussian seaman and a lascar, whom he had left there thirteen years earlier; the lascar had a silver sword-guard, which with other European artefacts had been brought from 'Mallicolo'—Vanikoro. Dillon could not make Vanikoro itself, but in Calcutta he gained official support for a follow-up in a little ship aptly named the *Research*. After some misadventures, by September 1827 he was back at Tikopia and Vanikoro, and here was a rich harvest; copper plates and pots, a silver vessel with the *fleur de lis*, bells, guns... The sea had yielded up its mystery; indubitably, La Pérouse and his ships had met their end at Vanikoro.[43]

A note on Baudin, Bass and Flinders

Although belonging to Australian rather than Pacific maritime history, the voyage of 1800–4 by Nicolas Baudin in the *Géographe*, with Jacques Hamelin in the *Naturaliste*, demands some attention as the last of the great eighteenth century navigations; when large-scale official expeditions (other than that of Krusenshtern and Lisianski in 1803–6) were resumed after the Napoleonic Wars, conditions navigational, scientific and political were vastly changed.

Baudin, who had experience of scientific voyaging in Austrian service, was himself the initiator.[44] As might be expected from its Napoleonic auspices, the expedition was well-equipped scientifically; but whether it had any concrete political aims is not clear. Certainly there were neither plans nor means for settlement, and Sydney, the obvious key point for a political reconnaissance, was not included in the instructions—the visit to Port Jackson was not planned but enforced by accident. But it was thought that New Holland might be not one landmass but two or more, in which case the western one(s) might be open to French colonisation, and it was important to know whether the British had establishments in Torres and particularly Bass Straits. Yet while 'Terre Napoléon' became dotted with Bonapartist names of capes and bays, and officers would be expected to keep their eyes open, like officers of any nation on such service, any actual espionage seems to have been free-lance.[45]

Like d'Entrecasteaux's, the voyage was riddled with dissension, the scientists again taking the lead; François Péron, the botanist who wrote the official account, only twice mentions his captain by name—in the nominal roll and in reporting his death near Timor—but his narrative and Baudin's journal are studded with venomous references to each other, and Péron is the source of Baudin's undeservedly poor repute.[46]

Most of the work was in Western Australia, the south coast of the continent, and Tasmania; on the southeast coast of south Australia—Terre Napoléon—Baudin and Matthew Flinders had an interesting meeting (8

April 1802) in Encounter Bay. The only strictly Pacific part of the voyage was a visit to Sydney. But the scientific results were immense; largely owing to Baudin's ill-requited devotion, the ships brought to France nearly 200 plant species, 600 types of seeds, over 100 living animals, some to adorn Josephine's gardens at Malmaison, though the main spread of eucalypts to many Mediterranean landscapes seems due to later introductions. Observations on the Tasmanian Aborigines just before they were overridden by sealing gangs and settlers constituted a precious record.[47]

Before Baudin, the suspected insularity of Van Diemens Land had been very strongly indicated by escaped convicts and by George Bass, who picked up some of them in the *Tom Thumb* (keel 2.5 metres, Bass himself 1.8 metres tall!). Final demonstration was made by Flinders and Bass who circumnavigated the island in 1798–9; it was on Flinders' recommendation that Bass Strait received its name. The Strait saved over 1100 km on the voyage from the Cape to Sydney.[48]

South Pacific interlude: the Bounty affair

The first voyage to the South Sea Islands with a clear and specific economic object was that of William Bligh in search of breadfruit. Perhaps no other gang of drop-outs has inspired so much both of myth-mongering and of devoted (if sometimes coterie and misguided) scholarship as the *Bounty* mutineers. Apart from the procreation of a Seventh Day Adventist community which, in its offshoot on Norfolk Island, can still give minor headaches to the Commonwealth of Australia,[49] and the deleterious effects on Tahitian society of a handful of the mutineers and their assistance in the rise of the Pomare dynasty,[50] the historical significance of the episode is slight. But the story is Byronic—in fact Byron built round it one of his less successful poems, *The Island, or Christian and his Comrades* (1823).

The idea that breadfruit might provide an admirable staple food for the West Indian slaves germinated in the fertile mind of Sir Joseph Banks, the seed perhaps planted by the report of a French ship captured on such a mission. When he had secured authorisation he arranged for the command to go to Bligh, who had shown himself a fine seamen and hydrographer as Master of the *Resolution* on Cook's last voyage.[51] The *Bounty* was a merchantman of 215 tons, too small for the job, fitted under Banks's direction with tiers for potted plants; the cramped conditions of this floating greenhouse may be imagined; Bligh collected 1015 breadfruit seedlings. More serious, he had no commissioned officer and no marines to act as ship's police, and was Lieutenant, not Captain, as he is always titled. The complement was forty-six, including a near-blind fiddler upon whom Bligh insisted to provide healthful recreation—nightly compulsory dancing. By current standards, Bligh was a light flogger, lighter than the almost worshipped Cook; but his care for his crew became

Plate IX. THE *BOUNTY MUTINY*. By Robert Dodd, 1790. By permission of National Library of Australia, Canberra.

an oppressive paternalism, and he never realised that a man could feel lacerated by the tongue as by the lash.

Bligh was to proceed by Cape Horn; final orders were inexcusably delayed, and when he sailed from Spithead on 23 December 1787 it was late for the Horn route. After a heroic struggle, for which he publicly thanked his crew, he had to turn for the Cape of Good Hope. At least until he reached Van Diemen's Land (21 August 1788) morale was good, though the boatswain's mate James Morrison was later to inflate or invent complaints about rations; as was normal in such a ship, Bligh was his own purser. He took all possible care for his crew's health and comfort, as he saw them, and that was probably part of the trouble. The lower deck liked to keep itself to itself and expected the quarter deck to do likewise, as slum-dwellers resent do-gooders; until near his end, Cook had the tact to carry things off, but Bligh was a compulsive nagger, and when angry, which was often, exceedingly foul-mouthed.

From Van Diemen's Land Bligh sailed south of New Zealand, discovering the Bounty Islands, to reach Matavai Bay on 19 September. From then until he left on 4 April 1789 he was too busy cultivating essential chiefly friendships and his precious plants to keep real control over the company, many of whom slept ashore, including Fletcher Christian, an old shipmate whom he promoted acting lieutenant. The lack of a commissioned staff was fatal, and by this time Bligh's foul temper had put him at odds with his warrant officers, who were slack and yet could not be displaced for lack of replacements. His rages were brief but constantly renewed, and he seems to have thought that smooth words could erase deeply wounding ones; especially was this so with Christian, a young man of good Manx family whose sensitivity verged on paranoia.[52] In contrast, his handling of 'King Tinah' or Otoo (Tu) was so tactful that the breadfruit were offered gratis.

Bligh has been blamed for spending over five months at Tahiti, but he had to wait until his seedlings were sufficiently advanced, and in this long stay more than passing amorous atachments were formed. All seemed glad to leave for Old England; but the delights of the New Cytherea were suddenly replaced by hard work. Trouble soon started; Bligh, with provocation, behaved outrageously, according to the received version publicly accusing Christian, a gentleman, of stealing coconuts, and tried to mend things by an invitation to dinner.[53] After discovering Aitutaki and calling at Nomuka, where there was an affray with the Tongans, Bligh was off Tofua when just before sunrise he was seized by Christian and his accomplices, and haled onto deck bound and in only his shirt.

The mutiny was not, as Bligh maintained, a long-maturing plot, but on the spur of the moment; Christian had simply had more than he could bear, and malcontents were not wanting. A basic motive seems to have been a yearning for the sweets of Tahiti—Christian himself had his 'Isabella', who was to go with him to Pitcairn and bear him three children; nor is this surprising in an age when Dr Johnson could compare shipboard life, unfavourably, with a jail. Those who see Christian's action as that of a cast-off lover forget that in the Age of Sentiment men often said 'love' where we should say 'liking', and both he and Bligh were heterosexual. But whatever the motivation, there is no doubt as to his bitterness towards his old friend and patron: 'That,—Captain Bligh,—that is the thing,—I am in hell—I am in hell.'[54]

After much confusion, Bligh and eighteen men were put into the launch; four at least of those who remained on the *Bounty* did so unwillingly, Bligh promising to do them justice in England; one of those with him, the carpenter William Purcell, was a troublemaker whom neither party wanted.

The 7-metre launch was very poorly provisioned and so grossly overloaded that its freeboard was only about 18 cm. Bligh had a sextant, a compass and some nautical tables, but no charts and no firearms; four cutlasses were grudgingly handed over. The standard daily ration for most of his boat journey was 18 grams of 'bread' (ship's biscuit) meticulously weighed on improvised scales of coconut shell with bullets for weights, and one gill (142 ml) of water, three times a day, and at intervals 30 or 45 grams of salt pork; wine and rum were doled out by the spoonful on emergent occasions. These short commons were supplemented by occasional seabirds and shellfish.

Bligh's first thought was to get water and victuals at Tofua; he did get some coconuts and breadfruit, but lost one man to an attack by the islanders. This savage reception ruled out further landings on inhabited islands; the only recourse was to make for Timor—Sydney was in existence, but Bligh could not know that. He passed between Vanua Levu and Viti Levu in Fiji, the first European sighting of the latter, and on 28 May was off the Great Barrier Reef (Fig.17). Next day a passage was found and the party landed on Restoration Island, named both for their deliverance and the return of Charles II, and feasted on oyster stew.

Bligh went up the coast, producing a remarkably good chart. With the relief from danger, discipline slipped and was only restored when Bligh, unsupported by his Master John Fryer, challenged Purcell to a cutlass duel; in Fryer's narrative, as convincing as the Captain's, the latter does not appear as quite the heroic master-spirit of his own version, yet the substance is much the same. Early in June the launch passed through Prince of Wales Channel into the Arafura Sea, and Bligh increased the rations, but very slightly lest he should miss Timor; characteristically, he still had eleven days in hand when, on 14 June, the pitiable group landed at Coupang (Koepang).[55] They were hospitably received; Bligh bought a small schooner which he called the *Resource* and made his way, still troubled by Fryer and Purcell, to Batavia and by Dutch shipping to England.[56]

Bligh's later career was honourable but chequered. Returning to a hero's welcome, he sailed again for breadfruit, and came back to face vilification from Christian's connections. In the Nore mutiny he was respected by his men, and after it stood up stoutly for some of them unjustly put into jeopardy after pardon;[57] he fought well at Camperdown and Copen-hagen; and was effectively finished when as Governor of New South Wales he tangled with the land-sharks of the New South Wales or Rum Corps. But as Post-Captain, Governor (another Banks job!), and Admiral, he never stood so high as when in command of a score of starvelings on a voyage which for skill and resolution has rarely been equalled.

Back at Tofua they pitched the nuisancy plants overboard and Christian asserted his leadership. To settle at Tahiti, however delectable, was to invite capture; even had Bligh not survived to tell the tale, search would begin there; Tubuai, seen by Cook in 1772 and 480 km to the south, seemed a possible haven.[58] They reached it on 24 May 1789; despite some Tubuaian hostility, it looked promising, but there were no pigs or poultry. It was decided to return to Tahiti to stock up, and by 7 June they were back at Matavai Bay, where Christian explained that Cook (whose death had been kept secret) had met Bligh and taken him to colonise Aitutaki or New Holland. By 26 June the *Bounty* was at Tubuai again, with 460 pigs.

The mutineers became on friendly terms with the strongest of the three chiefs, Tamatoa; unluckily they chose a site, paid for with red feathers, in the domain of a rival chief, Taroatohoa, which offended Tamatoa and the third chief Tinarou. However, a fort was built, loyally named Fort George; but there were inevitable quarrels over women and the pigs ravaged native gardens; later, the Tubuaians realised their value and resented Christian's attempts to collect them. The two alienated chiefs joined in a massive attack; it was defeated, but the island no longer seemed healthy. By sixteen votes to nine it was decided to return to Tahiti; they sailed on 15 September. So ended the first European settlement on a South Sea Island since the days of Quiros.[59]

Back on Tahiti (20 September) the party split; those who had wished to go with Bligh decided to await events and if taken to stand on their innocence, others simply wanted a *dolce far niente* life on the island. Christian stayed only two nights; when she sailed the *Bounty* carried nine mutineers, six Polynesian men and nineteen women, with one child—all but four or five kidnapped.

Rather aimlessly sailing west, they discovered Rarotonga and reached Tongatapu and southernmost Fiji; but these were relatively travelled seas. For security, they needed isolation; brooding over Hawkesworth's *Voyages*, Christian hit upon Pitcairn Island, not seen since Cartaret found it in 1767 and desirably upwind from Tahiti. They reached it on 15 January 1790. Within ten years all the Polynesian men, treated as slaves, were dead, and all but one of the whites, mostly by violence; but a new mixed generation was growing up, not revealed to the world until 1808, when the American skipper Matthew Folger was to his amazement greeted in English by Thursday October Christian, Fletcher's son, and met the mutineer John Adams, now a venerated patriarch. Born in lust and blood, Pitcairn grew into a peaceable pietistic community.[60]

Christian's instinct for isolation was correct; when Bligh arrived in England the Admiralty, despite the Nootka crisis, fitted out the 24-gun frigate *Pandora* under Edward Edwards, who seems to have been the sadistic Bligh of legend in frightful reality. Mortimer of the *Mercury* had also reached England with tales picked up on Tahiti (while the mutineers were at Tubuaii) about a visit by the *Bounty* under 'Titreano', clearly Christian. Tahiti was thus even more obviously the place to start the search.

Edwards sailed on 7 November 1790 by Cape Horn.[61] He passed near Pitcairn and reached Tahiti on 23 March 1791. There was quite a race by the loyalists to give themselves up, but though Bligh had exonerated four by name, that made no difference; they were put into irons. Another group, in a schooner built by Morrison, also surrendered, and the rest, except for two who had 'gone native' and got killed, were rounded up with the help of John Brown, left behind by the *Mercury*. Edwards had now fourteen 'pirates'; he immured them in a roundhouse, 'Pandora's Box', on the deck: 3.35 by 5.5 metres. They were not even allowed out in ones or twos for exercise.

On 8 May Edwards left Tahiti, with the schooner as tender, for Endeavour Straits, which he was instructed to examine. He wandered by the Tokelaus, Samoa and Tonga, losing the inadequately provisioned tender, which made her way to Java; *en route* her people became the first Europeans to land in Fiji and contact Fijians.[62] Edwards on 8 August discovered Rotuma, and on the 13th saw smokes on Vanikoro, very probably from La Pérouse's survivors. On the evening of the 28th the *Pandora* struck on the Barrier Reef east of Cape York.

The ship beat over the reef and was eleven hours in sinking. Three mutineers whom Bligh had absolved were released to help with the pumps; Edwards had been ordered to preserve his captives' lives for legal vengeance, but so far as he was concerned all but another three were left to drown. Four, and thirty-odd of the crew, did drown; the rest escaped only by the last-minute action of the boatswain's mate in unbolting the hatch of the Box. The survivors gathered on a little cay; the mutineers were barbarously refused even a sail to protect them from the sun.[63]

Despite the time available, the four boats were very scantily provisioned, though the rations were not so short as Bligh's. They reached Coupang on 15 September; not until they were put on board HMS *Gorgon* at the Cape were the prisoners treated with any decency. They arrived at Spithead in June 1792, to face inevitable court-martial.

Great interest was made for some, notably Midshipman Peter Heywood, who had good naval connections and had taken no part against—or for—Bligh; under seventeen, he claimed to have been overwhelmed by events, and the blackest mark on Bligh's name in the harsh letters he wrote to Heywood's relatives. Four whom Bligh absolved were acquitted; Heywood and Morrison were convicted but pardoned; one escaped on a technicality; three were hanged.

The vast publicity surrounding the mutiny has obscured the fact that, with good ships and offices, Bligh successfully carried out a second breadfruit voyage.[64] When he sailed from Spithead on 3 August 1791, he had the *Providence*, 420 tons, and the 110-ton *Assistant* under Nathaniel Portlock. The *Providence* had three lieutenants and twenty marines; her eight midshipmen included Matthew Flinders. Probably no ship under Bligh could be completely happy, and there was muted friction with the First Lieutenant, Francis Godolphin Bond, but nothing like the hatreds of the *Bounty*.[65] When the *Providence* was paid off, her crew cheered their Captain.

Bligh reached the Cape in November 1791 and sailed by St Paul Island to anchor in Adventure Bay; leaving Van Diemen's Land on 24 February 1792 he sailed south of New Zealand and well to the east before making north. He was in Matavai Bay on 9 April and spent fourteen weeks gathering breadfruit; he found the people sadly corrupted by the evil communications and 'vile expressions' (from Bligh!) of the mutineers.[66] He renewed old friendships with 'King' Tynah, now styled Pomare, and his queens—he seems to have been more tactful with Tahitians than with his own kind—and when he left on 20 July he had 2126 breadfruit and 472 other plants, and thirty-six 'curiosity plants'.

He sailed by Aitutaki to check Dalrymple's report of Maurelle's discoveries, and thence to Fiji. On his boat voyage he had produced a fragmentary chart; now in one week (5–11 August) he placed on the map most of the islands around the Koro Sea, Fiji's Mediterranean. There was now no doubt that these were the islands that Tasman had seen and Cook, at Tonga, surmised.[67]

By 1 September Bligh was on the eastern approaches to Torres Strait. His passage through the treacherous reefs and islands was a triumph of navigation,[68] greatly assisted by Portlock scouting ahead in the *Assistant* but impeded by brushes with the Islanders, whose fingers were very light on their 2-metre bows. The Straits are still dotted with the names he gave, and his passage north of Banks and Mulgrave Islands is still Bligh Channel. He reached Coupang on 2 October, and once refreshed set out for the West Indies via St Helena. St Vincent was reached on 22 January 1793; here he left 544 breadfruit. The remaining 623 went on to Jamaica; the survival rate of 55 per cent attests Bligh's almost obsessional care for his charges.

The planters of Jamaica voted Bligh 1000 and Portlock 500 guineas. They may have wished their money back when 'AFRICA'S dark sons', far from 'Teach[ing] children yet unborn to venerate thy name', ungratefully rejected as insipid the fruit brought to them with so much effort and anguish.[69]

Return to the North: the fur traders

Since this chapter is concerned with geography rather than economics, it would be pointless to try to particularise the many fur trading voyages, criss-crossing both in time and space, to the Northeast Pacific. While some captains did valuable work, notably Nathaniel Portlock and George Dixon, both of whom had sailed with Cook, others did not care to be too precise about their movements.[70] They amply warrant the epigraph to this chapter.

After Cook's third voyage, prompt exploitation of the Northeast Pacific as a fur supplier to China was inhibited by the American War. First to take advantage of the new opening was James Hanna in the *Harmon*, from Macao in 1785; he brought back pelts fetching $20,000. A rush began, with seven ships in 1786. The first non-Russian ships to winter on the coast were the Bengal Fur Company's *Nootka* and *Sea Otter* under John Meares, who decided to stay in Prince William Sound lest his crew should jump ship in Hawaii, already a forward base for the trade. He settled down on 7 October 1786 and had a hard time with scurvy, until in May 1787 he got some supplies from Portlock and Dixon, who made a tough bargain; as Meares was interloping and their company had virtuously got licences from both the EIC and the SSC, they made him bond himself in £1000 not to trade on the coast. Meares lost half his crew and the *Sea Otter* vanished at sea.[71]

Portlock and Dixon had been sent from England in the *King George* and *Queen Charlotte* by R. C. Etches's King George's [Nootka] Sound Company, which had plans for settlement both on Magellanic Staten Land and at Nootka.[72] They came out by Cape Horn and Hawaii and were in the Cook Inlet-Prince William Sound area in August 1786 (Fig.18). Moving against Cook's track, they failed to enter Nootka Sound and wintered in Hawaii. They were back at Prince William Sound by 23

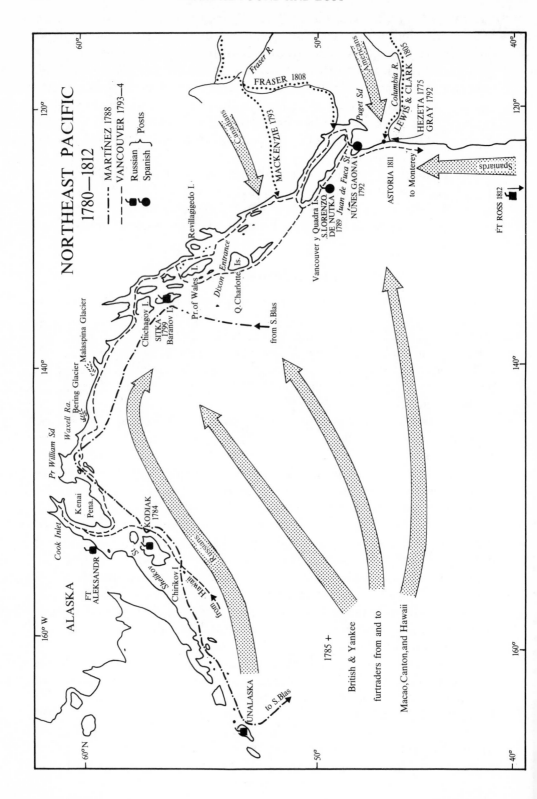

NORTHEAST PACIFIC
1780—1812

- · — · — MARTÍNEZ 1788
- · · · · · VANCOUVER 1793–4
- ■ Russian ⎫ Posts
- ● Spanish ⎭

Fraser R.

FRASER 1808

MACKENZIE 1793

Canadians

Puget Sd

Columbia R.

LEWIS & CLARK 1805

HEZETA 1775
GRAY 1792

Americans

Vancouver y Quadra I.
S.LORENZO
1789 DE NUTKA
Juan de Fuca St.
NÚÑES GAONA
1792

ASTORIA 1811

to Monterey

Spaniards

FT ROSS 1812

Revillagigedo I.

Dixon Entrance
Pr. of Wales I.
Q.Charlotte Is.

from S.Blas

Chichagov I.
SITKA
1799
Baranov I.

Malaspina Glacier
Bering Glacier
Waxell Ra.

Pr William Sd

Kenai
Pena.

Cook Inlet

ALASKA

FT
ALEKSANDR

KODIAK
1784

Chirikov I.

Shelikov St.

Russian

from Hawaii

UNALASKA

to S.Blas

1785 +

British & Yankee

furtraders from and to

Macao, Canton, and Hawaii

60°

120°

50°

40°

120°

140°

140°

160°

160° W

60° N

50°

40°

April 1787, and after hearing from Meares of likely competition agreed to separate.

Portlock stayed in the north until 22 August, when he bore away for Hawaii, spending most time at Port Etches on Hinchinbrook and Portlock's Harbour on Baranof Island. Dixon went south; off Nootka he met two more Etches ships (*Prince of Wales*, James Colnett; *Princess Royal*, Charles Duncan). On his way he had named the Queen Charlotte Islands and had found Dixon Entrance north of the group, although he did not enter Hecate Strait between these islands and the mainland. The ships rejoined in Canton River on 25 November.

The outer verge of the gap which Cook had left between Nootka in 49°33′N and his next landfall in 55°20′ was now seen to be a screen of islands; but the megalomania of John Meares gave a new though brief lease of life to the Bartholomew de Fonte fantasy of waterways to Hudson's Bay. Sailing from Macao under Portuguese colours[73] in the *Felice* (or *Feliz Aventureiro*), Meares was at Nootka on 13 May 1788, where he was joined by William Douglas in the *Iphigenia Nubiana*. Meares sent Douglas on a northern cruise; he himself negotiated with chief Maquinna (Maquilla or Ma-Kwee-na) for a little plot at Nootka, where he launched the schooner *North West America*, the first European craft built in these waters. On a southern cruise Meares named Mount Olympus and sent his longboat into Juan de Fuca Straits, allegedly for 'near thirty leagues' with a clear view fifteen leagues further east—thirty leagues would have taken the boat across Whidbey Island and miles into the mainland.

Not content with this mild exaggeration, Meares included in his book a map showing the track of the American sloop *Washington* from Juan de Fuca Straits to the ocean north of the Queen Charlottes; to the east of this imaginary track was shown sea with land visible at one point only. John Strange had discovered in 1786 Queen Charlotte Strait north of Vancouver Island and may have thought it de Fonte's opening, and Hoskins and Haswell of the *Columbia* also believed in his Straits; but Meares's special pleading, playing tricks with longitudes, was a conscious resurrection of that most fictitious Admiral.[74] Other trading voyages added fragments to the evolving map. The *Iphigenia* sailed through Dixon Entrance, giving Meares a pretext for renaming it after Douglas;[75] Duncan filled in the east coast of the Queen Charlottes; in 1787 Charles Barkley in the *Imperial Eagle* (Ostend-registered, another subterfuge) identified the passage between Vancouver Island and Cape Flattery as indeed Juan de Fuca's Straits.

In September 1788 the *Columbia*, John Kendrick, and *Washington*, Robert Gray, arrived in Nootka Sound, the first of many Americans.[76] Next

◀ *Figure 18.* NORTHEAST PACIFIC 1780–1812. Tracks generalised. Alternative names: Sitka, Novo-Arkhangel'sk; Núñez Gaona, Neah Bay. A geopolitical convergence is indicated by the Anglo-Russo-Spanish toponymy.

year Gray ranged north to Bucareli Bay and demonstrated the insularity of the Queen Charlottes, only inferred by Dixon; he also went some 50 km up Juan de Fuca Straits. Kendrick took over the *Washington* and misappropriated her in China; Gray in the *Columbia* returned to Boston on 9 August 1790 with Canton tea—the first American circumnavigation. The *Columbia* sailed again only seven weeks later and reached Nootka in June 1791; the most notable result of this voyage was the discovery (11 May 1792) of the great Columbia River—Hezeta in 1775 had noted and passed it by, Gray went 35–40 km upriver.[77]

What was now needed was a systematic programme to assemble correctly the patches and scattered tiles of this great archipelagic mosaic.

Later Spanish voyages; Alejandro Malaspina

The Spanish attempts at such an effort were made with poor resources and interrupted by the dispersal of the experienced San Blas officers for service in the American War; but reports from Concepción that La Pérouse had a map showing Russian posts down to Nootka, and Cook's account of them at Unalaska, evoked renewed concern in Madrid.[78] If more incentive were needed, it was provided by the fur traders.

On 8 March 1788 Estéban José Martínez, who had been with Pérez, left San Blas in the *Princesa*, accompanied by Gonzalo López de Haro in the *San Carlos*. By 10 June they were at 'Puerto Santiago', Port Etches; Martínez wished to return, but the winds forced them southwest. Haro met the factor Evstratii Delarov near Kodiak and Martínez, at Unalaska, Potap Zaitov. The Russians were very free with information, including their expectation of two frigates from Kamchatka to occupy Nootka next year;[79] an obvious warning-off which did not stop Martínez from unblushingly taking possession at several places, including Unalaska itself; he also produced a map of Aleutian islands, from Russian sources but with Spanish names. They cleared the islands on 27 August and Haro returned separately; there had been much dissension.

The most important result was political—the decision to occupy Nootka. Martínez strongly recommended this, and in anticipation of Madrid's sanction he and Haro sailed again in the same ships, on 17 February 1789, reaching Nootka on 5 and 12 May. The post was abandoned, owing to supply problems, after six months, time enough for Martínez to make arbitrary seizures which brought Britain and Spain to the verge of war.[80]

For 1790 Bodega y Quadra, in command at San Blas, projected a voyage to reclaim or reinforce Nootka via Hawaii, but resources for an oceanic voyage were lacking. Instead, Francisco Eliza was sent in February 1790, with three ships, to reoccupy Nootka more firmly. From Nootka he sent Salvador Fidalgo in the *San Carlos*, with a Russian-speaking pilot, to contact the Russians and examine the Bucareli Bay area; this he could not do owing to contrary winds, but he met Delarov at Kodiak and received a letter from Billings, in English and hence unintelligible. Meanwhile Manuel Quimper in the *Princesa Real*—ex-*Princess Royal*, one of Martínez's captures—spent June and July exploring the south of Vancouver Island; he examined Neah Bay on the southern shores of Juan de Fuca Strait, later (May–September 1792) a short-lived Spanish outpost.[81] In 1791 Eliza, after failing to make his way north against strong head winds, spent two months in the waters between the present Victoria and Vancouver, exploring Haro and Rosario Straits east and west of the San Juan group, still regarded as one island.

It was not to be expected that the Spain of Carlos III, with its enthusiasm for the scientific study of its vast domains, should not seek to emulate the great voyages of the French and British; the expedition of Alejandro Malaspina did not sail until six months after the King's death, but it was emphatically a product of his age. It was designed to round off a great hydrographic and scientific survey of all the Spanish possessions. Preparations were meticulous; twin corvettes of 306 tons, with complements of 104 each, were built under the commander's eye; they were not named as of old for saints but for discovery and daring—*Descubierta* and *Atrevida*. Scientists, artists, crews were specially picked; provisioning was thorough; they had six chronometers by Berthoud and Arnold and sixteen sextants by such makers as Ramsden, Troughton and Dolland; there was also a harpsichord.

  Malaspina was born in 1754 in Parma, then Spanish (Carlos III began his career as its Duke), and was a true son of the Enlightenment, which in the end brought him no good. The voyage was great in scope, but too late to add greatly to strictly geographical knowledge. For nearly a century its record lay buried in Spanish archives, until in 1885 Pedro Novo y Colson resurrected and promptly re-buried it in a folio of 681 pages, 573 of them double-columned, with no index and not even a table of contents.[82] With such presentation, it is not surprising that Malaspina's is the least-known of all the great Pacific voyages, barely and often inaccurately mentioned in most accounts. (Fig.16)

The ships sailed from Cadiz on 30 July 1789 for Montevideo and the Falklands, and reached Chiloé on 4 February 1790. They proceeded up the coast; Malaspina's often unflattering comments on the ports from Valparaiso to Sonsonate sometimes seem a re-write of those by Juan and Ulloa forty years earlier—Panama for instance had grass growing in the streets and costly fortifications now barely fit to keep off the Darien Indians.[83] In March 1791, at Acapulco, Malaspina received new instructions from Madrid, to investigate the passage through North America allegedly discovered by Lorenzo Ferrer Maldonado in 1588. This story, like its author discredited in his own day, had recently been revived, with some panache, by Philippe Buache in France and the Duque de Almodóvar in Spain. Such a passage, and Spanish priority in it, would make the Spanish position on the northwest coast firmer and facilitate occupation.[84]

Malaspina therefore sailed from Acapulco for the north on 1 May, and by 23 June was in sight of Cabo Engaño, Cook's Cape Edgecumbe on Baranof Island, and thence to Port Mulgrave (Yakutat Bay) where he made a very fair determination of the height of Mount St Elias; the great glacier stretching from the mountain to the bay now bears his name. He turned back for Nootka on 17 July; this, the last Spanish voyage to the far north, had little to show. He reached Nootka in 12 August and Monterey a month later, arriving at Acapulco in mid-October.

More significant locally was the work of two of Malaspina's officers, Dionisio Alcalá Galiano and Cayetano Valdés, in the 45-ton schooners *Sutil* and *Mexicana*. They left Acapulco on 8 March 1792 and after calling at Nootka and Neah Bay, where Fidalgo was setting up a post, went up Rosario Strait and on 22 June met Vancouver, with whom they sailed in company for three weeks. They carefully examined many inlets on the mainland before crossing to Vancouver Island and returning to Nootka on 1 September.[85]

Malaspina was sure that Maldonaldo's opening did not exist—his *Disertación* not only demolished that legend but scouted the idea that any useful passage could be found—but Colnett had hinted that de Fonte's strait might lie between 53° and 55°N. At last attempt to find it was made by Jacinto Caamaño in June–September 1792. He filled in much detail around Bucareli Bay, but naturally did not find the suppositious strait; he thought that if it did exist it must be Hecate Strait, which he duly labelled with the apocryphal Admiral's name. But it was clear that none of the inlets around 53°N could lead to Hudson's Bay.

There were still gaps in Spanish knowledge of these waters. Galiano wished to continue work in the distant north, but others opined more realistically that Vancouver was already in the field with superior resources. There had been some leap-frogging; the nearer coast from San Francisco to Juan de Fuca was still imperfectly known, and here Gray's discovery of the Columbia River might be followed up. Vancouver's second in command Broughton had gone up it, in boats, for at least 135 km in October 1792, and taken possession; possibly its sources lay in or near New Mexico, and it was important to guard this potential entry. Hence Eliza was sent in the *Activa* and Juan Martínez y Zayas in the *Mexicana*, sailing on 30 April 1793. Eliza got no further than 44°N, well south of the Columbia, but Martínez on 10–12 August penetrated the river for about 20 km. But for a visit to Nootka in 1796, the Spanish story in the Northeast Pacific ends with this feeble performance.

To the victor the spoils; the Spanish achievement was overshadowed by Vancouver's; much of it was in ethnography, and such valuable 'contact' documents as J. M. Moziño's *Noticias de Nutka* long remained unpublished.[86] Except for Malaspina and his officers, Spanish training and instrumentation were inferior; until their arrival, positions were apparently fixed by latitude and dead reckoning only; the ships were wretchedly cramped even for their day, and badly provisioned; scurvy was rife. On Admiralty charts and the widely-used maps of Aaron Arrowsmith, Vancouver's versions were naturally standard in an age when British and American shipping dominated the seas; yet Humboldt thought that on the whole Malaspina's determinations were better than his rival's, and his authoritative *Carte de la Nouvelle Espagne* (1802–4, published 1811) was based on Spanish sources.[87] But Vancouver's surveys were far more comprehensive and coherent, Cook's extended much farther north.

The strictly Pacific phase of Malaspina's voyage began with his departure from Acapulco for the Marianas on 20 December 1791. Rather unenterprisingly, he followed the Manila Galleon track, reaching Guam on 12 February 1792. Cabo Espíritu Santo was sighted on 2 March, and he spent three weeks threading the islands to Cavite (25 March). The *Atrevida* spent April on a visit to Macao, the *Descubierta* carried out local surveys, and for once the scientists could not complain of being rushed; Malaspina did not leave Cavite until 15 November, after the typhoon season. He cruised down to Zamboanga on Mindanao, and then struck eastwards on a course parallel to but north of those of Cartaret, Bougainville and Mourelle.

In theory this was correct, in practice it led to nothing; the ships were too far north and east of the Melanesian island screen. No land was seen before Eromango on 10 February 1793; on the 21st they were off New Zealand, near Dusky Sound, but strong northeasterlies forced them offshore, and it was decided to bear up for Botany Bay. Entrance to Port Jackson was easier, and they anchored there on 11 March.

The Spaniards were warmly received; the colony, little over five years old, made a very favourable impression, especially on a jaunt to see the infant but rising agriculture at Parramatta; in a short time a well-ordered settlement had been created from nothing. The day was still distant, however, when the colony would not have to rely for its subsistence on a voyage right round the globe, but the colonial officials were deploying every means to obviate this. From another point of view the impression was less favourable, indeed ominous; Malaspina wrote a 'Political Examination of the English Colonies in the Pacific', correctly seeing in them a likely menace to the Spanish position across the Ocean, through smuggling and privateering or piracy, but less realistically he saw some prospect of good if there could be co-operation in the spirit of Enlightenment and free trade.[88]

After an agreeable month in Sydney, Malaspina sailed on 11 April for the 'Mayorga Archipelago', discovered by Mourelle in February 1781 during a voyage from Manila to San Blas.[89] It was correctly identified with the Tongan islands that Cook had heard about at Tongatapu and Nomuka, the Vavau group; the purpose of Malaspina's visit was to confirm the Spanish claim to priority by an act of possession, rather against his Enlightenment principles. He spent three weeks (19 May–11 June) at Vavau, where there were careful astronomical, linguistic, botanical and ethnographic studies, most of them still in the archives.[90] Malaspina spent some days around adjacent islands (Late, Kao, Tofua) and sighted Tongatapu before leaving the Friendly Islands for Peru; he sailed steadily eastwards on 30°S before making northing but saw no islands; another unfruitful traverse. On 24 July the ships anchored at Callao; in October they sailed for Talcahuano and the Horn, reaching Cadiz on 21 September 1794.

Malaspina had sailed two weeks after the fall of the Bastille, he returned eight weeks after 9 Thermidor; his Enlightenment world of liberalising despotism had been turned upside down, from initial euphoria to the Terror and the reaction against it. At first he was well received, instantly promoted and encouraged to prepare for publication, at enormous cost, seven lavish volumes of reports. But these were often scathing in their criticism of Spanish colonial policy and radical in their proposals for reform on the lines of autonomy and truly free trade; there were dangerous appeals to British and (in 1795!) French practices.[91] Malaspina rashly tangled with Godoy, certainly politically by challenging his *far niente* attitude, very likely also personally as a rival not only for the favour but also the favours of Queen Maria Luisa; he was induced to put his dangerous thoughts into writing and to leave them in her care; she betrayed him.

In November 1795 Malaspina was arrested and condemned to ten years imprisonment; only fragments of the immense documentation of his voyage escaped seizure. Eight years later he was released on Napoleon's intervention, but banished to Italy; he died in 1810.[92] And so one of the mightiest scientific enterprises of the century was wrecked after reaching port, 'bound in shallows and in miseries' of political and personal intrigue, its stores of knowledge lost in dusty archives.

The end of dreaming: Vancouver

The last and far from the least of the century's Pacific voyages was that under Vancouver in 1791–5. Its genesis lay in the British reaction to the first sketchy reports of Martínez's seizures at Nootka; the mere private projects (albeit backed in high places) of operators like Etches would become government policy; British fur traders were to be protected by an official establishment on the sea-otter coast. The plan was global; two ships were to sail from England to Port Jackson, there to pick up personnel from the infant for the embryo colony, and rendezvous in Hawaii with a frigate from India.[93] After the mobilisation of the 'Spanish Armament' had brought the Dons to heel, the settlement of the crisis involved the formal restitution of the British holding at Nootka—John Meares's post—and the officer sent to receive it could also carry out the second part of the original plan, a survey of the whole Northeast Pacific coast to ascertain whether there were any waterway which might facilitate commercial intercourse with the British possessions on the Atlantic side of North America. The instructions included the examination of the coast between 30° and 60°N, and, on the return, of the Chilean coast south of Chiloé, if possible.[94]

The command was given to George Vancouver, another graduate from Cook's school; he sailed from Falmouth on 1 April 1791 in the *Discovery*, 340 tons, with William Broughton in the *Chatham*, 135 tons, crank and deep-drafted for her size, not the best choice for tricky inshore work, of which there would be plenty. The ships went by the Cape to southwest New Holland, where they discovered King George's Sound (Albany), reaching Dusky Bay, New Zealand, on 2 November. After sailing on the 23rd they were at once separated by a storm; Broughton found the Chatham Islands and reached Matavai Bay on 26 December, where Vancouver joined him four days later, having discovered Rapa in the Austral group. They sailed again on 24 January 1792 and on 29 February sighted Hawai'i. In Tahiti Vancouver had been pained by the decline in traditional arts, already working for the sailors' tourist trade, and dependence on European artefacts; in Hawaii he was still more grieved by the constant demand for muskets, which he neatly evaded by declaring them tapu'd by King George.

On 16 March Vancouver sailed from Niihau; a month later he made landfall at 39°50'N, near Cape Mendocino, and stood north. On 27 April discoloured water suggested a large river nearby; two days later the first sail met in eight months was by a striking coincidence the *Columbia* under Robert Gray, who was astonished to be shown the *Washington's* track credited to him by Meares. He also told Vancouver of a river which he had been unable to enter; this was the Columbia, surmised only two days before, which Gray himself was to penetrate and name twelve days later.[95]

On the 30th the ships entered Juan de Fuca Strait and the survey proper began; in May Lieutenant Peter Puget explored the hitherto unknown maze of waterways connected with Puget Sound. On 22 June the meeting with Galiano and Valdés took place, and Vancouver learned that Bodega y Quadra was awaiting him at Nootka. Spaniards and British sailed together until 13 July and parted amicably; it was the former who found the best passage to Queen Charlotte Strait and the Pacific north of Vancouver Island. Vancouver stood north until on 17 August he was told by a fur trader that his storeship *Daedalus* had reached Nootka. He accordingly turned for the Sound, arriving on 28 August, three days before Galiano and Valdés; these were the first known circumnavigations of what Vancouver named 'the Island of Quadra and Vancouver'.

This name happily, if clumsily, symbolised the personal relations of the two men, but not the political. Even had John Meares been an honest man, it would probably have been impossible to ascertain exactly how much land he had acquired from Maquinna; Quadra was prepared to hand over only the tiny triangle where Meares had built his post, and Vancouver, left throughout the voyage without any political guidance, could not accept this. It was agreed to disagree, referring the problem to Europe; Lieutenant Zachary Mudge was sent to Macao with despatches, on a Portuguese fur trader, and on 12 October Vancouver sailed south. He had found the Nootka people also changed for the worse; 'Iron was a mere drug', and as in Hawaii the demand was for muskets.

On 14 November Vancouver reached San Francisco, where he was joined by Broughton, who had been detached to explore the Columbia River; their reception was most cordial, but they were taken aback to find no sign of a town except the isolated Presidio. Things were better at Monterey, where all three ships were briefly united. The *Daedalus* was sent to Sydney, with a gift of livestock from Quadra, and from Vancouver a request that Governor Phillip should send her to Nootka with a year's supplies for the other two ships (the colony was just emerging from semi-starvation). Broughton was ordered home with despatches, travelling with Quadra as far as San Blas, and on 14 January 1793 Vancouver sailed for Hawaii, with Puget commanding the *Chatham*.

On the way he sought, as fruitlessly as had La Pérouse, for the 'los Mayos' islands shown in a chart given him by Quadra.[96] On this second Hawaiian visit Vancouver became ever more concerned over the destitution of the people by wars and the demands of the fur traders for supplies, which they were too willing to pay for with muskets; a cycle of impoverishment. He did what he could to recommend peace, and dropped the first hints of cession to Britain as a solution.

Leaving at the end of March, Vancouver reached Nootka on 20 May; the *Chatham*, sent on ahead from Maui, had arrived in mid-April and left on 18 May. Vancouver noted that the Spaniards had strengthened their hold by building a fort carrying eleven guns. He spent only a couple of days in port; on 26 May he met the *Chatham* near Fitzhugh Sound, on the mainland north of Queen Charlotte Strait. From then until 8 September he pressed on to the north of Prince of Wales Island, and his boats went further to about 57°30′N. Coincidentally, Alexander Mackenzie was approaching the coast on the first transcontinental crossing just as Vancouver was working his way up it; they missed meeting by a month or so.[97]

It is impossible to summarise his 'perplexing, tedious, and laborious' movements in this labyrinth of channels; at one point 'we had been almost intirely confined to the boats for twenty-three days; in which time we had traversed upwards of 700 geographical miles [1300 km] without having advanced our primary object, that of tracing the continental boundary, more than 20 leagues [111 km] from the station of the vessels.'[98] Much of this work was in cold and rainy weather, some of it on short commons. Vancouver felt that de Fonte's name could now be erased from the map, but he was generous in bestowing compliments—apart from British not-ables and the House of Hanover, he honoured Behm, Caamaño, Revilla Gigedo, Chirikov, even [Ambrosio O']Higgins.

On his return to Nootka on 3 October, Vancouver was disappointed to find neither the *Daedalus* from Sydney nor new instructions. He pressed on to continue the survey, as originally instructed, 'on the southern parts of [Drake's] New Albion' to 30°N. Spanish policy and personnel had changed, and his reception was ungracious, although subordinate officials and the mission Fathers were more helpful. The *Daedalus* caught him up between San Francisco and Monterey; Vancouver called at two or three missions—at Los Angeles, founded in 1781, the view from the sea showed '[n]either habitation or inhabitants'—and San Diego, leaving Baja California in 30°19'N, on 14 December.

He made a quick passage to Hawai'i, reached on 8 January 1794. He was warmly welcomed by Kamehameha (Tamaahmaah'), with whom he had established most cordial relations on his earlier visits, so cordial indeed that he acted as a marriage counsellor, reconciling the King and his estranged wife Kaahumanu ('Tahow-man-noo'). More in keeping with the normal role of a Captain R.N. was his negotiation of the cession of Hawai'i to the British Crown, really as a protectorate since there was to be no interference with religion, government, or 'domestic oecon-omy'.[99] Vancouver's genuine concern over the calamities of gun-running and internecine warfare was indubitable, but he was not of course unmind-ful of Hawai'i's strategic and commercial potential, nor was Kamehameha unmindful of the value of a 'special relationship' to his own hegemonic ambitions; but the cession had minimal practical effect.

For his last campaign in the Northeast Vancouver reversed his approach, sailing direct from Niihau on 14 March to reach Chirikov Island on 3 April and thence working east and south. He visited the Russian posts in Cook's River, which he restyled Cook Inlet; ice and snow were added to the normal impediments. The season's work, again marked by the most painstaking boat surveys, included Prince William's Sound, Cross Sound, the Chichagof and Baranof Islands (Vancouver's King George III Archipelago), and the channels between these and the main. By mid-

August Vancouver and Puget had linked up with their 1793 explorations; they were back at Nootka on 2 September.

In three seasons, a little over thirteen months, they had surveyed the coasts from Chirikof Island to Puget Sound, over 16° of latitude embracing most intricate mazes of islands and channels, and there were also the extensions to Hawaii and California, and on the return journey visits to the Galápagos and Juan Fernández groups. As an explorer Vancouver was the greatest of Cook's pupils.

The return was by the Horn; Vancouver left the *Discovery* in Ireland in September 1795 and she anchored in the Thames on 20 October. There had been only six deaths, none from scurvy, out of 146 men in a voyage lasting over four and a half years; but the *Discovery* was not always a happy ship. Vancouver seems to have been harsh and irascible; as with the later Cook, there were probably physiological reasons for this.[1] He survived his wearing voyage for less than three years, dying at forty-one. He had most worthily concluded a great era of primary exploration.

His work marked the end of a dream which had held the mind of Atlantic man for three centuries, the dream of a waterway, practicable for ships under sail, through temperate North America. Between them Cook and Vancouver had demonstrated that any passage linking Europe with Cathay must lie well beyond the Arctic Circle.

Chapter 9

SCURVY AND SCIENCE

Thus hath it fared with many Heroes and most worthy
persons, who being sufficiently commendable from true
and unquestionable merits, have received advancement
from falsehood and the fruitfull stock of fables.

The mountains wooded to the peak, the lawns
And winding glens high up like ways to Heaven,
The slender coco's drooping crown of plumes,
The lightning flash of insect and of bird,
The lustre of the long convolvuluses
That coil'd around the stately stems, and ran
Ev'n to the limit of the land, the glows
And glories of the broad belt of the world,
All these he saw ...

In 1757, seven years before Byron opened the great series of circumnavigations which ended with Vancouver in 1794, the amiable but minor
poet and painter John Dyer published a striking forecast of the coming
day when all the realms from California to Japan should be clothed with
good British woollens, and also the green South Sea isles which 'Not
yet are figured on the sailor's chart'.[1] He was oddly wrong in detail;
it was not so much a matter of clothing the Chinese in British cloth
as in American furs and of lighting the houses of Europe with whale
oil (and stiffening her ladies' corsets with whalebone); and 'proud Japan'
was to remain proudly closed. Yet the thirty years after Byron did see
revolutionary change in the Pacific; the Ocean was not only explored
but figured on the sailor's chart, and for the first time Europeans began
not just to traverse the South Sea but to *use* it. Dyer was sufficiently
impressed by the Power of Trade to grasp the heart of the matter: the
Pacific was to be brought into the world market.

Although by 1794 the fur trade in the northeast and whaling in the
southeast were only a few years old, the North Pacific was no longer
empty save for the annual Galleon between Manila and Acapulco but
was crossed by an active shipping which was already developing its own
node in Hawaii; in the South Pacific, Tahiti was a familiar, and seductive,

---

Sir Thomas Browne, *Pseudodoxia Epidemica* (1646), Book IV Ch. XII;
Alfred Tennyson, *Enoch Arden* (1864). The application of the first
quotation is to Cook and scurvy.

home from home for European seamen. In what had been New Holland, Sydney had been founded, to become a centre for entrepreneurial activity over a great arc from the New Hebrides through Fiji and Tahiti to New Zealand. All these elements were in their infancy; but they had been born, and were revolutionary in import. A positional geography had been established, an economic geography was taking shape.

This change in geographic values, from emptiness to use, itself was linked with technological changes in varying balances of cause and effect. The chronometric revolution was not yet for the common run of captains, naval as well as merchant, owing to the high cost of timepieces; it had to wait till well into the next century for its full effect; but it began with Cook's second voyage, and Malaspina sailed in 1789 with six chronometers. The preparation for voyages of long duration grew ever more sophisticated; gone were the days when Dampier and Cartaret could be thrown round the world in the wretched *Roebuck* and *Swallow*; now ships were chosen, or specially built, with careful attention to their proposed tasks. Care for the health of seamen was for the first time put on a quasi-scientific footing, with striking savings in mortality.

In the field sciences, immense gains were made, and at least the beginnings of ethnography are to be found in these three decades. And only just outside the thirty years lay the initiation of a movement which in time was to revolutionise much in the manner of life and mode of thinking of Pacific Islanders: the London Missionary Society was founded in 1795, and Tahiti became its first base in the South Seas in 1797.

Not only was the image of the Pacific changed; in its avatars of the Tahitian Venus and the (so-called) Noble Savage the image itself contributed powerfully to changing the sensibility of the age. While it is true that 'The "completed" geographic world of Cook and La Pérouse marks the arrival of positive geography whence dreams and utopias would be pitilessly banished',[2] this is only half the story. Certainly there was no room in this new physical world for the ancient geographical myths, Terra Australis the 'Great Sea of the West', de Fonte and Maldonado; but alongside or even coextensive with it was a human 'New World' analogous to that which Columbus found,[3] a vast new field for imagination and speculation, engendering new myths of its own, myths which still survive, utterly debased, in the touristic or novelistic picture of the South Seas.

The Pacific enclosed and displayed

The great burst of exploring activity of these years is comparable only with that which succeeded the voyages of Columbus and Vasco da Gama. Vague or hypothetical outlines were replaced by reasonably accurate plottings of coasts; wandering island groups—the Solomons, the Marquesas—were fixed, their 'various capes' increasingly 'figured on the sailor's chart'; bounds were set to the Ocean: northwards from California to the Arctic and in the mysterious sea-marches between Kamchatka, Japan and Tartary, while in the south Cook had skirted its icy limits. Nor had the variation of the magnetic steel—Dyer's phrase—been neglected or the currents left unmarked. Estimation was more and more replaced by precise determination; a fundamental datum was established by Bougainville's astronomer Véron, whose observation of a solar eclipse in New Ireland provided an accurate figure for the breadth of the Pacific. With the introduction of lunar distances and chronometers the number of such precise determinations proliferated.

Hawkesworth's narratives of the earlier voyages, from Byron to Cook's first, doctored as they were to appeal to a rather florid contemporary taste, had a catalytic effect similar to that of Dampier's *New Voyage round the World* three-quarters of a century earlier: *Voyages* poured from the presses, and became a specialism of some publishers: John Stockdale for example succeeded to the mantle of James Knapton in Queen Anne's day. The volumes have a striking family resemblance; there was in fact almost a standard form, which makes them easy to use compared with the less routinely structured earlier narratives. Although few of the later authors, if any except George Forster, have the charm of Dampier or his readability, the nautical content of their books is more consistent and coherent, their charts and plans as a rule much more sophisticated than those of their predecessors. In some of the more elaborate and official accounts complete suites of precisely determined positions were published, either as an integral part of the original publication, as in Rossel's *Voyage de Dentrecasteaux*, or as a separate work like *The Original Astronomical Observations* from Cook's second voyage, by William Wales and William Bayly. These serried masses of figures were obviously not for the general reader, then or now, but were invaluable to the marine cartographer, and they testify to the advance in scientific sophistication.

The first half of the eighteenth century added very little indeed to the map of 1700. The landfalls of Bering and Chirikov were hardly assimilated intelligibly into the corpus of geographical knowledge before Müller's maps of 1754–8, if indeed then,[4] and apart from these, discoveries were limited to Dampier Strait; Tobi or Helen Reef and Palau in the Carolines (and these may have been seen by the Portuguese in the sixteenth century); and Roggeveen's Easter Island, Makatea, three atolls in the Tuamotus, and glimpses of Borabora and Maupiti and in the Samoan group:[5] a very thin haul for half a century. Byron found four Tuamotuan atolls; Cartaret did better, but his most notable find—Pitcairn—was uninhabited and became notable only through a later historical accident. But when Wallis reached Tahiti he found not only one of the most attractive South Sea Islands but a productive and (once terrorised) a friendly base for further exploration.

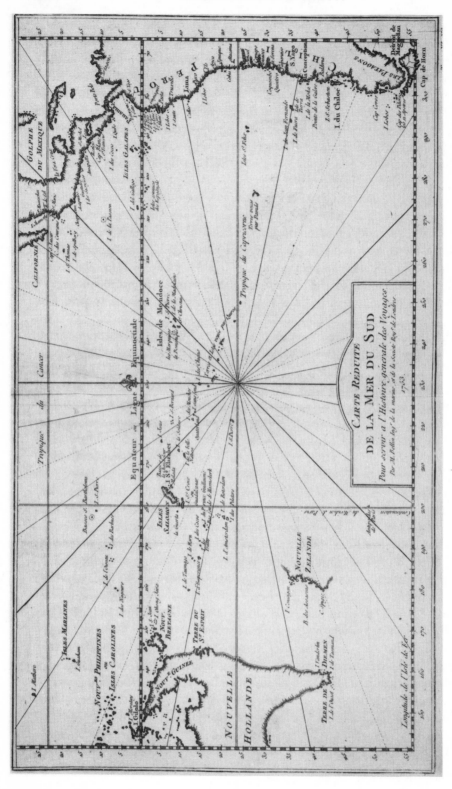

Plate X. THE PACIFIC IN 1753. Bellin's Carte Réduite de la Mer du Sud. Note the impaction of Quiros's Terre Australe du St Esprit into New Holland, and the separation of the Solomons and actually adjacent New Britain by over 30° of longitude; well might Bougainville complain 'O Bellin combien vous nous coûtez!'. By permission of National Library of Australia, Canberra.

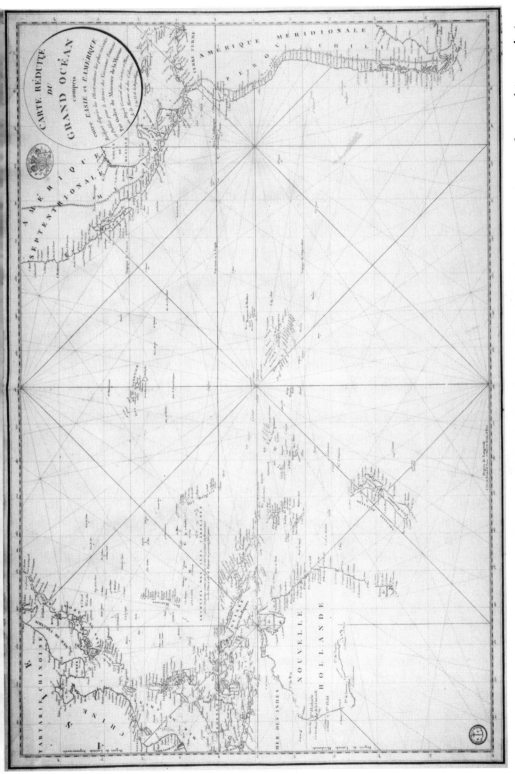

Plate XI. THE PACIFIC IN 1799. Poirson's Carte Réduite du Grand Océan. The Pacific has taken on its true form and its wandering islands have become fixed. By permission of National Library of Australia, Canberra.

This was indeed a key factor. As J. A. Williamson pointed out,

> Byron, Wallis, Cartaret, and Bougainville had all sailed with the quest of the southern continent as one of their primary objects. They had all failed to close with the problem... [because] when they approached the scene of action their crews had become too sickly and their ships too feeble in hull and gear to permit of a struggle with the tempestuous weather of the south temperate zone.[6] All had therefore edged northward for supplies and repairs.

It seems, however, too simple to follow Williamson in ascribing Cook's success, where his predecessors had failed, solely to his own superior personal qualities, real as these were. He had the great advantage over them of knowing exactly where to go for the rest and refreshment which enabled him to keep the seas, and that indeed was where he was instructed to go to observe the Transit. It was Tahiti, supplemented in the south by Queen Charlotte Sound, that enabled him not just to traverse but to quarter the South Pacific and, to adapt Numa Broc, to crumble Terra Australis into archipelagoes; and in the North Pacific, Hawaii was to provide a like service for himself and his disciple Vancouver, as well as a base for the fur traders.

'While Cook was gathering the richest harvest, the French were wrangling over the crumbs from the feast... Towards 1775, only one great geographical problem remained to be solved in the Pacific, that of the Northwest Passage',[7] which of course from a Pacific point of view is the Northeast. Broc perhaps overstates: there was still a great deal of confusion on the fog-bound northwestern shores of the Ocean, the mysterious land of Yezo or Jesso and its relations with Tartary on the one hand and Japan on the other. This must be admitted a sizeable crumb; the problem was solved by La Pérouse in 1787 and his solution was confirmed by Broughton ten years later, although the insularity of Sakhalin was not absolutely established for Europeans until the next century.

On the opposite shores, Cook set the general bounds of the Ocean but he perforce left a large gap north of Vancouver Island, and here took place the last rally of the Fonteans and the Fucoids. The work of the Spaniards, the fur-traders, and Vancouver filled this void, and with this the Pacific was enclosed. By the end of the century, the lineaments and much, if not most, of the detail of all the island groups had been displayed, more or less accurately, on the charts. And also the seal had been set on 'what is far more important to meteorology... the numerical relations of land and water on the face of our planet [were finally] freed from the highly erroneous views with which they had hitherto been regarded.'[8]

Long before, this great sector of the earth's surface, overwhelmingly more sea than land, had been the last of the world's realms to be occupied by men and women, in the superb diaspora of the Polynesians. In its limited and strictly sporadic environment they had built complex cultures, from it a rich mythology; and now European man had marked it down on paper with precise physical co-ordinates. For both Islanders and Europeans, the psychological bearings of this achievement were imperfect and imprecise.

A revolution postponed: the 'conquest' of scurvy

Few myths about James Cook have been so enduring or so widespread as that which claims that he 'conquered' scurvy. He did not; he evaded it, a considerable though not entirely unprecedented achievement, for which he received the Royal Society's Copley Medal. But the true way to the conquest of scurvy had been shown by James Lind fifteen years before the *Endeavour* sailed. It is rather difficult to believe that Cook had never heard of Lind's work, since Palliser, Cook's patron, had been very effectively advised by Lind;[9] and if he did know of it, his disregard for it must appear unscientific and opinionated. His constant search for greenstuffs as anti-scorbutic was anything but a novelty—it had been an almost instinctive practice of sailors for centuries—while on the other hand his insistence on useless prophylactics such as the wort of malt meant that his 'voyages delayed rather than hastened the introduction of the true cure' of the disease which 'killed more men and paralysed more fleets than any series of naval actions'.[10]

No better comment on this last dictum could be imagined than the experience of Anson's fleet: of its estimated 1410 deaths—73 per cent of the original force—997 are ascribed to scruvy, against four killed in action.[11] The description in *Anson's Voyage* was indeed to become classic:

> large discoloured spots over the whole surface of the body, swelled legs, putrid gums, and above all, an extraordinary lassitude ... [which] at last degenerates into a proneness of swoon on the least assertion of strength, or even on the least motion ... a strange dejection of spirits ... with shiverings, tremblings, and a disposition to be seized with the most dreadful terrors on the slightest accident ...[12]

There could be few more loathly ways to die: ghastly ulcers developed, teeth fell from stinking rotting gums, wounds healed years before broke out afresh, there were internal and external haemorrhages; that there should be a 'dejection of the spirits' does not seem strange. The magnitude of Anson's disaster was, it is true, exceptional; he had had an unusually frightful passage round the Horn, psychologically as well as physically, and his 259 veteran pensioners were guaranteed victims, sent to their horrible deaths by bureaucratic callousness.

It is now well known that scurvy is due to a deficiency of vitamin C, which is found in fresh vegetables and especially in citrus fruit.

Completely fresh meat, the less cooked the better, has some anti-scorbutic tendency. Scurvy was endemic amongst the poor in winter in many parts of northern Europe, owing to the complete lack of fresh vegetables, let alone fruit, but tended to clear up in spring as greenstuffs of some sort became available. Naval ration scales were quantitatively generous, probably much more so than the average diet of the poorer classes, urban or rural, and in terms of calories were very adequate: a daily intake of 4500 calories in the British navy, 4000 in the French, and the latter at least was reasonably balanced between carbohydrates, fats, and proteins.[13] But even if the supplies were of the first quality, which happened most rarely, the diet might almost have been designed to bring on scurvy.

The British official ration was confined to hard ships' biscuit (flour would not keep, so baking at sea was rare), beer (a gallon a day per man), salt beef and pork, dried peas, oatmeal, butter, and cheese; plus the sacred tot of grog. On the whole the French diet had more variety in dried vegetables and was better cooked and dressed, but British salted meats seem to have been preferable to French.

However excellent the provisions when packed, preservation for more than a few months was very difficult indeed in the 'sweaty' conditions below deck in wooden ships; and victuallers often supplied bad provisions poorly packed. The only containers were sacks, casks, and barrels, not all of which were completely air-tight; butter in particular rapidly became rancid, and could be used to lubricate rigging blocks, though conversely the cheese could become hard enough to be carved into buttons. Ships' biscuit had to be softened before it could be eaten, and was often infested with the larvae of weevils. It is not surprising that Bougainville wrote 'The provisions... had so cadaverous a smell, that the hardest moments of the sad days we passed, were those when the bell gave us notice to take in this disgusting and unwholesome food.'[14]

This was written when Bougainville's officers had been reduced to the same ration as the lower deck, which was not the normal case. Officers carried their own preserved provisions, liquid and other, and the staff commissariat often included live animals, sometimes almost a small farm-yard—Dr Johnson wrote a Latin distich, which Boswell Englished, on the goat which furnished Cook with milk on two circumnavigations, more fortunate than her sister Amalthée, who was tearfully sacrificed for Bougainville's starving crew.[15] The livestock of course did not add to shipboard salubrity, and their feeding and watering presented problems; but officers were much better fed than seamen and had a markedly lower incidence of scurvy. Decent officers helped the sick from their private stores, and in real emergencies, such as Bougainville's in New Guinean waters, it was share and share alike—including, on the *Boudeuse*, the officers sharing (on payment) the rats caught by the crew: no less a personage than Prince Charles-Nicolas-Othon d'Orange et de Nassau-Siegen ate them with pleasure—and with more profit than he knew, for rats synthesise a little vitamin C, enough to prevent or at least hold in check the worst forms of scurvy.[16]

While vitamin C deficiency is basic, a sufficient cause of scurvy, other factors helped to make men more susceptible to its attack—dirt, foul air, cold, wet clothing, stress, fear, incessant fatigue; Anson hinted at psychological as well as physical strain as a component of the scurvy syndrome, Lind called the factors listed 'predisposing causes'. Of most of these there was an abundance on almost any voyage entering the Pacific, especially by Cape Horn. It was indeed the appalling experiences of Anson's voyage, both here and between Mexico and the Marianas, which—as well they might—gave the impetus for James Lind's critically important *A Treatise of the Scurvy*,[17] dedicated to the Commodore himself, now Admiral and First Lord.

Not that there were not plenty of treatises before Lind—he himself enumerates sixty-one authors between 1534 and 1753, presenting a wide choice of alleged causes and cures; but most of these were based on antiquated medical theory, 'the humours' and the like, or on poor obser-vation and merely impressionistic empiricism. Lind brought to bear, for the first time, a truly *scientific* empiricism; in fact, in 1747 he carried out what is generally regarded as the first medical experiment with a proper control on record. This consisted of taking twelve scurvy cases, 'as similar as I could have them', in identical conditions of food and lodging, dividing into couples, and treating each pair with one of the standard remedies (which included 'elixir of vitriol'!). One pair received daily two oranges and a lemon each, and these two showed 'the most sudden and visible good effects', one man being fit for duty in six days. In general, 'nothing will avail where the patient cannot have vegetables or fruits', though spruce beer, raw onions, pickled cabbage, bottled goo-seberries, cresses grown on shipboard, and cider were seen as having some value, and indeed only cider contain no vitamin C; but Lind returns again and again to the superior virtue of citrus.[18]

The main difficulty was preservation of the juice; Lind gave directions for making a 'rob' or syrup of lemons by heating, which would have destroyed much of their vitamin C, as J. R. Forster suspected. He himself swore, erroneously, by sauerkraut and wort. Later it was found that adding 10 per cent of alcohol acted as a preservative while retaining the full antiscorbutic value.[19]

Citrus was by no means new; Lind cited a dozen medical writers who had reported or recommended its use, as prophylactic or cure, and practical seamen had used it for both purposes since the sixteenth century at least. But other captains pinned their faith on other remedies, including burying to the neck in warm sand, Bishop Berkeley's beloved panacea tar-water, and of course grog; until Lind there had been no sustained gathering and evaluating of the evidence by a man of critical powers. Yet there was plenty of experience. Richard Hawkins in 1593 found oranges and lemons 'a certaine remedie for this infirmitie'; James Lancaster, on the first Indies voyage by the EIC (1600–2), kept his ship's company in pretty good health by lemon juice while his three consorts, without it, lost heavily—an undesignedly controlled experiment! Le Maire in 1615–16 did suffer from scurvy in mid-Pacific, but in a voyage of seventeen months lost only three men, only one of them—Jan Schouten—to that disease, and owed this good record to thousands of lemons bought in Sierra Leone.[20] Another notable pre-Cook voyage was that of Palliser to the East Indies in 1748–50: over fourteen months with a single death ('in a Salivation for Pox')—and before sailing Palliser had been advised by Lind.[21]

Thus when Cook sailed there should have been ample warrant for a test of Lind's methods. The issue was clouded, however, by the insistence of the physician David MacBride on the surpassing antiscorbutic value of wort (infusion) of malt. In fact, it had no such value; but MacBride had contacts with Palliser and Sandwich and despite initial adverse reports a test at sea was authorised. It was carried out on the *Jason's* voyage to the Falklands by Captain John MacBride RN, David's brother and hardly an unprejudiced witness, and was farcical; the one scurvy patient treated with wort also ate apples and oranges. MacBride's claims were nevertheless accepted, and despite a further unfavourable report by Cartaret, Cook was instructed to try the wort as well as 'portable soup' in glue-like blocks, sauerkraut, and Baron Storsch's carrot marmalade. These had some nutrient value and added some variety—not always welcomed by the British tar!—to diet, but were of little or no use against scurvy.[22]

Although Cook's own ships had some scurvy, there is no doubt that its incidence was minimal, as shown by the contrasting records of his well-run *Resolution* and Furneaux's *Adventure* on the second voyage. Much of this success was due to preventive measures on Lind's lines; Wallis had led the way, with marked effect, in applying what now seem the most elementary of rules. Like him, Cook insisted on cleanliness, saw that the men had warm and as far as possible dry clothes, and on Wallis's advice put them on three watches instead of the usual two, thus giving longer rest periods than were customary.[23] On his first two voyages he had picked crews; selection was not so good on the third, owing to the demands of the looming American War, and this was perhaps a contributory factor to the more stressful atmosphere of this voyage. But his prophylactic rules were excellent, and were faithfully followed by his pupils such as Bligh and Vancouver. Cook's island-hopping progress also meant, for large sectors of his traverses, short passages and many stops, many opportunities to seek out fresh vegetable foods.

While Cook thus escaped scurvy, as a test of antiscorbutics his voyages were failures; so many nostrums were tried, without controls, that it was like killing a bird with a shot-gun: impossible to say which particular pellet was fatal, but this was masked by the general effect. The report of the *Endeavour's* surgeon William Perry, forwarded by Cook to the Admiralty as an official professional verdict, was virtually self-contradictory:

> It is impossible for me to say what was most conducive to our preservation from Scurvy so many being the preventives used: but . . .
> I shall not hesitate a moment to declare my opinion, viz. that the Malt is the best medicine I know, the inspissated Orange & Lemon juices not even excepted.

This in face of the fact that Banks had actually cured himself of an attack of scurvy by using lemon juice—not, one would imagine, a feat he would have kept quiet about.[24]

On the second voyage Cook seems to have taken little interest in the rob (syrup) of oranges and lemons, remarking that this was 'wholy under ye Surgeons care', but affirmed his faith in sauerkraut, and especially in the wort of malt as a preventive. He thought that malt would seldom prove a cure, but 'we have been a long time without any, without feeling ye need of it, which might be owing to other Articles'; his surgeon James Patten was equally firm on the virtues of malt and equally vague on specific reasoning.[25] And finally Cook in effect delivered the *coup de grâce* in a letter to Sir John Pringle, President of the Royal Society:

> I entirely agree with you that the dearness of the rob of lemons and oranges will hinder them from being furnished in large quantities. But I do not think this so necessary; for though they may assist other things, I have no great opinion of them alone.

Indeed, with fresh water and strict cleanliness 'a ship's company will seldom be afflicted with the scurvy' even without antiscorbutics.[26]

One cannot of course blame Cook for not grasping and applying modern scientific principles, in a field not his own; yet, tragically, these words and those of his surgeons held back the general recognition of the true cure of scurvy and thereby, all unwittingly, spelled death for hundreds if not thousands of seamen in the American War. It was not until 1795 that the persistent pressure of Lind's disciples Sir Gilbert Blane and Thomas Trotter brought the Admiralty to make a regular compulsory issue of lemon juice.[27] In 1760, when the authorised enrolment of seamen and marines was 70,000, the Haslar naval hospital treated 1754 scurvy cases; in 1806, with an enrolment of 120,000—just one.[28] The revolution in the health of seamen had been long delayed, and was not at the hands of Cook; but it had come. Despite the setback of 1846, when for economic reasons the Admiralty supplanted lemon juice by the much inferior lime (thereby adding a word to the American language), James Lind had done his work well.

Banks and botany

Anson's refuges from scurvy, 'The happy isles of Tinian and Juan Fernández, doubly linked with the literary fortunes of *Robinson Crusoe* and *la Nouvelle-Héloïse*, furnished the dreams of a whole generation'; the latter's hyper-sentimental hero Saint-Preux is indeed represented as a companion of Anson. As well as shipping Julie's lover to the South Seas, Rousseau called for 'a veritable mobilisation of the philosophic tribe': if men of the calibre of Montesquieu, Buffon, Diderot, d'Alembert were to undertake world-wide voyages ('not forgetting the Patagonians, true or false'), and to write 'the natural, moral and political history of what they had seen, we should see a new world arise from under their pens, and we would thus learn to know our own world'. These 'prophetic lines' were written in 1754; twelve years later ' "Philosophy" embarked with Bougainville for the shores of the Pacific...'.[29] But it was Joseph Banks who brought in the first scientific harvest.

The twins astronomy and geography, the oldest branches of human knowledge dependent on exact observation and record and so the first sciences, were the prime though not the exclusive concerns of the navigators; the three kingdoms, animal, vegetable and mineral and their overlord Man,[30] those of the naturalists they carried with them. The South Seas were not rich mineralogically, though there was the engaging geomorphological problem of the myriads of coral islands; the vertebrate terrestrial fauna, apart from birds, was scanty. Much the most prominent land animal was *Homo sapiens*, and it is probably not too much to say that the beginnings of serious field ethnography are to be found in the observations of Cook, Banks, and the Forsters; there were inevitable misunderstandings some of which will be discussed in later chapters. Of the field sciences, in that time and place botany was much the most fruitful.

Although Bougainville's was the first voyage to carry an official naturalist, this seems to have been with the ulterior motive of identifying spice plants for introduction to Ile de France. The naturalist, Philippe Commerson, was a competent scientist and had wider views, but he left the expedition at Ile de France and through the 'combined negligences' of himself and the royal officials at the Jardin des Plantes his notes and collections were dispersed. Commerson's contribution is thus negligible, and he is best known today for the roses and raptures of his absurd eulogy of Free Love, Tahitian style. This is a pity, as his 'Summary of observations in natural history'—an agenda, not a report of things actually observed—is comprehensive and sensible, quite in the Forsterian vein; there is some high-flown Enlightenment, but not very much, and most interesting ecological and even evolutionary hints—'an insensible transition from man to quadrupeds.'[31]

As Taillemitte remarks, the contrast with the harvest of Cook's first voyage is overwhelming (*écrasante*); Banks was able to report to the Académie des Sciences that he had brought back about 1000 species of plants hitherto undescribed, 500 birds, 500 fish: little wonder that on the Continent the voyage was often credited to the names of Banks and Solander. Despite the expenditure by Banks of perhaps £10,000 on engravings and other illustrations, the projected ten grand folios never appeared; it has been customary to ascribe this to the dilatoriness of his chief assistant, the too-sociable Swede Danial Carl Solander, but it seems at least as likely that the final cost appeared prohibitive.[32] There were over 950 botanical and nearly 300 zoological watercolours and drawings, mostly by Sydney Parkinson, and engravings were made of about 740 of them.[33]

The lack of formal publication did not mean that the collections were left to fust unused; rather they were constantly enhanced by contributions from Banks's protégés and colleagues in many parts of the world, and were readily accessible at his house in Soho Square, which became the centre of an extremely active information system. Much published work drew on his stores; in fact, the first specifically botanical publication from Cook's voyages, the Forsters' *Caracteres Generum Plantarum... Maris Australis* (1776) laid them open to charges of plagiarising Solander. While they may have made rather too free use of his material, their strained relations with Banks after the second voyage make it unlikely that they had sufficient access for the full charge to hold up.[34] Banks's own publications are few and rather slight, but he was far more than a dilettante; although he was not himself a great scientist, he was 'a scientific man of affairs... an amateur botanist of the highest calibre... an unusually discriminating patron of some very distinguished scientists.'[35]

Banks was then a magnificent organiser of research, for forty-one years from the commanding position of President of the Royal Society and for twenty-three as a full member of the royal Privy Council. It is an index of his power that 'within a year of Bligh's return from the catastrophe of the first breadfruit expedition', which he had initiated, 'Banks had prevailed on the government to send out a second, and that under the same luckless commander.'[36] He was as responsible as any man for the choice of Botany Bay as the first emplacement of a European society in what was to become Australia. He had probably the most widespread international reputation of any scientist before the later Humboldt, but amidst concerns which ranged over India, Africa, the Americas, he retained his interest in the continent he had trod as a young man with Cook; the Admiralty, the old row over the *Resolution* ignored, granted him virtually a free hand in the planning of Matthew Flinders's great circumnavigation which gave Australia its name. Well might Cook's companion James King look up to Banks as 'the common Center of we discoverers.'[37]

The Forsters: prickly pioneers

'My object was Nature in its greatest extent; the Earth, the Sea, the Air, the Organic and Animated Creation, and more particularly that class of Beings to which we ourselves belong'—such was Johann Reinhold Forster's ambitious programme when he and his son George set sail with Cook.[38] This was of course before the study of nature had crystallised out into bounded special disciplines, when 'A naturalist was anyone who subscribed to the study of the variety of the processes of the earth... right across its range. In the eighteenth century the test of mastery was breadth, not depth.'[39] Science was then not so separate from humanism and the arts as it became in the next century; moralising and elevated 'fine writing' were not considered incompatible with sober scientific observation and analysis. The Forsters certainly fitted the bill; they were in part inheritors of a German moralising pietistic tradition, in part men of the Enlightenment, in part avant-garde Romanticists. They ministered both to the scientific demands of the Enlightenment and to the emotional demands of the Age of Feeling.

They have had a generally bad press, at least in English, with extenuating circumstances being proffered for George as the victim of his father's ambition. This is too simple a view, but there can be no possible doubt that Johann Reinhold was usually difficult and sometimes impossible as a man and a colleague; the list of his faults and failings is not short. But his crabbed personality is no warrant for denigrating his virtues and achievements as a scientist, and these also were not few; yet this is what Beaglehole does in an uncharacteristically imperceptive and ungenerous note on Forster's *Observations*, while his portrait of the man does indeed 'seem simply caricature'. Even when he admits, as he must (not 'where we can'!) Foster's 'learning, the breadth of his interests', it is done most grudgingly: a lamentable lapse for a man of such humanity and attainment as Beaglehole.[40] A closer study shows Forster as a man of great devotion in the pursuit of knowledge and of no mean intellectual grasp.

Admittedly it is difficult not to type the Forsters, especially the father, as standard Teutonic Herr Doktor Professors, and this not from Beaglehole or the attacks of William Wales,[41] but from their own writings, which are often enough priggish and pompous to a painful degree. But the self-satisfaction, arrogance, and inordinate touchiness are generic rather than specific to the Forsters, not so much national traits as functions of a period when professional scientists were still struggling for acceptance in a milieu of genteel amateurism or open ridicule and hostility from very rude detractors.[42] There was a high index of prickliness; alongside the Forsters we must place Steller, Péron (much more vicious than ever Johann Reinhold was), Labillardière, perhaps even Archibald Menzies, though here the failing seems rather in Vancouver than in his naturalist. Nor was George Forster, at least, always on stilts: there is charm and geniality in his accounts of forest walks and 'marooning parties' in New Zealand, and humour (if rather heavy) in the comparison of cod-pieces, New Caledonian and European Renaissance, and in the Tahitian tale of the lady and the sheets.[43]

Plate XII. THE FORSTERS IN TAHITI. Painting by Rigaud of Johann Reinhold and George in the field. By courtesy of Herr Peter Rheinberger, Vaduz, Liechtenstein. Photo ANU.

Both Johann Reinhold's *Observations* and George's *Voyage* have their full share of the literary vices of the age—sentimental moralising and rhetoric taken to mawkish extremes, premature generalisation from limited data, tiresome girding at the corrupt luxury of Europe; but they have also much serious observation, shrewd commonsense, and pointed comment on the human condition. As a travel record the *Voyage* must be rated very high indeed; even Beaglehole admits that it has 'a force and charm beyond the reach of a great number of English professional writers of the time', and the great Alexander von Humboldt is glowing: 'all that can give truth, individuality, and distinctiveness to the delineation of exotic nature is united in his works.'[44] The *Observations* were the first general survey of both the physical and the human aspects of any oceanic area—and what an area, from Easter Island through the Marquesas, Tahiti, Tonga, the New Hebrides, to New Zealand and right round Antarctica! It was a review by a competent naturalist who 'combined a passion for empirical observation with a delight in philosophical speculation'; and indeed the *Observations* that Beaglehole rejected were to be built into the foundations of modern geography.[45] Besides Michael Hoare's avowedly rehabilitatory work, the Forsters are treated with respect, as pioneers of human and environmental science, by Glyndwr Williams and Clarence Glacken.[46]

The *Observations* are indeed wide-ranging, and over two-thirds of their 649 pages are devoted to 'Remarks on the Human Species in the South-Sea Isles'. The physical geography is naturally strongly influenced by Buffon, but at times Forster takes issue with that master, especially on the formation of sea-ice, on which his views are cogent. He is interesting on the formation of atolls and better on that of atoll islets, though here there is a striking example of the teleology which crops up from time to time: 'The animalcules forming these reefs, want to shelter their inhabitants [apparently 'the finest fish'!] from the impetuosity of the winds, and the power and rage of the ocean...'. Indeed there is a good deal of 'Natural Religion' in both the physical and the human sections of the book. George also has a wonderful blending of Natural Theology and Priestcraft, beautifully Enlightenment in a Voltaire-and-water manner.[47]

On the peopling of the Pacific, J. R. Forster distinguishes two races, an eastern and a western, corresponding to Polynesians and Melanesians (he does not of course use these terms), and, mainly on linguistic grounds, has no doubt of the ultimately Asian origins of the former, while the western isles were settled from New Guinea or thereabouts.[48] The marked contrast, in skin colour and in degree of culture, between two peoples living in the same latitudes gives Forster some trouble, since he inclines towards a sort of thermal determinism: in the vegetable and animal kingdoms there is an ascending scale from the empty horror of South Georgia through still horrible Tierra del Fuego and harsh New Zealand to the 'queen of tropical isles', Tahiti, where 'nature and art have united their efforts' to superb effect; and human types and societies fall into the same pattern.[49] But the Melanesians, though much better off than the wretched Pecherai of Tierra del Fuego, do present a break in the continuum. The anomaly is resolved with some plausibility by making the Melanesians stem ultimately from the small black hill tribes of the Malayan and Indonesian jungles—our Aeta, Sakai, Semang and so on— pushed into less favourable environments by the more numerous and more civilised littoral peoples.

Forster thinks that man was originally settled in the Tropics where food and shelter were easy to come by, and that 'the nations inhabiting the frozen extremities of our globe [are] degraded and debased', as is shown by the dreadful state of the Pecherai and the inferiority of the Maori in South Island to those in North. This shows his independence of thought; it is a striking shift from the fixation on temperate lands (Europe understood!) as the *juste milieu* for the flowering of civilisation, an idea which goes back at least as far as Aristotle and comes forward to Ellsworth Huntington in this century.[50]

Climate of course is a main factor in this, but in view of the Melanesian/ Polynesian contrast it cannot be the only cause. Forster sees the marginal peoples as forced out of the more favoured areas, progressively split into small and smaller groups which became confined simply to the search for necessities, especially food, and so gradually forgot 'the work of ages, and the result of the reason and the wits of thousands'. All human achievement 'ought to be considered as *the sum total of the efforts of mankind ever since its existence*'; but these pathetic relicts, the Pecherai for example, have lost all touch with the sources of civility and true happiness—'hardly a few sparks remain.'[51]

An eloquent passage, an interesting sociological theory of history leaving little or no place for the Noble Savage, a remarkable breakaway from the then conventional wisdom of a linear progression from hunting through pastoralism to agriculture and commerce, the current orthodoxy of the 'Four Stages';[52] but in its simplicity doomed to fallacy for lack of adequate data. So too with the sustained attempt to grasp and present the nature of Tahitian society. Here there is much useful information, but after all, Forster is trying to sort out, in a few weeks and with inadequate command of the language, ramifications which linguists and anthropologists have not yet unravelled to their own complete satisfaction. The wonder is that so much was achieved.

The Forsters' work is shot through with ambivalence. The picture of the South Seas is often idyllic, but realism will break in; conversely, the obsession with an imputed primitive simplicity of life and morals contraposed to the polished corruption of Europe makes them talk Rousseau's language despite themselves. 'The first view will convince the unprejudiced observer of the great happiness which reigns at O-Taheitee and the Society-isles. All the inhabitants are of an agreeable temper, and lovers of mirth and joy', and so on with prejudices apparent in every line. Yet, though *le mirage tahitien* exerts its innocent spell, even in this happy isle the trustful philosophic heart is shocked and grieved to find inequality and corruption, including an 'unexpected scene of immorality and selfishness'—the chief Potatou's offer of his wife to Cook, in exchange for red feathers—which quite damped the spirits of both Forsters.[53] George contrasts the Tahitians and Tongans—the latter 'seem to be ignorant of vices, which can only have arisen from a superior degree of opulence'; but a few pages after this impeccably Rousseauist sentiment the Malekulans, though the most intelligent people met in the South Seas, by their physique, chatter and grinning,

> often provoked us to make an ill-natured comparison between them and monkies. We should be sorry, however, to supply Rousseau, or the superficial philosophers who re-echo his maxims, with the shadow of an argument in favour of the orang-outan system. We rather pity than despise those men, who can so far forget and abuse their own intellectual faculties, as to degrade themselves to the rank of baboons.[54]

Voltaire would have approved.

Again, despite the corruption and vices bred by opulence, the savage and the barbarian live in a 'state of intoxication', their happiness being 'founded on mere sensuality, is transitory and delusive', and a man of any rationality must be glad to be born into a civilised society. Progress induced by European introductions—iron, livestock—will take much time, and there had been no opportunity to enlarge the Tahitians' minds with science or to improve their morals by instilling 'the spirit of charity, attachment, and disinterested love of the community'. But 'a nation's years are a man's moments', and there may be some hope even for the Pecherai from such contact. This is Johann Reinhold's view; George is less hopeful: the desire for luxuries and unrestrained indulgence in 'the impulses of nature'—sex—with resulting pressure of population could break up the easy-going patriarchalism of Tahitian society, leading to class conflict, even revolution. 'If the knowledge of a few individuals can only be acquired at such a price to the happiness of nations, it were better that the South Sea had still remained unknown to Europe and its restless inhabitants.'[55]

Enough has been said to give some idea of the temper and flavour of two books perhaps the most remarkable to come out of the eighteenth century Pacific. For all his flaws of personality, for all the extravagances of his writing, for all the theoretical fallacies which belonged to his age and which we see with hindsight, Johann Reinhold Forster's *Observations* is a comprehensive and courageous effort at understanding a new world, while his *Journal* is at once the documentation of a human tragi-comedy, a great if sad story of aspiration and frustration, and intellectually valuable as giving us an insight into a considerable mind, not obscurantist or behind the times but yet not in the forefront of the Enlightenment, but still in contact with a wide range of learned spirits, not a small figure in the Republic of Letters. And alone of the great theoreticians of terrestrial nature before Humboldt, he had seen that whereof he spoke.

The Forsters' botanical harvest was not so rich as that of Banks, who was first in the field in Tahiti and New Zealand and alone in New Holland, but it amounted to seventy-five new genera and at least 220 new species.[56] There were also extensive zoological collections, especially of course of birds and fish; but again, as with Banks, grandiose plans for publication came to nothing. There was, however, some sectional publication.

British expeditions after Cook's second voyage did not carry scientists as such, but reverted to surgeons—William Anderson on Cook's last voyage, Archibald Menzies with Vancouver; the latter pair carried on the tradition of strife between seamen and scientists. Both were competent botanists; it must be remembered that some botanical instruction was still often part of a medical training—the pharmacopia was still largely herbal.[57] La Pérouse and Malaspina had full complements of scientists, but shipwreck, literal in one case and political and perhaps amatory in the other, destroyed or dispersed their collections, although by devious ways some of those from Malaspina's voyage fell into the worthy hands of the great botanist Augustus de Candolle.[58] War and revolution also interfered with the publication of Labillardière's collections, though he regained them thanks to Banks's efforts, and only those of Baudin's expedition, but marginally of the century and of the Pacific, came home intact and secured adequate presentation.

The Oceanic contribution

The unveiling of this new world of wonders and delights could not fail to make a strong impact on an age much given to assiduous cultivation of its sensibilities, aesthetic and emotional. Bernard Smith's *European Vision and the South Pacific* renders any attempt to discuss the impact on the graphic arts superfluous, though it may be noted that one of his themes— the rendering of South Seas episodes in accordance with neo-classical ideas of decorum—was to some extent anticipated by J. R. Forster.[59] In any case, the impact was probably greater in the sphere of feeling than in that of taste, and this was the Age of Feeling. Sterne's *Sentimental Journey* and Mackenzie's *Man of Feeling*, its every chapter bathed in tears, appeared in the opening and the closing years of Cook's first voyage.

Early visitors to Tahiti might verbally repudiate Rousseau,[60] as did Geroge Forster and (privately) Bougainville,[61] but even without Commerson's uninhibited rhapsodies, there was enough in more sober reports for the ordinary reader to think that Jean-Jacques's imaginings had come true. Diderot's *Supplément au Voyage de Bougainville* was the most eminent but far from the only use of this material for direct attacks on the conventions and artificial *bienséances* of European society, by projecting Tahiti as an idyllic community where natural goodness reigned and natural desires were free. *Le mirage tahitien* was thus a powerful formative factor in that complex of feelings and idealisations that we call Romanticism and especially so in its avatar of the Tahitian Venus—

> Thus where pleased VENUS, in the southern main
> Sheds all her smiles on Otaheite's plain,
> Wide o'er the isle her silken net she draws,
> And the Loves laugh at all but Nature's laws.[61]

This euphoric image could not last. To some extent it rested on sheer exoticism, and was bound to dwindle as visits to the South Seas became more frequent, as the Heroes of Navigation were replaced by vulgar skippers trading in pork and sea-slugs. (It still survives after a fashion, in tourist brochures and on airport bookstalls.) With more evidence of the darker side of Island life—'treacherous natives', brutal warfare, human sacrifice, even cannibalism—the revolution of feeling was succeeded by a revulsion, which peaked in the Evangelicals' blanket damnation of the culture of an Oceania 'Where ev'ry prospect pleases And only man is vile'—nor was woman left out.

The three decades from Byron to Vancouver marked a crucial change in the frequency and intensity of European visitations. For the first time all the island groups were visited, and for the first time since Quiros contacts were more than fleeting; stays were marked not in hours or days but in weeks or months. After Quiros in 1606, Le Maire in 1616, Tasman in 1643, there was a blank of nearly six decades until Dampier in 1700; a few islands may have been picked up in the Marianas and western Carolines, but most of these had probably been sighted before

Figure 19–21. PACIFIC OUTLINES 1500–1600, 1600–1700, 1700–1800. Note the differences in periodisation of the three maps. There was very little European discovery in the Pacific between 1650 and 1725, and none at all in the next twenty-five years, except by the Russians in the north. About four-fifths of the island discoveries in Polynesia were made in 1750–75, as well as the filling-in of the coasts of New Zealand and eastern Australia. By 1800 all the shores of the Ocean were known, and all the archipelagos, though in them a large number of atolls were left for the nineteenth century. For Oceania, the maps are of necessity impressionistic, given the limitations of scale and the difficulties of island identification and of ascertaining priorities, but the rich harvest of 1750–75 is evident.

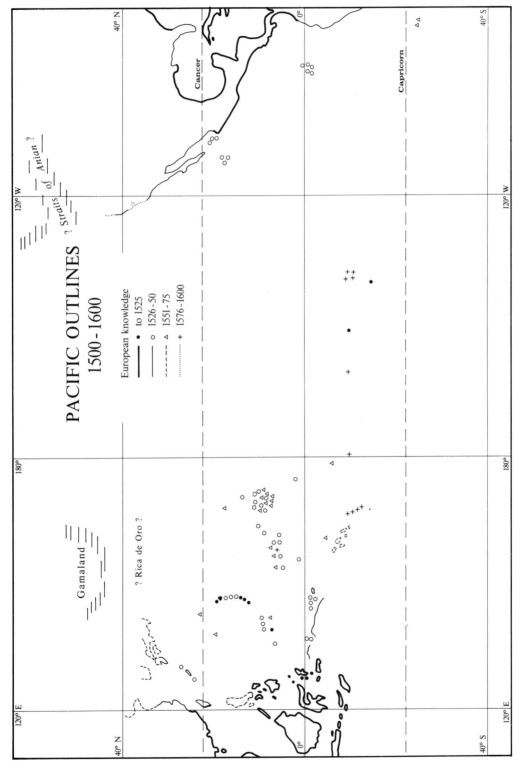

PACIFIC OUTLINES
1500 - 1600

European knowledge
•   to 1525
∘   1526 - 50
△   1551 - 75
+   1576 - 1600

? Straits of Anian ?

Cancer

Capricorn

Gamaland

? Rica de Oro ?

120° E
180°
120° W

40° N
40° S
0°

Figure 19.

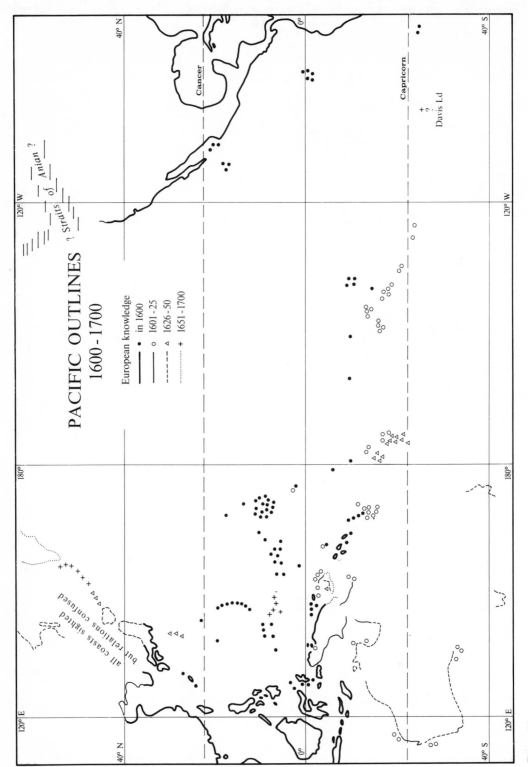

Figure 20.

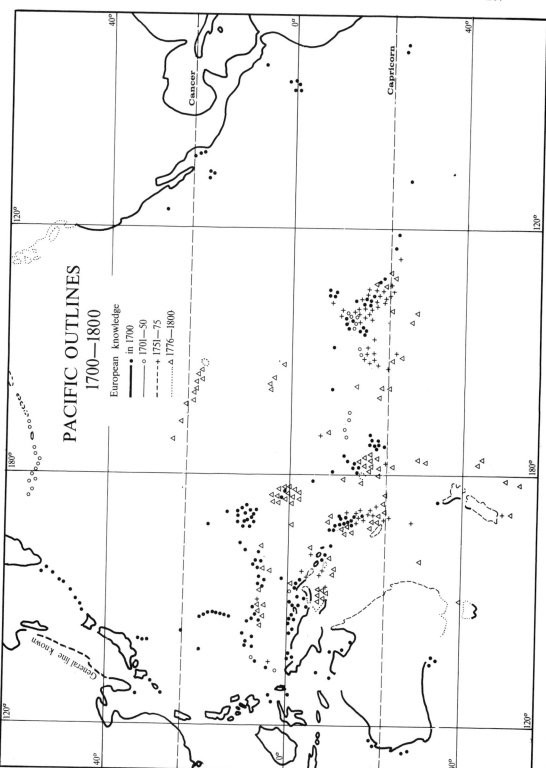

PACIFIC OUTLINES
1700—1800

European knowledge

● in 1700
○ 1701—50
+ 1751—75
△ 1776—1800

Cancer

Capricorn

General line known

Figure 21.

1606. Buccaneers and Malouins had nothing to do with the insular Pacific, save for Edward Davis's dubious land- or cloud-fall. There were twenty-two years between Dampier and Roggeveen, and then nearly twice as many before Byron reached the Pacific.

Only four significant explorations in 160 years, but then the rush: the longest interval between important voyages between 1764 and 1796 was five years, and at times there were two or three substantial expeditions in the South Seas simultaneously. Coupled with the longer stays, this was indeed a leap from quantity into quality, of revolutionary significance in the life of the Island peoples.

After 1795 one can no longer proceed by counting voyages; the fur trade, whaling and sealing, missionary activities, the rise of Sydney and Honolulu meant for the Ocean a criss-cross of voyaging, and for the Islanders a time of *Sturm und Drang*; but the Islands lost much of their magic. With exceptions—Melville, Stevenson, Gauguin—it was no longer a question of the mighty movement of Romanticism, but of petty romances and commercialised myths.

Although by the turn of the century the Islanders had contributed such important generalising concepts as *tapu* and *mana*, that freshness of the original impact of Oceania could not come again. In the world of learning the massive civilisations of India and China had a greater impact, though it may be doubted that they spoke so closely to the popular, not to say vulgar, heart of the West as did the South Seas. Yet Oceania has an important place in the growth of the field and even more the human sciences, in the European apprehension of the physical world and of mankind, and ideologically in the rise of Romanticism and in the acceptance of cultural relativism, this last perhaps its major contribution. In the thirty years after Byron's inept beginning, the Oceanic role was to act as a leaven, a ferment, in the revolution of sensibility; a creative contribution, buried for a while under the tides of commerce and Evangelicalism, but since Herman Melville and Paul Gauguin holding an assured place.

Chapter 10

CONDITIONS OF HUMANITY

The precious Gifts, whose boasted Aid we feel
Of pointed Iron, and of polish'd Steel, —
Boast tho' we may, to judge them by the past,
These Gifts may prove our fatal Foes at last.
By piercing Steel tho' proudest Forests fall
And take new forms at Man's Imperial Call,
By Steel too Man his Fellow Man destroys,
It tempts to plunder, and as Death destroys,
The dangerous Wealth exotic Wants inspires
Where equal Nature levell'd all Desires,
And, social Freedom sapp'd by envious Strife,
We risk at once our Morals and our life.

These enterprises familiarised the South Sea Islanders
to European persons, and manners, and traffic...
having discovered the Ahooa Indians... of Nootka
Sound, who had so far advanced from their savage state
as to refuse to sell to Mr. Strange, at any price,
the peltry which they had already engaged to Mr.
Hanna, these enterprises have ascertained this
exhilarating truth to mankind, that civilisation
and morals must for ever accompany each other.

The 'Fatal Impact?'

The Rev. Gerald Fitzgerald's very poor poem, in form an epistle from 'Queen Oberea' (Purea) to Captain Samuel Wallis, is subtitled 'The Influence of Art upon the Happiness of Nature'. Its theme was an ancient commonplace, strongly current in the Age of Feeling. Fitzgerald had been anticipated, in the year of Byron's voyage, by Charles Churchill in the vigorous opening of his satiric Utopia *Gotham*; Horace Walpole 'abominate[d] Mr Banks and Dr Solander, who routed the poor Otaheitans out of the centre of the ocean, and carried our abominable passions amongst them!'[1] But there were more witnesses than the poets and dilettantes: the explorers themselves.

In a famous passage, Cook wrote that the apparently wretched natives of New Holland were in reality 'far more happier than we Europeans',

G. Fitzgerald, *The Injured Islanders* (London 1779), 4; N. Portlock,
A Voyage... to the North-West Coast of America (London 1789), 3–4.

lacking knowledge of what they lacked, the conveniences and superfluities of Europe. Similarly Banks wrote of 'these I had almost said happy people' and moralised on the ease with which debilitating 'Luxuries degenerate into necessaries.'[2] Hawkesworth shifted the argument from New Holland to Tierra del Fuego.[3] His change of emphasis was subtle, but to the contemporary casual reader, if the equation of rude simplicity with happiness, or at least contentment, were true for the poor Fuegians, how immeasurably more true for those simple yet not rude Tahitians!

The Forsters were not 'soft primitivists'; they insisted on the superiority of civilisation over barbarism, *a fortiori* over savage life.[4] Yet the society of Tahiti appeared on the whole harmonious, and George Forster had forebodings: it was sincerely to be wished that intercourse with Europe might cease before civilised corruption reached 'that innocent race... fortunate in their innocence and simplicity... how much the introduction of foreign luxuries may hasten that fatal day, cannot be too frequently repeated.' His father thought that the Islands had too little to offer Europeans, and would probably be completely neglected by them; that Cook's people could not meet the Tahitians' demand for iron tools was as well, since otherwise they would forget how to fashion their own 'substitutes of stone.'[5]

What Cook and Banks hinted and the Forsters forebode, Bligh and Vancouver observed. On his second breadfruit voyage Bligh lamented that the filthy language the Tahitians had picked up from the mutineers was matched by the filthy European cast-offs they now wore; 'they are no longer clean Otaheitans, but in appearance a set of ragamuffins...'. Owing to the wars, 'the Matavai people are fled... the whole plain desolate which I have seen replete with cheerfulness and wealth.' The Tahitians had now nearly fifty muskets and pistols, and loved liquor.[6]

Bligh exaggerated, but Vancouver in his turn noted the rapid ousting of traditional by European tools; in Tahiti he saw very few bone or stone artefacts, and 'those offered for sale were of rude workmanship... solely intended for our market, by way of curiosity'—so quick off the mark was the tourist trap! He thought also that with a very small import of European textiles the already neglected 'culture of their cloth plant... will be intirely disregarded.' He concluded, like Cook before him, that 'it manifestly appears that Europeans are bound, by all the laws of humanity, regularly to furnish those wants which they alone have created'—a conclusion surely not meant cynically but as surely highly convenient to Manchester and Birmingham. More disturbing still was the rabid avidity with which chiefs, both in the North Pacific and the South, sought muskets; at Hawai'i Kamehameha had put a tapu, with pain of death, on all victualling except in exchange for arms and ammunition. Vancouver countered by declaring that the great chief George III had tapu'd his guns and powder.[7]

As the Age of Feeling was swamped by the tsunami of the French Revolution and gave way to that of evangelicanism and mundane *embourgeoisement*, as the explorers were succeeded by missionaries and traders, this tradition of idyllic communities shattered by European greed and brutality was severely shaken; with familiarity with Islands life came contempt. On a close look, Islands society seemed much less harmonious and attractive than it had to the dazzled firstcomers. To the missionaries, natural man and woman were depraved beings under sentence of damnation; the robustly materialist traders found their account in appealing to the more materialistic elements in Islands society, especially the chiefly lust for conspicuous consumption and distribution, or even mere accumulation.[8]

But the legend, as is the manner of legends, never quite died; indeed, it was caught up by a new romanticism—Melville, Stevenson, Gauguin, Jack London, Rupert Brooke, *Moana of the South Seas*, Margaret Mead. It is enshrined in Alan Moorehead's popular *The Fatal Impact*, and has recently received extreme expression in Trask's paper in which the dazzling whiteness of Hawaiian society is contrasted with the unrelieved blackness of European.[9] Yet it is also under attack from writers denying the fatality and asserting the resilience and continuity of Oceanic ways and values.

This is a reaction against the old colonialist historiography, rarely empathetic and sometimes arrogant, which saw 'natives' as mere pawns and supers in epics of empire: British policy, French expansion, American trade, German intervention—these were the sole active agents, Islanders mere patients. It was time that this tradition should be broken.[10] True, the outsiders named the Ocean, gave it bounds, and in a not trivial sense 'the Pacific' as a concept is a Euro-American artefact.[11] But it was not just 'made in Europe'; the local materials were not inert.

The Islanders were not bits of plastic to be twisted about at will by the intruders, who were 'manipulated' far more often than they realised. Polynesian chiefs had nothing to learn about the arts of politics, however sophisticated. But their actions, often admirably subtle and adroit, were at bottom reactive, enforced adaptations to a startling new factor in life. This new element as well as dangers offered opportunities, and these were seized upon—but too often for tribal or personal (normally chiefly) advantage.

'European guns and personnel were used for Polynesian and Micronesian goals'[12] that is, for the slaying or subjugation of other Polynesians and Micronesians. The intruders were often seen as potent auxiliaries to be exploited in immediate local struggles, not as a standing threat to Oceanian politics. The proponents of the 'manipulation' school have turned from the Good, Noble or Romantic Savage to the Politick Indigene, but in recording local tactical victories they lose sight of long-term strategic defeats. At the end of the game, the likely losers were both the local rivals. Sometimes the manipulation argument seems to topple under its own weight: when we are told that 'The extreme submission and complaisance of that fortnight was a *strategy* [my italics] for getting rid of the visitors sooner' (what else could be done, facing cannon?) we may ask how this differs from Toynbee's *pax oecumunica* as a term for seventeen years of constant war, 1797–1814; 'one is inclined to ask if words have the same meaning... as for the rest of us.'[13]

The Island reaction, however successful in specific instances, could have decisive weight only in detail or in the short term, at most in a middling range of action,[14] in Tahiti or Hawaii; the one lasting success, in Tonga, was at least precarious, and probably due to the lack of commercial temptation and to Anglo-German jealousy. The reason is obvious—the societies were too small and too fragmented, geographically and politically, for defence in depth. There is certainly no discredit in this; the vastly greater structures of eastern Asia until this century fared not much better, with the great exception of Japan and the minor one of Thailand; but Thailand survived as a buffer state, and even for triumphant Japan the process was an enforced reaction; with the Opium and the Arrow Wars her rulers had read the writing on the Chinese wall.

It is no longer possible, fortunately, to write world history in terms of a virtually automatic and basically beneficient spreading of European institutions and values; but for some three centuries the initiative, the driving enterprise, did come from the West, with the early economising and relative secularisation of its societies, its thorough-going eye to the main chance, its single-minded materialism. Even where commercial profit was not the primary motive in penetration, there was a blind belief in one, and only one, road to salvation, spiritual and worldly, and hence a blind rejection of any but Judaeo-Christian values; whatever their theological beliefs, the early missionaries were Calvinist in temper and drive and devotion to work: *laborare est orare* for their neophytes as for themselves.

What could the Islanders oppose to this dynamism and massive persistence of money and a militant Creed? In numbers they were only a tiny splinter of humanity split up into many tinier slivers living on crumbs of the earth's land surface. Euro-American numbers in the field were smaller still, but they were shock troops, and Islanders were brought to realise that behind these forward patrols lay immense reserves with undreamt-of technological power, the weight of modern states and capitalist enterprises. The end result was the total economic subjugation of the Islands, and political subjugation complete but for the limited exception of Tonga; and Tonga may be balanced by the Marquesas, the first group to suffer the European impact. Here, on any showing, the impact was indeed fatal—in effect, the achievements of the Marquesans survive in museums, not in their own islands.[15]

The full establishment of Western power, however, took a long time, and until its consummation Islanders—or at any rate their chiefs—had scope for actions, or inactions, which were often enough tactically successful for the nonce; and even if in the longer perspective the game was lost, much of the Islanders' manners and customs survived. They displayed remarkable syncretic powers, especially perhaps in religious matters, and became adept in living on two levels, adopting and adapting new techniques, while retaining much of their own traditional ethos, and were eventually able to take full advantage of the surge of anti-colonisation in our own times. Despite a notable faltering of morale in the later nineteenth century, with wide-spread fears of utter depopulation, whatever degree of fatality there was, and it was probably rather greater than the new school of historiography allows, it was not final; even the Marquesans are now increasing in numbers.[16]

Many of the successes in the Islanders' long delaying action were due to European ignorance and misunderstanding of South Sea societies. Conversely, many failures were due to the Islander's ignorance of European habits and rationales. It is thus not surprising that seemingly amicable intercourse might be suddenly and seemingly inexplicably disrupted. Once friendly relations were established, usually by gift exchanges, each side would assume that the other knew the norms of civilised behaviour and would respect the rules. But this was often a false assumption; an unconscious trespass could appear a deliberate offence. The standard European reaction to any hostilities not clearly defensive (as opposing an uninvited landing) was to cry treachery; and the converse must often have been true. When symbols which were thought to be universal had actually very different connotations to the parties concerned, the wonder is that there was not more violence.

Receptions and misconceptions

Apart from distant Hawaii and New Zealand, the island groups of Oceania were not individually closed worlds. The arrival of strangers might be infrequent but it was far from unknown, if not in living memory then in tradition, and there were rules for dealing with them in peace or war. Nevertheless, it is difficult to conceive of the shock of meeting large companies of very outlandish men, in novel and complicated craft equipped with the strangest devices. These weird people were organised by no known rules, except the quickly grasped equation of officers with chiefs; they had large appetites, wanton ways, and, most unnaturally, no women.[17]

The newcomers brought with them dazzling material wealth in unimagined forms, and at first were often taken for gods or spirits or ancestral ghosts: *papalangi*, 'people from the sky', in western Polynesia, *pakeha* in New Zealand, *haole* in Hawaii, *atua* or *etua* in the Marquesas; at least the first and the last of these terms imply a celestial origin. This fallacy did not long survive closer contact, and in any case did not necessarily impute benevolence or responsibility to these heaven-descended beings. Rather the reverse; god were more powerful than compassionate, spirits were tricky or malicious; in general they had to be cajoled and propitiated or, if possible, matched trick for trick.[18]

In Polynesia at least the first meeting was usually friendly—Melanesians were quicker on the draw—except on atolls with very few resources. Green branches were frequently presented and white flags displayed, and taken by Europeans as signals of amity, which they often were; the Forsters were particularly taken by this symbolism; which they thought universal. But for the Marquesans it had nothing to do with friendship and peace; in Dening's words, it was a ritual to bring these 'Gods from Beyond the Skies... under their control.' Gesture could also be misleading; a Marquesan assurance of friendship appeared to Krusenshtern as close to a threat, a Tongan expression of thanks was transmuted by a European engraver into a menace. When Islanders brought a captain to a 'good harbour' which was only a good beach for canoes, suspicion of ill intent was natural enough. Nor was the forthcoming behaviour of women always what it seemed.[19]

In European eyes, the white flag imposed a tapu on aggressive or unfriendly acts, and any breach was automatically branded as treachery; but converse assumptions by Islanders meant that 'In terms of their own preconceptions, each side was given ample proof of the other's treachery.' European and indigenous accounts of confrontations differ strikingly, since each party saw its own behaviour as normal and correct,

> while stressing the oddity and unpredictable nature of the other side's reactions. The 'savage treachery' on one side of the coin thus becomes on the other an understandable and praiseworthy retaliation for infractions of the local code too atrocious for any right-thinking person to condone.[20]

Unsuspected changes in local conditions could also cause trouble. Grass Cove in Queen Charlotte Sound was uninhabited in early 1773, but when Furneaux returned to it in December it was occupied by the chief Kahura; it was no longer available for the free gathering of fodder and anti-scorbutics. Add that the man in charge of Furneaux's grass-cutting party was contemptuous of the Maori, and the result was massacre.[21]

But even improper or irrational behaviour could be turned to account. Captains induced chiefs to impose tapu in their favour, to secure supplies or to guard against theft. An extreme example was the action of the fur-trader Simon Metcalfe at Maui to revenge the theft of a boat and the murder of a seaman. By representing the port side of his ship as *kapu* (= tapu in Hawaii), he brought a large number of trading canoes to starboard, where his guns were loaded with musket balls and scrap-iron; about a hundred Hawaiians were killed.[22] But again conversely, since the outsiders had their own gods and were exempt from penalties for breach of tapu, chiefs could induce them to take useful action barred to Islanders.

The Europeans had their own rituals of control—rights of conquest, Acts of Possession. This carry-over of Western ideas and usages was also displayed in the persistent search for 'the King'. In the long run this became self-fulfilling; if kings did not exist, they must be created. Although in Tahiti 'nobody in the decade of discovery had the right to be regarded as king', yet 'If one is treated as a king by influential outsiders, it may become difficult to refrain from regarding oneself as a king. So it was, in the end, with Tu', founder of the Pomare dynasty.[23]

European intermeddling, naval or missionary or beachcomber, assisted or enabled families such as the Pomares and in Tonga the Tupous to attain control over a whole group, or, as in Samoa, to preside over never-decisive intrigues and wars for such control. In Hawaii Kamehameha, a very different man from the timorous Tu, needed no encouragement; here, with greater resources and a developed hierarchical administration, centralisation may well have been an independent process; but it was aided by European advice and arms.

Kings in the European sense did not exist; the possible exception, Tui Tonga, seems to have been a Dalai Lama rather than a secular monarch. By Cook's time there was a triad of 'kings', with Tui Haatakalua as nominal head of state and Tui Kanokupolu as the executive, but other chiefs had authority which seemed to rival Tui Tonga's; the system of ranking was most intricate.[24] Cook thought that the government 'resembles the feudal system', but confessed himself baffled, and no wonder. Similarly, in Melanesian Tanna 'to give presents to seven or eight chiefs was to offend seventy or eighty "petty chiefs" '[25]—a point made long before by Sir Robert Walpole, and doubtless long before him.

In Tahiti, Cook on his first visit thought he had found two rival kings, but neither they nor the chiefs seemed to have much real authority; there was 'a kind of volantry obedience... these people seem to enjoy liberty in its fullest extend'. Banks was more realistic—'the Greater part of the Society are immersed in the most abject Slavery'—and pointed out that Tu, who by mere geographical accident was given undeserved prominence by British visitors, 'Calld himself King of both [parts of Tahiti]... as most European Monarchs usurp the title of king over kingdoms over which they have not the least influence.' Unfortunately Banks gave the orders of society as '*Earee ra hie* which answers to King; *Earee*, Baron; *Manahui*, Vassal; and *Toutou*, Villain [*sic.*].' This misleading correspondency was taken over by Hawkesworth, and, regrettably, J. R. Forster elaborated on it, though he thought that 'the kind of feudal system' had 'much of that original patriarchical form, blended with it'.[26] This is a very early example of 'feudalism', perhaps indeed its launching on its long career of fallacious usage.

Given the circumstances in which the explorers had to grapple with complex societies whose subtleties are still debatable, such confusions were inevitable. On the surface the relationships of high chiefs, *arii rahi* and so on, with subordinate chiefs, and perhaps of the latter with *raatira* ('gentry'), did bear some resemblance to feudal vassalage, especially in mobilisation for war and levies for great public events such as noble marriages. But kinship ties were more significant than in European feudalism, reaching much further down; and the analogy founders on the cardinal point of land ownership.

In fact 'the idea of an out and out sale of land seems to have been unknown to the native mind prior to contact with white men.'[27] Apart from conquest, land could be transferred, but usually within a group and for specific temporary purposes; rights were by usage, in commonalty, and garden land could be occupied by prescription rather than actually owned— 'a little less than *dominium*, a little more than usufruct.'[28] In general, the head of a kin group, great or small, was the titular 'owner', but his ownership 'was of a fiduciary character.[29]

The first Europeans to confront this situation, on a permanent basis, were the *Duff* missionaries in 1796, who in consideration of the inestimable benefits they were bringing demanded sizeable blocks of well-stocked land for their stations. With calm immodesty, they held that as their motives were so altruistic, 'we did not think ourselves under the least obligation to them for permitting us to settle in their country'. They got what they wanted, though in Tonga the as yet untutored chief 'could not divest himself of the idea of conferring a favour, in receiving and afterwards maintaining' the messengers of Grace. In Tahiti also, despite the 'pains taken to make things plain... as Otoo [Tu] appears to be a vacant-looking person, I doubt whether he understood the half of it, though he signified... that we might take what land we pleased.'[30]

Such was the title of the 'cession' of Matavai; it is clear that the clerics also understood only the half of it. Eight years later came the beginning of wisdom, when they informed the Directors of the London Missionary Society that

> the district of Matavai, which [you] have hitherto supposed to be purchased of Pomarre by Captain Wilson, the inhabitants do not consider as belonging to us... excepting the small sandy spot we occupy with our dwellings and gardens: and even as to that, there are persons who claim the ground as theirs... we are certain that if any of the natives were removed from their lands to make room

Plate XIII. THE CESSION OF MATAVAI, 1797. Engraving from painting by R. Smirke, in W. Ellis, *Polynesian Researches*, 1829. Photo ANU.

for us, it would occasion a great deal of murmuring, if not a war ...
it appears that we must purchase all the ground we wish to occupy,
not only of the chief but of those also who claim it as their hereditary
or possessive right.[31]

European pressure, essentially the bribing of chiefs to sell what was
not theirs to sell, eventually broke down indigenous control of the land
in many island groups; only Tonga remained completely unscathed. In
Hawaii full political subjugation waited until the 'revolution' of 1893,
but this coup merely placed the seal on the Kingdom's loss of even the
semblance of economic independence fifty years earlier through the Great
Mahele or 'land reform', really a great dispossession giving free rein
to foreign interests; by 1900 'white men owned four acres of land for
every one owned by a native'.[32] But 'civilisation and morals must for
ever accompany each other ...'.

'a devilish propensity to theiving'

So wrote Charles Clerke of the Tongans; he was particularly hurt that
'these good Fellows, with all their Benevolence, Hospitality & social
Qualities', had stolen his cats but left him the rats. He might have been
translating a journal he never saw; Louis Caro, at Tahiti with Bougainville,
had written 'il sont volleurs comme des diable [sic]'. La Pérouse, whose
landing party was left with hardly a hat or a hanky by the Easter Islanders,
thought they were hypocrites as well as thieves. Not so Commerson;
determined to see nothing but good in his Utopia, he adopted a somewhat
Proudhonian line: Property was not exactly theft, but a mere convention.[33]

Melanesians were not very often visited before the turn of the century,
and had a good name for honesty—this, and female chastity, were about
the only points held in their favour. But there is practical unanimity
in the explorers' reports that by and large the Polynesians were the most
expert, ingenious, impudent and persistent thieves in the world; a people
subject to a sort of Kleptomania Oceanica. Yet it was recognised that
amongst themselves theft was regarded as immoral or criminal.

It was particularly irritating that many thefts were of objects essential
to the visitors but of no possible use to the robbers. The *Duff* missionaries
thought the Marquesans too stupid even to think of using the tools they
stole, 'therefore they set but little value on what we have, except they
can steal it, which always enhances the worth of the article.' True, sextants
and so on were useless in themselves to the Islanders; but they doubtless
appeared highly prestigious or even magical cult objects—were they not
handled with great care, almost reverence, by officers (chiefs or priests)
only, so that their possession alone might confer mana? Or perhaps the
mere thrill might warrant the 'souveniring' of a volume of Fielding's
Tom Jones. If Europeans collected stone adzes, ludicrously useless to owners
of steel tools, why should not Tahitians collect 'artificial curiosities' such

Plate XIV. 'A DEVILISH PROPENSITY TO THEIVING'. Field work, with distractions, on Easter Island. From *The Voyage of La Pérouse*, 1798. Photo ANU.

as *The Statutes at Large*, whose new owner, a high priest, 'placed as much value [on the volume] as some of us do on a brass Otho, a petrified periwinkle . . .'.[34]

Those Europeans who attempted to rationalise this prevalence of thieving usually ascribed it to intense curiosity about the strange objects so abundantly displayed, and a simple lust to possess them: 'That this is their true motive . . . appears from their stealing everything indiscriminately at first before they are sensible it can be of the smallest utility'; the writer added his doubts that many Europeans could withstand similar temptation. Another suggested factor was resentment at the commandeering of food supplies by Europeans.[35]

More fundamental were customs governing the arrival of strangers. 'Traditionally, the Gilbertese believed that anything which came to the shore of their island belonged to the island people.'[36] In Tonga an arriving canoe and its contents were offered to the island's gods, but the newcomers, if they respected protocol, would be treated as guests and given canoes and stores for their homeward journey. Europeans knew nothing of such rules and 'recognised no such understanding'; continued theft, after agreed exchange of provisions and services for European goods, appeared to them a breach of faith. Ideas of property and propriety were at variance, and when this gave rise to dispute there was always the European 'consciousness of having superior weapons.'[37]

After a few hard lessons, the Islanders also were conscious of this superiority. European efforts to establish controlled barter were often successful, to the benefit of both sides; but resistance to intrusion, or even a show of resistance, could be taken as giving licence to pillage. At Takapoto the theft of a jacket and some canoe movements, which on Byron's own showing may have been merely defensive, were sufficient reason that his '*honest Englishmen* made no scruple to load their boats' with scurvy-grass and coconuts; and yet James Marra, who made this condemnatory remark, could also write, within three pages, 'after being in this manner intimidated'—by cannon fire—'without which nothing can be done with these people, they brought in their boats 27 cocoanuts . . .'.[38] Demands for supplies backed by a display of superior weaponry are perhaps not very easily distinguishable from highway robbery.

To the Aborigines of Endeavour River that improving landowner Joseph Banks, Esq., of Revesby Abbey, Lincs., must have appeared no more than a poacher of their turtles.[39] Theft for theft, is there any comparison between Tahitian pilfering and Wallis's taking of their whole island 'by right of conquest', or Bougainville's surreptitious Act of Possession under cover of night? This is not mere anachronistic judgement by the standards of a later age; Swift, Churchill, Diderot, La Pérouse, Malaspina, bore witness against this grotesque arrogance.[40]

How to deal with natives

Don't send a boat out of sight of your ship or of the range of its guns; have a great gun ready, loaded with grape, though the firing of an unshotted gun 'puts a terror on the natives'; don't let a landing party scatter, since

> The boat is left to the mercy of the Indians, and European sailors are very apt to commit trespasses that these people don't like... And, above all things, I recommend to avoid any Quarrels and not to be alured distant from the boat by young women. Remember the fall of Adam, who was deceived by a woman.[41]

Such was the advice of Edward Robarts, a deserter from an English whaler, after five years as a beachcomber in the Marquesas. It admirably reflects the mixture of nervousness and high-handedness, so often allied states of mind, with which Europeans in general approached the Islanders; although its precepts were often disregarded, especially the last misogynist warning, which was itself less than fair, since Robarts was very happily married to a Marquesan lady whom he first saw as she was leaving her bath in the costume of Eve.

The main preoccupation of captains was to find a suitable place for watering, victualling and repairs. Alongside these needs was that for the safety of their crews, who were frequently unhelpful in this matter; their main preoccupation was too often women, and as a rule they had scant regard for security, relying on their own toughness to cope with inferior breeds.

To the Islanders, the sudden influx of relatively large bodies of consumers, well-armed and under prestigious chiefs who needed conciliating, had a grossly distorting effect on the economy; it could have been ruinous on small atolls, but the newcomers as a rule made for the larger islands where supplies were more likely. We have seen the strong notions of property and quick grasp of trading principles of the Nootka people; in the Islands, though often the people probably thought initially in terms of prestations or symbolic gift exchanges, rather than of trade in the European sense, they too rapidly developed a lively appreciation of supply and demand. Tahiti, followed by Tonga and Hawaii, early became leading centres for refreshment; New Zealand, close to the Australian colonies, was soon to some degree commercialised in areas such as the whalers' haunts in the Bay of Islands, as was Fiji on the sandalwood coast.

Apart from its obvious risk of proliferating squabbles, uncontrolled trading by crews meant pilfering of ships' stores. At Tahiti in 1767 Wallis's men traded 'every cleat on the Ship' and the nails that held up their hammocks, so that many paid for the pleasures of the bed by sleeping on the deck. It also meant inflation; in a month the price of provision, mainly in terms of nails, doubled. The 'old trade' in sex was itself of course subject to inflation; the *Dolphin*'s crew 'had a tryall amongst them,

Plate XV. THE FIGHT AT DILLON'S ROCK. This was the affray in which the beachcomber Charlie Savage was killed and eaten by Fijians in 1813. From P. Dillon, *Narrative of the Discovery of the Fate de La Pérouse*, 1829. Photo ANU.

and six was condemd for spoiling the old trade by giving large Spick [spike] nails ... but two cleard themselves by proving that they got double value...'.[42]

Trading had therefore to be disciplined by establishing a market, at least for major transactions until victualling was assured. This involved the negotiation or the unilateral imposition of a boundary; Wallis 'gave strick Orders to the Gunner not to let any of our men go across the River, nor to allow more than two or three of the natives to come on our side'. Forewarned by Wallis, Cook issued in advance a set of rules which included a ban on the exchange of iron, in any form, except for provisions.

He had also to find a secure site for his observatory; whether or not the Tahitians understood his request, they seemed to raise no objection to the planting of 'Fort Venus', armed with two guns and six swivels. On his second visit, an area about 55 by 27 metres was guarded by 'only 4 Centinals, with no other lines to assist them but a rope... often so slack as to lay upon the ground', and this sufficed to prevent trespass in the midst of hundreds of people. But William Wales adds perceptively 'so terrible did Captain Wallace [sic] make the sight of a gun to the Inhabitants of Otahitee!'.[43] Always, behind the Europeans' tapu, was the latent firepower.

However, concepts of boundaries, including flags as markers, were well entrenched in the Islands, and the recognition of 'off limits' was simply an extension of tapu, if not indeed an integral part of it.[44] The setting of *ad hoc* boundaries, by either party or by both, is a recurrent event in the accounts of European landings. Although such *ne plus ultra* lines were generally respected, perhaps more generally by Islanders than Europeans, they did not always work. On Tutuila, de Langle's cordon of soldiers around his watering point was broken; he had given presents to the wrong people, and there was no control on the Samoan side.[45]

Instructions to commanders invariably enjoined fair and considerate treatment of indigenes, and the avoidance of violence; and there is no doubt that with very few exceptions, honourable efforts to comply were made by captains whether British, French or Spanish—indeed, the Spaniards of this period had a singular record of pacific behaviour.[46] The most violent action by a commissioned naval officer was Wallis's, which resulted in many Tahitian deaths, and here he was under serious attack.[47]

But a captain could not be everywhere, and subordinates, including junior officers, were often too quick to fire in face of real or fancied menaces, and were sometimes aggressive; it was the unauthorised action of Cartaret's Master in cutting down a coconut palm which involved him in his most serious affray, though he himself later, when his men without orders fired into rather than over a canoe, 'was not sorry, as

I hoped it would have brought them to reason'.[48] We have seen what happened on Moorea when Cook was under stress, and his seizures of hostages. But in general there is no doubt of the sincerity of the laments or indignation when shooting led to the loss of Islanders' lives.[49] The decision to fire or not to fire could be agonising, the more so as warning shots were often unheeded by people who had never met gunfire in earnest, but often, probably, there was less conscious thought than guts reaction to a real or seeming emergency.

Many officers shared the humanitarian sentiments proper to gentlemen in the Age of Feeling. Apart from this, captains knew that there was now, much more than in previous centuries, a general European public feeling against wanton outrage; would not the Most Christian King, Louis XVI, 'consider it as one of the happiest successes of [La Pérouse's] expedition, that it should terminate without costing the life of a single man', indigenes clearly included?[50]

With exceptions such as Corporal Ledyard,[51] the lower deck had fewer scruples; on the whole the ordinary rating viewed his ability to dispense death by gunshot with some abandon. When 'a boy, a midshipman' ordered firing and was 'obeyed, with the greatest glee imaginable, as if they had been shooting wild ducks' it was not only the sensitive Quaker Sydney Parkinson who deplored this light-hearted callousness. The Forsters, though devoted to the sentimental ethos, are ambivalent; very quick to deplore the brutality of the common seaman and the arbitrary severities of Cook, they were equally quick to censure him for lenience when their own persons or property were at risk; in which inconsistency both the writer and the reader of these lines, the case arising, might have found themselves at one with them.[52]

There are less sentimental witnesses. Cook himself spoke with deeply outraged feeling of a shooting on Tanna; Rickman, one of his lieutenants, summed up—'the common sailors were very apt to forget, that the life of an Indian was of any account.'[53] Some of this apparent blood-lust may be attributed to the heat of action—'let's have a crack at 'em, boys'; and even George Forster paid tribute to the British tar's rude virtues— 'rough, passionate, revengeful, but likewise brave, sincere, and true to each other.'[54]

As for the traders who followed the explorers, their record is mixed; they had their psychopaths such as Simon Metcalfe, but tendencies to atrocity were attenuated by the necessity of securing indigenous co-operation if they were to get their cargo, at any rate more than one cargo. The comments of John Boit, mate, and John Hoskins, supercargo, on the Boston fur-trader *Columbia* are revealing. Both denounced, in their private journals, the violences 'upon a level with the savage' of their fellow-traders, including their own captains Gray and Kendrick, and made sensible remarks on the mutual miscomprehensions of sailors and Indians—

'each deem[ing] the other insult[ing], a quarel ensues'; but clashes were inevitable—'I was sorry we was oblig'd to kill the poor Divells, but it cou'd not with safety be avoided.' It was with a bewildered sense of shock that Hoskins reacted to a plot to seize the ship; had his people ravaged towns or ravished women, this would be understandable, but since the Indians had 'been treated by us as christians and brothers' their action was one 'which nothing but a savage heart is capable of conceiving'. Yet Boit, sent against Opitsatah, laments that 'This fine Village, the Work of Ages, was in a short time totally destroy'd' to satisfy Gray's revengeful passion.[55]

In the last resort the most realistic assessment of the situation is I. C. Campbell's, that it was a question of power:

> Necessity occasioned tolerance and co-operation; opportunity demonstrated bigotry, intolerance, hostility, and violence... The quality of race relations, therefore, was not governed by romantic views or disinterested hospitality... Whichever party was dominant was able to show its true character; where neither party was dominant there had to be compromise.[56]

It must be added that as time went on, the balance of power, as in Asia, swung ever more in favour of those with ample reserves of guns and money and staying power, the Euroamericans.

How to deal with papalangi

Whatever naivety they might show in their initial reactions to such weird devices as watches and writing,[57] by and large the Islanders' endeavours to cope with the new factor in their lives were more subtle and varied than the converse actions of the Europeans. Polynesian high chiefs were at least as sophisticated politically as the captains, often more adroit; the newcomers, even if not mortal men (which they were soon found to be), might be alarming and dangerous, but they brought great stores of novel riches. They might have to be propitiated, but they could be used; it was only in the longer term that their subversive effects on society became patent.

There was of course no such thing as 'the Islander', with a few set responses, but some perennial and widespread traits and motifs are discernible, and generalisation is a cruel necessity. On smaller islands, the first reaction was as like as not to be either timorous avoidance or open hostility; or an initial welcome might be succeeded by mistrust and attacks. Closer acquaintance with the strange beings might also breed contempt and anger; an American captain who had a 'kind and hospitable reception' in Fiji in 1808 lost five men to Fijian attack in 1812: 'The natives told him, that... they had become acquainted with the whites, and had resolved to show no mercy to them.'[58]

On the whole hostility was more likely in Melanesia than in Polynesia; even discounting the bad press that Melanesians normally received (they were after all 'lower in the scale' than light-skinned Polynesians), one gets the impression that they were perhaps as arrow-happy as the Europeans were trigger-happy. Possibly this reflected differences in polity; warfare was endemic in both Melanesia and Polynesia, but in the latter political structures extended to more than a handful of villages and war had its formalities; in the former it was less disciplined, more a matter of raids and ambushes; not that the antithesis was complete. Again, in both realms outsiders eager for a share of European goods might be the instigators or perpetrators of violence, and some attacks were simply for loot.

The Europeans appeared as great consumers of Islands produce and conversely as purveyors of exciting novelties, whether of practical or prestigious value—one must not in the Pacific context say *merely* prestigious value. One did not of course wish them to stay too long, that would drain local resources; on the other hand, while they were around one did not wish rival groups to lay hands on the precious goods or to share in the prestige of harbouring such august guests.

Both aspects are beautifully illustrated in the finessing of Finau, who for a time impressed Cook by his claim to be 'King' of 153 islands, all Tonga. He induced Cook to sail from Nomuka not for Tongatapu, where his regal pretensions would not last long, but for Haapai, where he could act as the open-handed dispenser of largesse—but not to go further on to his own particular domain Vavau, whence he promised to draw supplies which were allegedly lost at sea. The game went well until the arrival of the real Tui Tonga; well might William Anderson remark that Finau was 'no stranger to good policy'. Piquancy is added by William Mariner's story, on the testimony amongst others of Finau's son, that at Lifuka (Haapai) that chief had plotted the massacre of Cook and his people, and desisted only through pique at his fellow-conspirators' disagreement on the timing.[59]

The chiefs had the authority, sometimes by placing a rahui on pigs or other produce, to organise the bulk supply of provisions, and later of trade items such as sandalwood and bêche-de-mer. Much prestige attached to the entertainment of guests in a chiefly manner, and also of course the lion's share of the curious gifts in exchange. Instead of waving the visitors on, chiefs might compete for the honour, and the profit, of supplying the papalangi. A notable if rather later example of reaction to first contact, which by exception can be checked both by European documents and local tradition, is provided by the experience of a ship at Rarotonga in 1814—an experience which gained for her captain's consort, Ann Butcher, the sinister distinction of being the only white woman definitely known to have been eaten by Polynesians.[60]

After its sighting by the *Bounty* mutineers, so far as is known Rarotonga was not seen again by Europeans until 1813. The next year the *Cumberland*, Captain Philip Goodenough, called in search of sandalwood; her super-cargo, W. C. Wentworth, later to be famous in Australian history, was travelling as a partner and also for his health. He was to find Rarotonga less than healthy, and there was no sandalwood; they fell back on the root of the *nono* plant, which provided a yelllow dye that Wentworth thought, wrongly, might have some commercial value in Sydney.

Rarotonga was divided into three districts; of these Arorangi does not enter the story except as the victim of a small raid by a Tahitian and a Maori from the *Cumberland*, at the behest of a chief of the Avarua district. Goodenough first attempted a landing at the harbour of Ngatangiia in the Takitumu district. The reception was rowdy but not ill-meant; 'the savage, yet delighted, natives rushed to the boats, and made attempts to secure each one, a white stranger.' Goodenough disengaged himself by firing over the Rarotongans' heads (they replied with sling-stones) and went on to Avarua, where he was received in a friendly but less boisterous fashion. However, the anchorage was exposed, so he went back to Ngatangiia, where sixty Rarotongans were engaged to dig and load nono roots; they were paid with axes and so on, and so far all was well.

However, some of the *Cumberland*'s men were living ashore, and they made far too free with pigs and coconuts. In view of the prestige which the visitors brought them, the leading Takitumu chiefs Pa and Kainuku turned a blind eye on minor rapine, and in particular they did not mind depredations in Avarua. Sexual liberties were also tolerated until they were extended to the wives of chiefs. But sacrilege was added by digging up nono roots from various marae, and at last the stores of the friendly Avaruan high chief Makea were looted, and his marae desecrated. Two Maori of the *Cumberland*'s company had a hand in this provocation, which aroused even Takitumu.

Two Europeans, and the Maori, primarily concerned in this outrage were killed at once; Wentworth escaped, pistol in hand, to become generally regarded as the father of Australian representative government. The unfortunate Ann Butcher became, whether by force or choice is unknown, the consort of a Rarotongan whose kin boasted of their *bonne fortune* and so roused the jealousy of another lineage which had received neither prestige nor profit from the *Cumberland*'s visit; they settled the score by eating her. Meanwhile, it was business as usual for Ngatangiia men loading the nono, and Pa and Kainuku were reconciled with Goode-nough and Wentworth by the traditional pressing together of noses.

This little case-history encapsulates a number of persistent motifs: the misunderstood initial reception; the desire of chiefs and clans to have 'their own' European; the attempt to enlist the strangers against traditional rivals; the tolerance of rapine so long as it was at the expense of commoners and of rival groups; on both sides, contempt born of familiarity; reconciliation using traditional forms; the sometimes ambiguous representations of indigenous interpreters. Obviously intermediaries were all but essential for worthwhile dealings, and their role was often undertaken by the strange tribe of beachcombers.

Beachcombers

The Oxford English Dictionary defines a beachcomber as 'a settler on the islands of the Pacific [multiplex man!], living by pearl-fishing, etc., and often by less reputable means'; conformably to this inadequate description, the modern image is of a poor white, possibly a remittance-man, hanging about sleazy bars on the fringes of white society in the Islands. This leaves out the historical dimension; the classic beachcombers of contact times were isolates, voluntary or involuntary, *from* white society, to varying degrees integrated into indigenous society. They had often a significant role as innovators and as mediators between the two cultures. Their books are invaluable records of the contact phase; Maude's *catalogue raisonné* lists twenty-one. The importance of these records lies in the fact that, unlike explorers and traders whose transient visits were exciting and disrupting events, they *lived* with the people day-to-day for long periods, and unlike the missionaries, their domestic life was not aloof, a thing apart from the indigenous life around them.[61]

They were a very mixed lot; they included psychopaths and scoundrels, but also thoroughly decent men—one cannot fail to love William Mariner; and a deserter from a whaler wrote a book still frequently reprinted: Hermann Melville's *Typee*. The one missionary on the roll, George Vason of the *Duff*, who horrified his colleagues by losing his faith, 'going native', and marrying (trigamously) in Tonga, ended as Governor of Nottingham Town Gaol.[62]

Some beachcombers were genuine castaways from wrecks or survivors of massacres to whom a chief took a fancy, as Finau did to Mariner; some were deserted rather than deserters, left behind by accident on the hurried departure of their ships or virtually marooned, sometimes left by consent, as with stowaway convicts from Botany Bay. Most, however, volunteered, escaping a tyrannical captain or hard work on short commons, and gambling on securing some months or years of ease with an Islands wife or wives. The first few days were critical and might make the difference between a nasty death and a comfortable career as the trusted client of a chief.

Islanders had a touching faith in the skills of papalangi as artificers, especially as fixers of muskets and as boat-builders, which must have been awkward for some simple seamen, and for reasons both of utility and prestige chiefs were anxious to acquire them as retainers; indeed, a stranger was virtually the property of the local chief, or of a stronger one who grabbed him.[63] For a skilled, versatile, adroit and tactful man with strong nerves, the rewards could be great—John Young and Isaac Davis rose high in the military service of Kamehameha I, the former, trusted by both the King and Vancouver, becoming Governor of Hawai'i (there were obvious advantages in having an outsider rather than a local tall poppy in this post). There were risks, of course; becoming a chief's retainer committed oneself to his feuds. And those with no skills and poor personality lived on sufferance, a life poor, nasty, brutish, and like enough short.

Without a ship's guns behind them, beachcombers could hardly insist on racial superiority. Survival depended on rapid adaptation, and they soon accepted indigenous modes and mores; clothing or the lack of it, war-paint, tattooing were adopted readily, polygamy avidly—their demographic input was substantial, one boasting of forty-eight offspring. Maude's 'cardinal principles of successful beachcombing' are respect for their hosts, deference to chiefs, learning the local rules, avoiding aggressive behaviour, and helping their patrons in war, as 'masters of ordnance', organisers of victory, shock troops.[64] Examples are many: the *Bounty* men in Tahiti; Mariner and his comrades in Tonga; Young, Davis and others in Hawaii; most notorious of all Charlie Savage in Fiji, the victims of whose 'cruelty and ambition'—and markmanship—were allegedly 'so numerous that the survivors piled up the bodies of their dead friends' as breastworks.[65]

It must be added that beachcombers sometimes tried to avert massacre of the vanquished, and the one point in the Island code against which they set their faces was cannibalism; they could rarely prevent it, but sometimes risked publicly denouncing it, and even the bloodthirsty Savage is said to have shot Fijians he caught in the act.[66] There were nastier brutes than Savage, but they tended to get killed by the Islanders—or each other.[67]

Beachcombers were also valuable lubricants in early trading. They knew the best harbours and watering-places, and acted as pilots; Robarts brought Krusenshtern into port, found him wood and water, suggested rules for the Russians' behaviour ashore, presented the 'royal family'.[68] As interpreters and guides to custom and local politics they were invaluable, organising not only wood and water but commodity exchanges and helping to recruit labour for the sandalwood and bêche-de-mer trades; Haggerstein, 'Peter the Swede', played a part in the Tahitian pork trade to Sydney—which incidentally brought about the first export of Australian manufactures, twelve pounds of soap sent by Governor King to Pomare I. Of course they exploited their intermediate position but generally it was to their interest to ensure fair dealing; if the Islanders found out that they had been grossly cheated, as sooner or later they well might, it would be the beachcomber who paid. In the Carolines they acted almost as *ad hoc* compradores, channeling trade goods to the chiefs.[69]

Technological innovation by beachcombers was not confined to the maintenance of modern weaponry, though this was highly regarded and rewarded; they also did general smithery and carpentry, and sometimes passed on know-how, at least to their sons. Archibald Campbell pioneered the weaving of canvas for sail-making in Hawaii; however, he bore witness to a general reluctance to share precious knowledge with the Islanders, lest they learn too much and set up on their own account; mechanical arts should remain in a double sense a 'mystery', as indeed they were in traditional craft societies. It did not always work; already on Cook's last voyage an unhealthy interest in the armourer's forge led Hawaiians to try their hands at home-made daggers.[70] A deleterious innovation was the art of distilling, the product of which was consumed with abandon by both parties; a general alcoholic haze enshrouds beachcombing life. Beachcombers in the Carolines introduced coconut toddy, distilling, and more innocently nine-pin bowling; but one built a chapel.[71]

There were less tangible importations:

> Not the least interesting among our occupations and amusements on the islands was conversation with the natives, and watching the avidity with which they swallowed whatever we told them, and the dexterity with which they applied the information thus given to the improvement of their arts...

O'Connell took advantage of this curiosity to implant an idea of the power of England and America, by geography lessons with bark for a blackboard. General knowledge of the outside world was thus diffused; by 1850 a girl on Kusaie in the Carolines could talk, doubtless hazily, of ice and snow.[72] Story-telling was in demand, and lucky the beachcomber who had a book or two, or a retentive memory. In Fiji tales from *The Arabian Nights* were rewarded with two fat pigs, and a shipwrecked crew amused themselves 'by parsing passages out of Pope's *Essay on Man*, hardly a pastime that would corrupt the Fijians.'[73]

Missionaries naturally did not like beachcombers; initially they had to use men like Peter the Swede as interpreters and advisers, but with misgivings which were sometimes—not always—justified by events.[74] Since they denounced excessive drinking, swearing, and polygamy, dislike and harrassment were often mutual. And yet some beachcombers tried in their crude way—perhaps not much cruder than some Evangelical offerings—to interpret Christianity as well as mundane aspects of the outer world; the *Bounty* mutineers on Tahiti always hoisted their ensign and read prayers on Sundays, telling the Tahitians that it was Mahana 'Atooa (Gods Day)', with which information they seemed pleased. The beachcombers' disapproval of cannibalism, their relative disregard of tapu

and 'contempt for the local gods . . . created a general spirit of scepticism'
and showed that there was another way of doing and thinking—a solvent
of traditional beliefs that must have indirectly and inadvertently facilitated
the missionaries' labours.[75]

It was a necessary condition of the beachcombers' existence that they
should be relatively free from feelings of racial superiority, should see
Islanders not as savages noble or ignoble but as fallible human beings
like themselves. Taken altogether, the good and the bad, they were a
lubricant on the grinding edge where two cultures met. The bad among
them, and they were many, rotted themselves to death or were killed
off; the good, and they were not few, left their temporary homes with
very mixed feelings. Mariner 'felt all the sweet bitterness of parting
from much loved friends'; Lockerby, despite 'strong motives' for leaving,
'could not help feeling considerable pain at parting'; Robarts 'took my
leave of my dearest adopted relations with the greatest weight of sorrow.'[76]

Firearms

Testimony to the lust, there is no other word, of Island chiefs for firearms
is all but universal; perhaps the only exception, a partial one, was in
the Loyalty Islands, where muskets were in less demand than tomahawks.
This in Melanesia, where generally speaking chieftainship was not strong
and pitched battles were often limited to confrontations with little mortality;[77] but for Polynesia the evidence is overwhelming.

Vancouver, as early as the 1790s, repeatedly denounced the musket
trade, and the compounding of wickedness and folly by selling dangerously
unreliable weapons. Really powerful chiefs amassed sizeable arsenals, part
effect and part cause of their power. By 1806 Kamehameha I is said
to have had 2000 stand of muskets, later (in the 1850s) Cakobau of Fiji
at least claimed 5000, with ammunition and accessories.[78] Kamehameha
had also a little European-style flotilla, with cannon, served and serviced
by such as Young and Davis. 'Muskets and cannon were of little value
without someone familiar with their use and servicing, and it is at this
point that the beachcomber comes into his own.'[79] The management of
firearms gave an assured place in chiefly polity to beachcombers with
the right skills.

Even in the tribally fragmented Marquesas there were several thousand
muskets by 1833; the Maori were also avid for them. The demand was
lively in Micronesia and the Northeast Pacific, where one chief is said
to have received from John Kendrick 200 muskets in 1789, doubtless an
exaggeration.[80] Writers concerned to scale down the effects of European
musketry cannot but admit the extent and intensity of the Islanders' desire
to possess it.

There is no question of the effectiveness of cannon—where they could
be brought to bear—for terror if not for lasting domination. Even light

guns like boat-swivels, which were readily transportable, could be devastating; Lockerby's Fijian friends, inclined to be scornful of muskets,
were convinced when they entered the enemy fort and saw the slaughter
wrought by grape-shot from a 4-pounder and a swivel.[81] But in bush-
fighting (especially in wet weather), European small-arms often proved
less effective than clubs, spears, arrows, and stones hurled by hand or
sling, with which last many Islanders were deadly. Well-posted and with
loaders, a good shot with a good musket could do much execution on
a mass target, even though tales of Charlie Savage's prowess were highly
coloured in memory; and so could a small formed body behind defences
or in an open field. In the Islands these conditions were often lacking,
especially where the preferred local tactic was ambush. The advantages
of muzzle-loading firearms varied with circumstances, 'from very great
to little or none at all.'[82]

Their great initial advantage was the shock effect of a mere stick
that flashed fire and smoke with disconcerting noise, and inexplicably
killed or wounded at a distance. Obviously, however, surprise could wear
off. The great disadvantage of the musket was the time spent in reloading;
one volley, and a small group might be overwhelmed by numbers. Islanders
soon learned to draw the first fire, and Europeans rarely had the numbers,
or the good muskets, for effective platoon firing, nor often the discipline.
Musketry thus was not to be used lightheartedly; with his usual solid
sense Cook summed up:

> too frequent use of [firearms] would have excited a spirit of revenge
> and taught them that fire Arms were not such terrible things as
> they had imagined, they are very sensible of the advantage they
> have over us in numbers and no one knows what an enraged multitude
> might do.[83]

By a sardonic twist, he was to find out, at Kealakekua Bay.

All this presupposes that the powder was dry and the flints good, as
they were not at the Morai in Kealakekua Bay. Trade muskets, perhaps
rejected for sophisticated sale or the cast-offs of armies, were notoriously
unreliable, sometimes blowing up in the faces of those using them. Why
then the insatiate craving for such crude weapons?

One obvious reason was of course pure prestige; guns were the most
spectacular of European artefacts, and their mere possession conferred
mana. An overlooked factor here is sheerly psychological: a soldier takes
great comfort from his gun,[84] and one need not be an orthodox Freudian
to see its potency as a symbol of masculinity in action, as macho as
could be. Even if the effect of firearms were no more than psychological,
and it could be material as well, that was an important effect for both
friend and foe. A more practical consideration has also been overlooked;
firearms might not be enough for victory if their possessors were faced

by greatly superior numbers with the 'conventional weapons' of the Islands; but what if indigenous numbers were supplied to back up a small shock force of musketeers? The case was altered, and the great chiefs could supply the numbers.

The depopulating effect of the new armaments has been grossly exaggerated, to the point of legend—the 'Fatal Impact', so far as it existed, was far more a matter of disease than of bullets. In the Carolines, battle casualties seem to have diminished rather than increased.[85] That does not mean that firearms can be discounted as a factor in social and political trade. An essential for an ambitious chief was control of a customary port of call, and so of the import of muskets. These given, and the adroitness to foster a little corps of beachcomber retainers, even chiefs not originally in the first rank might achieve extensive power; the pre-existing balance of offence and defence was subverted in their favour, and the possibility of larger and viable political structures was thus laid open. There can be no reasonable doubt of the role of firepower in the rise of Finau, Pomare, Kamehameha, Cakobau.[86]

Collaborations

The thought-provoking generalisations of Mannoni's *Prospero and Caliban* may not be so universally valid as he seems to claim, but at any rate we may agree that 'colonization has always required the existence of the need for dependence.'[87] But until far into the nineteenth century there was no true European colonisation in the Pacific, except on its continental margins and in Guam and Australia, and these were different stories. In the Oceanic Pacific, 'dependence' worked both ways.

In many aspects the intruders were dependent on the Islanders; this is obvious for beachcombers, and is also striking for early traders. Except for Vancouver in Hawaii, the first real paternalists in Mannoni's sense were the missionaries, and they and the traders took parallel lines: secure the chiefs, and their followers would follow. The difference was that the missionaries sought, and largely secured, religious monopoly; the traders would have liked exclusive spheres, but they were not permanently on the ground like the missionaries and so were open to competition. But conversely chiefs became increasingly dependent on the outside suppliers of arms, and their retainers on what to Europeans were mere trade goods, but to Islanders luxuries essential to a man's standing in society.

Affrays between Islanders and traders were many, and bulk large in the literature; but 'good news is no news' held then as now, and, overall, co-operation was the norm. Despite the likes of Simon Metcalfe, it was obviously impossible to sustain trade at gun-point. The co-operation of chiefs was essential to mobilise the labour for the collection and curing of bêche-de-mer and the gathering of sandalwood; the former trade eventually needed smoke-houses up to thirty-five metres long and hutments for up to 350 people. After an abortive start in 1790–1, the Hawaiian sandalwood trade took off about 1810, and twelve years later missionaries on Oahu 'saw two thousand persons, laden with faggots of sandalwood, coming down from the mountains to deposit their burdens in the royal store-houses.'[88] Clearly such trades would have been impossible without a symbiotic relationship between chiefs and traders to exploit the reserves of forced labour.

Whalers and sealers relied heavily on local victualling, especially on pigs and potatoes produced, largely under mission influence but on their own account, by the Maori; already in 1803 eight tonnes were sent to Sydney, and later 'potatoes and girls both constantly figure in whaling logs and journals, often in the same entry.'[89] This was perhaps the most notable instance of Islanders' entrepreneurial activity, but everywhere they displayed a keen commercial sense and a keen eye for prices. So did the Indians of the Northeast Pacific; we have seen Cook's remarks on the Yankee smartness of the Nootkans. Laments on the inequity of trading valuable spars from the unsuspecting Maori for a few axes leave out of account the comparative values of axes in New Zealand and spars in New South Wales.[90]

Islands labour was not land-bound; indeed there was something like a new Polynesian diaspora. The forerunners Aotourou and Omai were soon outstripped; one would like to know more about the Tahitian who lost an arm at Waterloo.[91] Hawaiians especially went down to the sea again; they were readily recruited by traders to the Northeast Pacific, being regarded as competent and courageous seamen and unequalled boatmen. Some engaged with land-based fur-trading companies and went inland, as far east as Lake Superior;[92] others found their way to the Atlantic shores of North America on whalers. Nor were Tahitians and Maori far behind; Peter Dillon had eight European and four Tahitian seamen on the *Calder*. Islanders were in great demand for whalers and sealers long before Queequeg shipped with Captain Ahab.[93] Many small South Sea schooners were largely manned, and some were partly officered, by Islanders. As with the later labour trade, this seeing the world was not only a way of getting material goods and discovering new if cloudy horizons for many young Islanders, but almost a diploma of manhood; and like the earlier impact of the beachcombers, the new images of the world brought back by the wanderer served as another solvent of traditional mores.

These were Islander contributions to the Euroamerican economy; what of the intruders' contributions to Island polities? The military role of the beachcombers was not that of active agents but of mercenaries, but from an early stage there were attempts to involve Europeans and their arms in local politics. Cook's emphasis on Tu (Pomare I) as 'King' was certainly a factor in the rise of that family, and while he avoided direct involvement in the Moorean war, he went so far as to threaten 'to retaliate it upon all who came against him [Tu] when I returned to the island' should a threatened attack eventuate.

Cook did not return, but Bligh faithfully followed his old commander's lead:

> There is a great deal due from England to this Man and his Family, by our connections with him and them we have brought him numberless Enemies . . . was it not for the particular trust that is imposed on me to complete the [breadfruit] Undertaking I am sent on, I would certainly adopt such means as to oblige those [enemies] to repent of their incursions . . . I think it is the business of any of his Majesty's ships that may come here to punish any such attempt.

And in Douglas Oliver's view the firepower and tactical guidance of Bligh's mutineers were decisive in the fighting which led to Pomare's dominance. This tradition of support for a more or less respectable 'monarchy' was a legacy to the missionaries of the *Duff* and their successors.[94]

In Hawaii things went further. Essentially pacific as Vancouver's intentions and actions were, and justified as attempts to check European lawlessness and local war, the fact remains that their upshot was a cession of Hawai'i to Great Britain. To Kamehameha this meant an enhancement of prestige, and advantage in dealing with assorted foreigners, by alliance with a superchief far enough away not to interfere but with a name inspiring respect. Nothing came of this diplomatic exploit, but immediately it fostered Kamehameha's ambitions.[95]

Vancouver's peace-making efforts seem to have been entirely secular in motive; to him succeeded the emissaries of the Prince of Peace, bearing glad tidings of 'CHRISTIANITY . . . to communicate that inestimable gift, with all its happy effects, to these unenlightened regions.'[96] There must be questioning of the missionaries' understanding of their own world, let alone of the Island world, but none of their sincerity, their devotion, their courage, and particularly that of their wives.[97] Yet they too had to come to terms.

We have seen how they got their first foothold in Tahiti through an indifferent chiefly complaisance. The first effort of the London Missionary Society, that of the *Duff*, in Tonga lasted only from 1797 to 1800–1; three brethren found martyrdom. On Tahiti the stronger group of twenty-three men and women was seriously depleted by 1801 when the second party arrived;[98] but they held on. Despite the moral deficiencies of Pomare II—drunkenness and homosexuality—the fortunes of the Tahitian mission were closely linked to his.

As the missions took root and grew, increasingly the note of this-worldly wisdom crept in. Modest plantations and trading enterprises intended to help meet expenses risked becoming full-fledged commercial operations in which the original intent yielded to the pursuit of profit. This seduction reached its height in Hawaii, where men who set out to serve God ended by serving Mammon; a friendly commentator is constrained to admit 'the embarrassing circumstance that the missionaries who arrived to save the souls of the natives came to possess, in the persons of their relatives and descendants, title to much of the Island's worldly goods.'[99] On occasion also the name of the Prince of Peace became the badge of war. 'Ye are the salt of the earth: but if the salt have lost his savour, wherewith shall it be salted?'[1]

The true story is thus at some variance with the hagiographical literature; there were backsliders as well as saints and heroes. Yet despite some unlovely aspects, despite uncharitable sectarian feuds, despite bigotries and extravagances which call forth scornful laughter, the evangelisation of the Islands was indeed a great, often heroic, work. Unlike the explorers and the beachcombers and the traders, who by and large took things as they found them, the missionaries were determined on fundamental change and 'cherished the hope of revolutionising almost every aspect of [Islands] life.'[2] Their success was not total; many traditional attitudes and customs survived, sometimes wrapped in ill-fitting Christian garb, and there were (and are) strange outbreaks of syncretic cults.

The basically secularising influence of colonial administrations cannot be overlooked; but, all discounts made, it seems safe to say that until very recently no outside intellectual force has had the intensity and persistence of the Christian missions. The Islanders today retain plenty of their ancient hedonism, and in the larger islands have acquired plenty of the new hedonism of pop culture, and there are still enclaves of honourable paganism: but essentially their *Weltanschauung* has a Christian basis. Whatever one's personal creed, one must recognise this as a very remarkable achievement. But it would not have been possible without the collaboration not only of chiefs, but also of humbler folk, an unsung army of indigenous pastors and teachers, 'reconnaissance scouts, expendable if necessary', who faced danger and sometimes death as the forerunners of more formal mission activity.[3]

These great changes, the rise of whaling and sealing, of bêche-de-mer and sandalwood, the preliminary probes of imperialism, the 'missionary kingdoms' (the term may not be precisely accurate, but is symbolically appropriate)—all were to have their flowering in the nineteenth century. But their seeds were firmly planted in the revolutionary decades spanning the voyage of the *Endeavour* and that of the *Duff*.

Chapter 11

THE TAHITIAN VENUS AND THE GOOD SAVAGE

> ...they acknowledge no Gods but Love. Every day is sacred
> to him, all the island is his temple, all the women are his
> altars, all the men his priests... There neither shame nor
> modesty exercises its tyranny, the flimsiest veil drifts at
> the will of the wind or of desire: the act of creating one's
> own kind is an act of religion, its beginnings are encouraged
> by the wishes and the chants of all the people assembled...
> every stranger is invited to partake in these happy mysteries
> ... so that the good Utopian enjoys endlessly either the
> sensation of his own pleasures or the spectacle of those of
> others.
>
> ... the people of PELEW, who, though they appear to be
> Philosophers in adversity, Stoics in pain, and Heroes in
> death, yet, in the more delicate feelings of the human heart,
> they possessed all the amiable tenderness of a woman.

A paradise of sensual delights

Bougainville really launched the legend, by his naming of Tahiti as
Nouvelle-Cythère, the new Isle of Venus. Before him, Wallis had been
greeted by girls 'with their Coats pulled up who made a thousand antick
tricks' to induce his men to land. This did not work, but when amity
was restored after the initial clashes, the old men ranked young girls
for the sailors to choose and 'made signs how we should behave to the
young Women, this all the boats crew seemed to understand perfectly
well'; the 'old trade' was soon in full swing. There were limits; an 'honest
Carpenter' wanting nails 'would have given all that he hade except his
handsom wife'; but the lady ingeniously managed to render the necessary
service without his knowledge.[1]

The strangers, and not only those from the lower deck, responded
readily to the invitation to partake in these happy mysteries. After the
Boudeuse was boarded by the Venus whose naked presence ensured the
heaving of the capstan with alacrity, Prince Nassau-Siegen remarked that
'the King's ordinance, which doubtless had not envisaged such a situation,
prevented us from responding to her polite attention'; the royal command

---

P. Commerson, *Post-Scriptum sur l'isle de la Nouvelle-Cythère ou Tayti*
(1769); G. Keate, *An Account of the Pelew Islands* (London 1789), 366.

237

did not prevent him from enjoying, ashore, a nude party with six girls. But he was dismissed smartly when he tried to caress the wife of a chief, and even Fesche, whose descriptions were of a lubricity befitting a *roman libertin*, admitted that married women were 'of exemplary fidelity', while Commerson contradicted himself by saying that once married or 'at least in a settled attachment' they 'no longer thought of having connection with others'; there might even be the death penalty for adultery. Fesche lamented the corruption of manners that made it difficult for Europeans to copulate in public, but added that several overcame this prejudice.[2]

So much might be expected from frivolous Frenchmen, but some British officers and gentlemen ran them hard, and as for their 'physically-repressed, prostitute-accustomed' crews, 'The sons of Neptune were only too glad to be received into the arms of the Graces at the price of a spike nail.'[3] Cook himself was irreproachably austere, declining chiefly proffers such as that which quite damped the elder Forster's spirits at such an 'unexampled scene of immorality',[4] but Banks may have gone beyond flirtation. Hawkesworth was wrongly accused of dwelling unduly on Tahitian sexual *mores*, but he was not one to spoil a good story, and there was enough in his account to give the more salacious wits of London a field-day, though their main target—Banks' supposed affair with Oberea (Purea)—was misjudged, since her alleged paramour remarked that 'was I as free as air her majesties person is not the most desireable.'[5] But there can be no doubt that the rollicking Welsh surgeon on Cook's *Discovery*, David Samwell, and his friends were joyous partakers in the happy mysteries, not only in Tahiti but also in Tonga, Hawaii, and even amongst the more modest Nootkans (once the girls had been well scrubbed) and Unalaskans. Spanish comments are in a much lower key, in keeping with Samwell's gibe at 'flesh-subduing Dons', but then they were only seven weeks from home comforts; even the Padres took a relaxed view of such dancing as they saw.[6]

If Samwell's temperament led him into completely participant observation, Johann Reinhold Forster's blinded him to the facts of life. He compared, most unfavourably, not only the moral but even the physical qualities of Tongan and Tahitian womanhood with 'the Virtue, Elegance & beauty so superlatively united in Britannia's fair Daughters', and could say mildly that 'Among the Chiefs, instances of matrimonial infidelity are to be met with, which seem therefore, as in Europe, to be the vicious prerogative attached to rank and dignity'. He expatiated mawkishly on mutual love and, ambiguously, on matrimonial complacency; though he had to admit lewdness.[7]

Forster's son George was under nineteen when he landed on Tahiti, in the heyday of the blood, and one wonders if now and then he did not wish in his heart that Johann Reinhold was farther off. Like his father, he lost no chance of showing himself a Man of Feeling. He was almost obsessional in his revulsion against the debauchery of the common sailors, yet now and then he relaxed and made allowances for the 'impulses of nature' and the attractions of Tahitian life to uneducated men whose passions came before their reason; and he stressed that the 'prostitutes' who boarded the ships were also from the common people.[8] His comparisons with Europe are as diverting as his father's; the gestures of the dance 'sometimes might be construed into wantonness' but were not so grossly indecent as European opera, while the miming of childbirth in a Tahitian farce 'according to the simplicity of their ideas, had not the least indecency', and the ladies could enjoy the play unconcerned, 'not obliged, like some dames in Europe, to peep through their fans.' The Tahitians were 'not wholly plunged in sensuality, as former voyagers have falsely represented them' but displayed 'the most generous and exalted sentiments'.[9]

But the Moon-Goddess whom the Tahitian women adored was not chaste Diana but rather the Phoenician Astarte, and if Europeans had no right to cast the first stone for adultery, there remained the heart-rending problem of the Arioi and their infanticide. In George's opinion Europe was much more given to sexual debauchery, but had not a society practising 'a particular refinement of sensuality' and evading responsibility by calculated and regular child-murder—and yet, there were the horrible advertisements of abortionists in the London press. The Forsters attempted a rationalisation—the Arioi society was originally a warrior caste, vowed to abstinence from venery to maintain their boldness of spirit; but the impulses of nature were too strong and so infanticide was adopted to keep down the numbers of chiefs. George tried to play down its incidence: 'the votaries of vice have no cause to triumph, in supposing a whole nation accustomed to commit unnatural murders, without a sense of wrong.'[10] But try as these innocents abroad might, it remained a dreadful mystery of evil.

An earthy paradise

So far we have a picture of nudity and sexual licence, deplorable or delightful according to taste, mitigated by marital fidelity. But our witnesses were transient visitors, and as James Morrison of the *Bounty* remarked, the Tahitians' 'whole system was overturned by the arrival of a ship, their Manners were then as much altered from their Common Course, as those of our own Country are at a Fair'[11]—and indeed in our own century the arrival of a naval force for 'Rest and Recreation' has been known to conduce to moral laxity. Morrison *lived* in Tahiti, without a ship behind him, for nearly eighteen months, mingling widely with the people, and he was a very good observer, presenting an unsensational picture.

It is clear that the Tahitians regarded sex as a very important part of the business of life, not only very pleasurable but also praiseworthy. Coition began early in life and youthful desire had full play, but 'both marriage and upper-class status tended to restrict, up to a point, a woman's sexual liberty'—a nicely qualified summing-up.[12] The customs governing divorce and the custody of children given by Morrison would seem eminently reasonable and humane to most modern Westerners not strictly adhering to traditional Roman Catholic or Fundamentalist teaching.[13] There was institutionalised homosexuality in the retinues of some chiefs; Pomare II was a notable offender.[14] But by and large Tahitian society seems to have been joyously heterosexual, perhaps not very different in *mores* from our own younger generations, in whom pre-marital indulgence is often followed by settling-down after marriage.

As regards 'indecency', the public copulation noted by Cook and Bougainville seems to have been exceptional. Morrison said that despite the unpartitioned houses, 'they cannot be charged with holding Carnal Conversation in Publick and like privacy in such cases as much as we do', though it seems likely that breaches were less shocking than in our own society. Nor were the Tahitian ladies so lacking in modesty as startled, or delighted, observers would suggest.

All are agreed on the fastidious personal cleanliness of the Islanders, extraordinary by contemporary European standards, and this was maintained by frequent and often mixed bathing. But 'bark cloth dissolved like blotting-paper in water', and before the missionaries brought in Mother Hubbards some nakedness was inherent in bathing and surfing. But the genitals were carefully covered. Morrison thought that 'they are more remarkable for hiding their Nakedness in Bathing then many Europeans' and there was more 'decency than levity' in mixed bathing, although 'A woman is not ashamed to show her limbs at a dance, or when bathing, if they are perfect'. He was confirmed by John Wilson, a naval surgeon on Tahiti in 1801, who could not be sure of his facts on venereal disease since, despite 'obscenity' in dances and games, 'at any other time... they are much more dexterous in concealing and infinitely more reluctant in exposing these parts than Europeans'—though of course in this case there may have been other reasons than decency.[15]

There were of course exceptions, of a ceremonial or social nature, such as the formal disrobing of a girl on the presentation of bark cloth to Banks, or in the dance. Body movements in some dances were explicitly sexual, and young women then exposed themselves 'with their fore part Naked to the Company making many lewd gestures'; but this was not 'Wantonness but Custom, and those who perform thus in Publick are Shy and Bashful in private, and seldom suffer any freedom to be taken by the Men on that account.' But some male dances were obscene by any outside standard.[16]

The private life of the Tahitians had thus more normal domesticity than the first accounts would suggest. Adultery might not be taken lightly; a formally adopted friend (*taio*) had of right the enjoyment of his fellow-taio's wife, but others caught in the act risked losing property, or life, and a husband might 'punnish his Wife with Stripes'. Along with infanticide on a large scale,[17] there was a remarkable respect and tenderness for surviving children.

The intrusion of strange sex-starved men, bringing wealth in new forms, was disruptive. Given the Tahitian predilection for fair skin colour, the whiteness of the strangers was attractive as well as curious,[18] but the seemingly spontaneous abandon with which the young women sought the embraces of their guests had its share of calculation: 'it is probably safe to say that most of the sexual encounters experienced by Europeans had to be purchased'.[19] Payment was usually in nails, cloth, and European gadgetry, and in Tahiti the coveted red feathers; it is clear that girls were designedly used by chiefs, and their own relatives, to procure such valuables. In European eyes this was prostitution, and sometimes they seemed to detect fear and reluctance on the part of girls; in Polynesian eyes it might be a natural service to be rendered by dependants.

There were other uses for girls, for enticement or to divert attention— Wallis's 'thousand antick tricks', George Forster's 'thousand lascivious gestures' to put a man off guard. The tactic could be effective; on Tutuila women tried to pass through La Pérouse's thin line of soldiers and met little resistance: 'Europeans who have made a voyage round the world, especially Frenchmen, have no arms against such attacks'. Chiefs restored order on this occasion, but the experience was disturbing, and was soon followed by de Langle's massacre.[20]

Prostitution, in this not quite formal sense, there undoubtedly was; sometimes youthful wantonness; sometimes, even on short stays, mutual affection. We may let Morrison sum up; he equated the Tahitian lust for iron with the European lust for gold—

> some, as fine Weomen as any in Europe, are said to prefer it to Virtue, and yet we upbraid these untaught and uncontrould people with such actions as we ourselves help them to Commit ... However the Ladys who act these parts are not to be taken as a standard for the Whole no more than the Nymphs of the Thames or Syrens of Spithead are to be taken as Samples of our own fair Country Weomen.

Here the hard-bitten Morrison and the young romantic George Forster spoke as one: 'It would be singularly absurd, if o-Mai were to report to his countrymen, that chastity was unknown in England, because he did not find the ladies cruel in the Strand.'[21]

Facts are reputed to be stubborn things, but it is doubtful that they are as stubborn as legends; in the prostitutions of tourism, the Islands are still Isles of Love, faery-lands of romance, the anxieties and agonies of existence smoothed away. Gauguin's terrible last years peel off the mask of legend; they end with a blind old Marquesan woman groping his body and, finding that he had not the scar of supercision on his penis, turning away with a scornful *'Pupa'*—White Man.[22] Yet humanity is marvellously resilient; the Islanders may no longer be, if they ever were, 'the Happiest on the Face of the Globe'; but they retain a singular gaiety, grace and charm, laced with the sorrow of the human condition.

Venus syphilitica

A worm was brought into this Eden—or lurked there?—the spirochaete or treponeme, the twisted bacillus of syphilis, and of yaws.

Even today, clinical distinction between these two diseases can be most difficult, in some circumstances impossible; their bacilli are usually given different specific names but are indistinguishable by the microscope, their initial lesions and many later manifestations are very similar, and they respond to the same treatments. There is however a significant difference in their modes of transmission, syphilis overwhelmingly by sexual contact, not commonly so for yaws.[23] Moreover, yaws, which is not congenital, gives a considerable degree of immunity from syphillis.

If confident diagnosis is often so difficult today, the confusions possible to a century often unclear even on the distinction between syphilis and gonorrhea may be imagined; the great John Hunter may have thought that they were different manifestations of the same 'morbid poison'.[24] Yaws is believed to have been endemic in many island groups, often regarded as an automatic disease of children and even desirable as an inoculation, since recovery is usually spontaneous.[25] But the sight of its horrible sores 'at some island could make one captain furiously self-righteous at the expense of a predecessor', while a naval surgeon remarked that the missionaries 'did not hesitate to pronounce, that almost every tumour or ulcer, had its origin in a veneral source.'[26]

Naval commanders were aware of a responsibility; they tried to confine suspected men to the ships (though there was often plenty of contact with girls aboard). Wallis thought his crew clear of venereal disease when he passed the Straits of Magellan at the end of 1766, though the Master, George Robertson, said in his log that there were still three 'Damn'd Inveterate Poxes and Claps'. At Tahiti in June 1767, his surgeon opposed a suggestion to keep liberty men on board on the sound ground that anything that oppressed their spirits would injure their health, or as Robertson put it, again in his log, he was 'afraid to impair the health of his reconvalescents [from scurvy] if deprived from the pleasures of love'; they themselves declared that they would do much better with a girl's nursing than with the doctor. In reply to 'a very necessary Question' the surgeon 'Affirmed upon his Honour that no man onb[oard] was affected with any sort of disorder' communicable to the Tahitians;[27] but pay could be stopped for venereal infection, a motive for concealment. The fact remained that Bougainville's men and Cook's contracted a sexually transmitted disease, probably gonorrhea, from women of Tahiti: how did it get there?

Banks, Cook, his surgeon Anderson, King, the Forsters, Bligh, were all gravely concerned with the problem; even the irresponsible Samwell was sufficiently sobered to convince himself that there was 'every reason to believe' that the Hawaiians were afflicted with venereal disease before the discovery, despite the fact that none was seen on Cook's first visit while it was rampant on his return.[28] For Anderson and the Forsters the concern was truly agonising. Anderson felt that no torture could be devised sufficient for the man who had wrought such misery on a whole nation for endless generations. In New Zealand Johann Reinhold 'cannot dwell longer on this Idea, my heart is revolted to reflect further' (he reflected for a further twenty-four lines), while his son denounced the execrable crime through which the savage but generous Maori found that 'love, the source of their sweetest and happiest feelings, is converted into the origin of the most dreadful scourge of life.'[29]

One way out was to make the scourge antedate the arrival of the Europeans, and this the Forsters strove valiantly to do, Johann Reinhold in an elaborate argument that syphilis was known in Europe long before Columbus, so that it would be no wonder if it were in Tahiti before the Europeans arrived. George in New Zealand thought that venereal disease could not have been brought to Queen Charlotte Sound by Cook's ships, nor was there time for it to have spread from the north of North Island since the visits there of Surville and Marion in 1769 and 1772, so that it was highly probable that it was indigenous. In Tahiti again he drew the charitable conclusion that the disease noted was 'a kind of leprosy ... such as the elephantiasis, which resembles the yaws'.[30] But the more usual recourse was to accuse a rival nation. The compulsion to blame somebody else is shown by the very nomenclature of syphilis: *morbus gallicus*, the Neapolitan disease, the Spanish pox.

The Spaniards however were let off lightly. J. R. Forster confused the *Aguila*'s 1773 visit with Bougainville's, and his *apaè-o-Paèope* or 'Spanish sore' seems to have been an influenza; Edward Riou thought that Spanish predecessors of Cook might have brought venereal disease to Hawaii. More recently a much earlier introduction to Tahiti has been somewhat cursorily suggested, by sixteenth century Spaniards via the Marquesas.[31] But the real controversy revolved around Wallis, Bougainville and Cook.[32]

Bougainville was told by a surgeon that he had seen signs of smallpox (probably the scars of yaws) and took precautions—unspecified—against infecting the Tahitians with 'the other', that is great pox or syphilis. When, after leaving Tahiti, he found that some of his men had contracted venereal disease there, he commented mildly that he did not know whether this was owed to his predecessors, Wallis's men. This was in the first edition of his *Voyage*, 1771, but in his second, 1772, he was crisper: 'the illness... we could suspect more justly was communicated to [the Tahitians] by M. Wallas's crew.' Cook's reaction was blunt: 'they call the venereal disease *Apa no Pretane* (English disease), though they, to a man, say it was brought to the isle by M. de Bougainville'; he got over the Tahitians' awkward label by saying that they knew of no European country except Britain and took all European ships as coming thence.[33]

Yet Cook himself half-suspected that 'this, or some disease which is near a kin to it' was of much longer standing (he also drew attention to possible confusion with scrofula), and Bougainville's surgeon Vivès said that venereal disease could not have been brought by the French since 'it appears certain that it has reigned in this country for some time.'[34] But the French could not have become familiar with the language in their few days' stay and, as Dunmore remarks, Vivès's 'quelque temps' need not have been a very long time, perhaps only the nine months between Wallis and Bougainville.

Peter Pirie raises an interesting environmental point. Yaws is a disease of hot and humid climates, with a narrow tolerance of microclimatic variation, and Matavai Bay, on the drier leeward side of Tahiti, is an area where yaws would be least likely to be prevalent. Here, then, there might have been yaws-free women for Wallis's men to infect, but the general population of the island having had yaws would have been imune from syphillis and an epidemic would have been unlikely. It is largely from the absence of firm evidence for an epidemic that van der Sluis draws his conclusions that the venereal disease(s) noted by visitors after Bougainville would be mainly gonorrhea, though not excluding some syphilis and chancroid brought by the French ships, and that in the next century the yaws gradually evolved towards syphilis.[35]

This is fine-drawn reasoning on all sides, and Howard Smith and Sir James Watt firmly ascribe the introduction of venereal disease to Wallis, though the latter thinks that it was gonorrhea and that Bougainville brought syphilis. Another kink in the puzzle is provided by recent skeletal research which strongly suggests that not, surprisingly, in America but 'only in Australia was there positive evidence of a pre-Columbian treponemal infection, which was probably yaws.'[36]

Fixation on the Wallis-Bougainville-Cook controversy has diverted attention from other island groups, notably New Zealand, where there was no yaws, and Hawaii, where its presence seems rather doubtful, and here we cannot acquit Cook's men. And fixation on venereal disease has diverted attention from other scourges. Immemoriably sheltered by the seas, the Islanders had no immunity to measles, smallpox, tuberculosis, which also slew their thousands or tens of thousands.[37] And as a final ironic note, the traffic was soon two-way: 'It is just as likely that a relatively innocent farm boy from New England [on a whaler] caught the disease from a Maori girl on his first sexual encounter...'.[38]

'Rousseau's Noble Savage'?

English writing on the Enlightenment or Arcadian view of the South Seas often invokes the so-called 'Noble Savage', very frequently with the fatal particularity 'Rousseau's Noble Savage', a misnomer if ever there were one. The term itself seems to come from Dryden; the hero of *The Conquest of Granada* declaims

> I am as free as nature first made man,
> Ere the base laws of servitude began,
> When wild in woods the noble savage ran.

Dryden tells us that his models for Almanzor were Homer's Achilles, Tasso's Rinaldo, and La Calprenède's Artaban; not a very primitive pedigree.[39] The elaboration of the concept was predominantly by French pens,[40] though with a British input from Cook and Banks, or rather Banks and Solander via Hawkesworth, and with British echoes such as Meares's fancy portrait of Tyanna (Kaiana) and Keate's Abba Thule and Lee Boo.[41] It should be noted that the French term is not the noble but *le bon* or *le beau sauvage*.

The Noble Savage was not the brain-child of Jean-Jacques Rousseau; he had enough as it were legitimate bastards without having this fictitious one fathered on him. It is astonishing that some sixty years after Fairchild's *The Noble Savage* and Lovejoy's essay, reputable authors can go on repeating this time-dishonoured cliché.[42] To begin with, it may well be true that Rousseau's disclaimer of dealing with facts of *vérités historiques* was no more than 'the usual lightning-rod against ecclesiastical thunderbolts', but he made it clear that he was writing of a hypothetical model— 'a condition which no longer exists, which has perhaps never existed.'[43] So far as his *homme sauvage* bore any perceptible relation to reality, he was not a man at all, but an ancestral primate, a missing link; Rousseau went so far as to invoke the gorilla and the orang-utan.[44]

Commentators on Rousseau are not noted for unanimity, but they seem in accord on one point: his primal natural man is 'an amoral and fundamentally uninteresting beast'; 'neither good nor bad, merely amoral, and above all isolated'; 'going about neither in groups or couples... *un promeneur solitaire*'[45]—so isolated in fact that one wonders how this loner managed to reproduce himself; we do not hear of *la femme sauvage*. But, by one of Rousseau's magnificent beggings of the question, in some unexplained manner this solitary has the gift of compassion,[46] and through this loophole entered hordes of *bonnes sauvages*. It is not clear upon what this isolate exercised his compassion; but the *bon sauvage* was at the minimum not only a compassionate but a generous being, and can one have generosity without a society?

Fairchild sums it up: Rousseau 'did not in any sense invent the Noble Savage idea'.[47] It must in justice be said of Jean-Jacques that despite gibes running back to Voltaire,[48] he did not wish people to crawl about on all fours and retreat to caves; society once started had to be carried on; else why write that blue-print for an ideal society, *Le Contrat Social*?[49] In justice also to his followers, it must be said that it is easy to see how in a deadly formal society, wrapped in arbitrary conventions, policed and artificially polished, the young and ardent could be seduced by that lucid, unornate but eloquent prose, and seize upon his supposed primitivism as a solution. What Rousseau stood for, on one side of his excessively complicated personality, has a permanent appeal; hippies, flower children, followers of 'alternative life styles' are Rousseauists without knowing it. And of course Rousseauism did not rest on formal discourses alone, but as much, or much more, on his emotive fictions, *Emile* and *La nouvelle Héloïse*. It was this side of Rousseau that coupled with the voyagers' reports to engender *le mirage tahitien*.

Pedigree of the Good Savage

From this point it seems appropriate to speak of the Good rather than the Noble Savage. The term Noble Savage, if used at all, is better reserved for the tougher North American varieties of the genus 'Savage', the Hurons, Iroquois, Mohicans of the Jesuit relations and Fenimore Cooper; men capable of chivalry and generosity but also of ruthlessness, Spartan in suffering, delighting in war. The Pacific facies of the concept was dominantly Arcadian rather than Spartan, 'soft' rather than 'hard'; the contrast between 'a rude and heroic primitivism and a hedonist primitivism'.[50]

In the early contact years, formative for the romantic vision of the Pacific Islanders, the only 'hard' primitives met in the Pacific were the Maori. The Australian Aborigines, like the Fuegians, might be considered hard, but were generally seen as too low in the scale of humanity to enter the moral picture, despite Cook's 'far more happier than we Europeans'. Later European reactions were usually at best a contemptuous and pitying tolerance, at worst vicious hostility.[51] It has been left to our own age to resurrect the Good Savage in the Aborigine.

The Good Savage was not an eighteenth-century discovery, the concept reaches very far back indeed, according to Henri Baudet to 'earliest times', to classical yearnings for the lost Golden Age.[52] In his modern phase, the Good Savage comes on stage with Columbus; the Arawaks he first met 'seem to live in that golden world of which old writers speak, wherein men lived simply and innocently without enforcement of laws ... content only to satisfy nature.' The people whom Gonneville met in 1503 are described in strikingly similar terms; they were probably Brazilians, and it was meeting with three Brazilians at the sophisticated and corrupt Court of Charles IX which inspired Montaigne to write those remarkable essays in cultural relativism (and much else!), *Of Coaches* and *Of Cannibals*; from the latter Shakespeare drew his Utopia in *The Tempest*—'No occupation, all men idle, all'.[53]

The Good, even the Noble, Savage really came into his own with the French penetration of Canada. Only eight years after Champlain founded Quebec (1608), Père Pierre Biard SJ anticipated Cook: 'But if we sum all up and compare their goods and ills with ours, I do not know whether in truth they have not good reason to prefer, as they do, their happiness to ours'.[54] Of course not all writers took this roseate view, especially when the Jesuits found cruel martyrdoms amongst the Iroquois;[55] yet many Fathers sought a soul of goodness in things evil. What might reasonably be called the French copyright in the American Good Savage, and his highly influential career in French literature, are fully documented by Gilbert Chinard.[56]

It is a long traverse, beginning with Jesuits and buccaneers, through Deistic Utopians to philosophes and sentimentalists; two points only need be noted. One is the equation of Indians with Spartans, alike by Champlain's comrade the *bon buvant* lawyer Lescarbot (1609) and the Jesuit Lafitau (1724), who dedicated his *Moeurs des Sauvages Américains* to the very unsavage and unmoral Regent Philippe d'Orléans; there was a classic as well as a romantic image of the savage, Pacific as well as American, and we find elements of a classicising tendency in English as well as in French writing and graphic art.[57] And the Baron de Lahontan's *Dialogues avec un sauvage* (1703) not only prefigured Rousseau but outdid him: Religion and Divine Right, the scourges of France, are but manifestations of the single evil—Property; lacking these, the Indians 'are born free, and we are slaves'.[58] Lahontan's Good Savage Adario lurked in the background of much sentimental and more or less consciously subversive writing.

The Good Savage in the Pacific: the French tradition

For our region, there can be few better brief delineations of the genus Good Savage, Pacific species, than George Keate's Pelew Islanders— Philosophers, Stoics, Heroes, yet with delicacy and 'all the amiable tenderness of a woman.' It had unluckily to be admitted that the Palauans killed their war captives, but Keate goes to ludicrous lengths to explain away this inconvenient anomaly; they had to be essentially Good, regardless, and the killing was human weakness, not wickedness.[59]

Plate XVI. ARCADY IN THE SOUTH SEAS. A romantic view in the wallpaper 'Les Peuples de l'Océan Pacifique', 1805, designed by J. -G. Charvet and manufactured by J. Dufour. Despite a hint of realism — the death of Cook is faintly sketched in the background — the general effect is of a 'soft' Utopia. By courtesy of the Australian National Gallery, Canberra.

This is a late statement, English not French, but it is typical of much Enlightenment opinion on both sides of the Channel; such full-blown rhetoric was made in Europe, of Pacific materials. The voyagers themselves, with exceptions such as Commerson, were less ecstatic; yet they were often sufficiently carried away by their experiences to provide raw material for plausible if extravagant idealisations of Pacific society and personages, female and male.

How much 'invisible baggage' in the form of Rousseauist concepts of the natural goodness of 'primitive' man did they take along with them, to colour their observations?[60] Were the travel accounts effects rather than causes of the philosophical movement?[61] Giraud says roundly

the explorer invents ... objectivity is his least concern ... His vision is conditioned by the image that he carries within himself, to the point that things are distorted [*dénaturés*] without his even perceiving the changes he has made them undergo ... he seeks, more or less confusedly, the confirmation of theories on the golden age, the good savage, natural societies.[62]

How far is this true? These are questions that can hardly be resolved in a general history, but that must be asked.

We can see a refashioning in accordance with the 'collective demand'—Mauzi's phrase—in the variants between Bougainville's shipboard Journal and his published *Voyage*. A distinguished mathematician, Fellow of the Royal Society at twenty-seven, a man of culture, he was very naturally touched on the nerve by Rousseau's insulting demand that voyages should be put in the hands of such Enlightened persons as Buffon, D'Alembert and Diderot, and not left to *voyageurs grossiers* of whom it was a question whether they were men or beasts; hence several acid remarks in the Journal were edited out of the *Voyage*.[63]

There are more serious variations. On the one hand lyrical passages in the *Voyage* comparing Tahiti to Eden and the Elysian Fields, were not in the Journal; on the other, the very Commersonian remark that there was no blood on Tahitian altars, unless that of lost virginities, was virtuously unpublished, though 'every tribute paid to [Venus] is a feast [*fête*] for the whole nation' was allowed to stand. In the Journal, the Tahitians are a united people 'knowing the mine and thine enough for there to be the distinction of ranks necessary to good order' but not sufficiently stratified to have poor people or ne'er-do-wells [*fripons*]; in the *Voyage*—after talk with Aotourou—it would appear that while all had an equal right to basic necessities, 'Flesh and fish are reserved for the tables of the great; the commmonalty live upon mere fruits and pulse', while that reasonable distinction of ranks has become 'very great ... and the disproportion very tyrannical. The kings and grandees have power of life and death over their servants and slaves' and perhaps over commoners, who were called 'vile men' and certainly used for human sacrifice—so much for those altars unstained but for virgin blood! There was thus an ambivalent balancing: some literary embellishments added, classical in form but romantic in feeling; some notes of harsh realism.[64]

Perhaps this was a wasted effort; despite Martin-Allanic's claim—not backed by his usual superfluity of minute detail—that Bougainville's *Voyage* was a success from the start, Taillemitte has shown—with detail—that apart from a review by Diderot (unpublished) there was virtually a conspiracy of silence amongst the intellectuals. No matter; Bougainville had been anticipated by Commerson, whose fantastically glowing 'Post-Scriptum' on Tahiti appeared in the *Mercure de France* in November 1769, eighteen months before the *Voyage*. Diderot's *Supplément au Voyage de Bougainville*, a key document in the formation of the myth of Tahiti, though not published until 1796 circulated under the counter from about 1773. Certainly Tahiti was the talk of Paris salons, but that was mainly due to the presence of Aotourou. Even in France the star of Bougainville paled before the dazzling sun of Cook.[65]

Commerson's erotic extravaganza has deflected attention from his interesting schema of natural history, which referred to 'antropomorphes' which 'establish the imperceptible [*insensible*] transition from man to the quadrupeds.'[66] But Bougainville, and one suspects also Commerson, lit the fuse for Diderot's explosive *Supplément*.'[67] One must begin, like Rousseau in the *Discours sur l'inégalité*, by 'setting aside the facts'; Diderot's Tahiti is an inspired caricature. Central to his thesis is the argument that the miseries of civilised men and women sprang from failure to conform to Nature's laws, from the arbitrary restraints placed on human relations (especially but not solely sexual relations) by religion, man-

Plate XVII. A VIEW IN TAHITI. Attributed to Augustus Earle, *c.* 1820; the Arcadian vision lingers on. By permission of National Library of Australia, Canberra.

made laws and the convention of lasting romantic passion. It is not a plea for unlimited sexual licence; according to the Tahitian spokesman, Orou, there should be no sex before maturity (set for males at twenty-two!), nor for women past child-bearing. More than Commerson, or Voltaire in *Les Oreilles du Comte de Chesterfield*, Diderot takes the act of public swiving seriously and invests it with a religious aura, since its end is to produce new citizens for a happy people, strong in the strength of numbers.[68]

There is a spirited defence of incest, in which the poor Chaplain who represents civilisation is hopelessly outmatched (when he is allowed to put a word in) by Orou's superior dialectic skill, and ends by sleeping on successive nights with three sisters—and their mother—exclaiming the while 'But my Religion! But my Orders!'. This comedy, and that of the delicious closing passage of the essay,[69] cannot mask the vehemence of Diderot's attack on the barbarity of European colonisation, in the passionate warning of the Old Man to the Tahitians to reject the intruders and their fatal gifts. They 'have buried in our soil the title-deeds of our future slavery', infected our blood with venereal disease, and ruined innocent enjoyment by bringing ideas of sin and shame: 'our young men hesitate, our girls blush...'.[70] Diderot goes further, to assault European society in its very foundations of Authority, religious and secular, and Property.

And yet he hedges; as a whole the *Supplément* is an eloquent plea for Anarchism; obeying only Nature's laws, 'The entire island offered the image of a single numerous family'.[71] But in the last resort the interlocutor who speaks for Diderot himself dares not say that he prefers the state of nature '*brute et sauvage*'. It is too late to turn back; in Tahiti do as Tahiti does, in France as France, and work for reform.[72] A rather lame conclusion after the power of the denunciation and dialectic refutation of the conventional *mores* of Europe.

After Diderot there was a long train—Taitbout, Poncelin de la Roche-Tilhac, Madame de Monbart, Abbé Baston, even Sade in *Aline et Valcour*. Chinard has traced his influence as far as Pierre Loti, and since then he has been paid the tribute of happy parody in Jean Girardoux's *Supplément au Voyage de Cook*. But nothing shows the spell of Tahiti more than the last letter of the Dantonist Camille Desmoulins, awaiting the guillotine, to his wife: 'Oh my beloved Lucile, I was born to make verses, to make you happy, to defend the unfortunate, and to form, with your mother and my father and a few kindred hearts, an Otaiti.'[73]

The responsibility of John Hawkesworth?

It was not enough that the Good Savage should lead an innocent and simple life; countless shepherds and shepherdesses had done that in pastoral Arcadias from Sir Philip Sydney on, or long before him, and by about

1720 the convention was faded and only feebly alive. Something more exciting was needed, an environment more naturalistic and yet exotic.

As we have seen the French found suitable milieux in Canada and the Caribbean; there seems to have been no English counterpart. Dampier and Wafer were too objective to offer much raw material, and the buccaneers in general were not believers in anybody's virtue. There are perhaps elements of the Good Savage in Crusoe's Man Friday, but he lacks the essential requisite of freedom. The Caribbean is indeed the setting for Aphra Behn's *Oroonoko*, and this hero has too often been seen as the original Noble Savage. Noble he may be, but not in the least Savage; he is in fact as polished a Prince as ever trod a Restoration stage, and before becoming a slave he had been a slaver.[74] Ms Behn's Caribbean local colour was first-hand, but it is of more interest that the highly successful play which Thomas Southerne made out of *Oroonoko* was revised by John Hawkesworth;[75] and it is with Hawkesworth's *Voyages* that the British contribution to the concept of the Good Savage in the South Seas has generally been taken as beginning; a view strongly criticised by W. H. Pearson, cogently as to Hawkesworth's actual writing, perhaps less cogently as to his undesigned effect.[76]

In our day, the main count against Hawkesworth is his editorial rather than sexual licence, not his rejection of Providential intervention to save the *Endeavour* from the reefs nor his alleged libertine writing, things which roused the ire of John Wesley amongst others.[77] This is anachronistic; the age had not our reverence for the text, the whole text, and nothing but the text. A sailor's tale needed an editor to make it palatable—as late as 1798 Vancouver apologised for his 'plain unvarnished' narrative—and there was no pedantic demand that the editor should necessarily have authoritative knowledge of the subject. Hawkesworth must have seemed an excellent choice, a man with a reputation almost on a par with Dr Johnson's, which 'ironically was destroyed by a book which also preserved his name for posterity'. Although Cook himself was dissatisfied with Hawkesworth's work and took good care to write the account of his second voyage himself, he also took care to enlist the editorial assistance of the Rev. Dr John Douglas, later doubly a Bishop and presumably above the accusations of infidelity and immorality which embittered Hawkesworth's last years, and were said to have shortened his life.[78]

In his General Introduction Hawkesworth made his method clear. The narration was to be in the first person, to give what is now called 'immediacy' for the reader; but to avoid 'exhibit[ing] only a naked narrative' he reserved the right to interpolate opinions and sentiments of his own, submitting them for approval to the writers of the journal on which his book was based. These interpolations 'are not indeed numerous, and when they occur, are always cursory and short'. This economised

on the truth; the book is studded with them, and Hawkesworth's interpretation of 'cursory and short' can run to three solid pages. What was
truly cursory was the opportunity given to commanders to check the
text; Cartaret was disgusted by the account virtually issued in his name,
and Cook denied having either perused his section—two whole volumes—
or having heard it read as a whole.[79] The necessary dovetailing was deftly
done, and the general effect was to accompany the narrative with a
mildly philosophising running commentary.

Given the taste of the age, most of Hawkesworth's variations seem
innocuous enough. Sometimes he even toned down or simplified his
original, but more often he smoothed and heightened, and pointed the
moral with sententious reflections. Some pages of philosophising are added,
for instance on moral relativism, human capacities as shown by Tahitian
surfing, exposure of the dead (replete with classical allusions), intem-
perance and disease, cannibalism, man's discovery of fire.[80]

As regards his treatment of the Savage, there was no problem with
Byron and Carteret, whose contacts were few and brief, but Wallis's
spare dry narrative gave little opening for Hawkesworth's skill in embel-
lishment. He did his best, heightening the account of the Tahitian reaction
to Furneaux's ritual of taking possession to convey an impression of British
magnanimity, and using Robertson's lively journal to supply some comic
relief, and some charm to Wallis's few and rather impersonal lines des-
cribing Purea's tears at his departure.[81]

The claim made for Hawkesworth as the godfather of the British version
of the Good or Noble Savage really hinges on his handling of Cook
and Banks. The most notorious of the alterations—the switching of Cook's
'far more happier' passage from New Holland to Tierra del Fuego—
is explained by Pearson as due to a desire to disagree with their views
on the happiness of savages without directly contradicting them, especially
Banks whom he seemed anxious to 'manage', and whose journal showed
strong Arcadian elements—on first landing in Tahiti he met 'the truest
picture of an arcadia . . . that the imagination can form.'[82]

This divergence could be tactfully indicated by referring the reflections
on the Australians to the Fuegians, whom all observers agreed were very
low on the scale of humanity; the argument is ingenious but not altogether
convincing, since the change left a gap in the account of a most striking
discovery. Be that as it may, Pearson does show that here and elsewhere
Hawkesworth actually toned down his originals, and he makes out his
case that Hawkesworth was not a primitivist, hard or soft. The intent
of the alterations was not to idealise the Savage, Good or Noble, but
rather British actions and attitudes in the New World, to create

> one heroic character, designated only as 'I', who is consistent in
> his behaviour and admirability, but not distinctly recognisable as
> Byron or Wallis or Cartaret or Cook . . . the prototype of that hero

of Victorian boys' sea fiction, the magnanimous British commander . . . a national hero.[83]

The debate cannot rest there. The very fact that Pearson has to argue so strenuously, after two hundred years, suggests that there must be something behind so persistent a misinterpretation, just as there was with 'Rousseau's Noble Savage'. It is what an author can plausibly be *seen* as saying that counts in the forming of such myths, and those who were conditioned by the trend of the times to look for the Good Savage could find him. Very few readers can have combed Hawkesworth (and none his sources) with Pearson's thoroughness; and despite the disapproval of the godly and of professional critics, there were many readers. His *Account* appeared in June 1773, and was reprinted—three large volumes—before the end of the year. Eighteen months later there had been unauthorised editions in Dublin and New York and four in France, as well as Dutch and German versions. By 1800 there had been at least eight English-language editions, six French, three German, not to mention paraphrases, with or without acknowledgement, and piracies, such as David Henry's obvious and anonymous crib of 1774.[84]

The reader predisposed to Good Savagery might not linger over Hawkesworth's ponderous moral reflections, but there were sufficient 'human interest' stories, moral relativism, and in Tahiti hints, and more, of innocent sexuality, to provide the specks of dust to crystallise out a saturated solution, especially in France where the number of editions is significant. Pearson himself draws attention to one incident—the affecting distress of the Tahitians at Cook's flogging of a sailor who had stolen from them— which 'was not overlooked in France.' Voltaire makes a direct reference to 'le docteur Jean Hakerovorth' in his salacious account of the Tahitian mode of worship, and there is a striking parallel between Hawkesworth and Diderot on the balance of good and ill in human societies.[85] Despite Hawkesworth's personal stance, and here Pearson is right, he and Banks must still stand as reluctant godfathers, along with the less reluctant Bougainville and the enthusiastic Commerson, to the myth of Tahiti.

Specimens: Aotourou and Omai

Paris and London did not have to rely solely on the voyagers' reports for their notion of the Good Savage; they had in their midst real life examples, both Tahitian, Aotourou and Omai.

Aotourou was a chief's son and seems to have had a genuine zeal to see the world, though he was naturally astonished to find how much of it there was; he was so impressed by the little Dutch post of Boero that he asked if Paris was as fine, but once in that metropolis he quickly adapted, shopping and visiting the Opera by himself. Bougainville thought him intelligent, given to raillery and mimicry, possesing finesse but timid and lazy. Some of his officers were less impressed—'as great a rascal as the other savages'—but all agreed on his amorousness. 'Our Indian greatly desired to stop at all these islands, solely to sacrifice to Venus'; he even tried to turn the helm for islands where he said there were plenty of fine girls; but the surgeon Vivès shrewdly remarked 'he well knew that was our foible.'[86]

Bougainville incurred the displeasure of some philosophes for snatching Aotourou from his happy island to be corrupted by French society; others found the savage less noble than stupid for no better reason than his difficulty in learning French. Bougainville defended himself and his protégé, on the sound grounds of culture shock and the immense differences between Tahitian and French, though he admitted Aotourou's mental indolence.[87] Not all philosophes were critical; Diderot was a friend, and La Condamine—perhaps more savant than philosophe—with Pereire, a pioneer in the treatment of deaf-mutes, made a careful study of Aotourou's speech habits.[88] The Duchesse de Choiseul, wife of Bougainville's patron the minister, made much of Aotourou, who was presented to Helvétius and d'Holbach, as well as Louis XV and the royal family. 'The Parisians had discovered, after the Turk, the Persian, the Huron or the Iroquois, a Tahitian'.[89]

All this came to nothing with Aotourou's death on the return journey to Tahiti. Nevertheless, after his season as a sensation for the salons, Aotourou contributed to the fixation on Tahiti as the seat of the good society.

Omai (properly Mai) was brought to England by Furneaux; Cook at first thought him 'not a proper sample', and not only on account of his lowly birth.[90] Omai's reception in England tells as much of the foibles of polite society as of himself; on the whole the attentions paid to him seem rather shallow. He was presented to the King and Queen, but probably enjoyed a trip to Scarborough with Banks much more. His portrait was drawn and painted by Nathaniel Dance, William Parry and Sir Joshua Reynolds, whose final version invested him with more nobility and dignity, almost those of a youthful Oriental sage, than he normally displayed.[91] Banks and his sister were patronising, Sandwich and his friends trivial, Fanny Burney (whose brother James sailed with Furneaux) twittery in her praises. Mrs Thrale took him up, and Dr Johnson was impressed by his table manners—with their backs to the light, Omai was hardly distinguishable from Lord Mulgrave—but gruffly dismissive of voyaging in general. There is no more devastating comment on the ephemeral frivolity of the whole show than the fact that even that amateur of celebrities, James Boswell, though he discussed Omai with Cook seems to have made no attempt to meet him face to face; so quickly did sensation fade.[92]

Plate XVIII. OMAI, BANKS, AND SOLANDER. Painting by William Parry, *c.* 1776, in the Collection at Parham Park, Sussex. By courtesy of The Hon. Clive Gibson, London.

Only the Evangelicals seem to have had a real concern for Omai's betterment, and their concern was not exactly disinterested. The anti-slavery crusader Granville Sharp took up the task of instructing him in English literacy and sound religion, with the aim of using him to spread 'Christian light over a new race of men', but he was sadly impeded by Omai's crowded social calendar. He cannot have brought his pupil very far in fifteen lessons, but he claimed to have made Omai understand the 'gross injury' caused by the adultery of Lord S[andwich] and Miss W[ray].[93]

Cook and the Forsters also were seriously anxious over the results of the experiment. George Forster, who rightly thought that Tupaia would have been a better choice than Omai, denounced the useless round of socialising and the merely curious nature of many of the presents given

Omai for Tahiti, an electrical machine and so on, as well as the failure to give him any practical instruction in useful arts and (ignorant of Sharp's efforts) 'in our exalted ideas of virtue, and the sublime principles of revealed religion.'[94] His forebodings were to be justified.

When Omai was landed by Cook in Huahine he was certainly not monarch of all he surveyed. The peerage of the Society Islands offered even fewer opportunities for upwards mobility than that of the British Isles, and despite his travels and accomplishments, his hand organ and his electrical machine, Omai remained at best in a middling station. He gained some prestige from his muskets, but according to the missionary William Ellis, not perhaps an entirely impartial witness, they brought him a posthumous ill-repute. By Bligh's visit in 1788 he was dead, apparently from natural causes.[95]

His name however lived on. Omai was, to mix metaphors, a very handy peg for a number of hobby-horses, and he appeared in a variety of genres—scurrilous couplets against Sandwich, Utopian science fiction, the sequel to Raspe's *Baron Munchausen's Travels*, Loutherbourg's spectacular pantomine *Omai: Or, a Trip Round the World*, the quiet but fanciful moralising of Cowper's *The Task*.[96] Surely for once the cliché 'meteoric' is in order: a bright flash, but fleeting; then an immortality of a kind, a name used merely to point a dubious moral or adorn a dubious tale. This for Europe; for Tahiti, he was only a ripple on the sand.

There were two other specimens, of later date and lesser fame. One of them, John Meares's 'Tyanna' (Kaiana) from Kauai, never reached England, but he made a great impression on the European society of Macao and Canton, in 1787, striding about in the full regalia of a Hawaiian chief, polychromatic feather cloak and helmet; he disliked the Chinese seclusion of women, but behaved most properly at English church services. Vancouver, who knew him in his native habitat, was less impressed: 'his countenance displayed those designing, ambitious, and (I believe I may with justice add) treacherous principles, that apparently govern his turbulent and aspiring disposition.'[97]

'Prince' Lee Boo, brought to England by Captain Henry Wilson after his wreck at Palau in 1783, was a less ambiguous character. An intelligent young man of a genuinely simple and outgoing nature, he like Omai 'became the darling of the dinner circuit'; unlike Omai, whom Banks took care to inoculate early, he died of smallpox after about six months in England, to be sentimentally memorialised by Keate. He was honoured by an epitaph on his tombstone, erected by the East India Company, and by some tears in a poem by Coleridge, both very poor.[98] These two were the last, and rather faded, representatives of the Good Savage in the flesh.

Neutrals and dissenters

The Forsters must be counted as neutrals in the debate; they betrayed an obsessive concern to denounce the vices and luxuries of European society, but this is counterpoised by a deep respect for the intellectual life which they found 'savages', however seemingly happy, to lack.

There is an ambivalence which at times passes almost into selfcontradiction. Nothing can be more direct than the attack on 'Rousseau and the superficial philosophers who re-echo his maxims',[99] yet there is a strongly Rousseauist comparison of the Tongans with the Tahitians. The former are active and industrious, but polite rather than cordial; 'their peculiar propensity to trade seems to have substituted this insincere civility, in the room of real friendship' shown by the Tahitians, who are indolent and 'too hearty in their affections to confine them to outward show and specious appearances.' True, the Arioi of Tahiti are luxurious and seem to be 'somewhat depraved', but the Tongans 'seem to be ignorant of vices, which can only have arisen from a superior degree of opulence.' This is perhaps the Rousseau of the *Discours sur les Sciences et les Arts* rather than of *Inégalité*, but it is Rousseau none the less. Then again, the philosophers are attacked for their insistence on the greater happiness of peoples in a state of nature, yet with all our superior knowledge, 'our civilized communities are stained with vices and enormities, unknown to the wretch, who, compared to ourselves, is next to a brute'.[1]

There are no doubts, however, as to the poor Pecherai of Tierra del Fuego, who are examples of the degeneracy which follows when tribes are 'driven from the benevolent influence of the sun' and sink almost into animalism, herding together by custom: 'sensuality, and the enjoyment of the few wants of nature, make the whole field of their brutish desires'. They think themselves happy, but this is only 'a state of intoxication', happiness 'founded on mere sensuality is transitory and delusive.'[2]

The Maori are in better case: 'A race of men, who amidst all of their savage roughness, their fiery temper, and cruel customs, are brave, generous, hospitable, and incapable of deceiving', and even war and cannibalism have their progressive aspects. Rather quaintly, the Maori taste for music, superior to that of other Islanders, affords 'stronger proofs, in favour of their heart, than all the idle eloquence of philosophers in their cabinets can invalidate. They have violent passions, but it would be absurd to assert that these only lead them to inhuman excesses.'[3] Yet the superiority of civilisation is shown by the improvements made at Dusky Bay by a few men working part-time for four weeks, which five hundred Maori could not have made in three months: 'All around us we perceived the rise of arts, and the dawn of science, in a country which had hitherto lain plunged in one long night of ignorance and barbarism!'.[4] The Forsters were not simple primitivists.

Tahiti is a test case—

> Let us now turn our eyes to O-TAHEITI, the queen of tropical
> isles... The first view will convince the unprejudiced observer, of
> the great happiness which reigns... All the inhabitants are of an
> agreeable temper, and lovers of mirth and joy; I never saw any
> one of a morose peevish, discontented disposition... they all join
> to their chearful temper, a politeness and elegance which is happily
> blended with the most innocent simplicity of manners... a degree
> of felicity... which is here still more enhanced by the generality
> with which it is diffused over whole nations

and so on for over three pages of unmitigated rapture. Even though
the government is quasi-feudal, it is founded on principles of kindness
and benevolence, and on that 'primitive simplicity, which bears always
the stamp of perfect undegenerated nature.'[5] Here at last, surely, we
have found the Good Savage, directly observed in his native perfection.

However, this is emotion recollected in tranquillity; in their more
objective phases both Forsters, but perhaps especially George, were constrained to admit large cracks in this mirror of perfection. When he
wrote the *Observations*, Johann Reinhold seems to have forgotten his
outbursts against the audacious Huahineans, when he had written that
if there were a third robbery, 'it would be necessary to avenge it in
such a manner, as would deter others from doing the like... in case
one were shot dead... it would cause more honesty among them, &
greater Security for Europeans.'[6]

The flaws included marital infidelity among the higher classes, lewdness
and prostitution in the lower; the mystery of the Arioi and the immolation
of infants, which could not quite be rationalised away by an appeal to
hypothetical history; 'the specious politeness of the court and courtiers,
who fed our hopes with empty promises' (true virtue seems a middle-
class prerogative!); gluttony such as the revolting spectacle of a chief,
'a picture of phlegmatic insensibility', being fed by a woman—

> We had flattered ourselves with the pleasing fancy of having found
> at least one little spot of the world, where a whole nation, without
> being lawless barbarians, aimed at a certain frugal equality... we
> saw a luxurious individual spending his life in sluggish inactivity,
> and without one benefit to society, like the privileged parasites of
> more civilized climates, fattening on the superfluous product of the
> soil, of which he robbed the labouring multitude.[7]

And in the last resort the daily round, from the morning to the evening
bath, 'the artless tale, the jocund dance', were not enough. One accustomed
to an active life, possessing treasures of knowledge to which the Tahitians
were strangers, thinking before and after and seeking the causes of things,

would soon tire of 'an uninterrupted tranquility and continual sameness, suited only to a people whose notions are simple and confined.'[8]

The Forsters could see clearly enough the idealisation of the Islanders by others; they criticised quite sharply, for example, artists and engravers who depicted them with 'fine floating draperies' striking classically heroic poses 'in finest Greek style';[9] But while they themselves were possessed by a touching desire to play down the less pleasing, sometimes repulsive, features of Tahitian life, realism would break in. Their minds were divided; they longed to present the picture of Paradise, but facts were against them, and they naively expressed their disillusion. Omai and Tupaia sailed with the British with the motive of getting firearms; there was no economic rationale for the Boraboran desire to conquer Raietea, which could be due to nothing but the spirit of ambition—'Such a spirit ill agreed with the simplicity and generous character of the people, and it gave us great pain to be convinced, that great imperfections cannot be excluded from the best of human societies.'[10] Paradise had been found, and lost.

The loss of the paradisical view is strikingly illustrated by the experiences and reflections of Frenchmen in the South Seas after Bougainville. The first of these, Surville, felt indeed no loss, since his expectations were low, at least on the human plane; although they had at least the first volume of the *Encyclopédie* aboard, he and his second Guillaume Labé seem to have had pragmatic minds, little affected by the literary culture of the day.[11] Surville at least approached new peoples with a compound of wariness and desire for fair dealing—'it is always better to make one's way patiently and gently rather than through force and violence which anyway seems to me unfair towards people who are in their own home and have never thought of going to bother you in yours.'[12]

At his first encounter with Islanders, in the Solomons, Surville's men were attacked in what seemed a wanton and treacherous manner; hence his name 'Arsacides' after the old Assassins of Syria, though one Frenchman had died and at least thirty Islanders.[13] With this incident and Tasman's Murderers' Bay in mind, Surville approached New Zealand with apprehension. Despite total ignorance of the language, he got on good terms with the Maori, taking care to respect local custom, so far as he could make it out, and to get permission for tree-felling. Until the very end of his fortnight's stay things went far better than he had expected; then the theft of his yawl led him to take reprisals, destroying canoes and houses—but no life was lost, French or Maori.

It was far otherwise with the next Frenchman, Marion du Fresne.[14] Surville had not known what to expect, and feared the worst; Marion knew all about Tahiti, and expected the best. At Ile de France he was well primed by Commerson, self-styled *adorator perpetuus* of Nouvelle-Cythère, who had wished to come on the voyage; an intriguing thought.

From Commerson, Marion, unlike Surville, had the advantage of possessing a basic Polynesian vocabulary.

When he reached the Bay of Islands, Marion was well received and settled his men in three camps, one of them, for timber-getting, in the bush. All seemed amiable, and the Frenchmen rambled about at will. Marion himself gave no thought to 'security'; when an officer expressed anxiety at what seemed nightly spying on the camps, Marion, conscious of his own good intentions, simply asked 'How can you expect me to have a bad opinion of people who show me so much friendship?'. As the days went by there came minor frictions, thefts by the Maori, unwitting breaches of tapu by the French. The strangers showed no signs of leaving; the officer, Roux, who had tried to alert Marion to possible risks said later 'I am persuaded that they firmly believed we were to remain there for always.' The upshot of Marion's belief in the goodness of the natural man was the killing of himself and some thirty of his company, and an unknown number of Maori.

His lieutenant Crozet drew the inference: there was no such being as the Good Savage, the simple Children of Nature were simply nasty vicious children, ferocious as wild beasts. His editor, the Abbé Rochon, attempted a rationalisation; treachery was the only recourse for the weak, the only way in which the Maori could punish the French for their injustices. Crozet, according to Anders Sparrman, who met him at the Cape, had personally given Rousseau details (doubtless lurid) of the massacre and the Maori character; Jean-Jacques could only ask 'Is it possible that the good Children of Nature could be so wicked?'.[15]

The decline of the Good Savage was sharply pointed up by La Pérouse. He was relatively tolerant at Easter Island; the 'Indians' of the South Seas were not savages, they had made very great progress in civilisation and corruption—'The most hardened rogues in Europe are not such hypocrites as these islanders; all their caresses were feigned...'. The Indians of northwest America stiffened his tone; doubtless it was impossible that a society should possess no virtues, but 'I had not the sagacity to perceive them.' Closet philosophers writing by their firesides might protest, but he himself had voyaged for thirty years and 'seen the bad faith and deceits of these people, whom they depict as so good because they are very close to Nature', but one cannot come to decent terms [*faire société*] with such men 'because they are barbarous, wicked and scoundrelly.'

The massacre in Samoa naturally provoked him to further bitterness. In so enchanting a place, it might seem that only happiness could reign, but the scarred bodies of the men bore witness to frequent wars and fights, while

> their features proclaimed a ferocity... which Nature had doubtless stamped upon them as a warning that, despite the academies which

award the crown to the paradoxes of philosophers, the almost savage
man, living in anarchy, is a being more malicious [*méchant*] than
the wolves and tigers of the forest.[16]

The voyage only confirmed La Pérouse in the settled opinion of years.
Even the few and feeble 'Indians' of Botany Bay were like all savages—
wicked; they threw spears after having received caresses, and would have
burned the ships if they could. But

> I am however a thousand times more angry with the philosophers
> who so exalt the savages than with the savages themselves. This
> unfortunate Lamanon, whom they massacred, said to me on the eve
> of his death, that these men were more worthy than ourselves. A
> rigid observer of the orders given in my instructions, I have always
> treated them with the greatest consideration, but I assure you that
> if I were to make a new voyage of this kind, I would demand different
> orders. A navigator, on leaving Europe, ought to consider the savages
> as enemies . . . .[17]

There were other factors in the decline of the idea of the Good Savage
than the fact of more frequent and closer contacts with the realities
of Islands life, and the fact that such contacts were increasingly in the
hands not only of more or less instructed and gentlemanly explorers,
but also of tough hard-headed, often hard-hearted, trading captains. The
climate of opinion changed with the reaction against the French Revolution, which was often simplistically attributed to Rousseauist ideas, and
with the rise, often allied with the reaction, of Evangelicanism.

To the missionaries, the heathen, whatever superficial virtues he or
she might display, was quite simply and in the fullest sense reprobate;
theologically, as plunged in darkest ignorance of the one truth, the Gospel;
humanly, for the very aspects which had appealed to the Enlightenment,
a happy indolence and a frank delight in the pleasures of fleshly love.
In their compulsion to present a stereotype of the ignoble savage, as
false as the idealisation they were combating, the pious were not above
the conscious production of mean distortions, using pictorial representation
not to idealise but to demean.[18] It was shabby and crude, but effective.

Then too the Pacific version of the Good Savage had been a 'soft
primitive', an eminently social being. The Romantics still had a use for
picturesque savages, but they tended to be 'hard', individualistic to the
point of being self-consciously, even aggressively, anti-social, Byronic
villain-heroes. The metamorphosis was not complete, but the softer side
was transferred to the gentler sex. The gentle generously loving Island
girl lived on in fiction and later in film, but in our day increasingly
relegated to the subliterature of exotic kitsch. It is a far cry from George
Keate's stoic and heroic philosophers.

Chapter 12

EXPLOITATION OF THE EXPLORATIONS

> Britain! behold the world's wide face;
> Nor cover'd half with *solid* space,
> Three parts are *fluid*, empire of the sea!
> And why? for commerce, Ocean streams
> For *that*, through all his various *names*:
> And if for commerce, ocean flows for thee.

The Yankees

Chauvinistic teleology notwithstanding, even Britannia, ruler of the waves, had to share the Ocean, *mare liberum*, with others, and most of all with her own rebellious sons the New England Yankees. Untrammelled by East India or South Sea Company monopolies, and until 1812 unhampered by war,[1] captains from Boston and Salem and Nantucket scoured the seas and shores of the Pacific in search of whales, seals, sea otters, sandalwood, bêche-de-mer, and cargoes and markets of opportunity. Whaling apart, the ultimate objective of these activities was mainly the Canton market; China was the magnet, and in default of silver and manufactures of her own the young Republic pillaged the Ocean for products to exchange for tea and silk. On 22 February 1784, within six months of the signing of the Treaty of Paris, the *Empress of China* cleared New York for Canton;[2] by January 1787 there were five American ships in that port, in 1789 fifteen, and in 1799–1806 the Yankees lifted nearly one-quarter as much tea as the EIC itself.[3]

The British were first into the Pacific for whaling, and first in the fur trade of the North Pacific, but the Americans followed hard in their wake; two years after the Enderbys of London sent the whaler *Emilia* (largely manned by Nantucketers) into the South Sea in 1789; three years after James Hanna, from India via Macao, opened the sea otter trade at Nootka in 1785. In both cases, it was not long before the Yankees took the lead. Simon Metcalfe had the *Eleonora* and his son the *Fair American* at Hawaii in 1790; the first American trader at Sydney was the *Philadelphia* in 1792, and by 1811 fifty-seven had visited the struggling colony, which

---

Edward Young, *Imperium Pelagi. A Naval Lyric* (1730), a
grotesquely strident expression of a mercantile chauvinism
which persisted throughout the century and much of the next.

'depended upon them for a wide range of commodities otherwise unobtainable', despite the doubtful legality of trading in face of the British Navigation Acts; after the War of 1812 their stricter enforcement practically ended this involvement.[4] Americans preceded colonial sealers at various points on the south coast of Australia.[5] Across the Ocean Yankees played an important part in the revivification of the Spanish Pacific shores from Chile to California, like the Malouins a century earlier and like them largely by smuggling.[6]

These New Englanders were 'an active, busy band, sagacious to discover and eager to improve every promising opportunity';[7] a magnificent breed, not only as seamen. Against the scoundrelly Simon Metcalfe and the shady John Kendrick must be set men of humanity and honour such as Edmund Fanning and Amasa Delano. Consider the voyagings of Richard Cleveland in 1797–1804, largely in very small vessels which he bought and sold *en route*: Le Havre-the Cape-Batavia-Amoy-Norfolk Sound (near Sitka)-Hawaii-Canton-Calcutta-Mauritius-Copenhagen-Rio de Janeiro-Valparaiso-Galápagos-San Blas-California-Hawaii (with the first horses

Plate XIX. THE EAST INDIA MARINE HALL, SALEM. By courtesy of the Peabody Museum of Salem.

seen there)-Canton-the Cape-Boston. Fanning took the brig *Betsey*, under 100 tons, round the world and at seventy-one, distrusting the Navy's competence, appealed to Congress for aid in fitting out a flotilla to rival the official United States Exploring Expedition. Delano (Fig.24) was a man of disconcerting candour, with moral as well as maritime courage; he denounced that profitable Yankee hobby, privateering, as 'licensed robbery' and offered a qualified defence of the Lima Inquisition. There is something of Dampier in Delano; while never neglecting commercial opportunity he had eyes for more than Trade.[8]

These captains have an enduring monument in the beautifully pro-portioned building of the East India Marine Society at Salem, Massachusetts (Plate XIX). The Society was founded in 1799 for Salem captains and super-cargoes 'who shall have actually navigated the Seas' of either Cape, Good Hope or Horn; and, like a little Royal Society, it directed its members to note, in standard form, not only nautical memoranda but also 'Whatever is singular in the measures, customs, dress &c. of any people' and to collect artefacts and natural productions. The result is the treasury of the Peabody Maritime Museum—ship models, figureheads, scrimshaw, paintings of ships and ports, portraits of Salem captains with tough Calvinistic character in every face, and ethnographic collections, that from Fiji one of the world's finest.[9] Truly a noble memorial to a most remarkable company of mariners and merchant adventurers.

The China trade

On a global scale, Vincent Harlow's 'swing to the East' may have been 'not particularly effective'; British exports to Asia doubled in value between 1772 and 1798, but this brought their share of expanding total exports only from about 8 to about 9 per cent. Regionally, there was a marked shift in terms of trade; in 1772–7 the ratio of value of imports from India and China into England and of British exports to those countries was 74:26, but in 1792–8 it was 42:58. The average annual value of exports to those countries had risen from £513,000 to £3,466,000 sterling, of imports from them £1,941,000 to £5,986,00.[10] This leaves out of account the direct trade between India and China in such things as cotton and opium, carried in scores or hundreds of multiracially owned and manned 'country ships'. Canton, with its gatehouse Macao, was the greatest city of the Pacific rim, the major magnet and motor of Eastern trade. Regionally then the shift was a significant reality.

The year 1784 saw two events of critical importance. The peace settle-ment with the Netherlands after the American War conceded to British subjects the right to navigate freely in those 'Eastern Seas' which the Dutch had tried to maintain as *mare clausum*, or at least one in which foreign sailors had to explain themselves, often with difficulty, as Cartaret had learnt.[11] It is true that British trade, as distinct from navigation, was still barred from the Archipelago; but the Dutch writ did not run through all its islands, and the long history of contraband in Spanish America could hardly have reassured the Netherlanders as to the practical effect of this most reluctant concession. Significantly, Penang, at the northern entrance to the Malacca Straits, was taken over by the EIC in 1786; almost simultaneously it was decided to establish a convict settlement at Botany Bay. Designedly or not, the founding of Sydney in 1788 was to open another door to Cathay through the Eastern Seas. Anglo-Dutch relations long remained tense.[12]

The second event of 1784, in appearance a simple matter of internal fiscal policy, was Pitt's Commutation Act, which cut the duty on tea from 119 to 12.5 per cent. In England this amounted to a minor social revolution, bringing tea 'from the palace to the cottage'. The vast structures of contraband which supported the continental India Companies were undermined. While in 1783 the EIC brought 1877 tonnes of tea to Europe and other national Companies 6635 tonnes, in 1795 the figures were respectively 10,765 and—1877! Although under pressure of war the tea duty was raised in stages until it reached 100 per cent in 1819, consumption was hardly affected.[13] All would have been rosy in this comfortable near-monopoly had it not been for the unforeseen Yankee intrusion—unforeseen, for it had been rashly assumed that 'It would be hardly to the interest of the Americans to go to Canton, because they have no articles to send thither, nor any money.'[14]

There were of course other factors than Pitt's Act in this dominance of the EIC—the European wars, and the success of the search for alternatives to the forced reliance upon silver. These were Indian cotton and opium and—at last—British woollens. Between 1785 and 1788 cotton exports from Bombay and Surat to Canton increased over nine-fold; there was an eight-fold increase in Indian opium exports, some three-fifths of them going to China, the rest to the East Indies.[15] These commodities were left by the EIC to private 'country traders', largely managed by 'Agency Houses' in India; in the 1790s there were said to be 795 country ships based in Calcutta alone, most very small but with a few up to 1000 tons. If their trade could be quantified, the British dominance would appear even more overwhelming. Country exports to the Far East greatly exceeded imports thence; the differential was largely absorbed by buying EIC bills of exchange on London, thus obviating the direct use of silver; in fact, the silver drain was reversed.[16]

The opium trade brought immense profits and carried immense risks. Apart from the constant attentions of Malay pirates, it was illegal, at least for foreigners, in the Dutch sphere, and in theory absolutely barred in China. Nothing illustrates the symbiosis between the EIC and country traders better than the opium traffic, which became 'an indispensable part of the structure of the company's tea trade'. Smuggling of course was beneath the propriety and dignity of the Honourable Company, but not the supplying of the smugglers with their staple: 'the whole crop had been grown by the Company, mainly with a view to sale in China, and was now in other hands mainly for the sake of decency or safety.'[17] *La belle époque* of opium, if that is the right term for such a trade, was however later, from 1820 onwards.

Other commodities in the China trade were lead and Cornish tin; drugs and spices from the East Indies; and from the Pacific, Chilean copper, sandalwood, bêche-de-mer, furs and sealskins. The Americans were well placed to supply Pacific products. They began with ginseng, a root with aphrodisiac properties which grew both in Manchuria and in North American forests; but both quality and supply of the American product were variable,[18] and the great American staples were furs and sealskins. The net effect was to tie China more closely to the Pacific; as a motor for penetration of the Ocean, 'to the myth of the Austral continent... succeeded the reality of China, a vast market whose prospects demanded the exploitation of the Pacific.'[19]

Several factors contributed to the American impact on the China trade. One was sheer necessity; there was a 'crisis of demobilisation', especially of privateersmen, at the end of the War of Independence, and the shipping of the one-time Thirteen Colonies was now cut off, by the Navigation Acts, from legal trade with the British West Indies, previously perhaps the most flourishing branch of American commerce. This trade was too valuable to the local British interests to stop, but it had to continue on the more precarious footing of contraband,[20] and there was still the need to conquer fresh fields, including China.

Once at Canton, the American methods of work provided distinct economies in competition with the European Companies. Organised by small *ad hoc* syndicates, they had not the capacity, and did not feel the need, to emulate the pomp and panoply of the giant East Indiamen. They used smaller ships, with much smaller crews and lighter rigging for ease of working; their turnarounds were remarkably quick. Their success 'seems to lie in the informality of their methods and consequent slight overhead.'[21] The expensive display of the EIC was not really necessary; Samuel Shaw of the *Empress of China* reported a conversation with a hong merchant who much preferred this 'second sort of Englishmen' to the arrogant old breed, but added shrewdly 'All men come first China very good gentlemen, all same you. I think two three time more you come Canton, you make all same Englishman too.'[22]

The Americans came to China from both east and west. They were active in the Indian Ocean, and Ile de France (from 1814 British Mauritius) was a favourite waystation. But the furs, sandalwood, bêche-de-mer, pearl and tortoise shell—all these came directly from the Pacific. Of course they were not brought by Americans only; but—aided by the almost constant European wars from 1793 to 1815—the Yankees were soon dominant in the most important trade, that in furs; and it was they who made Honolulu a great node on the seaways between the opposite shores of the Ocean. (This fixation on the Pacific approach to the Orient, contrasting with the British way by the Indian Ocean, was to become a perennial motif, with an effect on the conduct of World War II in Asia).

But there was another entry into the China Seas, antedating the foundation of New South Wales but in its development closely associated with it.

New ways to the East

Whatever political weight may be attached to the British 'swing to the East', navigationally there was a physical eastwards shift in the routes from the Cape to China, if not the supplanting of the old tracks then at least a significant supplement to them.[23] In 1758 William Wilson of the EIC ship *Pitt* found himself too late, in mid-September, to catch the SW Monsoon in the China Seas, where it is replaced in October by the winter NE Monsoon. But south of the Equator, further from the great foci of alternating high winter/low summer barometric pressure in continental Asia, winds are still from the SE, and by making athwart them one could gain sufficient easting to work north into the NE Monsoon.[24] This Wilson duly did, calling at Batavia and sailing south of Celebes (Sulawesi) and past the Vogelkopf, the northwestern protrusion of New Guinea, and finally north of the Philippines to Macao.

There was at first no particular inducement to take such a route; the navigation of Pitt and Dampier Straits[25] off the Vogelkopf was tricky (Fig.22), as was that of Torres Strait for ships coming round, later on, from Sydney. But by 1793 about thirty ships had taken it, and it is clear that Parkinson's remarks that Wilson 'had discovered some such possibility' as an Eastern Passage and that EIC captains 'kept to a beaten track' are far too dismissive.[26]

There was some associated British activity between Gilolo and New Guinea. In 1774–6 Thomas Forrest sailed in a Malay prau from Dalrymple's settlement at Balambangan in Sulu, to look for spices beyond Dutch control, and reached Dorei Bay on the northeast coast of the Vogelkopf.[27] John McCluer of the EIC's Bombay Marine was sent from India in 1790 with two ships, to search for a reputed passage through western New Guinea 'which, if practicable for an East Indiaman, would be the most eligible Passage for our ships to China at a late Season'. Sailing by Benkulen (Fort Marlborough, Sumatra), Macao and Palau, he explored McCluer Gulf, which almost cuts off the Vogelkopf from the main mass of New Guinea.

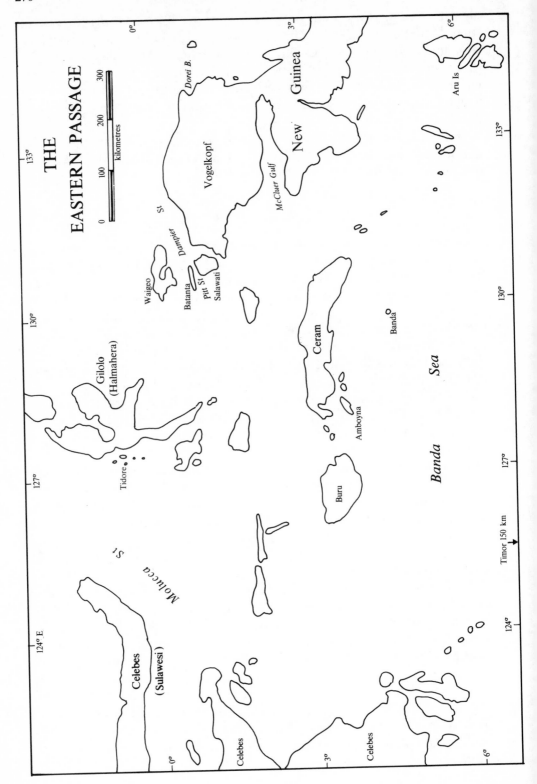

THE

EASTERN PASSAGE

kilometres

0   100   200   300

New Guinea

Dorei B.

Vogelkopf

McCluer Gulf

St

Dampier

Waigeo

Batanta
Pitt St
Salawati

Aru Is

Ceram

Banda

Amboyna

Buru

Banda   Sea

Gilolo
(Halmahera)

Tidore

Molucca St

Celebes
(Sulawesi)

Celebes

Celebes

Timor 150 km

This was an official EIC expedition; returning to the region in 1794, McCluer found that a private enterprise under John Hayes, also of the Bombay Marine, had settled at Dorei Bay, and taken nominal possession of much of the north coast of New Guinea by the name of 'New Albion', perhaps in reaction to D'Entrecasteaux's recent passage along the coast. Dorei Bay was exceedingly unhealthy, and there were native attacks; political reasons—first the desire to keep the Dutch from a French alliance and then war with them—prevented official acceptance of this far too isolated outpost, and in May or June 1795 it was abandoned.[28] In all this, it goes without saying, Alexander Dalrymple took a lively interest.

Despite the predictable failure of attempts at a lodgement hereabouts, the Eastern Passage continued in use and took new forms with the founding of Sydney. The first passage to China southabout Australia was, however, independent of this; on 30 December 1787 the *Alliance* of Philadelphia arrived at Whampoa 'out of nowhere'; she had come east of Australia through the Solomons and by Ponape. The EIC supercargoes thought that this might be 'a very good passage... very eligible' for an East Indiaman sailing late.

Just three months after Sydney was founded on 26 January 1788, Governor Phillip gave three transports 'leave to proceed to China', and in July four more followed them on the voyage on which John Shortland sailed through the Solomons and by Palao, Mindanao and Sulawesi. But already in May ships had left Port Jackson to establish tracks yet farther afield: Thomas Gilbert and John Marshall to Batavia through the islands named after them; even more to the east, Captain Sever to Macao via Tahiti (Fig.23).[29]

The New Directory for the East Indies (1780) says nothing of the Eastern Passage, but James Horsburgh, Dalrymple's successor as EIC Hydrographer, included it, as well as 'the passage round New Holland by the Pacific Ocean; in his authoritative *Directions for Sailing to and from the East Indies, China, New Holland...* of 1808–11. So far Howard Fry has traced about 180 ships, a hundred of them East Indiamen, which used some variant of the Passage by 1810; and this does not include ships passing through the Philippines or to China via Sydney.[30] Parkinson's 'some such possibility' was a reality.

The Manila trade

'This Colony would become far more flourishing in possession of any other Power, but the dronish disposition of the present possessors keeps them from turning to the most profit this rich & fertile country.'[31] As applied to the Spanish community long rooted in the Philippines, Nathaniel

◀ *Figure 22.* THE EASTERN PASSAGE. *P*, Pitt, *D*, Dampier Straits.

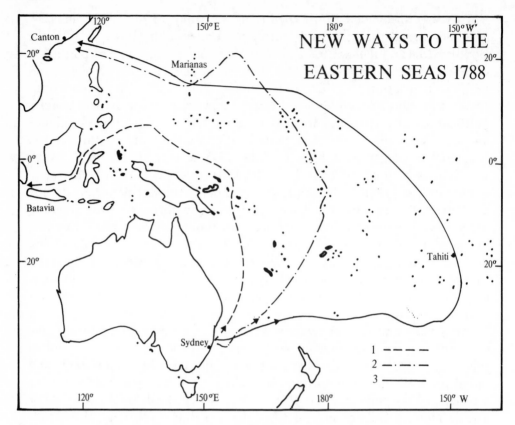

Figure 23. NEW WAYS TO THE EASTERN SEAS 1788. 1, Shortland in *Alexander*, 14 July–17 November; 2, Marshall in *Scarborough*, 7 May–8 September; 3, Sever in *Lady Penrhyn*, 6 May–19 October. Are these three courses, between them covering such a wide global arc, mere chance of weather or captain's caprice, or designed reconnaissance?

Bowditch's reproach, like La Pérouse's before him, was doubtless just; but its timing in 1796 was unkind. The Real Compañía de Filipinas was struggling to create a real economy by diversifying production and trade, against the bitter opposition of the 'City and Commerce of Manila', now represented by the Consulado formed in 1769 and so closely interwined with the moribund Galleon trade to Acapulco.

In the long run the RCF was to fail, at least in part owing to the European wars and the Napoleonic usurpation in Spain; but it had some local and temporary successes and left some ferment to enliven the traditional torpor. Perhaps the most notable success, for once in agreement with the Consulado, was the opening of the port of Manila in 1785 to the shipping of 'nations properly Asiatic', in 1790 to European ships but for trade in Asiatic goods only. A startling defiance of the ancient fear of contraband, but no more than the mighty EIC could the upstart RCF ignore the need for country traders as feeders.[32]

The supply of Chinese silks and porcelains for trans-shipment by the Acapulco Galleons had from the beginning been in the hands of the loathed but so necessary Sangleys, the Chinese traders of Manila; and there was some Indian trade, largely carried on by Armenians, British Indian subjects whose house flags could be considered 'Moorish'. This however was hardly enough, and the RCF's direct trade between Spain and India was the most lucrative of its many branches, which extended to New Spain and Peru. At Manila, however, the Chinese trade was always dominant over the Indian.[33] The RCF was still hampered by restrictions—Madrid was as ever desirous of reconciling irreconcilable interests—and from 1796 to 1808 it was subject to the vicissitudes of war with Britain. It had to its credit the expansion of Filipino production of cotton, sugar and indigo, the last of better quality than the Bengal product; and in 1787 it shipped the first Filipino manufactured export—835 pieces of cotton goods.[34]

The wars barred British shipping from Manila, but the Yankees were at hand to fill the gap; there were several American ships at Manila before the *Astrea* of Salem in 1796, often said to have been the first. The *Astrea*'s supercargo was the remarkable Nathaniel Bowditch, whose *New American Practical Navigator* was published in 1802 and in 1958 reached its seventieth edition.[35] Bowditch's trade at Manila was successful, if not legal; although his brandy and hats did not sell well, and the market for wine had been glutted by two RCF ships, there was a good demand for iron, lead and copper, cutlery and stationery, and glassware; and he took away a profitable cargo of local sugar, pepper, indigo and hides.[36] Hemp, later the staple Philippines export, did not become important until the 1820s; Bowditch does not mention it.[37]

'Manilla-men' were significant as recruits for yankee traders, although according to Delano they were distrusted as 'peculiarly savage'. Manila was involved in the initiation of the South Seas sandalwood trade; the first American ship to gather it in Fiji was probably the *Fair American* (not Simon Metcalfe's) in 1801; the same ship took thirty-seven head of cattle from Manila for New South Wales. Only two of these reached Sydney, but they were accompanied by some 5000 gallons of Filipino rum.[38] Manila had ceased to be a mere wharf for exchanging Chinese silks against Mexican silver; it had become a regional centre of diversified trade.

The China fur trade

When Cook's *Resolution* and *Discovery* reached Macao in November 1779, 'The rage with which our seamen were possessed to return to Cook's River, and, by another cargo of skins, to make their fortunes, at one time, was not far short of mutiny'; sea otter skins 'bought with only a hatchet or a Saw' fetched up to £15.15s.0d. James King himself sketched a plan for a voyage from Canton to northwest America, rather naively relying on EIC help; but his main objective was to fill the gap between 50 and 56°N, where Cook had been blown off the coast, and the furs were a secondary consideration to defray expenses. But he thought that the fur trade might 'become a fixed object of Indian Commerce' and gave practical advice on sailing times and trade goods.[39]

Others had a more exclusive eye to the main chance. John Ledyard, Cook's contact man with the Russians at Unalaska, failed to get support for an expedition in America and also in France, where he and the American naval hero John Paul Jones planned to send two ships to Nootka and set up a factory. Frustrated but never daunted, Ledyard set out on his remarkable journey from St Petersburg to his arrest at Iakutsk, which in his dreams was to be completed by sailing to Alaska and walking right across North America. A dream only, but it influenced Thomas Jefferson in planning the great Lewis and Clark transcontinental expedition, and, more immediately, Ledyard's account of Cook's last voyage was the direct impetus to the pioneer American venture to the Coast by Gray and Kendrick.[40]

There were other false starts,[41] but the first ships actually to reap the harvest sailed from India and Macao. James Hanna's *Harman* landed 560 skins at Macao in March 1786 and sold them for $20,000; hard on his heels were the *Captain Cook* and *Experiment* from Bombay and John Meares from Calcutta with the *Nootka* and *Sea Otter*. Meares was the first to winter on the coast, but he had to be succoured, at a price, by Portlock and Dixon.[42]

These two, companions on Cook's last voyage, were sent out by the King George's [Nootka] Sound Company, whose inspiring spirit was the assertive entrepreneur Richard Cadman Etches. Etches had prepared the ground thoroughly, with grudging permission for the voyage from the EIC and licenses from the SSC for the American side. The schemes were grandiose; trade with Japan, whaling and sealing as back-ups to the fur trade, Hawaii as a base, and a hint at the Northwest Passage. Factories were to be set up; the ships sailed by the Horn and may have made a short-lived settlement on Staten Island.

While fitting out the ships were visited by high officials and—a most significant touch—Portlock was told to send his despatches 'Care of George Rose, Esq. Treasury'. For a simple trading voyage, one might have expected a more mercantile accommodation address, say Lloyd's; and Rose was no mere clerk but Secretary to the Treasury and Pitt's right-hand man in finance. The very names of the ships attest the highest approval: *King George* (Portlock) and *Queen Charlotte* (Dixon), and on a later voyage *Prince of Wales* (James Colnett) and *Princess Royal* (Charles Duncan). It is hard to see why David Mackay should say that 'the government... had been at best luke-warm to the fur-traders who were interested in the area.'[43]

One also wonders whether his Majesty's Government was quite as surprised and shocked as it claimed when Colnett at last got himself arrested by the Spaniards at Nootka.

By the time Portlock and Dixon reached Canton, late in 1787, serious competition had set in. Meares had sold at $40 per skin in July, but he was under Portuguese colours and sold on his own account, while Etches's men had to sell through the EIC and made only $19 per skin. The Coast became a great haunt of interlopers, men with itchy feet and sticky hands, in ships like the mysterious French *Flavie*, Marchand's legitimate *Solide*, the *Imperial Eagle* under Austrian colours but a British captain (and wife), Meares's *Felice* (or *Feliz Aventureiro*) and *Iphigenia Nubiana* flying the Union Jack or Portuguese flag as best suited him, J. H. Cox's *Mercury* which doubled as the *Gustavus III*, a Swedish privateer against the Russians. In autumn 1788 the American vanguard arrived, Gray and Kendrick in the *Columbia Rediviva* and *Lady Washington*. By 1792 there were at least a score of ships on the Coast: eleven British, six American, one genuine and two pseudo-Portuguese (Meares's), one French, one 'Swedish'. The European wars, if not Yankee enterprise, prevented the British from maintaining this lead; before 1795, thirty-five British and fifteen American ships came to the Coast; in the period 1795–1805 the respective numbers were nine and sixty-eight. Between 1791 and 1795 the British brought 59,376 pelts (including seals) to Canton against 15,306 by the 'Bostonmen'; in 1801 the figures were 42,650 British and 444,807 Yankee.[44]

As for the original claimants to the Coast, the Russians and the Spaniards, the latter never succeeded in breaking into the trade substantially; Vicente Vasadre's scheme for getting Chinese mercury for the mines of New Spain was wrecked by RCF obstruction. There was some Spanish sea otter trade from California, but it did not amount to much.[45] With the Russians it was a different story; they, not the Spaniards, exploited the Farallons, within sight of San Francisco.

Grigorii Ivanovich Shelikov was a man of vision and indefatigable intrigue. In 1788 he proposed to Catherine the Great the chartering of a company which should end the anarchy of family firms and tiny syndicates which was ruinously exploiting the Alaskan fur trade, and might extend its activities to 'Japan, Korea, India, the Philippines' and even California.[46] He died in 1795, but his scheme came to fruition with the chartering in 1799 of the Russian-American Company. The RAC relieved the Imperial government of direct responsibility for Russian settlements in America and acted as a front for expansionist designs; plates intimating prior Russian possession were secretly buried as far south as San Francisco.[47] But this was a remote frontier, and Imperial policy was vacillating.

The disastrous depletion of fur-bearing animals along the Aleutians compelled longer voyages, and these squeezed out men with little capital. By 1820 the RAC had some fifteen settlements from Bering Strait to Fort Ross only 100 km north of San Francisco, but they were very thinly held—the largest, Novo-Arkhangel'sk (Sitka) had only 222 Russians—and away from their generally wretched hutments the coast was free for all, especially the Yankees, who often bought cheap from the Russians and sold dear in Canton. Despite two able administrators, Aleksandr Baranov and Shelikhov's son-in-law Nikolai Rezanov, the RAC seems always to have been a rickety and rackety affair. Its financial management was to say the least unsound; twice as much was spent on the Petersburg office as on the settlements; the capital value of its ships was grossly inflated by adding to the prime cost that of repairs, with no allowance for depreciation, so that 'an old, half-rotted ship would, after a few years' be reckoned as an asset at more than the value of a new one![48]

Corruption was rife both at St Petersburg and in the field; reading Okun's dry pages one feels that the old unreformed EIC was comparatively a model of purity. The naval officers who from time to time reported to the Imperial government were loud in their denunciations of the inefficiency and slovenliness, moral and physical, of the RAC's agents, and their gross brutality to the natives. At Novo-Arkhangel'sk Baranov's house, with a fine library and 'masterly paintings', made a good impression on foreign captains; but there was no school, no hospital, no medical store and—despite the RAC's repeated play with the opportunity it created for bringing Christianity to the natives—no priest.[49]

Although theoretically the RAC might seem to have had an advantage in the relative proximity of its bases in Petropavlosk and Okhotsk, this was offset by the miserable state of its marine, both ships and men; of the nineteen ships written off until 1820 (one a year) sixteen were wrecked 'especially because of the carelessness and lack of skill ... of the Okhotsk pilots.'[50] The RAC never succeeded in establishing direct trade to Canton and thus obviating the costs of the roundabout land journey from Okhotsk to Kiakhta; for Canton it relied on foreign shipping, especially American, and in fact even the supply of the posts depended largely on the Yankee traders; there was a symbiosis between Baranov and some Bostonmen. This was dangerous; the Americans swarmed along the Coast outside the RAC's nerveless grasp, they paid the Indians better—and they sold them firearms.

There were sometimes decent relations between the Russians and the Coast peoples, but the record was grim. The RAC was marginally less barbarous than the old private traders, but it relied on ruthless exploitation of Russian contract labour and often on sheer terrorism of the Indians. The Tlingit or Kolosh of the Novo-Arkhangel'sk hinterland were however much tougher than the Aleuts, and hit back; indeed, in 1802 they sacked the town, not without suspicion of British connivance. Baranov obtained arms and ammunition by a bargain with the Boston trader O'Cain, who was given skilled Aleut hunters to take sea otter as far as Baja California on half-shares with the RAC. Even so it took a full scale attack by I. F. Lisianski in the Imperial ship *Neva* to retake the town. Between 1806 and 1813 there were twelve joint ventures similar to O'Cain's.[51]

From 1797 to 1818 the RAC shipped 80,000 otter and 1,495,000 seal pelts. But practices were crude; curing was inefficient, markets were overstocked, and many thousand sealskins had to be burned. Yet the reckless overkill went on. It was accompanied by the degradation and drastic decline in numbers of the Coast peoples, especially the Aleuts.[52]

Despite the renown of the sea otter, based on the surpassing beauty of its pelt, quantitatively the bulk of the China fur trade was in sealskins, and sealing carried on after the otter was virtually wiped out. This elimination was aided by the fact that the female bore only one cub a year, and while diving for food would leave it on the kelp beds; if the cub was taken she returned to defend it.[53] As stocks declined in the north, the Russians pushed south, meeting the British and Americans working north, until their Aleuts were taking otter from the Farallons.

The trade could be brutal, and the Tlingit was not the only tribe willing to fight to avenge violence or swindling. Attacks on boats, sometimes even ships, were not uncommon; there were treacheries and stratagems on either side. Simon Metcalfe of Hawaiian ill-fame was trading peacefully when he was killed in the Queen Charlottes.[54] There may have been little to choose between Britons and Yankees in the reckless business of arming the Indians, so feelingly lamented by Vancouver. Of course, for every instance of outrage there must have been more of amicable trading.

After the outbreak of the European wars the Americans made the running; in 1801 Boston had fourteen of the sixteen ships on the Coast, which could be picturesquely described as 'a commercial suburb of Boston'.[55] But under Baranov the Russians' activity was becoming more coherent, and by 1816 their posts were 'highly prejudicial to American commerce'; and the Hudson's Bay Company was firmly planted on the Pacific. John Jacob Astor's settlement of Astoria, at the mouth of the Columbia, designed as an entrepôt for furs and an advanced base for the China trade, was badly timed; founded in 1811, it was caught up in the War of 1812 and virtually still-born. But the trade was dying of its own success. In 1821–7 the British brought no otter pelts to China, the Americans only 1500, and 105,000 sealskins, respectively 10.5 and 41.5 per cent of the numbers they had brought in 1799–1806. The handful of American ships which visited the Coast after this were mainly engaged in supplying Novo-Arkhangel'sk and the Hudson Bay Company posts.[56]

The killing cycle was over for the sea otter; a few of these most beautiful animals survive in carefully protected colonies—and James Colnett had said that it would take 'two centuries to destroy them so they could anyways be miss'd.'[57] The sea-hunters had found new worlds to conquer, the great seal rookeries of the southern oceans, where they massacred on a scale which put the North Pacific slaughter in the shade.

The quarry of the Ocean: whaling and sealing

A great work of art has fatally distorted our perspective on the very hard-headed (and as it seems today hard-hearted) trade of whaling; *Moby Dick* does not figure among the sources of Alexander Starbuck's sober history, but its quintessential Romanticism set the tone for far too many whaling 'histories' which are really repetitive anthologies of moving accidents by wreck, mutiny, fire and ice, without form and void. Yet Melville also pointed unerringly to the vast sweep of whaling enterprise, its cosmopolitanism, and its catalyctic economic and social role in the Pacific.

It is difficult to appreciate today the surpassing importance of whale and seal oil before the large-scale production of vegetable oils and the domestication of petroleum. They were far the best sources, before coal-gas, of artificial light; of especial value was the oil from the head of the sperm whale, a great buoyancy tank, as distinct from that rendered down from the blubber of that and other species. Sperm oil was also the finest lubricant known, in an age when precision engineering was more and more essential in manufacturing industry, and was used in textile and leather finishing. The numerous species of toothless whales—right and blue whales, rorquals—provided 'black oil' from blubber and 'whale-bone' or baleen, which formed a sieve within their mouths to retain the masses of tiny crustacea which were the food of these giants. Baleen is extremely light, tough and flexible; its best-known uses were for corsets and the hoops of crinolines, but it had at least thirty others, mostly for articles of minor convenience now made of plastic.[58] As a bonus there *might* be chunks of ambergris, a waxy concretion formed in intestinal ulcers of sperm whales; of high value in perfumery, in China it fetched up to £143 per ounce as an aphrodisiac. Finally, sperm whale teeth provided excellent ivory, not only for the scrimshaw engraving practised by whalemen in their waiting periods but also for billiard balls and so on. Whale meat and bones were used as early as 1812 for fertiliser.[59]

Figure 24. TRADERS & SEALERS: BASS, BISHOP, DELANO, CLEVELAND. 1, ▶ Charles Bishop in *Ruby*, 1794–6; 2, Bishop in *Nautilus*, 1797–8; 3, Amasa Delano in *Perseverance*, 1799–1802; 4, George Bass and Bishop in *Venus*, 1801–2; 5, Amasa Delano in *Perseverance*, 1803–7; 5a, Samuel Delano in *Pilgrim*, 1804–5; 6, Richard Cleveland, various ships, 1797–1804. Tracks are approximations only. C, Callao; E, Easter I.; H, Hawaii; JF, Juan Fernández; M, Macao; PP, Petropavlosk; S, Sydney; T, Tahiti; V, Valparaiso. Inset: minor passages in southeast Australia.

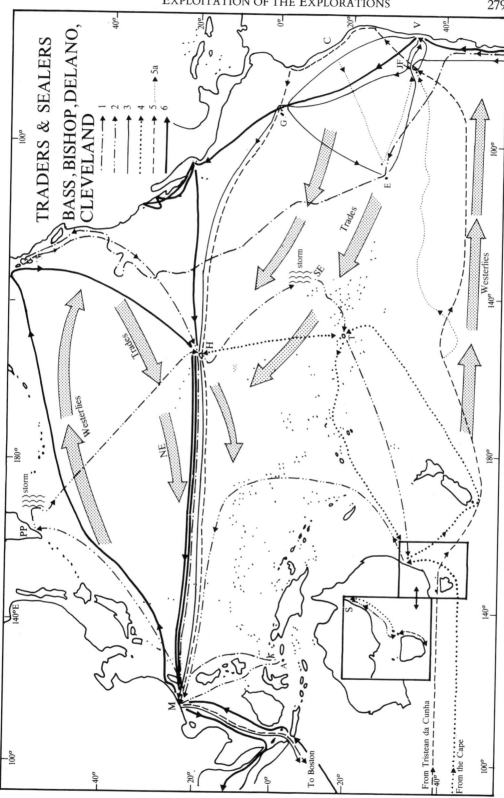

TRADERS & SEALERS
BASS, BISHOP, DELANO,
CLEVELAND

1
2
3
4
5 —— 5a
6

With the exception of shore whaling in Australia and New Zealand, Pacific whaling in our period was mainly for sperm, which are found mostly in tropical and warm temperate waters. The first known taking of a sperm whale was by a Nantucketer in 1712; this species yields more and better oil than the Arctic blue (rorqual) and right whales which had been hunted in the North Atlantic for centuries, and by the 1780s was being fished out even in the south. The London firm Enderbys then took the plunge by sending the *Emilia* round the Horn in 1788–9.

Licences from the SSC were easy, but the EIC was ever fearful of any possible approach to its sacred shores; as Harlow put it, 'The dog in the manger was barking furiously', but Pitt and Hawkesbury, President of his Committee for Trade, were determined to 'sustain the Southern Whalers as pioneers of commercial penetration in the South Seas'. The Company succeeded in banning British whaling in the Indian Ocean east of Madagascar, but in 1790 was forced to allow it in the Pacific east of 180° and south of the Equator.[60] The Yankees of course suffered no such restrictions; already in 1775 Edmund Burke had exclaimed 'Falkland Isles, which seemed too romantic and remote an object for the grasp of national ambition, is but a stage and resting-place in the progress of their victorious industry.'[61] With Independence even wider fields were open to them.

The Nantucketers soon made the running. Their tiny scrap of land off Massachusetts was totally dependent on whaling, and they tried, naturally in vain, to stay neutral during the American Revolution; after it, their search for security led to the formation of little Nantucket colonies in Dartmouth (Nova Scotia), Milford Haven in Wales, and Dunkirk, France. Under any of three flags, Nantucketers had an extraordinarily high proportion of those highly skilled technicians the harpooners—in 1789, perhaps three-quarters.[62] The British naturally found more difficulty in using South American west coast ports than the Americans, even before war with Spain in 1796, and until the check of the War of 1812 New Englanders were in the van of the spread of whalers over the Pacific. After 1814 the Yankees again took the lead; it has been calculated that between 1775 and 1844 there were 2153 British and 13,027 American sperm whaling voyages, the great majority to the Pacific.[63]

Whaling expansion was extraordinarily rapid (Fig.26). Starbuck, of a Nantucket family whalers since 1755, gives the reason: 'new fields must be opened up to supply the demand that had become rapacious... this crusade against the whale was relentlessly pursued.'[64] As early as 1793 the Enderbys, with government backing, sent James Colnett, recovered from his Nootka adventure, up the American coast as far as California; he found the rich grounds around the Galápagos Islands. The Yankees reaped the harvest; in 1818 a Nantucketer found the 'Off-Shore Grounds' west of the Galápagos, and in two years over fifty ships were exploiting them; another Nantucket captain, in an Enderby ship, reached the Japan Grounds in 1820, and again thirty ships followed in two years. Barzillai Folger, of a famous Nantucket family, initiated the North Pacific fishery by taking a right whale off Kodiak in 1836; in under half a century since the *Emilia*, the vast Ocean had been overrun.[65]

Several of the transports in the First Fleet to Botany Bay were whalers on charter to the government; it was impossible to sail south of Australia without sighting whales—one captain reported 'more in one day than off the coast of Brazil in six years'—and some having dumped their convicts went about their old business. The Enderbys had their sights on New South Wales from the beginning, and they along with the EIC were obstructive when the first ship carrying an export cargo, Robert Campbell's *Lady Barlow* in 1805, reached the Thames with seal oil and skins. As late as 1831 fishery products—whale oil and whalebone, seal oil and pelts—outranked wool in New South Wales exports, with 30 per cent of the total including re-exports.[66]

Sealing was dominant in the beginning, but already in 1804 five ships were said to have carried cargoes of sperm oil averaging £13,500 each. In that year the first right whale was taken in the Derwent, and Hobart on that river was set to become a great whaling port. Australian whaling, however, was carried on in boats from shore stations for right whales, which bred close inshore, and the southern coasts of Australia were soon dotted with look-out posts. Reckless slaughter of calving females cut this bay whaling to modest proportions.[67]

If whaling was important for the early economy of Australia, it was all-important for that of New Zealand, where the Bay of Islands harboured an odd colony of whalemen and missionaries in uneasy coexistence. The

Figure 25. EUROPEAN ECONOMIC ACTIVITY *c.* 1700–25. For key to symbols, see caption to Fig. 26. The Malouin trade with the South Sea was illicit after the Treaty of Utrecht, 1715, but not effectively checked until 1717. Altogether sixteen French ships crossed to China by the Galleon track 1707–14, ten making forgotten circumnavigations.

Figure 26. EUROPEAN ECONOMIC ACTIVITY *c.* 1800–1825. 1, sea-otter trade to China; 2, sperm whaling grounds with dates of entry; 3, bay whaling; 4, sealing; 5, sandalwood; 6, main trading routes in Eastern Seas; 7, new approaches to Eastern Seas; *posts and ports*: 8, Spanish (Fig. 25) or ex-Spanish; 9, still Spanish in 1825; 10, Russian; 11, Portuguese; 12, Dutch; 13, British; 14, Canadian (not Hudson's Bay Co.); 15, American Fur Company (J. J. Astor); 16, 'international' (Canton, Honolulu). There was obviously a vast difference in style between rigidly regulated Canton and utterly informal Honolulu, but both were open to all, as were Macao and by this time Manila. Some of these posts had a very brief existence — the Russians in Hawaii, the British in northern Australia — but have been included to show the geographical range of interests.

One might entitle this map 'The Economic Projection of Captain Cook'.

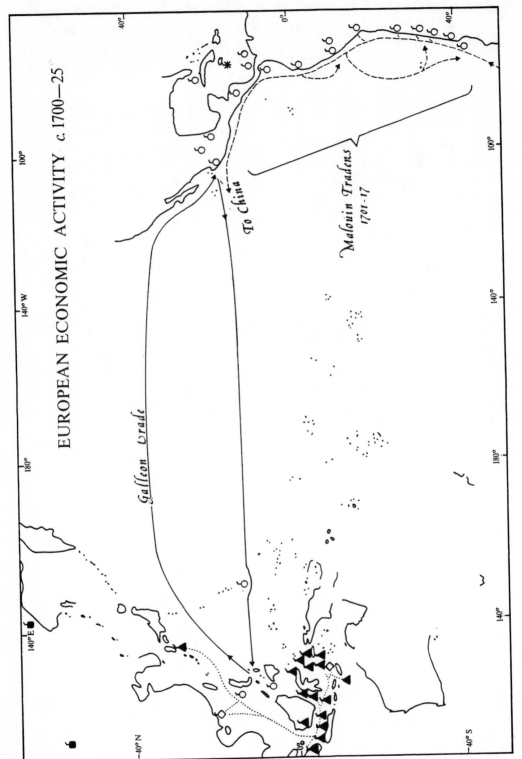

EUROPEAN ECONOMIC ACTIVITY c. 1700—25

Galleon trade

To China

Malouin Traders
1701-17

Figure 25.

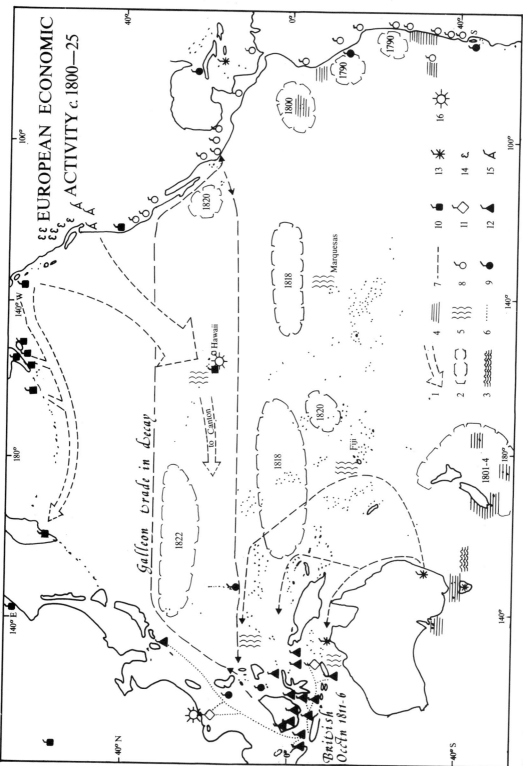

EUROPEAN ECONOMIC ACTIVITY c. 1800—25

Galleon trade in decay

To Canton

Hawaii

Marquesas

Fiji

British Ocean 1811-6

Figure 26.

whalers' relations with the Maori, despite some incidents of extreme violence, were symbiotic; the Maori were quick to take to farming and provided essential supplies, especially pigs, potatoes and onions; the whalers provided a lucrative market. Maori took to the sea by hundreds, becoming expert whalemen, some as junior officers. There was also the 'old trade', girls for guns—for the numerous shore whalers, often on a more or less permanent marital basis. 'Mission, Maori, and whaleship interests were interdependent in the 1820s'.[68]

The colonial duties which hampered Australian whalers were removed in 1823, and they could now compete with the British, though they lacked the resources to do so very effectually with the Americans; a by-product of American competition was the transfer of some British ships to Australian interests. The Americans had tended to avoid New Zealand until the missionaries had rendered the Maori more tractable, and New Zealand was never the major ground for Yankee whalers, though it remained the most important market for provisions and recruits.[69]

The whaleman's life, like the soldier's, was one of long stretches of boredom—the voyage out and home, the intervals between sightings—punctuated by spells of intense activity and risk of death or disablement; a life fostering *élan* and team spirit. Payment of the crews was by 'lays', percentages of the take, which provided incentive, though of course this was often offset by charges for food and clothing deducted from men's accounts; some owners were completely unscrupulous. Merchant seamen, badly paid and treated as they were, generally were better-off, and were not attracted by whaling—after all, taking to the boats was the last resort for the merchantman, the very first for the whaleman; and many captains preferred a core of skilled men and for the rest green hands whom they could knock into shape. Discipline, especially on American ships, was often very tough, desertions frequent, mutinies not unknown.

While some writers make a whaler's foc'sle seem almost a cosy parlour, those less determinedly romantic are apt to paint it as a hell-hole.[70] There seems a sharp decline in decency after about 1825, as the dominance of Quaker Nantucket lessened and the youth of New England anticipated the classic advice 'Go west, young man, go west' and was replaced by the crimped scourings of Sailortown. Paradoxically, the 'better elements' in later whaling were often Cape Verde or South Sea Islanders.[71] While the impact of the whalemen on Island people was often devastating enough, it was not without its positive aspects, as Morton has shown for New Zealand at least.[72] With the passing of unmechanised whaling, a great saga was ended.

It is possible to glamourise whaling, with its moments of high hazard, but hardly sealing, with slaving one of the most repulsive of trades. In sealing the skills and daring of the whale hunt were replaced by the mere bludgeoning of creatures who had left their native element for breeding and were helpless on land. Men could be reduced to a brutish existence, marooned often for months, sometimes years, in the drear desolation of sub-Antarctic islands. Yet the profits for entrepreneurs could be great, on little capital expenditure; an ideal breakaway from the starveling existence of the gaol around Sydney Cove.

As well as its use for lighting and lubricating, seal oil was used in textile processing and in foodstuffs, being free of the disagreeable taste of whale oil, and as a medium for paints; there was always the Chinese demand for fur sealskins, and although those of the hair seal or sea-lion were not wanted at Canton, they had a market in America. Sea-elephants were also hunted for oil; weighty monsters, they could fight back. Sealing in the Southern Oceans began on both the western and eastern approaches to the Pacific. In the Indian Ocean, George Mortimer of the ambiguous *Mercury* was at St Paul and Amsterdam in 1789, and American sealers were there and at Kerguelen in 1792–3. The first Yankee sealing at the Falklands was in 1784, and in 1788 Simon Metcalfe took the first Falkland skins to Canton.[73]

The Pacific itself offered richer fields. Already in 1684 Dampier had noted that at Juan Fernández 'Large ships might here load themselves with Seals-skins, and Trane-oil', and at Mas Afuera Cartaret found seals 'so numerous . . . that if many thousand were killed in a night they would not be missed in the morning.'[74] It was a century before Dampier's hint was taken up; when it was, Cartaret's opinion was more than confirmed, and a rush began. When Captain Mayhew Folger raised Cartaret's Pitcairn Island, he was looking for seals, not the *Bounty* descendants whom he found.[75]

The first sealer at Mas Afuera was the *Eliza* of New York in 1782; she took 38,000 skins and was followed in 1798 by seven ships. Despite the Spaniards, who cleared sealers from the island in 1801 and again in 1804–5, and a complete absence of harbours, this slab-sided chunk of lava, about twenty-one by six km and with hardly any coastal plain, became a temporary home of sorts to hundreds of American seamen. When the first wave of sealers arrived it was said that there were half a million seals on Mas Afuera, and more skins were taken thence to Canton than from all other rookeries combined. The coasts of Chile and Peru were also ransacked.[76]

The experiences of Fanning and Delano were typical. The former arrived in the *Betsey* in January 1798; in nine weeks the brig's hold, cabin and forecastle were packed, leaving just room to move about, and 4000 skins were cached ashore. Delano in 1800 found fourteen ships in the offing and himself carried away 100,000 skins; he estimated that about 3,000,000 were taken to Canton in seven years.[77] It could not last; the trade was killing itself when the Spaniards moved in, and in 1815 another American captain found a few ruined huts, and no seals.

In the long spells ashore at Mas Afuera, the sealing gangs were able to set up a simulacrum of civil society, with vegetable gardens and spirited celebrations of the Fourth of July; and in New Zealand the sealers, like the whalers, had to come to terms with the Maori around them. Things were ruder and rougher in the remote sub-Antarctic outposts—Campbell, Macquarie, and the Antipodes Islands—and in Bass Strait. Here the struggling infant colony of New South Wales found its first export outlet; a poor thing, but its own. Seals could be taken by small craft without the specialised gear and crews of the whalers, and while the gangs were left ashore the ships could double as coastal traders.

In October 1793 an American whaler arrived in Sydney from St Paul; her master expressed surprise that local craft were not exploiting the seals along the coast. Nothing happened until the *Sydney Cove*, en route to Bengal, was wrecked near Cape Barren Island, in the east of Bass Strait, in January 1797; reports of survivors, and of Matthew Flinders, sent to their assistance, again drew attention to the wealth of seals on Tasmanian offshore islands. The first exploitation was by Charles Bishop, who in late 1798 took 9000 skins from Cape Barren Island.[78] Local petty entrepreneurs, and the solid India-based merchant Robert Campbell, entered on the trade with avidity, if on a small scale—in 1806 the eight sealers registered in the colony averaged 26.6 tons and 5.5 men. Campbell's Bengal connections were invaluable, since trade to Canton had still, officially at least, to go by India.[79]

It was not to be expected that the Yankees would overlook these rich grounds; the name American River on Kangaroo Island, South Australia, attests their probable priority. There were physical clashes with the 'banditti' of the Strait, many escaped convicts, and both parties abducted and brutalised aboriginal women.[80] Almost minute as the Australian activity was alongside the American, it was a major input to an embryonic economy; one emancipist partnership, Kable and Underwood, brought in 26,282 skins in a single year, and another ex-convict, Simeon Lord, was an active participant. Between 1801 and 1806 a total of 98,271 skins were exported from Sydney; between 1805 and 1810, London received 217,791 and paid £33,735 for four-fifths of them; of course not all of this sum accrued to the shippers, freight and insurance charges were high. Sealing and supply to whalers had a modest multiplier effect through their demand for shipbuilding and repairing, salt, cooperage and chandlery.[81]

Once more the crudely extractive nature of the trade carried the seeds of its self-destruction, as Nicolas Baudin had warned Governor King at the start. Already towards the end of King's time (1800–6) depletion of the Australian rookeries was forcing the sealers farther afield, to New Zealand (where a tentative probe to Dusky Bay had been made in 1793) and the islands south and east—Macquarie, Auckland, Campbell, Antipodes, Chathams (Fig.26). On such bleak outposts gangs might be left, by accident or callous negligence, for as much as four years. The old story was repeated; Macquarie, which had yielded over 100,000 skins in one season, produced only 6000 in 1815; 50,000 were taken from Campbell in eight months of 1805–6, a gang left there in 1835 took a derisory 170 in four years.[82] This was not the first nor the last, but surely one of the most striking of those cycles of devastation which have marked man's rifling of his environment.

The Islands trades

The first export trade developed by Europeans from the Pacific Islands was unromantic: live pigs and salt pork. It began when in 1793 Vancouver's storeship *Daedalus* brought eighty pigs from Tahiti to Sydney. The *Duff* missionaries also reported the prevalence of pigs in Tahiti. Governor King saw an alternative to the costly procurement of salt pork, for convict and official rations, from Britain. In 1801 King sent a government ship for pork; his present to Tu (Pomare I) included 5.5 kg of Australian-made soap, presumably the country's first export of manufactured goods. With curious precision, Phillip's instructions had referred to the Pacific Islands between 10°37′ and 43°39′S (the extreme latitudes of New South Wales) as 'dependencies' of the colony. The trade could thus be regarded as intra-colonial to which EIC prohibitions did not apply, and so was a legitimate field for colonial entrepreneurs, and one involving little risk or capital.

In 1802 Charles Bishop and George Bass led the way, and by 1805 some 158 tonnes of salt pork had been imported, and sold at a price little more than half that of British pork. The trade was lively until about 1820–5, with fluctuations due to shortage or political disturbance in Tahiti or diversion of shipping to the sandalwood trade. It had been of considerable economic advantage to New South Wales, and in Tahiti pork traders and missionaries gave significant support to the Pomares in their rise to power, the former at times with arms.[83]

The Tahitian pork trade was an Australian affair; it was not profitable enough to attract the Yankees. This did not hold for the trade in sweet-smelling sandalwood, which was in great demand in China, especially for ceremonial burning as incense. In 1801 the Spanish prize *El Plumier*, now of Sydney, was seeking bêche-de-mer in Tonga when her master learned of the indigenous importing of sandalwood from Fiji; there he picked up a shipwrecked American, Oliver Slater, who guided him to the 'Sandalwood Coast' of Bua on Vanua Levu. *El Plumier* and her sandalwood were taken by the Spaniards near Guam, but in 1804 Slater arrived in Sydney from Manila, and his news touched off a minor rush to Bua. The enterprising Simeon Lord sent him off ostensibly to New Caledonia for bêche-de-mer but actually to Bua for sandalwood.

Pacific wood was not so good as that from Malabar and Timor, but could fetch £40–65 per tonne in Canton.[84] It was one thing to trade within the extensive technical limits of New South Wales, quite another to ship Islands products direct to China, and Sydney traders were soon entangled in EIC regulations. These could be got round by selling more or less surreptitiously to Americans at Sydney or in Fiji, but naturally sandalwooding fell more and more into American hands.

It was a risky trade—Fijians had a fearsome reputation as cannibals—and depended on the co-operation of local chiefs, who drafted labour for felling, haulage and sawing. Often enough this meant involvement in local feuds, in one of which Charlie Savage was eaten. It was also a brutally extractive trade; by 1813 the Fijian stands were being worked out—Peter Dillon, who had seen Savage killed, came back in 1825 and got only 227 kg where in 1808 he had taken 150 tonnes, and in 1840 Wilkes's expedition could hardly find a few scientific specimens. It was the same story in the Marquesas, where the first known cargo, 200 tonnes, was lifted by the Boston ship *Hunter* in 1810. The British blockade of American shipping at Canton in the War of 1812 kept news of this find from Boston and Salem, and Sydney moved in. With peace there was an American revanche; by 1821 the Marquesas also had been stripped.[85]

In Hawaii, where Yankee monopoly was nearly complete, there were interesting variants. The trade really took off in 1811, when three Boston traders carried cargoes to Canton, partly on account for Kamehameha I, who on their return granted them a ten years' monopoly on the export of sandalwood which he would supply, taking a quarter of the profits. Again the War of 1812 put an end to this early experiment in 'partnership for development', but with peace the trade became lively. Kamehameha retained the monopoly of supply until his death in 1819, when the trade was thrown open to lesser chiefs, who worked on the same lines, with the natural results—rapid depletion of the resource and ruthless exploitation of the commoners' forced labour. Apart from drastic over-working of the commoners, which may have contributed to their numerical decline, the trade led to a fantastic accumulation of often useless consumption goods in chiefly storehouses; from Kamehameha down, chiefs had a passion for possessing European-style vessels, and the exchange of sandalwood for sometimes unseaworthy small craft was common.

In 1817 Kamehameha sent a cargo to Canton under his own flag. Hawaiian sandalwood was rather poor, but sales at low prices sometimes glutted the market, and there was a serious slump in 1821. Revival led

to the bizarre venture of chief Boki in 1829. Inspired by the elimination
of sandalwood in Hawaii and true reports of good stands in the New
Hebrides, he set out with two brigs and over 400 men for Eromanga;
he disappeared in one, the other limped home with only twenty survivors.
The Eromanga finds touched off another wave of sandalwooding, longer-
lived but confined to Melanesia.[86]

Little need be said of the minor products of reef and lagoon—pearl-
shell, 'tortoise-shell' (really that of the hawksbill turtle), and bêche-de-
mer or trepang or (more descriptively) sea-slug, of which the last was
most important. Traders turned to these as the sandalwood became
exhausted, and pearl-shell, largely from the Tuamotus, was a useful side-
line; turtle-shell was a later development in the Pacific. Bêche-de-mer
was a highly valued delicacy in China, and its preparation in big smoke-
houses needed a large local labour force; again chiefly assistance was
essential. There was some exploitation in the Palaus and on the Great
Barrier Reef (only trifling) in 1804–5 and in Fiji and the Tuamotus in
the 1810s, but the real take-off was about 1820, especially in Fiji, a major
producer, and once again the trade had marked social and (through its
demand for fuel) ecological effects on the Islanders and the Islands.[87]

New nodes of trade: Sydney and Honolulu

'Before the hinterland of New South Wales had been penetrated for
fifty miles her settlers had established commercial contacts with the Pacific
Islands, India, China and South America'[88]—one might add the Cape
and Ile de France (Mauritius). Although it is rightly becoming more
generally accepted that commercial and strategic considerations were not
absent from the motives which led the British Government to found
the penal settlement, its nature as a gaol hindered normal commercial
development: 'The readiness of the convict population to put to sea for
distant parts in almost anything that would float' impelled Governor
Hunter to issue in 1797 a strict prohibition of the building of any private
boats whatsoever.[89]

Inevitably, this blanket ban was soon flouted, in fact discarded—the
very next year permission, carefully circumscribed, to build locally was
perforce granted. It would have been simply impossible to carry on the
life of the colony without an active cabotage between Sydney and its
widely scattered offshoots—Norfolk Island, Newcastle with its coal, the
agricultural heart of the colony on the Hawkesbury River (under 60 km
distant by land but much more accessible by water) (Fig.27), and after
1813 Van Diemens Land for meat, potatoes and grain. And Governors
desperate for some source of wealth encouraged sealing.

It is therefore not really surprising that the first private industry, other
than the making of petty consumption goods, was the building of small

vessels. By 1804, seven years after Hunter's ban, there were twenty-two privately owned cutters, schooners and sloops, all but one locally built. They were tiny—they totalled only 452 tons and the largest was only thirty-eight; it was a great step forward when in 1805 the first fully-rigged ship, the *King George*, was launched. There were between 100 and 120 colonially registered bottoms in the period 1800–20, about 100 of them locally built. Poor construction and seamanship brought heavy losses; of 112 definitely identifiable, no fewer than forty-three were wrecked.[90] But a foundation had been laid.

Despite the necessities of colonial life, there were still governmental inhibitions. That the official nervousness about convicts escaping was not unjustified was shown by the exploit of William and Mary Bryant, who with seven others (and their two infant children) stole the Governor's cutter in 1791, and sailed it to Timor, where they were picked up by Edwards of the *Pandora*. It is good to know that those reaching England, who included the indomitable Mary, were pardoned, mainly at the instance of James Boswell.[91] Less spectacular but more serious was the constant leakage of convicts stowing away, with or without connivance, on merchant ships.

Another constant was the nervousness of the EIC. In one aspect, the early history of British commercial enterprise in the Pacific is one of continuous but always grudging acquiescence by the Company in the erosion of its monopolistic claims—not the actual exercise of its legal monopoly of Pacific trade outside the territorial limits of New South Wales and the SSC's sphere, for that it never attempted, but the exclusion of any activities which might conceivably impinge upon its sacred preserves in Asia.

The first slight crack came with the Second Fleet to Botany Bay (1790), when a proposal that EIC ships should transport the convicts on charter to the government was met with the argument that private contractors could do the job more cheaply if the Company chartered their ships and allowed them to load for the return voyage in China or India, on their own account.[92] The EIC reluctantly accepted this arrangement, which would avoid locking up its own ships while allowing it to control the trade in Asia. The pressure of whaling interests opened Australian and New Zealand waters to British whalers in 1798. In 1814 trade between the United Kingdom and places within the EIC limits was thrown open to British subjects in ships of over 350 tons, though licences were still required for some areas and the tea trade at Canton was reserved to the Company. The 350–ton limit effectively barred colonial shipping from direct trade with Britain, until in 1819 it was lifted.[93]

François Péron, at Sydney with Baudin in 1802, gave an almost lyrical description of the shipping in Port Jackson: 'In the harbour were assembled a number of vessels, recently arrived from different parts of the globe, the greater part destined for new and hazardous voyages'—whaling on the 'wintry shores' of New Zealand, to the Cape and India with coal, to Bass Strait for sealing, to Peru to establish by force a contraband trade, to Northwest America for furs, to the South Sea Islands for salt provisions.[94] The picture is a little too glowing; although his plan of Sydney shows gallows ancient and modern (Plate XX), Péron does not mention the most significant sector—the import of men and women in chains.

Transports were the biggest ships entering, averaging 427 tons for the years in which complete tonnage figures are available, 1800–7, 1810–24. For these years they had 23 per cent of entries but 44 per cent of tons entering.[95] Convicts and their supplies were thus the largest bulk imports, and there was obviously no bulk return cargo; consequently transports had to double as traders going to India or Canton to pick up return cargoes, or as whalers.

Nearly all the ships represented in Table 12.II were British or British Indian owned, except for some colonial sealers and the Americans. These were shut out, first by the War of 1812–14 and then in 1816 by the strict enforcement of the Navigation Acts, over Governor Macquarie's anticipatory protest that it had been 'the Constant Usage and Custom' to admit American ships in peacetime and his pointed reminder that 'No regular Commercial Intercourse is Yet established between Us and the Mother Country'.[96] But the easing of restrictions in 1814 and the lifting of the 350-ton limit met his point; there was soon an active intercourse, especially when wool was added to oil and skins as a bulk return cargo.

Some points in Table II call for mention. The earlier contacts with South America were by smugglers (in 1803 George Bass disappeared on a smuggling venture) or privateers and their prizes; the first ship from South America, in 1799, was a prize usefully laden with sugar, flour and spirits. The revival in 1821–5 was due partly to whaling, more to the opening of ex-Spanish ports after Liberation; by 1825 the trade in wheat from Valparaiso had made a good start.[97] The increase in sailings to Batavia after 1811 is notable. The British occupied the Dutch East Indies in that year, but British trade in the Archipelago, as distinct from navigation, was restricted from 1815 to 1824 when it was opened by the Anglo-Dutch Treaty.[98] This increase was accompanied by a sharp decline in direct sailings to China, but presumably most ships clearing for Batavia went on to Canton or India. The first peak in traffic with the South Sea Islands was associated with the pork and sandalwood trades; there was a falling-off due to Yankee competition, the exhaustion of sandalwood, and heavy duties on imports to the colony, but a revival with the bêche-de-mer trade and some pearling when the duties were lifted in 1819. Not shown in Table 12.II are a few ships in transit to Northwest America for furs in the earlier years, and a handful trading with Manila.

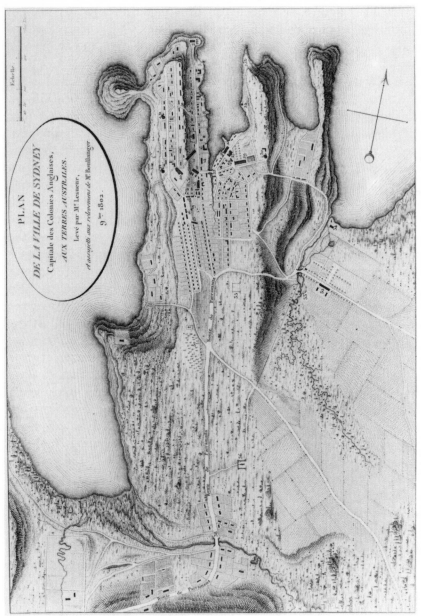

Plate XX. SYDNEY IN 1802. From F. Péron and L. -C. -D. Freycinet, *Voyage de Découvertes aux Terres Australes*, 1807–16. The Tank Stream, decisive of the site, enters the cove at extreme right; the first gallows in New South Wales '(Ruinée)' and the gallows 'en activité' can be seen east of the Parramatta Road. Photo ANU.

Table 12.II. OVERSEAS SHIPPING AT SYDNEY, 1791–1825

Years	Entries	Tons	Trans-ports, E	Whaling/sealing, E and D		American colours E	India		China		Batavia		I. de France		South Sea Islands		Chile, Peru	
				W	S		E	D	E	D	E	D	E	D	E	D	E	D
1791–95	47	?	18	19	4	9	7	20	0	12	1	1	0	0	0	0	0	5
1796–1800	61	?	10	13	0	9	6	10	0	20	0	0	1	0	1	0	1	0
1801–05	113	30,124	14	33	7	18	11	7	1	27	1	3	3	3	4	3	5	3
1806–10	134	211,152 (3 years)	16	57	19	15	19	15	1	10	0	0	1	0	15	21	4	2
1811–15	105	31,997	21	26	6	3	30	40	1	16	2	13	2	2	5	8	0	0
1816–20	169	54,147	66	13	3	7	38	74	3	4	1	45	11	4	2	3	3	2
1821–25	306	89,689*	56	30	43	1	21	17	5	4	7	44	20	24	14	19	8	7
TOTALS	935	227,109	201	191	82	62	183	147	11	93	12	106	38	33	41	54	21	19

Key:
E—Entries from; D—Departures to.
Tonnages before 1800 not available; * figures for 34 entries in 1825 missing from records.
Ships of war and on exploration not included; whaling includes off-shore New South Wales; colonial vessels excluded except for trading voyages to India and South Sea Is. and sealing outside Australian coastal waters, but colonial sealing to Macquarie I. and islands lying off New Zealand is included.

Sources: J. S. Cumpston, *Shipping Arrivals and Departures, Sydney, 1788–1825* (Canberra 1977), but transport numbers from 1801 from C. Bateson, *The Convict Ships* (Glasgow 1959), 288–96.

Although the table shows remarkable progress, even with the withering away of governmental restrictions all was not plain sailing. In 1807 Jefferson's Embargo Act blocked the American demand for British hats and hence cut into the market for sealskins. The tiny Sydney market was easily glutted by speculative shipments of consumption goods from India, and in 1813–15 was itself sharply diminished by the reduction of the British garrison from 1600 to 900. The decade after 1810 was for the most part a difficult time: there were droughts and floods; the colony suffered from the backwash of depression in Britain and the concomitant tightening of credit by Indian agency houses; there was a constant shortage of money in circulation. Leading colonial entrepreneurs were hard hit; the most eminent and respectable, Campbell & Co., collapsed, but Simeon Lord, a sharp practitioner, dubiously survived a sea of turbulent litigation.[99]

In 1819 the horizon brightened. Trade to Britain was now open, and drawbacks were allowed on import duties paid on sandalwood, pearls, bêche-de-mer, whale and seal oil, sealskins. The effect can be seen in Table II, a revival of whaling, sealing, and the Islands trade. By 1823, when the Australia-born William Charles Wentworth, whom we have met on Rarotonga, published his Cambridge prize poem *Australasia*, it could with truth be claimed that a New Britannia was arising in the southern seas.[1]

If Sydney was over-regulated, Hawaii was a free-for-all. The islands were magnificently situated as a cross-roads. Near the northern limit of the Northeast Trades, they lay central to the main whaling grounds in the North Pacific and close to the Equatorial grounds much used in the winter months when the boreal seas were stormy; they were well placed for the rest and refreshment of ships plying between America and Asia.

Within Hawaii there was not initially the concentration on one port as in New South Wales; Kealakekua Bay on Hawai'i continued to be used for some time, and Lahaina on Kauai was long a rival to Honolulu— in some years it had more foreign shipping. But the harbour of Honolulu, discovered in 1794 by the British fur trader William Brown, was much the safest anchorage, and by 1810 Archibald Campbell, speaking from a European point of view, could call Oahu 'the most important island of the group', and sixty Europeans of very varied respectability were living there.[2] Kamehameha I made it the base for his conquest, with beachcomber assistance, of Kauai, and under his successor Kamehameha II the royal court, though remaining to some degree peripatetic, tended to oscillate between Lahaina and Honolulu, far from the dynastic origins in Hawai'i.[3] When in 1817 Kamehameha I shipped a cargo of sandalwood to China and his captains blamed the resultant loss on heavy port charges at Canton, the King took the hint and began the formal organisation of the port of Honolulu by imposing harbour dues.[4]

The islands began to be of commercial significance when the fur traders used them for wintering; naturally refitting and repairing trades grew up—already in 1794 Vancouver had built the 36-foot schooner *Britannia* as a gift for Kamehameha I, and carpenters and ironworkers were sure of a ready welcome from Hawaiian chiefs.[5] After 1815 fur trading yielded to sandalwood and more general trading; Honolulu was becoming an entrepôt for American activities in the North Pacific—the American agent there described it as 'the only safe and commodious harbor in these seas to which ships can resort to be repaired, hove out, coppered &c'.[6] The Russian voyages of exploration and supply to their northern settlements used Hawaii, and in 1815 there was a rather *opera bouffe* attempt to form an RAC base on Kauai, disowned by St Petersburg.[7]

Honolulu's activities as a base for shipping of course demanded supplies of copper, iron, ships' gear and supplies, chandlery. (Equally of course, they demanded grog shops and brothels.)[8] The reckless and highly eclectic taste of Hawaiian chiefs for exotic luxuries and gadgetry had also to be catered for. Initially these demands were met by individual speculative shipments, but by about 1820 American business houses, including J. J. Astor's, were setting up resident agents at Honolulu, and one of these, John C. Jones, was in 1820 appointed United States 'commercial agent' and usurped consular functions, which must have led to a certain conflict of interests.[9] All these developments were vastly stimulated by the mass arrival of the whalers.

The first arrival was from New Bedford in 1819 or a Nantucketer in 1820—and the Japan grounds were discovered in the latter year. Only two years later agent Jones reported 'not less say than sixty' in Honolulu. Kuykendall gives an annual average of 104 at Honolulu and Lahaina in 1824–7; about one-third should be deducted to get the number of ships, many making two visits a year, in spring and autumn.[10] Although the number of white residents remained small—perhaps a hundred of more or less fixed abode and occupation, and about the same number of transient deserters and discharged or disabled seamen—Hawaii had to adjust to a biannual influx of hundreds, if not thousands, of sailors, mostly American, temporarily on the loose, with obviously disruptive effects.[11] And, also in 1820, a new element, more reputable but in the long run quite as subversive, was added by the arrival of the first missionaries. By the end of the decade Hawaii had taken the first steps—or had been pushed onto them—to becoming a *de facto* American colony.

Figures 25 and 26 depict a revolutionary transformation of locational values. The Pacific had ceased to be an emptiness traversed only by the

Manila Galleon and a few Malouin traders and had become the theatre of a very lively and diversified trade, crossing the Ocean in all directions, linking its shores from North to South, from East to West. In absolute quantitative terms it was minor; the China fur trade was transitory, whaling and sealing were the only activities of global significance. The traffic was a mere fraction of that in the North Atlantic; Sydney might be a great node in the South Pacific, Honolulu in the North, but they were puny beside scores of ports in Europe, Asia and Atlantic America. The commerce of the Pacific was peripheral to the global economy.

Perhaps the real significance of Pacific commerce lay not in its quantitative significance, which was slight, but in its role as a shaker of monopoly. The Galleon trade had indeed fallen of its own weight and through political revolution, but without these it must soon have yielded to the more efficient competition of British and American shipping. The fur trade, whaling, the necessities of the new colony in Australia played no small part in the erosion of the EIC's monopoly; nothing could be more *laissez-faire* than the aggressive thrust of the Yankee traders. Alexander M'Konochie's passionate plea for a great Pacific free trade emporium was met, in the year after his book was published, when Raffles founded Singapore in 1819; and in Hawaii, which he had favoured as the locus for such a port, Honolulu played a similar role, though not in British hands.[12] A vast new theatre had been opened to world commerce, by and for Free Trade.

Chapter 13

BOTANY BAY AND NOOTKA SOUND

> ... what continuance of happiness can be expected, when the
> whole system of European empire can be in danger ... by a
> contention for a few spots of earth, which, in the deserts of
> the ocean, had almost escaped human notice, and which if they
> had not happened to make a sea-mark, had perhaps never had a name.

> ... extent of empire demands grandeur of design.

> But if the King of Spain ... should PERSIST in WRONG! It must
> be remembered, that the *ALMIGHTY* hardened the heart of Pharaoh,
> to bring forth Israel FREE with a strong hand and an outstretch-
> ed arm! ... I shall not despair, before the conclusion of the
> present century ... to find the standard of Freedom displayed,
> in every quarter of the New World!

Prologue: the first Falklands crisis

After Anson's raid and the taking of Manila, the first Great Power
confrontation concerned with the Pacific took place in the South Atlantic.
This was the 'escrime à trois',[1] a three-cornered fencing match between
Britain and Spain backed by France under the Bourbon Family Compact,
over the Falklands, which in 1770–1 came very close indeed to war. It
is now most notable as having sown the seed for an armed conflict 211
years later, and for having inspired one of the most eloquent pleas ever
written for peaceful solution of a crisis, Samuel Johnson's *Thoughts on
the LATE TRANSACTIONS respecting FALKLAND'S ISLANDS*. Johnson
was abundantly right in saying of the Islands that 'the expence will be
perpetual, and the use only occasional', but wrong in dismissing them
as insignificant. True, the French Foreign Minister Choiseul said that
in themselves 'they were not worth the fitting-out of a corvette', but
to Spain they could be in British hands not only Johnson's 'nest of smugglers'
and 'refuge of future boucaniers', but a standing menace: the British
hawk Egmont, First Lord of the Admiralty, was not alone in seeing them
as 'the key to the whole Pacific Ocean' which 'must command ... all
the Spanish Territory upon that sea.'[2]

S. Johnson, *Thoughts on the LATE TRANSACTIONS respecting
FALKLAND'S ISLANDS* (London 1771), 1; W. Tench, *A
Narrative of the Expedition to Botany Bay* (London 1789), 103; A.
Dalrymple, *The Spanish Pretensions Fairly Discussed* (London 1790), 5–6.

From his bitter experience off the Horn Anson grasped their potential as an advanced base for operations beyond that cape, and as First Sea Lord projected an expedition to the Falklands in 1749. Any plan for settlement was carefully disclaimed, but the Spanish Minister Carvajal had also read Anson's *Voyage* and asked, very pertinently, what else could be the point, since the Islands were already amply known (a gross exaggeration!), and protested against the British being 'planted directly against the mouth of the straits of Magellan'.[3] The project was dropped, but in 1764 Byron was directed to search for 'His Majesty's Islands called Falkland's Islands', most erroneously alleged to have been taken into possession by Ambrose Cowley in 1686—it was not clear whether the Falklands and the Malouins or Malvinas, and even Pepys's Island (nonexistent) were not one and the same. In January 1765 Byron duly located them and made marks of possession at Port Egmont (his name) on West Falkland; his surgeon left 'a pritty little garden' walled with turf.[4] He did not know that he had been forestalled by nine months.

On the rebound from the failure of the Seven Years' War, Choiseul gave Bougainville authority for a modest revanche, a private settlement in the Falklands. In February 1764 Bougainville set up his colony in East Falkland at Port-St-Louis, so named for a Malouin ship which had called in 1707. Initially there were only two colonist families, but the thing was done in Gallic style: a turf fort for fourteen guns, an obelisk with a medallion of Louis XV.[5] The Spanish reaction was immediate: the Malouins were as notorious smugglers as the British, and if the French were allowed to settle in islands deserted but in proximity to La Plata (the Continental Shelf was not yet thought of), how to keep the British from the deserted coasts of Patagonia? Within a year it was agreed that Bougainville should hand over his settlement against financial compensation, and this he did on 1 April 1767. He sailed on around the world; the Spaniards were taken aback to find that the colony established with such panache consisted of three dozen wretched hutments.[6]

Meanwhile, Byron had been followed up by an expedition under John MacBride. He built a little fort at Port Egmont in January 1766; not until December did he find the French at Port Louis and politely give them notice to quit, which of course they politely disregarded. The Spaniards had bought out the French easily enough, but had bought into a much tougher problem. Their position was somewhat strengthened by the fact that they had taken over an antecedent holding and did not have to rely on outmoded claims to imperium over the New World; paradoxically, the British could not assert first occupation and had to fall back on shadowy claims of discovery.[7]

Into the mazes of the four years of tripartite negotiations we need not go far; behold, are they not written in stupefying detail by Martin-Allanic, and more concisely by Goebel? All parties were hampered by domestic politics—Carlos III had the Jesuit expulsions on his hands, George III had John Wilkes, Choiseul had Madame Dubarry. The British demand to a ransom for Manila and an Anglo-French dispute over Chandernagore in Bengal confused matters. Fiscal difficulties made for peace, affronts to national and royal honour for war. The British cabinet contained both doves and hawks, and went in fear of the Opposition, particularly the terrible William Pitt, Lord Chatham, out of office but far from disarmed. The French and Spanish were willing enough for war, but unsure of when they would be ready—1768? 1769?—and alternately spurred on and reined in each other: at one point Louis XV wrote personally to his good brother Carlos III that they must wait until French finances were in order, which realistically meant never.[8]

Matters came to crisis point when in February 1768 orders were sent to the energetic Captain-General of Buenos Aires, Francisco Bucareli, to evict the British, when he should find them. The Governor of the Malvinas had in fact located Port Egmont in November 1769, and once more a polite eviction order was disregarded. Bucareli's overwhelming force—six ships with 134 guns and hundreds of troops—arrived in February 1770, and the British—one frigate and twenty-five marines—had no option but to depart quietly.[9]

All three parties were arming heavily, and war seemed inevitable. But Lord North, who became Prime Minister in February 1770, justly feared that war would mean his overthrow by Chatham; Choiseul's temporising showed Spain that the Family Compact was fragile. The problem was to find forms of words: how to disavow Bucareli without too blatantly saying so (his action could be passed off as excessive zeal); how Port Egmont might be returned to the British without waiving Spain's right to the Malvinas. Mutual declarations, somewhat tortuously worded, were exchanged, and there seems to have been a verbal agreement that the British reoccupation would be strictly temporary. In September 1771 formal restitution of Port Egmont was made; the Spaniards stayed on at Port Louis, which they called Port Soledad. The British government was in no hurry to carry out a politically dangerous evacuation, but in May 1774 they quietly did so, alleging the time-honoured excuse of expense. They left a flag flying and a plate asserting British right to the Islands: in Johnson's words, a conclusion in which nothing was concluded.[10]

The Spaniards abandoned their settlement in 1811, and the would-be-United Provinces of La Plata, as the successor state, took over the Malvinas in 1820. By 1829 they had a promising little colony, but its Governor's efforts to control Yankee sealing led to its wanton destruction by an American warship in 1831. In 1833 Britain moved in and the Malvinas became once more the Falklands.[11] Argentina would seem to have a good legalistic claim, the British a good prescriptive right based on 150 years

of effective though disputed occupation. In 1982 the Argentines threw
their case away by an unprovoked act of violence; the British reaction
had the paradoxical, if undesigned, result of restoring democracy to
Argentina. Johnson's prognosis—occasional use, perpetual expense—seems
correct.

For the sake of completeness we may mention two minor episodes of
Pacific geopolitics. One was the Spanish reaction to the discovery of
Tahiti; as we have seen, this meant that the Tahitians were taken into
possession, without their understanding or consent, three times in eight
years. There was no official follow-up; further contacts were conspicuously
informal until the French takeover in the 1840s.

The other episode was a non-event, a fantasy probably stemming from
the over-heated brain of the Polish adventurer Benyowski, but it was
taken seriously by the French Ambassador in St Petersburg and his Minister
Vergennes. It was nothing less than an Anglo-Russian descent on Japan
in 1776, in which Captain Cook was to have a part; ulterior aims included
California and the Philippines. The year 1776 was hardly a propitious
one for Britain to indulge in such far-flung adventurism.[12]

Why Botany Bay?

In marked contrast to the bitter dispute over the poor wind-swept Falklands, the British takeover of the whole continent of Australia was without
crisis—so quiet in fact that in 1826 Governor Darling could blandly affirm,
for the benefit of expected French visitors to as yet unsettled Western
Australia, that there could be 'no doubt of the whole of New Holland
being considered within this Government [at Sydney], any division of
it ... under the designation of New South Wales, being merely ideal';[13]
this despite the fact that Arthur Phillip's commission of 1788 had bounded
his jurisdiction by 135°E—a boundary which ultimately stretches back
to the Tordesillas line of 1494! To the east however there was no bound:
'all the islands adjacent in the Pacific Ocean' between 10°37' and 43°39'S
were claimed, and Governors King and Macquarie, in 1801 and 1814,
appointed magistrates for Tahiti.[14] This is a very liberal reading of 'adjacent', before which the Spanish claim to the Falklands as belonging to
La Plata pales, and is surely a very long reach were the colony intended
merely as a penal settlement.

Contemporary Spaniards were under no illusions as to the innocent
nature of the colony. Malaspina pointed out its possible use as a waystation
on new routes to the East Indies and China, but was more deeply concerned
with the menace of two or three thousand bandits only two or three
months' easy sailing from 'our defenceless shores' in South America;
transporting convicts must have been not the end but the means to secure
domination in the Pacific; Watkin Tench had lifted the veil with his
remark 'extent of empire demands grandeur of design.' Malaspina was

echoed by another commentator, who forebode a new North America in New Holland.[15] Allowing for Spanish hypersensitivity in perceiving threats, their fears were not without reason. Spanish prizes were indeed to be brought into Sydney, and in the Nootka Sound crisis it was intended that a few troops and convict settlers for a small post on Vancouver Island should be drawn from the infant establishment at Botany Bay.[16]

Although in the centennial year 1888 E. C. K. Gonner had urged the inadequacy of the traditional view that Australia was founded simply as a dump for convicts, this opinion still ruled until quite recently.[17] American Independence meant the closure of a useful outlet for British undesirables, and there is no doubt that the convicts, piling up in insanitary hulks in the Thames and other ports, presented a real and urgent problem. Transportation was the traditional way of disposing of them.[18] In 1779, with the American War in full swing, a House of Commons committee advised the building of penitentiaries—an Act was passed but not implemented on the score of cost; it thought that sending young convicts to 'a colony or colonies' in distant parts and

> in new discovered countries where the climate is healthy and the means of support attainable ... might prove in the result advantageous both to navigation and commerce.

Unlike a penitentiary, a convict colony might produce some return. Transportation was recommended; but whither? After various places in Africa and North America had been canvassed, and one attempt in the Gambia ended in fiasco, Das Voltas Bay, between the Portuguese and Dutch holdings in southwest Africa, was a strong favourite, until a survey expedition returned with a negative report.[19]

How deliberate was the choice of Botany Bay? Was it anything more than a *pis aller*, all other options having been closed? Was it intended simply as a place to shovel convicts out of sight and mind, or were there larger motives, commercial and strategic? Since 1952 there has been animated debate on these questions; on the whole the trend in Australia has been away from the traditional view, regarded as simplistic in the geopolitical context of the times. (The motivation for this trend sometimes suggested outside Australia, that it stems from a desire to wipe out the 'convict stain' may be safely discounted.)[20] But the revisionists have not had it all their own way; the issues are tangled, and many arguments can cut both ways.[21]

The traditional view is straightforward: there is nothing in the official documents to indicate that the British government had any ulterior motive in throwing an expedition, in many respects ill-found, half-way round the world, or had in view anything more than a gaol. True, the potential of Botany Bay as a colony of settlement had been urged on the government by James Matra in 1783, in the usual glowing terms of projectors. He drew attention to New Zealand as a source of excellent flax or hemp for canvas and cables, and its wealth of timber for masts and spars, 'within a fortnight's run' of New South Wales. A settlement would 'enable us to carry on this [northwest fur] trade with the utmost facility', and would be essential if Britain were to take full advantage of the mooted Dutch concession of free navigation in the Molucca Seas, while it might 'powerfully annoy' Holland or Spain were there war with either. He cited Banks's 'high approbation of the scheme'. Labour might be drawn from China; later, after a conversation with Lord Sydney, Home Secretary, he added that Botany Bay would be 'a very proper region for the reception of criminals'—whether the observation was his own or Sydney's is not clear. Similar elements occur in proposals of 1784 by John Call and Sir George Young.[22] Banks's public statement to the 1779 committee was reasonably supportive.[23]

All eighteenth century governments must have been wearied by the unending flow of more or less hare-brained projects that poured into their offices, and the traditionalists point out, truly enough, that these proposals were made with private ends in view, jobs or profitable speculations for their promoters, and that the government did not accept them. That does not mean that they had absolutely no effect. The 'Heads of a Plan' for Botany Bay that Sydney presented to the Treasury say nothing of strategic or commercial advantages—except for a stress on New Zealand timber and flax, with a direct although unacknowledged quotation from Matra. It also included the suggestion that 'gross irregularities and disorders' could be obviated by importing women from the South Sea Islands to balance the sex ratio amongst the convicts.[24]

The government however had some reason to play down commercial motives, if it had them; the EIC was jealous of anything which might bring adventurers and interlopers nearer to its sacred shores, and had to be managed. Alexander Dalrymple, the vocal defender of the Company's rights, saw the point; like the Spaniards, he saw Botany Bay as a likely nest of pirates, but preying on China, not Peru.[25] *A fortiori*, the government would not wish to risk leakage of any hint of strategic advantage in the Eastern Seas; the Dutch in particular needed very careful handling at this time when the struggle between the Stadtholder, backed by Britain and Prussia, and the French-supported Patriots had not yet reached a decisive crisis. It did so while the First Fleet to Botany Bay was at sea, and French influence was eliminated; but in the meantime the conflict carried with it the menace of *de facto* French control at the Cape, Ceylon, and Batavia.[26] A base in New Holland could realise de Lozier Bouvet's old dream of taking the Dutch in the rear and wresting the spice trade from them.[27]

The virtual absence of reference to ulterior considerations, other than flax and timber, in official papers, is the weakest point in the revisionist case. It is not to the point to argue that the government tried to cut costs and failed to provide Botany Bay with a garrison adequate to beat off a serious attack;[28] as the Falklands had shown, even a token force was sufficient to stake out a claim for effective occupation, and 200 marines, even if meant for internal security, formed quite a substantial token. Of course the government tried to run the colony on the cheap; it did so for all colonies, and these were the days of Pitt's Economical Reform and later of the vast expenses of the Revolutionary Wars. At the worst this distant outpost was expendable, to be fought over at the treaty; but where was a serious attack to come from, so long as Britain held the seas? On the other hand, the occupation of New South Wales meant its denial to other powers; and La Pérouse was known to be sailing on a vast reconnaissance of the Pacific. It is not likely that the government was naive enough to believe that his objectives were just the advancement of science.

From Sydney's reference to flax and timber in the Heads of a Plan, and Phillip's instructions to occupy Norfolk Island, reported by Cook to abound in both—points stressed by Matra, Call, and Young—Geoffrey Blainey evolved a neat theory: 'Norfolk Island was [to be] the plant nursery; Australia was to be the market garden and flax farm surrounded by gaol walls.'[29] Naval stores were naturally an obsession with the maritime powers; traditional British sources in the Baltic were largely at the mercy of sometimes erratic Russian policy. However, Earl Howe, First Lord of the Admiralty, scouted both the urgency of the need for flax, hemp and timber, and the likelihood of supply from Australia, as well as the value of a settlement for the China trade, which at least shows that the latter came under official cognisance.[30] Despite the instructions to occupy Norfolk Island, no serious steps were taken to make it possible to exploit its resources; there seems to have been nobody capable of dressing hemp amongst the convicts sent out, who were indeed scarcely selected with any regard to skills, which should occasion no surprise given eighteenth century carelessness in such matters. When in 1793 two Maori were brought to Sydney to instruct convicts in the art, the pair, a chief and a priest, scorned it as women's work, and commoner women's at that.[31]

It seems then that flax and timber may have been no more than afterthoughts, perhaps window-dressing to put a good face on a costly enterprise. Had naval stores been a prime factor, a settlement on New Zealand would seem more logical; but the tradition of Tasman's Murderer's Bay had been reinforced by Cook's observations on Maori toughness and Furneaux's loss of men at Grass Cove, not to mention Marion Dufresne. Norfolk Island was uninhabited, and therefore free of cannibals.

There is still the hard fact that only three weeks after his arrival at Botany Bay, Phillip split his small force to occupy Norfolk Island. But in May-June 1785 the British ambassador in Paris had informed his government that it was reported that La Pérouse 'was to establish a small settlement in New Zealand for the exploitation of the timber resources.' Phillip's instructions stated explicitly that his occupation was to forestall any European power, and La Pérouse's arrival at Botany Bay, two days after Phillip's, gave urgency to these instructions. La Pérouse had in fact already tried, unsuccessfully, to land on the island.[32]

Yet there was an attempt to establish a small canvas industry, which failed—the fibre was too long, and too hard to separate. As for the tall Norfolk pines, so attractively straight and branchless for half their length, they were difficult to lift from an island with no good landing, and many proved rotten in the core. Blainey's plea that it is the intent rather than the event which should count seems rather feeble, the more so as on the China trade revisionists reverse these criteria.[33]

It is an undoubted fact that Botany Bay was only settled upon when Das Voltas Bay was found unsuitable. But strategic and commercial factors were considerations in the tentative decision for Das Voltas Bay—the Beauchamp Committee on Transportation (1785) thought that a settlement here might 'promote the Purposes of future Commerce or of future Hostility in the *South Seas*.' Its inquiries linked New South Wales and southwest Africa as alternates. Is it likely, then, that Commerce and Hostility should be entirely out of mind when considering Botany Bay? Nor had all hope of other sites been abandoned. Dalrymple suggested Tristan da Cunha; Cape Breton Island, Newfoundland (where convicts were actually sent by the then autonomous Irish government in 1789), the almost empty north coast of New Brunswick were possibilities; the last had excellent masting timber, which undercuts the Blainey theory: why send to the other side of the world for supplies which could be had on the other side of the Atlantic? Against this, security to prevent convicts escaping would obviously be easier in New Holland than in the Atlantic.[34]

There remains the question of the relation of Botany Bay to China. In case of war with the Netherlands, or the extension of French influence over the Dutch East Indies, a possibility to be reckoned with from 1784 to 1787, an alternative route to China would clearly be useful, if not essential, at least until Britain herself could take over the Dutch bases, as happened from 1810 onwards. The securing of Penang in 1786 is relevant in this respect.[35] Also relevant geopolitically is the fact that at least two of the sites considered before the Botany Bay decision, Das Voltas Bay and Kaffreria (near Port Elizabeth), had obvious strategic significance on the Cape route to India. It would be strange indeed if no such considerations were in the minds of the rulers of an empire dependent on the security of its great seaways, even were their proximate concern the disposal of convicts.

In 1784 Sir George Young, a naval officer who had also served in the EIC's Marine, informed the government, after consulting East Indiaman captains, that ships sailing for Canton by Botany Bay and thence either north or south of New Ireland 'would find the passage... more short, easy, and a safer navigation than the general route of the China ships through the Streights of Malacca'; and Matra asked Evan Nepean to pass this information to his superior in the Home Ministry, Lord Sydney.[36] (The route is not in fact shorter, but with the Westerlies and the Southeast Trades it might be quicker.)[37] The government thus had knowledge, from an informed if not disinterested source, of the advantages of this route, even in peace, let alone in times of war in the Eastern Seas.

The EIC took a different view, expressed with his usual vehemence by Dalrymple in his *Serious Admonition*, which lists the 'Proteus-like forms' in which the project had been for some years in agitation... just as the Temper of Ministers was supposed to be inclined to receive a favourable impression.' They included points dear to the revisionists—'a half-way house to China', the Spaniards and the Acapulco trade, hemp and cordage, the northwest fur trade.[38] Dalrymple was a well-informed man, and the government can hardly have been unaware of the commercial aspects of such a development as Botany Bay. But it was not to its interest to publicise them, in view of the EIC's sensitivities. 'Although Botany Bay lay within the area of the East India Company's monopoly, the Directors of the Company were kept completely in the dark about the Government's plans', as Dalrymple complained.[39]

If security prevailed as to commercial aspects, *a fortiori* it would apply to any strategic intentions. There is indeed an instance of what seems suspiciously like censorship in the deletion from the second edition of *The History of New Holland* (1787) of 'a perhaps too revealing passage' which hinted that the Spaniards might not have followed up their South Sea Islands discoveries for fear that weak outlying posts 'would not but serve other powers to dispossess them, and... fix themselves perhaps in a situation commodious for annoying either their American dominions, or the Philippine islands, in the most effectual manner...'.[39] Projects for descents on Pacific Spanish America had proliferated throughout the century; from the mid-1780s, New South Wales increasingly enters into such calculations as an advanced base.

In the last resort, the question seems to be whether Pitt and his colleagues were far-sighted statesmen with wide imperial views, as the revisionists claim (with the weighty shade of Vincent Harlow in the background), or whether they were short-sighted bunglers grasping desperately at any straw, as Mackay's study, the weightiest recent contribution to the traditionalist case, seems to imply—he speaks of Botany Bay as 'a reckless act on the part of a desperate ministry.'[40] Certainly there was bungling in the detailed planning—eighteenth century administration could almost guarantee that; but to maintain that 'Commerce and Hostility' played no art in the decision for Botany Bay seems to impute singular short-sightedness to a body of men who as a whole were not 'amateur, dis-organised, ignorant or dilettante in their handling of the national interest.'[41]

Whether His Majesty's Government intended Botany Bay as a mere convict dump or as a base for the commercial penetration and domination of the Pacific, it very soon became the latter, although the Ocean had to be shared with the irrepressible Yankees. Neglected the colony may have been during the long years of war nearer home after 1792, but it developed its own dynamism, with whaling, sealing, and the Islands trades; in this emancipated convicts like Simeon Lord, Henry Kable and James Underwood played a prominent part. Commercially speaking, the shipping figures in Table II suggest that Mackay's remark about the 'striking irrelevance' of Botany Bay to India and the new routes to China is itself strikingly irrelevant.[42]

The disposal of convicts was a necessary condition in the decision for Botany Bay; but a sufficient one? We may recall the 1779 committee's reference to 'new discovered countries' where a convict settlement 'could be advantageous to navigation and commerce.' What other new discovered country was there? To see the rise of Botany Bay to commercial dominance in the South Pacific as containing elements of deliberate policy and not essentially an accident of the disposal of convicts may be hindsight, a case of the *post hoc ergo propter hoc* fallacy; but it seems in accordance with the geopolitical dynamics and the temper of the times.

The founding

The First Fleet which Captain (later Admiral) Arthur Phillip took to Botany Bay was delayed at starting by a sailors' strike, which some may see as a portent of Australia's history. Phillip promptly broke the strike, and on 13 May 1787 cleared Spithead with two King's ships, the *Sirius* and the brig *Supply*, six chartered transports and three storeships; three of the transports were to go on to China under EIC contract.[43] The voyage out took them to Teneriffe and to Rio de Janeiro, where Phillip, who had served with credit in the Portuguese navy, was very well received. On 13 October they anchored in Table Bay, where the welcome was more reserved, but provisions and livestock were obtained at a price. From the Cape Phillip went ahead—perhaps spurred by news of La Pérouse—in the *Supply* with his three fastest transports, to make prep-arations for landing. On 18 January 1788 the *Supply* reached Botany Bay, all the rest on the two following days. It took Phillip only a few hours to decide that Botany Bay, despite Banks's recommendation, was quite unsuitable for a settlement: no water, except the drainage from an unhealthy-looking swamp. He personally reconnoitred Port Jackson, seen but not entered by Cook, where the Tank Stream (long since lost underground) entered Sydney Cove and promised an eligible site. They were in process of moving when La Pérouse arrived.

On 26 January the landing took place, and New South Wales began with about 740 convicts, 200 marines, a score of officials and some three-score women and children. We can be more precise about the livestock: one stallion, six mares and colts, two bulls, five cows, forty-eight sheep

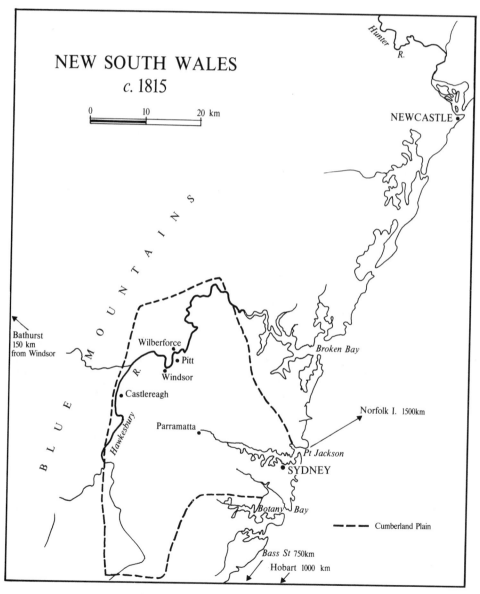

Figure 27. NEW SOUTH WALES *c.* 1815.

and goats, seventy-four swine, 291 assorted poultry, and five rabbits. The sheep and rabbits were given short shrift by convicts and Aborigines; the cattle, unlike the convicts, could live off the country; they went bush, and when the naturally increased herd was found a few years later it was promptly protected as an essential food reserve. There were two people with any knowledge of agriculture (and Phillip himself, who had farmed in Hampshire)—but it was British agriculture. They had few suitable tools, no plough or harrow, and Phillip was moved to write that a few good spades would be a saving of frying-pans. The first two or three years were miserable; more than once the colony nearly starved; the first supply ship was wrecked on the way out, off the Cape, and when after thirty months (and weeks on half-rations) a ship was sighted she brought 'so unnecessary and unprofitable a cargo' as 222 female convicts, many 'loaded with the infirmities incident to old age'.[44] Luckily the other transports of the Second Fleet were not far behind.

Somehow they survived. Captain Watkin Tench of the Marines, who seems to have been the intellectual of the colony, could even write 'To proceed upon a narrow, confined scale, in a country of the extensive limits we possess, would be unpardonable: extent of empire demands grandeur of design.'[45] As the extensive empire consisted of the huts of Sydney and about a dozen hectares of soil so poor and so poorly cultivated that it barely raised next year's seed, this looks like irony (Malaspina took it solemnly enough); and certainly many of his companions thought they had come to the worst of all possible worlds.

Not so Phillip, who never quite reconciled himself to the thought that his little kingdom was to be nothing but a cell of bandits under surveillance; he looked to a future of free farmers who would make the colony economically viable. Of German descent, he had not had an outstanding naval career, but seems to have had some claim on the government for secret service work which could not be publicly acknowledged.[46] His reign in New South Wales showed him a man of ability, resource, and above all quiet dogged courage in most discouraging circumstances. He was not well supported by all of his subordinates, some of them of a mediocrity equalled only by their vanity and quarrelsomeness; Robert Ross, commandant of the Marines, was openly unco-operative.

A major problem was relations with the Aborigines. Official policy of course recommended humane and fair dealing, something most difficult to accomplish with complete incomprehension on both sides and an unruly population of convicts. Phillip himself, unarmed, was wounded by a spear; 'depredations' by the Aborigines led him to lead a deterrent or punitive expedition, to the disgust of Lieutenant William Dawes, sent out with the important tasks of fixing the position of Sydney with astronomical precision.[47] Given the cultural gulf between the intruders and the Aborigines, reconciliation was hopeless; only one or two of the latter, notably

Bennelong, showed the slightest interest in becoming candidates for civilisation; and he in time went back to his old ways. The original owners of the soil soon became marginal, the first 'fringe-dwellers'.

Nevertheless, Phillip's quiet determination kept the infant colony on an even keel. After he retired, worn out, in December 1792, his successors were also naval officers, honest in the main but more competent on the quarter-deck than in guiding economic development and handling the specially-raised New South Wales Corps which provided the most permanent and the toughest official cadres in this enclave of exiles; with war raging in Europe, the best material was not likely to volunteer for or be drafted to New South Wales. The Governors on the whole did their best; as we have seen, the third, Philip King, took a lively interest in the maritime trades which were the life-blood of the colony until the rise of wool provided a bulk export commodity. Slowly progress was made; the ex-convict James Ruse showed that it was possible to farm successfully, and a small agricultural community of emancipated or free settlers, always in debt to the officers and merchants of Sydney grew up on the fertile flats along the Hawkesbury. And at last, in 1813, the narrow confines of 'the gaol', the little lowland behind Sydney, were broken. By abandoning the European habit of following the valleys and instead taking to the more open ridge-tops, the heavily-wooded Blue Mountains, riddled with blind canyons, were crossed. Beyond lay wide savannahs where in 1815 Bathurst was founded—a year after Cleveland, Ohio, five years before Indianapolis.

We need not go into the often sordid detail, a story of land grabs, the monopolistic ring run by the Corps with rum as a currency, the use of legal forms for lawless ends, the perpetual nasty bickering of cliques in this little society so isolated, so locked-up, so claustrophobic but for the merchant adventurers and the sealers. It culminated in the Rum Rebellion when James Macarthur and the Corps deposed Governor Bligh. When Lachlan Macquarie came out in 1809 to replace Bligh as Governor—with his own regiment—and cleared up the mess, a phase of stability and expansion set in. The colony was still tiny—about 10,500 in 1810, plus 1500 in Van Diemens Land and Norfolk Island. But already Sydney was becoming more than a gaol and a barracks; it was almost a little city-state whose merchants were struggling for independence and ultimately a local dominance in the South Pacific.

The clash at Nootka Sound

The imbroglio over Nootka Sound tied together the European Pacific; not only East and West, Macao and San Blas, but North and South, Nootka itself and Botany Bay. The protagonists were Britain and Spain, backed respectively by the Netherlands and France, the Portuguese of

Macao played a minor but important role, and the Russians gave the signal for the rising of the curtain. In the wings the Americans and the Indians were interested spectators, and in the event, by a wry twist, the adroit Indian chief Maquinna was left in possession of the stage.[48]

In January 1788 John Meares left Macao in the *Feliz Aventureiro* (usually referred to as the *Felice*), with William Douglas in the *Iphigenia Nubiana*, which had been the *Nootka* of Meares's 1786 voyage to the Northwest Coast. He sailed under Portuguese colours, as befitted the names of his ships, obviously to evade the EIC monopoly, and he had with him two Portuguese as nominal captains and one of his Macao backers, João Carvalho, as supercargo.[49] Meares arrived in Nootka Sound on 13 May and bought, or at any rate amicably acquired, a small area at Friendly

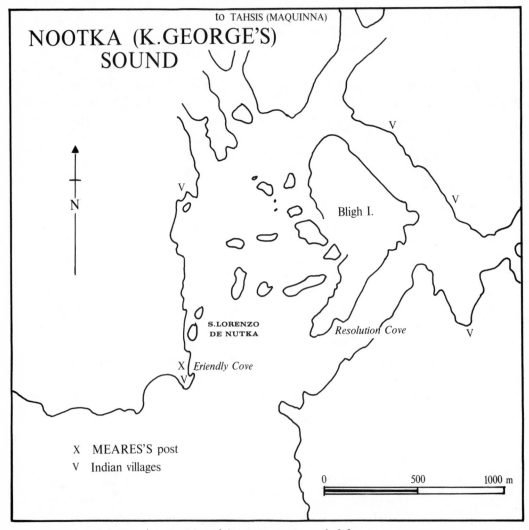

Figure 28. NOOTKA (K. GEORGE'S) SOUND. Compiled from contemporary sources.

Cove from the chief Maquinna (Ma-kwee-na). Here he built a house and on 20 September launched a little schooner, the *North West America*, the first European craft built on the Coast. This was a festive occasion, on which Meares displayed his true colours, the Union Jack; it would have been impossible to deceive the Americans on the spot in the *Lady Washington*. There is, however, unimpeachable evidence that on 16/17 September both his ships were under the Portuguese flag.[50]

Meares returned to Macao, and there in January 1789, under two years since his less than amicable meeting in Prince William Sound with Portlock and Dixon of the Etches company, he joined forces with the rival group. It was an Etches ship whose seizure precipitated the Nootka crisis, but it was Meares's dubious activities which formed the basis for the wide British claims which followed.

On 26 April 1789 Colnett sailed from Macao for Nootka in the *Argonaut*, for the Etches-Meares combination; he had an SSC licence, and later claimed to be commanding an SSC ship. The group knew that they were trespassing: the licence covered trade 'to the most northerly part of America in all the territories, islands and places that are looked upon as belonging to the Crown of Spain.' Colnett carried with him all that was needed, including twenty-nine Chinese artisans, to set up 'a solid establishment, and not one which is to be abandoned at pleasure... which you will name Fort Pitt.'[51] They did not know that three weeks after these instructions were given Estéban José Martínez had arrived at Nootka to plant a settlement which he also meant to be solid and permanent.

The immediate spur to the Spanish occupation was, however, not so much British activity as renewed fears of the Russians. From Chile Ambrosio O'Higgins had passed on alarmist reports derived from talk with La Pérouse's officers, and in summer 1788 Martínez and López de Haro, sent to investigate, met with Russians at Unalaska and near Kodiak, and were fed with information which they took to mean that their hosts would send two frigates to occupy Nootka next year. These became four frigates in Martínez's report, and the future Viceroy Revillagigedo was to add fears of transcontinental infiltration by the Yankees; that would be 'an enterprise for many years', but forestalling action was needed now, 'and the more so since we see that the Russian projects and those which the English may make from Botany Bay... already menace us.'[52]

Accordingly on 6 May 1789 Martínez arrived in Nootka with the *Princesa*, 26 guns, and was joined on the 13th by the *San Carlos*, 16. He met the Boston furtrader *Columbia* on the way in, and was told that the *Iphigenia* was in port, still in her Portuguese disguise; she had Francisco Viana as (nominal) captain and William Douglas as supercargo. Martínez's relations with the Luso-British were friendly enough at first, but examination of the ship's papers naturally aroused his suspicions, and he arrested her; but the prisoners would be a drain on his resources, and he released her under written obligation to be redelivered to the Spaniards should the Viceroy of New Spain deem her lawful prize. Martínez ensured that the *Iphigenia* had enough stores to make Macao, but once out of sight Douglas 'had no idea of running for Macao' with only a few skins, and sailed north for some successful trading; this belies his claim that his ship had been robbed of everything of value.[53]

This was only the first brush. Douglas sailed at the end of May, hoping to meet the *North West America* which was also trading to the north. He missed her, and on 8 June she came into Nootka and was promptly arrested. The next arrival, a week later, was the Etches ship *Princess Royal*. Her captain, Thomas Hudson, concealed the fact that the Etches and Meares interests were now allied, and pleaded distress. His papers showed no Portuguese connection, and he was allowed to leave on 2 July, even taking the furs from the *North West America* for consignment to Macao. He too disregarded the injunction against further trading. That evening James Colnett entered in the Etches *Argonaut*.

Like Hudson, Colnett was taken aback to find a regular Spanish garrison. According to Martínez, he tried to bluff it out, in a bullying manner: he was governor of the official British establishment to be set up at Nootka, the Coast belonging to Britain by virtue of Cook's discoveries; the *Iphigenia* and *North West America* had been transferred to the 'Company of Free Commerce of London' which because of Carvalho's bankruptcy had taken over Meares's claims. Colnett's version naturally said nothing of all this, but it did show that he tried to pass off his EIC and SSC permits as being a royal 'Grant and License'.[54] Martínez said that he would give permission to water and barter for supplies, even to pitch a tent ashore, but anything more was out of the question.

There is no doubt that both Colnett and Martínez were hot-tempered men; there is Spanish evidence that the latter could be violent and overbearing. Both were probably not too sure of their ground. Colnett seems to have been unbalanced; he himself says that after his arrest he was 'distracted' for five days and nights; he threw himself overboard, and his second officer said that he was in 'a high state of insanity'; later, in Mexico and admittedly trying circumstances, he seemed almost paranoid.[55] His military and naval stores, the parts to build a 90-foot sloop, and the Chinese artisans left no doubt that he intended a serious lodgement in the very port that Martínez held for his King.

There seems to have been ill-blood between the two men from the start.[56] Colnett did not observe protocol—to him it was not a foreign port—and hoisted a broad pennant which seemed to indicate commodore's rank. At first there was some attempt at preserving civility, but perhaps drink, very probably linguistic misunderstandings, led to a violent quarrel, hands on swords, which ended in Colnett's forcible arrest and the armed seizure of his ship.

Martínez decided to send the *Argonaut* to San Blas with a prize crew; she was about to sail on 13 July when Hudson rashly reappeared in the *Princess Royal*; he too was immediately arrested. Martínez had now too many prisoners on his hands for his own comfort; Hudson and his men were allowed to stay on the *Princess Royal* once her arms were removed, but Colnett and his people were shipped off in the *Argonaut*.

In all this the Americans of the *Columbia* and *Lady Washington* were interested if not totally impartial witnesses. Though they were technically just as illegal as the British, they had no aim but trade, and Martínez tolerated them—they were useful as intermediaries with both British and Indians and they were always careful to respect his authority. Colnett and Duffin claimed that Martínez had asked for the *Columbia*'s guns to be loaded and trained on the *Argonaut*; if so, it was an excess of caution, since he had forty-two guns and his enemy two swivels mounted. There is no doubt of the cordial relations between Americans and Spaniards, but when the *Columbia* eventually reached Macao she was carrying the crew of the *North West American*, who promptly made a deposition to add to Meares's documentation of his claim for compensation, and also Duffin's letters detailing the seizure of the *Argonaut*. The Americans were allowed to stay for a couple of months, and sent on their way to Macao with a warning not to trade on the Coast without a Spanish pass. As a matter of course they disregarded this; the *Lady Washington* fell in with Simon Metcalfe's *Eleanora* well north of Nootka. Martínez learned of this when Metcalfe's son Thomas came into Nootka in the *Fair American*, which Martínez added to his bag. When he left Nootka to convoy her to San Blas, the *Eleanora* and the *Fair American* sighted and recognised each other, but father and son could make no contact.[57]

Apart from his round of seizures, Martínez had been actively building up the settlement; Colnett's Chinese artisans were a valuable addition to his labour force. He had altered and repaired the *Santa Gertrudis*, ex-*North West America*, built the 'Castillo de San Miguel' and a battery, the commandant's house and a hospital, with other buildings, and had planted wheat and rice.[58] All for nothing: only eight days after he had sailed from San Blas, the Viceroy Manuel Antonio Flores had sent him a letter stating that he had intended Nootka as only a temporary pretence, to stake a claim, and that owing to shortage of shipping it was impossible to send further supplies—'you may consider your commission concluded.'[58] On 27 July Martínez had sent López de Haro with the *San Carlos* and *Princess Royal*, renamed *Princesa Real*, to seek supplies at Monterey; the prisoners and the Chinese had been an unexpected drain on his stores. A few hours after Haro had sailed the *Nuestra Señora de Aranzazú* arrived; she carried orders for Martínez to finish the season by sending a party to explore northwards—and then to abandon Nootka. He hung on as long as he dared, hoping for the return of the *San Carlos* with supplies and perhaps new orders. Bad weather prevented Haro from making Nootka, and at the end of October Martínez sailed for San Blas, arriving in December.

This was not the end of San Lorenzo de Nuca. On 14 April 1789 a royal order was sent to Flores approving its occupation, which was to be maintained. Martínez on arriving in New Spain naturally protested vigorously against the abandonment and advocated a 'forward policy'; he even proposed the occupation of Hawaii and put forward a programme for ships, missions and presidios far beyond the resources of the Viceroyalty. It was left to the incoming Viceroy, Revillagigedo, to carry out the royal order; on 1 April 1790 Francisco de Eliza came to Nootka and re-established the post on a far firmer footing than before. His fort was stronger than Martínez's, and despite serious hardships in the first couple of years considerable agricultural progress was made. When Vancouver came in 1792, he found the governor Bodega y Quadra living in some style, with 'a superfluity of the best provisions.'[60]

The influx of prizes and prisoners set Revillagigedo a problem. At first he inclined to think that the seizures were unjustified and that ships and men should be released; he did release the *Fair American*, and Thomas Metcalfe sailed away to be massacred in Hawaii. The prisoners brought to San Blas were well treated and given a fair degree of liberty at the port's 'hill-station', Tepic, but it was not until July 1790 that they were released and the ships delivered to their officers.[61] By that time the action had shifted to Europe.

Nootka: the European crisis

In January 1790 Anthony Merry, Consul-General in Madrid, gave the British government its first, and rather vague, news of the seizures, soon confirmed by the Spanish Ambassador. The Cabinet agreed that the affair needed to be treated with 'a high hand'. The government had taken a lively interest in the Etches scheme; its ships had prestigious names— *King George, Queen Charlotte, Prince of Wales, Princess Royal*—and the first two were seen off by such notables as Sir Joseph Banks and George Rose, Secretary to the Treasury. Portlock's instructions were approved by Ministers, and he was told to send his despatches 'and inclose them, under cover, to George Rose, Esq., at the Treasury, London.' One might think the Lord Mayor or Lloyd's a more fitting accommodation address for a private commercial venture.[62] Not exactly a provocation, it may have been a probe.

Advantage might therefore be taken of this event, which was perhaps not quite such an unexpected shock as has been assumed—the position of Rose is surely significant. There was a sharp diplomatic exchange between London and Madrid; by March the Spanish Foreign Minister,

Floridablanca, although irritated at the British tone, making demands before discussion, had ordered the release of the ships. But the opportunity of raising the wider issue of access to shores claimed as Spanish was too good to be passed over; 'The British were buoyantly and aggressively engaged in a multiple invasion of the Pacific and its markets and were at last breaking through the walls of Spanish-American commercial monopoly.'[63] An unstated motivation, at least in the public mind, must have been the settling of accounts with Spain for her intervention in the American War. As a preparatory naval move, orders were sent for the *Gorgon* and *Discovery* to rendezvous at Hawaii with a frigate from the East Indies, after they had called at Port Jackson.[64] Before that, in February, Pitt was asking the exiled Venezuelan revolutionary Francisco de Miranda to put into writing his plans for subversion in the event of war.[65] For her part, Spain was soon to start naval preparations, alleging as pretext the dangerous revolutionary situation in France, and Merry reported Spanish soundings for an anti-British coalition of five powers—Spain, France, Russia, Austria and the United States—soundings which found no bottom.[66]

The situation was thus delicately poised when, early in April, John Meares arrived in London, armed with the material he had received at Macao from Duffin and the crew of the *North West America*. His arrival touched off a furiously chauvinist campaign in the public prints, reminiscent of those over Jenkins's Ear and the Falklands, with the difference that this time the Ministry was far less halfhearted at the prospect of hostilities. Meares was a rogue with some gift for patriotic and humanitarian rhetoric, which he exploited in his *Voyages*. Immediately, he presented to the House of Commons a *Memorial*, a most mendacious document which the Ministry accepted as authentic; it was published at government expense.[67] He was backed anonymously by John Etches in two ranting pamphlets, and Alexander Dalrymple weighed in with two rather bizarre productions.[68]

Colnett's arrest added force to the attack; Etches and his group carried considerable political weight. The Spanish reply to representations merely said that the release of the prisoners was an act of courtesy, and mentioned nothing about reparations. But indeed British diplomatic aims far transcended the possession of the rain-swept shores of Nootka Sound; the basic Spanish concept of dominion over areas claimed but never actually occupied was to be challenged. In particular, rights of whaling and sealing off Chile and Patagonia, which involved at least temporary landings, came to the fore.

On 5 May Meares's *Memorial* was published; on the same day Pitt read to Parliament the King's message setting out the British case. The Speech avoided reference to Meares's ships and 'settlement' at Nootka, while demanding reparation for the *Princess Royal* and *Argonaut*; but its heart was a declaration that the Spanish claim to exclusive trade and navigation was 'the most absurd and extravagant that could be imagined', and must be surrendered. The Commons duly voted £1,000,000 for sixty ships, and simultaneously there was a 'hot press' of men for the Navy. The Netherlands were called upon for naval assistance—the Anglo-Prussian intervention of 1787 against the Patriots was paying off—and eventually a sizeable Dutch contingent joined the 'Spanish Armament' at Spithead.[69] Two entrepreneurs, one at least of them shady, and two arrogant seamen had brought Europe to the edge of war.

Pitt hoped that such a strong show of force would enable him to gain a vast concession without war. British demands were far-reaching: the Southern whale fishery to be secured, Meares's post at Nootka to be returned, the northwest Coast to be opened to settlement by all European nations (Spain claimed all south of the Russian limits in 61°N), Britons and Spaniards to be allowed to trade freely in each other's settlements,[70] and no new settlements to be formed by either in southern South America unless a third power intervened. In Madrid, Merry was replaced by the experienced diplomat Alleyne Fitzherbert; his opening bid was the modest one that Spain should give up her claims to everything north of 31°N— that is, all modern California![71] He was on sounder ground in pointing out that Spain's tacit acceptance of the Russian sphere north of 61°N weakened her case.

In view of the worsening situation in France, Floridablanca desperately proposed 'intimate concert and union' with Britain against this new danger; as W. L. Cook drily remarks, 'a gambit that did nothing to weaken Fitzherbert's stance.' It did nothing but advertise the weakness of Floridablanca's position. Already in May he had begun to call on the ancient ally for aid under the Bourbon Family Compact. That had proved a broken reed in 1770; now, with Louis XVI under popular surveillance in the Tuileries and the National Assembly demanding a say in matters of war and peace, it had even less chance. The Assembly did leave the King the right of proposing war and peace, but subject to its veto; treaties would need its ratification, and offensive war was repudiated. In August the Assembly did indeed vote forty-five ships, in the hope of influencing a peaceful settlement, but while Louis assured his brother of Spain that they would be fitted out 'with the greatest activity possible', his foreign minister assured the British ambassador that it would be with 'the greatest possible slowness'. In any case, the Revolution meant that French dockyards and arsenals were in chaos, naval discipline was crumbling, and morale, especially among the aristocratic officer class, dwindling away. Carlos IV saw the writing on the wall and wrote a secret and pathetic letter to Louis, admitting implicitly that the Assembly now ruled in France and that the Compact was dead.[72]

Fortified by victory in a jingoistic general election in June-July, the British government maintained its pressure. A Spanish proposal for arbitration by a neutral monarch was rejected, and the surrender of sovereignty at Nootka insisted upon. Floridablanca offered to concede equal trading and settling rights in a littoral strip from Nootka to 61°N, and fishing rights on the South American coasts beyond a certain distance from any Spanish settlement. It was politically impossible for the British government not to insist upon Nootka itself, and by July Floridablanca was forced to yield. Agreement was reached, as in the Falklands affair, for mutual declarations, Spain promising satisfaction for Martínez's actions. By the end of July the declarations had been signed, by each party without prejudice to its right to set up or maintain an establishment at Nootka. For a short time the crisis seemed over.

However, little was definitely concluded by these declarations; the key points, Nootka itself and southern whaling, were still for negotiation. Floridablanca naturally wished to keep his concessions as vague and general as possible; the British as naturally insisted on precision. In September the former put forward proposals which were promptly rejected—they evaded the Nootka issue and as regards whaling would have prohibited landings. The British fleet was ordered to sea under Howe, and Fitzherbert was told to present an ultimatum with a 10-day limit. A royal junta desperately appealed for all-out resistance—'This means nothing less than ceding the Indies to the English.' But the facts of power were too strong, and on the day that these words were written to Floridablanca, 18 October 1790, he and Fitzherbert signed the Nootka Convention.[73]

Nootka: the Convention

The Convention—the first international treaty arising from a European dispute in the Pacific since Zaragoza in 1529—was a diplomatic triumph for Great Britain. Article I provided for the restoration of the buildings and land of which British subjects had been dispossessed at Nootka. (In fact, Martínez found no buildings at Nootka—if they had been there he would certainly have noted them—and if not dismantled by Douglas before he left, they would as certainly not have long survived the attentions of the Indians, judging by the speed with which they utterly destroyed the far more substantial Spanish buildings on the final withdrawal.)[74] Articles III and IV affirmed the rights of both parties to navigate, trade and settle on the Pacific shores, beyond ten leagues from any existing Spanish settlement, Britain undertaking to see that this should not be used for contraband—an undertaking which on past form would be much more honoured in the breach than in the observance. A verbal ambiguity in Article V left it unclear whether free access to both nations should extend from north of San Francisco or of Nootka, but in the event this was of no significance.[75] There was still room for conflicting interpretations.

In the Commons debate on the Convention, Henry Dundas asserted, with truth, that 'We are not contending for a few miles but a large world...'.[76] In essence, the hard fact was that Spain had at last been forced to yield her secular claim, based on prescriptive right, in face of the almost equally long-standing British doctrine of effective occupation. There had been inconsistencies in British practice, and certainly the specific case of Nootka was a shoddy one. But in the north, whether above San Francisco or only Nootka, Britain now had equal rights in an area that Spain had considered inalienable; in the south, although new settlements south of existing Spanish ones were barred to both sides, the essential whaling and sealing rights were secured, and the limitations on them could not be effectively policed.

A squabble in a remote and desolate harbour had thus been adroitly used to obtain sweeping concessions, and given British maritime and commercial superiority, Spaniards were quite right in foreboding the crumbling of their dominion. Whether this was part of a coherent British policy, or merely brilliant exploitation of an opportunity has been debated, but is not perhaps very relevant in the long run, though either way one must agree that 'The British Government adopted the "new principle of colonial sovereignty" to give a gloss of respectability to a ruthless act of expropriation.'[77] Yet in a way the whole affair was itself to become a giant irrelevance: Nootka would in all probability have had far-reaching consequences in the subversion of the Spanish American empire, but in actuality it was tossed aside in a few years as Britain and Spain were plunged, first as allies then enemies, into the maelstrom of the Revolutionary Wars. Not Nootka but the Napoleonic usurpation in Spain was to loose the avalanche of Latin American independence.

After the Convention; loose ends

No more than the Falklands did Nootka end tidily. The settlement included compensation to the Etches-Meares group for their losses. Meares originally set them at 153,433 Spanish dollars for direct losses, padded by a minimum of 500,000 for cargoes that might have been obtained in 1790–1, about £365,000 in all. He later raised the claim to £469,865. But after the settlement his marginal utility had obviously diminished; a Second Convention scaled the claim down to £50,000, and 'the subtility of Spain' managed to postpone payment until the matter was lost to sight in the wars. The rogue's reward was not a single dollar.[78]

The actual rendition of Nootka was much more drawn out than had been expected. George Vancouver, sent with the *Discovery* and *Chatham* to explore thoroughly the northwest Coast and to carry out what was thought to be a formality, in August 1792 found Bodega y Quadra waiting for him at Nootka, Quadra had been making his inquiries, of the Indians

Plate XXI. FRIENDLY COVE, NOOTKA SOUND. The letters A and B indicate the slip of ground which was all that Quadra was willing to hand over as the site of Meares's post. From G. Vancouver, *A Voyage to the North Pacific Ocean*, 1798. Photo ANU.

and of the Americans Gray and Ingraham, who between them had wit-
nessed both Meares's activities in 1788 and the arrest of Colnett and
who had since returned to the port. To Quadra's query as to what
establishment Meares had had when Martínez arrived, they answered
'in a word, *None*.' The house 'or rather a hut' had been 'pulled to pieces'
by Douglas; and Maquinna and other chiefs denied selling land to Meares.'[79]
Such evidence was not of course conclusive, but in the circumstances
it was enough for Quadra to offer no more than the little strip where
the house had stood, and this was much less than the inadequately instructed
Vancouver could accept.

In September Robert Duffin, who had been on board both the *Felice*
and the *Argonaut*, arrived as supercargo of the Portuguese *São José o Fénix*
and gave a much more impressive account of Meares' installation, but
admitted that nothing was left of it at the time of Colnett's seizure.
Quadra scouted him as a prejudiced witness, and Maquinna again denied
selling to Meares.[80] Letters of vast politeness and inconclusiveness passed
between Quadra and Vancouver, who were on the most cordial terms—
the latter even gave the present Vancouver Island their joint names—
but no agreement was reached except to remit the matter to London
and Madrid. Vancouver never did receive adequate instructions, and when
in October 1794 he sailed from Nootka for the last time no handover
had taken place.

On his homeward journey Vancouver learnt at Monterey that a new
commissioner had been appointed. Lieutenant Thomas Pearce and Brig-
adier José de Alava, who had succeeded as commissioner on Quadra's
death, sailed together in a Spanish ship from San Blas to Nootka, and
at last on 28 March 1795 Alava handed over the site of Meares' house,
where the British flag was run up. A third Nootka Convention had agreed
that both powers—now in brief alliance against revolutionary France—
should evacuate for ever the site of so much dispute. Pearce gave the
Union Jack into Maquinna's keeping, and Nootka Sound was left to the
Indians—and, so long as the fur trade flourished, the Yankees.[81]

Between the reestablishment of San Lorenzo de Nuca in 1790 and 1794,
Nootka Sound was a place of much resort by the fur traders; eleven
ships called in 1794–5, two of them genuine Portuguese under Viana.
Despite a few violent incidents, the Indians by and large were thoroughly
accustomed to their visitors, and friendly to all comers from whom they
could get European goods. The very severe winter of 1793–4 however
caused much hardship to both Indians and the garrison, which in May
was on half-rations, a sad change from the palmy days of 1792 when
Quadra had dined the *Columbia*'s officers with five changes of silver plate.
In the next winter there may have been no more than a skeleton guard
at San Lorenzo.[82]

Until the terms of the Third Convention were known, it was thought that even without Meares' site the Spaniards might still control the fortified entrance and so the Sound; this seems to have been Quadra's view. But there was much debate as to the real value of such an isolated and expensive post. Moziño thought that it would be better to give up everything north of San Francisco and build up the fur trade from a strong base in California, using cheap ships and crews from Manila and replacing New Spain's dependence on the Galleon's silver by the profits from fur sales in China: 'As the Spanish traders along the coast increase in numbers, necessity itself will make the English and other foreigners retire'; a touching optimism. Quadra used much the same arguments to justify retaining Nootka as a centre for the trade; the copper, abalone shell and cloth from California and New Spain were the Indians' preferred trade goods and would enable the Spaniards to undercut other traders.[83]

The Viceroy Revillagigedo was more realistic. Clearly he regarded the fur trade as a wasting asset, given the increasing competition and the increasing adroitness and bellicosity of the Indians. He had no faith in the ability or even the willingness of Spaniards to compete effectively with the British and Bostonmen; they preferred mining investment in New Spain, then in a boom. Against waning prospects in the trade must be set the heavy costs and risks of holding on to a coast which could not be properly controlled. A number of experienced officers supported his submission to Godoy in February 1792, that effort should be concentrated south of Juan de Fuca Strait, where the little outpost of Núñez Gaona (Neah Bay) led a troubled existence from May to September of that year. It was essential to guard against British designs on the long coast between the Strait and San Francisco.[84]

Any hankering after maintaining a presence on the Northwest Coast yielded to the demands of war, at first against and from 1796 on the side of revolutionary France. W. L. Cook points to Spanish logistic advantages—the resources of Mexico and California near at hand, the established Galleon route to Pacific markets for furs—but these were outweighed by the costs of Spanish dominion with its cumbersome inherited style of governance, which made the Coast 'a parasitical colony, a gigantic white elephant' helpless against the self-sufficient entrepreneurial vigour of the British and Bostonmen.[85] The race was to the strong and swift at sea.

Time's revenges

In 1924 the British Columbia Historical Society unveiled a memorial cairn on a rocky islet in the entrance to Nootka Sound. The area was and is an Indian reservation, only 175 km from Vancouver but inaccessible by land. The last stage of the party's journey was by scow, and as the rock was small and slippery, the speeches were made in the scow, which was greeted as of old by chants of welcome from the Nootkan canoes. Amongst those speaking, at some length and in his own tongue, was Chief Napoleon Maquinna, a direct descendant of the Maquinna of Meares' day. Speeches were followed by sight-seeing and souvenir-hunting, the Indians 'as keen at a bargain as their ancestors had been in the days when the fur trade was in its glory.' Some bricks were salvaged from the Spanish bakehouse.[86]

In 1978 Simon Fraser University held a conference on 'Captain James Cook and His Times'; the programme included a well-booked visit to Nootka. The current Chief Maquinna and his people were heavily involved in the movement for Indian and Inuit (Eskimo) rights, and their village displayed a big sign warning off outsiders. The party spent an hour or so, in a bitter cold rain, cruising past the sites of San Lorenzo, Cook's anchorage and Meares' post; Friendly Cove was distinctly unfriendly.[87] The wheel had come full circle; by something like a miracle in the history of imperialism, Maquinna and his clan were still in possession of the place where Spain and Britain, Martínez and Colnett, had clashed so long ago.

Coda: a prospective epilogue

Four hundred years after Magellan first crossed it, the Pacific was becoming economically integrated into the world market, but it was still not integrated into the modern states system. The Napoleonic Wars had little direct impact in the Pacific, though they left the neutral Americans with a freer field than they might otherwise have had. There were no naval operations of significance except the British occupation of the Dutch Indies and the commerce-raiding of the American David Porter in the War of 1812, from a Marquesan base.

Nootka eliminated Spanish claims to the Northwest Coast, but in the year of Napoleon's march on Moscow the Russians leapfrogged to Fort Ross, only 100 km north of San Francisco.[88] The Tsar's ukase of 1821 promulgated a Spanish concept of dominion: 'The pursuit of commerce, whaling and fishery, and of all other industry, in all islands, ports, and gulfs, including the whole of the Northwest Coast of America beginning at Bering Strait and down to 51°N ... are exclusively granted to Russian subjects.' Britain and the United States protested strongly, and in 1825 an Anglo-Russian Convention fixed the southern limit of Russian claims at 54°40'—the source of the American slogan 'Fifty-four forty or fight' in the Oregon dispute of the 1840s with Britain.

In 1819 a treaty between the United States and Spain fixed the northern limit of Spanish claims at 42°N, the present northern boundary of California. The 'Oregon country' between 42 and 54°40' was open to joint occupation by British and Americans; infiltration by both led to acrimonious disputes, even risk of war, until the 1846 treaty which established the present boundary between Canada and the United States.[89] In the same year, with the Mexican War, the 'Bear Flag' revolt by American infiltrators and a small naval force brought California into the United States.

The Pacific rim, except for southernmost Chile, was now fully occupied by organised states, Asian, Russian, British, American, Spanish American. But in between the Ocean was still, in European terms, a political vacuum. There was one internationally recognised and seemingly fairly solid state, Hawaii, and 'missionary kingdoms' struggling to consolidate themselves in Tonga and Tahiti. With the Treaty of Waitangi in 1840 and the French 'protectorate' over Tahiti, New Zealand and the Society Islands became effectively British and French possessions. From the 1840s, then, the insular Pacific begins to have a political history in the European sense, as well as a cultural history of its own and a shared economic history. By that time Christianity was firmly grounded in Hawaii, Tahiti and Tonga, and was making headway elsewhere; the spiritual activities of the Messengers of Grace, Protestant or Catholic, were far from unconnected with the sometimes forcible conquests of materialistic commerce and colonialism. From now on the Islands were to become the small change of Euroamerican empires, sucked into the world market to subsist, poor relations, on its periphery. Paradise had been found, briefly even in seeming, then parodied in the tourist trade. The Islands of romance became the theatre of oceanic war, some even the testing grounds for atomic weaponry. Yet something of the ancient arts and graces survived; even under the heavy burdens, anxieties and stresses of the modern world, the Islanders are ever resilient.

NOTES

Notes for Chapter 1

[1] C. de Brosses, *Histoire des Navigations aux Terres Australes* (Paris 1756), I.78, 86; for the gradual adoption of the name 'Pacific', see O. H. K. Spate, 'From "South Sea" to "Pacific Ocean" ', *JPH* 12, 1977, 205–11.

[2] J. Golson, 'The Pacific Islands and their Prehistoric Inhabitants', in R. G. Ward (ed.), *Man in the Pacific Islands* (Oxford 1972), 5–33 at 7 ['Pacific Islands']. On Melanesia, see A. Pawley, 'Melanesian Diversity and Polynesian Homogeneity...', in J. Hollyman and A. Pawley (eds.), *Studies in Pacific Languages and Cultures* (Auckland 1981), 269–309 ['Diversity']—'It would be a boon if the word "Melanesia[n]" could be forgotten completely' (note 46)—and J. Guiart, 'A Polynesian Myth and the Invention of Melanesia', *JPS* 91, 1982, 139–44.

[3] S. A. Wurm, 'Languages of the Pacific', *Scientific Australian* 4, 1980, 26–33 at 26 ['Languages']; see also Wurm and Shiro Hitori (eds.), *Language Atlas of the Pacific Area*, Part I (Canberra 1982). Useful introductions to the mysteries of glottochronology and lexicostatistics may be found in P. Bellwood, *Man's conquest of the Pacific* (Auckland 1978), 117–34 [*Conquest*], and R. Clark, 'Language', in J. D. Jennings (ed.), *The Prehistory of Polynesia* (Canberra 1979), 249–70 [*Prehistory*].

[4] Wurm, 'Languages', 31–2; P. Bellwood, 'The Peopling of the Pacific', *Scientific American* 243, 1980, 174–85 at 180 ['Peopling'].

[5] H. Hale, 'Ethnography and Philology', in C. Wilkes, *Narrative of the United States Exploring Expedition* (Philadelphia 1846, reprint Ridgewood, NJ, 1968), VI.229–93 *passim*; [*US Ex. Ex.*] Beaglehole, I.169, 286–8, III.264. But according to Pawley this homogeneity is often exaggerated—'Diversity', 291 and note 39.

[6] J. H. Birdsell, 'The recalibration of a paradigm for the first peopling of Greater Australia', in J. Allen, J. Golson and R. Jones (eds.) *Sunda and Sahul: Prehistoric Studies in Southeast Asia, Melanesia and Australia* (London 1977), 113–68 at 115–16, 121–30; J. Chappell and B. G. Thom, 'Sea levels and coasts', ibid., 275–91 at 275–7, 282; and see below, 0–0.

[7] Beaglehole, I.cxci; A. Howard, 'Polynesian Origins and Migrations: A Review of Two Centuries of Speculation and Theory', in G. A. Highland et al., *Polynesian Culture History: Essays in Honor of Kenneth P. Emory* (Honolulu 1967), 45–102 at 45 [*Culture History*]; this and the following four paragraphs are based mainly on Howard's admirable essay. W. Howells, *The Pacific Islanders* (New York 1973), 3–7, [*Islanders*] cuts through the obfuscating concepts of 'Pure Race' and 'Long Migration'.

[8] Ibid., 252–63, and 'Computerised Clues Unlock a Door to Polynesia's Past', *Pacific Islands Monthly* (Sydney), May 1972, 67–9; but see reply by R. C. Green and J. M. Davidson, ibid., September 1972, 73, 113.

⁹ R. von Heine-Geldern's views are presented in H. D. Skinner, 'Migrations of Culture in South-east Asia and Indonesia', *JPS* 66, 1957, 206–7, and also in Howard's article in Highland, *Culture History*, 83–4, along with a similar theory by R. C. Suggs. For Sinic possibilities, see N. Barnard (ed.), *Early Chinese Art and its Possible Influences in the Pacific* (New York 1972) [*Influences*]; though many of the essays are hardly to the point of the title, those by C. Schuster, M. Badner, and D. Fraser have a more definite bearing. As to the North Pacific, harpoons in the Marquesas and New Zealand 'may hint at a contribution from this source'—Golson, 'Pacific Islands', 16.

¹⁰ F. M. Salzano, 'The peopling of the Americas as viewed from South America, in R. Kirk and E. Szathmary (eds.), *Out of Asia: Peopling the Americas and the Pacific* (Canberra 1985), 19–29 at 27 [*Out of Asia*].

¹¹ In *American Indians and the Pacific* (London 1952), a vast and confusing compilation [*American Indians*]; *Sea Routes to Polynesia* (London 1968), more succinct [*Sea Routes*]; and *Early Man and the Ocean* (London 1978) [*Early Man*]. As with Somervell's abridgement of Toynbee, it is not I think unfair to say that the more the argument is stripped down, the more the weaknesses stand out.

¹² I hope I have not done Heyerdahl wrong, but, with all good will, it is difficult to keep one's bearings with an author so voluminous and so repetitive.

¹³ Ellis, *Polynesian Researches* (London 1831), II.46–52; R. C. Suggs, 'The *Kon-Tiki* Myth', in T. G. Harding and B. J. Wallace (eds.), *Cultures of the Pacific* (New York 1970), 29–38 at 30. This is perhaps the most full-blooded of all attacks on Heyerdahl, but Suggs himself falls into the trap of polemical dogmatism; some of his points, for example that pre-Columban South Americans did not use sails, have been refuted.

¹⁴ This demonstration does not depend just on the *Kon-Tiki* voyage; indeed in 1947 Heyerdahl was not fully aware of the potentialities of centre-board sailing. It was confirmed *inter alia* by the Ra expeditions from North Africa to the Caribbean.

¹⁵ *Early Man*, 163, 172.

¹⁶ My discussion is largely based on the valuable survey in C. L. Riley et al. (eds.), *Man Across the Sea: Problems of Pre-Columban Contacts* (Austin 1971) [*Across the Sea*]; the book has a general but balanced diffusionist tendency. For Heyerdahl's views, see *Early Man*, 214–36.

¹⁷ S. G. Stephens, 'Some Problems of Interpreting Transoceanic Dispersal of the New World Cotton', in Riley, *Across the Sea*, 401–15.

¹⁸ T. W. Whitaker, 'Endemism and Pre-Columban Migration of the Bottle Gourd, *Lagenaria siceraria*', ibid., 320–7; Heyerdahl, *Early Man*, 218–19, 253–63; R. C. Green, review of *Across the Sea*, *JPS* 82, 1973, 108–12. On coconuts: G. S. Hope and M. J. T. Spriggs, 'A preliminary pollen sequence from Aneityum Island, Southern Vanuatu', *Bull. Indo-Pacific Prehistory Asstn* 3, 1982, 88–94; R. G. Ward, The Dispersal of the Coconut: did it float or was it carried? (unpublished, quoted by permission), and Ward and B. J. Allen, 'Viability of Floating Coconuts,' *Science in New Guinea* (Port Moresby) 7, 1980, 69–72. Ward doubts the validity of coconuts on the Costa Rican Cocos Island and thinks that the distribution is circumstantial evidence for a west to east crossing of the Pacific; cf. C. O. Sauer, *The Early Spanish Main* (Berkeley 1966), 255, 269. But J. Sauer, 'A Reevaluation of the Coconut as an Indicator of Human Dispersal', in *Across the Sea*, 309–19, thinks that it is 'cosmopolitan' and irrelevant. *Quot homines tot sententiae.*

¹⁹ D. E. Yen, 'The Development of Agriculture in Oceania', in R. C. Green and M. Kelly (eds.), *Studies in Oceanic Culture History*, Pac. Anthro. Records (Honolulu) 11–12, 1971, II.1–12 at 12, [*Studies*].

[20] D. E. Yen, *The Sweet Potato in Oceania* (Honolulu 1974), 249–60, 329–30 [*Sweet Potato*]; D. Brand, 'The Sweet Potato: An Exercise in Methodology', in Riley, *Across the Sea*, 343–65, and the comments of H. G. Baker at 433–5.

[21] P. J. O'Brien, 'The Sweet Potato: its Origin and Dispersal', *Amer. Anthropologist* 74, 1972, 342–65; she opts for introduction by drift voyages from South America, suggesting several ingenious mechanisms for this. It is of course impossible in a work like this to go through all the immense literature on this and other specialised topics; one would never emerge from the delectable but tedious tuber.

[22] For New Zealand, see Yen, *Sweet Potato*, 287–308, and J. Davidson, *The Prehistory of New Zealand* (Auckland 1984), 116–27 [*New Zealand*].

[23] Brand, in Riley, *Across the Sea*, 359–63.

[24] J. W. MacNab attempts to get round this awkward fact in 'Sweet Potatoes and Settlement in the Pacific', *JPS* 76, 1967, 219–21, but an accompanying note by R. Duff strongly suggests that his timing is impossible.

[25] See J. Golson, 'The Remarkable History of Indo-Pacific Man', *JPH* 7, 1972, 5–25 at 9–11; D. E. Yen, 'The Southeast Asian foundation of Oceanic agriculture: a reassessment', *Jnl Soc. des Océanistes* 66–7, 1980, 139–46, which suggests an almost independent role for New Guinea; H. C. Brookfield, *Melanesia* (London 1971), 77–93. The range of adaptation is strikingly displayed in Brookfield's analysis (94–123) of forty-four distinct examples.

[26] R. I. Murrill, 'A Study of Cranial... Material from Easter Island', in T. Heyerdahl and E. N. Ferndon, *Reports of the Norwegian Expedition... to Easter Island*, (Stockholm 1961–5, London 1966) II.255–331 at 318; R. T. Simmons, 'Blood Group Genes in Polynesians...', *Oceania* 32, 1962, 198–210 (reprinted in *Reports*, II.323–43). Howells gives a concrete illustration of loss of genes by 'accidental shifts' on Tench Island—*Islanders*, 54–5. For recent general discussions, see Howells, 'Physical Anthropology', in Jennings, *Prehistory*, 271–85, and Bellwood, *Conquest*, 32–7. Here, as with linguistics, I am acutely aware of my limitations in disciplines of labyrinthine complexity.

[27] R. A. Langdon, *The Lost Caravel* (Sydney 1975), 11–62. Many other lines of evidence are adduced in this well-argued book, but Langdon's extension of Spanish influence from the demographic to the cultural realm is more open to question.

[28] H. E. Maude, *Of Islands and Men* (Melbourne 1968), 134–69; N. McArthur, 'Essays in Multiplication: European Seafarers in Polynesia', *JPH* 1, 1966, 91–105.

[29] S. J. Serjeantson, 'Migration and admixture in the Pacific: insights provided by Human Leucocyte Antigens', in Kirk and Szathmary, *Out of Asia*, 133–46.

[30] M. Spriggs, 'the Lapita cultural complex...', in ibid., 185–206 at 188 ['Lapita complex']; R. C. Green, 'Lapita', in Jennings, *Prehistory*, 27–60 at 45 ['Lapita']; and the reply to Howells cited in note 8 above.

[31] Howells, *Islanders*, 241–65; maps at 256–9.

[32] J. M. R. Gibbon and F. G. A. U. Clunie, 'Sea Level Changes and Pacific Prehistory: New Insight into Early Human Settlement of Oceania', *JPH* 21, 1986, 57–82.

[33] Ibid., 82.

[34] J. Golson, 'Both Sides of the Wallace Line', in Barnard, *Influences*, III.533–96 at 578–84, and in Ward, *Pacific Islands*, 15–16. Incidentally, it is passing strange that while we are cheerfully dealing in millenia, the first Lapita excavations were only about four decades back (1952), and yet Golson confesses that the ware was named 'by whom pecisely I have never been able to discover'—'Lapita Ware...', in Green and Kelly, *Studies*, II.67–76 at 67.

[35] Spriggs, 'Lapita complex', 186.

[36] Ibid., 196; Green, 'Lapita', 45–7; W. R. Ambrose, 'The Loneliness of the Long Distance Trader in Melanesia', *Mankind* (Sydney) 11, 1977–8, 326–33 ['Loneliness']; J. Allen, 'Sea traffic, trade and expanding horizons', in Allen *et al.* (eds.), *Sunda and Sahul*, 387–417 at 389–90.

[37] J. M. Davidson, 'Samoa and Tonga', in Jennings, *Prehistory*, 82–109 at 87–91; L. M. Groube, 'Tonga, Lapita Pottery, and Polynesian Origins', *JPS* 80, 1971, 278–316 at 293–5 ['Tonga'].

[38] Cf. for example the diagrams of Groube in 'Tonga' and Green in Barnard, *Influences*, II.667; Groube emphasises the littoral orientation, which Green tends to discount. For another view, see Ambrose, 'Loneliness', 331–2.

[39] Groube, 'Tonga', 311–13; Green, 'Lapita complex', 197–201; J. P. White, 'Melanesia' in Jennings, *Prehistory*, 352–77 at 373–4.

[40] This is the Maori version, for which see Buck, *Vikings of the Sunrise* (Philadelphia 1938), 263–6 [*Vikings*], or K. Sinclair, *A History of New Zealand* (Harmondsworth 1959), 13–15.

[41] Buck, *Vikings*, 50–3, 267–8; cf. the story of Tahiti, 73–6.

[42] Rev. John Dunmore Lang, *View of the Origins and Migrations of the Polynesian Nation* (Sydney 1877), xvi. Lang was a more than ordinarily combative divine, and few things in this fantastic volume are more amusing than his spluttering charges of plagiarism against the Rev. William Ellis of *Polynesian Researches*.

[43] *Vikings*, 268–75; but for a devastating analysis of the story, see D. R. Simmons, The *Great New Zealand Myth* (Wellington 1967) or his 'A New Zealand Myth: Kupe, Toi, and the "Fleet" ', *NZ Jnl of History* 3, 1969, 14–31. The Fleet story is now regarded as an 'unreal synthesis' of regional traditions—Davidson, *New Zealand*, 10. There is an admirable survey in M. P. K. Sorenson, *Maori Origins and Migrations: The Genesis of Some Pakeha Myths and Legends* (Auckland 1979); the subtitle is significant: Pakeha is the Maori term for European(s).

[44] Hale, in *US Ex. Ex.*, VI.121.

[45] S. P. Smith, *Hawaiki: The Original Home of the Maori* (Christchurch, 6th ed. 1904), 45–7, 50.

[46] *American Indians*, 169–78, 733; G. R. Lewthwaite, 'Geographical Knowledge of the Pacific Peoples', in H. R. Friis (ed.), *The Pacific Basin: A History of Its Geographical Exploration* (New York 1967), 57–86 at 65 ['Knowledge'].

[47] P. Bellwood, 'Dispersal Centres in East Polynesia...', in Green and Kelly, *Studies*, I.93–104 at 93 ['Dispersal']; cf. the discussion in I. Goldman, *Ancient Polynesian Society* (Chicago 1970), 244 [*Society*].

[48] Y. H. Sinoto, 'The Marquesas', in Jennings, *Prehistory*, 110–34 at 120; they may be imports from Fiji. For general accounts of East Polynesian archaeology see the relevant chapters in Jennings, and Bellwood, *Conquest*, 317–416. Bellwood's *The Polynesians: Prehistory of an island people* (London 1978) is a lucid and well-illustrated introduction [*Polynesians*].

[49] Bellwood, 'Dispersal', 93–4; at 100 he gives an extreme example of micro-diffusion on Rarotonga, where the chance visit of a Tahitian woman led to 'the building of a *marae* to Jehovah and Jesus Christ'. For the converse, see Finau of Tonga's astute remarks on the misfortune of Europeans in having, and being subservient to, money— Goldman, *Society*, 476, or better J. Martin, *Tonga Islands: William Mariner's Account* (original ed. London 1817, 4th ed. Neiafu, Vava'u Press 1981, which cited) 153–6. This Tongan

edition has an introduction by Mariner's great-great-grandson, Denis Joroyal McCulloch, dated from Wallingford, Berkshire—a pleasing example of ancestral piety which should appeal to Polynesians.

50 Bellwood, 'Dispersal', 96.

51 'A Re-examination of East Polynesian Marae: Many Marae Later', in Kelly and Green, *Studies*, I.73–92.

52 Goldman, *Society*, 177; the largest in Hawaii was 162 metres long—ibid., 211.

53 But Bellwood paints a gruesome picture of a small wind-blown group living and finally dying in this loneliness—*Conquest*, 356; in *Polynesians*, 100–1, he allows periodical visits.

54 K. Shawcross, 'Fern-root, and the Total Scheme of 18th Century Maori Food Production . . .', *JPS* 76, 1967, 330–52; Davidson, *New Zealand*, 128.

55 L. M. Groube, 'The Origin and Development of Earthwork Fortification in the Pacific', in Kelly and Green, *Studies*, I.133–64 at 134 ['Fortification']; J. Golson, 'Culture Change in Prehistoric New Zealand', in J. D. Freeman and W. R. Geddes (eds.), *Anthropology in the South Seas* (New Plymouth 1959), 29–74 at 44 [*Anthropology*]; E. Schwimmer, *The World of the Maori* (Wellington 1966), 72–3. See also D. R. Simmons, 'Economic Change in New Zealand Prehistory', *JPS* 78, 1969, 3–34.

56 Davidson, *New Zealand*, 223–4.

57 L. Lockerbie, 'From Moa-Hunter to Classic Maori', in Freeman and Geddes, *Anthropology*, 75–110 at 81.

58 Groube, 'Fortification', 134–5.

59 Ibid., 156; Davidson, *New Zealand*, 116–17.

60 Ibid., 127; D. E. Yen, 'The Adaptation of the *kumara* by the New Zealand Maori', *JPS* 70, 1961, 338–48.

61 Groube, 'Fortification', 156–7.

62 Ibid., 159–63; cf. the general remarks in Goldman, *Society*, 486–9; though for the Maori he seems to take the simple view that there was a lot of land available, without due attention to land in relation to technique.

63 A. P. Vayda, *Maori Warfare* (Wellington 1960), 111–16.

64 K. A. Wittfogel, *Oriental Despotism* (New Haven 1957), 240–6; Goldman, *Society*, 200, 204–12.

65 Bellwood, *Conquest*, 353; H. D. Tuggle, 'Hawaii', in Jennings, *Prehistory*, 167–99 at 181. My account is drawn mainly from this chapter and from Bellwood, 353–61.

66 Bellwood, *Polynesians*, 102–3.

67 The islanders' own name is 'Te Pito o Te Henua', which according to T. S. Barthel means 'the fragment of the earth' and not as usually rendered the earth's navel or centre—*The Eighth Land: The Polynelsian Discovery and Settlement of Easter Island* (Honolulu 1978), 5 [*Eighth Land*]—a detailed analysis of local legend.

68 Goldman, *Society*, 95; cf. 'one of the most misunderstood and misinterpreted areas of its size in the world'—P. C. McCoy, 'Easter Island', in Jennings, *Prehistory*, 135–66 at 136 ['Easter'], an excellent short account.

69 Heyerdahl has an admirable historical and geographical account in *Records*, I.21–99. In what follows his Sea Routes is often quoted rather than the earlier *American Indians*.

My treatment, simplified as it is, may seem out of scale with the rest of the chapter, but seems warranted by the wide interest in Heyerdahl's ideas.

70 W. Mulloy, Foreword to Fr Sebastian Englert, *Island at the Centre of the World* (London 1970), 15 [*Island*]. This is a beautifully illustrated account, 'popular' but not sensationalist,

as is also J. Machowski, *Island of Secrets* (London 1975) [*Secrets*].

[71] Since Roggeveen (1722) and González (1770) mention no overthrown statues, Heyerdahl draws a dramatic picture of devastation between 1770 and 1774 (*Sea Routes*, 184); the extermination of the Long-ears but for one man was about 1680, on both radiocarbon and traditional evidence. R. I. Murrill, in his study of skulls (*Reports*, II255–319) asserts a continuous Polynesian racial type and scouts Heyerdahl's Caucasoid Peruvians, for whom see *Early Man*, 99–112. The linguistic study is R. Langdon and D. Tryon, *The Language of Easter Island* (Laie, Hawaii, 1983); but see review by R. Clark, *JPS* 92, 1983, 419–25.

It may be noted that 'Long-ears' and 'Short-ears' may be misnomers for 'slender' and 'thick-set' people—Barthel, *Eighth Land*, 280–1.

[72] H. E. Maude, *Slavers in Paradise* (Canberra 1981), 12–20, 159–60; J. D. Porteous, *The Modernization of Easter Island* (Victoria, BC, 1981), 158.

[73] *Sea Routes*, 79–82, 84–5; *American Indians*, 567–9; *Early Man*, 178–87.

[74] *Sea Routes*, 92–171; C. R. Edwards, *Aboriginal Watercraft on the Pacific Coast of South America* (Berkeley 1965), 66–79.

[75] V. I. Voikov and D. D. Tumarkin, 'Navigational Conditions of Sea Routes to Polynesia', in W. G. Solheim (ed.), *Archaeology at the 11th Pacific Science Congress* (Honolulu 1967), 89–100. This important paper gives little countenance to Heyerdahl's idea of a British Columbia-Hawaii link.

[76] Compare Fig.7 in Heyerdahl's *Early Man* with Fig.36B in M. Levison, R. G. Ward and J. W. Webb, *The Settlement of Polynesia: A Computer Simulation* (Minneapolis 1973) [*Settlement*]. Their computer maps in Appendix 2 seem decisive.

[77] This is well brought out in McCoy, 'Easter', 159–61.

[78] See Bellwood, *Conquest*, 374–6, and K. P. Emory, 'Easter Island's Place in the History of Polynesia', *JPS* 81, 1972, 57–69 at 58–9 ['Easter Island']'. The complicated problem of ahu-dating is ably discussed in J. Golson, 'Thor Heyerdahl and the Prehistory of Easter Island', *Oceania* 36, 1965–6, 38–83 ['Heyerdahl'].

[79] G. Figueroa and E. Sanchez, in *Reports*, I.201; Emory, 'Easter Island', 60–1.

[80] Ibid., 62–3; except on the peppers, Emory's botanical criticism is not too convincing, but see also Yen, *Sweet Potato*, 308–11, and for *Scirpus*/totora, McCoy, 'Easter', 144.

[81] As one of the very few boys of school age living in Bloomsbury in the mid-1920s, I can still recall their spell, and my frustration when I failed to find a book on Easter Island in the local library. Since then I have found too many.

[82] J. Dunmore and M. De Brossard, *Le Voyage de Lapérouse 1785–1788* (Paris 1985), I.223; Goldman, *Society*, 101–3; Heyerdahl, *Sea Routes*, 149–82, *American Indians*, 347–424 passim, and *Aku-aku: The Secret of Easter Island* (London 1958), 142–52. Heyerdahl himself cites the great trilithon on Tongatapu as an example of the method, but hints at a Peruvian connection—*American Indians*, 368–9, 403–5.

[83] For Rapanui traditions about the overthrowing, see Barthel, *Eighth Land*, 278–86.

[84] Emory, 'Easter Island', 63–6. Heyerdahl's views are given in *American Indians*, 625–37, and 'The Concept of RONGORONGO', *Reports*, II.345–6. The 1770 'signatures' to the Spanish 'treaty', crude glyphs, are reproduced in Machowski, *Secrets*, 38.

[85] N. A. Butinov and Y. V. Knorozov, 'Preliminary Report on the Written Language of Easter Island', *JPS* 66, 1957, 5–17.

[86] H. Marshall, *The Easter Island Script: A Definitive Decipherment and Study of its Origins* (Quebec 1978), 187. Marshall places an Egyptian naval base in Tonga in 250 B.C., associated with an expedition to Chile ('of course annexed to Egypt') to verify Era-

tosthenes's calculation of the diameter of the earth (146); he also refers to a Treaty of Vaitagi in 1891, 1892 and 1893, which may mean the Treaty of Waitangi 1840, but who can tell?

[87] 'Heyerdahl', 62, 81.

[88] *American Indians*, caption to Plate XC and the last lines of the text, 763.

[89] *The Oxford English Dictionary*, s.v. The standard work on the very numerous types is A. C. Haddon and J. Hornell, *Canoes of Oceania* (Honolulu 1936–8); more succinct accounts are in H. Morton, *The Wind Commands* (Vancouver 1975), 48–67, and D. Lewis, *We, The Navigators: The Ancient Art of Landfinding in the Pacific* (Canberra 1972), 253–75 [*Navigators*]; for Micronesia, see T. Gladwin, *East is a Big Bird* (Cambridge, Mass., 1970).

[90] Lewis, *Navigators*, Plates IX–XI.

[91] Ibid., 168; personal information from Mr F. G. A. U. Clunie, Fiji Museum. Cf. G. Parsonson, 'The Settlement of Oceania', in J. Golson (ed.), [*Poly. Navigation*], especially the quotation from Anson. This volume is 'A Symposium on Andrew Sharp's Theory of Accidental Voyages', first put forward in 1956; I quote from Sharp's revised version, *Ancient Voyagers in Polynesia* (Sydney 1963) [*Voyagers*]. See also the essays by D. Lewis, M. McCoy, S. H. Riesenberg and others in B. R. Finney (ed.), *Pacific Navigation and Voyaging* (Wellington 1976) [*Pac. Navigation*].

[92] Sharp, *Voyagers*, 71–2; Lewis, *Navigators*, 274–5.

[93] Lewthwaite, 'Knowledge', 81–3, and his 'The Puzzle of Tupaia's Map', *New Zealand Geographer* 26, 1970, 1–19. See also R. Duff, *No Sort of Iron* (Christchurch 1969), 15–18; Lewis, *Navigators*, 293–8; J. Kirk *et al.*, *Captain Cook's Problem: An Experiment in Geographical Semantics* (Lisse, Belgium, 1975).

The Cook/Banks copy of the map in the British Library has drawings of European ships at Tahiti, Raiatea, and another island, and a fourth with a caption indicating a ship larger than the *Endeavour*—R. A. Skelton, *Charts and Views* from Cook's voyages (Cambridge 1955), Plate XI and J. C. Beaglehole's note. R. A. Langdon, in a well-argued paper, sees this *more suo* as evidence of a visit by the *San Lesmes*, lost from Loaysa's fleet in 1526—'The European Ships of Tupaia's Chart: An Essay in Interpretation', *JPH* 15, 1980, 225–32. Much of the argument hinges on whether Tahitian *tupuna* = 'grandfather' (Beaglehole) or 'ancestor(s)' (Langdon), a matter on which I must decline judgement. There is a lively polemic between Langdon and H. A. H. Driessen in *JPH* 19, 1984, 239–57, arising from the latter's suggestion of a possible Dutch referend (to Roggeveen's expedition of 1722) in 'Outriggerless Canoes and Glorious Beings: Pre-contact prophecies in the Society Islands', ibid. 17, 1982, 3–28.

[94] Levison et al., *Settlement*, especially Figs.26–32 and 34.

[95] G. Dening, 'The Geographical Knowledge of the Polynesians', in Golson, *Poly. Navigation*, 102–31 at 129; cf. G. Heyen, 'Primitive Navigation in the Pacific', ibid., 64–79 at 75. The two sea-captains contributing to this volume, Heyen and Brett Hilder, take opposite sides, the latter supporting Sharp. Cf. also the notable NW-SE voyage, with no island-hopping, of the whaler *Essex's* boat, from 0°40′S to Juan Fernández— E. D. Merrill, *The Botany of Cook's Voyages*, Chronica Botanica 14 (Walthem, Mass., 1954), 216.

[96] Sharp, *Voyagers*, 70–1.

[97] Ibid., 33.

[98] B. Durrans, 'Ancient Polynesian Voyaging: Cook's View and the Development of Interpretation', in T. C. Mitchell (ed.), *Captain Cook and the South Pacific* (London 1979),

137–59 at 145–50, and his remarks on 'motive', 152, 155. See also J. M. Davidson, 'The Polynesian Foundation', in W. H. Oliver and B. R. Williams, *The Oxford History of New Zealand* (Oxford 1981), 3–27 at 5–6.

[99] Lewis, *Navigators*, 87, and for 'island blocks' 153–60.

[1] For the success and misadventures of the first of these see B. R. Finney, *Hōkūle'a: The Way to Tahiti* (New York 1979), and for Lewis's voyages *Navigators, passim*. Sharp comments in 'David Lewis's Experimental Voyage', *JPS* 75, 1966, 231–3.

[2] Finney, in *Pac. Navigation*, 9; Sharp, *Voyagers*, 53; G. K. Chesterton, 'The Song of Quoodle' (a dog): 'And goodness only knowses/ The noselessness of man.'

[3] See the critique by Heyen, in which Sharp appears as the 'theorist', a favourite term of his for his critics, in Golson, *Poly. Navigation*, 68–9, 73. At one point Sharp seems to mishandle evidence by citing John Williams's failed attempt to find Rarotonga but omitting any mention of a second and successful voyage in which Williams followed a course set by a chief on Atiu, which 'proved to be as correct as if he had been an accomplished navigator'—ibid., 83. Ironically, this instance is given by Sharp's only supporter in the volume, Hilder.

[4] P. Buck, *Arts and Crafts of Hawaii* (Honolulu 1957), 183–4; Sharp, *Voyagers*, 33. The calabash seems to have been a container for clothes, and vertical angles could be estimated more reasonably by using the fingers—K. Åkerblom, *Navigation and Astronomy in Micronesia and Polynesia* (Stockholm 1968), 41–2 [*Astronomy*].

[5] Levison *et al.*, *Settlement*, 62–4; cf. Åkerblom, *Astronomy*, 92–6, for some thoughtful remarks on motives and risk-taking, based on Raymond Firth's Tikopian experience.

[6] Levison *et al.*, *Settlement*, 53–6.

[7] B. R. Finney, 'Voyaging', in Jennings, *Prehistory*, 323–51 at 349; G. V. Scammel, *The World Encompassed: The first European maritime empires c. 800–1650* (London 1981), 6–7.

Notes for Chapter 2

[1] W. L. Thomas, 'The Variety of Physical Environments among Pacific Islands', in F. R. Fosberg (ed.), *Man's Place in the Island Ecosystem* (Honolulu 1963), 7–38 at 11 ['Environments']; see also 'Le Cadre Physique' in J. Doumenge, *L'Homme dans le Pacifique Sud* (Paris 1966), 7–108 [*L'Homme*]. The Naval Intelligence Division *Geographical Handbook Pacific Islands* (n.p. 1945) is still a useful reference [*NID Handbook*].

[2] Thomas, 'Environments', 11–12; H. C. Brookfield, *Melanesia: A Geographical Interpretation of an Island Realm* (London 1971), 21–32 [*Melanesia*].

[3] H. J. Wiens, *Atoll Environment and Ecology* (New Haven 1962), 41–3 [*Atoll Environment*]— an excellent study based mainly on the Carolines and Marshalls.

[4] It seems needless to go into detail about origins, but briefly, though the lower limit of reef-builders is about 45 metres below sea level bores have gone down to 1400 metres before reaching the volcanic base; the atolls have been formed mainly by coral growth keeping pace with gradual subsidence. This was Darwin's theory, which still stands on the whole, modified by R. A. Daly's glacial control theory to allow for the rise of sea level as the ice-sheets melted—ibid., 92–103; Doumenge, *L'Homme*, 46–54; H. W. Menard and E. L. Hamilton, 'Palaeogeography of the Tropical Pacific', in J. L. Gressit (ed.), *Pacific Ocean Biogeography* (Honolulu 1963), 193–218 at 211 [*Biogeography*].

⁵ Wiens, *Atoll Environment*, 317–21, 329.

⁶ Ibid., 317–21; Thomas, 'Environments', 33–5; NID *Handbook*, I.81–3.

⁷ Wiens, *Atoll Environment*, 171–86, 474–8; Doumenge, *L'Homme*, 18–23.

⁸ P. Privat-Deschanel, *Océanie* (*Géographie Universelle*, Tome X, Paris 1930), 7; for good illustrated descriptions of the vegetation see Brookfield, *Melanesia*, 45–53; Doumenge, *L'Homme*, 59–68; NID *Handbook*, I.118–67; Wiens, *Atoll Environment*, 363–403. For origins and dispersal, see R. F. Thorne, 'Biotic Distribution Patterns in the Tropical Pacific', in Gressitt, *Biogeography*, 311–54 at 313–14, 319–21.

⁹ E. J. H. Corner, 'Ficus in the Pacific Region', ibid., 233–45 at 234, Fig.1; but his reliance on land-bridges, which would have to be swing-bridges, is geomorphologically impossible, at least on the scale proposed—see E. C. Zimmerman, ibid. 477–8, for a *reductio ad absurdum*. See also Doumenge, *L'Homme*, 59–60; E. D. Merrill, *Plant Life in the Pacific World* (New York 1956), 215–18.

¹⁰ NID *Handbook*, 212–17; R. H. Black, 'The Geographical Distribution of Malaria in the South-west Pacific', *Austrn Geogr.* 4/2, 1955, 32–5. G. S. Parsonson calls 170°E 'the great cultural divide of the southern seas'—'Artificial Islands in Melanesia: The Role of Malaria . . .', *New Zealand Geogr* 22, 1966, 1–21 at 21.

¹¹ On high islands today people growing traditional foods on a cropped area of 8–10 hectares for 100 persons can have a daily intake of 2600–3000 calories each—Doumenge, *L'Homme*, 228–30; for 'intensity' see Brookfield, *Melanesia*, 88–92.

¹² P. Snow and S. Waine, *The People from the Horizon* (Oxford 1979), 157 [*from the Horizon*]; but I have always found it an agreeable stimulant—see O. H. K. Spate, 'Under Two Laws: The Fijian Dilemma', in *Let Me Enjoy* (Canberra 1965), 46–65 at 52–3.

¹³ J. Barrau, 'L'Humide et le Sec: An Essay on Ethnobotanical Adaptation . . . in the Indo-Pacific Area', *JPS* 74, 329–46 at 336–8 ['L'Humide']; cf. the Chinese Yin-Yang dichotomy. See in general Barrau's *Les Plantes Alimentaires de l'Océanie: Origines, distribution et usages* (Marseilles 1962) [*Plantes*]; Doumenge, *L'Homme*, 301–10; and as a sample study, G. R. Lewthwaite, 'Man and Land in Early Tahiti', *Pacific Viewpoint* (Wellington) 5/1, 1964, 11–34. Hawaiian planting methods are described in S. M. Kamakau, *The Works of the People of Old* (Honolulu 1976) [*The Works*].

In accordance with the aim of this chapter, the past tense is used in the text, though many practices and beliefs noted survive to this day; care has been taken to avoid references to European introductions.

¹⁴ Barrau, L'Humide', 331–5

¹⁵ G. Dening, *Islands and Beaches . . . Marquesas 1774–1880* (Melbourne 1980), 48, 59–60 [*Marquesas*]; W. Ellis, *Polynesian Researches* (London 1831), I.363–7 [*Researches*]; Beaglehole, *Banks*, II.330 (my commas)—this is Banks's 1773 revision of his more often quoted journal jotting of 1769 (I.341), the love interest being added 'to amuse the Princess of Orange.'

¹⁶ Barrau, *Plantes*, 195–201.

¹⁷ *Researches*, II.27; trepanning is the operation of removing a fractured part of the skull and replacing it with a silver plate or other cover to protect the otherwise exposed brain.

¹⁸ Brookfield, *Melanesia*, 86–7.

¹⁹ Beaglehole, *Banks*, I.192–3; the young Joseph was commendably willing to try every-thing once.

²⁰ D. Oliver, *Ancient Tahitian Society* (Honolulu/Canberra 1974), I.270–8 [*Tahitian Society*]; P. McCoy, 'Easter Island', in J. D. Jennings (ed.), *The Prehistory of Polynesia* (Canberra

1979), 135–66 ; at 140; Janet M. Davidson, 'New Zealand', ibid. 222–48 at 229.

[21] Ellis, *Researches*, II.285–99 (source of all direct quotations on fishing); G. R. Lewthwaite, 'Man and Sea in Early Tahiti', *Pacific Viewpoint* 7, 1966, 28–53; Oliver, *Tahitian Society*, I.281–314

[22] J. L. Fischer, *The Eastern Carolines* (New Haven 1957), 98–100.

[23] See the vivid account of Tahitian bonito fishing by Charles Nordhoff, cited in Oliver, *Tahitian Society*, I.294–303, from *JPS* 39, 1930, 137–73, 221–62.

[24] B. Anell, *Contribution to the History of Fishing in the Southern Seas* (Uppsala 1955), 189, 237–40, 243–6, and the maps. For the amazing variety of hooks, see the 192 plates in H. G. Beasley, *Pacific Islands Records, Fish Hooks* (London 1928). One rather wonders why these books are catalogued under 'primitive' fishing.

[25] For details on turtles and crabs, see Wiens, *Atoll Environment*, 422–39; for octopus, Kamakau, *The Works*, 67–71, or more romantically, with the author as bait, A. Grimble, *A Pattern of Islands* (London 1952), 112–18.

[26] P. S. Bellwood, 'Settlement Patterns', in Jennings, *Prehistory*, 308–22 at 309; for New Guinea, Brookfield, *Melanesia*, 221–8, especially Figs 9.1, 9.2.

[27] *Researches*, II.65–6; but after nights in Fijian *bures*, I felt a little cramped on returning to the neat little boxes of rooms in a European house. Ellis himself admits (I.390) that Tahitian houses 'exhibit no small degree of invention, skill, and attention to comfort'.

[28] Cook's phrase, in his rules for trading at Tahiti—Beaglehole, I.75–6; exception must be made for some drift iron in Hawaii. For a comprehensive and detailed survey of the artefacts of a major group, see Te Rangi Hiroa (Sir Peter Buck), *Arts and Crafts of Hawaii* (Honolulu 1957).

[29] *Researches*, II.172–81; but to initiates there could be 'a pleasing sound... like the cooing voice of a *lale* bird'—Kamakau, *The Works*, 108–16 at 109.

[30] See i.a. T. Barrow, *Art and Life in Polynesia* (London 1972) [*Art and Life*]; P. Gathercole et al., *The Art of the Pacific Islands* (Washington 1979) [*The Art*]; A. Kaeppler, '*Artificial Curiosities' [from the] Voyages of Captain James Cook R. N.* (Honolulu 1978).

[31] C. A. Schmitz, *Oceanic Sculpture* (London 1962).

[32] R. W. Williamson, *Religion and Social Organisation in Central Polynesia* (Cambridge 1937), 42, 173, 252 [*Religion*]—the second half of this book is virtually by its editor, R. Piddington; Katharine Luomala, *Voices on the Wind: Polynesian Myths and Chants* (Honolulu 1955), 176–7 [*Voices*].

[33] B. Malinowski, *Coral Gardens and their Magic* (London 1935), *passim*; R. Firth, *Economics of the New Zealand Maori* (Wellington 2nd ed. 1959), 264–8 [*Economics*]; Williamson, *Religion*, 42, 247–51, 295–6.

[34] R. W. Williamson, *The Social and Political Systems of Central Polynesia* (Cambridge 1924), II.407–8 [*Social Systems*].

[35] Ellis, *Researches*, I.287–305; as Oliver remarks, it is odd that neither bows and arrows nor javelins were used in Tahiti for war, despite skill in their sporting use—*Tahitian Society*, I.319–20.

[36] Some idea of the range and high quality of Polynesian oral literature can be gained from J. F. Stimson's interpretations in *Songs of the Sea Kings* (Salem 1957) and Luomala, *Voices*.

[37] Ibid., 16–17.

[38] Barrow, *Art and Life*, 12.

[39] *Tahitian Society*, II.1067–70; for the prevalence and devastating ferocity of Tahitian wars, ibid., I.375–95.

[40] Snow and Waife, *from the Horizon*, 162–3.

[41] A Fijian local official, cited in O. H. K. Spate, *The Fijian People: Economic Problems and Prospects* (Suva 1959), 10 [*Fijian People*].

[42] Ibid., 11; this refers to Fiji, but this general cast of tenure was wide-spread.

[43] *Melanesia*, 226–7 (cf. 'eminent domain'?); see also Williamson, *Religion*, 298, and *Social Systems*, III.236–40, for Samoa. Of course most generalisations in this section, or indeed chapter, are subject to exceptions.

[44] Ibid., III.279–84.

[45] I. Goldman, *Ancient Polynesian Society* (Chicago 1970), 508–14, 555–8 [*Society*]; M. Sahlins, *Social Stratification in Polynesia* (Seattle 1958), 13–16, 22–6 [*Stratification*]. In the early days of European contact, this high degree of political sophistication, together with its nodal position, ensured to Hawaii a brilliant but contaminated role.

[46] In 1944 a European member of the Legislative Council gravely congratulated the Fijians on having long ago attained a state of society which the Soviet Union was struggling to approach—Spate, *Fijian People*, 77. For the risible remarks of Elsdon Best see Firth, *Economics*, 364–5: one of Best's criteria of communism was public rejoicing over a high-ranking birth. Dare one mention Lady Diana?

[47] 'Poor Man, Rich Man, Big-Man, Chief: Political Types in Melanesia and Polynesia', T. G. Harding and B. J. Wallace (eds), *Cultures of the Pacific* (New York 1970), 203–15 [*Cultures*]; cf. C. A. Valentine, 'Social Status, Political Power . . . in Oceania', ibid., 337–84. Sahlins's paper first appeared in *Comparative Studies in Society and History* 5, 1963, 285–303, and is the source of direct quotations in this and the next paragraph.

[48] *Stratification*, xi, 109–10.

[49] *Society, passim*; for a spirited critique, Sahlins, *Stratification*, 130–1, while Dening discounts Sahlins but supports Goldman—*Marquesas*, 283–6.

[50] J. Friedman, 'Notes on Structure and History in Oceania', *Folk* (Copenhagen) 23, 1981, 275–95 at 276–8 ['Notes']. I am indebted to Dr Friedman for a copy of this most interesting paper.

[51] B. Douglas, 'Rank, Power, Authority: a Reassessment of Traditional Leadership in South Pacific Societies', *JPH* 14, 1979, 2–27 at 4, source of direct quotations in this paragraph unless otherwise indicated; see also A. Chowning, 'Leadership in Melanesia', ibid., 66–84.

[52] Firth *Economics*, 108, 132. Indeed, it has been said that in affairs transcending his immediate kin-group, the Maori chief 'did not stand at the apex of a hierarchy of command but rather in the position of *primus inter pares*'—R. S. Oppenheim, cited in Douglas, 'Rank', 21.

[53] 'Rubbish-Man Commoner, Big-Man Chief? Linguistic Evidence for Hereditary Chieftainship in Proto-Oceanic Society', in J. Siikala (ed.), *Oceanic Studies: Essays in Honour of Aarne A. Koskinen* (Helsinki 1982), 33–51 at 47, and 'Melanesian Diversity and Polynesian Homogeneity', in J. Hollyman and A. Pawley (eds.), *Studies in Pacific Languages* (Auckland 1981), 269–309 at 297–8.

[54] 'Notes', 276–8; *Stratification*, 112, 164–5; *Tahitian Society*, I.26–34.

[55] 'Notes', 284; Friedman's own theory to explicate differentiations both between and within Melanesia and Polynesia is most interesting but too complex for presentation here.

[56] H. G. Cummins, 'Tongan Society . . .', in N. Rutherford (ed.), *Friendly Islands: A History of Tonga* (Melbourne 1977), 63–89 at 64–6; N. Gunson, 'The *Hau* Concept of Leadership in Western Polynesia', *JPH* 14, 1979, 28–49; Williamson, *Social Systems*, I.418–21 and

R. Piddington in his *Religion*, 278–92; Goldman, *Poly. Society*, 282–5, 313–15. But see *contra* I. C. Campbell, 'The Tu'i Ha'atakalau and the Ancient Constitution of Tonga', *JPH*, 17, 1982, 178–94.

57 Sahlins. *Stratification*, 92–106.

58 'The Stranger-King or Dumézil among the Fijians', *JPH* 16, 1981, 107–32; but cf. Oliver, *Tahitian Society*, II.777–82.

59 Ibid., II.769–71; Goldman, *Society*, 189–90, 213, 250–2; Sahlins, *Stratification*, 14.

60 A. Kaeppler, 'Aspects of Polynesian Aesthetic Tradition', in Gathercole *et al.*, *The Art*, 77–100 at 81–2. The rest of this paragraph draws mainly from Oliver, *Tahitian Society*, II.854–60, 1102–3, and Barrow, *Art and Life*, 58–9; see also Sahlins, *Stratification*, 115–9, and cf. Goldman, *Society*, 492–5.

61 Piddington, in Williamson, *Religion*, 302–3.

62 E. de Bovis, *Tahitian Society before the Arrival of the Europeans* (1855; trans. R. D. Craig, Honolulu 2nd ed. 1980), 47 [*before the Arrival*].

63 Piddington, in Williamson, *Religion*, 288–90.

64 Goldman, *Society*, 552; on priestly tohunga, Firth, *Economics* 300–3.

65 de Bovis, *before the Arrival*, 46; Williamson, *Social Systems*, III.55–63, 138, and Piddington in *Religion*, 236–8, 286–900; Oliver, *Tahitian Society*, II.869–76.

66 Goldman, *Poly. Society*, 520–1; Williamson, *Social Systems*, III.89–96; Oliver, *Tahitian Society*, II.921.

67 Firth, *Economics*, 246–63, a very lucid discussion; Goldman, *Poly. Society*, 11.

68 Williamson, *Social Systems*, III.80; for a general account of tapu, *Religion*, 130–47.

69 B. Malinowski, *Argonauts of the Western Pacific* (London 1922), 64.

70 Dening, *Marquesas*, 50–3.

71 Firth, *Economics*, 258–63; for specific cases, see his *We, the Tikopia* (London 1936), 377–8, and *Primitive Polynesian Economy* (London 1939), 201–12, as well as Barrau, *Plantes*, 60–1. Cf. Williamson, *Social Systems*, III.322–9.

72 From the list of 'Meanings' in R. Firth, 'The Analysis of *Mana*: an Empirical Approach', in Harding and Wallace, *Cultures*, 316–33 at 317 [*'Mana'*]. See also Goldman, *Poly. Society*, 10–13; Oliver, *Tahitian Society*, I.68–9, II.1047; R. Bowden, *'Tapu* and *Mana*: ritual authority and political power...', *JPH* 14, 1979, 50–62; R. M. Keesing, 'Rethinking Mana', *Jnl of Anthro. Research* (Albuquerque, N. M.) 40, 1984, 137–56.

73 *'Mana'*, 325, 331–2.

74 Oliver, *Tahitian Society*, I.69, 139; I am irreverently reminded of the (now defunct?) English schoolboy game of conkers.

75 Firth, *Economics*, 391–2.

76 Oliver, *Tahitian Society*, II.635–6, 1004–5; Williamson, *Social Systems*, III.344–55.

77 M. Sahlins, *Stone Age Economics* (Tavistock ed. London 1974), 134–7, 140 [*Stone Age*]; Firth, *Economics* 131–4, 304–7.

78 C. Ivens, cited in Sahlins, *Stone Age*, 130.

79 Firth, *Economics*, 326–35; cf. Goldman, *Poly. Society*, 499–501. Cf. O. H. K. Spate, 'Progress at Mbanakoro', in *Let Me Enjoy* (Canberra (1965), 66–87 at 81.

80 Sahlins, *Stone Age*, 169; see 'The Spirit of the Gift', 149–84. But then, how 'primitive' was Polynesian society? In what sense was it not a 'civil' society? For a criticism of the Maussian ideas which Sahlins is discussing, see Firth, *Economics*, 419–21.

81 Ibid., 417, 422–30; Sahlins, *Stone Age*, 187–9; Oliver, *Tahitian Society*, II.636–7.

82 Ibid., II.1007–8, 1064–73; Sahlins, *Stone Age*, 143–6, 257–9, 272–3; R. Firth, *Social Change in Tikopia* (London 1959), 81–3, 90–3.

83 Goldman, *Society*, 76–80, 150–2 (the last phrase is from Peter Buck); Sahlins, *Stratification*, 171–8. What follows is drawn mainly from Oliver, *Tahitian Society*, I.375–405, and R. W. Williamson, *Essays in Polynesian Ethnology* (Cambridge 1939), 3–50 [*Essays*]; for New Zealand, see A. P. Vayda, *Maori Warfare* (Wellington 1960).

84 For an account by a participant observer, see G. Dening (ed.), *The Marquesan Journal of Edward Robarts 1797–1824* (Canberra 1974), 78–85; but (by his own account) Robarts took it upon himself to supply the missing generalship.

85 Firth, *Economics*, 247–8; Dening, *Marquesas*, 55–6, 248–9; Oliver, *Tahitian Society*, I.534 note 42. For an appeal of 1836 for the rescue of 'the poor, idolatrous, war-loving, man devouring FEEJEEANS' see R. Tannahill, *Flesh and Blood* (London 1975), 147–9.

86 W. Arens, *The Man-Eating Myth: Anthropology and Anthropophagy* (New York 1979), *passim*; he scores many witty points, but it is perhaps significant that there is no reference to the Maori and only one jocular and irrelevant one to Fijians. For a prime example of the stuff which is still peddled about, see R. Villeneuve, *Histoire du Cannibalisme* (Paris, n.d. but 1964+), 36–8—as late as the 1960s I was told by an Australian Broadcasting Commission official in New Guinea that the only occasions on which aircraft could be chartered without reference to Sydney was in response to reports of cannibalism or head-hunting.

87 Dening, *Marquesas*, 167–8; he gives an obviously incomplete list of thirty-eight gods mostly connected with illness or accidents.

88 Firth, *Economics*, 269–70; see the whole chapter 'Magic in Economics', 245–81.

89 Williamson, *Essays*, 113–53; Oliver, *Tahitian Society*, II.913–64, 1106–8. The one-fifth may be exaggerated, but about a fifth of the membership was female.

90 *Researches*, I.311–28; Ellis refers specifically to 'a Mahometan paradise'. The general sexual *mores* of the Islanders are discussed below, Chapter 11.

91 For attempts to suggest a rationale for this practice, see Oliver, *Tahitian Society*, II.938–44.

92 Williamson, *Essays*, 124, 128–9; C. Marlowe, *Hero and Leander* (London 1598), I.143–4.

93 J. A. Moerenhout, *Voyages aux Iles du Grand Océan* (Paris 1835), quoted in Williamson, *Religion*, 22–3; cf. Matthew, 10.29.

94 K. Luomala, *Maui-of-a-thousand-tricks* (Honolulu 1949), *passim*.

Notes for Chapter 3

1 This conventional view has been challenged by R. A. Langdon, in *The Lost Caravel* (Sydney 1975), who argues that the survivors of Loaysa's *San Lesmes*, lost in the Tuamotus in 1526 left lots of babies and had far-reaching cultural influence.

2 Gage's *The English-American* (1648; ed. A. P. Newton, London 1928), is a lively account of New Spain and Guatemala, by a renegade Benedictine; A. -F. Frézier's *Relation du Voyage de la Mer du Sud* was at once translated as *A Voyage to the South-Sea* (London 1717), significantly dedicated to George, Prince of Wales—and Governor of the South Sea Company.

3 R. A. Langdon, European Castaways in the Pacific before Captain Cook, unpublished seminar paper, ANU, 1969.

[4] A. Sharp, *The Discovery of the Pacific Islands* (Oxford 1960), 13–42, 86–8 [*Islands*]; G. Williams, 'Seamen and Philosophers in the South Seas in the Age of Captain Cook', *Mariner's Mirror* 63. 1979. 3–22 at 4–5.

[5] C. de Brosses, *Histoire des Navigations aux Terres Australes* (Paris 1757), II.198–9 [*Histoire*]; only Clipperton had to fight. In keeping, the Governor of Guam in 1898, unaware of war with the United States, prepared a courtesy salute for the cruiser which came to seize his island—P. Carano and P. C. Sanchez, *A Complete History of Guam* (Rutland, Vermont, 1964), 170–5.

[6] O. H. K. Spate, *The Pacific since Magellan: I. The Spanish Lake* (Canberra 1979), 139–41, 323; C. Jack-Hinton, *The Search for the Islands of Solomon 1567–1838* (Oxford 1969), 175–83, 222, 239–42.

[7] Sharp, *Islands*, 1–93 *passim*.

[8] J. A. J. de Villiers (ed.), *The East and West Indian Mirror . . .*, HS 2nd Ser. 18 (London 1906), 214; de Brosses, *Histoire*, II.437, 374–5. For Gonneville, see below, oo–o.

[9] G. de la Roërie, *Histoire de la Marine: Navires et Marins* (Paris 1946), II.11 [*Navires*]; see 22–34, 185–6, for masting and rig. Other useful accounts include B. Landström, *The Ship* (London 1961), 154–79; G. P. B. Naish, 'Ships and Shipbuilding', in C. Singer *et al.* (eds.), *A History of Technology* (Oxford 1957–8), III.471–500 ['Ships']; R. Davis, *English Merchant Shipping . . . in the Seventeenth Century* (London 1975), 7–17 [*Merchant Shipping*]; C. E. Gibson, *The Story of the Ship* (New York 1948), 122–7. H. I. Chappelle, *The Search for Speed under Sail* (London 1968) is admirable, but speed was not a prime desideratum on exploring voyages.

[10] Landström, *The Ship*, 171; Davis, *Merchant Shipping*, 8.

[11] Except on occasion the big well-gunned East Indiamen.

[12] D. Macintyre, *The Adventure of Sail 1520–1914* (London 1979), 24; de la Roërie, *Navires*, II.24. For the importance of headsails and the emergency use of 'the Flaps of our Coats' as substitutes, see W. Dampier, *A Discourse of Trade-Winds* (3rd ed. London 1725), 63–5.

[13] J. H. Parry, *Trade and Dominion: The European Overseas Empires in the Eighteenth Century* (London 1971), 208–9 [*Trade and Dominion*].

[14] Ibid., 207; Naish, 'Ships', 475–6, 497–8; illustrations in Landström, *The Ship*, 122–3, 156–7, and P. Kemp, *The Oxford Companion to Ships and the Sea* (London 1976), 937–8 [*Companion*].

[15] Parry, *Trade and Dominion*, 211–12; H. Morton, *The Wind Commands* (Vancouver 1975), 108, 204–13; for the favourable dockyard reports on the *Dolphin*, see H. Carrington (ed.), *The Discovery of Tahiti*, HS 2nd Ser. 98 (London 1948), xxx–xxxiii.

[16] Beaglehole, II.10, 524. Byron had found such a machine to 'answer very well', but this was only twenty-three days out from Plymouth and he does not mention it again—R. E. Gallagher (ed.), *Byron's Journal of his Circumnavigation 1764–1766*, HS 2nd Ser. 122 (Cambridge 1964), xxiii–xxiv, 16.

[17] E. Taillemitte (ed.), *Bougainville et ses Compagnons autour du Monde 1766–1769* (Paris 1977), I.301–3, 491–7 [*Bougainville*]. For Spanish distilling as far back as the 1560s, see J. de Zulueta and L. Higueras, 'Health and navigation in the South Seas: the Spanish experience', in J. Watt *et al*, *Starving Sailors* (London 1981), 85–100 at 90.

[18] Beaglehole, II.671–2, (and 922, 925–6, 954 for Priestley), III.91, 96; C. Lloyd and J. S. L. Coulter, in J. Keevil, *Medicine and the Navy, 1714–1815* (London 1961), III.90–2; L. Roddis, *James Lind* (London 1951), 94–103; Lind, in C. Lloyd (ed.), *The Health of Seamen*, Navy Records Soc. 107 (London 1965), 63–9.

[19] C. Van Doren, *Benjamin Franklin* (New York 1938), 156–73; for the comic controversy over blunt or pointed conductors, in which George III 'sharp conductors changed for blunt' and the now rebel Franklin scored 'By keeping to the point', see H. C. Cameron, *Sir Joseph Banks* (London 1952), 120–1.

[20] Kemp, *Companion*, 810; all the types mentioned in this section are identified in this volume.

[21] Beaglehole, II.xxix, 685; C. Lyte, *Sir Joseph Banks* (Newton Abbot 1980), 151–2.

[22] Beaglehole, I.cxxiii–cxxiv, II.xxiv–xxv, III.lxviii–lxxi; but for an assertion 'that, at the time, only Cook would have selected such a ship' see A. Villiers, *Captain Cook, the Seamen's Seaman* (Harmondsworth 1969), 95–7. A. P. McGowan, 'Captain Cook's Ships', *Mariner's Mirror* 65, 1979, 109–18, seems decisive against both this claim and Dalrymple's, for which see H. T. Fry, 'Alexander Dalrymple and Captain Cook', in R. Fisher and H. Johnson (eds.), *Captain James Cook and His Times* (Canberra 1979), 41–58 at 46. See also J. A. Williamson, *Cook and the Opening of the Pacific* (London 1946), 92–8.

[23] Taillemitte, *Bougainville*, I.28; J. E. Martin-Allanic, *Bougainville navigateur et les Découvertes de son Temps* (Paris 1964), II.891; C. Gaziello, *L'Expédition de Lapérouse 1785–1788* (Paris 1984), 95–6.

[24] H. Chevigny, *Russian America* (New York 1965), 33–4, 38–40; G. Barrat, *Russia in Pacific Waters, 1715–1825* (Vancouver 1981), 45–6, 61.

[25] M. E. Thurman, *The Naval Department of San Blas* (Glendale 1967), 52–9, 68–9; W. L. Cook, *Flood Tide of Empire* (New Haven 1973), 56–7, 550.

[26] N. Broc, *La Géographie des Philosophes* (Paris 1974), 37–43, 280 (quotation) [*Géographie*].

[27] E. G. R. Taylor, *The Haven-finding Art* (London 1956), 200–02, 230–1 (quotation), 236–8 [*Haven-finding*]; J. B. Hewson, *A History of the Practice of Navigation* (Glasgow, revised ed. 1963), 153–7 [*Practice*]. In fact, intervals between knots of forty-eight rather than fifty-two feet were preferred, as this indicated a position some way ahead of the true one, thus providing a safety margin when nearing a coast.

[28] W. Bligh, *A Voyage to the South Sea* (London 1792, reprint Adelaide 1969), 261–2.

[29] William Bourne (1574), cited in Hewson, *Practice*, 97–8; W. E. May, *A History of Marine Navigation* (Henley-on-Thames 1973), 17 [*Navigation*].

[30] Ibid., 53–77.

[31] Ibid., 67–9; Beaglehole, I.clxix, 631–2—the copper-bottomed bigotry, 'matchless in all other professions [?]' is a *cri de coeur* by a Captain Lecky (1887), in Hewson. *Practice*, 105.

[32] E. G. R. Taylor, *Navigation in the Days of Captain Cook* (Greenwich 1974), 2; for details see Hewson, *Practice*, 79–84, and May, *Navigation*, 140–8. A similar instrument was simultaneously produced by Thomas Godfrey of Philadelphia; such things were 'in the air'.

[33] Parry, *Trade and Dominion*, 229–31; developments can be followed in D. Howse and M. Sanderson, *The Sea Chart* (Newton Abbot 1973) and A. H. W. Robinson, *Marine Cartography in Great Britain* (Leicester 1962) [*Cartography*]. See also the essays in N. J. W. Thrower (ed.), *The Compleat Plattmaker* (Berkeley 1978) [*Plattmaker*].

[34] Robinson, *Cartography*, 48–66; quotation at 57.

[35] N. J. W. Thrower, Introduction to *The Three Voyages of Edmond Halley in the Paramore 1698–1701*, HS 2nd Ser. 156–7 (London 1981), 55–66. Thrower refers to a manuscript isogonic chart of 1630 (57) but not to the Portuguese chart of *c.* 1585 showing rough isogonic lines and, like Halley's, made in the hope that longitude and variation might

be associated—A. Cortesão and A. Teixeira de Mota (eds.), *Portugalliæ Monumenta Cartographica* (Lisbon 1960), III.71–2 and Plate 363. The delusion lingered on until the 1740s—see J. Campbell in his edition of J. Harris, *Navigantium atque Itinerantium Bibliotheca* (London 1744), I.xv.

[36] Thrower, 'Edmond Halley and Thematic Geo-Cartography', in *Plattmaker*, 195–228 at 202–7; Halley, 'An Historical Account of the trade winds, and monsoons', *Philosophical Transactions* 16, 1686, 153–68 [not seen]; W. Dampier. *A Discourse of Trade-Winds* (London 1699).

[37] Taylor, *Haven-finding*, 245–63; Hewson, *Practice*, 223–51; May, *Navigation*, 156–71. See also D. Howse, *Greenwich time and the discovery of the longitude* (Oxford 1980), 1–80 [*Greenwhich time*]—a book as entertaining as instructive—and H. Quill, *John Harrison: the Man who found Longitude* (London 1966).

[38] This was apparently largely due to the prodding of Charles II's mistress Louise de Kéroualle on behalf of a compatriot; judging from her portrait, an example of the Influence of the Spheres on temporal affairs—Howse, *Greenwich time*, 20, 24–6.

[39] May, *Navigation*, 27–8; E. G. Forbes, *The Birth of Navigational Science: Tobias Mayer* (Greenwich 1974), 1 [*Mayer*].

[40] Taylor, *Haven-finding*, 261.

[41] Forbes, *Mayer*, 12–14; Mayer died at thirty-nine and his widow received £3000.

[42] Beaglehole, II.692, and 'Eighteenth Century Science and the Voyages of Discovery', *NZ Jnl of History* 3, 1969, 107–23 at 116–17.

[43] P. Bonnichon, 'Eléments de connaissance géographique de l'Océan indien en France au temps de Bougainville', in M. Mollat in E. Taillemitte (eds.), *L'Importance de l'Exploration Maritime au Siecle des Lumieres* (Paris 1982), 125–50 at 136–9; Broc, *Géographie*, 280–3; M. de Brossard and J. Dunmore (eds.), *Le Voyage de Lapérouse 1785–1788* (Paris 1985), I.176–9.

[44] C. H. Cotter, *A History of Nautical Astronomy* (London 1968), 14, 195–205; Forbes, *Mayer* 6–10; R.-Ch. Duval in Taillemitte, *Bougainville*, I.490–1.

[45] E. G. R. Taylor, *Navigation in the Days of Captain Cook* (Greenwich 1974), 3–7.

[46] Hewson, *Practice*, 238. There is a depressing description of working conditions at sea in H. Richard, *Le Voyage de d'Entrecasteaux* (Paris 1986), 150–61.

Notes for Chapter 4

[1] G. A. Wood, *The Discovery of Australia* (1922, revised ed. by J. C. Beaglehole, Sydney 1966), 1–11; see also Beaglehole, I.xxiii–xxxi.

[2] A. Rainaud, *Le Continent Austral: Hypothèses et Découvertes* (Paris 1894), 3, 294–318 [*Continent*]; there were few dissentients. This very erudite work is still, to my knowledge, the fullest history of Terra Australis.

[3] O. H. K. Spate, 'Between Tasman and Cook: Bouvet's Place in the History of Exploration', in J. Andrews (ed.), *Frontiers and Men* (Melbourne 1966), 174–86 at 175–7 ['Bouvet's Place']. Gonneville's Land turns up in French speculation until at least 1783; it was almost certainly in southern Brazil.

[4] B. Varenius, *A Compleat System of General Geography* (4th English ed. from the Latin of 1712, London 1765), I.172, 177–8, 220, 395, 417–18 [*Geography*]. Varenius did have

a place for 'Special' or regional geography—see J. N. L. Baker, 'The Geography of Bernhard Varenius', in his *The History of Geography* (Oxford 1963), 105–18.

⁵ For the contrast, see E. H. Bunbury, *A History of Ancient Geography* (Dover ed., New York 1959), II.213, 217, 548. Strabo hints at a Terra Incognita—ibid., 223–4.

⁶ R. Porter, 'The terraqueous globe', in G. S. Rousseau and R. Porter (eds.), *The Ferment of Knowledge: Studies in the Historiography of Eighteenth Century Science* (Cambridge 1980), 284–324 at 288–94 ['The globe']; N. Broc, *La Géographie des Philosophes: Géographes et Voyageurs français au XVIIIᵉ Siècle* (Paris 1974), 10–11 [*Géographie*].

⁷ Spate, 'Bouvet's Place', 174–80; Rainaud, *Continent*, 395–405; M. Emmanuel, *La France et l'exploration polaire* (Paris 1959), I.220–42.

⁸ Broc, *Géographie*, 176–9; Rainaud, *Continent*, 407–10; J. E. Martin-Allanic, *Bougainville navigateur et les Découvertes de son Temps* (Paris 1964), I.30–3 [*Bougainville*]; de Brosses's work (Paris 1756) will be referred to as *Histoire*.

⁹ Broc, *Géographie*, 177–9, and for Buffon's general ideas 193–201. The only edition of Buffon's *Théorie de la Terre* (1749) available to me is in the edition of his *Oeuvres* (Paris An VIII); it repeats his advice to sail west from Valdivia in 50°S (after Cook's second voyage) but admits that there is not likely to be anything useful beyond that latitude—I.281–7. He modified his views on southern cold—Martin-Allanic, *Bougainville*, II.1155–6.

¹⁰ *Observations made during a Voyage around the World* (London 1778), 69–102; Rainaud, *Continent*, 5–6, 476–7.

¹¹ Broc, *Géographie*, 179–81 and Plate 7, *Carte Physique de la Grande Mer*. From a (literally!) microscopic examination I think that Broc is too generous in crediting Buache with 'astonishing prescience' in linking South America with Antarctica; he shows a short straight ridge south from Tierra del Fuego, not the true linkage by the Falklands arc.

¹² A. C. Taylor, *Le Président de Brosses et l'Australie* (Paris 1938) [*Président*]; see also his 'Charles de Brosses: the Man behind Cook', in B. Greenhill (ed.), *The Opening of the Pacific* (Greenwich 1971), 3–13, and W. P. Friederich, *Australia in Western Imaginative Prose Writings 1600–1960* (Chapel Hill 1967), 29–53 [*Australia*].

¹³ J. A. Williamson, 'Exploration and Discovery', in A. S. Turberville (ed.), *Johnson's England* (Oxford 1933), 88–124 at 104 ['Exploration'].

¹⁴ *Navigantium atque Itinerarium Bibliotheca* (London 1744–8) [*Navigantium*], originally published by John Harris in 1705 and often referred to as 'Harris's *Voyages*', Campbell's name nowhere appearing despite his large additions.

¹⁵ *Histoire*, I.79–81.

¹⁶ M. Bouchard (1929), cited in Broc, *Géographie*, 182.

¹⁷ *Histoire*, I.13–16, 76; Dalrymple, 'Investigation of what may be further expected in the South Sea', 13–16, in his *Historical Collection* (note 35 below).

¹⁸ *Histoire*, I.47–76.

¹⁹ Ibid., I.79; Varenius, *Geography*, I.107.

²⁰ For Purry, see G. Mackaness (ed.), *Some Proposals for Establishing Colonies in the South Seas* (Sydney 1943, reprint Dubbo 1976), 12–20 (but 'La Terre de Nuyts' is not best translated 'The Land of Nights'!). Bowen's map is in *Navigantium* at I.324–5; cf. I.62–3, 271. Campbell gives a clear explanation of 'climates' (I.iv–vi), 'the most Useful Invention of the Ancients in Geography', and in fact the concept goes back to Hipparchus (*fl.* 162–125 B.C.)—E. H. Warmington, *Greek Geography* (London 1934), 241–7. It crops up as late as 1785 in Sir George Young's proposal for settlement in New South Wales—G. Martin (ed.), *The Founding of Australia* (Sydney 1978), 19.

21 Taylor, *Président*, 47, 59; J. Dunmore, *French Explorers in the Pacific* (Oxford 1965–9), I.46 [*Explorers*]. For comment on Campbell, see Taylor, 34–7; Beaglehole, I.lxxiv–lxxvii; Williamson, 'Exploration', 100–1; and G. R. Crone and R. A. Skelton, 'English Collections of Voyages and Travels, 1635–1846', in E. Lynam (ed.), *Richard Hakluyt and his Successors*, HS 2nd Ser. 93 (London 1946), 63–140 at 93–7 ['Collections'].

22 Broc, *Géographie*, 182; Campbell, *Navigantium*, I.284, 332–4. The VOC had indeed colonised, but this might be the difference between a bourgeois republic, or indeed a bourgeois monarchy like William III's, as against Louis XIV's absolute monarchy—cf. de Brosses, *Histoire*, I.8–9.

23 Cf. ibid., I.47–76, II.215–16 (ice); I.307, II.359–63 (Quiros); II.364–7 (Juan Fernández); II.368–9, 380–8 (New Britain); I.431, 437 (Dutch), with respectively *Navigantium* I.263; I.230, 271, 324–5 (map), 332; I.318–19, 334; I.333; I.330. Apart from its omission of Africa, Campbell's agenda (I.336) is practically as that in Maupertuis's *Lettre*, eight years later.

24 *Histoire*, I.76, II.185 (Robinson Crusoe), II.333–7; de Brosses speaks always in the highest terms of Dampier—'Where will we find navigators like unto Dampier?', our best guide (I.437, II.59). For Bouvet's plan, see Spate, 'Bouvet's Place', and Fig.9 below, and for the Espíritu Santo/New Holland conflation Spate, *The Spanish Lake* (Canberra 1979), 140 and references given there.

25 *Navigantium*, I.320, 333–4. Yet Campbell can put up a spirited defence of the despised Hottentots, who have 'Noble and generous Sentiments, despite their Grease and their Sheep-skins!'—I.362–3.

26 *Histoire*, I.16–21, II.393–405.

27 Ibid., II.393.

28 Ibid., I.22–9, 42.

29 Ibid., I.30–9, 41

30 Moll transported as a thief, Manon as a prostitute—D. Defoe, *Moll Flanders* (London 1722); Abbe A. -F. Prévost, *Manon Lescaut* (*c.* 1731; Harmondsworth 1949).

31 *Terra Australis Cognita, or Voyages to the Terra Australis* (Edinburgh 1766–8), I.i [*Terra Australis*]. See Crone and Skelton, 'Collections', 119–21.

32 A crucial section of de Brosses's work on fetishism (he coined the word) comes from Hume's *Dialogue on Natural Religion*, with prudential amendments and only a reference to an eminent foreign writer; but it would never have done for a high magistrate to name so notorious an enemy of religion, and Hume, a friend, quite understood—F. E. Manuel, *The Eighteenth Century Confronts the Gods* (Cambridge, Mass., 1959), 187– 8.

33 *Terra Australis*, I.ii, III.745.

34 E. H. McCormick, *Tasman and New Zealand: A Bibliographical Study* (Wellington 1959), 26, 31–4. In an unguarded moment Beaglehole seems to equate the Hero with Dalrymple (IV.121–2), but H. T. Fry points out that this is incompatible with the dates—'Alexander Dalrymple and James Cook…', in R. Fisher and H. Johnston (eds.), *Captain James Cook and His Times* (Canberra/Vancouver 1979), 41–58 at note 23.

35 The preliminary *An Account of the Discoveries made in the South Pacifick Ocean* was privately printed in 1767, but the two volumes of *An Historical Collection of the Several Voyages and Discoveries in the South Pacific Ocean* were not published until 1770–1 (London; reprint in one volume Amsterdam 1967)—see H. T. Fry, *Alexander Dalrymple and the Expansion of British Trade* (London 1970), 107–13, 121–6, and 'Alexander Dalrymple and New Guinea', *JPH* 4, 1969, 83–102 at 85–7. The wonderful charter is in *A Collection of Voyages, Chiefly in the South Atlantick Ocean* (London 1775). See also Beaglehole, I.ci–cv, clx–clxiv, 377–

87, 410–11. Cook himself refers only to de Brosses.

[36] Taylor, *Président*, 50, 156–60; but cf. Dunmore, *Explorers*, I.50.

[37] Ibid., I.202–49; Beaglehole, III.43; Martin-Allanic, *Bougainville*, II.1335–7, 1353–4, 1413–16. The account in L. R. Marchant, *France Australe* (Perth 1982), 50–67, is marred by a curious derangement of dates. A more sympathetic view is given by M. de Brossard, *Kerguelen: Le Découvreur et ses Iles* (Paris 1970), Tome I *passim*.

[38] Martin-Allanic, *Bougainville*, I.42, 63, II.973; Broc, *Géographie*, 185; Taylor, *Président*, 117, 141–51 (Anson also inspired Bougainville, but he read him in de Brosses); E. Taillemitte (ed.), *Bougainville et ses Compagnons autour du Monde 1766–1768* (Paris 1977), I.8–10 [*Bougainville*].

[39] Taylor, *Président*, 45, 48—with a shade of difference.

[40] G. Williams, ' "Enlarging the Sphere of Contemplation": The Exploration of the Pacific 1560–1800', in P. J. Marshall and G. Williams, *The Great Map of Mankind* (London 1982), 258–98 at 260.

[41] O. H. K. Spate, 'De Lozier Bouvet and Mercantilist Expansion in the Pacific in 1740', in J. Parker (ed.), *Merchants and Scholars* (Minneapolis 1965), 223–37 at 223–4.

[42] Porter, 'The globe', 301; A. C. Crobie and M. Hoskin, 'The Scientific Movement', in *The New Cambridge Modern History* VI 9 (1971), 37–71 at 38–42; N. J. B. Plomley, *The Baudin Expedition and the Tasmanian Aborigines 1802* (Hobart 1983), 4–12.

[43] Broc, *Géographie*, 280–3.

[44] H. Woolf, *The Transits of Venus* (Princeton 1959), 135–40, 182–7.

[45] M. L. A. Milet-Mureau (ed.), *The Voyage of La Pérouse round the World* (Stockdale ed., London 1798), I.li–cxii; J.-M. Degérando, *The Observation of Savage Peoples* (London 1969), a remarkable questionnaire for Baudin's expedition; L. Barber, *The Heyday of Natural History 1820–1870* (London 1980), 30—the supersession was not of course total, T. H. Huxley began as a naval surgeon.

[46] Broc, *Géographie*, 287, 290–1; J. C. Beaglehole, *The Endeavour Journal of Joseph Banks 1768–1771* (Sydney 1962), I.396.

[47] Broc, *Géographie*, 292; M. Hoare (ed.), *The Resolution Journal of Johann Reinhold Forster 1772–1775*, HS 2nd Ser. 152–5 (London 1982), II.233–4, 251, III.438–9, 444–9, 550–01, IV.611–13 [*JRF Journal*]—a shocking litany of woes; O. H. K. Spate, 'Ames Damnées: Baudin and Péron', *Overland* (Melbourne 58, 1974, 52–7).

[48] Porter, 'the globe', 302–4; C. E. Carrington, *The British Overseas* (Cambridge 1950), 200; Martin-Allanic, *Bougainville*, 295–455 *passim*—this author has not the ghost of an idea of selectivity. J. C. Beaglehole, 'Eighteenth Century Science and the Voyages of Discovery', *NZ Jnl of History* 3, 1969, 107–23 at 115, singularly plays down the politics of Bougainville's voyage.

[49] This imbroglio is explicated in Beaglehole, II.cxlviii–cli, IV.461–2, 465–70, and from a differing viewpoint by M. E. Hoare, *The Tactless Philosopher: Johann Reinhold Forster* (Melbourne 1976), 152–69, and *JRF Journal*, I.61–73. Of course George Forster's own contributions to his *A Voyage round the World* were considerable; see his version, Liv–vii.

[50] J. P. Faivre, 'Savants et Navigateurs: Un aspect de la cooperation international entre 1750 et 1840', *Cahiers d'Histoire Mondiale (Jnl of World History)* 10, 1966, 98–124.

[51] Sir Gavin de Beer, *The Sciences were never at War* (London 1960), *passim*; for the efforts of Banks and Bougainville on behalf of Flinders, 112–20, 140–3, 167. Sir Gavin's title seems a large and dubious generalisation indeed! For the Spanish orders, see W. L. Cook, *Flood Tide of Empire* (New Haven 1973), 90–1.

52 Williamson, 'Exploration', 101, 124.

53 J. Meyer, 'Le contexte des grands voyages d'exploration au XVIIIe siècle', in M. Mollat and E. Taillemitte (eds.), *L'Importance de l'Exploration Maritime au Siècle des Lumières* (Paris 1982), 17–59 at 37–8.

54 Martin-Allanic, *Bougainville*, II.1430–3.

55 O'Higgins in B. G. Corney (ed.) *The Quest and Occupation of Tahiti by the Spaniards*, HS 2nd Ser. 32, 36, 43 (London 1913–19), II.414–20 at 418–19; La Pérouse's military engineer Monneron, in J. Dunmore and M. de Brossard, *Le Voyage de Lapérouse 1785–1788* (Paris 1985), I.226–7, and La Pérouse himself similarly on the Philippines, II.269–71. See also J. Muñoz Perez, 'La Pérouse en Chile', *Estudos Geográficos* (Madrid) 66, 1957, 169–76.

56 Not, as G. Chinard says, with Magellan—*L'Amérique et le Rêve Exotique* (Paris 1934), 190 [*L'Amérique*]. For speculation on the site, see M. L. Berneri, *Journey through Utopia* (London 1950), 59 [*Journey*].

This section has been greatly expanded in O. H. K. Spate, 'The Pacific: Home of Utopias', in E. Kamenka (ed.), *Utopias.* (Melbourne 1987)

57 'Post-Scriptum sur l'isle de la Nouvelle-Cythère ou Tayti', in Taillemitte, *Bougainville*, II.506–10. Commerson derives the name Utopia from Greek *ous* = 'happy' instead of *ou* = 'not'; though More may have intended this play upon words, and Bougainville also uses Eutopie—Martin-Allanic, *Bougainville*, II.685.

58 See the list in J. Garagnon's valuable 'French Imaginary Voyages to the Austral Lands in the Seventeenth and Eighteenth Centuries', in I. Donaldson (ed.), *Australia in the European Imagination* (Humanities Research Centre, ANU, Canberra 1982), 87–107 at 106–7 [*European Imagination*].

59 Ibid., 93–5, 101; Chinard, *L'Amérique*, 194–5; Broc, *Géographie*, 259–68.

60 J. W. Johnson, 'The Utopian Impulse and Southern Lands', in Donaldson, *European Imagination*, 41–58 at 43–6.

61 A. L. Morton, *The English Utopia* (Seven Seas ed., Berlin (GDR) 1958), 126–7.

62 For our group, these are excellently characterised by Garagnon in Donaldson, *European Imagination*, 96–101. Of the vast literature on Utopianism, I have found most stimulating F. E. Manuel (ed.), *Utopias and Utopian Thought* (Boston 1966), especially his own essay 'Towards a Psychological History of Utopia', 69–98.

63 Accounts of and excerpts from these works may be found in Chinard, *L'Amérique*; Friederich, *Australia*; Berneri, *Journey*; G. Atkinson, *The Extraordinary Voyage in French Literature* (New York, 1920, 1922, reprint Burt Franklin, New York n.d.); and F. E. and F. P. Manuel, *French Utopias: An Anthology of Ideal Societies* (New York 1966). Foigny was a defrocked monk, Vairasse and Tyssot Huguenots; for the latter, see A. Rosenberg, *Simon Tyssot de Patot* (The Hague 1972). A modest pride makes me add that I have conscientiously struggled through the originals.

64 For this underground genre in general, see M. C. Jacob, *The Radical Enlightenment* (London 1984).

65 E. von der Mühll, *Denis Veiras* [Vairasse] *et son Histoire des Sévarambes* (Paris 1938), 270–2. The English translation of *Jacques Massé* ascribed that book also to that arch-sceptic 'the Celebrated Monsieur Bayle'—Friederich, *Australia*, 123. For Vairasse and Rousseau, see Chinard, *L'Amérique*, 349.

66 [G. F. Coyer], *A Supplement to Lord Anson's Voyage* (The Hague 1749, London 1750); 'Hendrick Schouten', *The Hairy Giants: or, a Description of Two Islands in the South Sea* (London 1766); *The Travels of Hildebrand Bowman* (London 1778), a fictitious survivor

of the Maori massacre of Tobias Fueneaux's men—see E. H. McCormick, *Omai: Pacific Envoy* (Auckland 1977), 304–6; Anon., *Fragmens du dernier Voyage de la Pérouse* (Quimper An IV).

67 1781: 'Imprimé à Leipsick: Et se trouve à Paris' (reprint Slatkine, Geneva 1979) [*Découverte*]. I first met this, serendipitously, in 1956, looking in the British Library catalogue for Diego de Couto.

68 M. Poster, *The Utopian Thought of Restif de la Bretonne* (New York 1971), 39; A. Viatte, *Les Sources Occultes du Romantisme* (Paris 1965), I.251–62; Restif, *Découverte*, II.460–8.

69 Ibid., II.539–56.

70 Ibid., I.36–8, II.483, 493, 532–6, 544. Franklin (too busy), Voltaire (too old), and Buffon were also on the short list for political adviser.

71 Fulke Greville, Lord Brooke, 'Chorus Sacerdotum'; in *Mustapha* (1609).

72 Y. Girard, 'De l'exploration à l'Utopie: notes sur la formation du mythe de Tahiti', *French Studies* (Oxford) 31, 1977, 26–41 at 37, which led me to *Aline et Valcour*. The reader will be glad to know that Sainville eventually found his Leonore, still chaste after the most horrendous adventures.

73 In Donaldson, *European Imagination*, 102.

Notes for Chapter 5

[Notes are not normally given for statements of narrative fact, since these can be readily checked in the main sources, references to which are by author's or editor's name only. The official accounts of British voyages up to and including Cook's first are in J. Hawkesworth, *An Account of the Voyages undertaken by the order of his present Majesty for making Discoveries in the Southern Hemisphere* (London 1773)].

1 Byron's names, in sequence: Isles of Disappointment, King George's, Prince of Wales's, Islands of Danger, Duke of York's. The main source is R. E. Gallagher (ed.), *Byron's Journal of his Circumnavigation 1764–1766*, HS 2nd Ser. 122 (Cambridge 1964).

2 Gallagher (111) and H. E. Maude, *Of Islands and Men* (Melbourne 1968), 91–2 say that this is Nukunau, A. Sharp that it is most likely Tabiteuea, possibly Beru, least likely Nukunau—*The Discovery of the Pacific Islands* (Oxford 1960), 104 [*Islands*]. But Sharp is wrong in stating that Byron's course after leaving the island was NW—it was much nearer N by W, an error material to his argument.

3 O. H. K. Spate, *Monopolists and Freebooters* (Canberra 1983), 258. [*Monopolists*].

4 Gallagher, lviii–lxii; incidentally, the *Dolphin* returned 'in excellent condition'—lxiv.; so much for those disabled ships.

5 After Le Maire, only A. -F. Frézier seems to believe in the Giants, but from hearsay—*A Voyage to the South-Sea* (London 1717), 84–7. See Helen Wallis's authoritative and amusing account in Gallagher, 185–96, and annexed documents including a skit by Horace Walpole. The main sources for Wallis's voyage are his MS Journal, Mitchell Library, Sydney; H. Carrington (ed.), *The Discovery of Tahiti* (Journal of *Dolphin*'s Master George Robinson), HS 2nd Ser. 98 (London 1948); and H. Wallis, (ed.) *Cartaret's Voyage Round the World 1766–1769*, HS 2nd Ser. 124–5 (Cambridge 1965).

6 Ibid., lxiv–lxxi; Beaglehole, I.xc–xci; Carrington, xxii–xxiii—but it is odd that the last should say that Surville and Marion 'found that the only practical method of entering

the Pacific Ocean was from the west'; what of all the navigators from Magellan to the Malouins in the Spanish Succession times?

7 As the *Dolphin*'s barber put it in rollicking if uninspired verse, 'Whose Height from six feet, reach'd to ten'—to which Wallis (S.) appended the useful gloss 'Six Feet Ten Inches'—Mitchell MS.

8 See the judicious discussion in H. Wallis, I.22–49.

9 Wallis's names, in sequence: Whitsunday, Queen Charlotte's, Lord Egmont's, Gloucester, Cumberland, Prince Henry's.

10 Wallis's names: in the Societies, Osnaburgh (Mehetia); King George III's (Tahiti), Duke of York's (Moorea), Sir Charles Saunders (Tapuaemanu), Lord How(e)'s (Mopihaa), Scilly Is. (Motu One); in Tonga, Boscawen, Keppel; Wallis (Uvea); Rongerip was not named.

11 Which H. Wallis accepts as 'almost certainly correct'—I.50–3; but see *contra* Spate, *Monopolists*, 151, 372.

12 The atolls were Mururoa (or according to Sharp Tematangi—*Discovery*, 110), Cartaret's Bishop of Osnaburgh and the Duke of Gloucester's group). In the Santa Cruz group ('Queen Charlotte's Islands'); these Hanoverian duplications are annoying. Cartaret gave the first firm report of Vanikoro, but it had probably been seen by Mendaña's people in 1595. In Hawkesworth's maps Cartaret's names are supplemented by a suite drawn from the Channel Islands (he was a Jerseyman), Lord Egmont's Island becoming New Guernsey and so on; see H. Wallis, Plate X adn II.337–9. At least Cartaret's toponymy, unlike Wallis's, is drawn from his shipmates as well as the top brass.

13 Cf. H. Wallis, I.260–74, with Hawkesworth, *Voyages*, I.348–63. Tetanus rather than poisoning was probably responsible for the deaths.

14 These are Cartaret's Gower's, Cartaret's and Winchilsea's. He also discovered Kilinailau atoll ('Nine Islands'), which he took to be Tasman's Ontong Java. For Cartaret in these waters, see C. Jack-Hinton, *The Search for the Islands of Solomon 1567–1838* (Oxford 1969), 247–54 [*The Search*].

15 Cartaret lamented 'the great destruction of these usefull trees', cut down for the growing shoots at the top; these were boiled, to the detriment of their anti-scorbutic value.

16 See Figure 12 in Spate, *Monopolists*, 162.

17 A murky tangle of intrigue, unravelled in H. Wallis, I.76–93, and documented in II.365–437.

18 There was however chat between the crews, from which George Forster may have drawn his untrue assertion that Bougainville had visited Juan Fernández—*A Voyage round the World* (London 1777), x [*Voyage*].

19 The major sources are E. Taillemitte (ed.), *Bougainville et ses Compagnons autour du Monde 1766–1769* (Paris 1977) and J.-E. Martin-Allanic, *Bougainville navigateur et les Découvertes de son Temps* (Paris 1964). Both these massive works, which total 2698 pages, are indispensable. Martin-Allanics book is a work of more scholarship than skill; over two pages are devoted to the death-bed of Louis XV, and there is not a single map. Taillemitte edits, most meticulously, all the journals and has plenty of maps, including ten of Bellin's—but not his Pacific chart of which Bougainville complains, though there are six colour plates of New Guinea Highlanders, not seen by white men until the 1930s! See also L. D. Hammond (ed.), *News from New Cythera* (Minneapolis 1970) for the first published account of the voyage. M. Ross, *Bougainville* (London 1978) is elegant but not always accurate.

[20] J. Meyer, 'Le contexte des grands voyages d'exploration du XVIIIe siècle', in M. Mollat and E. Taillemitte (eds.), *L'Importance de l'Exploration Maritime au Siècle des Lumières* (Paris 1982), 17–39 at 33, 37–8; Nassau–Siegen, in Taillemitte, II.412–13; N. Broc, *La Geographie des Philosophes* (Paris 1974), 293 [*Géographie*].

[21] Vahitahi (Quatre Facardins), Akiaki (Lanciers), Hao (Ile de la Harpe), Marokau, Reitoru, Haraiki, Hikueru, Anaa (all unnamed). Dunmore doubts the sighting of Anaa; only Hao had been seen by Europeans—see Sharp, *Islands*, 114–16, and J. Dunmore, *French Explorers in the Pacific* (Oxford 1965–9), I.71–7 [*Explorers*].

[22] For the next thrilling instalment see below, 'The Tahitian Venus'.

[23] She had maintained her role as a young man impeccably to this point, though Commerson must have known her sex, and was clearly, unlike Kerguelen's Louison, a decent girl; but she was not, as is sometimes said, the first woman known to have sailed round the world. She left at Ile de France and married respectably. The fullest, and rather salacious, account is by the surgeon Vivez in Taillemitte, II.237–40, 267–8.

[24] There were signs of land—sea-weed, pieces of wood—and some thought they had seen distant hills, but this seems unlikely.

[25] Which J. R. Forster turned into 'probable' in his translation of Bougainville—*A Voyage round the World* (London 1772, reprint Amsterdam 1967), 307. On contemporary knowledge of Torres Strait, see Beaglehole, I.clvii–clxiv; Jack-Hinton, *The Search*, 175–83, 239–42; O. H. K. Spate, *The Spanish Lake* (Canberra 1979), 140–1, 323.

[26] 'Amalthée' was less lucky than the goat which sailed twice around the world with Cook, and was honoured with a Latin distich by Samuel Johnson—Beaglehole, IV.291.

[27] Taillemitte, I.388.

[28] H. Wallis, *Cartaret's Voyage*, I.179.

[29] Taillemitte, I.393.

[30] M. Devèze, quoted in Taillemitte, I.106–8; Broc, *Géographie*, 294.

[31] Commerson's 'Post-Scriptum sur L'isle de la Nouvelle-Cythère ou Tayti' (Taillemitte, II.506–10) was published in 1769, Diderot's *Supplément au Voyage de Bougainville* not until 1796, but had circulated in MS 'sous le manteau' from 1773—Martin-Allanic, 1388 note 88. See also Voltaire, *Les Oreilles du Comte de Chesterfield* (1775; in *Romans et Contes*, Pléiade ed. Paris 1979, 577–95)—Commersonian but avowedly based on 'Jean Hakerovorth' (Hawkesworth!).

[32] On this affair see Beaglehole, I.civ–cviii, IV.102–4, 126–7; but *contra* H. C. Fry, *Alexander Dalrymple and the Expansion of British Trade* (London 1970), 113–22, 275–7, and his 'Alexander Dalrymple and Captain Cook', in R. Fisher and H. Johnston (ed.), *Captain James Cook and His Times* (Canberra 1979), 41–57 at 42–7 [*James Cook*]. Fry disposes of Hawke's legendary antipathy to Dalrymple, but I cannot see that the latter was really well-fitted to command the expedition. Direct quotations in the Cook sections are from his journals unless the context shows otherwise. See also J. C. Beaglehole (ed.), *The Endeavour Journal of Joseph Banks 1768–1771* (Sydney 1962).

[33] Beaglehole, I.cvi, cxliii–cxlv; but see J. Waldersee, '*Sic Transit*: Cook's Observations in Tahiti', *Jnl Roy. Aust, Histl Soc.* 55, 1969, 113–23; Sir Richard Woolley (Astronomer Royal), 'The Significance of the Transit of Venus', in G. Badger (ed.), *Captain Cook: Seaman and Scientist* (Canberra 1970), 118–35; and W. H. Robertson, 'The Endeavour Voyage and Observation of the Transit of Venus', in J. V. S. Megaw (ed.), *Employ'd as a Discoverer* (Sydney 1971), 109–16. L. Woolf, *The Transits of Venus* (Princeton 1959), is interesting but little to our point. See also C. E. Herdendorf, 'Captain James Cook and the Transits of Mercury and Venus', *JPH* 21, 1986, 49–55.

34 Beaglehole, I.151; the name now covers the entire Tahitian Archipelago.

35 L. Fitzgerald, 'Point Hicks to Cape Howe', *Vict. Histl Mag.* 42, 1971, 489–96, concludes that Cook's Cape Howe was a point 6 km SW of the Cape's position on modern maps.

36 Plugging a leak by lowering over it a canvas loaded with oakum and yarn.

37 This was a situation more desperate than that on Endeavour Reef and for once Cook's wonted laconism deserts him—Beaglehole, I.377–8.

38 Ibid., I.388—the 'south' seems an afterthought. See also J. Bonwick, *Captain Cook in New South Wales or the Mystery of the Naming of Botany Bay* (London 1901)—much ado about little.

39 O. H. K. Spate, 'Between Tasman and Cook: Bouvet's Place in the History of Exploration', in J. Andrews (ed.), *Frontiers and Men* (Melbourne 1966), 174–86 at 182–3 ['Bouvet's Place']. Had Bouvet got his two ships, he might well have anticipated Cook in 'Nouvelle Galles du Sud' or rather, since his roots were in St Malo, 'Nouvelle Bretagne'. Main sources for this voyage are Beaglehole, II; G. Forster, *A Voyage round the World* (London 1777); M. E. Hoare (ed.), *The* Resolution *Journal of Johann Reinhold Forster 1771–1775*, Hs 2nd Ser. 152–5 (London 1982).

40 For Wales, see B. Smith, 'Coleridge's Ancient Mariner and Cook's Second Voyage', *Jnl of Warburg and Courtauld Inst.* 19, 1956, 117–54, and his *European Vision and the South Pacific* (2nd ed. Sydney n.d. [1985], 56–82. The Banks fiasco is documented in Beaglehole, II.704–18, including the Admiralty's caustic demolition of Banks's claims. For J. R. Forster see M. E. Hoare's admirable biography *The Tactless Philosopher* (Melbourne 1976), a telling title.

41 This was left to George Bass and Matthew Flinders in 1797–8. See R. Furneaux, *Tobias Furneaux* (London 1960), 108–9, and Beaglehole, II.729–45.

42 Cook's Doubtful, Furneaux and Adventure Islands; he also saw Tauere, discovered by Boenechea the year before.

43 G. Forster, I.503–4, 518–23; J. R. Forster, III.426–7 and his *Observations made during a Voyage round the World* (London 1778), 325–35—all remarkable rhetoric, with some sense.

44 See B. Hooper (ed.), *The Private Journal of James Burney* (Canberra 1975), 95–9, and for analysis of the complex story D. W. Orchison and L. C. Horrocks, 'Contact and Conflict: The Rowe Massacre', *Histl Studies* 16, 1975, 518–38. This incident is not mentioned in W. Arens, *The Man-Eating Myth* (New York 1979).

45 See A. G. Price, 'Further Notes on Captain Cook's Possible Discovery of the Antarctic Continent', *Geogr. Rev.* 66, 1956, 283–5. It is however very unlikely that Cook saw the continent, even refracted, and his achievement scarcely needs Price's gilding of the lily; see A. G. E. Jones, *Antarctica Observed: Who Discovered the Antarctic Continent?* (Whitby 1982), 34, 53–4.

46 J. R. Forster, III.443–7; cf. 438–9. To be fair, the food was awful, he was in a leaky cabin and suffering from rheumatic fever, probably influenza, and at times toothache; and he still observed the bird life.

47 Except for Quiros's and Bougainville's islands in the north, Cook retained the indigenous names, or presumed names, in variant spellings, but for Efate, which he called Sandwich Island.

48 This incident gave rise to much debate on the ship, but otherwise even J. R. Forster does not condemn the use of firearms; Melanesians always had a bad press.

49 Perhaps New Caledonia might be taken as the 'last remains' of Quiros's and Dalrymple's

mighty continent—[J. Marra], *Journal of the Resolution's Voyage* (London 1775), 282.

⁵⁰But no indecent familiarities, 'an innocent recreation . . . and not destitute of ingenuity'—
G. Forster, II.402–3, 418; there is also (II.383–4) some heavy humour about penis-cases
and European codpieces, but even here there is a moral to be rubbed in.

⁵¹ Discovered, if not by Antoine de la Roche in 1675, by the Spanish ship *Léon* in
1756, which is the more likely—Beaglehole, II.617.

⁵² Seen by an Enderby sealer in 1808, Bouvet Island was not firmly located until the
visit of the German surveying ship *Valdivia* in 1898—Spate, 'Bouvet's Place', 180.

⁵³ Clerke succeeded to overall command at Cook's death, 14 February 1779, Lt John
Gore taking over the *Discovery*. From Clerke's death, 22 August 1779, Gore returned
to the *Resolution* in command of the expedition, with Lt James King as commander
of the *Discovery*. The main source for Cook's last voyage is Beaglehole, III.

⁵⁴ Cook to his old employer, John Walker, in Beaglehole, IV.445. For the background,
ibid., IIII.xxii–lxviii; G. Williams, *The British Search for the Northwest Passage in the Eighteenth
Century* (London 1962), *passim* [*NW Passage*]; H. T. Fry, 'The Commercial Ambitions
Behind Captain Cook's Last Voyage', *NZ Jnl of History*, 7, 1973, 186–91, stressing the
roles of James Blankett and our old friend John Campbell.

⁵⁵ Beaglehole, III.lxi–lxv; Spate, *Monopolists*, 232–3, 246–50; Williams, *NW Passage*, 179–
83.

⁵⁶ G. Lefèvre-Pontalis, 'Un Project de Conquête du Japon par l'Angleterre et la Russie
en 1776', *Ann. de l'Ecole Libre des Sci. Politiques* 5, 1889, 533–57; C. E. Chapman, *The
Founding of Spanish California* (New York 1916), 221–5, 232, 376–9; E. Vila Vilar, 'Los
Rusos en América', *Anuario de Estudos Americanos* (Seville) 22, 1965, 569–672 at 597–
9, 610–14. The Polish adventurer Benyowsky was probably responsible for the canard—
G. V. Blue, 'A Rumor of an Anglo-Russian Raid upon Japan, 1776', *Pac. Histl Rev.*
8, 1939, 453–63.

⁵⁷ William Anderson, the *Resolution's* surgeon, in Beaglehole, III.823–4, 849, 858; Anderson
had criticised Cook's seamanship on an isolated occasion in the Cape Verdes, ibid.,
736–7. Lt John Rickman on the *Discovery* was less balanced—Anon. [Rickman], *Journal
of Captain Cook's Last Voyage* (London 1781, reprint Amsterdam 1967), 78–81, 96, 147.

⁵⁸ The Frenchman du Clesmeur, returning from Marion's disaster in New Zealand,
had seen the group, but his sightings are not certainly identifiable; Cook 'gave the
first firm record of Uoleva, Lifuka, Foa, and Haano'—Sharp, *Islands*, 122–3, 140.

⁵⁹ J. Martin, *An Account of the Natives of the Tonga Islands* (London 3rd ed. 1837, II.71–
2; Vava'u Press, Neiafu (Tonga), 279–80). This book is based on the experiences of
William Mariner, one of two survivors of the Port-au-Prince massacre of Lifuka in
1806, who lived in Tonga for four years.

⁶⁰ Beaglehole, III.cvii–cviii, cxiv, 162–4.

⁶¹ Omai's prosperity was brief; he died, of natural causes, some thirty months after
Cook's departure—E. H. McCormick. *Omai: Pacific Envoy* (Auckland 1977), 261–94,
and M. Alexander, *Omai: 'Noble Savage'* (London 1977), 203–9.

⁶² A plot to kidnap Clerke and Gore as counter-hostages was denounced in time by
an officer's mistress—Beaglehole, III.246–50.

⁶³ J. K. Munford (ed.), *John Ledyard's Journal of Captain Cook's Last Voyage* (Corvallis,
Oregon, 1963); first ed. Hartford (1783), 72 [Ledyard, *Journal*]. Much of this book is
cribbed from Rickman, and there is much sentimental rhetoric, but it is not so worthless
as Beaglehole suggests (III.ccviii–ccix); it does give us the sometimes critical lower
deck view. Ledyard was that unlikely combination, a New England romantick, who

later travelled from Stockholm to St Petersburg by land, without passport or much money, and got as far as Iakutsk before the police caught up with him; he died in Cairo (1789) preparing to lead an African expedition; Jefferson admired him. As he remarks of the Nootka Indians, 'that hardy, that intriped [*sic*], that glorious creature man'!

64 On Cook's possible or probable prior knowledge of Spanish visits to the coast, see H. R. Wagner, *The Cartography of the Northwest Coast of America to the Year 1800* (Berkeley 1937), I.183–5.

65 Ledyard, *Journal*, 91–100; Beaglehole, III.448–58.

66 Ibid., III.456; G. Williams, 'Myth and Reality: Cook and the Theoretical Geography of Northwest America', in Fisher and Johnson, *James Cook*, 58–80 at 69–79.

67 For a bitter complaint, see Ledyard, Journal, 102.

68 King's journal entry, 2 February 1779–Beaglehole, III.517. Cook's own journal ended on 17 January, and was carried on by King. The circumstances of Cook's death are discussed in Chapter 7.

69 This was on the earlier visit, in May—David Samwell, in Beaglehole, III.1248.

Notes for Chapter 6

1 J. Dunmore (trans. and ed.), *The Expedition of the* St Jean-Baptiste *to Pacific 1769–1770*, HS 2nd Ser. 158 (London 1981), 17–31 [*Expedition*]; this volume produces the journals of Surville and Labé from the Bashi Islands to leaving New Zealand. See also Dunmore, *French Explorers in the Pacific* (Oxford 1965–9), I.114–65 [*Explorers*], and his *The Fateful Voyage of the St Jean-Baptiste* (Christchurch 1969). My debt to Professor Dunmore will be obvious.

2 Robertson, of Wallis's *Dolphin*, saw at Tahiti a man whom he thought very like 'the Jews, which are Scaterd through all the knowen parts of the Earth', and John Campbell's map of Dampier's New Guinea discoveries has a legend referring to people there suspected of being a remnant of the Ten Tribes of Israel—H. Carrington (ed.), *The Discovery of Tahiti* HS 2nd Ser. 98 (London 1948), 228; Beaglehole, I.lxxvii. This sort of thing could easily have become tavern talk at Batavia and the Cape and spread through the Sailortowns of the Indian Seas. The Lost Tribes had wandered far!

3 This is perhaps the place to mention, for completeness, the voyage of Felipe Tompson in the *Buen Fin* on an alternative route from Manila to Acapulco in 1773. This gave the first firm records of Helen Reef, Ngatik and Oroluk in the Carolines, which may have been seen respectively by Woodes Rogers, Saavedra and Arellano—A. Sharp, *The Discovery of the Pacific Islands* (Oxford 1960), 127–8 [*Islands*].

4 J. Dunmore, 'A French Account of Port Praslin, Solomon Islands, in 1769;, JPH 9, 1974, 172–82. The 'contact' aspects of Surville's voyage are discussed below, ooo–oo.

5 See the conspectus of discoveries 1767–95 in Maps XLIIa–b in C. Jack-Hinton, *The Search for the Islands of Solomon 1567–1838* (Oxford 1969), 328–9 [*The Search*].

6 Had Surville known of the Spanish garrison on Mas a Tierra, he could have received a welcome doubtless less than cordial, but at least some relief.

7 J. Stockdale (ed.), *The Voyage of Captain Philip to Botany Bay* (London 1789; reprint Adelaide 1968, Melbourne 1982), 185–221 at 202–03. On the controversy see Dunmore,

Explorers, I.162–5, and *Expedition*, 52–7, and the full discussion in Jack-Hinton, *The Search*, 266–307.

8 Paris 1790; English trans. London 1791. Ironically, the latter was published by Stockdale, who eats his humble pie gracefully enough—xv–xvi, 201–05.

9 *Considerations on M. Buache's Memoir concerning New Britain and the North Coast of New Guinea* (London 1790); C. Jack-Hinton, 'Alexander Dalrymple and the Rediscovery of the Islands of Solomon', *Mariner's Mirror* 50, 1964, 93–114.

10 B. G. Corney (trans. and ed.), *The Voyage of Captain Don Felipe González to Easter Island 1770–1771*, HS 2nd Ser. 13 (Cambridge 1913) [*Voyage*]. Amat's instructions to González are not in this volume but in Corney's *The Quest and Occupation of Tahiti by Emissaries of Spain during the Years 1772–1776*, HS 2nd Ser. 32, 36, 43 (London 1913, 1914, 1919), I.182–92 [*The Quest*].

11 Cited from Corney, *Voyage*, xlviii.

12 See Chapter 1 above.

13 Corney, *Voyage*, 140.

14 Ibid., 67; for Amat's confusions, 72–6.

15 The main source for this voyage is A. -M. de Rochon, *Nouveau Voyage à la Mer du Sud commencé sous les ordres de M. MARION* (Paris 1783); this is the narrative of Julien Crozet, Marion's second on the *Mascarin*, and is often referred to as 'Crozet's Voyage'. There is again an admirable discussion in Dunmore, Explorers, II.166–99.

16 J. E. Martin-Allanic, *Bougainville navigateur et les Découvertes de son Temps* (Paris 1964), II.1323 [*Bougainville*], followed by two long-winded pages with almost hourly bulletins from Aotourou's deathbed. A desire to avoid being anticipated by Kerguelen may also have hastened Marion's sailing.

17 There is a full and well-illustrated account in L. G. Kelly. *Marion du Fresne at the Bay of Islands* (Wellington 1951); the significance of the disaster is discussed in Ch. 10 below. This was a sad end for a man who had rescued Bonnie Prince Charlie after the '45—J. Dunmore, 'Marion du Fresne and the Young Pretender', *NZ Jnl of History* 3, 1969, 70–3.

18 Sharp, *Islands*, 122–3; Dunmore, *Explorers*, I.190–3.

19 Martin-Allanic, *Bougainville*, II.1377.

20 Of Corney's *The Quest*, volumes I and II.1–89 cover Boenechea's first voyage to Tahiti; the remainder of II is devoted to his second Lángara's, III is nearly all occupied by the Journal of Máximo Rodríguez.

Ironically, the *Aguila* had been built at Cadiz by a British shipwright seduced by Jorge Juan—*The Quest*, I.xliv; O. H. K. Spate, *Monopolists and Freebooters* (Canberra 1983), 408.

21 The *Quest*, I.8, 226–7, 231–5, 265; also Boenechea's Instructions, I.263–8, and those to the Missionary Padres, 278–83.

22 Boenechea's names, in sequence: San Simon y Judas, San Quintin, Todos Santos, San Cristobál.

23 *The Quest*, I.304–05, 307–08.

24 Gayangos's journal is in *The Quest*, II.103–08; Andía's, much more informative, at II.221–316. There is a reprint of the original, *Relación del Viaje hecho a la Isla de Amat, por otro Nombre Otahiti* (Barcelona 1947) [*Relación*].

25 He also saw Tekokoto, Hikuera and Motutunga, all discovered by Cook or Bougainville.

26 *The Quest*, II.143–52 (Gayangos), 299–300 (Andía), III.34–40 (Rodriguez).

27 Ibid., II.155–8.

²⁸ Ibid., II.290; 'La contemplación y dulzura con que nosotros tratamos a estes gentes, y el rigor y torpeza con que los trataron los ingleses'— *Relación*, 69.

²⁹ Lángara's rather cursory report is in *The Quest*, II.375–75, the Padres' puerile journal at 319–49, and Rodriguez's admirable account in III.1–210.

³⁰ Sinning to the lamentation 'Mais ma religion! mais mes Ordres!'—D. Diderot, *Supplément au Voyage de Bougainville*, in *Oeuvres* (Pléiade ed. Paris 1951), 993–1032 at 1021–2.

³¹ *The Quest*, III.175; a more modern French version, with an introduction by Robert Langdon, is in press with the Société des Océanistes, Papeete. For an appreciation, see C. Robineau, '... les Espagnols à Tautira et le Journal de Máximo Rodríguez', in M. Mollat and E. Taillemitte, *L'Importance de l'Exploration Maritime au Siecle des Lumîeres* (Paris 1982), 151–60.

³² Beaglehole, III.188; *The Quest*, II.422–9.

Notes for Chapter 7

¹ W. K. Beddie, *Bibliography of Captain James Cook* (Sydney 1970—xvi + 894 pages); M. Holmes, *Captain James Cook: A Bibliographical Excursion* (London 1952), 8 [*Excursion*].

The official account of the first voyage, much dolled up from the journals of Cook and Banks, is in Volumes II–III of J. Hawkesworth, *An Account of the Voyages... for Making Discoveries in the Southern Hemisphere* (London 1773 [*Voyages*]. Cook's own accounts are in J. Douglas (ed.), *A Voyage towards the South Pole...* (London 1777, reprint Adelaide 1970), and *A Voyage to the Pacific Ocean... for making Discoveries in the Northern Hemisphere* (London 1784; my quotations are from 2nd ed. 1785) [*Voyage to Pacific*], also edited by Douglas and from Cook's death written by Captain James King. Beaglehole has edited *The* Endeavour *Journal of Joseph Banks 1768–1771* (Sydney 1962) [*Banks*] and M. E. Hoare *The* Resolution *Journal of Johann Reinhold Forster 1772–1775*, HS 2nd Ser. 152–5 (London 1982) [Forster, *Journal*].

Other contemporary accounts are S. Parkinson, *A Journal of a Voyage to the South Seas* (London 1773) reprint Adelaide 1972); A. Sparrman, *A Voyage round the World with Captain James Cook* (London 1953, ed. O. Rutter) [*Voyage*]; C. Holmes (ed.), *Captain Cook's Final Voyage: The Journal of Midshipman George Gilbert* (Canberra 1982) [*Final Voyage*]; and above all G. Forster, *A Voyage round the World* (London 1777) [*Voyage*], which for all its moralising and bad temper is much the most vivid and vivacious narrative. The 1784 edition of Parkinson gives his book's publishing history; on the whole more interesting than the text itself; for criticism on Banks's part in this affair, see Smith and Joppien, *The Art* (Melbourne 1985), 51–4 (full reference in note 9 below).

Beaglehole's Introductions to Cook's *Journals* give a full survey of the manuscript materials, and his Appendices excerpts from the most important. See also H. Wallis, 'Publication of Cook's Journals: Some New Sources and Assessments', *Pacific Studies* 1, 1978, 163–94 ['New Sources'].

² *Zimmermann's Account of the Third Voyage of Captain Cook* (trans. U. Tewsley, Wellington 1926) [*Account*] and F. W. Howay (ed.), *Zimmermann's Captain Cook* (Toronto 1930); ingenuous, but nowhere else do we find such a considered account of Cook not by a fellow-officer. Anon. [J. Rickman], *Journal of Captain Cook's Last Voyage* (London 1781,

reprint Amsterdam 1967) [*Last Voyage*], is largely pirated, with additions by a lively if untutored mind, in J. Ledyard's book of the same title (Hartford, Conn., 1783) [Ledyard, *Journal*]; my quotations are from the edition by J. E. Munford (Corvallis, Oregon, 1963). Anon. [J. Marra], *Journal of the Resolution's Voyage . . .* [1772–5] (London 1775, reprint Amsterdam 1967) has a marked bias against Cook, but some of his independent remarks on Cook's contacts with Islanders are sensible; see Beaglehole, II.cliii–clv, 961–2. Anon. [J. Matra], *A Journal of a Voyage round the World . . .* [1768–71] (London 1771, reprint Adelaide 1975), is slight, and W. Ellis, *An Authentic Narrative of a Voyage performed by Captain Cook and Captain Clerke* (London 1782) is dull poor stuff.

3 Beaglehole, I.cl.

4 Beaglehole, 'Cook the Navigator', in J. V. S. Megaw (ed.), *Employ'd as a Discoverer* (Sydney 1971), 117–34 at 132 [*Discoverer*]; cf. Beaglehole, IV.699–701. On the choice of ships, see Sandwich's massive snub to Banks and Palliser's sensible comments, ibid., II.704–18.

5 G. S. Ritchie, 'Captain Cook's Influence on Hydrographic Surveying', *Pacific Studies* 1, 1978, 78–96 at 86; F, White, 'Cook the Navigator' in G. M. Badger (ed.), *Captain Cook: Navigator and Scientist* (Canberra 1970), 50–69 at 58, 61 [*Navigator*].

6 From the inscription, by Admiral John Forbes, on Palliser's monument to Cook's memory, a superb example of the century's mortuary style—*Geogl Jnl* 73, 1959, 101, 108, and Cook and King, *Voyage to Pacific*, liv, lxxxvi–lxxxix.

7 Ibid., lviii–lix; of the pioneers in this trade, at least Colnett, Dixon and Portlock had sailed with Cook.

8 Beaglehole, II.cvi–cvii, III.424–5; Forster, *Journal*, II.192–3, 198–201; J. R. Forster, *Observations made during a Voyage round the World* (London 1778), 69–102. For the Buffonian orthodoxy, see N. Broc, *La Géographie des Philosophes* (Paris 1974), 177–8.

9 The Hints are in Beaglehole, I.514–19; for comment see B. Smith and R. Joppien. *The Art of Captain Cook's Voyages* (Melbourne 1985), I.51–4 [*The Art*] and for Degérando, F.E. Moore's translation of his work (London 1969). Banks and the Forsters are further discussed in Chapter 9 below.

10 H. Wallis, 'Conclusion', in H. Cobbe (ed.), *Cook's Voyages and Peoples of the Pacific* (London/Canberra 1979), 129–52 at 30 [*Cook's Voyages*].

11 B. Smith, *European Vision and the South Pacific* (2nd ed. Sydney 1985), 1; see especially 37–58 on Hodges, whose work is well displayed in A. Murray-Smith, *Captain Cook's Artists in the Pacific 1769–1779* (Christchurch 1969). See also A. M. Lysaght. 'Banks's Artists . . .' in Cobbe *Cook's Voyages*, 9–80, and R. Joppien, 'The Artistic Bequest of Captain Cook's Voyages', in R. Fisher and H. Johnson (eds.), *Captain James Cook and His Times* (Vancouver/Canberra 1979), 187–210 [*James Cook*], especially 199–203 on the Charvet/Dufour wallpaper, Plate XVI of this volume. Finally there are the two superb volumes of Smith and Joppien, *The Art*, and a happy marriage of science and art in D. J. Carr (ed.), *Sydney Parkinson: Artist of Cook's* Endeavour *Voyage* (London/Canberra 1983).

12 See M. Pointon, 'Geology and landscape painting in nineteenth century England', in L. J. Jordanova and R. S. Porter (eds.), *Images of the Earth*, Brit. Soc. for Hist. of Science Monograph 1 (Chalfont St Giles 1979), 84–117 at 90.

13 *Cosmos: A Sketch of a Physical Description of the Universe* (trans. E. O. Otté, London 1864), II.371–2; cf. II.436–7. Hodges's paintings were not of the Pacific but of India, seen at Warren Hastings's house on a visit to England with George Forster, 1790.

[14] Biographical details are from Beaglehole, IV; see also his 'Some Problems of Cook's Biographer', *Mariner's Mirror* 55, 1969, 365–81 ['Biographer']. A major problem for later writers on Cook is to keep a respectable yet respectful distance from Beaglehole.

[15] IV.12; cf. J. A. Williamson, *Cook and the Opening of the Pacific* (London 1946), 68–71.

[16] Ibid., 73–4—'a free choice, natural to an able man of twenty-seven'—and *contra*, Beaglehole, IV.15–16—to the Navy a trained volunteer would be 'a prize indeed, with nothing against his intelligence' except the fact of volunteering. Far from taking umbrage, Walker, through his local MP, suggested to Palliser that Cook should be commissioned at once, which was against regulations.

[17] A relic of the days when many officers, appointed through influence or on account of military experience; had to rely on subordinates from the merchant marine for sailing, as distinct from fighting, their ships.

[18] 'Genius' in this context had not its full modern significance, but meant rather 'turn of mind, aptitude, special knack'—*The Oxford English Dictionary*.

[19] Guns from the *Endeavour* were indeed salvaged from the reef in 1969.

[20] Beaglehole, 'Biographer', 327, and IV.126–7.

[21] Ibid., 176–7, 310, 445, 474; for the swearing, Sparrman, *Voyage*, 51–2—flatly denied by Zimmermann (*Account*, 41), but Sparrman is more circumstantial and convincing.

[22] Beaglehole, 'Cook the Man', in Badger, *Navigator*, 11–29 at 18, 24.

[23] Beaglehole, III.151–4; the officer was the straight-laced John Williamson.

[24] S. McLachlan, 'Savage Island or Savage History: An interpretation of early European Contact with Niue', *Pacific Studies* 6, 1982, 26–51 at 28 (my italics).

[25] S. V. Benét, *John Brown's Body* (New York 1927), 171 (Oxford 1944, 182). The whole passage, some 170 lines, seems in several places curiously apposite to Cook.

[26] Cook to Walker, 17 August 1771, in Beaglehole, IV.276–7. For Bank's role in the Rio incident, see Beaglehole, *Banks*, I.37

[27] R. Hough, *The Murder of Captain James Cook* (London 1979), 42–4 [*Murder*]. Hough states, without giving his source, that Bligh, the Master, 'was amazed at this occurrence'; if so, it is very odd that in a letter from Cape Town, only ten weeks later, all Bligh says about the Cape Verdes is that they passed Port Praya but as the *Discovery* was not there they did not stop—G. Mackaness (ed.), *Fresh Light on Bligh*, Aust. Histl Monographs 5 (Dubbo, N.S.W. 1976), 13. Anderson's comments are in Beaglehole, III.736–7.

[28] In Megaw, *Discoverer*, 133.

[29] Rickman, *Last Voyage*, 80.

[30] Cf. Beaglehole, IV.547–8.

[31] Ledyard, *Journal*, 37–41.

[32] For details, see Beaglehole, III.228–33, IV.558–9. Other biographers, except Hough (*Murder*, 103–8), tend to slur over this incident, or to omit it.

[33] Zimmermann, *Account*, 41. The men accepted the proposal; a full allowance was half a pint (c. 300 ml) of brandy or rum—Beaglehole, III.189.

[34] Ibid., II.333–4, IV.640–3. Although Cook said that his only motive was to save spirits for the next northern cruise, Midshipman Watts reported him as saying that 'he did not chuse to keep turning & working among these Isles without having some Profit'— from purserage?

[35] Ibid., II.333–4, IV.370–1; there was no other fresh meat. J. R. oddly enough does not mention his 'Sacrifice to [Cook's] tender Stomack', but Cook does, and also George

Forster—*Voyage*, I.538, 547–18, II.3.

[36] Medical details from Surgeon Vice-Admiral Sir James Watt. (Medical Director General RN, retired), 'Medical Aspects and Consequences of Captain Cook's Voyages', in Fisher and Johnston, *James Cook*, 128–57 at 154–7—a most important paper. Acute infection of the gall-bladder has also been suggested. Cf. Hough, *Murder*, 248–50: 'pathology rather than psychology is likely to be our best guide.'

[37] 'The action of ranking, or fact of being ranked, among the gods; transformation into a god, deification'—*The Oxford English Dictionary*.

[38] Hikiau is 'the Morai' in contemporary accounts of Cook's last weeks. These are in fair general agreement; references will be confined to direct quotations and points of discrepancy or interpretation. Quotations not otherwise identified are from King, in Beaglehole, III.502–31, 549–69.

[39] Koah and Kareekeea in Cook and King, *Voyage to Pacific*, III.6–9.

[40] King, in Beaglehole, III.504–7; perhaps the most vivid account of the mass enthusiasm is in Ledyard, *Journal*, 102–7.

[41] G. Daws, *Shoal of Time: A History of the Hawaiian Islands* (Honolulu 1968), 11–27 at 26 [*Shoal of Time*]; also 'Kealakekua Bay Revisted', *JPH* 3, 1968, 21–4. The Lono/Cook parallel is worked out in detail in M. Sahlins, *Historical Metaphors and Mythical Realities: Structure in the Early History of the Sandwich Islands Kingdom* (Ann Arbor 1981, especially at 11–24 [*Metaphors*]; some of his inferences about later political history may be queried, but this is an important and richly suggestive book; for a critique, see J. Friedman, 'Captain Cook, Culture, and the World System', *JPH* 20, 1985, 191–201. G. Dening, 'Sharks that Walk on the Land', *Meanjin* (Melbourne) 41, 1982, 424–41, is an elegant presentation of Sahlins's view. There is an interesting interpretation in M. R. de Brossard, *Moana, Océan Cruel: les dieux meurent à la grande mer du sud* (Paris 1966), 289–319 [*Moana*]. And once one has suspended disbelief in a Cook who would allow Ledyard to argue Calvinist theology with him, there is much to reflect on in O. A. Bushnell's novel *The Return of Lono* (2nd ed. Honolulu 1971).

[42] Or Teriiopu, Tarei 'opu'u, Kalani 'op'uu, Kalei 'opu'a, Kala'i'opu'u, etc.—Beaglehole, III.508. Cook had already met Kalanipopuu, not knowing his rank, on Maui.

[43] Zimmermann, *Account*, 37; Cook and King, *Voyage to Pacific*, III.24.

[44] Ibid., III.25–6; Ledyard, *Journal*, 136–7 and note at 225–7; Zimmermann, *Account*, 37; S. Dibble, *A History of the Sandwich Islands* (Honolulu 1843, reprint 1909), 25 [*Sandwich Is.*]; T. G. Thrum, 'The Paehumu of Haiaua Non-Sacred', *Annl Report Hawaiian Histl Soc.* 35, 1927, 56–7. More modern references: Beaglehole, III.cxlvi, IV.326–7; Brossard, *Moana*, 304, 326–7; Daws, *Shoal of Time*, 15; Sahlins, *Metaphors*, 22, 25–6; and G. Kennedy, *The Death of Captain Cook* (London 1978), 26–7 [*Death*]—but his suggestion seems to overlook the fact that Lono was god of peace, not war.

[45] Sahlins, *Metaphors*, 16, 22.

[46] Sahlins, *Metaphors*, 22–4; see 24–7 for further development of the theme.

[47] Of contemporary accounts of Cook's last days. King's in *Voyage to Pacific*, III.35–82, is in places a cover-up (though the silence on Williamson's conduct was probably inevitable in an official account), and throughout is an exercise in subtle self-advertisement—see my note 'Splicing the Log at Kealakekua Bay', *JPH* 19, 1984, 117–20. David Samwell, surgeon of the *Discovery*, collated the evidence of his comrades in *A Narrative of the Death of Captain Cook* (London 1786) [*Narrative*], but while one cannot doubt his sincerity, his reverence for his Captain led him to palliate Cook's errors or failings. Ledyard is more vivid than reliable.

R. T. Gould has assembled 'Some Unpublished Accounts of Cook's Death', *Mariner's Mirror* 24, 1928, 300–19, and also 'Bligh's Notes on Cook's Last Voyage', ibid. 371–85 [Bligh, 'Notes'], which perhaps throw more light on Bligh's crabbed personality than on the event. For cogent comment on these accounts, see H. Carrington, *Life of Captain Cook* (London 1939), 280–1.

Two recent studies are those of G. Kennedy, *Death*, and R. Hough, *Murder*; the former is in my opinion the clearest and most careful reconstruction, unpretentious but much superior to Hough's.

48 Samwell, *Narrative*, 4, 19.

49 Kennedy, *Death*, 43–4. Most accounts agree that there were nine marines, not eleven as in Hough, *Murder*, 219, and they did not include Ledyard—see editorial note in Ledyard, *Journal*, 228–31.

50 R. S. Kuykendall, *The Hawaiian Kingdom* (Honolulu 1968), I.18–19. Hough's 'Murder' is an obvious misnomer for a death incurred through the attempted forcible seizure of a man regarded as a sovereign prince.

51 Bligh, and he only, says that the affray was over before this news reached Kowrowa—'Notes', 380. Kennedy (*Death*, 68–71) thinks it unlikely that the news triggered the attack, but it must have added to the confusion and agitation.

52 Gilbert, *Final Voyage*, 107.

53 Kennedy, *Death*, 77–8; for Phillips's reported statement, see A. Kippis, *The Life of Captain James Cook* (London 1883, original ed. 1788), 341. Samwell, in Beaglehole, III.1199–1201, is particularly severe on the failure to rescue the bodies.

54 Beaglehole, usually inclined to take King at face value, says 'There is no justification for the statement commonly made that he [Cook] was waving to the boats to cease firing'—IV.672. It is incidentally extremely difficult to see why Hough (*Murder*, at 49) should call John Zoffany's neo-classical painting *Death of Cook* 'probably the least fanciful version'; cf. Smith, *European Vision*, 119–20.

55 Beaglehole, III.540. Bligh's notes show that he must have been for violent measures. King is ambivalent; he favoured 'an early display of vigorous resentment' yet was not sorry to be overruled—it might have looked bad in the eyes of the world—*Voyage to Pacific*, III.59–61.

56 *Moana*, 308–10, 317, 327–8.

57 The most vivid account is Samwell's, in Beaglehole, III.1209–14; King's reflections (ibid., 561–3) on the brutality of common seamen are quite Forsterian; Bligh's comment on the beheadings was 'If this had not been done, they would never have been brought to submission'—'Notes', 383.

58 The Revd William Ellis, *Narrative of a Tour through Hawaii* (London 1826), 103–6 [*Tour*]. The bones of the marines were too widely dispersed to be reclaimed.

59 J. Burney, *A Chronological History of North-Eastern Voyages of Discovery* (London 1819), 263–6; Samwell, *Narrative*, 9–10; Ledyard, *Journal*, 144 (and cf. 136); Beaglehole, III.568; Clerke, ibid., 538–9.

60 Wallis, 'New Sources', 173. See W. H. Pearson, 'Hawkesworth's *Voyages*', in R. F. Brissenden (ed.), *Studies in the Eighteenth Century II* (Canberra 1973), 239–58, and 'Hawkesworth's Alterations', *JPH* 7, 1972, 45–72—there were eight editions in sixteen years. There is a sympathetic study in J. L. Abbott, *John Hawkesworth* (Madison 1983). For a stimulating survey see M. E. Hoare, 'Two Centuries' Perceptions of James Cook', in Fisher and Johnston, *James Cook*, 211–28. My following notes are inevitably highly selective.

61 A. Frost, 'The Pacific Ocean—The Eighteenth Century's New World', in W. Veit (ed.), *Captain James Cook: Image and Impact: South Sea Discoveries and the World of Letters*, II (Melbourne 1979) 5–49 at 32–3 [*Image*]; R. Leigh, 'Diderot's Tahiti', in J. P. Hardy and J. C. Eade (eds.), *Studies in the Eighteenth Century* V (Oxford 1983), 113–28 at 125 note 3.

62 C. Roderick, 'Sir Joseph Banks, Queen Oberea, and the Satirists', in Veit, *Image*, I (Melbourne 1972), 67–89, and E. H. McCormick, *Omai: Pacific Envoy* (Auckland 1977), 89–92, 121–4, 183–7, 301–4 [*Omai*]. Anon., *An Historic Epistle from Omiah to the Queen of Otaheite* (London 1775) is above the ruck in verse and feeling.

63 'Cook the Discoverer: an Attempt at a Memorial' (Berlin 1787); see M. E. Hoare in *Rec. Aust. Acad. Sciences* 1, 1969, 7–16 at 11. For the widely-ramifying 'Cook-Syndrome' see L. Bodi, 'Captain Cook in German Imaginative Literature', in Veit, *Image*, I.117–37.

64 R. Joppien, '... Loutherbourg's Pantomine "Omai" ...' in T. G. Mitchell (ed.), *Captain Cook and the South Pacific* (London/Canberra 1979), 87–137, a lavishly illustrated account; see also McCormick, *Omai*, 313–18, and Smith, *European Vision*, 114–19. The Paris production was M. Arnould, *La Mort du Capitaine Cook* (1788)—see Acte III Scene XXVIII.

65 Anna Seward, *An Elegy on Captain Cook* (London 1780); Cook 'quit[s] imperial London's gorgeous plains/Where, rob'd in thousand tints, bright Pleasure reigns' at the call of 'HUMANITY!', and when he presents Farmer George's civilising livestock to the Maori
>   Stern moves the Bull along th'affrighted shores,
>   And countless nations tremble as he roars.!

66 B. Smith, 'Cook's Posthumous Reputation, in Fisher and Johnston, *James Cook*, 160–86 at 161–8; of the eulogies discussed I have read only M. Gianetti's *Elogy* [*sic*] (Florence 1785) beautifully printed in English and Italian, a fine example of the eulogist's recklessness about facts—he alleges, falsely, that Cook could swim from infancy. For H. J. Pye, understandably one of the least-known of little-known laureates, see his *Naucratia, or Naval Dominion* (London 1798), III lines 9–76.

67 This is established by H. T. Fry, 'Alexander Dalrymple and Captain Cook', in Fisher and Johnston, *James Cook*, 41–57 to 50–02, 55–7; he explodes Frédéric Metz's myth, which misled commentators for 150 years or more, including E. T. Hamy in 'Cook et Dalrymple', Société de Géographie, *Centenaire de la Mort de Cook* (Paris 1879), 17–32.

68 J. Richard and F. Babié, *Voyages chez les Peuples Sauvages ou L'Homme de la Nature* (Paris 1801), II.371–95 at 385–6, 391—the authors, without knowing it, have adopted Omai's tenfold multiplication of Cook's devastation on Morea; for this curious work, see McCormick, *Omai*, 327–9. Cowper is quoted in J. C. Beaglehole, 'The Death of Captain Cook', *Histl Studies* 11, 1964, 289–305 at 289.

69 Ellis, *Tour*, 3–6; 100–12; Dibble, *Sandwich Is.*, 20–5; Bingham, *A Residence of Twenty-one Years in the Sandwich Islands* (Hartford, Conn., 1947), 65 (in fact, Cook lost face by refusing a princess); Stokes, 'Origin of the Condemnation of Captain Cook in Hawaii', *Annl Report Hawaiian Histl Soc.* 39, 1930, 68–104; S. M. Kamakau, *Ruling Chiefs of Hawaii* (Honolulu 1961), 92–104.

70 M. Letts, General Preface, Beaglehole, I.v.

71 Sir Joseph Hooker's edition of Banks's journal (1896) is licentious (Beaglehole, *Banks*, I.144–5), in the sense of infidelity to its original.

72 Holmes, *Excursion*, 62, 86; Royal Geographical Society, *Proceedings* (New Series) 1, 1879, 219–20—this apart there are just seven (7) references to Cook from 1870 to 1881,

all strictly *en passant*. Of course, the 'Great Game' in central Asia was in full swing, and the scramble in Africa was nearing take-off.

73 Details from J. Robertson, *The Captain Cook Myth* (Sydney 1981); not an attack on Cook but a refreshing polemic against the grosser hagiography, a few slips not affecting the argument. It should if possible be read alongside J. Carruthers, *Captain James Cook R. N.* (London 1930). I write under the shadow of the 1988 bicentenary.

74 I have seen the Omai but not the Cook passages in *Les Jardins* (Paris 1782); Baggesen is discussed in L. Albertsen, 'Trusting in the Antipodes', in Veit, *Images*, II.173–9.

75 O. H. K. Spate, 'Luso-Australia: in Maps and Verse', *Rev. da Universidade de Coimbra* 27, 1929, 219–37 at 214–37.

76 For Ingamells's poem (Melbourne 1951), ibid, 231–2; *Five Visions* is in Slessor's *Poems* (Sydney 1957), 57–62. Hume's memories were retailed by his son George in a very odd book, *Memoirs of an Aristocrat* (London 1838), 302–9.

77 See Marlies Thierch's very interesting 'Cook Plays Now and Then', in Veit, *Image*, I.43–53; Girardoux's *Supplément* is discussed, along with Diderot's to Bougainville, in J. Dunmore, 'The Explorer and the Philosopher', ibid. 54–66.

Notes for Chapter 8

1 So much the opposite number that in the Crimean War the two Companies, with the approval of their Governments, concluded a formal neutrality pact—S. B. Okun, *The Russian-American Company* (trans. C. Ginsburg, Cambridge, Mass., 1951), 234–53 [*RAC*].

2 For both exploits, see J. Mirsky, *The Westwards Crossings* (2nd ed. Chicago 1970) [*Crossings*], a stimulating book.

3 For Krenitzin and Levashov, see S. P. Pallas in J. R. Masterson and H. Brower (eds.), *Bering's Successors 1745–1780* (Seattle 1948), 50–61, and W. Coxe, *Account of the Russian Discoveries between Asia and America* (3rd ed. London 1787, reprint New York 1966), 205–33. On Billings, I have not seen M. Sauer, *An Account of [an]... Expedition to the Northern Parts of Russia* (London 1802), but have used G. Sarytschew [Sarychev], *Account of a Voyage... to Siberia, the Frozen Ocean, and the North-East Sea* (London 1806, reprint Amsterdam 1967) [*Account*]. See also G. Barratt's excellent *Russia in Pacific Waters 1715–1825* (Vancouver 1981), 56–66, 74–96 [*Pacific Waters*], and A. I. Alekseev, 'Joseph Billings', *Geogr. Jnl* 132, 1966, 233–8.

4 *A Chronological History of North-Eastern Voyages of Discovery* (London 1819, reprint Amsterdam 1969), 278–81; Mirsky, *Crossings* 235–6; but cf. Sarytschew, *Account*, 42–3.

5 This was the *Gustavus III*, a privateer with a Swedish commission but sailing also as the British brig *Mercury*, under J. H. Cox, who diverted her from raiding Russians into trading with them—G. Mortimer, *Observations and Remarks made during a Voyage on the Brig Mercury* (Dublin 1791) [*Observations*]; Pethick, *Nootka* (below, note 70); G. Cottez, 'Recherches historiques sur une expédition suedoise en Océanie', *Bull. Soc. Etudes Océaniennes* (Papeete) 8, 1951–2, 173–82, 425–53; Barratt, *Pacific Waters*, 80–3.

6 The expedition surmounted bad luck and terrible hardships, but when one recollects Vancouver it is very difficult to agree with Barratt (*Pacific Waters*, 76) that none of those who sailed on Cook's last voyage had a success 'larger or more brilliant' than Billings.

[7] J. Meares, *Voyages... from China to the North-West Coast of America* (London 1790, reprint Amsterdam 1967), 312 [*Voyages*]; there is a more interesting Russian version in A. I. Andreyev (ed.), *Russian Discoveries in the Pacific and North America* (Ann Arbor 1952), 108 [*Discoveries*]. For Shelikhov and Baranov, see *inter alia* Barratt, *Pacific Waters*, 99–104, 125–9; Okun, *RAC*, Chs II–III *passim*, especially 32–3, 44–5, 53–4; G. C. Hulley, *Alaska 1741–1953* (Portland 1953), 70–81, 111–32 [*Alaska*], unpretentious but lucid. Political background in G. P. Taylor, 'Spanish-Russian Rivalry in the Pacific, 1769–1820', *The Americas* 15, 1958, 109–117, and E. Vila Vilar, 'Los Rusos en América', *Anuario de Estudios Americanas* (Seville) 22, 1965, 569–672.

[8] R. Pierce, *Russia's Hawaiian Adventure, 1815–1817* (Berkeley 1965).

[9] Andreyev, *Discoveries*, 42, 53; C. E. Chapman, *The Founding of Spanish California... 1687–1783* (New York 1916), 228, 376–80 [*Founding*]; W. L. Cook, *Flood Tide of Empire: Spain and the Pacific Northwest, 1543–1819* (New Haven 1973), 58, 90–1, 130 [*Flood Tide*]; C. I. Archer, 'The Spanish Reaction to Cook's Third Voyage', in R. Fisher and H. Johnston (eds.), *Captain James Cook and His Times* (Vancouver/Canberra 1979), 99–119 at 99–100, 110–12.

[10] For the Spanish voyages I have followed H. R. Wagner, *The Cartography of the Northwest Coast of America to the Year 1800* (Berkeley 1937), I.172–236 [*Cartography*], meticulous in the identification of place names in this littoral labyrinth, and Cook, *Flood Tide*, 54–145, 271–326 *passim*, more vivid. Original accounts are hard to come by in Australia, but for Pérez see the diaries of his chaplains in D. C. Cutter (ed.), *The California Coast* (Norman. Okla., 1969), 135–278.

[11] It would have been greater still had Vancouver Island retained the name that its eponym generously gave it—'Island of Quadra and Vancouver'. The abbreviation is regrettable but understandable; as H. H. Bancroft cynically remarked, only one name was likely to remain, 'and that would depend entirely as to which nation the territory fell'—quoted in Lambe, Introduction to Vancouver's *Voyage* (note 94 below), I.106. Quadra was a Criollo, born in Lima, which may be why he was not originally in command. I use 'Quadra' instead of 'Bodega' in deference to Vancouver's contemporary usage.

[12] J. Dunmore, *French Explorers in the Pacific* (Oxford 1965–9), I.250–3 [*Explorers*]; J. Forsyth, 'Latouche-Tréville and his Proposal to Explore the South Coast of New Holland', *Mariner's Mirror* 45, 1959, 115–29; G. V. Blue, 'French Interest in Pacific America in the Eighteenth Century, *Pac. Histl Rev.* 4, 1935, 246–66 at 262.

[13] The official publication was M. L. A. Milet-Mureau (ed.), *Voyage autour du Monde de La Pérouse* (Paris 1797); two anonymous translations appeared in London in 1798, of which that published by J. Johnson, *A Voyage round the World... by J. F. G. de La Pérouse*, is rather better than J. Stockdale's and is quoted here [Milet-Mureau, *Voyage*]. Milet-Mireau was on the whole a good editor, tidying up the style but more faithful to his texts than Hawkesworth, but he had the delicate task of adjusting writings of the Ancient Régime to the Revolution. J. Dunmore and M. de Brossard have produced a splendid edition of La Pérouse's own Journal, with commentary and documents: *Le Voyage de Lapérouse 1785–1788* (Paris 1985) [Dunmore/Brossard, *Lapérouse*], while C. Gaziello, *L'Expédition de Lapérouse 1785–1788: Réplique française aux voyages de Cook* (Paris 1984) [*Expédition*] is an important study from the archives. For biographical detail, see M. de Brossard, *Lapérouse: Des combats à la découverte* (Paris 1978) [*Lapérouse: combats*] and J. Dunmore, *Pacific Explorer: The Life... of La Pérouse* (Palmerston North 1985). E. Scott, *Lapérouse* (Sydney 1912) is slight but has a certain period charm.

'La Pérouse' is favoured in English usage, but the current trend in France is for 'Lapérouse', which is how he signed his name.

14 See his sensible marginalia to the project in Dunmore/Brossard, *Lapérouse*, I.13–19.

15 Gaziello, *Expédition*, 169; the search expedition by d'Entrecasteaux took another million and a half, when the total naval budget was 30,000,000—Richard, *à la Recherche* (see note 33), 243–5.

16 Ibid., I.3–10; Gaziello, *Expedition*, 47–59—she may rather overplay Bolts, for whom see N. L. Hallwards, *William Bolts* (Cambridge 1920).

17 Milet-Mureau, *Voyage*, I.228–9, 523; Dunmore/Brossard, *Lapérouse*, I.53–4, II.57.

18 Quotations from Milet-Mureau, *Voyage*, II.99, and Dunmore/Brossard, *Lapérouse*, I.4; Monneron's cynical reports ibid., I.224–7, and Milet-Mureau, III.247–67.

19 Dunmore/Brossard, *Lapérouse*, I.270–1 (Tahiti), II.65–83, 322–3 (Easter Island); 86–7 (Hawaii), 109–59 (Port des Français).

20 Ibid., II.197, 209–11.

21 Ibid., I.221–2, 263–4; La Pérouse overestimated Spanish capability in the sea-otter trade, II.211–13.

22 Ibid., I.219–20, 271, II.261–71; he is particularly severe on the new tobacco monopoly. At this time, however, the Governor Basco y Vargas and the Real Compañia de Felipinas were making efforts to diversify the economy—O. H. K. Spate, *Monopolists and Freebooters* (Canberra 1983), 283–6.

23 Milet-Mureau, *Voyage*, II.374–5.

24 Dunmore/Brossard, *Lapérouse*, II.319.

25 W. R. Broughton, *A Voyage of Discovery to the North Pacific Ocean* (London 1804, reprint Amsterdam 1967), 64–6, 264–326—a resolute voyage, but Broughton's journal is one of the dullest I have ever read, which is saying much; J. J. Stepan, *Sakhalin: A History* (Oxford 1971), 24–7, 34–40 and map at 30. For the background to Broughton's voyage, see D. Mackay, *In the Wake of Cook: Exploration, Science and Empire, 1780–1801* (London 1975), 51–2, 112–18 [*Wake of Cook*].

26 de Lesseps identified the relics brought back by Peter Dillon—Dunmore/Brossard, *Lapérouse*, I.195.

27 Ibid., I.163, II.443–6—very vivid; cf. II.147; Lamanon's ill-timed remark is at I.279. There is some evidence that the assailants were outsiders from Upolu—Dunmore, *Explorers*, I.278–9.

28 Dunmore/Brossard, *Lapérouse*, II.505–8, with British reactions.

29 My account is based on that of Marchand's 'second captain' Prosper Chanal, in C. P. Claret de Fleurieu, *Voyage autour du Monde par Etienne Marchand* (Paris 1798; English trans. London 1801, reprint Amsterdan 1969). This contains a long historical survey by Fleurieu of voyages to the Northeast Pacific, despite a penchant for de Fonte still worth reading. I have not seen Marchand's own *Découverte des Iles de la Révolution* (Marseilles 1792). Dunmore as ever gives an admirable account, *Explorers*, I.342–53.

30 Ibid., I.349–50; A. Sharp, *The Discovery of the Pacific Islands* (Oxford 1960), 166–8 [*Islands*]. Nukuhiva became successively Federal or Franklin's Island, Ile Baux (after Marchand's backers), and Sir Henry Martin's Island; what's in a name?

31 Dunmore, *Explorers*, I.348.

32 The promoters had used La Pérouse in an unsuccessful ploy to get government backing— ibid., I.285. See also Pethick, *Nootka*, 134–5, 160–1, and R. Haswell, in Howay, 'Columbia', 341–2, 347 (full references in notes 70 and 73 below).

33 Another example of the perennial clash of seamen and scientists. The main sources are E. -P. -E. de Rossel, *Voyage de Dentrecasteaux envoyé à la Recherche de La Pérouse* (Paris 1808) [*Dentrecasteaux*] and J. -J. -H. de la Billardière, *Relation du Voyage à la Recherche de La Pérouse* (Paris 1798); I quote from the translation, *Voyage in Search of La Pérouse* (London 1800) [*Voyage*]—the Translator's Preface (viii–ix) anticipated by forty years Macaulay's New Zealander surveying the ruins of London Bridge. Rossel was a Royalist, la Billardière a Jacobin; the former's work is more to the point geographically and is nearly all d'Entrecasteaux's own journal. Dunmore has an admirable summary—*Explorers*, I.283–332.

34 Rossel, *Dentrecasteaux*, I.20–31; la Billardière, *Voyage*, 103–12; Dunmore, *Explorers*, I.295–6. Whatever Hunter may have said was undoubtedly misunderstood and/or heightened by the French captains, perhaps by a confusion of 'custom' with 'costume', but it is strange that while Hunter was in Cape Town when d'Entrecasteaux was making inquiries, he made no contact.

35 Oral traditions suggest that La Pérouse actually landed at or near Isle of Pines—G. Pisier, *D'Entrecasteaux en Nouvelle-Calédonie 1792 et 1793* (Nouméa 1976), 51, 95 [*Calé-donie*], an excellent local monograph. Despite specific instructions, d'Entrecasteaux neglected it on both visits—ibid., 58–61. In 1964–5 the discovery at Vanikoro of pieces of diabase and an axe, both from New Caledonia, confirmed La Pérouse's visit—Brossard, *Lapérouse: combats*, 598–9.

36 Rossel, *Dentrecasteaux*, I.132–40.

37 La Billardière, *Voyage*, I.261.

38 Dunmore discusses this at some length, *Explorers*, I.308–11.

39 Rossel, *Dentrecasteaux*, I.252–3—a lyrical passage which is pure Rousseau.

40 Ibid., I.113, 358; could teleology go further?

41 Dunmore, *Explorers*, I.326–31; Pisier, *Calédonie*, 127–34.

42 Ibid., 115–22.

43 P. Dillon, *Narrative and Successful Result of a Voyage to Ascertain the Actual Fate of La Pérouse's Expedition* (London 1829, reprint Amsterdam 1972), *passim*; for Dillon's rumbustious and pathetic career, see J. W. Davidson, *Peter Dillon of Vanikoro: Chevalier of the South Seas* (Melbourne 1975). Chapters 7–11 deal with his findings, which were confirmed by Dumont d'Urville in February 1828. Recent discoveries at Vanikoro are described in Brossard/Dunmore, *Lapérouse*, I.192–206.

44 The main sources are F. Péron, continued by L.-C.-D. de Freycinet, *Voyage de Découverte aux Terres Australes* (Paris 1807–16; reprint of 1804 English translation Melbourne 1975) and C. Cornell (trans.), *The Journal of Post Captain Nicolas Baudin* (Adelaide 1974)—astonishingly, the first printing in any language. A full study by Frank Horner of Canberra is in press. See also, Dunmore, *Explorers*, II.9–40, and J. -P. Faivre, *L'Expansion française dans le Pacifique de 1800 à 1842* (Paris 1953), 78–123. [*Expansion*]

It is a solemn thought that Alexander von Humboldt wished to join the expedition, and had he done so might have died on it—B. Botting, *Humboldt and the Cosmos* (London 1973), 57–8.

45 See the very balanced reviews of this question Faivre, *Expansion*, 109–13, and Dunmore, *Explorers*, II.9–11. L. R. Marchant, *France Australe* (Perth 1982), 101–202, is meticulous on local identifications but charges Ernest Scott with alleging political motives for the expedition (ix, 103, 105); Scott devoted over a chapter of his *Terre Napoléon* (London 1910) to refuting this view and Faivre calls him 'le principal négateur' (109 note 62, 112).

46 O. H. K. Spate, 'Ames damnées: Baudin and Péron', *Overland* (Melboune) 58, 1974, 52–7, and 'Baudin and Flinders', in R. W. Russell (ed.), *Matthew Flinders: The Ifs of History* (Flinders Univ., Bedford Park, S.A., 1979), 87–93.

47 N. J. B. Plomley, *The Baudin Expedition and the Tasmanian Aborigines 1802* (Hobart 1983), far superior to the near-hagiography of C. Wallace, *The Lost Australia of François Péron* (London 1984), who has Napoleon as Emperor 'request[ing] an audience with Péron' (156)!

48 Flinders, *A Voyage to Terra Australis* (London 1814, reprint Adelaide 1966), I.cvi–cxx, cxxvii–cxciii [*Terra Australis*]; A. Sharp, *The Discovery of Australia* (Oxford 1963), 191–232; K. R. Bowden, *George Bass* (Melbourne 1952), 57–68, 70–9. On the strategic and commercial significance of Bass Strait, see G. Blainey, *The Tyranny of Distance* (Melbourne 1966), 73–81.

49 As late as 1983 a mainland teacher on Norfolk could claim that he had been deported from the island for opposing the restriction of the franchise to descendants of the Pitcairners who were settled there in 1856. See also G.C. Ingleton, *Matthew Flinders: Navigator and Chartmaker* (Ivanhoe, Victoria, 1986), 20–34—a definitive study of Flinders with much of value on Baudin.

50 Douglas Oliver devotes a whole chapter to 'The Wars of the Bounty Mutineers'—*Ancient Tahitian Society* (Canberra 1979), III.1256–70.

51 There are many biographies, some worthless. Worthy are G. A. Mackaness, *The Life of Rear-Admiral William Bligh, R. N., F. R. S.* (Sydney 1932; I use the New York edition, n.d.) [*Life*], old-fashioned but valuable; O. Rutter, *Turbulent Journey* (London 1936) [*Journey*], reasonably balanced; and G. Kennedy, *Bligh* (London 1978), probably the best. H. S. Montgomerie, *William Bligh of the 'Bounty' in Fact and Fable* (London 1937) is a spirited and telling defence.

Bligh published two accounts: *A Narrative of the Mutiny on H.M.S. Bounty* (London 1790; ed. by R. Bowman under title *An Account...* Gloucester 1981) and *A Voyage to the South Sea* (London 1792, reprint Adelaide 1969, Melbourne 1979) [*Voyage*], which was edited by James Burney (see R. du Rietz, 'Three Letters from James Burney to Sir Joseph Banks', *Ethnos* (Stockholm) 1962, 115–25. This *Voyage* is the source of my quotations unless otherwise indicated.

Owen Rutter has edited *The Voyage of the Bounty's Launch* (London 1934), *The Log of the Bounty* (London 1936–7), and *The Journal of James Morrison* (London 1934) [*Journal*]; these are Golden Cockeral Press productions and the journal may be more accessible in the French translation, *Journal de James Morrison* (Musée de l'Homme, Paris 1966). This incomparably vivid journal, especially important for post-mutiny events, has been the subject of much disputes; in the *Pandora*'s pinnace, under the eye of Captain Edwards, Morrison cannot have kept notes; it is a *post facto* construction but carefully done.

There is a facsimile edition of the mutiny and launch voyage sections, edited by S. Walters under the title *The Mutiny of the Bounty* (Guildford 1981), and an abridged edition of the whole log, with often perspicacious notes, by R. M. Bowker: *Mutiny!!* [*sic*] *Aboard H.M. Armed Transport 'Bounty'* (Old Bosham 1978). Finally the National Library of Australia has produced a superb replica of the actual notebook used by Bligh on the launch—J. Bach, (ed.), *The Bligh Notebook* (Canberra 1986).

For the French precedent, see D. MacKay, 'Banks, Bligh and Breadfruit', *NZ Jnl of History* 8, 1964, 61–8 at 67, and E. Smith, *The Life of Sir Joseph Banks* (London 1911), 126.

[52] The mutiny itself has been analysed *ad nauseam*. The verbatim accounts in O. Rutter (ed.), *The Court-Martial of the "Bounty" Mutineers* (Edinburgh 1931), have an immediacy denied to later retellings, of which B. Danielsson, *What Happened on the Bounty* (2nd ed. London 1963) is one of the fairest. M. Darby, *Who Caused the Mutiny on the Bounty?* (Sydney 1965) seeks to establish a homosexual relationship between Bligh and Christian, with the help of some *non sequiturs*; see the amusing if somewhat solemn polemic in R. du Rietz, 'The Causes of the Bounty Mutiny' ['Causes'] and Darby's reply, *Studia Bountyana* 1 and 2 (Uppsala 1965, 1966). R. Hough, *Captain Bligh and Mr Christian* (New York 1973) also opts for homosexuality; vivid but with some tendency to move from inference into asserted fact. G. Christian, a direct descendant of Fletcher, in *Fragile Paradise* (London 1982) tries hard to be fair to Bligh, and rejects homosexuality (149–50) with very sensible arguments.

G. Mackaness reprints Bligh's *Voyage* and *Narrative*, S. Barney's *Report of the Court Martial* with Edward Christian's Appendix attacking Bligh and Bligh's *Answer to Edward Christian's Assertions* in his valuable *A Book of the 'Bounty'* (London 1938). One cannot complain of lack of material!

[53] But Kennedy points out that Christian does not appear in the first record of the incident—John Fryer's—and his prominence may be an afterthought of Morrison's— *Bligh*, 89–96.

[54] Bligh, *Voyage*, 161.

[55] Compare ibid., 165–238, with S. Walters (ed.), *The Voyage of the Bounty's Launch: John Fryer's Narrative* (limited facsimile, Guildford 1979), *passim*.

[56] O. Rutter (ed.), *Bligh's Voyage on the Resource* (London 1937).

[57] J. Dugan, *The Great Mutiny* (London 1966), 182–3, 321–2.

[58] H. E. Maude, 'In Search of a Home', in his *Of Islands and Men* (Melbourne 1966), 1–34: Morrison, *Journal*, 52–73.

[59] Juan Fernàndez, occupied by the Spaniards in 1749, after Anson hardly counts as a South Sea Island. The mutineers had a narrow escape from detection on 9 August, when the *Mercury* (note 5 above) saw lights on Tubuai.

[60] See *Inter alia* H. Shapiro, *The Heritage of the Bounty* (Anchor ed. Garden City, NY, 1962), 49–78. The island led the world in giving votes to women, 1838—I. M. Ball, *Pitcairn: Children of the Bounty* (London 1973), 308–9. See also the title essay in W. K. Hancock, *Politics in Pitcairn* (London 1947), 1–17.

[61] B. Thomson (ed.), *Voyage of H.M.S. 'Pandora'* (London 1915) contains Edwards's very routine reports and the surgeon George Hamilton's more lively (indeed salacious) *A Voyage round the World* (original ed. Berwick 1793); Thomson's introduction is justly criticised in G. Rawson, *Pandora's Last Voyage* (London 1963), 11–12, 94–5. See also Mackaness, *Life*, I.253–79, and Morrison, *Journal*, 119–34.

[62] H. E. Maude, 'The Voyage of the *Pandora*'s Tender', *Mariner's Mirror* 50, 1964, 217–35. She was not, as is sometimes stated, the schooner used by Broughton in 1797— A. C. F. Dodd, 'Broughton's Schooner and the Bounty Mutineers', ibid. 63, 1977, 207–14.

[63] Morrison, *Journal*, 128; he alone mentions this, but his journal was circulated (Heywood and Bligh himself saw it) and he could hardly get away with so atrocious a charge unless it had some substance.

[64] Not much has been written about this unsensational voyage; see I. Lee, *Captain Bligh's Second Voyage to the South Sea* (London 1920), [*Second Voyage*], which gives much of Bligh's and Portlock's journals; Mackaness, *Life*, I.314–69, II.1–31; Kennedy, *Bligh*, 176–94.

65 G. A. Mackaness (ed.), *Fresh Light on Bligh*, Aust. Histl Monographs New Series 5 (Dubbo 1976), 68–72; du Rietz, 'Causes', 26–31.

66 Lee, *Second Voyage*, 74–87.

67 See G. C. Henderson, *The Discoverers of the Fiji Islands* (London 1933), 149–72; Oliver in the *Pandora*'s tender may have seen some of the Koro Sea islands, but Bligh's is the first record—ibid., 241–54.

68 Flinders, *Terra Australis*, I.xix–xxix.

69 However, breadfruit is now grown and liked throughout the Caribbean. Connoisseurs of bad verse should not miss the ode to Bligh, here quoted, by George Keate, the eulogist also of Prince Lee Boo—Rutter, *Journey*, 169–71.

70 See in general Wagner, *Cartography*, I.206–13; P. C. Philips, *The Fur Trade* (Norman, Okla., 1961), II.36–61; D. O. Johansen and C. M. Gates, *Empire of the Columbia* (New York 1957), 40–7, 58–76. D. Pethick, *The Nootka Connection: Europe and the Northwest Coast 1790–1795* (Vancouver 1980) [*Nootka*] gives a year-by-year account of all voyages 1790–5.

71 Meares, *Voyages* (note 7 above), xii–xxxviii; G. Dixon [really W. Beresford], *A Voyage round the World... to the North-West Coast of America* (London 1789), 154–80, and N. Portlock's identically titled book (London 1789), 219–21; and the entertaining pamphlets in F. W. Howay (ed.), *The Dixon-Meares Controversy* (Toronto 1929, reprint Amsterdam 1979) [*Controversy*]. Dixon had decidedly the better of this flyting.

72 F. W. Howay (ed.), 'Four Letters from Richard Cadman Etches to Sir Joseph Banks, 1788–92', *Brit. Columbia Histl Qly* 6, 1942, 125–39; J. Etches, *An Authentic Narrative of All the Facts relative to NOOTKA SOUND* (London 1790), 4–6 [*Authentic Narrative*]. Commercial and political aspects will be discussed in Chapters 12 and 13. Etches and Meares, smart operators both, cry out for monographs.

73 To evade the EIC and SSC licences; Meares denied this, and the plates in his book show huge Union Jacks, but see Cook, *Flood Tide*, 136–43; F. W. Howay (ed.), *Voyages of the "Columbia" to the Northwest Coast* (Boston 1940, reprint Amsterdam 1969), 47–8 [*"Columbia"*].

74 Meares, 'Observations on the Probable Existence of a North West Passage, &c', in *Voyages*, xli–lxvi, especially lvi; Etches, *Authentic Narrative*, 8–10; G. Williams, *The British Search for a Northwest Passage in the Eighteenth Century* (London 1962), 215–30; Howay, *"Columbia"*, 99, 213, 233, and *Controversy*, 99–101—for the origin of the *Washington* tale see the latter, 13–15, 66–7. See also 'Autour de la Mer de l'Ouest' in N. Broc, *La Géographie des Philosophes* (Paris 1974), 152–65.

75 So 'stripping the silly Jay of his borrowed plumage'—in fact, Dixon's name had been bestowed not by himself but by Sir Joseph Banks—ibid., 68, 126–7.

76 Unless they had been preceded by Simon Metcalfe in the *Eleonora*—Howay, 'Columbia', x–xi. The ships were formally *Columbia Rediviva* and *Lady Washington*.

77 Ibid., 396–400, 435–8.

78 The best concise guide to a tangle of voyages is Wagner, *Cartography*, I.202–38 (source of most details); see also his *Spanish Explorations in the Straits of Juan de Fuca* (Santa Ana, Calif., 1933), and Cook, *Flood Tide*, 114–34, 271–326, 344–56.

79 Barratt, *Pacific Waters*, 96–8.

80 Cook, *Flood Tide*, 186–94; G. V. Blue, 'Why the Spaniards Temporarily Abandoned Nootka Sound in 1789', *Canadian Histl Rev.* 17, 1936, 168–72.

81 Quimper in the *Princesa Real* also made a reconnaissance voyage to Hawaii in 1791,

Martinez having proposed a settlement there—R. S. Kuykendall, *The Hawaiian Kingdom* (Honolulu 1966–8), I.21 [*Kingdom*].

[82] P. Novo y Colson, *Viaje Politico-Cientifico Alrededor del Mundo por las Corbetas Descubierta y Atrevida al Mando de... Don Alejandro Malaspina y Don José Bustamante y Guerra* (Madrid 1885) [*Viaje*]. In an unpaginated 'Nota Curiosa' Novo y Colson remarks that 'despite its size, this book can be considered as an extract or summary' of his materials. I have laboured through this wearisome volume, but have perhaps more generally used the more convenient version, largely using Malaspina's words, by one of his officers— F. X. de Viana, *Diario de Viage de las Corbetas españolas 'Descubierta' y 'Atrevida'* (Cerrito de la Victoria (Uruguay), Imprensa del Ejercito, 1849) [*Viage*]; I am indebted to Robert Langdon for the loan of the rare reprint, Montevideo 1958.

Depite Novo y Colson's 'Alrededor' this was not a circumnavigation, though much longer than many. It rates ten lines (and two errors) in Donald Brands's chapter on the Spaniards in H. Friis (ed.), *The Pacific Basin* (New York 1967), 109–44 at 141–2, and is not so much as mentioned in Ernest Dodge's survey of Pacific exploration after Cook, *Beyond the Capes* (Boston 1971).

See also D. C. Cutter, *Malaspina in California* (San Francisco 1960); T. Vaughan, *Voyages of Enlightenment: Malaspina on the Northwest Coast 1791/1792* (Portland 1977), mostly on the art of the voyage; I. H. W. Engstrand, *Spanish Scientists in the New World* (Seattle 1981), 44–75, 109–28.

[83] Novo y Colson, *Viaje*, 105; Viana, *Viage*, I.254–6; for Juan and Ulloa, O. H. K. Spate, *Monopolists and Freebooters* (Canberra 1983), 310–11.

[84] B. del Carril (ed.), *La Expedición Malaspina en las Mares Americanas del Sur* (Buenos Aires 1961), 21; H. R. Wager, *Apocryphal Voyages to the Northwest Coast of America* (Worcester, Mass., 1931), 43–56; P. Novo y Colson, *Sobre los Viajes Apócrifos... de Maldonado* (Madrid 1881)—an amusing book for which one almost forgives him for the editorial nightmare of the *Viaje*, Maldonado, unlike de Fonte, really existed, apparently an astrologer and forger, certainly a con man; his own *Relación,* Buache's *Memoria* of 1791 to the Académie Royale des Sciences and Malaspina's *Disertación* in refutation are given in *Viaje*, 137–49, 183–90.

[85] C. Jane (trans.), *A Spanish Voyage to Vancouver [sic] and the North-West Coast of America* (London 1930); D. C. Cutter (ed.), *The California Coast* (Norman, Okla., 1969), 131– 278—vivid account by the schooners' chaplains.

[86] Trans. and ed. I. H. Wilson (Seattle 1970).

[87] Wagner, *Cartography*, I.251–4.

[88] Novo y Colson, *Viaje*, 253–5; Viana, *Viage*, II.155–61; the Examen Político is Museo Naval, Madrid, MS. No. 318—I owe knowledge of this interesting if rather muddled document to Mr R. J. King of Canberra. See also [A. Grove Day, ed.], *The Spaniards at Port Jackson* (Sydney 1967).

[89] His account is printed in Milet-Mureau, *Voyage*, I.340–418; see also A. Sharp, *Islands*, 147–51, and comment in R. A. Langdon, 'The Maritime Explorers', in N. Rutherford (ed.), *Friendly Islands: A History of Tonga* (Melbourne 1977), 40–62 at 52–4.

[90] Ibid., 59–61; Novo y Colson, *Viaje*, 258–85.

[91] See his plan for an 'Examen politico de los dominios ultramarinas de España', ibid., xxix–xxi—his ideas bear some resemblance to those of the Conde de Aranda, the most overtly Enlightened of Carlos III's ministers—see M. Rodríguez, *La Revolución Americana de 1776 y el Mundo Hispanico* (Madrid 1976), 63–6.

[92] Novo y Colson, *Viaje*, ix–xix; Cook, *Flood Tide*, 314–20.

[93] G. Goodwin, *Vancouver: A Life 1757–98* (London 1930), 189–91 [*Vancouver*]; A. Frost, *Convicts and Empire: A Naval Question* (Melbourne 1980), 155–7. For the politics of Nootka, see below, Chapter 13.

[94] The main source is G. Vancouver, *A Voyage of Discovery to the North Pacific Ocean and round the World* (London 1798, reprint Amsterdam 1967) [*North Pacific*]; I quote from W. Kaye Lamb's Hakluyt edition, HS 2nd Ser. 163–6 (London 1984): the Instructions are at I.283–8. Much superior to Goodwin's *Vancouver* is B. Anderson, *The Life and Times of Captain George Vancouver: Surveyor of the Sea* (Washington paper back ed., Seattle 1966 [*Surveyor*]. See also Mackay, *Wake of Cook*, 42–5, 87–90, 96.

[95] Vancouver, *North Pacific*, II.503, 692–3, 748–69 (Broughton's report on the river). On Vancouver's initial failure to recognise the Columbia see Anderson's very sensible remarks, *Surveyor*, 74–5.

[96] Anderson argues plausibly that 'los Mayos' and 'la Mesa' may in fact have represented Hawaii, so that the Spaniards had priority—ibid., 128–34.

[97] Ibid., 156–7; J. L. Brebner, *The Explorers of North America 1492–1806* (Meridian paperback ed., Cleveland 1968), 380–1.

[98] Vancouver, *North Pacific*, III.1022.

[99] Ibid., 1157–60 (the Jane Austenish marriage comedy), 1160–4, 1178–83; Kuykendall, *Kingdom*, I.38–44.

[1] N. Tolstoy, *The Half-Mad Lord* (New York 1979), 17–38, deals with Vancouver's troubles with the aristocratic and thuggish Lord Camelford, first cousin to the Prime Minister William Pitt; see also Anderson, *Surveyor*, 217–23, who suggests (66–7) that Vancouver suffered from Graves's disease (hyperthyroidism).

Notes for Chapter 9

[1] *The Fleece* IV.673–85; the book is a brisk commercial epic—see O. H. K. Spate, 'The Muse of Mercantilism', in R. Brissenden (ed.), *Studies in the Eighteenth Century* (Canberra 1968), 119–31 at 128–30.

[2] N. Broc, *La Géographie des Philosophes* (Paris 1974), 312 [*Géographie*]. For 'positive' one might read 'positivistic'; Broc's section 'Le Pacifique et la solution des énigmes' (298–312) is very stimulating.

[3] A. Frost, 'The Pacific Ocean—the Eighteenth Century's "New World"', in W. Veit (ed.), *Captain James Cook: Image and Impact* (Melbourne 1972–9), II.5–49, which is also in T. Besterman (ed.), *Studies in Voltaire and the Eighteenth Century* 152 (Oxford 1976), 779–822.

[4] O. H. K. Spate, *Monopolists and Freebooters* (Canberra 1983), 247 [*Monopolists*].

[5] A. Sharp, *The Discovery of the Pacific Islands* (Oxford 1960), 13–16, 91–100. Since Dampier discovered his Strait in March 1700, it is not strictly an eighteenth century discovery.

[6] 'Exploration and Discovery', in A. S. Turberville (ed.), *Johnson's England* (Oxford 1933), 88–124 at 112. Actually a southern continent in the *Pacific* was not part of Byron's instructions, but he had it in his own mind—R. E. Gallagher (ed.), *Byron's Journal of his Circumnavigation 1764–1766*, HS 2nd Ser. 122 (Cambridge 1964), 3–7, 88–9, 105.

[7] Broc, *Géographie*, 306.

[8] A. von Humboldt, *Cosmos: A Sketch of a Physical Description of the Universe* (Bohn trans. London 1864), II.643–4 [*Cosmos*]. Humboldt was writing of an earlier period when knowledge 'began to be freed' from error, but the demolition of Terra Australis was the final stage.

[9] Beaglehole, IV.136. Cook's disregard of Lind may have been due to the influence of Sir John Pringle, President of the Royal Society and a MacBride supporter.

[10] C. Lloyd and J. S. L. Coulter, in J. Keevil, *Medecine and the Navy 1714–1815* (London 1961), III.293, 318 [*Medecine*]; cf. i.a. A Carré, 'Scorbut Marine et Biologie Moderne', *Comptes rendus du 104ᵉ Congrès Nationale de Sociétés Savantes* 4 (Paris 1979), 219–30 at 221 ['Scorbut']: 'Cook retardera ainsi de 25 ans le traitement rationnel de scorbut.' I owe this reference to Mr Frank Horner of Canberra.

[11] Sir J. Watt, 'Some consequences of nutritional disorders in eighteenth century British circumnavigations', in J. Watt et al. (eds.), *Starving Sailors: The influence of nutrition upon naval and military history* (London 1981), 51–72 at 57 [*Starving Sailors*].

[12] R. Walter or B. Robins, *A Voyage round the World... by George Anson* (ed. G. Williams, London 1974; original ed. London 1748), 105–7; see also Carré, 'Scorbut', 223.

[13] C. Lloyd, 'Victualling of the Fleet...', in Watt, *Starving Sailors*, 9–16 at 10–11; G. J. Milton-Thompson, 'Two hundred years of the sailor's diet', ibid., 27–34 at 29; A. Carré, 'Eighteenth century French voyages of exploration: general problems of nutrition ibid., 73–84 at 74–5; and graph in Watt's paper, ibid., 68.

[14] J. R. Forster (trans.), *A Voyage round the World... by Lewis de Bougainville* (London 1772, reprint Amsterdam 1967), 364.

[15] Beaglehole, IV.291; E. Taillemitte (ed.), *Bougainville et ses Compagnons autour du Monde 1766–1769* (Paris 1977), I.359 [*Bougainville*].

[16] Ibid., II.404; Carré, in Watt, *Starving Sailors*, 82.

[17] Edinburgh 1753; I use the reprint edited by C. P. Stewart and D. Guthrie (Edinburgh 1953) [*Treatise*].

[18] Lind, *Treatise*, 145–6, 160–4, 186; and see in the addenda the table of sources of ascorbic acid, 434.

[19] C. P. Steward, ibid., 405–6; Carré, 'Scorbut' 227; J. R. Forster, *Observations made during a Voyage round the World, on Physical Geography, Natural History and Ethical Philosophy* (London 1778), 610–13, 630–8 [*Observations*]. For 'Ethical' we should say 'Ethnological'.

[20] J. A. Williamson (ed.), *The Observations of Sir Richard Hawkins* (London 1913, original ed. 1622), 42, 54, 56; Lind, *Treatise*, 151–2; Spate, *Monopolists*, 22–4. There is a good general account in H. Morton, *The Wind Commands* (Vancouver 1975, 269–86 with plates).

[21] There was scurvy on Palliser's voyage, but this was overcome by changing the diet—Lind, *An Essay on the Health of Seamen*, excerpted in C. Lloyd, *The Health of Seamen*, Navy Records Society 107 (London 1965), 26–130 at 40 [*Health*].

[22] Lloyd and Coulter, in Keevil, *Medecine*, 308–10; Sir James Watt, 'Medical Aspects and Consequences of Cook's Voyages', in R. Fisher and H. Johnston (eds.), *Captain James Cook and His Times* (Canberra 1979), 129–57 at 137, 143–5 [*James Cook*]—this is already a *locus classicus*. I regret that the excellent and most comprehensive study by K.J. Carpenter, *The History of Scurvy and Vitamin C* (Cambridge 1986) came to hand too late for me to use it.

[23] Ibid., 130–50 *passim*; H. Wallis (ed.), *Cartaret's Voyage round the World 1766–1769*, HS 2nd Ser. 124–5 (Cambridge 1965), I.63–4, II.444–54—good comment on Cartaret's good report.

24 Beaglehole, I.632–3, and his *The* Endeavour *Journal of Joseph Banks 1768–1771* (Sydney 1962), I.250–1 [*Banks*]—it is astonishing that after contrasting wort with lemon juice in this passage, Banks could say (II.43) that MacBride's treatise 'can never be enough recommended.' But then, the wort had banished his constipation.

25 Beaglehole II.954; Lloyd and Coulter, in Keevil, *Medecine*, 31.

26 Ibid., 316; D. Guthrie and A. P. Meiklejohn, in Lind, *Treatise* 402–3—as they say, 'a remarkable example of a great man's failure to distinguish between essential and contributory factors.'

27 Lengthy excerpts from their writings are given in Lloyd, *Health*.

28 C. P. Stewart in Lind, *Treatise*, 404; cf. Lloyd and Coulter, in Keevil, *Medecine*, 326, 329, and Blane in Lloyd, *Health*, 198–201. Enrolments are from W. L. Clowes, *The Royal Navy: A History* (London 1897–1902), III.5, V.9.

29 M. Duchet, *Anthropologie et Histoire au Siècle des Lumières*, (Paris 1971), 60 [*Anthropologie*]; Rousseau, quoted in Broc, *Géographie*, 270–1. Duchet led me to Rousseau's suitably moralised account of Anson's voyage in *Julie, ou la Nouvelle Héloïse*, Liv. I Lettre IV (Pléiade ed. Paris 1961, 412–16).

30 And of course Woman; but despite my personal preference, it would be anachronistic to use equalising terms in a strictly historical discussion. The same applies to 'overlord', which also may raise hackles; for comment on Enlightenment aggressiveness towards the environment, see R. Porter, 'The terraqeous globe', in G. S. Rousseau and R. Porter (eds.), *The Ferment of Knowledge* (Cambridge 1980), 285–324 at 294–9, 316.

31 Taillemitte, *Bougainville*, I.105, II.514–22; Duchet, *Anthropologie*, 116–17. Some of Commerson's collections did reach France—F. A. Stafleu, *Adanson Labillardière De Candolle* (Lehre, West Germany, 1967), 19. [*Adanson*].

32 P. I. Edwards, 'Sir Joseph Banks and the Botany of Captain Cook's Three Voyages', *Pacific Studies* (Laie, Hawaii) 2, 1978, 20–43 at 25–6 ['Joseph Banks']; W. T. Stearn 'The Botanical Results of Captain Cook's Three Voyages...', ibid. 1, 1978, 147–62, and 'Sir Joseph Banks (1743–1820)', *Rec. Austr. Acad. Sci.* 2/4, 1974, 7–24.

33 W. Blunt, 'Sydney Parkinson and his fellow artists', in D. N. Carr (ed.), *Sydney Parkinson* (London/Canberra 1983), 14–45 at 24–5, 44; details of an almost indecently de luxe publication are given at 45. A complete set, in twenty-four 'Solander boxes' has been produced by the Alecto Press, London, at $90,000—not seen!

34 W. T. Stearn, 'The botanical results of the *Endeavour* voyage', *Endeavour* 27, 1968, 3–10, and especially E. D. Merrill, *The Botany of Cook's Voyages* (Waltham, Mass., 1954) (*Chronica Botanica* 14), 203–11; but *contra* Edwards, 'Joseph Banks', 31–2, and M. E. Hoare, *The Tactless Philosopher: Johann Reinhold Forster (1729–98)* (Melbourne 1976), 140–1 [*Tactless Philospher*]. A. C. and N. C. Begg, *Dusky Bay* (Christchurch 1968), 139–47, accept the plagiarism but pay glowing tribute to the Forsters' work.

35 J. C. Beaglehole's introduction to *Banks*, I.120–5; D. Walker's review of this, *Histl Studies* 40, 1963, 527–9. See also A. M. Lysaght's introduction to *Joseph Banks in Newfoundland and Labrador, 1766* (London 1971) [*Joseph Banks*].

36 D. Mackay, 'Banks, Bligh and Breadfruit', *NZ Jnl of History*, 8, 1974, 61–77 at 74. Pending the appearance of Harold Carter's fullscale study, there is no really satisfactory biography. H. C. Cameron, *Sir Joseph Banks... The Autocrat of Philosophers* (London 1952) is more substantial than C. Lyte, *Sir Joseph Banks...* (Newton Abbot 1980) [*Banks*] which divertingly defines 'the public stew' as 'being in a sweat and state of excitement' (209)—true in a sense, but—. J.H. Maiden, *Sir Joseph Banks, the "Father of Australia"* (Sydney 1909) has much undigested information, and although Lysaght (*Joseph Banks*, 42) calls

E. Smith, *The Life of Sir Joseph Banks* (London 1911) 'the most comprehensive life available', it is far too smooth on some issues and not always reliable on peripheral detail. The astonishing scope of Sir Joseph's activities can be gauged from W. R. Dawson's calendar of *The Banks Letters* (London 1958).

[37] Quoted in D. Mackay, 'A Presiding Genius of Exploration: Banks Cook, and Empire, 1767–1805', in Fisher and Johnston, *James Cook*, 21–39 at 29.

[38] *Observations*, ii.

[39] D. E. Allen, 'The lost limb: geology and natural history', in L. J. Jordanova and R. S. Porter (eds.), *Images of the Earth*, Brit. Soc. for History of Science Monograph 1 (Chalfont St Giles 1979). For acute comment on the Forsters as professional intellectuals and as romanticists, see B. Smith in B. Smith and R. Joppien, *The Art of Captain Cook's Voyages* (Melbourne 1985), II.23–4.

[40] Beaglehole, II.xlii–xlix, clii–cliii. I must admit to having myself discounted Forster, as geomorphologist, in the past—see Hoare, *Tactless Philosopher*, 80 n. 15, and my review of this most appositely entitled book, *JPH* 12, 1977, 247–8.

[41] W. Wales, *Remarks on Mr Forster's Account of Captain COOK's Last Voyage round the World* (London 1778); G. Forster, *Reply to Mr WALES's Remarks* (London 1778), both very vigorous. In my opinion Wales is rash, hasty, and too inclined to press trifles, Forster has good points but more bluster; on his charge that Cook fired on the 'Loo' (Ilhéu) fort at Madeira, I am informed by Major Rui Carita of Funchal that what Forster took for a bombardment was the courtesy of a salute!

[42] There was a long tradition of lampooning savants on the stage (Shadwell's *Virtuoso*, Pope and Gay's *Three Hours after Marriage*) and in more serious satire—Swift's *Laputa*, or Cowper's denunciation of the sciences in *The Task*, Book III—'Some drill and bore the solid earth...'. Cf. the cartoons of Banks and Solander, especially 'The great South Sea Caterpillar, transform'd into a Bath Butterfly' (on Banks's Knighthood) in Lyte, *Banks*, at 127, 142–3. See also J. M. Levine, *Dr. Woodward's Shield: History, Science, and Satire in Augustan England* (Berkeley 1977), 117–27, 238–50.

[43] *A Voyage round the World* (London 1777), I.127–8, 165–6, 260–2, II.383–4 [*Voyage*].

[44] Beaglehole, II.cxlix–cl; Humboldt, *Cosmos*, II.436–7.

[45] B. Smith, *European Vision and the South Pacific* (2nd ed. Sydney n.d. [1985]), 55; R. Hartshorne, *The Nature of Geography* (3rd ed. Lancaster, Pa., 1949), 42; D. R. Stoddart, *On Geography and its History* (Oxford 1986), ix, 33–5, 39.

[46] G. Williams, ' "Enlarging the Sphere of Human Contemplation": The Exploration of the Pacific', in P. J. Marshall and G. Williams, *The Great Map of Mankind* (London 1982), 258–98 at 276–83, and 'Seamen and Philosophers in the South Seas in the Age of Captain Cook', *Mariner's Mirror* 65, 1979, 2–22; C. Glacken, *Traces on the Rhodian Shore: Nature and culture in Western thought* (Berkeley 1967), 610–19, 702–95 [*Rhodian Shore*]. As well as Hoare's *Tactless Philosopher* and his introduction to *The Resolution Journal of Johann Reinhold Forster 1772–1775*, HS 2nd Ser. 152–5 (London 1982), I.1–122 [*Journal*], see for George L. Bodi, 'Georg Forster: The "Pacific Expert" of Eighteenth-Century Germany', *Histl Studies* 32, 1969, 345–63.

[47] *Observations*, 69–101 on ice, 148–51 on atolls; other instances of teleology at 334–5 (a very gushing invocation to Providence to kindle Promethean fire &c), 570–1, and in George's *Voyage* at I.308–09, II.153.

[48] *Observations*, 228, 276–83.

[49] Ibid., 36–7, 161–86.

[50] Contemporary references in Glacken, *Rhodian Shore*, 581, 603; Huntington, *Civilization*

and Climate (New Haven 1915, 3rd ed. 1924) and *Mainsprings of Civilization* (New York 1945), *passim*.

51 *Observations*, 286–300. The Forsterian views on the 'Noble Savage' and Tahitian morality will be considered in later chapters.

52 R. I. Meek, *Social science and the ignoble savage* (Cambridge 1976), 174, 178 and *passim*.

53 *Observations*, 389–92; other flaws in the pattern at 414–17, and in *Voyage*, I.295–7, 391–3, II.85–101. But there is a glowing tribute to the excellence of Tahitian life in *Observations*, 582–6.

54 *Voyage*, II.190–1, 207. I. C. Campbell, 'Savages Noble and Ignoble', *Pacific Studies* 4, 1980, 45–59 at 50–3, seems to me to make the Forsters more consistently rationalist than they are, and to miss their ambivalences.

55 *Observations*, 301–7, 333–4; *Voyage*, I364–8. George speaks of the 'impulses of nature' with a frequency very natural in a lad of twenty.

56 Hoare, in Forster, *Journal*, I.85–101; Preface (by J. R. F.) to *Characteres Generum Plantarum* by J. R. and G. Forster, translated E. Edgar, *NZ Jnl of Botany*, 7, 1969, 311–15.

57 Stafleu, *Adanson*, 17; Barber, *The Heyday of Natural History* (London 1980), 30; D. Mackay, *In the Wake of Cook...* (London 1983), 13. Menzies became President of the Linnean Society—B. Anderson, *Surveyor of the Sea* (paperback ed. Seattle 1966), 46; for Banks's elaborate instructions to him, see Mackay, 100–3.

58 I. H. W. Engstrand, *Spanish Scientists in the New World* (Seattle 1981), 182–3.

59 *Observations*, 395, 399.

60 Taillemitte, *Bougainville*, I.52, 269, 281–2.

61 *The Loves of the Plants* (1789), IV.487–90, in D. King-Hele, *The Essential Writings of Erasmus Darwin* (London 1968), 151.

Notes for Chapter 10

1 To William Cole, 15 June 1780, quoted in G. Williams, 'Enlarging the Sphere of Contemplation', in Williams and P. J. Marshall (eds.), *The Great Map of Mankind* (London 1982), 258–98 at 290.

2 Beaglehole, I.399, and his *The Endeavour Journal of Joseph Banks 1768–1771* (Sydney 1962), II.130 [*Banks*]; see G. Williams, 'Far more happier than we Europeans', *Histl Studies* 19, 1981, 499–512.

3 B. Smith, *European Vision and the South Pacific* (2nd ed. Sydney 1985), 37–8; W. H. Pearson, 'Hawkesworth's Voyages', in R. F. Brissenden (ed.), *Studies in the Eighteenth Century II* (Canberra 1973), 239–58 at 242–4.

4 J. R. Forster, *Observations made during a Voyage round the World* (London 1778), 286, 301–2, 381 [*Observations*]; G. Forster, *A Voyage round the World* (London 1777), I.177–80 [*Voyage*].

5 Ibid., I.302–3; J. R. Forster, *Observations*, 306.

6 I. Lee, *Captain Bligh's Second Voyage to the South Sea* (London 1929), 74–87 *passim*; D. Oliver, *Ancient Tahitian Society* (Honolulu/Canberra 1974), III.1284–6 [*Tahitian Society*]; but see also C. Newbury, *Tahiti Nui: Change and Survival in French Polynesia 1767–1945* (Honolulu 1980), 14 [*Tahiti Nui*].

7 G. Vancouver, *A Voyage of Discovery to the North Pacific Ocean* (London 1798, reprint Amsterdam 1967), but my references are to W. Kaye Lamb's Hakluyt edition, HS

2nd Ser. 163–6 (London 1984), II.470, III.800 [*North Pacific*], and other references to the mania for muskets (see below, note 78). Cook's anticipation of Vancouver is in Cook and J. King, *A Voyage to the Pacific Ocean* (London 1784), II.136.

[8] T. Morgan, *Hawaii: A Century of Economic Change 1778–1976* (Cambridge, Mass., 1948), 63–5 [*Hawaii*]; C. Ralston, 'Hawaii 1778–1854: Some Aspects of Maka'ainana [Commoner] Response to Rapid Cultural Change', *JPH* 19, 1964, 21–40 at 25–8 ['Hawaii 1778–1854']. For a broad survey of changing attitudes to the South Sea Islanders, see Bill [W. H.] Pearson, *Rifled Sanctuaries: Some Views of the Pacific Islanders in Western Literature to 1900* (Auckland 1984).

[9] Moorehead's subtitle is *An Account of the Invasion of the South Pacific 1767–1840* (Penguin ed. Harmondsworth 1968); H.-K. Trask, 'Cultures in Collision: Hawai'i and England, 1778', *Pacific Studies* 7, 1983, 91–117.

[10] For a good general statement of the newer islands-oriented case, see K. R. Howe, *Where the Waves Fall* (Honolulu 1984), 347–52 [*the Waves*]. Two major manifestoes are J. W. Davidson, 'Problems of Pacific History', *JPH* 1, 1966, 5–21, and G. Dening, 'Ethnohistory in Polynesia', ibid., 23–42 ['Ethnohistory']; Davidson, Foundation Professor of Pacific History in The Australian National University, was not doctrinaire, as are some of his followers. See also Howe's well-balanced survey, 'The Fate of the "Savage" in Pacific Historiography', *NZ Jnl of History* 11, 1977, 137–54.

[11] O. H. K. Spate, 'The Pacific as an artefact', in N. Gunson (ed.), *The Changing Pacific: Essays in Honour of H. E. Maude* (Melbourne 1978), 32–45, q.v. for the distinction between Oceanic and Insular history; cf. J. W. Davidson, 'History, Art or Game', *NZ Jnl of History* 3, 1971, 115–20 at 118.

[12] C. Ralston, *Grass Huts and Warehouses: Pacific Beach Communities in the Nineteenth Century* (Canberra 1977), 41 [*Grass Huts*]. Manipulation could work both ways; the history of Samoa suggests that 'Polynesian guns and personnel were used for European goals'.

[13] Pearson, 'Reception', 147–8 (see note 17)—the reference is to Schouten and Le Maire at Futuna; P. Geyl, 'Toynbee's System of Civilizations', *Jnl Hist. of Ideas* 9, 1948, 445–50.

[14] The attempt of W. M. Gibson, Minister of King Kalakaua, to cast the shield of Hawaiian protection over Samoa, Tonga and the Gilberts (Kiribati)—the 'Empire of the Calabash'—was too feeble to count—R. S. Kuykendall, *The Hawaiian Kingdom* (Honolulu 1967), III.304–39 [*Kingdom*]; G. Daws, *Shoal of Time* (Honolulu 1968), 235–9.

[15] This seems the inescapable conclusion from G. Dening, *Islands and Beaches: Discourse on a Silent Land Marquesas 1774–1880* (Melbourne 1980), 268–90 [*Silent Land*], a book of high quality in style, thought and feeling. Nukuhiva had the bad luck to become the first foreign combat base in the Islands, maintained with violence by Commodore David Porter USN in the War of 1812.

[16] N. McArthur, *Island Populations of the Pacific* (Canberra 1967), 320, 330–1.

[17] Ralston, *Grass Huts*, 1–8, gives an admirable concise summary of the nature of early contacts. Three important papers are I. C. Campbell, 'Polynesian Perceptions of Europeans in the Eighteenth and Ninetenth Centuries', *Pacific Studies* 5, 1982, 64–80 ['Perceptions']; W. H. Pearson, 'European Intimidation and the Myth of Tahiti', *JPH* 4, 1969, 199–218 ['Intimidation'], and his 'The Reception of European Voyagers on Polynesian Islands, 1568–1797', *Jnl Soc. Océanistes* 26, 1970, 12–54 ['Reception']. For Micronesia, see F. X. Hezel SJ, *The First Taint of Civilization... 1521–1885* (Honolulu 1983), 65–86 [*First Taint*]. P. Snow and S. Waine, *The People from the Horizon... the Europeans*

among the South Sea Islanders (Oxford 1979) is more than a coffee-table book but rather less than a serious study; two stools . . . .

18 Campbell, 'Perceptions', 65–9. When the first white men, the Leahy brothers, penetrated the New Guinea Highlands in the 1930s, defecation and copulation showed that they were not spirits but mere men—see if possible the remarkable film *First Contact*, by R. Connolly and R. Anderson.

19 Pearson, 'Intimidation', 201; M. E. Hoare, *The* Resolution *Journal of Johann Reinhold Forster 1772–1775*, HS 2nd Ser. 152–5 (London 1982), I.260–2 [Forster, *Journal*]; G. Forster, *Voyage*, I. 167–8; Dening, 'Ethnohistory', 35. For gesture, Dening (ed.), *The Marquesan Journal of Edward Robarts* (Canberra 1974), 230 [Robarts, *Journal*], and B. Smith and R. Joppien, *The Art of Captain Cook's Voyages* (Melbourne 1985), II.73 and Plates 59, 60. For the beach/harbour misunderstanding, see Edmund Fanning in W. Teller (ed.), *Five Sea Captains* (New York 1960), 146–50; Fanning admitted the error of his suspicions. The role of women in receptions is discussed in the next chapter.

20 R. Adams, *In the Land of Strangers: A century of European contact with Tanna, 1774–1874* (Canberra 1984), 14 [*Strangers*]; H. E. Maude, *Of Islands and Men: Studies in Pacific History* (Melbourne 1968), 343 [*Islands*].

21 D. W. Orchiston and L. C. Horrocks, 'Contact and Conflict: the Rowe Massacre . . .'. *Histl Studies* 19, 1975, 519–38 at 536–7.

22 Kuykendall, *Kingdom*, I.24–5; E. Joestling, *Hawaii: An Uncommon History* (New York 1972), 46–9. Metcalfe's son Thomas was killed in an unrelated incident on Hawai'i; four years later the father and another son were killed by Indians in the Queen Charlotte Islands. See also Vancouver, *North Pacific*, III.819–25.

23 Beaglehole, I.clxxxii.

24 H. G. Cummins, 'Tongan Society at the Time of European Contact', in N. Rutherford (ed.), *Friendly Islands: A History of Tonga* (Melbourne 1977), 68–89 at 64–9 [*Friendly Islands*]; Howe, *the Waves*, 125–6. See also N. Gunson, 'The *hau* concept of leadership in Western Polynesia', *JPH* 14, 1979, 28–49.

25 Beaglehole, III.cxix, 174–5; Adams, *Strangers*, 14, 21; J. Guiart, *Un Siècle et demi de contacts culturels à Tanna, Nouvelles-Hébrides* (Paris 1956), 9–10—this title is somewhat of a misnomer; of its 426 pages, twelve only are devoted to the first 101 years, but it has a valuable detailed account of the John Frum movement of the 1940s.

26 Beaglehole, I.133–4, and *Banks* 384–6; J. Hawkesworth, *An Account of the Voyages . . . for making Discoveries in the Southern Hemisphere* (London 1773), II.242–4; Forster, *Observations*, 352–8. George III was 'King of France' until 1802.

27 R. W. Williamson, *The Social and Political Systems of Central Polynesia* (Cambridge 1924, reprint Oosterhout/New York 1967), III.267, 286–7 [*Social Systems*]; the reference is to Tonga and Samoa but has much wider application.

28 B. Thomson, *The Fijians: A Study in the Decay of Custom* (London 1908), quoted in O. H. K. Spate, *The Fijian People: Economic Problems and Prospects* (Leg. Council Paper 13, Suva 1959), 11; see the chapter 'The Land: the Mataqali Problem', 10–15.

29 Williamson, *Social Systems*, III.275; see 229–319 *passim* for the many permutations.

30 [J. Wilson], *A Missionary Voyage in the South Pacific Ocean* (London 1799, reprint Graz/New York n.d.), xciv, 16–17, 104–5 [*Missionary Voyage*]—a splendid display of the bland and blind certainty of Evangelicanism.

31 Quoted in Williamson, *Social Systems*, III.227.

32 Daws, *Shoal of Time*, 124–8; Ralston, 'Hawaii 1778–1854', 30–1; for a Panglossian view, see Morgan, *Hawaii*, 130–9, and Kuykendall, *Kingdom*, I.259–98 is little better.

33 Beaglehole, III.1310–11; E. Taillemitte (ed.), *Bougainville et ses Compagnons autour du Monde 1766–1769* (Paris 1977), II.328 (Caro), 508 (Commerson) [*Bougainville*]; J. Dunmore and M. de Brossard, *Le Voyage de Lapérouse 1785–1788* (Paris 1985), II.75 [*Lapérouse*].

34 Wilson, *Missionary Voyage*, 136; William Wales, in Beaglehole, II.788–9; Lieut George Tobin, in G. Mackaness, *The Life of Vice-Admiral William Bligh, R.N., F.R.S.* (New York ed. n.d.), I.343–4; a brass Otho was a Roman coin.

35 William Anderson, in Beaglehole, III.929; Anon. [J. Marra], *Journal of the Resolution's Voyage* (London 1775, reprint Amsterdam 1967), 45–6 [*Resolution*]. Cf. Taillemitte, *Bougainville*, I.321.

36 Ahling Onorio, 'I-Matang: Early European Contacts', in *Kiribati: Aspects of History* (Suva/Tarawa 1979), 44–55 at 47–8; this is a cooperative production by indigenous authors.

37 Pearson, 'Reception', 122, 139–41.

38 Marra, *Resolution*, 170, 173; R. E. Gallagher (ed.), *Byron's Journal of his Circumnavigation 1764–1766*, HS 2nd Ser. 122 (Cambridge 1964), 98–101.

39 Beaglehole, *Banks*, II.96–9; Banks speaks of 'our Turtle', but one 'had an Indian turtle peg in it', surely a sufficient evidence of prior possession.

40 J. Swift, *Gulliver's Travels, Part IV: A Voyage to the Houyhnhms* (1726), Ch. XII; C. Churchill, *Gotham* (London 1764), I.7–44—splendid stuff; D. Diderot, *Supplément au Voyage de Bougainville* (written c. 1771–2; in *Oeuvres*, Pléiade ed. Paris 1951), 993–1032 at 1000; Dunmore/Brossard, *Lapérouse*, II.99—eloquent; F. X. de Viana, *Diario de Viage de las Corbetas españolas 'Descubrimiento' y 'Atrevida'* (Montevido 1958), II.165–6.

41 Robarts, *Journal*, 263; cf. 105–6, 113. When his wife died, years later, in Calcutta, he was heart-broken.

42 G. Robertson, *The Discovery of Tahiti*, HS 2nd Ser. 98 (London 1948), 207–9 [*Tahiti*]; cf. Vancouver, *North Pacific*, III.842–3.

43 Ibid., 169; Beaglehole, I.75–6, 520–1, II.794.

44 Oliver, *Tahitian Society*, I.194, 624, II.720; W. Ellis, *Polynesian Researches* (London 1829), II.286.

45 Dunmore/Brossard, *Lapérouse*, II.449–55; Dunmore, *Explorers*, I.277–9.

46 Perhaps the only notable exception—and not in the Islands—was the killing of a Nootkan chief by Estebán Martínez, who seems at times to have been unbalanced. This was condemned as 'barbaric' by a compatriot, perhaps prejudiced, but Martínez's own excuse does little to soften this verdict—J. M. Moziño, *Noticias de Nutka* (Seattle 1970), 74–7 [*Nutka*].

47 Robertson, *Tahiti*, 152–8; for analysis see Pearson, 'Intimidation', *passim*, and cf. G. Forster, *Voyage*, I.320–2. Wallis seems to have fired more than was needed to control the situation.

48 H. Wallis (ed.), *Cartaret's Voyage round the World 1766–1769*, HS 2nd Ser. 124–5 (Cambridge 1965), I.59–63, 161–7, 194. At least he paid tribute (164) to these 'Heroick defenders of their country'.

49 See for example Beaglehole, I.171, and *Banks*, I.257, 403—'the most disagreeable day my life has yet seen, black may be the mark for it'.

50 Dunmore/Brossard, *Lapérouse*, I.38. 'Feeling' in that age had the connotation that 'caring' has in ours.

51 J. K. Mumford (ed.), *John Ledyard's Journal of Captain Cook's Last Voyage* (Corvallis, Oregon, 1963), 38, 58.

52 S. Parkinson, *A Journal of a Voyage to the South Sea* (1784 ed., London, reprint London 1984), 15; J. R. Forster, *Journal*, II.354–5, III.515, 517–20, IV.586, 590, 611–13; G. Forster,

Voyage, I.513, 535–6, II.10–11, 124–6 (a contorted apology for taking part in a punitive raid, twisted into an attack on others' brutality), 254–8, 349–53, 425–8—ample documentation!

53 Beaglehole, II.498–500; but J. R. Forster, *Journal*, IV.611–12 blames Clerke, and Marra, *Resolution*, 277–8 gives a totally variant version—a good instance of the difficulty of untangling such incidents. Rickman's comment is in his *Journal of Captain Cook's Last Voyage* (London 1781, reprint Amsterdam 1967), 83.

54 *Voyage*, I.536; there is another spot of geniality at I.165–6.

55 F. W. Howay (ed.), *The Voyages of the "Columbia" to the Northwest Coast* (Boston 1941, reprint Amsterdam 1969), 271 (Hoskins), 377, 390–1, 395 (Boit). For an excellent discussion of 'Massacres and Motives', at a later stage but very applicable to the earliest traders, see D. Shineberg, *They Came for Sandalwood . . . 1830–1865* (Melbourne 1967), 199–214 [Sandalwood].

56 'Race Relations in the Pre-Colonial Pacific Islands: A Case of Prejudice and Pragmatism', *Pacific Studies* 8, 1965, 61–80 at 61, 78.

57 But Finau of Tonga devised, on the spot, an ingenious test to make sure that writing did what Mariner claimed for it, and acutely remarked that it would not do for Tonga, for fear of conspiracies, but would be useful if its use could be confined to himself and his inamoratas!—J. Martin, *An Account of the Natives of the Tonga Islands* (London 1817), I.116–20 (92–4) [Martin/Mariner, *Tonga*]. References in parentheses are to the edition published by the Vava'u Press, Neiafu, Tonga, 1981; this contains a biography of William Mariner, on whose recollections Martin's book was based, and who, adopted by Finau, survived the massacre of the Port au Prince in 1806.

58 O. von Kotzebue, *A Voyage of Discovery into the South Sea and Beering's Straits* (London 1821, reprint Amsterdam 1967), III.257–8; Marra has some sensible remarks on this reaction at Tanna—*Resolution*, 269–70.

59 Beaglehole, III.100–25 (Cook, 865, 868, 880–1 (Anderson), IV.532–7; Martin/Mariner, *Tonga* (3rd ed. Edinburgh 1827), II.71–2 (Vava'u ed. 279–80).

60 What follows is drawn from H. E. Maude and Marjorie Tuainekore Crocombe, 'Rarotongan Sandalwood', in Maude, *Islands*, 343–71.

61 My main sources are Maude, 'Beachcombers and Castaways', in *Islands*, 134–77; Ralston, *Grass Huts*, 20–43; Howe, *the Waves*, 102–8; F. X. Hezel SJ, 'The role of beachcombers in the Carolines', in N. Gunson (ed.), *The Changing Pacific* (Melbourne 1978), 261–72 ['beachcombers']—chronologically beachcombing in the Carolines, apart from Palau, was a later phenomenon than in Polynesia, but in terms of culture contact may be regarded as contemporary. See also T. Bargatzky, 'Beachcombers and Castaways as Innovators', *JPH* 15, 1980, 94–102, I have also read with advantage I. C. Campbell, European Transculturalists in Polynesia, 1789–*ca.* 1840 (Adelaide PhD thesis, 1976), solid, a little too solemn, but regrettably unpublished.

62 Maude, *Islands*, 174, 177, and cf. 161–5; N. Gunson, 'The Coming of Foreigners', in Rutherford, *Friendly Islands*, 90–113 at 99.

63 Cf. G. Mannoni, *Prospero and Caliban: The Psychology of Colonization* (New York 1956), 80–1, 86 [*Prospero*].

64 Maude, *Islands*, 137.

65 A. J. Schütz (ed.), *The Diaries and Correspondence of David Cargill 1832–1843* (Canberra 1977), 165–7 [*Diaries*]; R. A. Derrick, *A History of Fiji* (Suva 1946), 44–6 [*Fiji*]; Maude, *Islands*, 158–9. Cargill's account is at least twenty years after the event. Savage was killed and eaten on Vanua Levu in 1813—J. W. Davidson, *Peter Dillon of Vanikoro*

(Melbourne 1975), 28–41, 312–15, and P. Dillon, *Narrative... of a Voyage to the South Seas...* (London 1829), 1–31. J. G. Orr, *Savage of Bau* (Sydney 1977) is a '[melo]dramatized history'.

66 Ralston, *Grass Huts*, 37; Derrick, *Fiji*, 45.

67 Maude, *Islands*, 160–1; Hezel, 'beachcombers', 266.

68 Robarts, *Journal*, 129–39; at 262–4 he gives details of harbours. See also A. J. von Krusenshtern, *A Voyage round the World* (London 1813), I.110–12, 127–8, and V. Lisiansky. *A Voyage round the World* (London 1814), 68–77 (both reprinted Amsterdam, 1967, 1968). Kanakas also acted as pilots.

69 Ralston, *Grass Huts*, 30–1; Maude, 'The Tahitian Pork Trade', in *Islands*, 178–232 at 184, 187, and 'The Coconut Trade of the Gilbert Islands', ibid., 233–83 at 238–9; Hezel, 'beachcombers', 268.

70 Ralston, *Grass Huts*, 30–3; Maude, *Islands*, 150–5; A. Campbell, *A Voyage round the World* (Edinburgh 1816, but cited from the Honolulu 1967 reprint), 99–101; Beaglehole, III.1191–4.

71 Hezel, 'beachcombers', 270.

72 J. F. O'Connell (ed. S. H. Riesenberg), *A Residence of Eleven Years in New Holland and the Caroline Islands* (Canberra 1972, original ed. Boston 1830), 173; Hezel, 'beach-combers', 269.

73 Ralston, *Grass Huts*, 25, 34. This may seem the limit of the bizarre, but I myself claim to have been the first white man to read Mark Akenside's *Pleasures of the Imagination* (1744) in a Melanesian-manned launch in the Gulf of Papua; anyone can have a first if he/she tries hard enough.

74 Wilson, *Missionary Voyage*, 58–62, 98–107, 163–70, 256–71; Gunson, in Rutherford, *Friendly Islands*, 98–101. But a beachcomber was killed with the Tongan missionaries in 1799—ibid., 101.

75 O. Rutter (ed.), *The Journal of James Morrison* (London 1935), 83–4; Maude, *Islands*, 163.

76 Martin/Mariner, *Tonga*, II.34 (Vava'u ed. 267); E. im Thurn (ed.) *The Journal of Edward Lockerby 1808–1809*, HS 2nd Ser. 52 (London 1925), 71 [Lockerby, *Journal*]; Robarts, *Journal*, 159.

77 K. R. Howe, 'Firearms and Indigenous Warfare: a Case Study', *JPH* 9, 1974, 21–38 at 25–8 ['Firearms'].

78 Vancouver, *North Pacific* I.180–1, II.449, 470, 476, 612, III.797–800, 818, 1016, 1144, IV.1370; Maude, *Islands*, 152.

79 Ibid., 156.

80 Dening, *Islands*, 127–8; K. Sinclair, *A History of New Zealand* (Harmondsworth 1959), 40–1; Hezel, *First Taint*, 68–9, 125, 130; Vancouver, *North Pacific*, II.612; Moziño, *Nutka*, 16, 56, 70–1.

81 Lockerby, *Journal*, 52–7; for a similar incident in Tonga, see Martin/Mariner, *Tonga*, I.82–3 (Vava'u ed. 81–2).

82 D. Shineberg, 'Guns and Men in Melanesia', *JPH* 6, 1971, 61–82 at 62; see 78–80 for a debunking of Savage, and her *Sandalwood*, 170–5.

83 Beaglehole, II.398, at Tahiti.

84 As anyone will know who has served, or read C. S. Forester's *The Gun* or seen Sean O'Casey's unforgettable *The Silver Tassie*. For guns as 'the mark of a man' in the Solomons of this century, see R. M. Keesing and P. Corris, *Lightning Meets the West Wind: The Malaita Massacre* (Melbourne 1980), 18–20, 116–17.

[85] Hezel, *First Taint*, 130, 297–8. For litanies of 'Fatal Impact' remarks, see Shineberg, 'Guns and Men', 78 note 60, and Howe, 'Firearms', 21—though his conclusion at 38 does not necessarily follow.

[86] Maude, *Islands*, 156–60.

[87] *Prospero*, 85.

[88] R. G. Ward, 'The Pacific *Bêche-de-mer* Trade with special reference to Fiji', in Ward (ed.), *Man in the Pacific Islands* (Oxford 1972), 91–123 at 106–8; Kuykendall, *Kingdom*, I.85–6, 90. These trades are discussed below, Chapter 12.

[89] Howe, *the Waves*, 96; H. Morton, *The Whale's Wake* (Dunedin 1982), 187—see the whole chapter 'Maori Agriculture Adapts', 178–95. Both pigs and potatoes were European introductions—ibid., 183–4.

[90] Ibid., 216–17.

[91] Maud, *Islands*, 165; Mitchell Library, Sydney, MS A1677–3, 511–14.

[92] Howe, *the Waves*, 100–1; J. A. Lower, *Ocean of Destiny... the North Pacific, 1500–1978* (Vancouver 1978), 43–4; G. I. Quimby, 'Hawaiians in the Fur Trade of Northwest America', *JPH* 7, 1972, 92–103.

[93] G. Bayly, *Sea-Life Sixty Years Ago* (London 1885), 77–82; Morton, *The Whale's Wake*, 169–77, and *The Wind Commands* (Vancouver 1975), 394–6; H. Melville, *Moby Dick, or the White Whale* (1851), Chs. X–XII—Queequeg was from 'Kokovoko, an island... not down in any map'.

[94] Beaglehole, III.214; Bligh, quoted in Oliver, *Tahitian Society*, III.1253; ibid., III.,1249–50, 1256–90 *passim*.

[95] Kuykendall, *Kingdom*, I.38–44; Vancouver, *North Pacific*, I.127, III.836–9, 855–65, 1152–64, 1175–83.

[96] Wilson, *Missionary Voyage*, Dedication to George III.

[97] See for example the deeply moving account by David Cargill of his wife Margaret's death from dysentery and childbirth, *Diaries*, 180–91.

[98] Strictly speaking, the third party a second in the *Duff* having been captured by a French privateer—C. W. Newbury (ed.), *The History of the Tahitian Mission 1799–1830* (by John Davies), HS 2nd Ser. 116 (Cambridge 1961), xxxi. For the Evangelical missions in general see N. Gunson, *Messengers of Grace: Evangelical Missionaries in the South Seas 1797–1860* (Melbourne 1972), or for a somewhat caustic view L. B. Wright and M. I. Fry, *Puritans in the South Seas* (New York 1936).

[99] Morgan, *Hawaii*, 94–5.

[1] H. G. Cummins, 'Holy War: Peter Dillon and the 1837 Massacres in Tonga', *JPH* 12, 1977, 25–39; St Matthew, v. 13.

[2] Oliver, *Tahitian Society*, III.1288.

[3] H. E. Maude, 'Foreword' to R. G. and M. R. Crocombe, *The Works of Ta'unga* (Canberra 1968), xi–xii. One is reminded of the Saxon SS Boniface and Willibrord who brought the Gospel to Germany.

Notes for Chapter 11

[1] S. Wallis, MS Journal, Mitchell Library, Sydney, 22 June 1767; H. Carrington (ed.), *The Discovery of Tahiti* (by George Robertson, the *Dolphin's* Master), HS 2nd Ser. 98

(London 1948), 166–7, 180, 184, 196–200 [Robertson, *Tahiti*]—a *fabliau* for Boccacio or Chaucer in their looser moments.

2 E. Taillemitte (ed.), *Bougainville et ses Compagnons autour du Monde 1766–1769* (Paris 1977), II.384–7 (Nassau-Siegen), 80–5 (Fesche), 497, 506–10 (Commerson) [*Bougainville*].

3 Beaglehole, Iclxxxvi–clxxxviii—very level-headed.

4 Ibid., II.444; J. R. Forster, *Observations made during a Voyage round the World* (London 1778), 390–2 [*Observations*]; Lieut. John Elliot, in C. Holmes (ed.), Captain *Cook's Second Voyage* (London 1984), 31 [*Second Voyage*].

5 J. C. Beaglehole (ed.), *The Endeavour Journal of Joseph Banks 1768–1771* (Sydney 1962), I.279; cf. 254–5, 292 [*Banks*].

6 Samwell's Journal, in Beaglehole, III.987–1295—1030–1, 1044, 1054–5 (the Dons), 1085 (Hawaiian girls 'would almost use violence', hardly needed), 1093–6, 1143–5, 1181–2; B. G. Corney (ed.) *The Quest and Occupation of Tahiti by the Spaniards*, HS 2nd Ser. 32, 36, 43 (London 1912–19), I.333, II.330–1.

7 M. E. Hoare (ed.), *The Resolution Journal of Johann Reinhold Forster 1772–1775*, HS 2nd Ser. 152–5 (London 1982), III.390–1 [Forster, *Journal*], and *Observations*, 350–2, 365.

8 *A Voyage round the World* (London 1777, reprint London 1986), I.265–6, 277, II.54–5, 107–13, 469–70 [*Voyage*]. References are to the original edition.

9 Ibid., I.264–5, 383–6, 400; II.137–8.

10 Ibid., II.129–35, 151–2; Forster, *Observations*, 409–14.

11 O. Rutter (ed.), *The Journal of James Morrison* (London 1935), 235 [*Journal*]—country fairs were places where 'Many a green gown there was given'. All direct unreferenced quotations in this section are from Morrison, 185 (divorce), 225–38.

12 D. Oliver, *Ancient Tahitian Society* (Canberra/Honolulu 1974), I.350 [*Tahitian Society*]. See in general his Ch. 11, 'Sexuality', and B. Danielsson, *Love in the South Seas* (London 1956) [*Love*]—more serious than the title suggests.

13 For slightly critical comment, see Oliver, *Tahitian Society*, II.838–41.

14 Ibid., I.369–74; Danielsson, *Love*, 149–53.

15 Ibid., 60–3 (bark cloth); Wilson is quoted from van der Sluis, *Treponematosis*, 63 (see note 24 below). Of course other factors than delicacy, such as fear of sorcery, may be involved in this shielding of genitals; who knows how much of our own attitude may be due to taboos handed down at mother's knee through the ages?

16 Beaglehole, I.93, and *Banks*, I.275–65; Oliver, *Tahitian Society*, I.335–9.

17 Ibid. I.424–6—'there can be no doubt that a very large percentage of Moahi [Tahitian] infants were deliberately slain.'

18 Taillemitte, *Bougainville*, I.317, II.243–4.

19 Oliver, *Tahitian Society*, I.354–7.

20 Forster, *Voyage*, II.176–9; J. Dunmore and M. de Brossard, *Le Voyage de Lapérouse 1785–1788* (Paris 1985), II.445 [*Lapérouse*].

21 Morrison, *Journal*, 237; Forster, *Voyage*, II.54. The comparison with British whores was also made by Cook and William Wales (for once in agreement with George Forster!)—Beaglehole, II.239, 796–7.

22 G. Daws, *A Dream of Islands* (New York 1980), 271–2. To be fair, Gauguin's syphilis was contracted in Paris—ibid., 247.

23 J. C. Hume, 'Problems in Diagnosis of Syphilis and Other Treponematoses Throughout the World', in US Department of Health, *Proceedings of World Forum on Syphilis and other Treponematoses* (Washington 1964), 214–16; I must thank my colleague Dr F. B. Smith for lending me this volume. This is obviously delicate ground for a layman.

24 H. M. Smith, 'The Introduction of Venereal Disease into Tahiti: a Re-examination, *JPH* 10, 1975, 38–45 at 39–40 ['Venereal Disease']; G. Qvist, *John Hunter 1728–1793* (London 1981), 157–60—at 42–53 Qvist refutes the legend of Hunter's auto-inoculation with syphilis. S. R. Gloyne, *John Hunter* (Edinburgh 1950), 70–3, states that the difference between syphilis and gonorrhea was known in the eighteenth century, at least to Hunter. For some other confusions see the important monograph by I. van der Sluis, *The Treponematosis of Tahiti: Its Origin and Evolution: A Study of the Sources* (Amsterdam 1969), 60–9 [*Treponematosis*].

25 P. Pirie, 'The Effects of Treponematosis and Gonorrhea on the Populations of the Pacific Islands', *Human Biology* (Sydney) 1, 1971–2, 187–206 at 189 ['Effects']; cf. for Fijian attitudes to yaws as late as the 1890s C. M. Woodford in W. H. R. Rivers, *Essays on the Depopulation of Melanesia* (Cambridge 1922), 72–3.

26 Beaglehole, III.clix; John Wilson (1801) in van der Sluis, *Treponematosis*, 62, cf. 75.

27 Robertson, *Tahiti*, 167, 186; quotations from Robertson's log, not referred to in Carrington's rather slight editorial discussion (284–7), are from van der Sluis, *Treponematosis*, 21, and J. Watt, 'Medical Aspects and Consequences of Captain Cook's Voyages', in R. Fisher and H. Johnston (eds.), *Captain James Cook and His Times* (Vancouver/ Canberra 1979), 129–58 at 151 ['Medical Aspects'].

28 D. Samwell, 'Observations respecting the Introduction of Venereal Disease into the Sandwich Islands', in his *A Narrative of the Death of Captain James Cook* (London 1786), 30–4.

29 Anderson, distinguishing between an indigenous disease (yaws) and a 'most destructive' European one, in Beaglehole, III.926–7; J. R. Forster, *Journal* II.306–9; G. Forster, *Voyage*, I.237–40.

30 J. R. Forster, *Observations*, 492–4; G. Forster, *Voyage*, I.237–40, 369–70. There was however no yaws in New Zealand.

31 J. R. Forster, *Journal*, II.347–8; Beaglehole, III.474–5 note; H. Jacquier, 'Le mirage et l'exotisme tahitiens dans la littérature', *Bull. Soc. d'Etudes Océaniennes* 7, 1945, 3–27, 50–76, 91–114, at 64—a very uneven paper.

32 Useful discussions are Beaglehole, III.clix–clxi; Smith, 'Venereal Disease'; Watt, 'Medical Aspects', 149–54; and J. Dunmore, *French Explorers in the Pacific: I. The Eighteenth Century* (Oxford 1965), 86–90 [*Explorers*].

33 Bougainville, *Voyage autour du Monde* (Paris 1771, 232, and (1772) II.115–16, cited Dunmore, *Explorers* I.88); Beaglehole, II.231–2; Cook, *A Voyage towards the South Pole* (London 1777, reprint Adelaide 1970), I.152–3, 181–2.

34 Ibid., I.182; Taillemitte, *Bougainville*, II.244.

35 Pirie, 'Effects', 188–91; van der Sluis, *Treponematosis*, 69–74, 165 (if I read him aright).

36 Watt, 'Medical Aspects', 150–2.

37 J. A. R. Miles, 'On the observations on health in the Pacific by Cook', *Proc. Roy. Soc NZ* 97, 1969, 69–75. Norma McArthur, a determined deflator of exaggerated estimate, allows a morality of 20 per cent, probably over 25,000 souls, for the Fijian measles epidemic of 1875—*Island Populations of the Pacific* (Canberra 1967), 8–11.

38 H. Morton, *The Whale's Wake* (Dunedin 1982), 175.

39 Prefatory essay 'Of Heroic Plays' to *Almanzor and Almahide, or The Conquest of Granada* (1672; Mermaid ed., London n.d.), 28–36 at 34–5. The quotation is from Part I, I.i; cf. III.i, 'And yet there's something roughly noble there'.

40 Y. Giraud, 'De l'Exploration à l'Utopie: Notes sur la formation du mythe de Tahiti', *French Studies* (Oxford) 31, 1977, 26–41 at 26–7 ['De l'Exploration']; G. Chinard, 'Intro-

duction' to Diderot, *Supplément au Voyage de Bougainville* (Paris 1935), 72–8 ['Introduction'.].
[41] E. S. Dodge, *Islands and Empires: Western Impact on the Pacific and East Asia* (Minneapolis 1976), 50–2 [*Islands*].
[42] H. N. Fairchild, *The Noble Savage: A Study in Romantic Naturalism* (New York 1828) [*Noble Savage*]—Ch. IV is required reading; A. O. Lovejoy, 'The Supposed Primitivism of Rousseau's *Discourse on Inequality*', in his *Essays on the History of Ideas* (Baltimore 1948; the paper was first published 1923), 14–37 ['Primitivism']. See also M. Duchet, *Anthropologie et Histoire au siècle des lumières* (Paris 1971), 329–46 [*Anthropologie*].
[43] Lovejoy, 'Primitivism', 18 note 4; Rousseau, *Discours sur l'origine et les fondements de l'inégalité parmi les hommes* ('Amsterdam' 1755; in *Oeuvres*, ed. du Seuil, Paris 1971), II.203–68 at 209, 2121 [*Discours*]. For a view opposed to Lovejoy's, see R. Meek, *Social science and the ignoble savage* (Cambridge 1976), 78 note 46.

I am aware of the hazards of entering the minefield of Rousseau scholarship; can there really be a balanced view on a genius so great and so unbalanced?
[44] *Discours*, 254–6; Lovejoy, 'Primitivsm', 17–18.
[45] P. Gay, *The Enlightenment: II. The Science of Freedom* (London 1969), 95 [*Enlightenment*]; A. Sinclair, *The Savage: A History of Misunderstanding* (London 1977), 75; R. Mauzi, 'Représentations du paradis sous les tropiques', in M. Mollat and E. Taillemitte (eds.), *L'Importance de l'Exploration Maritime au Siècle des Lumières* (Paris 1982), 169–74 at 171 [*Exploration Maritime*]—a paper which leaves the Noble Savage dead and *le bon sauvage* at death's door.
[46] *Discours*, 223–4, 251 note i.
[47] *Noble Savage*, 139.
[48] See his satirical letter of thanks to Rousseau in *Discours*, 268.
[49] Cf. Gay, *Enlightenment*, 95: 'Rousseau directed his energies toward discovering not a state of nature without culture but a culture that would realize man's true nature ... his nostalgia was never for a primitive state of nature'; cf. J. Barzun, *Classic, Romantic and Modern* (Anchor Books ed., Garden City N.Y., 1961), 23–8.
[50] Chinard, 'Introduction', 71. Caribbean Good Savages were 'soft'.
[51] B. Smith, *European Vision and the South Pacific* (2nd ed. Sydney 1985), 5 [*European Vision*]; Bealghole, I.399.
[52] *Paradise on Earth: Some Thoughts on European Images of Non-European Man* (New Haven 1965), 11, 20–1.
[53] Peter Martyr, quoted in S. E. Morison, *The European Discovery of America: II. The Southern Voyages 1492–1616* (New York 1974), 67; *The Tempest*, II.i.
[54] *Relation de la Nouvelle-France* (1616), quoted in G. Atkinson, *Les Relations de Voyage et l'Evolution des Idées* (Paris 1924), 106.
[55] G. Williams, 'Savages Noble and Ignoble', *Jnl of Imperial and Commonwealth History* 6, 1978, 300–13 at 302.
[56] *L'Amérique et le Rêve Exotique dans la Littérature Française au XVIIe et au XVIIIe Siècles* (Paris 1934; original ed. 1913), passim [*L'Amérique*]; there are doubtless newer lights in C. J. Jaenen, *Friend and Foe: Aspects of French-AmerIndian Cultural Contact ...* (Ontario 1974), which I have not seen.
[57] Chinard, *L'Amérique*, 112, 139, 319, 324–5; Smith, *European Vision*, 37–43, 73–5, 119–20; Beaglehole, *Banks*, I.258–60.
[58] Chinard, *L'Amérique*, 167–87—cf. the opening of Rousseau's *Le Contrat Social*, 'Man is born free, but he is everywhere in chains'.
[59] *An Account of the Pelew Islands* (London 1789), 366 [*Pelew Islands*]; for the rationalisations,

215–16 ('my hand shrinks from the page'), 335–6.

[60] For differing views, see K. R. Howe, 'The Fate of the "Savage" in Pacific Historiography', NZ *Jnl of History* 2, 1977, 137–54 at 137–9, and I. C. Campbell, 'Savages Noble and Ignoble: The Preconceptions of Early European Voyagers in Polynesia', *Pacific Studies* 4, 1980, 45–59 ['Preconceptions'].

[61] R. Pomeau, 'Voyages et lumières dans la littérature française du XVIIIe siècle', *Studies in Voltaire* (Geneva) 57, 1967, 1269–89 at 1279 ['Voyages'].

[62] 'De l'Exploration', 27–8.

[63] Rousseau, *Discours*, 257; Taillemitte, *Bougainville*, I.46 note 3, 52, 269, 281–2, 359.

[64] Ibid., I.326–7; Bougainville, *A Voyage round the World* (trans. J. R. Forster, London 1772), 228, 244–5, 252, 269; Mauzi, in Mollat and Taillemitte, *Exploration Maritime*, 173–5—but he is beside the point in speaking of the 'derisory' payments to the Tahitians for supplies; to them, nails were as good as gold, or better.

[65] J.-E. Martin-Allanic, *Bougainville navigateur et lés Decouvertes de son Temps* (Paris 1964), II.1251, 1388 note 88 [*Bougainville*]; Taillemitte, *Bougainville*. I.111–21.

[66] Ibid., II.506–10 ('Post-Scriptum'), 514–22 at 514 ('Sommaire d'Observations d'Histoire Naturelle'—not real observations but the plan for them). Commerson spoils things by some startling teleology, but his geomorphological outline ('Observations Physiques', 520) could have given points to J. R. Forster. The first report of Bougainville's voyage, a four-page pamphlet of July 1769, is remarkably low-key—L. D. Hammond (ed.), *News from New Cythera* (Minneapolis 1970).

[67] I quote from the Pléiade edition in *Oeuvres* (ed. A. Bailly, Paris 1951), 993–1032. For discussion see *inter alia* Chinard, 'Introduction'; Duchet, *Anthropologie*, 407–75 especially 453–69; R. Leigh, 'Diderot's Tahiti', in J. P. Hardy and J. C. Eade (eds.), *Studies in the Eighteenth Century* 5 (Oxford 1983), 113–29. I have not been able to see Dieckmann's edition of the Supplement.

[68] *Supplément*, 1012–15; at times one seems to be reading a pro-natalist tract. Voltaire's *I es Oreilles* is in the Pléiade edition of *Romans et Contes* (Paris 1979), 579–95 [*Les Oreilles*].

[69] Ibid., 1022, 1032.

[70] Ibid., 1000–3.

[71] Ibid., 1023.

[72] Ibid., 1030–1.

[73] Chinard, 'Introduction', 78–96 (the Desmoulins letter is at 87); Giraud, 'De l'Exploration', 30–9; J. Gautier, 'Tahiti dans la Littérature française à la fin du XVIIIe Siècle: Quelques Ouvrages oubliés' (and why not?), *Jnl Soc. Océanistes* 3, 1947, 308–16. For the curious romance in which Omai becomes a Benevolent Despot, see H. Jacquier, 'L'abbé Baston', *Bull. Soc. Etudes Océaniennes* 79, 1947, 308–16, or E. H. McCormick, *Omai: Pacific Envoy* (Auckland 1977) 320–7, [*Omai*].

[74] *Oroonoko: or, the Royal Slave* (London 1688), in P. Henderson (ed.), *Shorter Novels of the Seventeenth Century* (Everyman ed. London 1967), 153, 155, 178, 187. 'Ms' seems more appropriate than 'Mrs' for the first woman to gain her living as a writer, a Founding Mother of feminism.

[75] *Oroonoko: A Tragedy* (London 1696), in J. Sutherland (ed.), *Restoration Tragedies* (Oxford 1977), 355–438; Fairchild, *Noble Savage*, 40–1, gives 1775 as the date for Hawkesworth's revision, presumably published posthumously to take advantage of the recent publicity.

[76] *An Account of the Voyages undertaken by the order of his present Majesty for making Discoveries in the Southern Hemisphere* (London 1773) [*Voyages*]. The following discussion is based on Beaglehole, I.ccxlii–ccliii, and W. H. Pearson's papers 'Hawkesworth's Alterations',

JPH 7, 1972 ['Alterations'] and 'Hawkesworth's *Voyages*' in R. F. Brissenden (ed.), *Studies in the Eighteenth Century* II (Canberra 1973), 239–58 ['*Voyages*']. See also O. H. K. Spate, 'Seamen and Scientists: The literature of the Pacific 1697–1798', in P. F. Rehbock and R. M. MacLeod (eds.), *Western Science in the Pacific* (Berkeley 1987) and J. L. Abbott, *John Hawkesworth: Eighteenth Century Man of Letters* (Madison 1983).

[77] For some choice invective, see 'A Christian', ibid., 161; Wesley thought that Tupaia knew of an island 1100 degrees in latitude from Tahiti!—Beaglehole, I.ccli.

[78] Vancouver, *A Voyage of Discovery to the North Pacific Ocean*, HS 2nd Ser. 163–6 (London 1984), I.290–1 [*North Pacific*]; H. Wallis, 'Publication of Cook's Journals', *Pacific Studies* 1, 1978, 163–94 at 167; Beaglehole, II.cxliii–cxlviii.

[79] Hawkesworth, *Voyages*, I.iv–v; Beaglehole, I.ccxlv–ccxlvii; H. Wallis (ed.), *Cartaret's Voyage round the World 1766–1769*, HS 2nd Ser. 124–5 (Cambridge 1965), I.3, II.504–9.

[80] Hawkesworth, *Voyages*, II.101, 136–7, 143–5, 231, III.41–3, 235–6; cf. Beaglehole, *Banks*, I.264, 283, 286, 373, II.12, 128.

[81] Wallis's Journal, 27 July 1767, Mitchell Library, Sydney; Hawkesworth, *Voyages*, I.257–8; Pearson, 'Alterations', 61–2, and '*Voyages*', 249–50, 252.

[82] Beaglehole, *Banks*, I.252; see W. Veit, 'On the European Imagining of the Non-European World', in I. Donaldson (ed.), *Australia and the European Imagination* (Canberra 1982), 124–56 at 127–31.

[83] Pearson, '*Voyages*', 253.

[84] Ibid., 239; [D. Henry], *An Historical Account of All the Voyages round the World performed by English Navigators* (London 1774)—volumes III.1–470 and IV.1–122 follow Hawkesworth closely.

[85] Pearson, '*Voyages*', 246; Voltaire, *Les Oreilles*, 589–90; Hawkesworth, *Voyages*, II.59, and Diderot, *Supplément*, 1030.

[86] Taillemitte, *Bougainville*, I.326, 331, 340, 406, II.249, 328; Martin-Allanic, *Bougainville*, II.964–72, and for Aotourou's last voyage II.1307–26.

[87] Bougainville, *A Voyage round the World* (trans. J. R. Forster, London 1772, reprint Amsterdam 1967), 262–7.

[88] Martin-Allanic, *Bougainville*, II.964–5; but he gives a misleading impression of La Condamine's general attitude towards 'Indians'—see Duchet, *Anthropologie*, 108–11.

[89] Girard, 'De l'Exploration', 30.

[90] McCormick, *Omai*, 182–3—an excellent and most comprehensive biography; see also M. Alexander, *Omai, 'Noble Savage'* (London 1977). T. B. Clarke's flashy sketch *Omai, First Polynesian Ambassador to England* (Honolulu 1969) has amongst other absurdities Sandwich explaining 'the new kind of transportation then exciting London' (21–2)—the balloon, in 1774, a mere nine years before the first Montgolfier ascent. Some paragraphs in this section are drawn from my review of McCormick, *NZ Jnl of History* 12, 1147, 85–7.

[91] McCormick, *Omai*, 174; all known portraits of Omai are reproduced in the book.

[92] Ibid., Chs 5–8 *passim*, especially 94–114, 124–5, 169–73.

[93] Ibid., 164–8; one would like the comments of Sandwich, hero of the Hell-Fire Club and the affair of Wilke's pornographic *Essay on Woman*.

[94] Ibid., 295–300; the incident figured in his controversy with William Wales—G. Forster, *Reply to Mr. Wales's Remarks* (London 1778), 21–3.

[95] Full details in McCormick, *Omai*, Chs 9–11.

[96] Ibid., Ch. 12, 'The Literary Heritage'; Cowper, *The Task*, Book I—one cannot quite

see Omai weeping 'honest tears, A patriot's for his country . . .'.

⁹⁷ J. Meares, *Voyages . . . from China to the North West Coast of America* (London 1790, reprint Amsterdam 1967), xxxix, 4–10, 341, 454—very flowery stuff; Dodge, *Islands*, 50–1; Vancouver, *North Pacific*, III.826–7, 845–6. Dodge curiously fails to mention Vancouver's verdict, but in general his book fails to live up to its ambitious subtitle.

⁹⁸ Keate, *Pelew Islands*, 339–65; Dodge, *Islands*, 48–50; F. X. Hezel SJ, *The First Taint of Civilization* (Honolulu 1983), 74–5, source of 'the darling'; Coleridge, 'Lines to a Young Lady, with a Poem on the French Revolution'.

⁹⁹ Quoted in full above, 202.

¹ G. Forster, *Voyage*, II.190–1, 503 (at Tierra del Fuego); there is another Rousseauist passage, on European education 'stifl[ing] the feelings of the heart', at I.417.

² Forster, *Observations*, 297–302, a richly rhetorical passage.

³ Ibid., 318–32; G. Forster, *Voyage*, I.240, II.478.

⁴ Ibid., I.177–80; J. R. Forster, *Journal*, II.265–6.

⁵ Forster, *Observations*, 293–4, 357–8, 582–6 (main quotation); cf. 347–52.

⁶ *Journal*, III.515, 517.

⁷ Ibid., III.390; *Observations*, 411–17; G. Forster, *Voyage*, I.295–7 (main quotation), 306–17.

⁸ Ibid., II.110–13.

⁹ Ibid., I.427–8; J. R. Forster, *Observations*, 395, 399; Smith, *European Vision*, 40–3, and 'Captain Cook's Artists and the Portrayal of Pacific Peoples', *Art History* 7, 1984, 295–312. Banks used such names as 'Hercules' and 'Lycurgus' for his Tahitian contacts until he learnt their real names—Beaglehole, *Banks*, I.258. See also A. Dalrymple, *A Letter . . . occasioned by some groundless and illiberal Imputations in* [Hawkesworth's] *Account of the late VOYAGES to the SOUTH SEAS* (London 1773), 26.

¹⁰ G. Forster, *Voyage*, I.391–3.

¹¹ Above, ooo–oo, and Dunmore, *Explorers*, 116–23.

¹² J. Dunmore (trans. and ed.), *The Expedition of the* St Jean-Baptiste *to the Pacific 1769–1770*, HS 2nd Ser. 158 (London 1981), 152–3.

¹³ Ibid., 96–8, 105–6.

¹⁴ Dunmore, *Explorers*, 180–9, and his papers 'Rousseau's Noble Savage: A New Zealand Case History', in W. Veit (ed.), *Captain James Cook: Image and Impact II* (Melbourne 1979), 160–72, and 'L'Image et le Réel: le mythe du Bon Sauvage de Bougainville à Marion du Fresne', in Mollat and Taillemitte, *Exploration Maritime*, 161–8. The '*adorator perpetuus*' is from the extraordinary Latin inscription which Commerson drew up to commemorate his visit—Taillemitte, *Bougainville*, 508–10.

¹⁵ A. M. Rochon (ed.), *Nouveau Voyage à la Mer du Sud commencé sous les Ordres de M. MARION* (Paris 1783), 141–6; Sparrman, *A Voyage round the World with Captain James Cook* (London 1953), 180–2, 185.

¹⁶ Dunmore/Brossard, *Lapérouse*, II.75, 147–9, 447—the allusion to the Dijon Academy's prize to Rousseau for his first *Discours* is oblique but pointed. Milet-Mureau, who edited La Pérouse's papers, made some slight variants, noted in Dunmore/Brossard, which 'point up the attitudes of the age' (II.446).

¹⁷ La Pérouse's last letter, to Fleurieu from Botany Bay, ibid., I.279.

¹⁸ Smith, *European Vision*, 317–25, and especially the progressive debasement of the Islanders, in some cases a literal denigration, shown in Plates 197–201, 209—with the concomitant provision of a 'more heavenly' countenance for the Rev. John Williams.

Notes for Chapter 12

[1] The undeclared maritime war with the French Directory in 1798–1800 hardly counts in the Pacific, though a frigate had brushes with privateers in the Sunda Straits— C. O. Paullin, *American Voyages to the Orient 1690–1865* (Annapolis 1971), 12–17 [*to the Orient*].

[2] The *Hornet*, a 55-ton sloop, had sailed from Boston for Canton in December 1783, but at the Cape exchanged her cargo of ginseng for EIC tea—S. E. Morison, *The Maritime History of Massachusetts* (Boston 1941), 44 [*Massachusetts*].

[3] L. Dermigny, *La Chine et l'Occident: le Commerce à Canton au XVIIIe Siècle* (Paris 1964), III.1162 [*Commerce*]; Paullin puts the figure at nearly one-third (*to the Orient*, 10–12) but has not Dermigny's precision. In 1787 Americans, Dutch and Macaoese had each five ships at Canton, all others except the EIC only six altogether—C. N. Parkinson, *Trade in the Eastern Seas 1793–1815* (Cambridge 1937), 93 [*Eastern Seas*]. See also F. R. Dulles, *The Old China Trade* (Boston 1930, reprint New York 1970), 4–12, 26, 210–11 [*China Trade*].

[4] J. Bach, *A Maritime History of Australia* (Melbourne 1976), 46 [*Maritime History*]; T. Dunbabin, 'New Light on the Earliest American Voyages to Australia', *American Neptune* 10, 1950, 52–64; G. Greenwood, *Early American-Australian Relations . . . to 1930* (Melbourne 1944), 117–41 [*Relations*].

[5] N. Wace and B. Lovett, *Yankee Maritime Activities and the Early History of Australia*, ANU Research School of Pacific Studies Aids to Research A/2 (Canberra 1973), 10. There is an immense bibliography (eight volumes) in R. G. Ward (ed.), *American Activities in the Central Pacific, 1790–1850* (Ridgeway, N. J. 1966–7).

[6] A. Ogden, 'New England Traders in Spanish and Mexican California', in Ogden and E. Sluiter (eds.), *Greater America* (Berkeley 1945), 395–413; E. Pereira Salas, *Los Primeiros Contactos entre Chile y los Estados Unidos* (Santiago 1971), 213–20, 305–14 [*Primeiros Contactos*].

[7] [A.] M'Konochie, *A Summary View of the Statistics and Existing Commerce of The Principal Shores of the Pacific Ocean . . .* (London 1818), 196–7 [*Pacific Ocean*]. The author is better known as the notable prison reformer Maconochie; see J. V. Barry, *Alexander Maconochie of Norfolk Island* (Melbourne 1958), which is however slight on the *Pacific Ocean*.

[8] R. J. Cleveland, *A Narrative of Voyages and Commercial Adventures* (Cambridge, Mass., 1842), *passim*; A. Delano, *Narrative of Voyages and Travels* (Boston 1817, reprint Upper Saddle River, N. J., 1970), 202–05, 495–8 [*Narrative*]; E. Fanning, *Voyages round the World* (New York 1933, reprint Upper Saddle River 1970)—a dull dog beside Delano, whose superb honesty on his feelings when it was a case of his own life or a shipmate's curiously shocked E. S. Dodge—Delano, 466–71; Dodge, *New England and the South Seas* (Cambridge, Mass., 1965), 70–1. There are well-edited selections from Delano, Fanning and Cleveland in W. Teller, *Five Sea Captains* (New York 1960), but the biography of Delano by J. B. Connolly, *Master Mariner* (New York 1943) is correctly written off by Teller (19) as Delano 'with all [his] flavor drained away and nothing authentic added.' Pereira Salas has a good chapter on these three, 'Los grandes capitanes-cronistas', *Primeiros Contactos*, 113–25.

[9] Morrison, *Massachusetts*, 116–18.

[10] J. H. Parry, *Trade and Dominion: The European Empires in the Eighteenth Century* (London 1971), 278, 362 note 7; Dermigny, *Commerce*, III.1046–7.

[11] The Sunda Straits, essential for access to Batavia and Canton, seem to have been regarded as an international waterway.

[12] The complicated story of the sparring for position may be found in N. Tarling, *Anglo-Dutch Rivalry in the Malay World 1780–1824* (St Lucia, Qld, 1962), and V. T. Harlow, *The Founding of the Second British Empire 1763–1793* (London 1964), II.190–5, 365–401 [*Second Empire*].

[13] Ibid., II.530–4; Parkinson, *Eastern Seas*, 93–5; cf. Dermigny, *Commerce*, III.931–2, 1052–4.

[14] Lord Sheffield, quoted in Dulles, *China Trade*, 115—unfortunately without either date or reference.

[15] Harlow, *Second Empire*, II.436–40; H. Furber, *Rival Empires of Trade in the Orient 1600–1800* (Minneapolis 1976), 176 [*Rival Empires*]; Parkinson, *Eastern Seas*, 346.

[16] Furber, *Rival Empires*, 176, 289–97; Harlow, *Second Empire*, II.534–40; Dermigny, *Commerce*, III.1207–12, 1341.

[17] Furber, *Rival Empires*, 244.

[18] Dermigny, *Commerce*, I.384–7, III.1148–9; J. Kirker, *Adventures to China: Americans in the Southern Oceans 1792–1812* (New York 1970), 6–7 [*Adventures*]; Dulles, *China Trade*, 5–6. Dulles appears to be in error in discounting the virile virtue of the root.

[19] Dermigny, *Commerce*, III.1129.

[20] Ibid., III.1132–6; efforts to enforce the law by Nelson and Collingwood met with stiff resistance from merchants, planters, and officials—T. Pocock, *The Young Nelson in the Americas* (London 1980), 189–92.

[21] Dermigny, *Commerce*, III.1132–6; B. Lubbock, 'Ships of the Period', in C. N. Parkinson (ed.), *The Trade Winds* (London 1948), 87–101 at 93; Dulles, *China Trade*, 116.

[22] M'Konochie, *Pacific Ocean*, 97–9, 243–4; Dulles, *China Trade*, 10–11—Shaw tells the story well, he was all in a glow at this compliment until 'Justice compels me to add' the merchant's disconcerting rider.

[23] Unless otherwise stated, this section is based on H. T. Fry, 'Alexander Dalrymple and New Guinea', *JPH* 4, 1969, 83–104 ['Dalrymple'], 'Cathay and the Way Thither', *Histl Studies* 14, 1971, 497–510, and 'The Eastern Passage and its Impact on Spanish Policy in the Philippines, 1758–1790', unpublished. I am grateful to Dr Fry for the typescript and for information from his current work. See also R. P. Crowhurst, 'The Voyage of the *Pitt*—A Turning Point in East India Navigation', *Mariner's Mirror* 55, 1969, 43–56, and especially R. Richards, 'The Easternmost Route to China and the Robertson Aikman Charts', *Great Circle* 8, 1986, 54–67, 104–16 ['Easternmost Route'].

[24] Modern atlas maps usually give winds for January and July only, thus missing the critical equinoctial changes. Plate VIII in M. F. Maury, *The Physical Geography of the Sea* (2nd ed. London 1868) is rather confusing, but see his text, 337–59.

[25] Not to be confused with the Dampier Strait between New Britain and the other end of New Guinea. Vogelkopf = Bird's Head, an apt name.

[26] *Eastern Seas*, 118, 219; cf. Table II in this volume.

[27] T. Forrest, *A Voyage to New Guinea and the Moluccas* (London 1780, reprint Kuala Lumpur/Melbourne 1969); for the background, O. H. K. Spate, *Monopolists and Freebooters* (Canberra 1983), 268–77, [*Monopolists*].

[28] Fry, 'Dalrymple', 95–101; G. Souter, *New Guinea: The Last Unknown* (Sydney 1965), 20–2; J. P. Hockin, *A Supplement to the Account of the Pelew Islands* (London 1803); I. Lee, *Commodore Sir John Hayes* (London 1912), 71–100, 137–8, 164–5, 172–85. Amasa Delano sailed with McCluer and gives a lively account—*Narrative*, 43–110, 152–93.

²⁹ Richards, 'Easternmost Route', 63–4; *The Voyage of Governor Phillip to Botany Bay* (London 1789, reprint Melbourne 1982), 97, and accounts of these voyages 183–266, with charts for Shortland and Marshall and detailed positions for all three in the Appendix, Tables VI–IX.

³⁰ Fry, personal communication.

³¹ T. R. and M. C. McHale, *Early American-Philippine Trade: The Journal of Nathaniel Bowditch in Manila, 1796*, Yale Southeast Asia Studies Monographs 2 (New Haven 1962), 40–1 [Bowditch, *Manila*].

³² The standard work is M. L. Diaz-Trechuelo Spínola, *La Real Compañia de Filipinas* (Seville 1965) [*Filipinas*]; for a brief account, see Spate, *Monopolists*, 284–9.

³³ Ibid., 90; S. D. Quiason, *English "Country Trade" with the Philippines, 1644–1765* (Quezon City 1966), 37–41, 88–9; M. L. Diaz-Trechuelo Spínola, 'Eighteenth Century Philippine Commerce', *Philippine Studies* (Manila) 14, 1966, 255–61, and her *Filipinas*, 60–75 (the restrictions), 211, 196–200, 228–35; P. Chaunu, *Les Philippines et le Pacifique des Ibériques* (Paris 1960), 267; Chaunu's tables of the movement of the port stop unfortunately in 1787. See also W. T. Cheong, 'Canton and Manila in the Eighteenth Century', in J. Ch'en and N. Tarling, *Studies in the Social History of China and Southeast Asia* (Cambridge 1970), 227–46.

³⁴ Diaz-Trechuelo Spínola, *Filipinas*, 264–75; exception might be made for the cigars sent by the Governor of the Philippines to the Viceroy of New Spain in 1641—O. H. K. Spate, *The Spanish Lake* (Canberra 1979), 222, 340 note 58.

³⁵ The McHales, 'Introduction' to Bowditch, *Manila*, 8, 16–18; from 1866 the book was published by the U. S. Hydrographic Office.

³⁶ Ibid., 34, 42, 63.

³⁷ Ibid., 'Introduction', 21; Morison says that Bowditch opened the hemp trade—*Massachusetts*, 94.

³⁸ R. Richards, 'The Manilla-Men and Pacific Commerce', *Solidarity* (Manila) 95, 1983, 47–57; Delano, *Narrative* 167; M. Steven, *Merchant Campbell: A Study of Colonial Trade* (Melbourne 1965), 90–2 [*Campbell*].

³⁹ J. King in Cook and King, *A Voyage to the Pacific Ocean* (London 1784), III.434–8; Beaglehole, III.714.

⁴⁰ S. D. Watrous (ed.), *John Ledyard's Journey through Russia and Siberia 1787–1788* (Madison 1966), 9–27, 91–5, 106–11; J. Mirsky, *The Westwards Crossings* (Chicago 1970), 223–37. A gallant adventurer!

⁴¹ Such as that of the shady Willem Bolts, founder of the Imperial Asiatic Company of Ostend and Trieste; see N. E. Hallward, *William Bolts* (Cambridge 1912). Another 'specialist in interloping', J. H. Cox of the *Mercury*, was involved with Hanna and used Prussian or Swedish colours as Meares used Portuguese—Dermigny, *Commerce*, III.950–2, 1154–5; 1240–3; D. Pethick, *The Nootka Connection* (Vancouver 1980), 43–4, 74–80, 198 [*Nootka*].

⁴² The more important voyages are outlined above, Ch. 8, with references. My general sources are Harlow, *Second Empire*, II.419–41; Dermigny, *Commerce*, III.1146–92; P. C. Phillips, *The Fur Trade* (Norman, Okla., 1961), II.36–66; Pethick, *Nootka*, passim. See also B. Gough, 'Canada and China: Early Trading Links by Sea' (how could they be by land or air?), *Proc. North American Soc. for Oceanic History* (Peabody Museum, Salem, 1977), 1–19, and F. W. Howay, 'The Fur Trade in Northwestern Development', in H. M. Stephens and H. E. Bolton (eds.), *The Pacific Ocean in History* (New York 1917), 276–86.

[43] Etches later tried to interest Alexander I of Russia in a filibustering expedition to the Red Sea. See G. Dixon (really W. Beresford), *A Voyage... to the North-West Coast of America* (London 1789, reprint Amsterdam 1968) [*Voyage*]; J. Etches, *An Authentic [?] Statement of the Facts Relative to NOOTKA SOUND* (London 1790); F. W. Howay (ed.), 'Four Letters from Richard Cadman Etches to Sir Joseph Banks', *Brit. Columbia Histl Qly* 6, 1942, 125–39—Rose named the ships (137 note 28); Harlow, *Second Empire*, II.420–33. Mackay's remark is in *A Place of Exile* (Melbourne 1985), 96—hard to reconcile with those in his *In the Wake of Cook* (London 1985), 62–4, 68. Political aspects of the Nootka affair are discussed in the next chapter.

[44] Pethick, *Nootka*, 88–147; Dermigny, *Commerce*, III.1177; M. E. Wheeler, 'Empires in Conflict and Cooperation: The "Bostonians" and the Russian-American Company', *Pac. Histl Rev.* 40, 1971, 419–51 at 422 ["Bostonians"].

[45] W. L. Cook, *Floor Tide of Empire: Spain and the Pacific Northwest, 1543–1819* (New Haven 1973)), 107–11 [*Flood Tide*]; A. Ogden 'The Californias in Spain's Pacific Otter Trade, 1775–1795', *Pac. Histl Rev.* 1, 1932, 444–68—an inflated view. Even Hawaii took a hand, with a 45-ton schooner built for Kamehameha I which traded successfully for skins in California—J. C. Kemble, 'The Cruise of the Schooner *Tamana*, 1805–1807', *Amer. Antiquarian Soc.* (Worcester, Mass.) 78, 1969, 283–98.

[46] G. Barratt, *Russia in Pacific Waters 1715–1825* (Vancouver 1981), 99–103 [*Pacific Waters*]. In general I follow this excellent study and S. B. Okun, *The Russian-American Company* (trans. C. Ginsburg, Cambridge, Mass., 1951) [*RAC*], detailed but deadly dull. Short accounts may be found in histories of Alaska such as H. Chevigny, *Russian America* (New York 1965) and C. C. Hulley, *Alaska 1741–1953* (Portland, Ore., 1953).

[47] Okun, *RAC*, 121.

[48] Ibid., 50, 55–7, 62–7 and *passim*.

[49] V. M. Golovnin in 1810, quoted in Barratt, *Pacific Waters*, 162–3—Barratt speaks aptly of Golovnin visiting 'from one area of maladministration to another'.

[50] Okun, *RAC* 99; cf. Barratt, *Pacific Waters*, 106, 110.

[51] According to Okun, British traders led the Tlingit attack—*RAC*, 54. In 1798 Rezanov feared, or told Tsar Paul that he did, that the English might infuse 'the gullible natives... with the spirit of republicanism'! This is too much even for Okun—ibid., 42. For friendly relations, see G. Vancouver, *A Voyage... to the North Pacific Ocean*, HS (2nd Ser. 163–6 (London 1984), IV.1308–9, 1337, 1352 [*North Pacific*], but *contra* Dixon, *Voyage*, 59–60, 66; for O'Cain, see Barratt, *Pacific Waters*, 125–9, and Wheeler, "Bostonians", 425–6.

[52] Okun, *RAC*, 58–61, 205.

[53] L. Cook, *Flood Tide*, 107; W. R. Hunt, *Arctic Passage... the Bering Sea 1697–1975* (New York 1975), 32–4.

[54] Pethick, *Nootka*, 199–200. See in general F. W. Howay, 'Indian Attacks upon Maritime Traders... 1785–1805', *Canadian Histl Rev.* 6, 1925, 287–309—on the whole the whites asked for it.

[55] Dermigny, *Commerce*, III.1177–8, quoting Howay.

[56] Ibid., III.1192–41; Morison, *Massachusetts*, 53, 260–1. For Astoria, G. W. Fuller, *A History of the Pacific Northwest* (2nd ed. New York 1938), 95–109; H. C. Franchère, introduction to G. Franchère, *Adventure at Astoria, 1810–1814* (Norman, Okla., 1967), xii–xxxi.

[57] F. W. Howay (ed.), *Colnett's Journal aboard the Argonaut* (Toronto 1942), 280–1; A. Couper (ed.), *Times Atlas of the Oceans* (London 1983), 210.

⁵⁸ The list included 'probangs' (surgical probes), busks, and tongue-scrapers—A. Starbuck, *History of the American Whale Fishery* (Washington 1878, reprint New York 1964), 155–7 [*History*]. For the commercial species of whales, see I. T. Sanderson, *Follow the Whale* (London 1958), *passim* [*the Whale*], and H. Morton, *The Whale's Wake* (Dunedin 1982), 21–9. Though Sanderson starts each of his sections with a reconstruction of a key event, both these excellent books are free from the anecdotage which infects the genre and is feelingly deplored in *the Whale*, 249–50. For the global importance of oil, see Harlow, *Second Empire*, II.293–5. There is an admirable bibliography—H. Forster, *The South Sea Whaler* (Kendall Maritime Museum, Sharon, Mass., 1985), comprehensive and annotated.

⁵⁹ Sanderson, *the Whale*, 211–12, 278; for scrimshaw, see C. W. Ashley, *The Yankee Whaler* (New York, 2nd ed. 1942), 111–16, and A. B. C. Whipple, *The Whalers* (Amsterdam 1979), 126–31.

⁶⁰ Harlow, *Second Empire*, II.307, 312, 319–23; K. M. Dallas, *Trading Posts or Penal Colonies: The Commercial Significance of Cook's New Holland Route to the Pacific* (Devonport, Tasmania, 1969), 57–86 [*Trading Posts*]; E. A. Stackpole, *Whales and Destiny: The Rivalry between America, France, and Britain for Control of the Southern Whale Fishery, 1785-1825* (n.p. [Univ. of Massachusetts Press] 1972), 116–18 [*Destiny*].

⁶¹ Speech on Conciliation with America, quoted at length in Starbuck, *History*, 60–2.

⁶² The best account of these Odysseys of the Nantucketers is in Stackpole, *Destiny*, *passim*.

⁶³ S. G. Brown, Introduction to T. Beale, *The Natural History of the Sperm Whale* (London 1839, reprint London 1973), v [*Sperm Whale*]—a main source for *Moby Dick*.

⁶⁴ *History*, 96, 171; for a concise conspectus, see R. C. Kluger, 'The Penetration of the Pacific by American Whalemen', in B. Greenhill (ed.), *The Opening of the Pacific: Image and Reality*, National Maritime Museum Monograph 2 (Greenwich 1971), 20–7.

⁶⁵ Stackpole, *Destiny*, 155–7; Starbuck, *History*, 96–7, 229; Beale, *Sperm Whale*, 150.

⁶⁶ W. J. Dakin, *Whalemen Adventurers in Southern Waters* (Sydney 1934, references to paperback ed. Sydney 1977), 8–13 [*Adventures*]; Morton, *Whale's Wake*, 88–104 ('British South Pacific Whaling Policies'); Steven, *Campbell*, 119–29 (Banks however supported colonial interests); G. J. R. Linge, *Industrial Awakening: A Geography of Australian Manufacturing 1788 to 1790* (Canberra 1979), 86, 89 [*Awakening*]. See also G. Blainey, *The Tyranny of Distance* (Melbourne 1966), 105–7.

⁶⁷ Dakin, *Adventurers*, 13, 21, 30–43, 61. See also K. M. Bowden, *Captain James Kelly of Hobart Town* (Melbourne 1964), 20–2, 62–72.

⁶⁸ Morton, *Whale's Wake*, 140; cf. 126–31, 169–222 *passim*, 250–60—most thoughtful discussions of race relations and Maori modernisation.

⁶⁹ Ibid., 155, 159, 163; for impediments to Australian whaling, 121–4—but did free trade end in the 1840s?

⁷⁰ Contrast the sombre picture in E. P. Hohman, *The American Whaleman: A Study of Life and Labor* (New York 1928), *passim*, with E. A. Stackpole, *The Sea-Hunters: The New England Whalemen... 1635-1835* (Philadelphia 1953), 436 [*Sea-Hunters*]. There is a favourable view of whaling life in F. A. Olmsted, *Incidents of a Whaling Voyage* (New York 1841, reprint New York 1969)—a young Yale man whaling for health, a prig but a good narrator.

⁷¹ Stackpole, *Sea-Hunters*, 250; Dakin, *Adventurers*, 65, 67–8, 71; Sanderson, *the Whale*, 261–2.

⁷² See also the chapter on 'The Whalers' Contribution to the Islands', with its surprising

tribute to the whalemen from the Anglican Bishop Selwyn, in Part II of R. Richards, *Whaling and Sealing at the Chatham Islands* (Canberra 1982), 49–51 [*Chathams*].

[73] Dakin, *Adventurers*, 86–90; Steven, *Campbell*, 106; Stackpole, *Sea-Hunters*, 199–205; Kirker, *Adventures*, 10–11, 16–17, 35–6, 50–64; R. Richards, 'The Maritime Fur Trade: Sealers on St Paul and Amsterdam', *Great Circle* (Nedlands, W. A.), 7, 1984, 24–42.

[74] W. Dampier, *A New Voyage round the World* (London 1697, Dover ed. New York 1968 cited), 69; J. Hawkesworth, *An Account of the Voyages... in the Southern Hemisphere* (London 1773), I.555–6.

[75] Kirker, *Adventures*, 61. Incidentally, there are thirteen Folgers and eleven Starbucks in the index to Stackpole, *Sea-Hunters*.

[76] Kirker, *Adventures*, 61; Stackpole, *Sea-Hunters*, 213–14, 218–27; there is a great mass of interesting detail in Pereira Salas, *Primeiros Contactos, passim*, especially 261–84, 'La vida marinera norteamericano en el Pacifico' and 'La curiosa vida de los loberos en las islas'.

[77] Fanning, *Voyages*, 108–19; Delano, *Narrative*, 306–7.

[78] D. Collins, *An Account of the English Colony in New South Wales* (London 1798, reprint Sydney 1975), I.268–9; C. Bateson, *Dire Strait: A History of Bass Strait* (Sydney 1978), 29–31 [*Dire Strait*]; M. Roe (ed.), *The Journal and Letters of Captain Charles Bishop*, HS 2nd Ser. 131 (Cambridge 1967), xl–xliii, 290–6, 310. Bishop's *Nautilus* was Bristol-owned and he was not an American, as stated in M. J. E. Steven, 'Exports other than Wool', in G. J. Abbott and B. Nairn (eds.), *Economic Growth of Australia 1788–1821* (Melbourne 1969), 283–305 at 288 [*Economic Growth*].

[79] Ibid., 288–9, and her *Campbell*, 106–21. Campbell built the first private wharf in Sydney, begun in 1800—ibid., 40–1, 54; C. Newman, *The Spirit of Wharf House* (Sydney 1961), 15–18.

[80] Bateson, *Dire Strait*, 39–45; D. R. Hainsworth, *The Sydney Traders: Simeon Lord and his Contemporaries 1788–1821* (Melbourne 1971), 137–8, 143–7 [*Traders*].

[81] Ibid., 131–3, 136; Steven, in Abbott and Nairn, *Economic Growth*, 131. 'Emancipists' were time-expired convicts.

[82] Morton, *Whale's Wake*, 105–24 (Baudin at 118–19); Hainsworth, *Traders*, 136–8; Richards, *Chathams*, Part I 23, 31, 71. Incidentally, the *Britannia's* people at Dusky Bay in 1793 did not build 'the very first [European] ship to be constructed in the south-west Pacific from scratch' (Morton, 106); that honour belongs if not to Mendaña's men on Santa Ysabel in 1593 then to the *Bounty* mutineers on Tahiti, who launched their schooner in 1791.

[83] H. E. Maude, 'The Tahitian Pork Trade: 1800–1830', in his *Of Islands and Men* (Melbourne 1968), 178–232 ['Pork Trade'] is an excellent detailed study.

[84] D. Shineberg, *They Came for Sandalwood* (Melbourne 1967), 7 [*Sandalwood*]; Hainsworth, *Traders*, 172–8; Steven, in Abbott and Nairn, *Economic Growth*, 295–8; Kirker, *Adventures*, 111–46 (rather too anecdotal).

[85] R. A. Derrick, *A History of Fiji* (3rd ed. Suva 1957), 39–53 [*Fiji*]; G. Dening, *Islands and Beaches... Marquesas 1774–1880* (Melbourne 1980), 115–22.

[86] R. Kuykendall, *The Hawaiian Kingdom: I. 1778–1854* (Honolulu 1968), 82–98 [*Kingdom*]; H. W. Bradley, *The American Frontier in Hawaii: The Pioneers 1789–1843* (Palo Alto 1942, reprint Gloucester, Mass., 1968), 28–32, 54–71, 111–20 [*Frontier*]; T. Morgan, *Hawaii: A Century of Economic Change 1778–1876* (Cambridge, Mass., 1948), 61–73 [*Hawaii*]. Dorothy Shineberg's admirable *Sandalwood* deals with the later, Melanesian, phase.

[87] Maude, 'Pork Trade', 199–200; J. J. Parsons, 'The Hawksbill Turtle and the Tortoise Shell Trade', in (ed. unknown), *Etudes de géographie tropicale offertes à Pierre Gourou* (Paris/La Haye 1972), 45–60; R. G. Ward, 'The Pacific *Bêche de Mer* Trade with special reference to Fiji', in Ward (ed.), *Man in the Pacific Islands* (Oxford 1972), 91–123; Derrick, *Fiji*, 65, 67–70; reluctant personal experience of sea-slug as a 'delicacy'. Cf. K. N. Chaudhuri, *Trade and Civilisation in the Indian Ocean* (Cambridge 1985), 20–21—but birds' nests are divine!

[88] Steven, 'Enterprise', in Abbott and Nairn, *Economic Growth*, 119–35 at 120.

[89] J. S. Cumpston, *Shipping Arrivals and Departures, Sydney, 1788–1825* (Canberra 1977), 6 [*Shipping*]—an indispensable compilation. Astonishingly, there seems no connected and intelligent history of the *port* of Sydney. P. R. Stephensen, *The History and Description of Sydney Harbour* (Adelaide 1966) is agreeable topographical antiquarianism rather in an eighteenth century manner; the quasi-official 'The Port of Sydney—Its History and Development', *Port of Sydney Jnl* 10, 1970, is useless.

[90] Cumpston, *Shipping*, 68; Hainsworth, *Traders*, 115–20; Linge, *Awakening*, 39–41; Bach, *Maritime History*, 70–92.

[91] C. H. Currey, *The Transportation Escape and Pardoning of Mary Bryant* (Sydney 1983).

[92] C. Bateson, *The Convict Ships 1788–1868* (Glasgow 1959), 75 [*Convict Ships*].

[93] Cumpston, *Shipping*, 5–7, 17, and map; Bach, *Maritime History*, 46–52; R. B. Joyce, 'Government Policy', in Abbott and Nairn, *Economic Growth*, 59–74 at 63–4.

[94] F. Péron and L.-C.-D. de Freycinet, *Voyage de Découvertes aux Terres Australes* (Paris 1807–16), I.374–5.

[95] Calculated from figures in Cumpston, *Shipping, passim*, and Bateson, *Convict Ships*, 288–94. The biggest ship entering was the *Dromedary*, 1100 tons, bringing Governor Macquarie in 1809. Complete accuracy is not claimed for Table II—the interpretation of Cumpston's necessarily compressed data is sometimes tricky—but it gives a substantially accurate view of the movement of the port.

[96] Cumpston, *Shipping*, 16–18; instructions to Macquarie to enforce the Acts and his protest crossed.

[97] E. Pereira Salas, 'Los primeiros relaciones entre Chile y Australia', *Boletin de la Academia Chilena de Historia* 22, 1955, 44–75—excellent and comprehensive; Greenwood, *Relations*, 159–66.

[98] D. G. E. Hall, *The History of South-East Asia* (3rd ed. London 1968), 509–11.

[99] Linge, *Awakening*, 27; Hainsworth, *Traders*, Ch. 6 *passim*; Steven, *Campbell*, Ch. IX *passim* and in Abbott and Nairn, *Economic Growth*, 178–84.

[1] The poem was placed second to W. M. Praed's; it ended '[May] Australasia float, with flag unfurl'd, A New Britannia in another world.'

[2] *A Voyage round the World* (Edinburgh 1816, but cited from reprint of 1822 American ed., Honolulu 1967), 109–13, 118–20 [*Voyage*].

[3] C. Ralston, *Grass Huts and Warehouses* (Canberra 1977), 49–52, 58; Kuykendall, *Kingdom*, I.73–4.

[4] Morgan, *Hawaii*, 79.

[5] Vancouver, *North Pacific*, III.1152–3, 1178–9; Campbell, *Voyage*, 118–19.

[6] Bradley, *Frontier*, 72–3.

[7] Kuykendall, *Kingdom*, I.56–9; R. A. Pierce, 'Georg Anton Schäffer, Russia's Man in Hawaii, 1815–17', in M. B. Sherwood (ed.), *Alaska and its History* (Seattle 1967), 71–81—based in part of information from a collateral descendant of Schäffer's, a professor in São Paulo!

[8] S. Hugill, *Sailortown* (London 1967), 271–7.

[9] Bradley, *Frontier*, 84–93; Kuykendall, *Kingdom*, I.92–5.

[10] Ibid., I.305–9; Bradley, *Frontier*, 79–82. B. Judd, *Voyages to Hawaii before 1860* (2nd ed. Honolulu 1974), 19–22, gives only twenty-five entries (five by warships) plus 'several whalers' for these years put together. I have not used this source.

[11] Bradley, *Frontier*, 82–4.

[12] *Pacific Ocean*, 217–23, 252–63. M'Konochie illustrates the Free Trade ethos at its most exalted; the great moral advance of the Hawaiians as against the Tahitians shows that Free Trade was a more effective civilising agent than Christian missions.

Notes for Chapter 13

[1] This apt phrase is from J.-E. Martin-Allanic, *Bougainville navigateur et les Découvertes de son Temps* (Paris 1964), II.1055 [*Bougainville*]. He details the course of the affair with immense particularity and tedium, I.71–106, 123–455, 532–49, II.921–1250—reading him is a necessary penance. J. Goebel, *The Struggle for the Falkland Islands* (New Haven 1927, reprint 1982), 229–410 [*Falklands*], is a full examination of the legal and political aspects, scholarly but with some anti-British bias. F. L. and O. M. Hoffmann, *Sovereignty in Dispute: The Falklands—Malvinas 1493–1982* (Boulder, Colorado, 1984) [*Sovereignty*] tend to follow Goebel's line. I regret that a Spanish case is not available to me.

[2] *Thoughts on the LATE TRANSACTIONS respecting FALKLAND'S ISLANDS* (London 1771), in *The Works of Samuel Johnson* (Yale ed. Vol. X, New Haven 1977), 346–86 at 369 [*Thoughts*] Egmont from V. T. Harlow, *The Founding of the Second British Empire* (London 1952–64), I.28 [*Second Empire*]; Choiseul in Martin-Allanic, *Bougainville*, II.1097.

[3] G. Williams (ed.), *A Voyage round the World... by George Anson* (London 1974, original ed. 1748), 96–9; Johnson, *Thoughts*, 355–6; Goebel, *Falklands*, 194–202.

[4] It is odd that Goebel (ibid., 233) does not see the significance of this garden, an extension of the ritualised gestures—cutting of grass and boughs, digging of turf, erecting gallows—which symbolised the transformation of a *terra nullius* into one changed by the hand of man—see H. R. Wagner, 'Creation of Rights of Sovereignty through Symbolic Acts', *Pac. Histl Rev.* 7, 1938, 297–326 at 299–303.

[5] Martin-Allanic, *Bougainville*, I.148–60.

[6] Ibid., I.225–39, 532–9.

[7] Hoffmann and Hoffmann, *Sovereignty*, 48–9; Goebel, *Falklands*, 268–9.

[8] Martin-Allanic, *Bougainville*, II.1098.

[9] Ibid., II.1014–18; Goebel, *Falklands*, 271–7.

[10] Ibid., 354–60. 407–10; Martin-Allanic, *Bougainville*, II.1221–45; Hoffmann and Hoffmann, *Sovereignty*, 52–60; *Rasselas*, Ch. xlix.

[11] Ibid., 64–86; Goebel, *Falklands*, 432–58.

[12] G. Lefèvre-Pontalis, 'Un Project de Conquête du Japon par l'Angleterre et la Russie en 1776', *Annales de l'Ecole Libre des Sciences Politiques* 4, 1889, 433–57; G. V. Blue, 'A Rumor of an Anglo-Russian Raid upon Japan', 1776', *Pac. Histl, Rev.* 8, 1939, 453–69.

[13] Quoted in J. Dunmore, 'Dream and Reality: French Voyages and their Vision of Australia', in I. Donaldson (ed.), *Australia and the European Imagination* (Canberra 1982), 109–22 at 118.

14 B. Gammage, 'Early Boundaries of New South Wales', *Histl Studies* 19, 1981, 524–31. R. J. King sees this assertion of extensive limits as a counter-claim to the Spanish doctrine of the South Sea as *mare clausum*)—'The Territorial Boundaries of New South Wales in 1788', *Great Circle* (Nedlands, W.A.) 3, 1981, 71–89. In the *Canberra Times* of 4 November 1978 'Public Servant' argued amusingly that by treaties from Madrid 1670 to Versailles 1783, eastern Australia should be legally regarded as part of the Republic of Chile.

15 Malaspina, 'Examen Político de las Colonias Inglesas en el Mar Pacifico', 1793, Museo Naval, Madrid, MS. No. 318; F. Muñoz, 'Reflexiones sobre los establecimientos ynglesas de la Nueva Holanda', 1790s, British Library MS 19264. I owe copies of these documents to the kindness of Mr R. J. King of Canberra; his ' "Ports of Shelter, and refreshment . . .": Botany Bay and Norfolk Island in British naval strategy, 1786–1808', *Histl Studies* 22, 1986, 2999–213 [' "Ports of Shelter" '], provides ample evidence of British aspirations as well as Spanish apprehensions. Cf. the French appraisal of Tench (1789) quoted in Dallas, *Trading Posts*, 124–7 (reference in note 21 below).

16 Harlow, *Second Empire*, II.438–41. Although of course the settlement was in Port Jackson, 'Botany Bay' seems appropriate in this section in view of its long life, especially in popular parlance, for the colony regarded as a place of convict exile.

17 'The settlement of Australia', in G. Martin (ed.), *The founding of Australia: the argument about Australia's origins* (Sydney 1978), 30–7 [*The founding*]—a useful collection of contributions to the debate.

18 For reasons well stated in D. Mackay, *A Place of Exile: The European Settlement of New South Wales* (Melbourne 1985), 10–13 [*Place of Exile*]—a hard-hitting restatement of the traditional view.

19 M. Steven, *Trade, Tactics and Territory: Britain and the Pacific 1783–1823* (Melbourne 1983), 106–7 [*Trade, Tactics*]; for Das Voltas Bay, Mackay, *Place of Exile*, 52–6 and M. Cullen, 'The Botany Bay decision, 1786: convicts, not empire', *Engl. Histl Rev.* 97, 1982, 740–66 at 749–54 ['Botany Bay']. See also G. Martin, 'The alternatives to Botany Bay', in *The founding*, 152–67.

20 Convict ancestry is an 'in thing' in Australia today, and seekers after genealogies sometimes impede academic workers in the archives. For a general discussion of transportation, see i.a. the earlier chapters of A. G. L. Shaw, *Convicts and the Colonies* (London 1966).

21 The debate began with K. M. Dallas's 'The first settlement in Australia . . . in relation to sea-power in world politics', *Tasmanian Histl Research Asstn Papers* 3, 1952; he expanded his views in *Trading Posts or Penal Colonies* (Hobart 1969) [*Trading Posts*].

22 Matra and Young are in Martin, *The founding*, 9–21; for Call, see A. Frost, *Convicts and Empire: A Naval Question* (Melbourne 1980), 24–6, 45–6 [*Convicts*]—a very full presentation of the revisionist case. Frost has edited a limited edition of Young's texts— *Dreams of a Pacific Empire* (Sydney 1986). For Matra, see A. Giordano, *A Dream of the Southern Seas* (Adelaide 1984).

23 C. M. H. Clark, *Sources of Australian History* (Oxford 1957), 67–9.

24 Ibid., 69–75, and Martin, *The founding*, 22–9. An enthusiastic correspondent of Banks suggested that 'without imitating the Violence of a Roman Rape . . . a set of the most beautifully formed Women that the Sun beholds' might be brought from Tahiti and people Botany Bay with 'Ornament[s] to Human Nature . . . a generation of social Benevolent Beings'—*JPH* 1, 1966, 105. The Lucky Country!

[25] *A SERIOUS ADMONITION to THE PUBLICK, on the Intended Thief-Colony at Botany Bay* (London 1786), 23, 27. This is vintage Dalrymple, and extremely rare; I cite from George Mackaness's reprint, Sydney 1943/Dubbo 1979 [*Admonition*]. See M. Roe, 'Australia's Place in the "Swing to the East", 1788–1810', *Histl Studies* 8, 1958, 202–13 at 213, and R. A. Swan, *To Botany Bay* (Canberra 1973), 138–41.

[26] This is a main theme in Swan, ibid.; see e.g. 12–13, 161–3, 166.

[27] O. H. K. Spate, 'De Lozier Bouvet and Mercantilist Expansion in the Pacific in 1740', in J. Parker (ed.), *Merchants and Scholars* (Minneapolis 1965), 219–37 at 229.

[28] Mackay, *Place of Exile*, 95–6; cf. his 'Far-Flung Empire: A Neglected Imperial Outpost at Botany Bay 1788–1801', *Jnl Imperial and Commonwealth Hist.* 9, 1981, 125–45 at 128–9.

[29] *The Tyranny of Distance* (Melbourne 1965), 27–37 at 33 [*Tyranny*]; extracts in Martin, *The founding* 79–90, with criticisms by G. C. Bolton, 'The Hollow Conqueror: Flax and the Foundation of Australia', 91–104 (from *Aust. Econ. Hist. Rev.* 8, 1968, 3–16), and A. G. L. Shaw, 'The Hollow Conqueror and the Tyranny of Distance', 122–30. See further Dallas, *Trading Posts*, 10–20, anticipating some of Mackay's points in *Place of Exile*, 61–5.

[30] Cullen, 'Botany Bay', 744.

[31] For the start that was made, see Blainey, *Tyranny*, 35–7. There is a balanced discussion of this question in G. Martin, 'Economic motives behind the founding of Botany Bay', in *The founding*, 237–51.

[32] Frost, *Convicts*, 140. Cf. G. C. Bolton, 'Broken reeds and smoking flax', in Martin, *The founding* 115–21 at 118.

[33] Blainey, *Tyranny*, 36.

[34] Frost, *Convicts* 43–4; Dalrymple, *Admonition*, 28–30, 32–8; G. Martin, in *The founding*, 156–65.

[35] H. T. Fry, 'Cathay and the Way Thither: The Background to Botany Bay', *Histl Studies* 14, 1971, 497–510 at 501–5 ['Cathay'].

[36] Ibid., 504; Young was *replying* to a query from the Attorney-General. This makes it difficult not to see some connection between Botany Bay and the China trade in the government's thinking.

[37] *Admonition*, 18, 20–1; on Botany Bay and Spanish trade, see B. Atkins, 'Australia's Place in the "Swing to the East", 1788–1810: An Addendum', *Histl Studies* 8, 1958, 315–18.

[38] Fry, 'Cathay', 508; Dalrymple, *Admonition*, 18, says that the Directors were not 'acquainted with this Scheme' until they saw the advertisement for transports in the newspapers. Steven suggests a deliberate policy of secrecy—*Trade, Tactics*, 116. Her final chapter, 106–28, is an able statement of the case for ulterior motives. See also A. Frost, 'The East India Company and the Choice of Botany Bay', *Histl Studies* 65, 1973, 606–11.

[39] Quoted in King, '"Ports of Shelter"', 199.

[40] Mackay, *Place of Exile*, 37.

[41] Steven, *Trade, Tactics* 68; and cf. Harlow, *Second Empire*, II.225–53 *passim*.

[42] Mackay, *Place of Exile*, 89.

[43] This section is mainly concerned with matters which 'every [Australian] schoolchild knows'; there is of course a vast literature, but specific documentation seems unnecessary on most points. Contemporary narratives include *The Voyage of Governor Phillip to Botany Bay* (London 1789, reprint Adelaide 1968, Melbourne 1982); D. Collins, *An Account*

of the English Colony in New South Wales (London 1798, with a second volume coming up to 1801, London 1802, both reprinted Sydney 1975) [*Account*], an immensely detailed chronicle; W. Tench, *A Narrative of the Expedition to Botany Bay* (London 1789) [*Narrative*] and *A Complete Account of the Settlement at Port Jackson* (London 1793) [*Complete Account*], both reprinted in L. F. Fitzhardinge, *Sydney's First Four Years* (Sydney 1961).

⁴⁴ Collins, *Account*, I.96 of reprint.

⁴⁵ Tench, *Narrative*, 103 (Fitzhardinge 57).

⁴⁶ There is a rather old-fashioned biography by G. Mackaness, *Admiral Arthur Phillip: Founder of New South Wales 1738–1814* (Sydney 1937), very full on New South Wales but sketchy and out-of-date on Phillip's earlier career; see A. Frost, *Arthur Phillip 1738–1814: His Voyagings* (Melbourne 1987).

⁴⁷ Collins, *Account*, I.32, 36, 110–12, 118–19; Tench, *Complete Account*, 58–60, 91–7 (Fitzhardinge 179–80, 207–11, and note at 319).

⁴⁸ The fullest and best account of the Nootka crisis known to me is in W. L. Cook's masterly study *Flood Tide of Empire: Spain and the Pacific Northwest, 1543–1819* (New Haven 1973), 65–396 passim [*Flood Tide*], which is especially good on the actual happenings in the Sound. For the diplomatic side, see Harlow, *Second Empire*, II.420–81, and W. R. Manning, 'The Nootka Sound Controversy', *Annl Report Amer. Histl Asstn for 1904*, 281–484 (reprint Ann Arbor 1966) ['Nootka Sound'], long regarded as the standard discussion but a little disappointing. There is a good short account in B. M. Gough, *Distant Dominion: Britain and the Northwest Coast... 1579–1809* (Vancouver 1980), 81–115. None of these have any pronounced bias, though Manning seems to regard Meares as much more of an authorised 'English' (why not 'British'?) agent than he was. References to Nootka in Spanish works available to me are slight.

⁴⁹ There were two sets of papers: the Portuguese showed Meares and Douglas as supercargoes, the English set as captains—Cook, *Flood Tide*, 137. That Manning could pass off this double-dealing as 'probably a harmless trick, meant to deceive the Celestials' baffles belief—'Nootka Sound', 360–1.

⁵⁰ Robert Haswell, second mate of the *Lady Washington*, in F. W. Howay (ed.), *Voyages of the "Columbia" to the Northwest Coast* (Boston 1941, reprint Amsterdam 1969), 47–8 ["*Columbia*"]. This artless private log carries more weight than the letter of the American captains to the same effect, which is not entirely impartial, although from internal evidence not collusive—R. Gray and J. Ingraham to F. Bodega y Quadra, Nootka Sound, 3 August 1792, ibid. 474–9. Meares's own account is in his *Voyages... from China to the North West Coast of America* (London 1790, reprint Amsterdam 1967), 180–286 [*Voyages*]. The dates given by British coming from China and Americans from New England differ by one day.

⁵¹ Cook, *Flood Tide*, 143–4; Meares's instructions to Colnett, in his *Voyages*, second Appendix II—there are two sets of appendices, neither paginated.

⁵² J. E. Baird, 'San Lorenzo de Nuca: Spain's Northermost Outpost' (Berkeley thesis ?1956, Bancroft Library mF 1089 N8 B15), 52, 59, 65–6 (Martínez's instructions) [San Lorenzo]; Revillagigedo to Valdés, Minister of Marine and Indies, 23 December 1788, in Manning, 'Nootka Sound', 502.

⁵³ For the detail of events at Nootka, see Cook, *Flood Tide*, 146–93. The obligation was signed by Douglas and Viana in the name of João Carvalho—Meares, *Voyages*, second Appendix IV.

⁵⁴ Cook, *Flood Tide*, 166–7; F. W. Howay (ed.), *The Journal of Captain James Colnett aboard the Argonaut...*, Champlain Society No. 26 (Toronto 1940), 54–63, 308–18 [*Colnett*].

Duffin's letter is in Meares, *Voyages*, Appendix XIII.

[55] Howay, *Colnett*, 61; Cook, *Flood Tide*, 175–7, 291. J. M. Moziño condemns Martinez for his 'barbarous resolution' of killing the Nootka chief Quelequem (Callicum, Ke-le-kum) for a 'slight affront' and ascribes the quarrel to the 'churlish nature' and 'uncultivated boorishness' of both men—I. H. Wilson (ed.), *Noticias de Nutka* (Seattle 1970), 74–6, 83 [Mozínos, *Nutka*].

[56] H. I. Priestley, 'The Log of the Princesa by Estevan Martínez', *Oregon Histl Qly* 21, 1920, 182–5.

[57] Cook, *Flood Tide*, 192–4; Manning, 'Nootka Sound', 330.

[58] Cook, *Flood Tide*, 185, 190–2; Baird, *San Lorenzo*, 80–2.

[59] Flores to Martínez, Mexico, 25 February 1789, text in C. L. Stewart, 'Why the Spaniards Temporarily Abandoned Nootka Sound in 1789', *Canadian Histl Rev.* 17, 1936, 168–72; Cook, *Flood Tide*, 186–8, 192–4.

[60] Ibid., 275–7; Baird, *San Lorenzo*, 90–2, 99–100; W. K. Lamb (ed.), *A Voyage of Discovery to the North Pacific Ocean . . . 1791–1795*, HS 2nd Ser. 163–6 (London 1984), II.660 [Vancouver, *Voyage*].

[61] Manning, 'Nootka Sound', 348–58; Cook, *Flood Tide*, 198–9, 205, 289–91.

[62] [John Etches], *An Authentic Statement of the Facts relative to NOOTKA SOUND*, 3, and *A Continuation of an Authentic Statement . . .* (both London 1790), 29—there is much that is not authentic in these pamphlets, but such statements could hardly have been risked if untrue. What becomes of Mackay's remark that the government 'had been at best luke-warm to the fur traders who were interested in the area'?—*Place of Exile*, 96.

[63] Harlow, *Second Empire*, II.444.

[64] J. B. Burgess, Under-Secretary in Foreign Department, *A Narrative of the Negotiations occasioned by the Dispute between England and Spain in the year 1790* (London 1790), but quoted from British Library MS Bft hmF 1089 N8B96) [*Narrative*], an official resumé apparently prepared for George III. The orders were withdrawn on 30 April when 'General Preparatons for Arming Commenced'.

[65] Cook, *Flood Tide*, 211; Manning, 'Nootka Sound', 370–1, 384–5.

[66] Ibid., 373–4; Cook adds Denmark to the prospective allies—*Flood Tide*, 117.

[67] N. B. Pipes (ed.), *The Memorial of John Meares to the House of Commons* (Portland, Or., 1933; also in Meares, *Voyages*, second Appendix I). The original edition (London 1790) was published by J. Debrett, who also put out John Etches's pamphlets. For the Government's payment for it, see J. M. Norris, 'The Policy of the British Cabinet in the Nootka Crisis', *English Histl Rev.* 70, 1955, 562–80 at 569 ['Nootka Crisis'] and for government reliance on it Burges, *Narrative*, 24–36, almost straight from the Memorial.

[68] Dalrymple's pamphlets are *The Spanish Pretensions Fairly Discussed* and *The Spanish Memorial of 4 June Considered* (both London 1790). George Dixon's attacks on Meares were not political—see Ch. 12.

[69] Harlow, *Second Empire*, II.447–51; Cook, *Flood Tide*, 213–17; Norris, 'Nootka Crisis', 572–4, who says that the credit was £ 2,000,000.

[70] A pseudo-reciprocity which reminds one of Anatole France: 'The Law, in its majestic impartiality forbids rich and poor alike to sleep under railway arches.' This summary is Harlow's, *Second Empire*, II.451.

[71] Manning, 'Nootka Sound', 432–4; Cook, *Flood Tide*, 224–6—an 'ambit claim' indeed!

[72] Ibid., 224–31; Manning, 'Nootka Sound', 428, 437; G. V. Blue, 'French Diplomacy in the Nootka Sound Controversy' (Berkeley Ph.D. thesis, Bancroft Library mF 1089

N8B5, no date), 152–66. Blue's 'Anglo-French Diplomacy during the Critical Phase of the Nootka Controversy', *Oregon Histl Qly* 39, 1938, 162–79, is slight.

[73] Harlow, *Second Empire*, II.458–64; Cook, *Flood Tide*, 231–49; Manning, 'Nootka Sound', 439–49, 454–6. The quotation on 'ceding the Indies' is in L. Mills, 'The Real Significance of the Nootka Sound Incident', *Canadian Histl Rev.* 6, 1925, 110–22 at 120 ['Significance'].

[74] Cook, *Flood Tide*, 140, 423. Norris notes that Meares's promise to Maquinna that he should have the house, and his orders to Douglas to winter in Hawaii, belie his claim to have intended a permanent settlement—'Nootka Crisis', 571.

[75] The point is argued with semantic skill in Cook, *Flood Tide*, 236.

[76] Harlow, *Second Empire*, II.464.

[77] Norris, 'Nootka Crisis', 580; for the 'colonial sovereignty' doctrine, Mills, 'Significance', *passim*. As Norris's use of quotation marks implies, it was not new.

[78] Meares, *Voyages*, unnumbered final Appendix; Harlow, Second Empire, II.462–3; Cook, *Flood Tide*, 409–19.

[79] For the knowledge of Meares's claims that Vancouver had, see Harlow, *Second Empire*, II.465–6; it was not too precise.

[80] Cook, *Flood Tide*, 379–80; Vancouver, *North Pacific*, II.679–80. Details of the negotiations are in Cook, 362–79, 391, 410–17, and Vancouver, II.663–9, 674–5, 681, IV. 1567–72, 1578–81.

[81] For the final scene, see Cook, *Flood Tide*, 421–3, and Baird, *San Lorenzo*, 164–6. Harlow's February date (*Second Empire*, II.480) is incorrect.

[82] Details in Baird, *San Lorenzo*, 130–63.

[83] Cook, *Flood Tide*, 390–1; Moziño, *Nutka*, 91–7—he refutes himself by pointing out an excellent well-armed Boston ship cost one-sixth as much as a San Blas frigate.

[84] Cook, *Flood Tide*, 400–5; for Núñez Gaona, ibid., 349–52, 382–3.

[85] Ibid., 526.

[86] British Columbia Historical Society, *Annual Report* 2, 1924, 17–26.

[87] Personal experience.

[88] For these developments see G. Barratt, *Russia in Pacific Waters 1715–1825* (Vancouver 1981), 209–19, 228–30; the quoted ukase is at 216–18.

[89] The 1846 boundary was unclear in the San Juan Islands of Juen de Fuca Strait, and was not finally settled until 1872.

INDEX

Merely 'marker' and *en passant* references omitted. References to modern authors, and in the notes, are given only when there is comment or additional information. A number of islands of little significance, mainly in the Tuamotus, are omitted. Abbreviation: *pm* = *passim*.

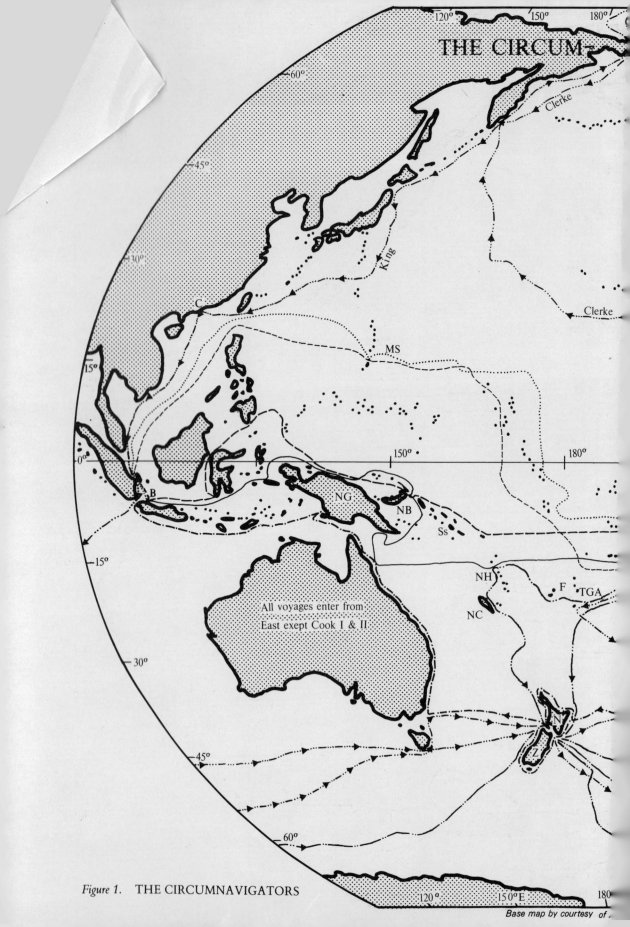

Clerke

Clerke

King

C

MS

180°

150°

0°

B

NG

NB

Ss

15°

NH

F

TGA

All voyages enter from
East exept Cook I & II.

NC

N

Z

30°

45°

60°

120°

150°E

180

Figure 1. THE CIRCUMNAVIGATORS

Base map by courtesy of